HUMAN EMOTIONS

EMOTIONS, PERSONALITY, AND PSYCHOTHERAPY

Series Editors:
Carroll E. Izard • *University of Delaware, Newark, Delaware*
and
Jerome L. Singer • *Yale University, New Haven, Connecticut*

HUMAN EMOTIONS • *Carroll E. Izard*

THE PERSONAL EXPERIENCE OF TIME • *Bernard S. Gorman and
Alden E. Wessman, eds.*

HUMAN EMOTIONS

Carroll E. Izard

Unidel Professor of Psychology
University of Delaware
   formerly
Professor of Psychology
Vanderbilt University

PLENUM PRESS · NEW YORK AND LONDON

Library of Congress Cataloging in Publication Data

Main entry under title:

Human emotions.

   (Emotions, personality, and psychotherapy)
   Bibliography: p.
   Includes index.
   1. Emotions. I. Izard, Carroll E. II. Series.
BF531.H78   152.4   77-1989 /
ISBN 0-306-30986-6

© 1977 Plenum Press, New York
A Division of Plenum Publishing Corporation
227 West 17th Street, New York, N.Y. 10011

Printed in the United States of America

PREFACE

In recent years—especially the past decade, in sharp contrast to preceding decades—knowledge in the field of emotions has been steadily increasing. This knowledge comes from many different specialties: Emotion is a truly interdisciplinary subject. Workers in the fields of physiology, neurology, ethology, physiological psychology, personality and social psychology, clinical psychology and psychiatry, medicine, nursing, social work, and the clergy are all directly concerned with emotion. Professions such as law and architecture have an obvious concern with emotions as they affect human motives and needs. The various branches of art, especially the performing arts, certainly deal with the emotions, especially with the expression of emotions. Constantine Stanislavsky, the Russian theatrical genius, revolutionized modern theater by developing a training method for actors and actresses that emphasized creating genuine emotion on the stage, the emotion appropriate to the character and the life situation being depicted. Indeed, one can hardly think of any human activity that is not related in some way to the field of emotion.

Since the contributions to the subject of emotions come from so many different disciplines, it is difficult to find the important common themes that can yield an understanding of the field as a whole. This volume will attempt to make that task easier, but I recognize that no one can treat all of the diverse material expertly and in detail. My aim will be to represent all important types of contributions and perhaps point the way for further and more intensive study of special topics.

One other qualification is needed about the coverage of the book. The first chapter will include a definition of *emotion* (or of *an emotion*), the definition that served as an organizing principle in selecting material for the book. The definition is general enough to include a wide variety of materials from the many disciplines named in the foregoing paragraph, but it will allow the exclusion of certain materials which are not specifically in the realm of emotions. For example, some research does not draw a clear distinction between drives and emotions or between arousal and emotion. Such contributions will be included only when they seem to have reasonably clear implications for human emotions as defined in Chapter 1. Also, there is now a great deal of research on visceral functions, or on activities of organs innervated by the autonomic nervous system. Many studies in this area include the term emotion in their title. Sometimes these contributions are relevant to the themes of this volume, sometimes they are not—and sometimes, quite frankly, it is impossible to say whether they are or not. In some cases the investigators are more concerned with the drive states (hunger, thirst, pain, sensory pleasure) than they are with the study of emotions per se. Some of this work, particularly that which throws light on the interactions of drives (e.g., pain and sex) with emotions (such as fear and joy), will be considered, but research focused solely on simple drive states will not be included.

In addition to presenting the theoretical and factual material necessary for a general understanding and overview of the field of emotions, another aim here is to provide a resource for students who want to better understand themselves and others through furthering their knowledge of the emotions. Those who fear that scientific analysis of the emotions will destroy their power and mystique (certainly a dreadful thing in the case of excitement and joy) may take solace in the fact that schools of art have not destroyed their subject matter (although the young art student sometimes thinks they surely will). The power and mystique of human emotions are such that they cannot be diminished by an attempt to better understand them, just as the fascination and attraction of the Mona Lisa or Michelangelo's David are certainly not lessened by a knowledge of the facts surrounding their conception and execution.

C. E. IZARD

Vanderbilt University

ACKNOWLEDGMENTS

In the years since the publication of *The Face of Emotion* (1971) and *Patterns of Emotions* (1972), I have learned to appreciate more fully the contributions from theoretical positions that differ from my own. This is probably a joint function of the quality of the competition and the mellowing of my own emotions. In addition to this constructive effect of rival theories, there has been a significant increase in the research literature on emotions. There has also been a broadening of perspectives as a result of contributions from those whose work successfully links emotion concepts to cognitive theory and research. Perhaps this has given me a better "affective-cognitive orientation." In any case, I am indebted to numerous scientists for enlightenment and intellectual stimulation, and their contributions to the field of emotions are noted in the pages of this book.

My understanding of emotions has also benefited from living and working in other cultures, and I am grateful for the learning experience provided by a recent National Academy of Sciences Exchange Fellowship with the Soviet Academy of Sciences. In addition to scientific gains from the laboratories, there were many occasions when my ineptness with the Russian language afforded me the opportunity to revive my keen appreciation of the transcultural messages of emotion expressions.

I have learned much about emotions from the arts, especially from the theater, where effective integrations of emotion, cognition, and action are stock in trade. Special thanks is owed to Barbara Izard, of the Department of Theatre of the University of Delaware, for the rich experiences we have shared while co-teaching our course on emotion expression and control.

I deeply appreciate the insightful questions and comments of the many undergraduate and graduate students who have taken my courses and seminars on human emotions. I am equally appreciative of the experiences I have shared with my psychotherapy clients, who challenge us to develop a science of emotions that will facilitate important human services.

Infants and children are the greatest teachers for the student of emotions. Nowhere are the emotions more evident than in the faces of the young and in no situation is the critical importance of emotion communication more convincing than in the infant-caregiver or infant-parent relationship. I have profited immeasurably from such relationships and from the consequent abiding friendships with Cal, Camille, and Ashley. I thank them and all the infants, parents, and caregivers who have participated in my research.

Part of the work for this book was supported by a Centennial Fellowship from Vanderbilt University and by funds provided by the Unidel Foundation. Dorothy Timberlake, Victoria Wofford, Anita Fields, Elsie Conte, Barbara Parker, and Dawn Downing provided excellent assistance in the preparation of the manuscript. To each I extend my heartfelt appreciation.

CONTENTS

THE EMOTIONS
IN LIFE AND SCIENCE

This chapter will present material relating to two broad questions: What are the emotions and the processes that describe their activation and their functions? What is the place of the emotions in life and in science?

Is there a need to study the emotions? There is a wide range of scientific opinion regarding the nature and importance of the emotions. Some scientists (for example, Duffy, 1962) have maintained that emotion concepts are unnecessary for the science of behavior. She, as well as others (e.g., Lindsley, 1957), suggested that the concept of activation or arousal has more explanatory power and is less confusing than emotion concepts. Others (Tomkins, 1962, 1963; Izard, 1971, 1972) have maintained that the emotions constitute the primary motivational system of human beings. Some say that emotions are only transient phenomena while others maintain that people are always experiencing some emotion to some extent or that there is no action without affect (e.g., Schachtel, 1959). Some scientists have maintained that for the most part emotions disrupt and disorganize behavior, and are primarily a source of human problems (for example, Arnold, 1960a,b; Lazarus, 1968; Young, 1961). Others have argued that the emotions play an important role in organizing, motivating, and sustaining behavior (Rapaport, 1942; Leeper, 1948; Mowrer, 1960a; Tomkins, 1962, 1963; Schachtel, 1959: Izard, 1971, 1972).

Some scientists have taken the position that the emotions are primarily a matter of visceral functions, activities of organs innervated by the autonomic nervous system (Wenger, 1950). In 1974, the twenty-sixth International Congress of Physiological Sciences held in Baku, USSR, was entirely devoted to "Emotions and Visceral Functions" (Gasanov, 1974). Other scientists have emphasized the importance of the externally observable behavior of the face and the role of the somatic nervous system, the part of the nervous system generally considered to be under voluntary control (Gellhorn, 1964, 1970; Tomkins, 1962, 1963; Ekman, Friesen, & Ellsworth, 1972; Izard, 1971, 1972).

Most clinical psychologists and psychiatrists describe problems of adjustment and types of psychopathology as "emotional problems," as conditions in which the emotions have created a problem (e.g., Dunbar, 1954). On the other hand, Mowrer (1960b, 1961) maintains that it is not the emotions that are at fault in problems of adjustment and psychopathology, but the person's thoughts, attitudes, and actions.

Some have argued that the emotions should be subordinate to cognition (and reason) and have maintained that when they are not something is wrong. Others have held that the emotions trigger and guide cognitive processes (that they always influence reasoning) and that the more important questions relate to the quality and intensity of the emotions involved. Some maintain that we alleviate psychopathological problems and human problems in general by deconditioning or extinguishing inappropriate emotional responses or by bringing emotion under control. Others maintain that psychopathological and other human problems are best treated by freeing the emotions to interact naturally and easily with the other subsystems of the personality—homeostatic processes, drives, perceptions, cognitions, motor acts.

Psychologists, as well as philosophers and educators, vary in their opinions regarding the place of emotions in life and human affairs. Some say we are essentially rational beings—our "reasons for being" are primarily cognitive–intellectual. Witness our occupation as students for twelve to twenty or more years of life. For almost everyone in our society and in many other societies education continues from early childhood through the years of growth to maturity; and education is most widely considered as the process of learning facts and theories, the amassing of information. Other psychologists, however, despite their respect for cognitive–intellective activities and their own devotion to the accumulation of knowledge, feel that people are essentially emotional or emotional–social beings. They say that our "reasons for being" are affective or emotional in nature. They surround themselves with the people and things to which they are emotionally attached. They feel that learning through experiences (both private and social) is as important or more important than the acquisition of facts and theories.

The foregoing questions and issues will be touched on in a general way in the following sections of this chapter and in more detail in the remaining chapters of this book. The status of the science of emotions will not permit definitive resolution of these broad, philosophically oriented issues. The more modest aim of this book is to organize the material in the field of human emotions so that we can see the current status of these issues and perhaps increase the precision with which we articulate and study them. The book aims to present a systematic view of the emotions and their roles in consciousness, cognition, and action in the individual personality and in human relations.

My view is that the emotions constitute the primary motivational system for human beings. The underlying theory for this position, the differential emotions theory or the theory of differentiated affects, will be presented in detail in Chapter 3. Early statements of this position (Tomkins, 1962, 1963; Izard & Tomkins, 1966) were considered by some to represent an extremist view (e.g., Sarason, 1967), though some psychoanalytic thinkers had been discussing the importance of emotions as motivational phenomena for a long time (Abraham, 1911; Rado, 1928; Brierley, 1937).

Actually a similar view of the importance of the emotions in behavior and human life had been stated earlier by a leading personality theorist (Leeper, 1948) and by a prominent learning theorist (Mowrer, 1960a). Mowrer stated that "the emotions play a central role, indeed an indispensable role, in those changes in behavior or performance which are said to represent 'learning'" (Mowrer, 1960a, p. 307). Mowrer went on to decry the widespread tendency in Western civilization to look upon the emotions with distrust and contempt and to elevate the intellect (reason, logic) above them. "If the present analysis is sound, the emotions are of quite extraordinary importance in the total economy of living organisms and do not at all deserve being put into opposition with 'intelligence.' The emotions are, it seems, themselves a high order of intelligence" (Mowrer, 1960a, p. 308).

Mowrer, Tomkins, and the present writer, though differing in some particulars of theory, agree that it is experiential affect or, as Mowrer terms it, the inner subjective field, that provides the ongoing motivational state that modifies, controls, and directs behavior moment by moment. A growing number of theorists and investigators (e.g., Nowlis, 1965; Singer, 1973, 1975; Schwartz, Fair, Greenberg, Freedman, & Klerman, 1974; Ekman, 1972; Savitsky, Izard, Kotsch, & Christy, 1974) have contributed to our understanding of the motivational and adaptive significance of differentiated affects.

Even though opinions of scientists vary widely regarding the nature and significance of this field, the theoretical and research contributions of the past dozen years have established the emotions as a legitimate area of scientific inquiry. Despite the varying opinions of scientists, virtually all people (scientists included) readily admit that they experience joy and sadness and anger and fear, and that they know the difference between these emotions and the differences in how they feel and how they affect them. But how many people have reflected carefully on the basic questions? What really are the emotions? What are the processes by which they occur and influence us? How do they influence other aspects of our lives?

What Are Emotions?

Most of the questions raised in this chapter—including the present one, the definition of emotions—will concern us throughout this book. The aim of the present chapter is to present synoptic answers or comments, a general picture of the field.

How Is Emotion Defined? Most theories either explicitly or implicitly acknowledge that an emotion is not a simple phenomenon. It cannot be described completely by having a person describe his emotional experience. It cannot be described completely by electrophysiological measures of occurrences in the brain, the nervous system, or in the circulatory, respiratory, and glandular systems. It cannot be described completely by the expressive or motor behavior that occurs in emotion. A complete definition of emotion must take into account all three of these aspects or components: (a) the experience or conscious feeling of emotion, (b) the processes that occur in the brain and nervous system, and (c) the observable expressive patterns of emotion, particularly those on the face.

How Do Emotions Occur? Most people know what kind of conditions or situations interest them or disgust them or make them feel angry or guilty. Almost any middle-class person would experience interest on seeing a space walk by an astronaut, disgust on seeing feces on a needed toilet seat, anger on being crudely insulted, and guilt on shirking responsibility to loved ones. Thus in a general way people know what brings about a given emotion. However, scientists do not agree on precisely how an emotion comes about. Some maintain that emotion is a joint function of a physiologically arousing situation and the person's evaluation or appraisal of the situation. This explanation of the causal process comes from a cognitive theory of emotion (e.g., Schachter, 1971). Some cognitive theorists (e.g., Lazarus & Averill, 1972) describe appraisal as a rather elaborate set of cognitive processes (consisting of primary, secondary, and tertiary appraisal), while Arnold (1960a,b) describes appraisal as essentially an intuitive automatic process.

Considering the problem at the neurological level, Tomkins (1962) maintains that emotions are activated by changes in the density of neural stimulation (literally the number of neurons firing per unit of time). This rather persuasive theory does not say much about the causes or conditions at the conscious level that trigger these changes in neural stimulation. However, Tomkins's ideas as to what kinds of things can change the density or level of neural stimulation and activate emotion go well beyond the cognitive theorists' concept of appraisal. Tomkins states that changes in neural stimulation, and hence the activation of an emotion, can occur as a result of an innate releaser, a drive state, an image, or another emotion. Conceivably, any of these phenomena could activate an emotion without the occurrence of an appraisal process.

Both Tomkins and Izard (1971) have emphasized the important role that perception and cognition can play in initiating emotion, but they also emphasize the two-way interactions between cognition and emotion and the important effects that emotion can have on perception and cognition. The differences in the physiological-arousal–cognitive model and the neurosensory model of emotion activation have important implications for the science of emotions. For example, the former emphasizes the role of the autonomic nervous system and sympathetic arousal and characterizes emotion as primarily a reaction or response; in particular, a response that follows from cognitive processes. The neurosensory model emphasizes the somatic nervous system and electrocortical arousal and characterizes emotion as an organized process that has significant experiential and motivational characteristics. It emphasizes the importance of the effects of emotion on perception and cognition, while recognizing the reciprocal nature of emotion–perception and emotion–cognition interactions.

Are Emotions Transient or Stable Phenomena: Emotion States or Emotion Traits? Do emotions come and go or are they always with us? To what extent are emotions determined by the situations and conditions of the moment and to what extent are they stable characteristics of the individual? Since the work of Cattell and Scheier (1961) and Spielberger (1966), many investigators describe emotion phenomena as having two forms: state and trait. Application of this typology to the traditional concept of anxiety has provided the most widely known examples of this research. There has been a great deal of theorizing and research aimed at distinguishing the meanings and effects of "state anxiety" and "trait anxiety." The terms "state" and "trait" are distinguished primarily in terms of time, the duration of an emotion experience. It is also conceded that state emotion has a greater range of intensity than trait emotion. State and trait do not imply differences in the quality of the experience. In this book the term "emotion state" (e.g., anger state) will refer to a particular emotion process of limited duration. Emotion states may last from seconds to hours and vary widely in intensity (see Figure 1-1). In extraordinary conditions an emotion state of high intensity may continue for an extended period of time, but chronically intense emotion or frequent episodes of intense emotion may indicate psychopathology.

The term emotion trait (for example, anger trait) refers to the tendency of the individual to experience a particular emotion with frequency in his day-to-day life. A complementary concept is that of emotion threshold (Izard, 1971). If a person has a low threshold for guilt, he probably experiences guilt frequently and thus would score high on a measure of trait guilt. Later chapters will discuss the evidence and arguments relating to a number of emotion traits.

Are Emotions Innate or Learned? The early work of Darwin (1872, 1877) and the more recent work of Ekman *et al.* (1972) and Izard (1971) has

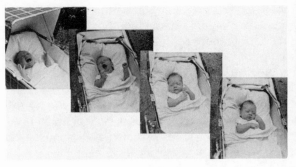

FIGURE 1-1. From distress, to joy and contented sleep in a seven-week-old infant girl in the span of a few seconds (left), and interpersonal interest that sustains a long conversation between two Uzbek men in Tashkent, Uzbekistan, U.S.S.R. (right).

shown that certain emotions, referred to in this book as fundamental emotions, have the same expressions and experiential qualities in widely different cultures from virtually every continent of the globe, including isolated preliterate cultures having had virtually no contact with Western civilization. The data presented in Tables 1-1 and 1-2 provide a sound basis for inferring that the fundamental emotions are subserved by innate neural programs. However, the fact that there are genetically based mechanisms for the fundamental emotions does not mean that no aspect of an emotion can be modified through experience. Almost anyone can learn to inhibit or modify the innate emotion expressions. While the innate expression of anger involves baring of the teeth as in preparation for biting, many people clinch their teeth and compress their lips as though to soften or disguise the expression. People of different social backgrounds and different cultures may learn quite different facial movements for modifying innate expressions. In addition to learning modifications of emotion expressions, socio-cultural influences and individual experiences play an important role in determining what will trigger an emotion and what a person will do as a result of emotion (see Figure 1-2).

As used in this book the terms "innate" and "learned" do not imply an absolute dichotomy. In the wake of the long standing controversy over the nature of intelligence or IQ, Murphy (1958) remarked that "nothing is innate, nothing is acquired." Most behavioral scientists tend to agree with Murphy in the sense that virtually any response or behavior pattern requires some practice or experience. Innate emotion expressions come as close as anything to being an exception to Murphy's rule. For example the prototypic distress expression (crying) appears at birth. The work of Dumas (1932, 1948), Fulcher (1942), Goodenough (1932), Thompson (1941),

TABLE 1-1

Percentage of Subjects Who Agreed on the Emotion Category of Photographs Selected to Represent Fundamental Emotions

	Cultural (national) group											
	American[a]	English[a]	German[a]	Swedish[a]	French[a]	Swiss[a]	Greek[a]	Japanese[a] (Tokyo)	Mexican[b]	Brazilian[c]	Chilean[c]	Argentinian[c]
N =	89	62	158	41	67	36	50	60	616	82	90	168
Interest–excitement	84.5	79.2	82.0	83.0	77.5	77.2	66.0	71.2				
Enjoyment–joy	96.8	96.2	98.2	96.5	94.5	97.0	93.5	93.8	97	97	90	94
Surprise–startle	90.5	81.0	85.5	81.0	84.2	85.5	80.2	79.2	54	82	88	93
Distress–anguish	74.0	74.5	67.2	71.5	70.5	70.0	54.5	66.8	61	83	90	85
Disgust–contempt	83.2	84.5	73.0	88.0	78.5	78.2	87.5	55.8	61	86	85	79
Anger–rage	89.2	81.5	83.2	82.2	91.5	91.8	80.0	56.8	86	82	76	72
Shame–humiliation	73.2	59.5	71.8	76.2	77.2	70.0	71.0	41.2				
Fear–terror	76.0	67.0	84.0	88.8	83.5	67.5	67.8	58.2	71	77	78	68
Average	83.4	77.9	80.6	83.4	82.2	79.6	75.1	65.4				

[a] From Izard, 1971.

[b] The Mexican data were obtained by Dickey and Knower (1941).

[c] The data from Brazil, Chile, and Argentina were obtained by Ekman and Friesen (1972). Ekman and Friesen also obtained data from a Japanese sample on the same six emotions they studied in South America, and they obtained somewhat higher percentages of agreement than those obtained by Izard.

TABLE 1-2

*Identification of Emotion Photographs from Orally Presented Emotion Stories
by Visually Isolated Preliterate Observers in New Guinea and Borneo* [a]

Emotion category described in the story	Percentage choice of the emotion expected in terms of agreement with the judgments of Western literate culture observers	
	Adults (N = 189)	Children (N = 130)
Happiness	92	92
Surprise	68	98
Sadness	79	81
Disgust	81	85
Anger	84	90
Fear		
Distinguished from anger/disgust	83	93
Sadness from surprise	43	—

[a]Table adapted from Ekman, Friesen, & Ellsworth, 1972, p. 161.

and Eibl-Eibesfeldt (1972) indicate that congenitally blind children express emotion in the same way as seeing children, although the expressions of the born-blind tend to deteriorate in quality with increasing age. The decrease in the quality of the expressions of the blind may be mainly a result of disuse, since changes in the expressive movements around the eyes are the most profound.

Is It Sufficient to Classify Emotions Simply as Positive or Negative? Scientists as well as laymen agree that there are both positive and negative emotions. While this very broad classification of emotions is generally correct and useful, the concepts of positiveness and negativeness as applied to the emotions require some qualification. Emotions such as anger, fear, and shame cannot be considered categorically negative or bad. Anger is sometimes positively correlated with survival, and more often with the defense and maintenance of personal integrity and the correction of social injustice. Fear is also correlated with survival and, together with shame, helps with the regulation of destructive aggression and the maintenance of social order. Unwarranted or overdetermined anger or fear usually has negative organismic and social consequences, but so may the emotion of joy if it is associated with derisive laughter or is combined with excitement and ulterior motives and becomes what Lorenz (1966) called "militant enthusiasm."

Instead of saying that emotions are simply positive or negative, it is more accurate to say that there are some emotions which tend to lead to psychological entropy, and others which tend to facilitate constructive behavior or the converse of entropy. Whether a given emotion is positive or negative in this sense depends on intra-individual and person–environment processes as well as on more general ethological and ecological considerations. For example, fear of certain elements in the environment (e.g., flying in airplanes, antibiotics, school) may have purely deleterious effects. The positive emotion of interest–excitement may play a role in activities as widely different as sexual assault and creative endeavor. Nevertheless, for convenience the terms positive and negative will be used to divide emotions into classes that are less likely and more likely, respectively, to have undesirable consequences.

How Do Emotions Affect Us?

The emotions affect people in many different ways. The same emotion has different effects on different people, even different effects on the same person in different situations. Emotion tends to affect all aspects of the individual, the whole person.

Emotions and the Body. Electrophysical changes occur in the muscles of the face during emotions (Rusolova, Izard, & Simonov, 1975; Schwartz,

FIGURE 1-2. A smile of joy on the face of a beautiful Indian girl working with an object (fresh cow dung) that might elicit disgust in Westerners. Her smile for the people who attracted her attention has an innate neural substrate, but her affective–cognitive responses to the object have their basis in her experience in a culture where handmade dung cakes are readily marketable as a fuel supplement.

Fair, Greenburg, Freedman, & Klerman, 1974). Changes occur in the electrical activity of the brain, in the circulatory system, and the respiratory system (Simonov, 1975). In strong anger or fear the heart rate may increase as much as 40 to 60 beats per minute (Rusolova *et al.* 1975). These dramatic changes in body functions during strong emotion suggest that virtually all of the neurophysiological systems and subsystems of the body are involved in greater or lesser degree in emotion states. Such changes inevitably affect the perceptions, thoughts, and actions of the person. These bodily changes may also contribute to medical and mental health problems. Emotion activates the autonomic nervous system, which changes the flow of glandular secretions and neurohumors. The mind and body are tuned for action. If the emotion-relevant cognitions and actions are blocked, psychosomatic symptoms may result (Dunbar, 1954).

Emotion and Perception. It has long been known that emotions as well as other motivational states influence perception. The joyful person is more likely to see the world through "rose-colored glasses." The distressed or sad individual is more likely to interpret others' remarks as critical. The fearful person is inclined only to see the frightening object (tunnel vision).

Emotion and Cognition. Just as an emotion affects body processes and the perceptual process, so too it affects the person's memory, thinking, and imagination. The "tunnel vision" effect in perception has a parallel in the realm of cognition. The frightened person has difficulty considering the whole field and examining various alternatives. In anger the person is inclined to have only "angry thoughts." In a high state of interest or excitement, the individual is curious, desirous of learning and exploring.

Emotions and Actions. The emotions or patterns of emotions that a person experiences at a given time influence virtually everything the person does—work, study, play. When really interested in a subject one is eager to study it and to pursue it in depth. If one is disgusted with a subject, one wants to reject it. Consider for a moment the difference in the educational experiences of students who are lucky enough to pursue mainly courses that interest and excite them and students who study primarily out of fear of failure and rejection.

Emotions and Personality Development. Two kinds of factors are important in considering emotion and personality development. The first is the person's genetic endowment in the sphere of the emotions. A person's genetic makeup probably plays an important role in establishing emotion traits or the thresholds for the various emotions. The second factor is the individual's experiences and learnings relating to the emotion sphere, in particular the way emotion expressions and emotion-related behavior are socialized. Observations of Russian infants (ages 6 months to 2 years) who were reared in the same social environment (an institution that provided a great deal of attention, warmth, affection, and educational opportunities) showed wide individual differences in emotion thresholds and emotion-related activities (Izard, Izard, & Makarenko, 1976). Anyone who doubts the significance of genetic influences on differences in emotion experiencing, emotion expression, and emotion responsivity, need only observe these children for a few hours.

However, when an infant has a low threshold for a particular emotion and experiences and expresses it frequently, this will inevitably lead to particular kinds of responses from other infants and from the surrounding adults. These interacting forces inevitably produce distinct and significant personality characteristics.

The individual's emotion traits also significantly influence social development, especially in infancy and childhood. The infant who has frequent temper tantrums, the one who frightens easily, and the one who oftens wears a smile, will each invite and receive different responses from peers and adults. Social interactions and hence social development will differ widely depending upon the emotions most frequently experienced and expressed by the infant. Emotional responsiveness not only affects personality characteristics and social development but intellectual development as well. The infant who is distressed much of the time will be much less inclined to explore and manipulate the environment than the child who has a low threshold for interest and enjoyment. Tomkins (1962) has maintained that the emotion of interest is as essential to intellectual development as exercise is to physical development.

Emotions and Sex. As early as 1935, Beach showed that copulation and fear are incompatible phenomena. His subjects were rats, but the fact that this generalizes to human beings is well established in clinical literature as well as by common sense. The sex drive virtually always interacts with some emotion. The sex drive interacting with anger and contempt may result in sadism or rape. The sex drive interacting with guilt may produce impotence or masochism. In love and marriage the sex drive can interact with excitement and joy and produce peak experiences of sensory pleasure and emotion.

Emotion, Marriage, and Parenthood. An individual's emotion expressiveness and responsitivity will be a factor in courtship and the selection of a partner in marriage. There is not much research evidence on the role of emotion traits in courtship and marriage, but research in other areas suggest that two kinds of factors may be operative. A person may select a mate whose emotion experiencing and expressiveness complements his or her own. Or an individual may select a mate who has a similar emotion profile—similar thresholds for experiencing and expressing the various emotions.

Just as the emotions affect sex life and marriage, so too do they affect parenthood. An individual's threshold for excitement, joy, disgust, or fear will play a significant role in his or her response to the child's interest, joy, disgust, or fear.

Do Emotions Alter Consciousness? Is emotion an altered state of consciousness? This question may have the ring of contemporaneity to the present day student, but the notion that an emotion may be considered as a separate or special state of consciousness is not a new one in science. The great nineteenth century biologist Herbert Spencer described "centrally initiated emotions" as follows: " . . . their beginnings and endings in time are comparatively indefinite, and they have no definite localizations in space. That is to say, they are not limited by preceding and succeeding states of consciousness with any precision; and no identifiable bounds are put to them by states of consciousness that co-exist" (Spencer, 1890, p. 172). Spencer's seminal idea did not have marked effects on the scientists of his day or those of the next seventy years. Beginning in the 1960s many lay people, especially young people, and a few scientists became interested in altered states of consciousness. These people generally have not considered emotion as an altered state of consciousness, nor have they described their experiences during altered states of consciousness in the language of discrete emotions. However, their descriptions often include discrete emotion concepts.

Our everyday language testifies to the reasonableness of considering an emotion state as an altered state, or perhaps more accurately, as a particular or special state of consciousness. An individual after doing something foolish often explains his or her behavior by saying, "I was not myself" or "I was out of my mind." Anyone who has experienced intense emotion realizes that this emotion experience is not one's ordinary state of consciousness.

The idea of distinctly different states of consciousness is evident in ancient Eastern thought. At least since the middle of the 19th century (e.g., Jackson, 1864), biological scientists have raised the possibility and presented some evidence for the notion that each of the separate hemispheres of the brain control a completely separate consciousness. A contemporary neurologist (Gazzaniga, 1967) concluded: "All the evidence indicates that separation of the hemispheres creates two independent spheres of consciousness within a single cranium, that is to say, within a single organism" (p. 100). He recognized that this conclusion would be disturbing to people who view consciousness as an indivisible property of the human brain.

Related to the notion that there may be more than one type or state of consciousness is the long-standing idea that there are many ways of knowing. In the 13th century Roger Bacon spoke of two modes of knowledge, one gained through argument, the other through experience. A number of contemporary scientists and philosophers (e.g., Ornstein, 1973; Tart, 1969:

Polanyi, 1958) speak of these different ways of knowing, these distinct types of knowledge. The kind that dominates in modern thought is typically described as logical and rational. The other type of knowing is described as intuitive, tacit knowing, or the receptive mode. Implicit, although not explicit, in the writing of these provocative thinkers is the notion that is presented here as a formal proposition. Special states of consciousness dominated by nonspecific interest or receptive joy, or some combination of these, set the stage for intuition, tacit knowing, and the receptive mode. Specific, focused emotion states set the stage for analytical, critical, logical, rational processes. It is proposed that certain nonspecific emotion states may be either directly identifiable with intuition or result in intuition with such immediacy as to preclude cognitive process in the usual sense of that term. One characteristic of emotion as a special state of consciousness that may be different from some other discrete or altered states of consciousness is the fact that emotion often, if not typically, co-exists with other states of consciousness. Consequently, emotion as a process continuously interacts with processes characteristic of other states of consciousness. A long time ago Spencer (1890) suggested that "only in those rare cases in which both its terms and its remote associations are absolutely indifferent, can an act of cognition be *absolutely* free from emotion" (Spencer, 1890, p. 474). Spencer also thought that no emotion was absolutely free from cognition. Spencer's main point seems valid; namely, that there are frequent and important interactions between emotion and cognition. The questions and issues raised in this section relating to emotion, special states of consciousness, and the different ways of knowing will be treated in greater detail in Chapter 6.

How Does the Field of Emotions Relate to Psychology and the Other Human Sciences?

The theory and research described in this book come from many different approaches and areas of investigation. The emotions constitute a truly interdisciplinary subject. The following paragraphs are only illustrative of the kinds of things that have been and can be contributed by the various branches of psychology and other life sciences.

Social Psychology. Social psychologists have made significant contributions to the study of the facial expression of emotion and to the topic of nonverbal communication, which often involves emotion communication (e.g., Ekman *et al.*, 1972; Mehrebian, 1972; Exline, 1972; Argyle, 1975). Eye contact, a form of nonverbal communication that definitely has emotion connotations, has been extensively studied by a number of social psychologists (e.g., Argyle & Dean, 1965; Kendon & Cook, 1969; Exline,

1972; Ellsworth & Ludwig, 1972; Ellsworth & Ross, 1974). Social psychologists (Berkowitz, 1969; Buss, 1971) have also made numerous contributions to the study of aggression and anger-related behavior. For example, they have demonstrated experimentally that anger may or may not be a factor in aggression.

Personality Theory and Research. As a general rule investigators in the field of personality have not studied the emotions in a direct and explicit fashion. Although their contributions are more indirect, they are in one respect quite significant. Many theorists and investigators in this field have made extensive studies of various motivational concepts—needs (Murray, 1938; McClelland, 1965), traits (Allport, 1961; Cattell, 1967), the self-concept (Combs & Snygg, 1959; Rogers, 1951; Fitts, 1971), self-control (Mischel, 1974). All of these motivational concepts have emotion connotations.

A few personality researchers have made significant contributions to the study of differentiated affects or moods. Nowlis (1965) developed a Mood Adjective Checklist (MACL) that measures several discrete moods or affective states. Nowlis and numerous others have used the MACL to study changes in affective states associated with drugs, stress, psychotherapy, and other phenomena affecting personality functioning. Other instruments for measuring affective states have been developed by Zuckerman (1960), Wessman and Ricks (1966), and Izard (1972), and some of the research utilizing them will be discussed later. Other personality investigators have shown that imagery-induced emotion has predictable effects on thought and action (e.g., Moore, Underwood, & Rosenhan, 1973).

Clinical Psychology and Psychiatry. Investigators in this area have made extensive contributions to the psychology of emotions, particularly in their studies of anxiety and depression. Many examples of the work on fear and anxiety can be found in Rachman (1974) and in the volumes edited by Spielberger (1966, 1972). Good examples of psychoanalytic contributions to the understanding of depression can be found in a volume edited by Galin (1968). A cognitive theory of depression and extensive research on the topic has been presented by Beck (1967). A number of these theorists and investigators specify fundamental emotions that are involved in anxiety or depression.

Recent research has shown the importance of nonverbal signals of emotion in psychotherapy. Haggard and Isaacs (1966) showed that patients in psychotherapy often express emotions on the face that may not be detected even by well-trained therapists who may be more keenly focused on the verbal communication. They found that the emotion expressed on the face sometimes contradicted what the patient was expressing with words. The work of Ekman and Friesen (1969) suggests that most therapists need special training in order to become efficient in "reading" the emotion messages of facial expression. Even facial expressions that can be readily recognized ("macro" expressions) often last less than a second. Micro expressions are much faster and often escape detection in ordinary interpersonal interactions.

Excellent analyses of the role of shame and guilt in healthy development and in psychopathology have been presented by Erikson (1956), Lewis (1971), Lynd (1961), and Tomkins (1963). Singer (1973, 1974) has related differentiated affect concepts to fantasy, imaginative play, and psychotherapy. Lazarus (1974) has considered the problem of ego defenses and other coping processes associated with negative emotions.

In her extensive review of psychogenically determined health problems, Dunbar (1954) cites numerous theorists and clinical investigators in support of the notion that "emotional factors" are involved in a wide variety of psychosomatic disorders. She argues that the interaction of personality factors and "emotional conflicts" contributes to the development of psychosomatic symptoms in the nervous system, cardiovascular system, respiratory system, gastrointestinal system, and virtually every other system of the body. Whether these problems are "caused" by the emotions or by the individual's thoughts and actions, as Mowrer maintains, there can be little doubt that the direct or indirect influences of the emotions on bodily functions are sometimes involved.

However, the cause of many of the psychosomatic symptoms can be attributed to hyperactivity, imbalance, or other malfunctioning of the autonomic nervous system, and this implicates undifferentiated arousal more than specific emotions. That the former may often be the source of the problem is consistent with the fact that undifferentiated arousal provides much less specific information for relevant thought and action than does a discrete emotion. The relatively more specific information from discrete emotions can be more readily processed and integrated in wholistic and effective personality functioning. Emotions and emotion-elicited autonomic nervous system activity are implicated in psychosomatic and other mental health problems when emotion-related cognitive and action tendencies are chronically blocked. Such is the case if one cannot clear one's conscience, resolve some frustration, or escape from a threatening situation and thus attenuate the guilt, anger, or fear.

Psychoanalysis. Psychoanalytic theory and practice, more than any other force, must be credited with making human motivation a concern of the behavioral sciences and professions. Freud (1938) conceptualized motivation in terms of drive, a combination of ideation and affect. While he had little to say about the role of differentiated affects (particularly the discrete emotions), some of his followers did (e.g., Rado, 1951; Schachtel, 1959). Schachtel revised the Freudian view of affects, placing emphasis on their organizing and constructive functions. He also attempted to relate affect to

perception, attention, memory, and action. Some contemporary psychoanalytic thinkers are making greater use of emotion concepts (Holt, 1970,
1976; Schafer, 1976), and one of them (Dahl, 1977) is developing a psychodynamic theory which treats emotions as fundamental motives in human
relationships.

Ethology. The studies of ethologists have contributed greatly to our
understanding of animal social behavior, including both prosocial and
aggressive activities. Some of the earlier ethological works made highly
interesting and provocative attempts to relate overt behavior to motivational mechanisms, including emotion mechanisms (Hinde, 1956; Tinbergen, 1951). The approach of contemporary ethologists (see Hinde, 1966)
excludes the use of motivational terms and emotion concepts and describes
behavior "objectively" in terms of body parts and motor patterns. "They
eschew inferential labels, such as 'threat face' and subjective adverbial
descriptions, such as 'frightened walking'" (McGrew, 1972, p. 19). Even
though they do not use emotion or motivational concepts in their descriptive analysis of behavior, their work continues to make significant contributions to the understanding of emotion and motivation. For example, instead
of describing a child as angry and aggressive (even a child who is beating on
another child) they describe the facial movements that constitute the anger
expression and the motor acts that constitute the aggression. Recent ethological studies of children such as those studies of McGrew and Blurton
Jones (1972) are rich resources that aid in the understanding of emotions
and emotion-related behavior in natural settings.

Neurology, Neurophysiology, Physiological Psychology. Some very
exciting and provocative findings are coming from research on brain and
emotion (e.g., Delgado, 1971; Simonov, 1975). Some of these studies are
pointing to the discovery of specific brain mechanisms that contribute to
emotion experiencing and emotion expression. However, one should be
cautious in evaluating the research reports that speak in terms of localized
emotion centers in the brain. A careful analysis of the research in this area
suggests that while there are certain specific brain mechanisms that contribute significantly (and more than certain other brain areas) to emotion, the
emotion process tends to involve many areas and systems within the brain.
It is possible that the whole brain participates in the emotion process, with
some mechanisms contributing more than others and playing different roles
in different emotions.

The work of Deglin (1973) suggests that the dominant and nondominant
hemispheres of the brain have different relationships to positive and negative emotions. The work of Papez (1937, 1951), MacLean (1954, 1968, 1970),
Arnold (1960a,b), Pribram (1970), and Simonov (1975) has made contributions to the understanding of the limbic system of the brain and the
relationship of its various mechanisms to the emotions. Schwartz and his

colleagues (e.g., Schwartz, Fair, Greenberg, Freedman, & Klerman, 1974) have launched a series of promising experiments on emotions and hemispheric functions and on the psychophysiology of "covert" expression (facial EMG activity). In the EMG studies, they have shown that even when gross changes are not readily observable in facial expression, EMG recordings from appropriately selected facial muscles differ for various fundamental emotions and between normal and depressed persons imaging a "typical day."

Biochemistry and Psychopharmacology. The more traditional contributions of biochemistry to the understanding of emotions and emotion-related behavior have been through the analysis of hormones, neurohumors, and the effects of these upon the individual's behavior. The contributions of some investigators in this area have been directly related to the emotions. For example, Gellhorn (1965) summarized evidence from a number of studies that showed that experimentally induced fear, in which no attempt is made to escape the situation, increased epinephrine without changing the norepinephrine level. A number of investigators (Wehmer, 1966; Brady, 1970) have shown that fear or "anxiety" is accompanied by marked changes in corticosteroid (17-OH-CS) level in the blood. The student interested in the biochemistry of depression is referred to the works of Schildkraut, Davis, and Klerman (1968), Kety (1970), Davis (1970), Sutherland (1970), and Cohn, Dunner, and Axelrod (1970). Some of the works of these and other investigators have been summarized by Izard (1972). In his view the most important contribution of biochemical changes to the emotion process is through their effect on sustaining a given emotion or combination of emotions over time.

Summary

The present book emphasizes the study of specific or discrete emotions and their interrelationships (emotion system), and the interaction of emotions with other subsystems of the personality. A complete definition of emotion must take into account neural, expressive, and experiential components. The emotions occur as a result of changes in the nervous system and these changes may be brought about by either internal or external events. Intense emotion states have captured the attention of scientists and nonscientists alike, but the science of emotions must go beyond the study of transient states. There are stable individual differences in the frequency with which people experience the various emotions, and these differences may be studied in terms of emotion traits or emotion thresholds.

Robust cross-cultural evidence supports Darwin's century-old thesis that the emotions as intraindividual processes are innate and universal.

This means that the emotions have innately stored neural programs, universally understood expressions, and common experiential qualities.

It is convenient to classify emotions as either positive or negative on the basis of their sensory/experiential characteristics. However, any emotion (e.g., joy, fear) may be positive or negative if the criteria for classification are based on the adaptiveness or dysadaptiveness of the emotion in a particular situation. Extreme excitement can create problems in a sexual realtionship, and joy over another's suffering can lead to sadism.

Emotions affect the whole person and each emotion affects the person differently. Emotion affects the level of electrical activity in the brain, the amount of tension in the muscles of the face and body, the visceral–glandular system, circulatory system, and the respiratory system. Changes in emotions can alter the appearance of our world from bright and cheerful to dark and gloomy, our thinking from creative to morbid, and our actions from awkward and inappropriate to skillful and effective.

Infants' individual differences in thresholds for the various emotions change the frequency with which they express these emotions, and this greatly influences the responses they invite from those around them. In turn the way others respond to the emotion expressions of infants and children will influence their expressive style and hence their personalities.

Emotion can be considered as an altered or special state of consciousness. Emotion may exist relatively independently of other states of consciousness but ordinarily interacts with and influences other co-existing states or processes in consciousness.

The field of emotions is a complex and interdisciplinary one. Social psychology contributes to the study of emotion as nonverbal communication. Personality psychology has suggested ways in which emotions may related to other motivational constructs such as the self-concept and psychological needs and has increased our knowledge of affective states and personality functioning. Clinical psychology and psychiatry have contributed to our understanding of the role of certain complex combinations of emotions in psychopathology and to our understanding of the need to deal with emotions in psychotherapy. The neurosciences have increased our knowledge of the role of various brain mechanisms in emotion, and biochemistry and psychopharmacology have shown the importance of hormones and neurohumors in emotion processes and emotion-related behavior.

THEORIES OF EMOTION AND EMOTION–BEHAVIOR RELATIONSHIPS

Although McDougall's theory (1908) linked emotions and ''conation'' and his work and Freud's (1938) laid the groundwork for relating emotions, motivations, and behavior, one of the persistent problems in the human sciences is that most theories of personality, theories of behavior, and theories of emotion have been created independently of each other. The majority of personality theories have typically not concerned themselves with the problem of emotion. Most personality theorists make use of one or more concepts of motivation, but they have very infrequently made use of discrete emotion concepts as motivational variables. On the other hand, investigators in the field of emotions have typically been concerned with one or more components of the emotion process—its neurophysiology, its expression, or its phenomenology—and with only a few exceptions (e.g., Tomkins, 1962, 1963), they have done little to relate their findings to personality or the behavior of the organism as a whole. This chapter will consider some of the major approaches to the study of emotion and discuss where possible the relevance of a given approach to the study of other functions of the organism or to personality as a whole.

Psychoanalytic Conceptions of Affect and Motivation

Freud (1930, 1936, 1938) and psychoanalytic theory occupy a special place in the history of psychology and behavioral sciences for many reasons—heuristic conceptions of the unconscious, dream dynamics, conscience development, defense mechanisms, repression, regression, resistance, transference, infantile sexuality, consciousness. The reason most relevant to this chapter, however, is Freud's pioneering analysis of personality functioning that opened up the field of human motivation, made it a significant part of modern psychology and launched the psychodynamic tradition (Boring, 1950). Of greatest interest here is Freud's conception of affects, but these must be viewed in the context of his more general theory of motivation.

The core of the classical psychoanalytical theory of motivation is Freud's theory of instinctual drives. As in other areas of psychoanalysis, Freud developed and changed his ideas in this realm several times. An accurate and systematic synthesis is difficult, and even Freudian scholars do not always develop the same picture. Rapaport's (1960) integrative summary is perhaps the most widely accepted, and it is the principal source for the following synopsis.

Rapaport cautions his readers to beware of the exaggerated claims and often overlooked limitations of the explanatory power of instinctual drives. For example, instinctual drives do not explain a range of behaviors, such as defenses and cognitive synthesis and differentiation, that are determined by the ego. Nor do they explain the role of external stimulation in behavior or functions of consciousness that result from attention cathexes relating to external stimuli. The determinants of such behaviors, however, are "causal" rather than "motivational," in the psychoanalytic sense of these terms.

An instinctual drive or motive is defined by Rapaport as an appetitive internal or intrapsychic force that is (a) peremptory, (b) cyclic, (c) selective, and (d) displaceable. These characteristics define the appetitive nature of drives or motives and help distinguish them from "causes," but some instances of this distinction appear arbitrary. For example, some "reasons" and "willings" are said to be motives or rationalizations of motives with all the aforesaid defining characteristics while other "reasons" or "rule-followings" are not motives because they lack displaceability or cyclicity. Further, curiosity and exploratory behaviors are a function of causes (not motives) since their determinants (largely external) do not show cyclicity, selectivity, and displaceability.

Rapaport maintains that the four defining characteristics of the appetitive nature of instinctual drives are continuous dimensions rather than dichotomous categories. Thus drives vary in the extent to which they are peremptory, cyclic, selective, and displaceable. Instinctual drives have four other defining characteristics: (a) pressure, or the amount of force and demand for work it represents, (b) aim, or discharge of energy that results in satisfaction, (c) object, or that which makes satisfaction possible, and (d) source, or underlying somatic process.

It is difficult to present a consistent treatment of affect in terms of classical psychoanalytic theory since Freud and his followers used the term rather loosely and prescribed different roles for it as the theory developed. In his early work Freud thought affect or emotion was the only driving force in mental life, and at various times in his later writings he "still spoke of affects or emotions as the intrapsychic factors which give rise to fantasies, wishes, and symptoms" (Rapaport, 1960, p. 191). Although the term affect was largely replaced by the concept of energy or cathexis, the standard psychoanalytic view is that an instinctual drive is represented in mental life as both idea and affect and both the idea and the affect are considered peremptory.

After reviewing psychoanalytic and other contributions, Rapaport reached the following conclusion:

> Of the various theories, the following theory of the mechanism of emotions emerges as not conflicting with known facts: an incoming percept initiates an unconscious process which mobilizes unconscious instinctual energies; if no free pathway of activity is open for these energies—and this is the case when instinctual demands conflict—they find discharge through channels other than voluntary motility; these discharge-processes—"emotional expression," and "emotion felt"—may occur simultaneously or may succeed one another, or either may occur alone; as in our culture open pathways for instincts are rare, emotional discharges of varying intensity constantly occur; thus in our psychic life, besides the "genuine" emotions described in textbooks—rage, fear, and so on—an entire hierarchy of emotions exists, ranging from the most intense to mild, conventionalized, intellectualized emotions. (Rapaport, 1961, p. 37)

The psychoanalytic literature distinguishes, though does not use consistently, three aspects of affect—the energy component of the instinctual drive representation ("charge of affect"), the discharge process, and perception of the final discharge (feeling or felt emotion). The discharge and feeling components are considered merely expressions, the communicative value of which was not generally recognized in psychoanalysis until the work of Schachtel (1959). However, Rapaport (1953) had noted that "affect as signals are just as indispensable a means of reality-testing as thoughts" (Rapaport, 1953, p. 196). The affect charge corresponds to the quantitative or intensity dimension of affect and the discharge processes are perceived or felt in qualitatively different tones.

Freudian theory and psychoanalysis in general are concerned primarily with negative affects arising from conflict, hence the prominent role of repression as a defense mechanism. Since affects are by their nature phenomena of consciousness, they are not subject to repression. Only the ideational aspect of an instinctual drive can be denied entry into consciousness. When repression is successful, there is a separation of the ideational and affective components of drive such that the instinct representations are denied their preconscious cathexes and their associated verbal images. In short the instinctual drive or motive can no longer be symbolized semantically. Repression thus may prevent conflict at one level (e.g., between libidinal interest and superego sanction) at the risk of neurotic or psychosomatic symptom formation at another. If repression fails, conflict occurs between the unconscious and preconscious systems and a qualitiatively distinct and symbolizable affect may emerge in consciousness. Since this affect is negative and associated with conflict-related ideation, it can constrict ego functions and contribute to mental health problems.

Freud's concept of motive as an ideational–affective representation in consciousness bears at least phenotypical similarity to the differential emotions theory concepts of ideo-affective organization (Tomkins, 1962, 1963) and affective–cognitive structure (Izard, 1971, 1972). These latter concepts will be discussed in more detail in Chapter 3, but it should be noted here that they are conceived not as representations of instinctual drives but as the structures or orientations of consciousness that result from the interaction of emotion (the primary motivational condition) and cognition.

Another Freudian notion, the wish or wish impulse, bears an even closer resemblance to the concept of affective–cognitive structure. Freud first discussed the wish ("craving fulfillment") as the motive power of the dream. In the unconscious the wish impulse is an instinctual demand and in the preconscious it becomes a dream-wish or wishfilling fantasy. "The wish, the affective organizing principle, uses the mechanisms of condensation, displacement, symbolism, and secondary elaboration to express itself—that is the latent content of the dream—in a form acceptable to consciousness" (Rapaport, 1961, p. 164). A difference between the Freudian wish impulse and the differential emotions theory concept of affective–cognitive structure is that the latter sees the affects rather than the ideational processes as the organizing principles. Both theories agree that some kind of combination or bond of affect and cognition constitutes a significant factor in human motivation.

A number of contemporary psychoanalytic theorists have presented modifications or alternatives to the Freudian conception of affects. Schachtel (1959) saw the limitations of Freud's negative view of affects and emphasized their organizing and constructive functions. He also disagreed with Freud's tendency to see affect and action on the outer world as mutually exclusive. "I believe there is no action without affect, to be sure not always an intense, dramatic affect as in an action of impulsive rage, but more usually a total, sometimes quite marked, sometimes very subtle and hardly noticeable mood, which nevertheless constitutes an essential background of every action" (Schachtel, 1959, p. 20). As already noted, Schachtel also attributed to affects a "tremendous role in communication" and thus a significant influence in social interactions. These conceptualizations of affect are not inconsistent with differential emotions theory.

Schachtel distinguished between embeddedness-affects and activity-affects. The former correspond to the negative affects as described by Freud, those arising out of conflict or frustration and characterized by helpless distress. Hope and "magic" joy (see Chapter 10) are also embeddedness-affects. Embeddedness-affect may occur in the hungry infant who can not obtain nourishment or in the depressed adult who loses interest in the surrounding world. Activity-affects are characterized by zestfulness, interested feeling tones, and positive tension. Activity-affects appear in the attentive looking of the infant and in the creative activities of adults. Schachtel's activity affects overlap conceptually with the positive emotions—interest, joy—of differential emotions theory.

Schachtel also distingushes between subject-centered or autocentric perception and object-centered or allocentric perception. In autocentric perception the emphasis is on how and what the perceiver feels. There is little or no objectification (subject–object independence); the perceiver is merely reacting to the object with pleasure or unpleasure rather than actively engaging it. The autocentric perceptual mode is the characteristic one for the "lower" senses of taste, smell, touch, pain, and proprioception. In classifying proprioception as autocentric, Schachtel implicitly raises the question of the autocentricity of emotion activation, since some theories hold that emotions are activated and differentiated through proprioceptive (facial) feedback. He unequivocally indicates that some affective experiences (e.g., sex, pain, disgust) are autocentric and thus characterized by pleasure–unpleasure boundedness, lack of objectification, and relatively greater environmental control.

In the allocentric mode the perceiver actively examines the object and "figuratively or literally, takes hold of it, tries to 'grasp' it" (1959, p. 83). Allocentricity is characteristic of the "higher" senses of sight and hearing. He views interest (which he calls an attitude rather than an affect) as allocentric. Developmentally, the shift from the autocentric to the allocentric mode of perception parallels the change from embeddedness–affects to activity–affects. Aside from the influence of ontogenetic factors, intense negative affects (associated with the struggle to separate from embeddedness or uterine-like security) interfere with allocentric perception, while positive affects tend to facilitate it. Schachtel's conception of the allocentric attitude as one of profound interest that leads to focal attention, active involvement in the environment, and creativity will be discussed in later chapters.

Schachtel notes that affect expression not only plays an important role in interpersonal communication but also in the individual's shift from embeddedness–affect to allocentric affect. His idea that changes in emotion involve changes in facial expression, posture, and muscle tone is reminiscent of Bull's (1951) hypothesis that emotion follows from changes in "involuntary motor attitude, maintained as readiness or wish" (pp. 5–6). Bull's theory, however, like Freud's and Rapaport's, is a conflict theory of emotion, while Schachtel sees positive emotions arising in nonconflict situations and motivating adaptive, even creative, action.

The move of a number of contemporary psychoanalytic thinkers away from the mechanistic, instinctual drive theory presented by Freud and systematized by Rapaport received considerable impetus from the work of Klein (1967; 1976). He developed the concept of peremptory ideation, maintaining that an affect once experienced tends to acquire meaning that goes beyond sensory pleasure or unpleasure. For example, a sensual experience is "etched in memory and concept." It becomes associated with positive and negative values and is "recorded in a cognitive structure or schema whose activation ever after helps shape sensual experience" (Klein, 1976, p. 26). The cognitive matrix of an affect becomes an important part of the "driving force" or motivation underlying behavior. The sequence of events in a "cognitive unit of motivation" occurs in a closed feedback loop that begins with a "primary region of imbalance" (PRI) (in a particular brain area) that facilitates relevant thought, affect, and action. Apparently some combination or interaction of affect and cognition is experienced as a specific desire, gratification of which provides the feedback that switches off the PRI. Klein proposed, in effect, that affect becomes embedded in a cognitive framework, resulting in peremptory, motivational ideation. In contrast to the Freudian drive-discharge, and ($s-r$ tension-reduction) model, Klein's approach allows for tension-seeking and tension-maintaining behavior. Thus Klein abandoned the Freudian concept of sex as an instinctual drive ("a linear force impelling itself against a barrier") and viewed it as appetitive activity within a set of cognitive structures or motivational meanings.

In his forthright rejection of instinctual drive theory, Holt (1976) develops a convincing conceptualization of affect and motivation. He places emphasis on the importance of external stimulation and perceptual–cognitive processes, but he also recognizes the significance of the experiential and expressive phenomena of the emotions.

Holt (1967), along with Kubie (1974), Rubinstein (1967), Peterfreund (1971) and others, holds that the concept of instinctual drive as psychic energy or appetitive internal force is completely without supporting evidence. He maintains that while sex, aggression, fear, or other affective phenomena may be innately determined ("though extensively modifiable") reactions, their arousal is largely dependent on awareness of external (sometimes limited or special classes of) *press*—the motivationally relevant aspects of a person's environment (Murray, 1938), defined in terms of consensually established meanings.

In moving toward a new theory of motivation, Holt (1976) builds on the early Freudian notion of *wish* and interprets it as "a cognitive–affective concept, framed in terms of meanings and potentially pleasant or unpleasant outcomes of possible courses of action" (p. 179). He sees his interpretation as closely related to Klein's model, but he replaces the PRI by "perceptual–evaluative mismatch." A mismatch is explained as a conscious, preconscious, or unconscious comparison of a perceptual (input) and a centrally generated pattern *and* a comparison of the value judgments attached to the two patterns. Phenomenologically this amounts to a comparison between an existing and a potential state of affairs, a process similar to the appraisal, monitoring, and evaluative processes discussed in the cognitively oriented theories of emotion (Arnold, 1960a; Lazarus, 1974; Pribram, 1970; Schachter, 1971). Thus a wish—the key motivational phenomenon—is initiated by a mismatch, "a cognitive–affective state something like dissatisfaction" (Holt, 1976, p. 182). A moderate degree of mismatch arouses mild pleasure and interest, while an extensive and sudden mismatch arouses startle and unpleasure. Holt's notion that different degrees of mismatch arouse different affects is similar to Singer's (1974) attempt to account for differential affect activation in terms of differential success in the assimilation of cognitive information. Both ideas bear some relationship to Tomkins's (1962) principle of density of neural stimulation, which will be discussed in later chapters. The mismatch may arise in the face of opportunity (and have positive implications) or in the face of threat (and have negative implications); and so to Klein's model, which is limited to negative feedback systems, Holt adds positive feedback systems, which are not regulated by "discharge" or "switch-off" mechanisms.

Holt's model assumes that people have biologically (innately determined) differences in readiness toward positive or negative evaluation and toward relevant (escape or coping) actions in the face of frustration or threat. Such inborn readiness is related to hormones and neurohumors that influence sex, aggression, and other affect-related phenomena. Although Holt characterizes his model as "protoneurophysiological," eventually translatable into anatomical and physiological language, it is, at present, described mainly at the phenomenological level. Units are defined primarily in terms of meanings and the key motivational concept—the wish—is a cognitive–affective structure and the affective component of this structure is strictly a phenomenon of consciousness. Although Holt's model has some features similar to the cognitive theories of emotion discussed in a later section, it also has important parallels with differential emotions theory (Chapter 3, this volume). For example, Holt recognizes the existence of discrete emotions and their contributions to motivation. His concept of wish as a cognitive–affective structure is similar to differential emotions theory concepts of ideo-affective organization (Tomkins, 1962) and emotion–cognition interaction or affective–cognitive orientation (Izard, 1971; Chapter 3, this volume). Holt and differential emotions theory are also in accord in recognizing the significance of emotion expression in social and clinical interactions.

Dahl (1977) is developing a theory of motivation that promises to make discrete emotion concepts a significant part of psychoanalytic thought. He agrees with Holt on the inadequacy of instinctual drive theory and conceives emotions as "fundamental motives" in human relationships. He renounces the efficacy of pleasure (drive reduction or decrease in quantity of tension) as an explanation of behavior and proposes that pleasure be redefined as satisfaction of a wish (as Holt defined this term) and unpleasure as nonsatisfaction of a wish. Dahl maintains that tieing pleasure–unpleasure to wish satisfaction calls for a look at the "qualitative characteristics of the experience of satisfaction and focuses our attention on the perceptual process." Qualitative characteristics are added by the perception (felt experience) of discrete emotions.

Dahl divides emotions into two classes, those that take objects (IT emotions) and those that do not (ME emotions). IT emotions are three-part phenomena consisting of (a) a distinctive perception (felt experience), (b) a wish, and (c) an expression (facial, gestural motor patterns, some of which are considered species-specific). The wish component may represent attraction to the object (love), repulsion to it (anger), attraction from it (surprise), or repulsion from it (fear). Negative ME emotions include anxiety and depression and positive ME emotions include eagerness and hopefulness. Both IT and ME emotions are considered as appetites, with appetitiveness characterized, according to Rapaport (1960), as peremptory, selective, displaceable, and in some cases cyclic. Thus it seems that in Dahl's system emotions take on essential characteristics of Freudian instinctual drives and require satisfaction in analogous fashion: escape from a fear-producing situation is to fear as eating is to hunger and as orgasm is to sex.

Dahl continues his description of emotions with a list of properties assembled by de Rivera (1962), some of which are consistent with cognitive theories of emotions discussed in the following sections and some with the differential emotions theory presented in Chapter 3. One important difference between Dahl's approach and differential emotions theory lies in Dahl's analogy between drives and emotions. These and other differences will become evident later. Nevertheless, Dahl's treatment of emotions as fundamental motivational processes rooted in phylogenetic adaptedness represents a significant possibility for interaction between some of the clinically derived observations of psychoanalysis and contemporary motivational theories of emotion.

The Dimensional Approach: Arousal, Activation, and Dimensions of Emotion and Behavior

Spencer (1890) was one of the early scientists to conceptualize emotions or feelings as dimensions or states of consciousness, and hence as dimensions of personality and behavior. Wundt (1896) extended the Spencerian tradition and proposed that the sphere of consciousness described by emotion or feeling could be accounted for by three dimensions: pleasantness–unpleasantness, relaxation–tension, and calm–excitement. As will be described below, Wundt's dimensions were revived by Woodworth (1938) and Schlosberg (1941) and their colleagues in a long line of successful research on the dimensions of emotion expression.

Emotion as Organismic Arousal. Building on the conceptions of Spencer and Wundt, Duffy (1934, 1941, 1951, 1962) proposed that all behavior can be explained in terms of a single phenomenon, organismic arousal, a concept having apparent similarity to Wundt's dimension of relaxation–tension. Duffy (1962) maintained that behavior varies in only two dimensions, direction and intensity. She defined direction in terms of selectivity of response, a selectivity based on the expectancies and goal-orientation of the organism and the relationships among the perceived stimuli. An individual goes toward or away from a situation depending on its incentive value or threat value. She considered her concept of directionality or "response to relationships" to be the same as Tolman's (1932) "cognitive maps" and Hebb's (1955) "cue functions."

Intensity was defined as general organismic arousal or energy mobilization, and level of arousal "as the extent of release of potential energy, stored in the tissues of the organism, as this is shown in activity or response" (Duffy, 1962, p. 17). According to Duffy, emotion is simply a point or range of points toward the high end of the arousal dimension. Hence emotion as such can vary only in intensity, there being no allowance for discrete types of emotion experience.

Duffy's ideas were among the influential forces that tended to exclude emotion concepts from psychological theory and research in the first half of the twentieth century. However, her conceptions helped to pave the way for activation theory which in turn helped facilitate the currently blossoming area of brain–behavior research. In recent years investigators in the latter group have initiated important lines of investigation on brain–emotion relationships.

Neural Activation, Emotion, and Behavior. Following Moruzzi and Magoun's discovery of certain functions of the brain stem reticular formation, Lindsley (1951, 1957) developed his activation theory of emotion and behavior. His theoretical formulation attempted to replace Duffy's (1962) broad and difficult-to-measure concept of organismic arousal with a concept of activation, defined as neural excitation of the brain stem reticular formation and concomitant changes in electroencephalographic patterns in the cortex. His explanation of emotion presupposes antecedent emotion stimuli, either external and conditioned or internal and unconditioned. Such stimuli initiate impulses activating the brain stem which, in turn, sends impulses to the thalamus and cortex. A hypothetical activating mechanism transforms these impulses into behavior characterized by "emotional excitement" and into cortical EEG patterns characterized by low amplitude, high frequency, and asynchrony.

When impulses initiated by a reduction of emotional stimuli influence the thalamus directly, synchronized, high-amplitude, low-frequency EEG patterns may be established. Under these conditions, Lindsley predicts observable behavior opposite to that seen in "emotional excitement": namely, "emotional apathy." Lindsley acknowledged that his theory could not elucidate the nature of discrete emotions. His primary concern was with the relationship between certain antecedent conditions, changes in electrical activity of the brain (as measured by the EEG), and observed behavior.

Dimensions of Emotion Expression. Since Darwin published his famous work on *The Expression of the Emotions in Man and Animals* in 1872, the complex field of facial expression of emotion has been treated by some investigators as virtually a discipline unto itself. Some of these workers made invaluable contributions to the analysis and understanding of facial expression but often did not integrate their important findings into the psychology of personality and social behavior.

The approach to the study of facial expressions with which we are concerned here was initiated when Woodworth (1938) proposed the first really successful system for classifying the facial expressions of discrete emotions. He showed that many different facial expressions could be reliably categorized by use of the following six-step linear scale: (1) love, happiness, mirth; (2) surprise; (3) fear, suffering; (4) anger, determination; (5) disgust; (6) contempt.

After applying the Woodworth classification scheme to various series of photographs of facial expressions, Schlosberg (1941) proposed that facial expressions could be more adequately described by considering the Woodworth scale as a circular surface with two axes or dimensions: pleasantness–unpleasantness (P–U) and attention–rejection (A–R). Later Schlosberg added a third dimension, sleep–tension, and thus came very close to adopting and verifying empirically the usefulness of the three dimensions of feeling originally proposed by Wundt in 1896.

Schlosberg's approach was similar to that in a psychophysical experiment where judgments are based on physical dimensions. His instructions required subjects to make their ratings on the basis of observable physical characteristics of the photographed expressions. In his earlier experiments

Schlosberg had his subjects rate each photograph of a facial expression on two nine-point scales: pleasantness–unpleasantness and acceptance–rejection.

For each picture, the average rating was computed for each dimension. With P–U and A–R scales represented by perpendicular lines intersecting at scale point 5, the circular surface can be represented by a circle connecting the ends of the P–U and A–R axes. Any given picture (expression) can be represented as a point on the space within a quadrant of the circle. By drawing a line from the origin (intersection of P–U and A–R) through the plotted point to the rim of the circle, one can determine the circular scale value and the emotion category of the particular expression (see Figure 2-1). The correlation between the circular scale values obtained via the

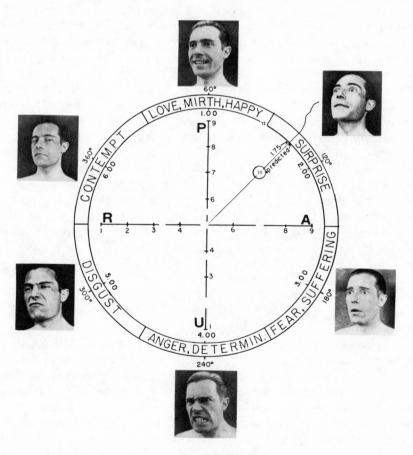

FIGURE 2-1. Predicting emotion categories from ratings on the dimensions of pleasantness–unpleasantness and acceptance–rejection. (Adapted from Woodworth & Schlosberg, 1954.)

category sorting technique and those determined or predicted by the dimensional ratings was .76. Thus facial expressions as represented in still photographs can be relatively accurately classified into discrete emotion categories on the basis of the P–U and A–R dimensional ratings.

Schlosberg and his colleagues (Engen, Levy, & Schlosberg, 1958) added the dimension of sleep–tension (S–T) because they became impressed by the work of Duffy and Lindsley and with evidence suggesting that a dimension of "activation" was important in emotion. With a specially developed series of facial expressions (the Lightfoot series) they demonstrated test–retest reliabilities of .94, .87, and .92 ($N = 225$) for the P–U, A–R, and S–T dimensions respectively. Triandis and Lambert (1958) applied Schlosberg's three dimensions in a cross-cultural study and showed that they were as valid for Greek subjects as for Americans. However, later investigators (e.g., Abelson & Sermat, 1962; Ekman, 1964) showed that the acceptance–rejection and sleep–tension dimensions were highly correlated (thus not independent dimensions) and raised the question of their meaningfulness as separate dimensions of emotion expression. Several other investigators made contributions to the dimensional approach to the study of facial expressions and emotion (Hofstatter, 1955–1956; Izard & Nunnally, 1965; Plutchik, 1962). Some of this research led to the development of new dimensions, such as control or deliberative–impulsive (Osgood, 1966), attention–inattention (Frijda & Phillipszoon, 1963), and self-assured–insecure (Frijda, 1970).

Osgood's extensive analysis of live expressions yielded three dimensions which he interpreted in terms of his semantic dimensions of linguistic signs. He concluded that his expression dimensions of pleasantness, activation, and control correspond to the semantic dimensions of evaluation, activity, and potency. Osgood's interpretation may be an important one for students of emotion–cognition interactions.

Cognitive Theories of Emotion and Personality

At least two broad classes of theories may be classified as cognitive: Self-theories and theories that view cognition as a cause or component of emotion. The central and overriding variable in self-theory is the self-concept. The individual's perceptions of and cognitions about the self as organized in the wholistic and integral phenomenon called the self-concept is given extensive explanatory powers (Snygg & Combs, 1949; Rogers, 1951; Combs & Snygg, 1959). For these theorists, behavior is a function of perception, in particular the perception of self.

Self-Theory, Feeling, and Emotion. The more the perception or cognition relates to the center or core of the self, the more likely it is to involve feeling or emotion. When the self-concept is attacked the individual becomes fearful and defensive; when the self-concept is accepted and approved the individual is likely to feel interested and joyful.

Self-theories consistently emphasize the importance of the "feeling content" as opposed to the strictly semantic content of the verbal expressions of the individual. They hold that it is particularly important for psychotherapists to understand and respond in terms of this principle when treating individuals with psychological problems. A similar principle has been adopted by several current approaches to psychotherapy and personal growth (e.g., T-groups, encounter groups, gestalt therapy). The impressive volume of research in the framework of self-theory deals with emotion or feeling in general terms and seldom makes use of discrete-emotion concepts.

Emotion as a Function of Cognition. Several contemporary theories treat emotion essentially as response or as a complex of responses determined by cognitive processes. These theories seem to have stemmed from some pervasive ideas about human nature that can be traced through Aristotle, Thomas Aquinas, Diderot, Kant, and other philosophers, and are deeply rooted in Western civilization. These ideas are: (a) man is first and foremost a rational being; (b) rationality is basically good, emotionality basically bad; (c) reason (cognitive processes) should be used as a control and as a substitute for emotion.

The most senior and comprehensive theory of emotion and personality in this influential tradition is that of Arnold (1960a,b). For Arnold, emotion results from a sequence of events described by the concepts of perception and appraisal.

Arnold used the term perception to mean "simple apprehension of an object." To apprehend something is to know what it is like as an object, independent of any effect on the perceiver. Before emotion can enter into the picture, the object must be perceived and appraised as having an effect on the perceiver. Emotion is distinct from appraisal, though it may include it as an integral or necessary part. To be precise, the emotion proper is the nonrational attraction or repulsion which follows upon the appraisal of something as good or bad for the perceiver.

These rather fine distinctions between emotion, perception, and appraisal were maintained despite the fact that the appraisal itself was characterized as direct, immediate, and intuitive. Appraisal is not the result of reflection or deliberation, but is almost as direct as perception. It immediately follows and completes perception and can be recognized as a separate process only upon reflection.

The sequence perception—appraisal—emotion is so closely knit that our every-day experience is never the strictly objective knowledge of a thing; it is always a knowing-and-liking, or a knowing-and-disliking . . . The intuitive appraisal of the situation initiates an action tendency that is felt as emotion, expressed in various bodily changes, and that eventually may lead to overt action. (Arnold, 1960a, p. 177)

Emotion has important residual or continuing effects. The action tendencies which follow an emotion organize and bias later perception and appraisal; the emotion "fascinates us and takes us captive" (Arnold, 1960a, p. 182). Further, the intuitive appraisal and emotion response tend to have constancy, so that the object or situation so appraised and responded to tends to evoke this appraisal and response "for all times to come" (Arnold, 1960a, p. 184). In addition, appraisal and emotion response to a given object tend to be generalized to the whole class of objects.

Arnold drew several distinctions between emotion and other motivational concepts. She defined feeling as positive or negative reaction to some experience or to something which affects our functioning. She also maintained that emotion is distinct from biological drives. More importantly, Arnold made a distinction between emotion and motive. Emotion is a felt-action tendency, while a motive is an action impulse plus a cognition. Thus motivated action is a function of both emotion and cognitive processes. "A motive seems to be an action impulse (a want) that is appraised as good for action" (Arnold, 1960a, p. 233). This want is typically an emotion, and the wanting becomes a motive "when we endorse it and let it lead us to action" (Arnold, 1960a, p. 238). Thus an "emotional motive"—action impulse plus cognition—develops only after the emotion has been favorably assessed.

Emotion as Physiological Arousal plus Cognition. Schachter and his colleagues (1966, 1971; Schachter & Singer, 1962) have proposed that emotion results from physiological arousal and a cognitive appraisal or evaluation of the situation that elicited the arousal. In short, some event, situation, or condition creates physiological arousal in the individual and the individual has a need to appraise or evaluate the context of the arousal, the situation that elicited it. The type or quality of emotion that an individual experiences depends not on the sensation arising from the physiological arousal but on how the individual evaluates the situation or conditon in which it occurs. The evaluation ("cognizing or sizing up") of the contextual situation enables the individual to label the arousal sensations as joy or anger, fear or distress, or whatever is appropriate to the situation as it is appraised. According to Schachter's position, the same physiological arousal may be experienced as joy or as anger (or as any other emotion), depending on the cognitions available in the situation. Mandler (1975) presents a similar view of emotion activation.

In one well-known experiment, Schachter and Singer (1962) tested their theory by injecting epinephrine to induce arousal in three groups and injected a placebo in a fourth. Then they manipulated the "appropriate explanation" or cognitive input by giving accurate, inaccurate, or no information as to the effects of the drug to independent groups. Immediately after the injection and explanation, all of the misinformed group and half of the subjects in each of the other groups were exposed to a stooge who modeled euphoric actions and verbalizations; the other half of each of the three groups were exposed to a stooge who modeled angry actions and verbalizations. They found that subjects who were given misinformation or no information about their arousal state were more likely to imitate the stooge's mood and behavior, whether it was euphoric or angry. Subjects who were given accurate explanations of the effects of epinephrine were relatively immune to the influence of the stooge. Among the subjects exposed to the euphoric model, the misinformation and no-information groups reported significantly higher happiness scores than did the correctly informed group, but they did not differ from the placebo group. Of those exposed to the anger model, the groups having received no information to explain their drug-induced arousal symptoms were rated significantly higher on "angry behavior" than the other groups, but again the placebo group did not conform to Schachter's model. It was no different from either the misinformed or the noninformed group on the anger self-report scale.

Schachter's theory and research has had considerable impact on the study of emotion, particularly within the field of social psychology. His formulation has generated a lot of research and a number of theoretical revisions. The study inspired considerable theorizing and research, but it has been criticized by a number of other investigators (e.g., Plutchik & Ax, 1967; Izard, 1971). Plutchik and Ax questioned Schachter's assumptions regarding the physiological effects of epinephrine and Izard raised the question as to whether the result on the psychological measures might not be adequately explained by the increased suggestibility of the misinformed and noninformed groups. These subjects were in a strange situation created by physiological events that were unexplained or misinterpreted to them. Mandler (1962, 1964), Mandler and Watson (1966), and Atkinson (1964) have argued that in such uncertain situations the subjects' apprehension or anxiety may lead them to choose anything rather than remaining uncertain. Further, if subjects followed the model (stooge) and unconsciously imitated the model's facial–postural expressions of euphoria or anger, the neural feedback from their expressive behavior could have triggered the observed emotion (Tomkins, 1962; Izard, 1971). The case for a causal role for differentiated sensory feedback from facial patterning seems more persuasive than the case for ambiguous signals from undifferentiated physiological arousal.

More significant, however, than any of the foregoing criticisms is the fact that two recent experiments representing the first reported replications of the Schachter–Singer experiment failed to replicate its findings (Maslach, unpublished; Marshall, 1976). Maslach showed that unexplained hypnotically suggested autonomic arousal tended to create a set to interpret internal conditions (feelings) negatively. Subjects were not equally likely to report anger or joy depending on the actions of the confederate. Marshall used the same drug-arousal technique as Schachter and Singer and found results similar to those of Maslach.

Emotion as a Complex Response System that Results from Appraisal. Lazarus and his colleagues (Averill, Opton, & Lazarus, 1969; Lazarus & Averill, 1972) have presented a theoretical framework in which each emotion is a complex response system composed of three distinct subsystems. Their explanation of the activation or cause of emotion is similar to the classical psychoanalytic theory of Freud and virtually identical with the scheme proposed by Arnold (1960a,b). The more distinct features of their theory is their description of the three major components of the emotion response system (ERS).

The first component consists of input variables or stimulus properties. The authors propose abandoning the traditional view of perceptions as compounds of simple sensations emanating from stimulus objects. Instead, they advocate the idea of Dewey (1895), that a stimulus is influenced by the response to the stimulus. They note that this idea has been elaborated in the test–operate–test–exit concept of Miller, Galanter, & Pribram (1960) and in the "obtained perception" concept of Gibson (1966). Extending this concept one step further, the authors note that an "emotional response" may also serve as a stimulus in its own right and thus be capable of contributing to the quality of the emotion experience.

The second component of the ERS is the appraiser subsystem. The appraiser subsystem is defined as a function of brain processes whereby the individual appraises and evaluates the stimulus situation. The authors liken it to the decider system of Miller (1965); it is also quite similar to Arnold's (1960a,b) concept of the estimative system.

According to Lazarus and his associates, primary appraisal serves to reduce the array of incoming information to a unitary or organizing concept such as threat. Such primary appraisal is a function of the stimulus properties, the motives and belief or psychological structure of the individual, and sociocultural factors such as norms, mores, values, and role demands. There is also a secondary appraisal which evaluates alternative modes of behavior that enable the organism to cope with the situation as perceived. The authors believe that the distinction between primary and secondary appraisal is of more heuristic than practical value since the two processes are often indistinguishable, either temporally or phenomenologically. These ideas, apparently developed independently, are very similar to those of Arnold (1960a,b).

The third component of the emotion response system consists of three types of response categories: cognitive, expressive, instrumental. Lazarus and colleagues regard the first of these, cognitive reactions, as essentially synonymous with what are normally discussed as defense mechanisms, such as repression, denial, projection; these have been more fully explored in the study of abnormal emotions and behavior.

Expressive responses consist primarily of facial expressions, which they consider as non-goal-directed behavior. They divide expressors into subcategories of biologic and acquired expressors.

The third type of response, instrumental reaction, may fall into one of three categories: symbols, operators, and conventions. All are goal-directed. Symbols function to signal the presence of some affect, when other forms of communication do not. Symbols may also conceal an unwanted affect. Operators are complex goal-directed instrumental acts such as aggression and avoidance. Conventions are culturally determined operators such as mourning rites, patterns of fighting, and courting.

Emotions as Derivatives of Biological Processes and Mixtures of Emotions as Personality Traits

Plutchik (1962) views the emotions as adaptive devices which have played a role in individual survival at all evolutionary levels. The basic prototypic dimensions of adaptive behavior and the emotions related to them are given below:

Prototypic Adaptive Pattern	Primary Emotion
1. Incorporation—ingestion of food and water	Acceptance
2. Rejection—riddance reaction, excretion, vomiting	Disgust
3. Destruction—removal of barrier to satisfaction	Anger
4. Protection—primarily the response to pain or threats of pain or harm	Fear
5. Reproduction—responses associated with sexual behavior	Joy
6. Deprivation—loss of pleasurable object which has been contacted or incorporated	Sorrow
7. Orientation—response to contact with new or strange object	Startle
8. Exploration—more or less random activities in exploring environment	Expectation or curiosity

Plutchik defines emotion as a patterned bodily reaction corresponding to one of the underlying adaptive biological processes common to all living organisms. He sees the primary emotions as transient and as usually, though not necessarily, triggered by external stimuli. There are physiological and overt expressive patterns of activity associated with each emotion and with each emotion mixture or secondary emotion (mixture of two or more primary emotions). However, the determination of patterns is strictly an empirical problem which can be worked out experimentally only by successive approximation. Discrete patterns for each of the primary emotions at the physiological and overt expressive level are defined as constructs whose true nature can only be inferred and approximated.

It is interesting to note that Plutchik's theoretical formulation tends to follow Wenger (1950), who like Lange emphasized the bodily state itself, rather than the perception of bodily changes and the subsequent feeling in consciousness, as did James. Plutchik also finds support for his concentration on bodily states in Fenichel's (1945) notion of affect as a substitute for voluntary action and in Gesell's (1950) description of emotion as patterned phenomena associated with patterns of tension, action, and organic attitude. Plutchik (1954) interpreted a number of findings to support the notion that the blocking or impeding of adequate motor responses in conflict or frustration gives rise to chronic muscular tension, often a characteristic of maladjustment.

Plutchik maintains that his emotion theory contains a number of implications for the study of personality and psychotherapy. He suggests that personality traits can be studied and analyzed in terms of mixed (or secondary) emotions, representing two or more primary emotions which may be in conflict. Plutchik points out that eight primary emotions lead to 28 dyadic combinations and 56 triadic combinations for a total of 84 different emotions at one intensity level. (While in Plutchik's view, primary emotions mix to form new emotions as primary colors mix to form new colors, Izard (1972) conceptualizes primary or fundamental emotions as interacting in patterns or combinations in which the fundamental emotions retain their qualitative identity.) Assuming even four discriminable levels of intensity, this would produce 336 new emotions. Plutchick thinks that understanding the way emotions mix increases understanding of many important emotion phenomena. For example, he writes the following formulas: pride = anger + joy; love = joy + acceptance; curiosity = surprise + acceptance; modesty = fear + acceptance; hate = anger + surprise; guilt = fear + joy or pleasure; sentimentality = acceptance + sorrow.

Social regulators (superego phenomena) can be understood in Plutchik's system as mixtures of fear and other emotions; anxiety, as fear and expectancy. Thus, for example, analyzing situations that lead to fear and determining one's expectations in regard to these situations increases understanding of the dynamics of anxiety.

Plutchik concluded that learning and experience influence emotions in only a very special sense:

> (1) An individual may learn to modify or inhibit some of the external expressive signs of emotions . . . ; and (2) an individual's experience will affect which of the prototypic patterns is most likely to be dominant in his behavior and which are most likely to fuse or interact. (Plutchik, 1962, p. 170)

Emotion as the Interaction of Need and the Probability of Goal Achievement

Simonov (1964, 1970, 1972, 1975) concludes that the degree of emotion experienced or degree of "emotional stress" (E) is a function of two factors: (a) the value of the motivation or need (N), as well as (b) the difference between prognostically necessary information for its satisfaction (I_n) and information available to the subject (I_a). This can be expressed by the formula: $E = f(N, /I, . . .)$, where $/I$ is $I_n - I_a$. The term "information" is used in its pragmatic sense—the change of probability of goal achievement based on a given information message.

According to Simonov's theory of emotions the occurrence of emotion due to the deficit of pragmatic information (when I_n is more than I_a) determines its negative character: distress, fear, anger, etc. Such positive emotions as joy and interest arise in the situation when the newly obtained information increases the probability of need satisfaction in comparison with the already existing prognosis—in other words, when I_a is more than I_n.

Simonov maintains that there is relative independence of neural mechanisms for need, emotion, and prognosis or probability of goal achievement, and that this relative independence of underlying mechanisms make for a variety of interactions among them. Activation of the neural apparatus of emotion will intensify need, and either a deficit or a surplus of information tends to affect need, for $N = E/(I_n - I_a)$. On the other hand, changing the intensity of emotion and need will affect the prognosis of the probability of goal achievement: $I_n - I_a = E/N$. Under either of these consequences the formula would predict complex interrelations of emotion and cognitive components of human behavior. Simonov (1972) gave the example of a study of space flight as an example of experimental confirmation of the informational theory of emotions. The "emotional stress" of a cosmonaut was estimated by his heart rate (HR) and the results of spectral analysis of his voice. The high motivation of a cosmonaut linked with his responsibility for the success of the flight, the novelty of the situation, and his desire to accomplish the task of the flight lead to "emotional stress" even in performance of operations which were several times performed on earth without pronounced emotions.

For example, seven minutes before the opening of the lock chamber for his space walk, Leonov's HR did not exceed his HR recorded during his training on earth. However, immediately after the opening of the hatch his HR began to rise and in six minutes reached 162 beats per minute. Four minutes after returning to the lock chamber his HR became normal again. Later the HR of the Captain, Belysev, increased as the result of an impairment in the automatic landing system. Belysev's "emotional stress" lessened after he obtained permission to start manual procedures, but during his decision to start the braking system it increased again. The liquidation of "emotional stress" as the result of skilled performance (the space craft approaches the earth, the engines are running all right) neutralized the effects of acceleration at the last stage of the flight and Belysev's HR decreased.

According to Simonov, these facts show that the most important condition for prophylaxis of "emotional stress" was the correct and valid choice of activity in the complicated situation, the level of skilled performance, and the readiness of the cosmonaut to face any of the surprises which are the inevitable companions of man exploring outer space.

A Cognitive–Affective Approach

Singer's (1973, 1974) original and incisive contribution to affect psychology reflects his background in psychoanalysis and his immersion in the scientific study of the cognitive processes of daydreaming, fantasy, and imaging. At the same time the kinship of his cognitive–affective approach to that of Tomkins (1962, 1963) and the present writer (Izard, 1971, 1972) makes his ideas as relevant to the Chapter 3 on differential emotions theory as to the present survey. Singer, like Tomkins, Izard, and Dahl, assumes that the emotions constitute the primary motivational system for human beings. His unique contribution lies in his clinical and experimental investigations that support his key proposition that fantasy processes, dreams, and imagery link cognition and affect and thus provide representations of major human motives.

According to Singer, the intimate relation between affect and cognition is rooted in the infant's early efforts at accommodation to its novel and ever-changing environment. He assumes, with Tomkins (1962) and Izard (1971), that environmental novelty activates the interest affect which in turn sustains efforts at exploration and accommodation. Mastery or successful accommodation reduces excitement and activates joy, whereas a complex mass of unassimilable material may produce startle, distress, or fear. Thus affective and cognitive processes are intertwined from the very beginning of life. As will be seen in later chapters, Singer's relating of cognitive assimilation to affect activation is similar in some ways to Hunt's (1965) ideas on information processing and to Tomkins's (1962) principle of variations in density of neural stimulation.

A significant outcome of Singer's research has been his innovative application of his knowledge about imagery and affects to the practice of psychotherapy (Singer, 1974). His approach is congruent with Izard's (1971) emphasis on the use of imagery and action (e.g., role-playing) in helping the patient achieve affect differentiation and thus a better basis for control of emotions, thought, and actions. Singer adds valuable insights on the effectiveness of developing the patient's imagery and fantasy capacities as a means of increasing his or her feeling of competency and self-control. His clinical case material suggests that the skilled therapist in traditions as widely separated as psychoanalysis and behavior therapy can make effective use of imagery and daydream techniques in improving patients' control of emotions and behavior. He makes use of both positive and negative emotion imagery, using one type to attenuate or inhibit the other depending on the patient's specific problem. For example, he successfully treated voyeurism by having the patient cross-up his fantasy life. The patient developed a series of noxious images and learned to substitute disgust-evoking images of skin diseased male nudes for guilt-ridden attempts to peep at partially dressed women in neighboring apartments. Positive emotion imagery involving women was used to counteract heterosexual fear and homosexual tendencies. These techniques were used in the framework of extended psychodynamic therapy which provided the necessary understanding for their skillful application.

Summary

As a general rule, theories of personality and behavior have failed to deal explicitly with the discrete emotions of human experience. Similarly, many popular theories of emotion have had little to say about the role of the emotions in the development of personality and in influencing thought and action. Most emotion investigators have been concerned with only one of the components of the emotion process. Some theories have attempted to work out some aspects of the relationship between emotion and cognition, action and the personality as a whole, but much remains to be done both at the theoretical and empirical levels.

Although classical psychoanalytic theory does not deal systematically with discrete emotion concepts, it emphasizes the importance of noncognitive phenomena or the "affects" in human behavior. Freud's early emphasis on the importance of affects as motivational variables launched the psychodynamic tradition in psychology and psychiatry. Although Freud's conception of instinctual drives as the wellspring of motivation has been severely criticized or rejected by some contemporary psychoanalytic thinkers, his seminal notion that motivational phenomena (including "wish impulses") are represented by bonds between ideas and affects still thrives in various forms and contexts. It can be seen in Klein's and Holt's concepts of the wish and it probably influenced Dahl's conception of emotions as fundamental human motives and Singer's views that draw both from psychoanalysis and differential emotions theory.

The dimensional approach links emotion and personality functioning less convincingly than does psychoanalytic theory, particularly the work of contemporary psychoanalysts. This approach began with Spencer's conceptualization of emotions or feelings as dimensions or states of consciousness and became established as a tradition in psychology when Wundt proposed that the sphere of consciousness described by emotion or feeling could be accounted for by the dimensions of pleasantness–unpleasantness, relaxation–tension, and calm–excitement. Building on the conceptions of Spencer and Wundt, Duffy proposed that all behavior can be explained in terms of organismic arousal (level of tension or energy). Emotion was seen as a point or range of points on the high end of the arousal dimension. That is, according to Duffy, emotion represents high levels of tension or energy in the tissues of the organism. This system, like that of Lindsley's, allows emotion to vary quantitatively but not qualitatively.

Woodworth and Schlosberg directed attention to the observable aspect of emotion and showed that the facial expressions of emotions could be reliably categorized and that these categories could be rather accurately predicted on the basis of ratings of the dimensions of pleasantness–unpleasantness, attention–rejection, and sleep–tension. Later research showed that attention–rejection and sleep–tension may not be independent dimensions, but several investigators found other reliable dimensions. The research in this tradition has yielded rather substantial evidence that qualitatively distinct emotions may be represented as points or clusters of points in multidimensional space. As shown by a study of Bartlett and Izard (1972), dimensional concepts such as pleasantness, tension, self-assurance, and impulsiveness can be useful in describing the subjective experience associated with various discrete emotions.

A number of theorists have explained emotion as a consequence of perceptual–cognitive processes. Such cognitive theories are rooted in rationalism and tend to view emotions as undesirable entities that disrupt or disorganize thought and action. Arnold's version of this approach defines emotion as a felt-action tendency and distinguishes emotion from biological drive on the one hand and motive (action impulse plus cognition) on the other. Schachter's version of cognitive theory defines emotion as undifferentiated arousal plus cognition. In his view the underlying physiological state is the same for all emotions and qualitative distinctions result from cognitive appraisal or evaluation of the situation that elicited the arousal.

Lazarus's version of the cognitive theory of emotion places emphasis on emotion as response and defines three types of emotion response categories: cognitive, expressive, and instrumental. Cognitive responses (of emotion) are essentially synonymous with defense mechanisms such as repression and projection. Expressive responses are seen primarily as facial expressions, and instrumental reactions may be characterized as symbols, operators, or conventions.

Plutchik defines emotion as a patterned bodily reaction corresponding to an underlying adaptive biological process. For example, the adaptive pattern of rejection gave rise to disgust and that of destruction to anger. Plutchik defined eight primary emotions and indicated that these eight primaries mix to form secondary emotions in much the same way as primary colors mix to form new colors. The mixing of the primary emotions, taking two or three at a time, results in hundreds of mixtures or new emotions. For example, pride = anger + joy, and modesty = fear + acceptance. Plutchik suggests that personality traits can be analyzed in terms of mixed (or secondary) emotions. For example, social regulators (superego phenomena) can be understood as mixtures of fear and other emotions.

Simonov defines emotion as the interaction of need and the probability of goal achievement. According to this view negative emotion occurs as the result of a deficit in pragmatic information necessary for adaptive and satisfying action. Thus the resolution of "emotional stress," in Simonov's terms, is a result of correct information and competent action based upon it.

Kagan (1972) presents a rather sophisticated cognitive theory of motives and motivation. He defines a motive as a cognitive representation of a *desired* goal that may or may not be associated with particular behaviors. A motive differs from other cognitive representations in that it includes a goal—a representation of a future event that will enable the person to *feel* better. Motivation is the mental set-like state that follows cognitive activation of a goal.

Though not so categorized by Kagan, his theory has some of the features of a cognitive–affective position. The italicized words in the foregoing paragraph are key words in Kagan's definition of motive and motivation and they clearly connote affect. Further, *uncertainty,* which gives rise to the important motives of achievement, affiliation, power, dependency, succorance, and nurturance, is seen as an *affect state* related to its derivative motives in the same way as "the affect state of anger and the motive of hostility" (Kagan, 1972, p. 58). On the surface, this sounds very much like the treatment of the concepts of anger and hostility in differential emotions theory (Izard, 1972, 1975). The latter theory, however, views emotion as motivation (and the emotions as constituting the principal motivational system for human beings), while Kagan does not take an explicit and consistent stand on this issue.

Kagan describes uncertainty both in terms of affect and in terms of cognitive conflict—an incompatibility of cognitive structures or a discrepancy between an experienced event and an existing schema. From his description of uncertainty as an "alerted affect state," one can easily infer that he is talking about an emotion–cognition interaction or an affective–cognitive organization and attributing motivational properties to emotion. He hints at the idea of viewing thought and action as a joint function of cognitive process (uncertainty, discrepancy) and the quality of the specific emotion that follows. If this is a valid interpretation, then he views affect as at least a component of motivation. Actually, however, he neither defines emotion nor elucidates his view of the relationships between affect, cognition, and action.

3

DIFFERENTIAL EMOTIONS
THEORY

Differential emotions theory draws from a rich intellectual heritage and claims kinship with the classical works of Duchenne, Darwin, Spencer, Kierkegaard, Wundt, James, Cannon, McDougall, Dumas, Dewey, Freud, Rado, and Woodworth and with the more contemporary works of Jacobson, Sinnott, Mowrer, Gellhorn, Harlow, Bowlby, Simonov, Ekman, Holt, and Singer and many others. All of these scientists, representing several different disciplines and points of view, have in common a belief in the central importance of the emotions in motivation, social communication, cognition, and action. However, the contemporary writer most directly responsible for the ideological foundations of the theory presented here is Silvan Tomkins, whose brilliant two-volume work—*Affect, Imagery, Consciousness*—will be cited frequently throughout this volume.

Differential emotions theory takes its name from its emphasis on discrete emotions as distinct experiential/motivational processes. The theory is based on five key assumptions. (1) Ten fundamental emotions (which will be briefly defined in Chapter 4 and discussed in detail in later chapters) constitute the principal motivational system for human beings. (2) Each fundamental emotion has unique motivational and phenomenological properties. (3) Fundamental emotions such as joy, sadness, anger, and shame lead to different inner experiences and different behavioral consequences. (4) Emotions interact with each other—one emotion may activate, amplify, or attenuate another. (5) Emotion processes interact with and exert influence on homeostatic, drive, perceptual, cognitive, and motor processes.

Emotions as the Principal Motivational System

Differential emotions theory assumes that emotion is a determinant in behaviors as widely different as rape and unpremeditated murder on the one hand and personal sacrifice and courageous ventures on the other. The emotions are viewed not only as the principal motivational system but, even more fundamentally, as the personality processes which give meaning and significance to human existence. The emotions are considered important both for behavior and for sensing, experiencing, and being.

The Six Subsystems of Personality

Personality is a complex organization of six subsystems: the homeostatic, drive, emotion, perceptual, cognitive, and motor systems. Each system has a degree of autonomy or independence but all are complexly interrelated. The homeostatic and drive systems are of primary importance in biological maintenance, reproduction, and the regulation of body functions.

The "homeostatic system" is really a network of interrelated systems that operate automatically and unconsciously. Chief among these are the endocrine and cardiovascular systems which are of importance to personality mainly through frequent interactions with the emotion system. Homeostatic mechanisms are considered auxiliary to the emotion system, but the hormones, neurohumors, enzymes, and other regulators of metabolism are important in regulating and sustaining emotion once it has been activated.

The drive system is based on tissue changes and deficits that create signals and provide information about bodily needs. The most common drives are hunger, thirst, sex, and comfort or pain-avoidance. Drives are obviously important when survival is at stake. Under normal circumstances (after survival and comfort needs are met) the drives (with the exception of sex and pain) are of little psychological importance, becoming significant mainly as they influence or are influenced by the emotions. The important exceptions, sex and pain, are drives that have some of the characteristics of emotion. These drives inevitably recruit and interact with emotions and it is the subsequent drive–emotion interactions that often make sex and pain important for personality and behavior.

The four systems most important in personality, social interaction, and higher-order human functioning are the emotion, perceptual, cognitive, and motor systems. These four systems jointly form the basis for uniquely human behavior. Effective behavior derives from the harmonious interaction of these four systems. Ineffective behavior and maladjustment result when systemic interaction breaks down or becomes faulty.

The Four Types of Motivational Phenomena

Differential emotions theory holds that the six subsystems of personality generate four major types of motivation: the drives, emotions, affect–

cognition interactions, and affective–cognitive structures. The drives result from tissue deficit or tissue change that is usually cyclic in nature. Emotions are experiential/motivational phenomena that have adaptive functions independent of tissue needs. An affect–cognition interaction is a motivational state resulting from the interaction between an affect or pattern of affects and cognitive processes. Such interactions are innumerable and they vary with the particular person–environment transaction. Affective–cognitive structures are psychological organizations of affect and cognition—traitlike phenomena that result from repeated interactions between a particular affect or pattern of affects and a particular set or configuration of cognitions. A complex affective–cognitive structure or an interrelated set of them may constitute an affective–cognitive orientation, a more global personality trait, trait complex, or disposition such as introversion. Any one of the four major types of motivation may dominate the individual and become for a time the primary determinant of behavior. A taxonomy of affects and affect interactions is presented in Table 3-1.

As can be seen from Table 3-1, the emotions and other affects give rise to a great diversity of motivational/experiential conditions. When high-order affect interactions and affective–cognitive structures and orientations are added, the schema for human motivation and experiential phenomena become extremely complex. Such complexity is required to establish a framework for understanding both the personalities and the social interactions of human beings.

A great diversity of affective–cognitive structures may result from affect–cognition interactions. The concept affective–cognitive structure is very similar to Tomkins's (1962) "ideo-affective organization," except that Tomkins uses affect to refer only to emotions. It is also similar to the concept of attitude as defined by Katz and Stotland (1959). They defined attitude as having an affective, cognitive, and behavioral component. They interpreted the affective component as "the central aspect of the attitude since it is the most closely related to the evaluation of the object" (p. 429). They defined the cognitive component of an attitude as the set of beliefs about the attitudinal object. The behavioral component was defined as the action tendencies in relation to the object.

The term affective–cognitive structure is used in differential emotions theory to underscore the importance of the interactive components of this type of motivation. It is considered important for psychological theory, empirical research, and applied psychology to maintain a conceptual distinction between emotions, drives, and the phenomena described as affective–cognitive structures. These affective–cognitive structures consist of a dynamic and relatively stable relationship between an affect (emotion, drive) on the one hand and certain cognitive processes such as ideas and beliefs on the other. For example, if a child is rewarded and made joyful for

TABLE 3-1
A Taxonomy of Affects and Affect Interactions

I. Fundamental emotions[a]

1. Interest–excitement
2. Enjoyment–joy
3. Surprise–startle
4. Distress–anguish
5. Anger–rage
6. Disgust–revulsion
7. Contempt–scorn
8. Fear–terror
9. Shame/shyness–humiliation[c]
10. Guilt–remorse

II. Drives/bodily feelings[b,c]

1. Hunger
2. Thirst
3. Fatigue–sleepiness
4. Pain (pain-avoidance: safety, comfort, etc.)
5. Sex

III. Affective–cognitive structures or orientations[b]

1. Introversion–extraversion
2. Skepticism
3. Egotism
4. Vigor
5. Calmness/tranquility

IV. Affect interactions[e]

A. Emotion–emotion

Dyads:
1. Interests/enjoyment[d]
2. Distress/anger
3. Fear/shame
(The ten fundamental emotions lead to 45 dyads.)
.
.
.
45.

B. Emotion–drive

Dyads:
1. Interest/sex
2. Interest/enjoyment/sex (To each fundamental emotion and to each dyadic emotion interaction can be added one or more of the drives.)
.
.
.

C. Emotion–affective/cognitive structures

Dyads:
1. Interest/introversion
2. Interest/enjoyment/introversion (To each fundamental emotion and each dyadic emotion interaction can be added one or more of the affective–cognitive structures.)

Triads:
1. Surprise/interest/enjoyment
2. Distress/anger/disgust
3. Fear/shame/guilt
   (The ten fundamental emotions lead to 120 triads.)

.
.
.
120.

Emotion triads and drive:
1. Pain/fear/shame/anger (To each triadic emotion interaction can be added one or more of the drives.)

.
.
.

Emotion triads and affective–cognitive structure:
1. Surprise/interest/enjoyment/egotism (To each triadic emotion interaction can be added one or more of the affective–cognitive structures.)

.
.
.

To each of the above affect interactions, can be added homeostatic functions, perception, cognition, and motor action. These complex interactions are exemplified by the following emotion–cognition interactions:

D. Emotion/cognition interactions
1. Interest/extraversion/thinking
2. Interest/enjoyment/introversion/imaging
   (Each of the fundamental emotions and each dyadic emotion interaction can interact in relation to affective–cognitive processes.)
3. Anger/disgust/contempt/extraversion/"hostile thoughts"
   (Each triadic emotion interaction can interact in relation to affective–cognitive orientations and ongoing cognitive processes.)

---

[a] Two terms are given for each fundamental emotion. They are intended to suggest that each emotion varies along a dimension of intensity. The first term represents a lower level of intensity, the second term a higher level of intensity. The terms are intended to represent a range along the intensity dimension rather than a specific quantity.
[b] These are not exhaustive lists.
[c] (Any other tissue change that has motivational properties may be termed a drive. Phenomena such as sensory pleasure and body contact may have drive characteristics or at least involve drive interactions.)
[d] There are some grounds for separating shame and shyness, but as yet there is no empirical basis for separation.
[e] Virtually any of the interactions listed in columns A–D can be either harmonious or conflictful.

assertiveness, including assertions about his powers and skills, he may invest much interest in the self, develop superiority feelings (contempt for others), and take on the affective–cognitive orientation of egotism.

A number of empirical studies of the major types of motivation have been conducted using the Differential Emotions Scale (DES) (Izard, Dougherty, Bloxom, & Kotsch, 1974). The DES has reliable scales representing the ten emotions and a number of drives and affective–cognitive orientations. (For examples of research with these scales see Izard, 1972; Marshall & Izard, 1972a; Izard & Caplan, 1974; Schultz, 1976; Schwartz *et al.*, 1976.)

The Emotions and the Emotion System

An important assumption of differential emotions theory is that the discrete emotions of human experience are important variables for the life sciences. It also assumes that the ten fundamental emotions, the drives, and the numerous affective–cognitive structures make the study of human motivation extremely complex. These assumptions are contrary to those underlying the approaches that treat emotion as a global, catch-all term.

Those concerned with the application of psychology, whether in industry, education, or clinic, sooner or later have to come to grips with specific discrete emotions. The people they work with feel specifically happy, angry, fearful, sad, disgusted, or excited, not simply "emotional." Recent practice is moving away from the use of such general terms as "emotional problem," "emotional disturbance," and "emotional disorder." The current trend is for the practitioner to try to analyze and treat the various discrete affects and affective patterns as distinct motivational phenomena in the life of the individual.

Definition of an Emotion. Differential emotions theory defines emotion as a complex process with neurophysiological, neuromuscular, and phenomenological aspects. At the neurophysiological level emotion is defined primarily in terms of patterns of electrochemical activity in the nervous system, particularly in the cortex, the hypothalamus, the basal ganglia, the limbic system, and the facial and trigeminal nerves. The cutaneous nerves in the face and the proprioceptors in the facial muscles also participate in emotion at the neurophysiological level. It is assumed that emotion proper is a function of the somatic nervous system (controller of voluntary actions) and that the somatically activated emotion recruits the autonomic nervous system (controller of involuntary functions such as glandular secretions and heart rate), which in turn may amplify or sustain the emotion over time. At the neuromuscular level emotion is primarily facial activity and facial patterning, and secondarily it is bodily (postural–gestural, visceral–glandular, and sometimes vocal) response. At the phenomenological level emotion is essentially motivating experience and/or experience which has immediate meaning and significance for the person. The experiencing of emotion can constitute a process in consciousness completely independent of cognition.

When neurochemical activity, via innate programs, produces patterned facial and bodily activities, and the feedback from these activities is transformed into conscious form, the result is a discrete fundamental emotion which is both a motivating and meaningful cue-producing experience. Phenomenologically, positive emotions have inherent characteristics which tend to enhance one's sense of well-being and to instigate and sustain approach toward, and constructive interactions or relations with, the involved persons, situations, or objects. Negative emotions tend to be sensed as noxious and difficult to tolerate and to instigate avoidance of and/ or nonconstructive interactions or relations. As already indicated, while certain emotions tend to be positive and others negative in import, these terms cannot be applied rigidly to the various emotion experiences without considering them in ecological perspective.

The Emotions as a System. Differential emotions theory refers to the emotion elements of personality as a system since, on the basis of both innate and learned characteristics, emotions are interrelated in dynamic and relatively stable ways. Largely because of the nature of the underlying innate mechanisms, some of the emotions are organized in a kind of hierarchical relationship. Darwin (1872) noted that attention may graduate into surprise and surprise into a "frozen astonishment" resembling fear. Similarly Tomkins (1962) has argued that the stimulation gradients which activate interest, fear, and startle represent a hierarchy, with the gradient for eliciting interest being the least steep and that for startle the steepest. A novel sound might elicit the interest of an infant or child. If in its first presentation the strange sound were quite loud it might elicit fear. If the sound were extremely loud and sudden it might evoke startle.

Another characteristic of the emotions which contributes to their organization as a system is the apparent polarity between some pairs of emotions. Observation and arguments for polarity extend from Darwin (1872) to Plutchik (1962). Joy and sadness, anger and fear are often considered as opposites. Other possible polar opposites are interest and disgust, shame and contempt. Like the concepts of positive and negative, the concept of polarity should not be considered as defining inflexible relationships between emotions, and the apparent opposition does not always denote an either-or relationship. Opposites are sometimes associated with or elicited by each other, as evidenced by the often observed "tears of joy."

Certain emotions other than the pairs of polar opposites tend to have fairly regular relationships, at least under certain circumstances. Interest may oscillate with fear as the organism explores some unknown (potentially exciting, potentially dangerous) object or situation. Contempt may graduate into or oscillate with joy and excitement to produce something like Lorenz's (1966) "militant enthusiasm." Regular or frequent occurrence of two or more fundamental emotions that interact with a particular set of cognitions may produce an affective–cognitive structure or orientation with traitlike characteristics. The descriptive term affective–cognitive orientation seems a particularly useful way of conceptualizing certain personality traits. For example, the interest–fear combination may be frequently associated with cognitions about risking and escaping danger for fun and thrills and result in the affective–cognitive orientation (or trait) of sensation seeking. However, the interest–fear combination may be associated with the risk-taking involved in exploration for the sake of discovery, and in this case the affective–cognitive orientation could be intellectual curiosity.

Several other factors help to define the emotions as a system. All emotions have certain characteristics in common. All emotions, as contrasted with drives, are noncyclical. One does not become interested or disgusted or ashamed two or three times a day in rhythm with ingestion, digestion, and metabolic processes. Emotions have virtually unlimited generality and flexibility as motivational factors. While only food and drink will satisfy the hunger and thirst drives, a person can learn to be joyful or contemptuous or afraid in response to a seemingly infinite variety of things.

All emotions influence or regulate the drives and other personality subsystems. One of the important and frequent functions of emotion is to regulate—to act as amplifier or attenuator in the various motivational systems. For example, drives which are not reduced to a level within the tolerance limits of the organism tend to instigate and recruit emotions, which in turn amplify the drive. The emotion of interest–excitement may bring the sex drive to high pitch; the emotions of disgust, fear, or distress may modulate, mask, reduce, or completely inhibit the sex drive. Even behavior motivated by homeostatic mechanisms is continually influenced by such emotions as joy, fear, distress, and anger.

Restrictions on the Emotion System. Tomkins (1962) has pointed out that there are certain inherent restrictions on the emotion system and these in turn affect the degree to which a person's behavior is apparently determined and the degree to which it is free. At the same time there are freedoms inherent in the nature of the emotions and the emotion system and these freedoms of the emotion system affect the freedom of the human being. (For a fuller discussion of the material in this and the next section see Tomkins, 1962, pp. 108–149.)

(a) The emotion system in comparison with the motor system is quite difficult to control. Emotion control (including "freedom" of emotion expression) probably is best achieved through its motor (striate muscle) component, facial expression, in combination with cognitive processes such as imagery and fantasy.

(b) Emotions instigated by and linked to drive conditions are restricted in freedom. An example of such an emotion–drive bond is the case of the individual who can experience joy only while eating or drinking. Another example is the person who experiences excitement only when sexually aroused.

(c) There is a restriction on the emotion system because of the syndrome character of its neurological and biochemical organization. Once an emotion is instigated all parts of the emotion system tend to be innervated at once in very rapid succession.

(d) Memory of past experience of emotion places another limit on emotion freedom. The human being has the mixed blessing of being constrained and pushed by the vividness of past emotional experiences that can be present in memory and thought.

(e) Another restriction on freedom of emotion can be imposed by the nature of the object of emotion investment, as in the case of the unrequited lover.

(f) Emotion communication is restricted by the taboo on looking at the face, particularly when this involves prolonged eye contact.

(g) Another factor restricting emotion communication is the complex relationship between language and the emotion system. We have not been taught to verbalize accurately our emotion experiences.

Freedoms of the Emotion System and the Freedom of Human Beings. Emotions are motives that are more free than drives. The problem of the freedom of the will and the general controversy concerning the freedom of human beings has stemmed in part from the failure to distinguish between motives that are more or less free. Tomkins has described the role of emotion in this sphere as follows: "Out of the marriage of reason with emotion there issues clarity with passion. Reason without emotion would be impotent, emotion without reason would be blind. The combination of emotion and reason guarantees man's high degree of freedom" (Tomkins, 1962, p. 112). Although most human beings never become able to control their emotions with a high degree of precision, it is the complexity of the emotion system that gives rise to man's freedom and competence. The emotion system has some ten types of freedom not characteristic of the drive system.

(a) The first of these is freedom of time; there is no essential rhythm or cycle as with the drives.

(b) Emotion has freedom of intensity; whereas drives characteristically increase in intensity until they are satisfied, the intensity curve or profile of an emotion may vary markedly in time.

(c) Emotion has considerable freedom in the density with which it is invested. Density of emotion is the product of intensity and duration. On the density dimension emotions may either be much more casual than any drive or much more monopolistic.

(d) The freedom of the emotion system is such that emotion can be invested in "possibility." Thus emotion underwrites anticipation, the central process in learning. It is the emotion of fear that enables the burnt child to avoid fire; he will avoid it only if he is afraid of it. Emotion can also be invested in positive possibility.

(e) The emotion system has freedom of object. Although emotions which are activated by drives and by special releasers have a limited range of objects, the linkage of emotions to objects through cognition enormously extends the range of the objects of positive and negative emotion. (See Figure 3-1.)

(f) Emotion may be invested in a monopolistic way in a particular mode of experience, such as in one of Jung's types. Emotion may be monopolistically invested in thinking, feeling (sensing), action, achievement, decision making, etc.

(g) Emotions are free to combine with, modulate, and suppress other emotions.

(h) There is considerable freedom in the way emotions may be instigated and reduced. As a general rule most people strive to maximize positive emotions and minimize negative emotions, but even different aspects of the same activity may instigate or reduce negative and positive emotions:

FIGURE 3-1. Most any object, whether fancy doll and tea set or an unadorned stick can elicit interest that motivates imagery, fantasy, and imaginative play, which in turn bring enjoyment and strengthen the affective–cognitive bond between child and plaything.

(i) Emotions enjoy considerable freedom in the substitutability of objects of attachment. It is the transformability of the emotions, not of the drives, that accounts for the Freudian concept of sublimation.

(j) Emotions have great freedom in terms of goal orientation or response-sequence alternatives, whereas drives as motives are quite specific in this regard. According to Tomkins "there is no strict analog in the emotion system for the rewarding effect of drive consummation. It is rather the case that emotion arousal and 'reward' are identical in the case of positive emotions: what activates positive emotions usually has a self-enhancing effect, and the situations and objectives that activate positive emotions are spatially widely distributed" (Tomkins, 1962, p. 139).

The Auxiliary Systems. Two other biological systems function in an auxiliary relationship to the emotion system: the brain stem reticular system (which controls changes in level of neural activation) and the autonomically innervated glandular–visceral system (which controls such activities as hormone secretion, heart rate, respiration rate, etc.). The glandular–visceral system helps prepare the body for emotion-determined and directed action and helps sustain the emotion and emotion-related actions. The reticular formation serves as regulator or control for the neural component of emotion, acting as an amplifier or as an attenuator.

The emotion system rarely functions in complete independence of other systems. Some emotion or pattern or emotions is virtually always present and interacting with the perceptual, cognitive, and motor systems, and effective personality functioning depends on balance and integration of activities of the different systems. In particular, since emotion of any substantial intensity tends to organize action of the organism as a whole, all physiological systems and organs are involved to some extent. The influence of emotion is readily observable in changes in the cardiovascular and respiratory subsystems of the glandular–visceral network.

The Neural Activation of Emotion. Neural activation refers to the changes in the nervous system that initiate the emotion process which culminates the subjective experience of a specific emotion. These neural changes are to be distinguished from those internal and external events and conditions that cause them. These latter phenomena are the ones typically referred to as the "causes" or "determinants" of emotion.

Tomkins (1962) has argued that the neural activation of all the emotions can be accounted for by variants of a single principle: the density of neural firing, "the product of the intensity times the number of neural firings per unit time" (p. 251). He maintained that some emotions are consistently elicited by stimulation increase, some by stimulation decrease, and some by the maintenance of a steady level of stimulation. According to Tomkins, the individual is thus equipped for emotion activation in relation to every major contingency. As noted in Chapter 2, Singer (1974) proposes to operationalize Tomkins's principle by translating it in terms of the relative assimilability of the information that the individual is processing.

In addition to Tomkins's principle of density of neural firing there is the possibility that the neural mechanisms relating to specific emotions may be genetically programmed to be selectively sensitive to certain inputs. It is assumed that selective sensitivity operates differently at different ages or stages of development, depending on the maturity of the individual's emotion mechanisms and the person's ability to cope with the emotion-eliciting conditions. The neurophysiological events that follow the neural activation (change in neurochemical activities) which leads to the emotion felt in subjective experience will be discussed in a later section on the emotion process.

The Causes of Emotion. In addition to the problem of neural activation, there is the question of emotion causation in a more general (meta-neural) sense; that is, what determines or "causes" emotion—what internal and external events and conditions bring about the changes in the nervous system that lead to emotion. Emotions have innumerable determinants. Since they will be discussed in more detail in the chapters dealing with the fundamental emotions they will be treated here only in a general fashion. Three types of person–environment interactions and five types of intraindividual processes that can cause emotion (or effect the neural activation of emotion) are listed below.

   A. Person–environment interactions that can cause emotion:
      1. Obtained perception—perception following stimulation derived from selective activity of a receptor or sense organ.
      2. Demanded perception—environmental or social event demands attention. The orienting reflex may be the first response to such a stimulus.
      3. Spontaneous perception—indigenous activity of a perceptual system.
   B. Intraindividual processes which can cause emotions:
      1. Memory:
         a. Obtained (active, sought).
         b. Demanded (something reminds).
         c. Spontaneous (autochthonous or indigenous cognition).
      2. Imaging.
      3. Imaginative and anticipatory thinking.
      4. Proprioceptive impulses from postural or other motor activity—the neuromuscular activity of posture and locomotion may help initiate, amplify, and sustain emotion.
      5. Endocrine and other autonomically initiated activity affecting neural or muscular mechanisms of emotion.

In differential emotions theory, facial expression and facial feedback play a highly important role in the emotion process and in emotion regulation or emotion control. Before considering these topics in greater detail the problem of facial vs. visceral feedback will be discussed. As we shall see, there are good reasons why people describe strong emotions in vernacular terms as "gut feelings" (referring to changes in the visceral–glandular system) rather than as facial feelings (referring to the proprioceptive and cutaneous impulses from the face).

Face vs. Viscera as Source of Sensations Felt in Emotions

Over a century ago, Charles Darwin (1872) laid the foundation for research on the role of facial patterns and feedback of facial sensations in emotion. From his observations one could conclude that expressive behavior could be either a consequence of an emotion or a regulator of emotion. Regarding its regulatory function, Darwin stated: "The free expression by outward signs of an emotion intensifies it. On the other hand, the repression, as far as possible, of all outward signs, softens our emotion" (p. 22). With this statement Darwin set the stage for an explicit facial feedback hypothesis—the face → brain feedback of sensations created by facial expression causes, or at least influences, felt (experiential) emotion.

Considering the nature of Darwin's early contribution to the field of emotion, one might expect continued and intensive study of the role of the somatic system and particularly facial expression, but this did not happen. Instead, the theorizing of William James (1884, 1890), the great pioneering psychologist, captured the imagination of psychologists and directed the attention of emotion researchers to the autonomic system and visceral functions.

The Original Feedback Hypothesis in Emotion Theory. James formulated the first feedback hypothesis in emotion theory, but it did not hold true to Darwin's lead. Generally, James's hypothesis about the cause of emotion has been interpreted as relating to feedback from "bodily changes," primarily visceral in nature. He defined emotion as the perception of the bodily changes brought about by the stimulus situation. That is, he considered emotion to be the individual's awareness of the sensations produced by such phenomena as a pounding heart and interrupted or rapid breathing. However, in the original statement of his famous theory, James (1884) clearly included voluntary striate muscle action in his concept of bodily changes. After describing certain visceral and glandular responses involved in emotion, James said:

> And what is really *equally* prominent, but less likely to be admitted until special attention is drawn to the fact, is the continuous cooperation of the *voluntary*

muscles in our emotional states. Even when no change or outward attitude is produced, *their inward tension alters to suit each varying mood,* and is felt as a difference of tone or strain. (James, 1884, p. 192)

The research and conclusions relating to James's notion were beclouded by the relationship that developed between James's ideas and those of Lange (1885). Lange took the position that emotion consisted of vasomotor disturbances in the visceral and glandular organs and that secretory, motor, cognitive, and experiential phenomena are secondary effects. This proved to be a very unfortunate mergence of ideas, for it concealed from most emotion researchers the fact that James thought that striate (voluntary) muscle feedback also played a role in emotion. Except for largely unnoticed clarifications and extensions of the concept by F. H. Allport (1924) and Jacobson (1929), the mainstream of science excluded (or neglected) the role of the somatic system and facial feedback for over seventy years. (For more detail on the history of the feedback hypothesis, see Izard, 1971, pp. 114–19; 401–06.)

The James–Lange theory, grew rapidly in popularity. Psychologists apparently enjoyed explaining that according to this theory, a person was "sad because he cried, afraid because he ran." Note that these examples of the theory's application depend on broad-gauged feedback phenomena, from both voluntary and involuntary muscles. Gradually, however, in the tradition of the James–Lange theory of emotion (see Lange, 1885; and Wenger, 1950), the concept of bodily changes in emotion became synonomous with visceral activity innervated by the autonomic nervous system.

The popularity of the James–Lange theory set the stage for an attack on the feedback hypothesis by the great physiologist W. B. Cannon (1927). After a series of successful experiments in which he denervated the visceral organs of experimental animals, he thought he had successfully disconfirmed the James–Lange theory of emotion. He claimed that his evidence showed that (a) total separation of the viscera from the central nervous system does not alter emotional behavior, (b) the viscera are too insensitive and too slow to be a source of emotional feeling, (c) the same visceral changes occur in different emotional states and in nonemotional states, and (d) artificial induction of the visceral changes typical of emotions does not produce emotions. Cannon's arguments and supporting evidence appear rather convincing, but they had no bearing on facial–postural (somatic system) feedback. In fact, the work of Cannon actually supports the facial feedback hypothesis and the position of differential emotions theory, which excludes visceral activity from the emotion process proper and relegates it to the role of an auxiliary system. Further, Cannon's argument that there can be sympathetic nervous system (visceral) arousal in *nonemotional* states is consistent with the differential emotions theory concept of the relative independence of emotion and visceral arousal—increased visceral arousal from exercise (or from sympathomimetic drugs) does not necessarily involve emotions, a point also made by Marañon (1924).

Mandler (1975) gives a detailed critique of Cannon's criticisms, disagreeing with the first two of Cannon's points and agreeing with the last two. In support of the autonomic nervous system (ANS) arousal–cognition view of emotion, he maintains that ANS arousal combined with cognitive interpretation of the arousal-eliciting conditions produces emotion and that it is the arousal that provides the "warmth" or "coloring" of emotion experience. His arguments against Cannon's first two points lack clear empirical support. In attempting to write off Cannon's point that emotion experience results more rapidly than (and hence prior to) ANS arousal (which has a one- to two-second latency), he suggested that "emotional stimuli are *familiar stimuli* that may directly produce some aspect of the emotional response" (p. 99, italics added). To support the notion that " 'emotional' responses can occur in the absence of arousal," he invoked the idea that such "familiar stimuli" could trigger "autonomic imagery" that could mediate "emotional responses." Aside from the fact that the notion of emotion without arousal is contradictory to the basic Schachter–Mandler position, it does not seem plausible in evolutionary perspective. If an organism had to form an association between stimuli and autonomic imagery before it could react rapidly in critical situations, its chances of survival would be substantially reduced.

The Somatic System, Facial Feedback, and Emotion Differentiation. Despite Cannon's devastating criticism of the visceral feedback hypothesis, most emotion investigators continued to study the autonomic nervous system and visceral processes. A significant exception was F. H. Allport, the first scientist to consider the somatic system and striate muscle feedback as the critical factor in determining what specific emotion would be experienced.

Allport (1924) maintained that the autonomic nervous system accounts only for the two broad classes of affective reactions—the pleasant, mediated by the parasympathetic division, and the unpleasant, mediated by the sympathetic division. Although this sharp dichotomy of sympathetic and parasympathetic functions in affective processes is no longer tenable, his concept of emotion differentiation has a more contemporaneous ring. The differentiation of positive and negative affective reactions into specific emotions was seen as a function of sensory stimuli from the somatic system. He stated his hypothesis as follows:

> We propose that the differentiating factor arises from the stimulation of the proprioceptors in the muscles, tendons, and joints of the somatic part of the organism, and that afferent impulses from these somatic patterns of response add to the autonomic core of affectivity the characteristic sensory complexes by which one emotion is distinguished from another of the same affective class. (Allport, 1924, pp. 91–92)

Since Allport's modification of the feedback hypothesis, a few theorists have focused on the role of striate muscle activity and the consequent sensory messages from proprioceptors (neural receptors imbedded in the muscles) and cutaneous receptors (receptors in the skin). More specifically, they have been concerned with facial expression, as first described in scientific literature by Duchenne (1876) and Darwin, and with face–brain feedback.

The special significance of the face, facial expression, and facial feedback was first emphasized by Tomkins (1962), and then by Gellhorn (1964). In the language of Tomkins (1962), the emotions are primarily facial responses. He maintains that proprioceptive feedback from facial behavior, when transformed into conscious form, constitutes the experience or awareness of emotion. Emotion-specific innate programs for organized sets of facial responses are stored in subcortical centers. Because the nerves and muscles of the face are much more finely differentiated than those of the viscera, facial activity and feedback are much more rapid responses than that of the viscera. Visceral responses play a secondary role in emotion, providing only background or accompaniment for the discrete expressions of the face. According to Tomkins, a specific emotion is a specific facial expression, and our awareness of that facial expression is the innately programmed subjective experience of emotion.

Gellhorn (1964) has offered a very detailed analysis of the relationship between proprioceptive impulses from facial and postural activity and the subjective experience of emotion. According to his neurophysiological analysis of discrete emotions, the proprioceptive and cutaneous discharges from the face contribute via the posterior hypothalamus to the cortical excitation that accompanies emotion. Thus "facial, proprioceptive, and cutaneous impulses seem to play an important role in facilitating the complex interactions between brain stem and limbic and neocortex which occur during emotion, and to contribute to the variety of cortical patterns of excitation which underlie specific emotions" (p. 466). In short, Gellhorn thought that feedback from facial contractions resulted in hypothalamic–cortical excitation which, in turn, influences the subjective experience of emotion. He was cautious in assigning a strictly causal role to the sensory stimuli from the face, but he appeared confident in the efficacy of the face as a regulator of emotion, as did Darwin, James, and Allport before him.

The Emotion Process in Terms of Differential Emotions Theory

Building on the work of Darwin, early James, F. Allport, Tomkins, and Gellhorn, Izard hypothesizes that facial patterning is one of the integral components of emotion. While facial expression is part of the emotion or emotion process, neither this nor any other single component constitutes emotion. In his theory, an emotion consists of three interrelated components: neural activity of the brain and somatic nervous system, striate muscle or facial–postural expression and face–brain feedback, and subjective experience. Each component has sufficient autonomy so that in certain unusual conditions it may be dissociated from the others, but the three components are characteristically interactive and interdependent in the emotion process.

Functions of the Somatic Nervous System in Emotion Activation. Differential emotions theory postulates the continual presence of emotion in consciousness. Therefore, the following description of the emotion process applies to the activation and experiencing of a new emotion. An internal or external event, as processed by the selectivity and organizing functions of relevant receptors changes the gradient of neural stimulation and the pattern of activity in the limbic system and sensory cortex. Impulses from either the cortex or from limbic structures (probably the thalamus) are directed to the hypothalamus, which plays a role in emotion differentiation, determining what facial expression will be effected. From the hypothalamus impulses go to the basal ganglia, which organize the neural message for the facial expression that is mediated by the motor cortex. In the case of a fundamental emotion, impulses from the motor cortex via the facial (VIIth cranial) nerve lead to a specific facial expression. The trigeminal (Vth cranial) nerve conducts the sensory (facial receptor) impulses, probably via posterior hypothalamus, to the sensory cortex. Finally, the cortical integration of facial-expression feedback generates the subjective experience of emotion. The emotion process probably also involves other complex interactions between neocortical and limbic structures, with the structures and nature of the interactions varying for different fundamental emotions.

Functions of the Visceral System. The three-component definition of emotion and the foregoing description of emotion activation (the events that lead from neural activation to experiential or "felt" emotion) apply to emotion proper, not to the activities of the autonomically innervated visceral organs. Differential emotions theory does not rule out the importance of homeostatic mechanisms or autonomic–visceral–glandular processes as auxiliary systems. Once an emotion is activated it typically involves virtually all the life-systems. The glandular–hormonal system, the cardiovascular system, and the respiratory system are particularly important in amplifying and sustaining emotion.

The fact that the glandular–hormonal system is typically aroused in emotion has contributed to the confusion about the role of visceral functions. Once an emotion has been activated and facial feedback has provided the differential data for a specific emotion experience, the individual may become acutely aware of such autonomic–visceral changes as a pounding heart, flushed ("hot") skin, "woozy" stomach or sweaty palms. Since changes in visceral activities are usually associated with emotion and since such changes can demand more of the individual's attention than impulses from the face, it is easy to infer that they are the real "cause" of emotion, or at least a part of the emotion process. Another factor contributing to erroneous attributions about the autonomic–visceral system is the fact that facial feedback plays its role in emotion activation in a rapid reflexive fashion and awareness of facial activity or facial feedback is actually our awareness of the subjective experience of a specific emotion. One does not ordinarily become aware of the proprioceptive and cutaneous impulses (as such) created by frowning or smiling; rather, one becomes aware of experiential anger or joy. Once angry or joyful the individual may become acutely aware of the accompanying changes in visceral functions, and misattribute causal or other nonveridical characteristics to them.

Visceral functions are often important auxiliaries or accompaniments to emotion. Changes in the autonomic–visceral system are necessary in organizing the body for emotion-related activity. They merit attention from the experiencing individual; to be heedless to situations that make the heart race may prove dangerous. They deserve the attention of scientists since their specific role in different discrete emotions remains unknown, but hopefully the setbacks due to the attribution of nonveridical characteristics to the autonomic–visceral system will diminish.

Somatic vs. Visceral Components in Emotion. Several features that distinguish differential emotions theory, which emphasizes the somatic system, from theories that emphasize the autonomic system and visceral functions warrant recapitulation. First, autonomic–visceral arousal can occur without emotion, and hence is not a perfect indicator of emotion. Second, the differentiation of specific emotions in consciousness (subjective experience) is dependent on the rapid and specific sensory feedback from the activity of the finely differentiated (somatic) muscles of the face as they form discrete facial expressions or corresponding covert patterns. The cortical integration of facial feedback produces the specific emotion experience. In short, the face provides the data for the activation of qualitatively distinct emotions, but it may be less critical in sustaining emotions. The activity of the striate muscles of the body and the smooth muscles of the viscera amplify and sustain emotion and tell us something about its intensity.

Emotion Experience without Facial Expression. A possible variation in the emotion activation process is exemplified when an emotion process is initiated (or anticipated) but the facial expression is partially or fully inhibited. Such expression inhibition may be willfully effected by an individual who knows he is about to face a frustrating anger-eliciting situation in which a show of anger is in violation of personal values and social norms.

For example, on a particular occasion Rafe makes a decision and a determined effort, including motor activity contrary to anger expression, in order to avoid displaying any behavior that would signal anger. His effort may be called volitional or willful inhibition. In this situation he can still experience anger in one of three ways. First, the anger expression may actually occur but occurrence may be limited to such rapid patterning of facial musculature that it would not ordinarily be perceived by the observer. Haggard and Isaacs (1966) have demonstrated the existence of such "micromomentary expressions." Such expressions could furnish the feedback required for generating the subjective experience. Further, studies by Schwartz, Fair, Greenberg, Freedman, and Klerman (1974) have suggested that subjects who visualize an emotion-eliciting situation show predictable changes in facial muscle tension (EMG) even when no marked expression appears on the face.

Second, Rafe could experience anger even though the motor message from the subcortical centers were entirely blocked at the final synapse in the pathway to the face, preventing any movement or change in the target muscles. In this case the activation of emotion is based on the assumption that the efferent (motor) message to the face, though prevented from stimulating facial muscles, triggers a sensory message that simulates the emotion-specific facial feedback that typically occurs with facial expression. Thus a reafferent or inner loop is substituted for the usual efferent–afferent (outer) loop via patterned facial muscles.

Third, through a process like classical conditioning, Rafe could have developed an association between the particular proprioceptive cutaneous pattern of stimulation (the "feeling") of an anger expression on the one hand and the subjective experience of anger on the other. In this case the "memory" or what it "feels" like to have an anger-expression on the face could substitute for the actual expression, and the emotion process would again be completed by a reafferent loop.

Suppression of facial expression in the presence of strong emotion-eliciting conditions calls for the nervous system to do extra work since it is blocking the normal emotion process (inhibiting facial expression) and executing a circuitous one. Chronic use of such an indirect emotion activation process might lead to psychosomatic or other psychological problems.

Facial Expression without Emotion Experience. Under unusual conditions the facial feedback from a discrete expression may not achieve consciousness (hence no new "felt" or experiential emotion) because of overriding demands already being made on consciousness or by virtue of some inhibitory process. The inhibitory process could be the existence in consciousness of a strong emotion. For example, a high intensity of the emotion of interest–excitement can sustain such intense cognitive activity, as in the pursuit of a scientific discovery, that a competing emotion would not achieve awareness. Inhibition could also result from an ongoing high-intensity drive. A starving person might not experience disgust because his intense hunger enables him to eat substances that would ordinarily disgust and repel him. Also, ongoing emotion–drive interactions, such as the interaction of the sex drive, excitement, and the emotions involved in romantic love can inhibit competing emotions or drives from achieving awareness.

Two corollaries follow the foregoing propositions. First, when the initial neural and expressive components of emotion fall short of full cortical integration and the achievement of awareness, unexpended energy exists in the nervous system. This energy may be directed to the brain stem reticular formation, with a resulting increase in nonspecific activation or arousal and increased activity in autonomically innervated organs. Chronic repetition of these effects can contribute to the development of psychosomatic symptoms. Second, if the neural and expressive components reach a certain level of integration, the nascent subjective experience may be stored as a unit in some type of memory system. In this case the subjective experience may be realized at a later time (a) as a function of the stimulus associated with the original experience, (b) by an active search-and-retrieval process, or (c) by spontaneous neural activity. This kind of delay of the emotion experience is similar to what Tomkins (1962) calls the postponement of emotion.

As already indicated, under ordinary conditions facial expression or a particular pattern of changes in the tension of the appropriate facial muscles leads to emotion experience. Situations in which discrete facial expression does not lead immediately to emotion are considered to be rare. An exception to this rule, however, is voluntary expression.

Voluntary Expression and Emotion. A voluntary expression displayed for purposes of social communication may fail to activate the emotion process either because voluntary and involuntary expression involve different neural structures and pathways or because the sensory feedback might be blocked by one of the inhibitory processes described above. The social smile is a good example of voluntary expression that may not activate joy and that may not even be veridical to ongoing emotion experience. Nevertheless, the open and deliberate use of a specific voluntary expression to activate the corresponding subjective experience may be effective if the individual wants the experience (e.g., to bolster courage) and if inhibitory processes are not too strong. There are both neurological and psychological grounds for such emotion activation. Even if there are different motor pathways for effecting voluntary and involuntary expression, both types could result in similar sensory feedback to the cortex, and the desire to experience the emotion should reduce the strength of inhibitory processes.

Facial Expression and the Regulation of Emotion Experience. It follows from the foregoing theory of the emotion process that facial expression, when sufficiently veridical to the expression of a fundamental emotion, can play a role in the control or regulation of emotion experience.

A number of prominent emotion theorists and investigators have reached a similar conclusion. Darwin maintained that the free expression of an emotion ("by outward signs") intensifies it, while suppression of overt expression attenuates ("softens") it (Darwin, 1872, p. 22). James thought that if a person refuses to express an emotion "it dies," and that one can "conquer undesirable emotional tendencies" if one will assiduously go through the outward movements of a contrary and desirable emotion. Similar opinions have been expressed by Dumas (1948), Jacobson (1967), and Pesso (1969), and Gellhorn (1964, 1970) has proposed a well-reasoned account of the neurophysiological bases for emotion control by means of the expressive system.

The notion supported by the scientists cited above is consistent with such folkways as whistling in the dark to convince oneself (and any potential adversaries) that one is happy and not frightened. Yet despite common belief and long standing scientific opinion that altering one's facial expression and posture alters one's emotion experience, there have been only two series of experiments testing aspects of this proposition (Laird, 1974; Kotsch & Izard, in preparation). In these studies, simple manipulation of facial muscles by experimenter instructions did not produce expression–experience correspondence. However, these studies did not rule out the possible effectiveness of self-determined expression or such expression in combination with relevant imagery, cognition, and action.

The Relative Independence of the Emotion Process. According to discrete emotions theory the emotion process can operate relatively independent of any cognitive process. However, cognition interacts with the emotion process almost continually. In addition to regular interactions that influence ongoing affective–cognitive processes, there are special interactions such as that which takes place when an individual makes the decision to inhibit a facial expression. This decision and the lack of expression may serve to decrease the intensity of the subjective experience of the discrete emotion of anger while increasing autonomic activity that may be experienced as "stress," "strain," or an even more vague sort of discomfort. As already suggested, a person can initiate and sustain cognitive and motor activities that can inhibit the facial-expression component of emotion. It is also possible that inhibitory processes can influence the feedback from a facial expression in such a way that it is never transformed into a conscious report. In this case the subjective experience of the discrete emotion would not occur. Thus, while cognition can influence the emotion process in important ways, cognition is not a necessary part of the process, and it ordinarily plays no part in the normal face–brain feedback. The neural messages from the patterned face follow innate pathways, and the cortical integration of this information is entirely sufficient to generate the subjective experience of the emotion without the influence of cognition.

Yet, the importance of cognition (via emotion–cognition interaction) in motivation and behavior can hardly be overestimated. After initiation of the emotion process the cognitive system quickly comes into play. Indeed, cognitive processes such as memory and imagination often result in emotion activation (Singer, 1974). Whatever the stimulus, memory and anticipation play a role in organizing the action of the organism as a whole. The influence between the emotion and cognitive systems is reciprocal, the balance between them or the dominance of one over the other helping to determine the appropriateness and effectiveness of personality functioning.

The motor system and emotion system interact in ways similar to the cognition–emotion interactions. As is the case with cognition, motor activity can also result in emotion activation. A success in one's favorite sport can lead to interest and enjoyment; a failure, to anger, shame, or self-contempt. There are a number of ways in which motor activity influences emotion; for example, fatigue may lower the thresholds of the negative emotions; relaxation, raise them.

Effective personality functioning results from balanced and harmonious interaction of the emotion, cognition, and motor systems and the necessary support of the auxiliary and other life systems. There is no fixed formula for balance and interaction among systems which guarantees effective functioning of the person as a whole; rather, optimal balance and interaction of systems is influenced by environment, particularly the social context, and adjusted by person–environment processes.

Definition of Key Terms in Differential Emotions Theory

As a partial summary and glossary for differential emotions theory, the definitions of some key terms are presented below.

Emotion (Fundamental, Discrete). An emotion is a complex phenomenon having neurophysiological, motor-expressive, and experiential components. The intraindividual process whereby these components interact to produce the emotion is an evolutionary-biogenetic phenomenon. For example, in the human being the expression of anger and the experiential phenomenon of anger are innate, pancultural, universal phenomena.

Patterns of Emotions. A pattern of emotions is a combination of two or more fundamental emotions which under particular conditions tend to occur together (either simultaneously or in a repeating sequence) and to interact in such a way that all of the emotions in the pattern have some motivational impact on the organism and its behavior.

Drives. A drive is a motivational state brought about by tissue change or tissue deficit. Drives are examplified by the common phenomena of hunger, thirst, fatigue, etc. The motivational intensity of all the drives except pain is cyclical in nature. Two of the drives, pain and sex, have some of the characteristics of emotions.

Affect. Affect is a general nonspecific term that includes all the foregoing motivational states and processes. Thus the affective domain includes the fundamental emotions, patterns of emotions, drives, and their interactions. The affective domain also embraces states or processes in which one of the affects (emotions, drives) is linked with or interacting with perception or cognition.

Emotion–Emotion Interaction. An emotion–emotion interaction is the amplification, attentuation, or inhibition of one emotion by another.

Emotion–Drive Interaction. These are motivational states characterized by the amplification, attenuation, or inhibition of drive by emotion or vice versa.

Affect-Interaction. An affect intensifies, deintensifies, blocks, or alters the quality of a percept (or a perceptual process), a concept (or a cognitive process), or an act (or activity).

Affective–Cognitive Structure or Orientation. An affective–cognitive structure or orientation represents a bond, tie, or strong association of one of the affects (or a pattern of affects) with images, words, thoughts, or ideas.

Affect Expression. Affect expression occupies a middle ground between an experiential/motivational state and behavior. For example, the patterning of the striate muscles of the face in the form of anger expression can be described as facial responses or facial behavior. However, the essential feature of a facial, vocal, gestural, or postural expression that is integral to the emotion process is its motivational property, not its behavioral structure. These definitions distinguish between experiential/motivational phenomena and behavior and thus narrow the meaning of the latter. Behavior includes perceptual and cognitive processes (perception, imaging, thinking, remembering, planning) as well as manipulatory and locomotor activity.

Action or Behavior. Behavior is a genral term that cannot be defined precisely without going against long standing tradition. Behaviorists use the term to refer to observable responses, but others use it to refer to any organismic function, whether affective, cognitive, or motor. The present author prefers to avoid the term behavior when a more precise or limited term (e.g., cardiovascular, perceptual, cognitive, motor) is applicable.

Because of the surplus meanings and ambiguities surrounding the concept of behavior, the interchangeable term, action, is preferred. Action refers to motor acts (including vocal activity or speech), other than those involved in the expressive component of emotion. Action is distinguished from affective states and processes. Thus emotions, emotion patterns, and drives are not considered as behavior or action, but as the motivational phenomena that produce behavior or behavioral tendencies. Action or behavior will refer mainly to activity of the individual as a whole, activity that follows from the experiential/motivational phenomena of affective processes and which may include activities of all nonaffective subsystems.

4

THE FACE,
THE FUNDAMENTAL EMOTIONS,
AND AFFECT INTERACTIONS

A number of different theories now implicitly (and sometimes explicitly) suggest that an emotion has three components: the neural, the expressive (mainly facial), and the experiential. Further, an increasing number of investigators in personality and social psychology, and practitioners in psychiatry and clinical psychology have been placing emphasis on the importance of the expressive component of emotion. There are a number of reasons for this emphasis. The face is the supreme center for sending and receiving social signals that are crucial for development of the individual, interpersonal communication, and the cohesiveness of the family and society.

Evolutionary-Biological Significance of Facial Expression in Social Communication

Facial expressions of the emotions have evolutionary-biological significance as well as psychological and social significance. Leading contemporary ethological theorists support Darwin's (1872) belief that facial expressions resulted from the evolutionary process. Darwin held that expressions evolved primarily from "serviceable associated habits" or what Tinbergen calls intention movements (Tinbergen, 1952)—the incomplete or preparatory phases of activities such as attack, locomotion, defense, and movements associated with respiration and vision. During the course of evolution facial expression developed into a system of social communication that conveyed information about the internal states ("intentions") of the

expressor and alerted fellow creatures to certain aspects of the environment. For example, a fearful face signaled the perception of danger and the
intention of the organism to flee or submit.

The field studies by ethologists (e.g., Blurton Jones, 1972; McGrew,
1972; Van Hooff, 1967) and some recent experiments by psychologists
(e.g., Miller, Banks, & Ogawa, 1962; Miller, Caul, & Mirsky, 1967; Miller,
Murphy, & Mirsky, 1959) have provided clear evidence of the significance
and validity of social communication via facial patterning.

The importance of facial expressions and facial movements in social
communication among primates has been noted by almost every student of
primate behavior (Altmann, 1967). While the whole body of the primate is
typically involved in a rapid movement of musculature providing a dynamic
visual signal (often accompanied by a vocal signal), certain parts of the
body seem to assume a particularly significant role in the visual aspect of
primate communication. Marler (1965) and Van Hooff (1962) agree that in
most species of primates the face is the most important part of the animal in
this respect. Hinde and Rowell (1962) have described various distinctive
facial patterns in the rhesus monkey that play particularly important roles
in the communication of threat, harassment, submission–fright, and pacifi-
cation. Elsewhere, these same facial patterns have been shown to be
closely associated with interanimal communication involved in establishing
and maintaining a social dominance heirarchy (Bernstein, 1970; Sade,
1967). While many authors (e.g., Altmann, 1967; Marler, 1965) have
emphasized the importance of considering multisensory, composite signals,
all have attested to the fact that facial patterns are integrally associated with
these communicative behavorial constellations in primates (Altmann, 1967;
Van Hooff, 1967).

The Evolutionary Perspective. A review of the theory and research on
the evolution of facial expression (Izard, 1971) led to the following
conclusions:

1. The facial neuromuscular mechanisms necessary for executing the
   basic expressions show continuity from the higher primates to man
   (Bolwig, 1964; Darwin, 1872; Huber, 1931) (see Figure 4-1).
2. Facial expressions in man bear close similarity to animal responses
   that originally served a function relating to defense of vulnerable
   areas, to vigorous respiration, and to grooming (Andrew, 1963,
   1965; Van Hooff, 1963).
3. Some facial expressions closely resemble reflexive reactions (and
   consequent spreading reactions) to nonsocial stimuli (Peiper, 1963).
4. At least some facial expressions are derived from responses that
   served to communicate to other animals. This concept was seen in
   the work of Darwin (1972) and Tinbergen (1952) and stated very
   strongly by Andrew (1963), who held that the communicative ele-

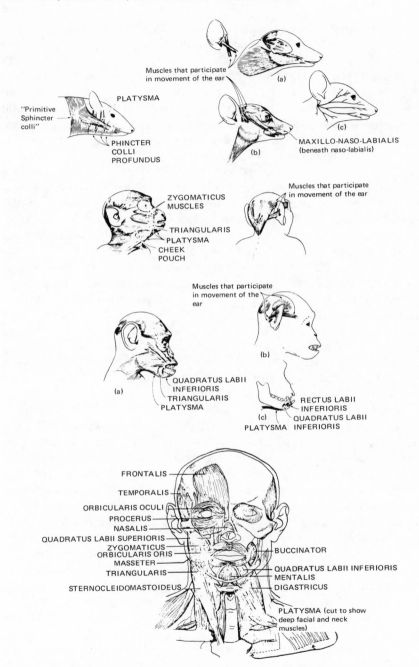

FIGURE 4-1. Continuity of facial muscle development and facial expressions in animals and human beings. (Nonhuman primate drawings adapted from Huber, 1931; that of the human being, from Izard, 1971.)

ment must be present before natural selection could begin to shape a response into a component of a display.

5. Some facial expressions may be the result of nonvoluntary "actions due to the constitution of the nervous system" (Darwin, 1872, pp. 28–29).

6. Emotion is adaptive in the life of the highly complex, social organisms (Izard, 1959, 1971; Izard & Tomkins, 1966; Leeper, 1948; Tomkins, 1962). The same argument can be made for the expression and recognition of the emotions.

The theory and evidence that led to the foregoing conclusions have a bearing on the question of the fundamental biologic character of the emotions and their facial expressions. Certainly if the human facial expressions are phyletically continuous with the displays of subhuman organisms, then evolutionary selection must have played an important role in the differentiation of the emotions and their expressions. If we assume that differentiated emotion expressions have an evolutionary-biological basis, then studies of their adaptive functions should prove rewarding. In their studies of how genetically programmed behavioral patterns and experience contributed to the adaptiveness and adjustability of the organism, many ethological investigators obtained an appreciation of the adaptive value of facial patterning. The studies of human ethologists like Blurton Jones (1972), Grant (1969), and McGrew (1972) point the way to ethological analysis of the expressive component of discrete emotions.

Working independently and following a rather different approach, Tomkins and McCarter (1964), Ekman, Friesen, and Ellsworth (1972), and Izard (1971) have presented strong evidence for the existence of genetically determined universal behavior patterns that represent several fundamental emotions. Their findings showed that significant aspects of emotion communication were based on genetically programmed and species-common behavior patterns—the facial expressions of the fundamental emotions.

All human social bonds or interpersonal relationships are based on emotions and the emotions are communicated one to another primarily by means of facial expressions. In the most fundamental social bond, the mother–infant relationship, facial expressions, as Darwin (1877) noted, play a significant role. The work of Bowlby (1969) and others has shown that failure to establish an affectionate mother–infant relationship can have serious consequences in the social and emotion development of the individual.

Evolutionary-Phylogenetic Changes in Emotion Components and Emotion Communication. The importance of facial as compared with postural activity in emotion, and particularly in emotion differentiation and emotion communication, increases with phylogenetic and ontogenetic development. In phylogeny, this change parallels the evolution of the facial muscles. In the invertebrates and lower vertebrates, there are no superficial facial muscles at all. These animals are not thought to have a very large repertory of emotions if, indeed, the term emotion can properly be applied to such animals. What is considered by some as emotion or emotional behavior in these animals is ordinarily labeled as aversive or attack behavior by the behavioristically oriented scientists who prefer not to infer emotional experience in animals.

Regardless of theoretical orientation, there is fairly wide agreement that the range of emotions or "emotional behavior" in the invertebrates and lower vertebrates is highly limited, and this may be considered a condition paralleling the absence or paucity of superficial facial musculature. Beyond the possibility of differentiating when the mouth is opening in preparation for attack and when it is opening for ingestion (when indeed these two are separable processes) the faces of many of the lower animals remain inscrutable.

Going up the phylogenetic scale to the level of birds, one can observe patterned expressions or displays involving head and facial features. There may be some question as to whether bird displays should be termed emotional, but there is good evidence that they play a significant role in social communication and social relationships (Smith, 1969). Candland (1969) cited a number of investigators (e.g., Guhl, 1956; Hale, 1948; Marks, Siegel, & Kramer, 1960) who have obtained evidence supporting the proposition that the head and facial features of the domestic chicken play a crucial role in maintaining the social dominance order. In these studies, alternation or removal of various facial features produced change in the dominance relationship.

Dominance, at least in certain species of birds and animals, is sometimes temporarily determined by the outcome of fights. One can easily infer that in higher species emotions such as anger and fear play a part in aggressive acts such as fighting. A less well-grounded though seemingly reasonable inference is that in evolution, as in the development and maintenance of social order, emotion displays became capable of deterring or short-circuiting aggression.

Among vertebrates, the facial ground plan varies from complete absence of superficial facial musculature to the well-developed musculature of the higher primates and the complex, finely differentiated facial muscles in man. The ethological evidence on classification of emotion expressions in primates as advanced as the rhesus macaque monkey suggests that postural activity remains an important ingredient in emotion. In Hinde and Rowell's (1962) careful analysis of emotion expression in the rhesus macaque, many of the facial expressions are described in context with particular postural or other motor activity. Van Hooff's (1967) work comparing facial displays of catarrhine monkeys and apes suggests that facial displays may become somewhat more independent of posture and locomotion in the anthropoid apes. For human beings the evidence indicates that facial patterns as communicative cues have gained considerable independence from posture, locomotion, and environment (Ekman, Friesen, & Ellsworth, 1972; Eibl-Eibesfeldt, 1972; Izard, 1971). Figure 4-2 shows some similarities between chimpanzee and human facial expressions.

The Social and Psychological Significance of the Face

Long before infants can speak a single word, their facial expressions convey messages that are crucial in binding mother and infant in an affectional relationship and in the maintenance of the infant's well-being. These messages have vital importance not only because they are infants' chief means of communication, but also because what they communicate is highly important. They indicate infants' emotional states. Their facial expressions tell us whether they are happy or sad, angry or frightened,

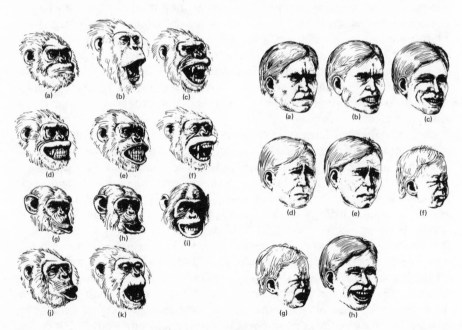

FIGURE 4-2. Continuity of facial expressions in chimpanzees and human beings (from S. Chevalier-Skolnikoff, Facial expressions of emotion in nonhuman primates, in P. Ekman (Ed.) Darwin and facial expression: A century of research in review. New York: Academic Press, 1973).

surprised or shy. If we could not "read" infants' faces, we could not understand their most important communications. We could not empathize with them or show them sympathy.

The Face as a Social Stimulus. The literature on the role of the face in the infant and child's social development has been reviewed by Charlesworth and Kreutzer (1973) and Vine (1973). Numerous studies show that the human face is an extraordinary social stimulus. A list of some of the more important findings will illustrate the significance of the face in interpersonal interactions.

Infants will focust their eyes on the eyes of an attending person in a true mutual gaze by the age of three weeks (Wolff, 1963).

The face (or a facial schema) is preferred by the neonate to various stimuli (Fantz, 1963; Stechler, 1964), and the more realistic the face the greater the visual fixation time of the infant (Fantz, 1965, 1966). (Other studies by Thomas (1965) and Kagan (1970) suggest that preference for the face as a stimulus varies with age and other factors. Fantz and Nevis (1967a,b) found that the most consistent overall preference between 0–24 months was for a bull's eye target. Definitive experiments on this problem are difficult because the measurement techniques in this area are complex and not entirely satisfactory.)

The face in comparison with several other stimuli (photographs of nursing bottle and panda bear, checkerboard, bull's-eye target) resulted in more visual attention and motor quieting (including decreased heart rate) in six-month-old infants (Kagan & Lewis, 1965; McCall & Kagan, 1967).

Some of the inconsistencies in the findings on the face as a visual stimulus in infancy undoubtedly result from problems of measurement. For one thing, it is difficult to obtain any one certain index of the infant's visual behavior. There is a question as to whether to measure duration of first look, frequency of looks, overall looking time, or to combine one or more of these with various psychophysiological measures. Although there are methodological problems and much yet to be learned about the affective aspects of the infant's response to facial and comparison stimuli, the weight of the evidence suggests that the human face is a potent stimulus in social development.

The Face, Emotion Communication, and Mother–Infant Attachment. Mother–infant attachment has been considered by many scientists as the foundation of social life, and the systems of behavior that constitute attachment are usually considered to be closely related to the emotions. John Bowlby, who has been a student of attachment for many years, devoted an entire volume to the subject. He concluded:

> No form of behavior is accompanied by stronger feeling than attachment behavior. The figures toward whom it is directed are loved and their advent is greeted with joy. So long as a child is in the unchallenged presence of a principal

attachment-figure, or within easy reach, he feels secure. A threat of loss creates
anxiety, and actual loss, sorrow; both, moreover, are likely to arouse anger.
(Bowlby, 1969, p. 209)

Although there are some similarities in attachment behavior across
species, attachment behavior in human beings shows substantial differences from that of nonhuman primates. For example, on the first day of life
the rhesus macaque infant can move to its mother and support its own
weight while clinging to her. It can perform these response-sequences
before it can discriminate its mother from other monkeys. Human infants
do not learn to discriminate their mothers from other people until the age of
about four months (see Figure 4-3), and it is yet another three months
before they can move to their mothers or do much in the way of clinging to
them.

Perhaps the first evidence of attachment behavior emerges at about the
age of four months when the infant discriminates his or her mother from
other people and shows his or her preference for mother by visually
tracking her as she moves through the field of vision. At about this age the
infant also begins to make proximity-maintaining responses (e.g., crying)
when the mother gets out of the infant's field of vision. By about the age of
six months infants not only cry when the mother departs but may attempt
to follow her on all fours (Ainsworth, 1967). At this age infants also perform
proximity-maintenance responses when the mother returns. They smile,
hold out open arms, and make vocal sounds associated with interest and
joy. All these actions become more regular and stronger in the period from
six to nine months. At the age of nine months infants cling to the mother

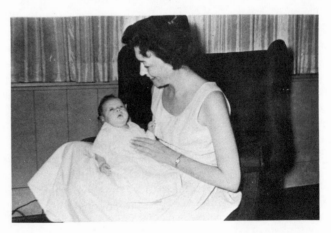

FIGURE 4-3. *A mother seeks face-to-face emotion communication with her five-week-old
infant, not yet old enough to "perceive" mother's face.*

when they are frightened, and they seek body contact with the mother when they are distressed.

The sequences of responses in attachment behavior continue with about the same frequency and intensity until the last quarter or so of the third year of life. Toward the end of the first year and throughout the second and most of the third year of life the infant shows the ability to anticipate the mother's intentions to depart, and it may perform proximity-maintaining responses before she leaves. After about four years of age, the frequency and intensity of sequences of responses in attachment behavior gradually decrease but by no means disappear.

As babies grow from infant to toddler, their facial expressions of emotion facilitate the development of play with age-mates and the establishment of the relationships that characterize their social life. Beginning with adolescence, attachment behavior begins to be directed more toward peers and less toward parents. Attachment may also be directed toward groups and institutions other than the family (e.g., school, college, work group, religious group). Despite the decrease in frequency and intensity of the responses in the behavioral systems of attachment, bonds with parents tend to be maintained throughout adolescence and adulthood and continue to influence the individual in many ways.

Thus, attachment can be described as a set of emotion ties that create a strong bond between two individuals. In infancy the establishment and maintenance of these ties depends in large measure on emotion communication via the facial–visual system. The vocal expression of emotions (cooing, babbling, crying, screaming) also plays a significant part in this special interpersonal relationship. The third important factor in developing and maintaining attachment is the sense of touch and the exercise of this sensory modality by body contact.

The hypothesis that attachment results from emotion communication via the visual, aural, and somesthetic (skin) senses is contrary to the view of classical psychoanalytic and social learning theorists who explain attachment as a function of the mother's role in gratifying the infant's "primary" needs. According to these theories the mother's presence and appearance take on a secondary reward value by virtue of the mother's association with need gratification. However, infants do not show attachment to other objects (e.g., nursing bottles) associated with need gratification, and such objects elicit neither smiling (Dennis, 1935), vocalization (Kagan & Lewis, 1965), nor attentional responses (Fantz and Nevis, 1967a,b). The work of Kistiakovskaia (1965) and Shaffer and Emerson (1964) shows that the person who fulfills the essential caretaking responsibilities for the infant is not necessarily the focus of the first and strongest attachment. Walters and Parke (1965) have made a strong case for the importance of the visual and auditory senses (distance receptors) in social attachment. It is difficult to explain the importance of these sensory modalities on the basis of the drive-reduction concepts of classical psychoanalytic and social learning theory. Their role in receiving the signals of emotion expression is obvious.

The emotion communication theory of social attachment does not rule out the role of learning, but the type of learning that is important may better be explained on the basis of the exercise of innate tendencies and perceptual development, which go hand in hand as the infant grows. This crucial exercise of functions is like learning in that growth and development of the relevant perceptual skills requires practice that results from "stimulation"—facial–visual, vocal–aural, and tactile interaction with the mother or principal caregiver. Further, through a learning process like classical conditioning the infant may learn to respond to certain idiosyncrasies in the mother's emotion signaling and consequently develop some idiosyncrasies of its own.

The emotion communication theory is not necessarily inconsistent with Bowlby's (1969) notion that much of the behavior in mother–infant attachment is instinctive. He used the term instinctive like contemporary ethologists (e.g., Hinde, 1959) to refer to a biological character that is environmentally stable—one that is little influenced during the course of its development by variations of the environment. On the basis of the evidence presented by Ekman, Friesen, and Ellsworth (1972) and Izard (1971) the facial expressions of fundamental emotions meet all the criteria of biological characters that are environmentally stable. Thus Bowlby's notion that the mother–infant attachment is based largely on instinctive behavior is consistent with the emotion communication theory of attachment. The latter holds that the infant's emotion communication system is based in large part on expressive responses whose morphology was determined through evolutionary–genetic processes.

The emotion communication theory of attachment is similar in some respects to that of Sears (1972) who views the response patterns in attachment as a product of maturation, a process that involves the emergence of behavior patterns and the result of interaction of genetic programs and experience. Sears pointed out that the suddenness, intensity, passion, and prolonged irreversibility of the response patterns in attachment are difficult to explain in terms of learning theory such as the $s–r$ functional analysis proposed by Gewirtz (1972).

Bowlby (1969) proposed that there were five important patterns or systems included in attachment behavior: sucking, clinging, following, crying, and smiling. Four of the five can be seen as functions of systems implicated by the emotion communication theory of attachment. Crying and smiling involve the vocal–aural and facial–visual systems. Sucking and clinging can be seen as functions of the sense of touch, since both include body contact.

With the emergence of language and the rapid increase in cognitive and social skills, involuntary (reflexive, spontaneous) emotion expression is no longer the only type of facial patterning that influences the mother–infant relationship. Probably as early as the last half of the second year of life the child is capable of two broad classes of facial expression. Any given emotion has an expression which occurs naturally or instinctively as a part of the normal emotion process. The same emotion can also be expressed willfully or voluntarily as in the case in which one wants to convey to another that one feels a certain emotion. Voluntary expressions may be considered as a social skill and people (from infancy to old age) vary widely in the degree to which they develop and use this skill.

Voluntary expression may vary from something like "making faces" to a situation in which an individual feels a little of an emotion but wants to show much more of it. In still other instances an individual may want to feel an emotion and may use the facial expression in order to facilitate the experience. While little is known about the relationship between ability to express emotions voluntarily and other personality characteristics, it appears to be a fruitful area for investigation.

Emotion Expression and the Sense of Touch

Although some investigators (e.g., Shaffer & Emerson, 1964) have suggested that tactile stimulation is not a critical factor in human social attachment, there has been little or no research on the function of touch as a means of communicating emotion. It is not possible to present empirical evidence relating to the problem, but some discussion of the sense of touch may help understand its possible role in emotion expression and communication.

Harlow's (1971) extensive work with rhesus monkeys led him to conclude that touch or body contact is a biological need, integral to attachment and love. Montague (1972) did an extensive review of literature on the sense of touch and concluded that touching itself was an emotion response. Even if the feeling or sensory impressions that derive from body contact do not constitute an emotion per se, most people can readily agree that touching and body contact in a mother–infant relationship as well as all other social relationships tend to elicit emotions.

The importance of the sense of touch in emotion communication (and hence emotion control) may be clarified by placing it in evolutionary-biological perspective. Touch or the sensory impressions (feelings) arising from body (skin) contact is apparently associated with a number of behavior patterns that in at least some species appear to be as environmentally stable as facial patterns of emotions. In some species certain types of touching behavior have important biological and social functions. It has not been clearly established whether touching serves similar functions in human beings, but it is apparent that touching, like facial expression, is subject to social norms and a set of taboos that vary from culture to culture. The social phenomena related to the concept of "personal space" (the distance typically maintained between individuals of a given culture in face-to-face contact) probably derives from the cultural norms governing touching.

The sense of touch is highly complex. Of the five senses it is the one that has most frequently been subdivided into "extra" senses. According to Geldard (1972) a fair claim to independent status has been established for the following touch-qualities: contact pressure, deep pressure, prick pain, quick pain, deep pain, warmth, cold, heat, and muscular pressure. The organ of touch, the skin, has many different kinds of sensitivities, subserved by a multiplicity of end organs and sensory fibers.

Attributing special importance to the skin of the face has a basis in the anatomy of the brain. A sensory homunculus that shows the amount of cortical tissue devoted to the various parts of the body makes it quite evident that the face region, including the mouth and tongue, claim a highly disproportionate amount of cortical tissue. In Chapter 3, it was noted that Tomkins (1962), Gellhorn (1964), and Izard (1971) make the assumption that the cutaneous impulses from facial skin make up part of the sensory feedback that leads to discrete emotions.

The importance of touching the face in both affectionate and hostile gestures is a well-known transcultural phenomenon (see Figure 4-4).

FIGURE 4-4. A seven-month-old baby explores her sister's face through vision and touch in a positive affective interchange.

Touching the face can be a most intimate and tender caress between mother and infant as well as between lovers. On the contrary, slapping the face with hand or glove is counted among the highest insults, in earlier times a signal for a dual. Another indication of the importance of the skin and the sense of touch comes from common expressions such as "rubbing people the wrong way," "a soft touch," "handle with kid gloves," "thick skinned," "gets under your skin," "skin deep," "get the feel of it," and "a touching experience." Most of these expressions connote emotion.

Most mammalian mothers except the great apes and human beings stimulate the skin of their newborn infants by licking them. The evidence reviewed by Montague (1972) suggests that such stimulation of the skin of the newborn animal is important for survival in that in some species the genitourinary system would not function in the absence of cutaneous stimulation. Animal research has shown that licking or stroking and gentling by use of the hands tend to improve the health and vigor of growing animals.

Montague speculated that there has been an evolutionary development from licking in lower mammals, to tooth combing in lower primates, to finger grooming in monkeys and the great apes, to hand stroking and caressing in human beings. He thinks the evolutionary perspective shows that hand stroking (or some form of cutaneous stimulation) is as important to human infants as the experience of licking and grooming in nonhuman mammals. After his extensive review of the literature on cutaneous stimulation , he concluded: "We are quite evidently speaking of a fundamental and essential ingredient of affection, and equally clearly of an essential element in the healthy development of every organism" (Montague, 1972, p. 31).

In his poem *In Memoriam,* Tennyson presents a poet's impression of the importance of the sense of touch in the mother–infant relationship and the emergence of the sense of self in the infant.

> The baby new to earth and sky
> What time his tender palm is pressed
> Against the circle of the breast,
> Has never thought that "this is I?"
> But as he grows he gathers much,
> And learns the use of "I and me,"
> And finds I am not what I see,
> And other than the things I touch.
> (cited in Montague, p. 229–230)

Day-to-day life experiences, Tennyson's poem, and a significant body of scientific literature indicate that the sense of touch and the emotions are intimately related.

Emotion Expression and Physiological Arousal

A number of studies (Prideaux, 1922; Landis, 1932; Jones, 1935; Block, 1957; Learmonth, Ackerly, & Kaplan, 1959; Buck, Savin, Miller, & Caul, 1969; Lanzetta & Kleck, 1970) have found an inverse relationship between physiological (internal) arousal and overt expression under various stimulus conditions. Lanzetta and Kleck's experiment illustrates this type of study. They had twelve college-age males view a sequence of equally spaced and randomly ordered red and green lights, which were followed by shock and nonshock respectively. Since the red light was always followed by electric shock, the experimenters assumed that the red light became a conditioned stimulus for affective arousal. During the session the subject's skin resistance was measured continuously and he was videotaped from the waist up, without his knowledge. Prior to the experiment the subjects were told that the experimenter was interested in physiological responses (changes in skin resistance) to an event signaling the advent of shock or an event signaling its absence.

In sessions 2 and 3 of the experiment the subject viewed his videotaped responses to the red and green light series of session 1, and he also viewed the responses of five other subjects. In sessions 2 and 3 the subject's task was to determine whether the person he was viewing in the video tape was responding to a red or green light. Thus, his task was to differentiate between shock and nonshock trials for the stimulus persons. The assumption was that the CS (red light) would be affect arousing and would result in nonverbal cues that would enable the subject to differentiate the shock (red light) trials and the nonshock (green light) trials. During the judging session the subject had a four-second period within which to make his response; if he failed to respond or responded incorrectly, the trial was terminated by shock. The principal dependent measure was the accuracy of the subjects in differentiating between the shock and nonshock trials on the videotape records of the stimulus persons.

The results showed that the judges performed more accurately than would be expected on the basis of chance. A further analysis showed the judges were no more accurate in judging their own nonverbal behavior than in judging that of others. A repeated-measures analysis of variance of the mean error data over stimuli showed that immediate feedback and punishment for errors apparently did not result in significant improvement in performance. Another finding of interest indicated that persons who are comparatively accurate in judging others are themselves difficult for others to judge. Conversely, those who were comparatively inaccurate as judges were relatively easy to judge. In summary, the subjects who were most accurate as expressors of affective cues were least accurate in perceiving the expressed affective cues of others. Apparently consistent with this finding was the fact that the subjects who showed the greatest changes in skin resistance during session 1 (the conditioning session) gave the best performances as the judges of externally expressed affective cues in sessions 2 and 3.

Lanzetta and Kleck review several possible explanations for the observed inverse relationship between physiological arousal and overt expressivity. Jones (1950) suggested that autonomic arousal and overt behavior are substitutional modes of reducing tension. Thus if one inhibits overt display of affect it will be internalized and dissipated physiologically. Conversely, if the individual expresses the affect externally there will be a minimum of internal activity. Block (1957) argued against Jones' explanation and maintained that tension can be reduced by motor behavior or cognition, but not by autonomic activity. Schachter and Latané (1964) argued that a certain type of subject (primary sociopath) fails to learn to apply emotion labels to states of internal arousal and thus, while physiologically extremely labile, are overtly nonemotional.

Lanzetta and Kleck added another possible explanation. They held that some individuals during socialization were punished for affect expression and thus learned to inhibit expressivity. These individuals come to experience response conflict between expressing and inhibiting expression in affect-arousing situations. The individual's physiological arousal level becomes a joint function of the arousal value of the stimulus situation and the conflict over expression or inhibiting expression. They explain the "internalizers' " better performance as perceivers of others' affective displays on the grounds that such individuals have become sensitized by virtue of their own conflict over affect display.

A study by Buck and his associates (1974) used a different experimental paradigm and extended the analysis of differences between physiological responding and overt expressiveness. Instead of electric shock, they presented the subjects with a series of slides that had been prerated on a pleasantness–unpleasantness continuum. The judges' task was to determine whether the expressor was viewing a pleasant or unpleasant slide. They used both male and female subjects and found the females to be better expressors (senders) then males. They repeated the earlier finding of a negative correlation between overt expressiveness and physiological responsiveness (skin resistance and heart rate). Buck et al. offered another possible explanation of this oft-repeated finding. They suggested that experiences associated with learning to inhibit overt expression tend to be stressful and threatening and that the stress, and not the inhibition per se, produces the increased physiological responding.

In another phase of their study Buck, Miller, and Caul (1974) attempted to validate the differences between good and poor expressors (nonverbal senders) in a nonlaboratory situation. They used an experimental situation to obtain scores on expressiveness (sending ability) and corre-lated this with teachers' ratings of a number of different observable responses. They found significant negative correlations between expressive (sending) ability and the following types of behavior: "is shy," "fears strangers," "is emotionally inhibited," "controls his emotions," "is quiet and reserved," "is cooperative," "is an introvert," They found sending ability positively correlated with the following types of behavior: "often shows aggression," "has high activity level," "has many friends," "expresses feelings openly," "is impulsive," "is often difficult to get along with," "expresses his hostilities directly," "tends to be rebellious and nonconforming," "is bossy," "often dominates other children," "is an extravert." While their findings are interesting and have important implica-tions, there are some difficulties with the study. The correlations are based on rather small samples (six girls, eight boys) and the types of behavior being rated by the teachers are often highly overlapping and even synony-mous. Despite these limitations the investigators have opened up a highly interesting and potentially fruitful line of investigation regarding the rela-tionship between overt expressiveness and autonomic arousal and between expressiveness and personality characteristics.

In their study of the personality characteristics of "internalizers" and "externalizers," Buck *et al.* showed that "internalizers" were more intro-verted and had lower self-esteem than the more extroverted "externaliz-ers." "Internalizers" were also more impersonal in their vocal descriptions of their emotions. One finding which stands in apparent contradiction to the others showed that "internalizers" had higher scores on sensitization on the Byrne (1961) repression–sensitization scale. The puzzle here is that previous studies have described sensitizers as individuals who express their emotions freely rather than denying them.

J. L. Singer (personal communication) suggests that "expression externalizers" and "repressors" (viewed clinically as hysterics who "wear their hearts on their sleeves") may share some common personality dynamics. The hysterics (repressors), who show a lot of spontaneous but superficial emotions, may be so preoccupied with the task of mastering their own emotions that they cannot be sensitive (or take the time to attend) to the emotion expressions of others. This interpretation is consistent with the Lanzetta–Kleck finding that "expression externalizers" are poorer judges of others' affective expressions than are "expression internalizers." This is a provocative finding but further research is needed in order to reach a better understanding of the internalizer–externalizer dimension.

Studies of expressiveness should probably allow for the possibility that voluntariness and involuntariness of expression, though commonly accepted as categorically different in terms of conscious control, actually vary on a continuum of awareness. Some voluntary (or partially voluntary, intentional) expressions, such as those that occur when one wants to show sympathy, may be performed at a low level of awareness. The same may be true of the child who willfully increases its expression of genuine distress in order to elicit the desired or needed help. The illustrative photographs in the following section are voluntary expressions obtained by asking individuals to express the particular emotion, but some of them used imaging or role-playing to self-induce emotion.

The Fundamental Emotions

Each of the fundamental emotions has unique motivational properties of crucial importance to the individual and the species, and each adds its own special quality to consciousness as it mobilizes energy for physical or cognitive adventure. An intense emotion may be considered as a special state of consciousness, experienced as highly desirable or highly undesirable.

Each of the fundamental emotions has an inherently adaptive function. They are termed fundamental because each of them has (a) a specific innately determined neural substrate, (b) a characteristic facial expression or neuromuscular-expressive pattern, and (c) a distinct subjective or phenomenological quality. No one of these three facets constitutes emotion; each is an emotion component. A complete emotion or complete emotion process requires all three, although socialization may greatly diminish the expressive pattern in both duration and intensity. In a sense, each fundamental emotion is a system made up of its three components and their interactions. Ten fundamental emotions have been identified and defined empirically (Darwin, 1872; Ekman, Friesen, & Ellsworth, 1972; Izard, 1971; Tomkins, 1962).

In addition to the three principal components of an emotion, there are a number of other organs and systems that become involved during emotion. Of particular importance are the endocrine, cardiovascular, and respiratory systems of the homeostatic network. For a long time it has been known that emotion is accompanied by changes in the autonomic nervous system and in the visceral organs which it innervates (e.g., heart, blood vessels, glands). Unfortunately, a great deal of research in the past has mistakenly treated autonomic–visceral processes as though they constituted emotion or were the best indexes of emotion. Some prominent investigators who once followed this trend now distinguish among emotions, drives, and visceral processes (e.g., Pribram, 1970). Some investigators still maintain that the fact that autonomic–visceral processes accompany emotion means that they can serve as relatively reliable indicators of the presence of emotion. However, such indexes actually signify only arousal (changes in functions of the autonomic nervous system). Such arousal is often a function of emotion, but it is difficult to use measures of arousal to identify a particular discrete fundamental emotion or a particular pattern of emotions. At present there is only tentative evidence for discrete emotion-specific autonomic–visceral patterns, and such evidence exists for only a few of the fundamental emotions. Autonomic–visceral patterns may be quite helpful in the study of discrete emotions when it is possible to obtain other data concurrently (e.g., facial patterning, including video and EMG records, and phenomenological self-report) to help identify the particular fundamental emotion or pattern of emotions.

Two kinds of phenomena make it difficult to study discrete emotions. First, emotion tends to involve the whole organism rather than to remain a process confined to a single system. For example, the activation of sympathetic mechanisms that accompany one emotion may activate other sympathetic mechanisms that subserve other emotions. Second, emotions tend to occur in certain combinations or patterns. Discrete fundamental emotions occur and are important in the life of an individual, but most of them usually exist separately for relatively short periods of time before other emotions are activated. Further, moments of experience characterized by a single fundamental emotion are rather difficult to obtain for sufficient duration and under conditions that are necessary for systematic study. These difficulties are substantial but not insurmountable, as evidenced by a growing body of literature on discrete emotions.

Although fundamental emotions are assumed to be innate, transcultural phenomena (and as shown in Tables 1-1 and 1-2, this assumption is supported by robust empirical evidence), it is recognized that idiosyncratic and sociocultural factors play a significant role in defining the antecedents and consequences of emotion expression. As Ekman (1972) puts it, each culture has its own "display rules" and their violation may have more or less serious consequences for the individual. These cultural rules may call for inhibiting or masking certain emotion expressions and the frequent display of others. Westerners often feel compelled to smile while experiencing distress and the Japanese are obligated to smile even in the face of grief.

Both cultural and sex-differences proscribe situations for laughing and crying. There are few occasions where American men can cry in public with impunity, as one recent presidential candidate well remembers. While such displays may be seen by a few as signs of "humanness" and empathic sensitivity, it is seen by many as an indication of weakness and untrustworthiness.

Associated with cultural display rules are significant cultural differences in attitudes toward emotion experiences (Izard, 1971). For example, Swedish men have significantly more tolerance for anger experience than

Greek men, whereas both these groups prefer to experience interest (in relation to joy) more than a number of other cultural groups.

The foregoing section defined the concept of fundamental emotion. The concept was emphasized and given specific definition by differential emotions theory, but a number of theories of emotion from Darwin to the present day have presented similar concepts. In the following overview, the fundamental emotions will be described only briefly and mainly at the phenomenological level, since each fundamental emotion will be treated in greater detail in subsequent chapters.

1. Interest–excitment (Figure 4-5), the most frequently experienced positive emotion, provides much of the motivation for learning, the development of skills and competencies, and for creative endeavor. Interest results from an increase in neural stimulation, usually brought about by change or novelty. In a state of interest the person shows signs of attentiveness, curiosity, and fascination. One feels caught up or captivated by the object of interest. Since people are the most changing and unpredictable aspects of our world, the interest activated by other human beings facilitates social life and the development of affective ties between individuals. The effort of the infant in tracking the movements of mother's face or a mobile and the artist's or scientist's pursuit of the novel or unknown are sustained by interest.

FIGURE 4-5. Interest–excitement. (The correspondence between emotion expressions and emotion categories in Figures 4-5 through 4-13 has been validated in many Eastern and Western cultures.)

2. Joy (Figure 4-6) is a highly desirable emotion, though not necessarily a state to be desired continually. Work, as well as adventure, requires interest–excitement; sympathy and concern for the problems of other individuals and the world are functions of distress. Joy seems to be more a by-product of events and conditions than a result of a direct effort to obtain it. In Tomkins's (1962) view, joy results from a sharp reduction in the gradient of neural stimulation. Joy together with interest guarantees that human beings will be social creatures. The smile of one person eliciting the smile of another is a reciprocal pattern that is observed in the infant–mother relationship and throughout life. An active state of joy is characterized by a sense of confidence, meaningfulness, and a feeling of being loved. Receptive joy, a state that is extremely difficult to describe, is a feeling of trust and acceptance of the surrounding world.

3. Surprise (Figure 4-7) has some of the characteristics of an emotion, but it is not an emotion in quite the same sense as the others discussed here. Unlike the other emotions, surprise is always a transient state. It results from a sharp increase in neural stimulation, typically brought about by a sudden unexpected event. Surprise serves the very useful function of clearing the nervous system of ongoing emotion and cognition so that the individual can respond appropriately to the stimulus situation and the sudden change he has experienced.

FIGURE 4-6. Enjoyment–joy.

FIGURE 4-7. Surprise–startle.

4. The act of birth, when the infant is physically separated from the mother, provides the first occasion for distress. Distress–anguish is pictured in Figure 4-8. Throughout the remainder of life, separation remains a common and profound cause of distress or sadness. Another important and common cause of distress is real and imagined failure to live up to the standards set by self or by others (e.g., parents). In distress a person feels sad, downhearted, discouraged, lonely, out of touch with people, miserable. Distress serves highly useful functions by communicating to the self and to others that all is not well and by motivating the person to do what is necessary to reduce the distress. Distress makes one responsive to one's own problems and to the problems of the world.

5. An angry face (Figure 4-9) may disturb or frighten the perceiver, and the control of anger or anger expression receives considerable attention in the socialization of the child. Anger often results from physical or psychological restraint, or from interference with goal-oriented activity. In anger the blood "boils" and the face becomes hot. Rapidly mobilized energy tenses the muscles and provides a feeling of power, a sense of courage or confidence, and an impulse to strike out, but as discussed in Chapter 13, the emotion of anger should be distinguished from acts of aggression. Although anger served useful functions in the evolution of human beings, its positive functions have become less conspicuous. Per-

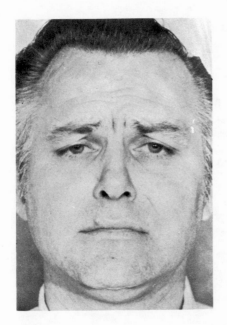

FIGURE 4-8. Distress–anguish. (From Ekman & Friesen, 1975.)

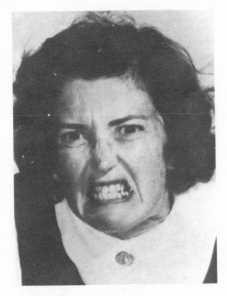

FIGURE 4-9. Anger–rage.

haps mild to moderate anger can be justified when it becomes the added source of strength and courage necessary for response to oppression or a life-threat. Anger expressed in words with enough tact to keep from angering the other person or cutting off communication with him may facilitate a needed defense of personal integrity and improve a relationship.

6. Disgust (Figure 4-10) often occurs together with anger but it has some distinct motivational–experiential features of its own. Physical or psychological deterioration ("anything spoiled") tends to elicit disgust. When disgusted one feels as though one has a bad taste in one's mouth, and in intense disgust one may feel as if one is "sick at the stomach." Disgust combined with anger may motivate destructive behavior, since anger can motivate "attack" and disgust the desire to "get rid of." However, disgust with pollution, the defacing of wilderness, and the wanton waste of natural resources may help provide motivation for a healthier atmosphere and ecology.

7. Contempt (Figure 4-11) often occurs with anger or disgust or with both. These three emotions have been termed the "hostility triad" (Izard, 1972). In evolutionary perspective contempt may have evolved as a vehicle for preparing the individual or group to face a dangerous adversary. Still today the situation in which the individual has a need to feel superior

FIGURE 4-10. Disgust–revulsion.

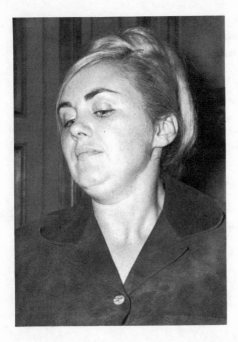

FIGURE 4-11. Contempt–scorn.

(stronger, more intelligent, more civilized) may lead to some degree of contempt. One of the dangers of contempt is that it is a "cold" emotion, one that tends to depersonalize the individual or group held in contempt. Hence it may help motivate "cold-blood killing," or, as in the case of war, large-scale annihilation of people. It is difficult to find any useful or productive function for contempt in contemporary life, unless one considers it appropriate to express it toward conditions that foster waste, oppression, crime, or war.

8. Fear (Figure 4-12) affects every individual. It tends to lock into the memory unforgettable experiences that can be re-lived through active recall or through dreams. Fear has great toxicity. It is actually possible to be "frightened to death." Fear is activated by a rather rapid increase in the density of neural stimulation, brought about by real or imagined danger. Apprehension, uncertainty, the feeling of a lack of safety and impending disaster accompany strong fear. Except for the rare and extreme fear that paralyzes, this emotion mobilizes energy and provides motivation for escape from danger. By anticipating danger and acting appropriately the individual often avoids intense fear like that portrayed in the photo.

9. Shame (Figure 4-13) may have emerged during the course of evolution as a result of man's social nature and the human need for social

FIGURE 4-12. Fear–terror.

FIGURE 4-13. Shame/shyness–
humiliation.

community. If the child deviates from the norms established by family and community he may be shamed. The active, curious child inevitably explores the forbidden, and the parent's scolding interrupts his interest and leads to shame. Shame occurs typically, if not always, in the context of an emotional relationship. The sharp increase in self-attention (and sometimes the increased sensitivity of the face produced by blushing) causes the person to feel as though he were naked and exposed to the world. Shame motivates the desire to hide, to disappear. Shame can also produce a feeling of ineptness, incapability, and a feeling of not belonging. Shame can be a powerful force for conformity, but if the individual's deepest loyalties and emotional ties are to "out groups," then shame can lead to rebellion. While strong and chronic shame can shatter human integrity, this emotion often stands as a guardian of self-respect. An individual will go to great lengths to develop self-respect, self-esteem, and hence a self-concept that is less vulnerable to shame. Shame avoidance can foster immediate self-corrective behavior as well as sustained programs of self-improvement.

10. Guilt often has a close relation to shame, and Tomkins (1963) considers shame, shyness, and guilt as different aspects (at the conscious level) of the same emotion. While shame may result from any misdoings (or mis-being), guilt results from wrongdoing (wrong-being) of a moral, ethical, or religious nature. Guilt occurs in situations in which one feels personally responsible. Shame is most typically elicited by the responses of others to the self, but guilt comes from one's own acts and from within one's self. In guilt people have a strong feeling of "not being right" with the person or persons they have wronged. For the religious person the act eliciting guilt may simply be wrongdoing in the sight of God. While shame befuddles one's thoughts temporarily, guilt stimulates thought and cognitive preoccupation with the wrongdoing. Intense and chronic guilt can cripple the individual psychologically, but guilt may be the basis for personal–social responsibility and the motive to avoid guilt may heighten one's sense of personal responsibility.

Some Common Patterns or Combinations of Affects

The pattern of facial activity or the image of the corresponding pattern of proprioception is a chief determinant of the specific quality of any felt emotion. If the pattern is that of an innately programmed fundamental emotion there will be a corresponding specific emotion experience. A fundamental emotion will be felt. If there are two or more fundamental emotions experienced simultaneously or in rapid sequence the face may show a blend of two or more emotion expressions and the experience will be a pattern or combination of felt emotions.

Two or more fundamental emotions which pattern frequently may produce over time a relatively stable, well-defined emotion characteristic of the person that may be considered an emotion trait. The development of such emotion traits is strongly influenced by the individual's genetic makeup and by his history. Through learning and experience certain types of relatively frequently experienced conditions come to elicit this combination of emotions (pattern of fundamentals) and its related cognitive–motor behavior. One possible result would be a pattern that could be called "trait anxiety," a complex trait subserved by a relatively consistent yet variable pattern of emotions and other affects. Conceiving such patterns as a variable combination of interacting fundamental emotions and other affective processes has important implications for personality psychology and for psychodiagnosis and psychotherapy.

Anxiety. Anxiety theory and research have suffered from inconsistent and inadequate definitions of the concept. Theorists and investigators have tended to think of anxiety as unidimensional despite the fact that clinical experience has always run counter to such a conception. The professional attempting to understand and help individuals has never been convinced that anxiety is a singular and simple thing, either in terms of its motivational qualities or in terms of its effect upon adjustment and behavior. A close look at experimental and clinical literature reveals that even authors who spoke of anxiety as unitary often included in their descriptions of anxiety two or more relatively independent components of some sort. Now it is becoming more widely recognized that anxiety is not unipolar, unidimensional, or unifactor in nature. The complexity of anxiety was recognized to some extent in Freud's theory, but this aspect of his thought was not followed up.

Differential emotions theory defines anxiety as a combination or pattern of fundamental emotions including fear and two or more of the emotions of distress, anger, shame/shyness, guilt, and the positive emotion of interest–excitement (Izard, 1972). These six emotions are considered as variable components of a complex pattern. The relative importance of these emotions in the anxiety pattern varies with the individual and his life situation. Individual variations in the pattern of emotions in anxiety are a function both of hereditary and experiential determinants. One of the problems in studying anxiety results from its great complexity. It is a variable combination of elements; it has no single, characteristic behavioral-expressive component; and it has no singular phenomenology. This formulation of anxiety has implications for psychodiagnostic assessment and psychotherapy and for the analysis and management of interpersonal and intergroup problems. In the framework of differential emotions theory, the term anxiety (without qualification) has very doubtful utility as a scientific concept.

Depression. The first psychodynamic explication of depression came from Karl Abraham, the German psychoanalyst. He saw anxiety and depression as having a relationship analogous to that between fear and grief. According to Abraham, anxiety results when an instinct strives for gratification and repression prevents the attainment of satisfaction. Depression follows when a sexual aim has to be given up without having obtained gratification; therefore, the depressed individual "feels himself unloved and incapable of loving and therefore he despairs of his life and his future" (Abraham, 1968, p. 27). The depressed cannot love because hostility feelings (or hatred) interfere. The hostility that was once part of an ambivalence toward a love object becomes both inner- and outer-directed hostility upon the loss of the love object.

In this brief but poignant picture of depression, Abraham laid not only the groundwork for Freud's later and more detailed comparison between mourning (grief) and melancholia (depression) but also a foundation for a differential emotions theory of depression. Abraham saw fear and anxiety as having a relationship similar to that of grief and depression. In the analysis of anxiety in terms of differential emotions theory, fear was found to be the key emotion of anxiety with which other important fundamental emotions interrelate and interact (Izard, 1972). Similarly, differential emotions theory posits distress–anguish, the emotion which predominates in grief, as the key emotion in depression and the one with which other fundamental emotions interact.

Differential emotions theory holds that depression is an even more complex pattern than anxiety. More emotions are activated and there are more possibilities for conflicts in the emotion—emotion dynamics. The fundamental emotions involved in depression are distress, anger, disgust, contempt, fear, guilt, and shyness. Anger, disgust, and contempt are expressed both toward the self and toward others. Since anger, disgust, and contempt may all be related to hostility, these components of depression may be termed inner-directed and outer-directed hostility.

Although the fundamental emotions are thought to be the primary and most important elements of depression, there are other affective factors which are frequently present—decreased physical well-being, decreased sexuality, and increased fatigue (Izard, 1972). These elements may be most properly considered as immediate effects or by-products of depression. Nevertheless, they have motivational properties and, consequently, influence the other components of the depression and its course.

Love. Love commands a place of prominence in every human life. The love of mother is sensed in early infancy and remains for many people the greatest influence in their lives throughout their formative years. Parental love is typically steadfast and resistant to erosion and decay. After parental love comes love of brother or sister and then love of friends. These loves, too, can be sources of enrichment and joy.

As childhood's joys and sorrows are replaced by adolescent dreams, romantic love (dominated by interest, joy, and the sex drive) becomes a compelling force that must be dealt with in one way or another. Romantic love tunes the whole body and the mind to a high pitch and makes the person open to excitement and ecstasy and vulnerable to the affective–cognitive orientations we call possessiveness and jealousy.

Each of these types of love has unique features. Each is a particular pattern of affects and cognitions. Although the differences among them are considerable, perhaps they have a common thread. Love of any type binds one person to another, and this affective bond has evolutionary-biological, sociocultural, and personal significance.

While fundamental emotions may have both state and trait characteristics, love seems best described as an aspect of a relationship. Love's ingredients include emotions and drives, but it may be best described as an affective–cognitive orientation.

Reciprocal love establishes a special bond and a special relationship that changes all other affective thresholds and alters perception, cognition, and action, particularly in relation to the loved one. Despite its great importance in human life, love has received far less attention from scientists than has anxiety and depression. In the past few years, however, some studies of romantic love have emerged.

Hostility and Hate. Hostility has been defined as the experiential/ motivational underpinning of aggression (Izard, 1975). Just as motivation does not always lead to overt behavior, hostility does not inevitably lead to aggression. The fundamental emotions of anger, disgust, and contempt interact in hostility, and the relative strength of these three emotions (together with cognitive and situational factors) probably determine the likelihood and the nature of aggression. For example, the greater the anger, the "hot" emotion in the hostility triad, the greater the probability of impulsive acts of aggression. Such impulsive "acting out" may be verbal or physical. The prominence of disgust in the hostility triad may prompt a person to hurt another by shunning or avoiding him. Contempt, the "cold" emotion in the hostility triad, contributes to the aggressive acts associated with racial prejudice. It causes people to hurt others through acts of indifference. Contempt characterizes the interracial rapist and the "cold-blooded" killer. It also characterizes the individual who sexually seduces a person for whom he has no affection.

Hostility has both state and trait characteristics. Intense hostility with strong anger illustrates state hostility. Such hostility occurs in love relationships as well as in chronically competitive relationships between unfriendly parties. Prejudice and indifference are examples of trait hostility, a "compartmentalized" form of hostility that may be apparent only to those for whom prejudice and indifference are felt.

Hate, the more common term in this area, has a close kinship with hostility as defined here. It may be thought of as an affective–cognitive orientation in which the affect consists of some combination of the emotions in the hostility triad.

Summary

The face provides immediate and specific information regarding human emotions. In addition to its neural and experiential aspects, each fundamental emotion has a characteristic facial expression. The face plays a crucial role in the social communication system that helps establish and maintain the mother–infant relationship as well as all other interpersonal affective ties.

Facial expressions are instinctive in the sense that they occur reflexively or automatically as a part of the emotion process. Only through learning and experience do individuals learn to inhibit or alter the facial expressions of emotions. The weight of the evidence indicates that the expressions of the fundamental emotions are hereditary and bear a close resemblance to the expressions of nonhuman animals, especially the nonhuman primates. Andrew (1965) has argued that the adaptive value of the communicative function of facial expression provided the basis for the process of natural selection to make emotion expressions a part of the genetic code.

A number of studies have shown that the face is an extraordinary social stimulus. Although there are some inconsistencies that result from measurement, there are stages in the development of the infant when the human face is preferred above all other stimuli. This fact alone may help account for the attachment that develops between the mother (or principal caregiver) and the infant, who spend many hours each day in face-to-face contact. Of course the attraction of the face has its roots in the importance of this area for communicating emotions. The facial–visual, vocal–aural, and somesthetic systems all play a role in the development and maintenance of human social attachments; the underlying emotion conveyed through these systems is the common denominator.

A number of recent experiments have suggested that emotion expression has other adaptive functions in addition to its role in social communication and the establishment and maintenance of interpersonal relationships. The evidence from this line of research indicates that emotion expression is inversely related to physiological arousal. One possible implication of this finding is that suppression of facial and somatic expression of emotions can lead to changes in personality characteristics, some of which may have implications for physical well-being—chronic suppression of overt expression and hence increased physiological arousal could lead to psychosomatic symptoms.

A fundamental emotion is defined as having neural, expressive, and experiential components. Each of ten fundamental emotions has been briefly described in this chapter. Interest provides motivation for learning and creative endeavor. Joy is associated with a sense of confidence and a feeling of being loved. Surprise clears the nervous system of ongoing emotion and cognition so that the individual can respond to the sudden change he has experienced. Distress makes one responsive to one's own problems and to the problems of the world. Anger may motivate destructive behavior, but it may also prove adaptive as a source of strength and courage when it is necessary to defend personal integrity or one's loved ones. Disgust can combine with anger in a dangerous blend of emotions, but it may help provide the motivation for maintaining personal standards, such as good body hygiene, as well as ecological standards, such as a cleaner atmosphere. Contempt can lead to prejudice and even cold-blooded killing and its only positive function comes into play when it is directed against the enemies of human welfare. Fear motivates the avoidance of danger situations. Shame can produce feelings of ineptness and isolation, but shame avoidance can foster self-corrective activities and self-improvement. Guilt can dominate and torment the mind, but the anticipation and avoidance of guilt can serve as the basis for the development of personal–social responsibility.

In addition to the fundamental emotions operating as discrete motivational phenomena, they sometimes combine or interact to form fairly stable patterns of emotions. Such patterns often have stable interactions with a set of cognitions that help give the complex a certain character. Anxiety, depression, love, and hostility are examples of such affective patterns. In anxiety the key emotion of fear interacts with distress, anger, shame, guilt, or interest. In depression the key emotion of distress interacts with anger, disgust, contempt, fear, guilt, or shyness.

A love relationship is dominated by interest and joy but at one time or another it may involve virtually every one of the emotions. Hostility results from the interactions of anger, disgust, and contempt. When combined with a particular set of cognitions it may develop into an affective–cognitive orientation which is commonly called hate.

Note Added in Proof

Emde, Gaensbauer, and Harmon (1976) have presented the results of an excellent longitudinal study of emotion expressions in infancy. Although they found considerable individual differences among infants with respect to the age of appearance of specific emotion expressions (e.g., social smile, fear), they concluded that such expressions emerge at a particular time primarily as a function of the development or maturation of underlying biological processes. In fact, the appearance of a given emotion may be a significant factor in the psychobiological shift from one stage of infancy to the next. An apparent weakness of their study was their failure to make a systematic analysis of the infants' facial expressions which is probably the only reliable method for distinguishing between such phenomena as "stranger distress" and "stranger fear."

5

BASIC PRINCIPLES
AND METHODS IN THE
PSYCHOLOGY OF EMOTIONS

This chapter is devoted to the description of some basic principles of emotion psychology and the various methods and techniques used in emotion research. These principles and methods will be illustrated with summaries of studies drawn from the growing body of literature in this area. The psychology of emotion and its methods emerged against a background of opposing forces ranging from inertia in psychological theorizing to outright rejection of emotion concepts by some of psychology's leading theorists and model builders. Perhaps a brief look at these forces may give the student a better appreciation of the status of emotion in contemporary science and of the relationship of emotion theory and research to other theories and other realms of investigation.

The term "behavioral sciences" has been for the past several years the most popular designation for the group of disciplines which focus on the individual and on the social behavior of human beings. This term calls attention to one of the problems relating to research in the area of emotions. Behavior as it is most commonly understood, and specifically behavioral science as described by such eminent psychologists as B. F. Skinner (1973), precludes emotional experience as a variable. By rejecting the experiential component, the behavioristic tradition excludes from its definition of science the study of the meaning, significance, and effects of "felt" or conscious emotion.

Of the many forces which have militated against the study of emotion, three stand out. The first of these, and perhaps the most important, has been the lack of a viable conceptual framework for the study of emotions. Earlier theories were not sufficiently complex and flexible to be adequate scientifically or were unacceptable to interested investigators. One of the chief aims of this chapter will be to present some basic principles for a general science of the emotions, principles that will be explicit enough to offer the possibility of consistency in defining and understanding emotion variables and sufficiently broad to allow for various theoretical approaches.

The second factor that has impeded the study of emotion has been the overriding concern of psychological and other life scientists with behavioristic learning theories and with perceptual and cognitive processes. These are very important areas of investigation that should continue to flourish. However, there is a great need for collaboration between investigators in these areas and investigators working in the domain of the emotions. A few scientists are conducting research that bridges the spheres of cognition and emotion and some of their work will be discussed in later sections. One of the aims of this book will be to discuss how the emotions interact with perceptual and cognitive processes and to present evidence showing the reciprocal influences among the perceptual, cognitive, emotion, and action systems.

The third force that has impeded the study of the emotions has been the attitude that the emotions cannot be studied objectively or systematically and do not yield to investigation by the usual methodologies and procedures of science. A related attitude has been that while it may be possible to study the emotions, their very nature makes the undertaking highly expensive and time-consuming. Another aim of this book and the present chapter in particular will be to refute these attitudes by presenting some methods of emotion study and to illustrate these with reports of actual experiments.

Principles of Emotion

Although emotion theorists and investigators differ in many particulars, there are some important principles that function as common denominators among a number of current approaches to the study of emotion. Most theories do not specify all of these principles, and one theory may place much more emphasis on some principles than on others.

These principles and their descriptions do not constitute a finished list. The study of emotions has only recently occupied an important place in contemporary psychology, neurophysiology, biochemistry, ethology, and other branches of the life sciences. Future research will revise and extend this list for many years to come. The present list is intended to help organize the knowledge that is available from many different disciplines. Perhaps the list will also facilitate emotion research by helping establish an acceptable taxonomy of emotion principles and variables. With greater consistency in the definition of emotion concepts and emotion variables the comparability of findings from different investigators will improve.

The Principle of Differential Emotions

According to this principle there are a number of discrete emotions that can be differentiated in terms of their neurophysiological underpinnings, their facial patterns, and their experiential/motivational characteristics. All people, including the most rigorous behavioral scientists, speak of phenomena such as joy, sadness, anger, fear, and shame. Common sense and personal experience also tell us that these emotions are existential reals and that their effects are discernible in thought and action.

Two boys, Rafe and Dalin, watch a bully intimidate and beat their friend. Dalin becomes frightened and runs away. Rafe empathizes with his friend in distress, gets angry at the unfairness of the fight, and goes to his friend's defense. Rafe and Dalin experienced different emotions and consequently behaved in highly contrasting ways, one courageously and the other cowardly.

In addition to the wisdom of common sense and experience, at least six different theories or approaches recognize discrete emotions and the need for studying them. Webb (1948) and Brown and Farber (1951) showed how frustration or anger could be treated as an intervening variable within the $s-r$ theoretical framework. Mowrer (1960a) acknowledged the existential reality of the subjective phenomena of fear and anger and related them systematically to his revised two-factor learning theory. Arnold (1960a,b) maintained that there were a number of distinct emotions, each with its own unique neurophysiological substrate and experiential characteristics. Gellhorn (1964) pointed out that different emotions exist and that one of the important differentials was striate muscle activity, particularly facial expression. Jacobson (1929, 1967) has also emphasized the role of striate muscle activity in different emotions. Lazarus and his colleagues (Lazarus & Averill, 1972; Lazarus, Averill, & Opton, 1970) have recognized the existence of different emotions and have emphasized their differentiation on the basis of response characteristics. Tomkins (1962, 1963) defined eight primary emotions and Izard (1971, 1972) defined ten discrete or fundamental emotions. The work of Allport (1924), Ax (1953), Funkenstein (1955), and Plutchik (1962) has contributed significantly to the development of the principle of differential emotions.

Each of the emotions affects the individual differently. Common sense and most of the current approaches to the study of emotions recognize that the feeling of joy is different from the feeling of sadness, and that our perceptions, thoughts, and actions when we are angry are different from our behavior when we are afraid or ashamed. In explaining these differences in behavior, some approaches look for differences in the situation as appraised by the individual, some for differences in response characteristics, some for differences in the subjective experience. In any case most of the theories discussed in Chapter 2 agree that different emotions are associated with different perceptions, experiences, expressions, cognitions, and motor responses.

The Principle of Interacting Emotion Components

Even a discrete fundamental emotion has more than one component. When we have the subjective experience of anger we may also be aware of a hot flushed feeling in our faces, tension in our muscles, and pounding of our hearts. Of necessity, both the subjective experience and the bodily changes have neural substrates. Several theories agree that an emotion has neural, expressive, and experiential components. Any one of the three components can influence (e.g., amplify, attenuate) the activity of the other two. The components are basically interactive. In the normal emotion process they operate in a feedback loop—the sensory messages from the face (expression) are integrated in the brain resulting in conscious ("felt") emotion.

There remains some disagreement over the definition of emotion in terms of three interactive components. One reason for controversy on this issue is that different approaches have focused solely on one or the other of the emotion components, and some have even defined emotion in terms of only one component (e.g., Duffy, 1962; Lindsley, 1951). Research on any one of these components may make valuable contributions, but it may not throw light on the overall emotion process as it affects individual and social behavior.

The Principle of Emotion Patterning

While it is highly important to recognize the existence of different emotions, each affecting our experiences and our actions differently, it is also important to recognize that day-to-day life situations often elicit more than one emotion and that one emotion can, in fact, elicit another. Some common patterns or combinations of emotions were presented in Chapter 3.

The kind of emotion patterning that can occur in everyday life is illustrated by an incident that occurred when Rafe was walking in a strange neighborhood and discovered he was being followed by three young boys. He became frightened, though not intensely so; he was also excited about his first date with a girl he was on his way to visit. The idea of being afraid of three such small boys made him ashamed. When he turned around and saw the young boys snickering he got angry. When he frowned and glared at the boys they started off in the other direction, and his excitement and anticipation rose to a new pitch.

The Principle of Emotion Communication

While the experience of an emotion is completely personal, its expressive component (particularly patterning on the face) is public and social. The question of the universality of emotion expressions was long a controversial subject in psychology. This controversy has recently been resolved. The work of Ekman and his colleagues (e.g., Ekman, Friesen, & Ellsworth, 1972) and Izard (1971) has shown conclusively that several discrete emotions are universal (pancultural) phenomena. Both the encoding and decoding of these emotion expressions are the same for people all over the world regardless of culture, language, or educational background. This finding points to the potential importance of the study of emotion and emotion communication in psychology, anthropology, biology, and other related fields.

The first really meaningful social interactions in the life of every individual is a function of emotion expression in the mother–infant relationship. The first exchange of smiles between the infant Rebecca and her mother was a truly joyous occasion. It profited Rebecca greatly; she was picked up, fondled, talked to, and taken to the next room to see her father.

Beginning in adolescence, social pressure tends to lead the individual to inhibit or conceal the veridical expressions of the emotions. However, suppression and disguise occur rarely in infants and young children, and they are rarely completely successful for adolescents or adults. Generally the child's emotions are written plainly on the face. More often than not the faces of parents or teachers also reveal emotions and convey a message, often more important than that conveyed by their words. And words that say one thing while accompanying expressions that say another can create conflict in the child.

The Principle of Emotion-Facilitated Personal Growth and Emotional Attachment

Emotion experiences of day-to-day life influence individual and social development and the formation of interpersonal ties in important ways. Spitz and Wolf (1946) argued that the emotions play a pioneering role in the development of the infant and in "every human activity, be it perception, physical proficiency, memory, inventivenss, or understanding" (p. 94).

Bowlby (1953) and Goldfarb (1955) have shown that institutionalized children who lack the positive emotion interactions of a normal mother–infant relationship suffer grave consequences. Kistiakovskaia (1965) found evidence that led her to conclude that the timely appearance of positive emotion responses in the infant is of great significance to the neural, mental, and physical development of the child. Walters and Parke (1965) reviewed research on the determinants of social responsiveness and concluded that vision and other stimulations such as vocalization and facial expression directed toward the infant played a much more important role than did the meeting of the infant's physiological needs. Wolff's (1963) work supported the notion that the positive emotion expression of smiling established a social bond between the mother and her offspring. His finding that the human face proves to be the generally most effective stimulus for eliciting a smile is consistent with the conclusion that facial expression as the public aspect of emotion constitutes the cornerstone of social responsiveness, emotion attachments, and meaningful interpersonal affective ties.

The Principle of Interactive Systems

According to this principle, activities within the emotion system (e.g., the activation of joy or distress) influence the functions of the homeostatic, drive, perceptual, cognitive, and action systems of the individual. Support for this proposition comes from many sources and many different theoretical orientations. Numerous studies have been concerned with the relationship between the emotions and homeostatic drive systems (Gasanov, 1974). Among other things these studies have contributed to knowledge of the long-term effects of negative emotion (emotional stress) on hormonal balance, the cardiovascular system, the alimentary system, and other visceral functions. Arnold (1960a,b), and most of the other cognitive theorists who deal with emotion, consider appraisal (a cognitive process) as the cause or as the initial step in the sequence of events that constitute emotion. Spitz (1965) has argued that affect precedes and paves the way for perceptual and cognitive development and that the development of perception remains closely linked with affect. He concluded: "Ultimately, affects (emotions, feelings) determine the relation between perception and cognition" (p. 85). A large body of experimental work on perception (for example, Bruner & Goodman, 1947; Levine, Chein, & Murphy, 1942; Sanford, 1936, 1937) showed that needs (some of which may be considered as affective in nature) intrude on and distort perception. More recently emotion theorists and investigators (Tomkins, 1962, 1963; Izard & Tomkins, 1966; Izard, 1971, 1972; Leventhal, 1974; Schwartz, Fair, Greenberg, Mandel, & Klerman, 1974; Singer, 1974) have presented both theory and empirical evidence relating to the interactions of emotion, perception, and cognition.

The Principle of Inherently Adaptive Functions and Psychopathology

A number of scientists from Darwin to present-day investigators have pointed out the functions of the emotions in the evolution of human beings. The fact that the emotions play a significant role in the evolutionary process supports the assumption that each of the emotions has an inherently adaptive function. This does not mean that one cannot have an inappropriate emotion nor that intense emotion cannot be involved in the motivational–experiential aspects of maladaptive functioning. It does mean that in some naturally occurring situations a given fundamental emotion experienced in proportion appropriate to the situation can facilitate adaptive action. The capacity to experience and express the fundamental emotions fosters optimal experiential and behavioral alternatives, allowing for actualization of the fully functioning person and the realization of different qualities of being or special states of consciousness.

Mowrer has proposed that emotional responses are not the real source of psychopathology. For example, he maintained that the individual becomes "guilt-ridden" because of his own "misbehavior" or "misconduct," not because guilt is "bad." Thus in Mowrer's view, it is not the emotions experienced by neurotics or psychotics that constitute their "craziness." Rather, he thought their problems resulted from the behavior they had engaged in. "Given their personal history and 'life style,' the presumption is that (in the absence of gross neurological reasons, toxic states, and humoral disorders) their emotions (however turbulent or painful) are, in an ultimate sense, reasonable and proper" (Mowrer, 1960a). Thus given the life style and the behavior of the person suffering a psychopathological condition, the emotions experienced and expressed may not be in any way unsuited to the circumstances.

Mowrer reasoned that it was incorrect to "blame" the emotions for psychological problems since the emotions are not a result of willful or deliberate choice. We can choose to behave or misbehave, but we "cannot choose or control our *emotions,* directly or voluntarily. Given the 'appropriate' ('condition') stimulus, *they* occur automatically, reflexly. So the question of control and choice exists only at the level of overt, voluntary behavior" (Mowrer, 1960a). Thus, behavior is a result of choice, is under voluntary control, and thus, unlike emotions, behavior can be judged "good" or "bad." Drawing from his earlier extensive reviews of the literature Mowrer concluded that:

> Stimuli never 'produce' or 'cause' behavioral (as opposed to emotional) responses in the manner implied by S–R connectionism or reflexology. A stimulus (S) may suggest (i.e., provide an image or memory of) a particular

> response (R) . . . but whether or not the individual responds to the suggestion
> ('yields to the temptation') is dependent on prudential factors (hopes and fears)
> which are complexly determined, by the individual's total life experience,
> knowledge (including that which is gained vicariously), and objective—in a
> word, by 'character.'

Mowrer's view that behavior is a result of choice, or in a broader sense the result of "character" is provacative but controversial. Psychoanalytic theory holds that much of behavior is unconsciously determined and behaviorism maintains that behavior is controlled by the contingencies of reinforcement. His view that emotions are always automatic and involuntary is incompatible with ideas dating back to Darwin and James. Further, recent experimental evidence has shown that emotions may be self-induced by imagery (Izard, 1972; Rusolova, Izard & Simonov, 1975; Schwartz, Davidson, Maer, & Bromfield, 1973).

Regardless of the opposing ideas and evidence, Mowrer's proposals called for a new way of looking at the emotions and the emotion system, a way that is compatible in some respects with differential emotions theory. Mowrer made the potentially important point that considering the emotions as the system at fault in psychopathological behavior is too narrow an approach, if not a wholly erroneous one. What may be equally or more seriously at fault are the cognitions and actions that are interacting with the emotion system.

The Principle of Emotion Contagion

Emotion is catching. The prototypical case of emotion contagion is reciprocated smiling in the mother–infant relationship. In certain stages of this relationship, the smile functions somewhat like an innate releaser or a stimulus that is environmentally highly stable (one to which the organism tends to respond with a specific behavior pattern despite changes in the environment). Throughout life the smile of one person remains a strong stimulus for the smiling response of the person to whom the smile is directed (see Figure 5-1). There are probably a number of other instances where one emotion expression is an environmentally stable psychological activator of a particular emotion in the other person. However, in most cases an individual's past experiences, affective–cognitive structures and orientations, and his characteristic and momentary emotion thresholds help determine whether or not he will "catch" the emotion displayed by the other person or persons.

The principle of emotion contagion can help explain the unity of feeling and the single mindedness that occurs in groups under widely different circumstances–parties, celebrations, athletic contests, street-gang encounters, "kangaroo courts," riots, war, or the spell cast by a demagogue or

FIGURE 5-1. Emotion contagion. The joy of
a proud father elicits smiles from mother and
daughter, and their smiles tend to evoke a
smile in the emphatic reader.

charismatic leader. For example, consider the behavior of the student
section of the gymnasium at a basketball game when the home team is
playing its arch rival for the conference championship. As time for the tip-
off approaches, interest builds to high excitement. When the home team
enters, a loud roar of approval, as though from a single high-pitched voice,
fills the gymnasium. When the opponents enter, the highly partisan crowd
may respond either with feigned indifference (contemptuous silence), or a
loud gutteral "boo" of disgust. As the home team goes, so go the emotions
of the rooting section. With one voice the students shout approval of
effective plays and moan loudly over setbacks. The cheerleaders' expressions can easily trigger consonant expressions from the group. A single
irate student spectator can shout "Go to hell, 'Winsocki'," and have the
entire student section chanting this epithet with seemingly considerable
feeling and conviction. In the heat of the contest an angry protest by the
opposing coach can send a wave of angry frowns across the faces of the
home team's rooting section and in some cases a bevy of missiles (angrily
crushed paper cups) to the gym floor.

Although these examples of emotion contagion are by some standards
"disgraceful" disruptions of the game that sometimes result in a technical
foul against the home team, they are generally quite harmless. According to
some theorists (e.g., Lorenz, 1966) they are even therapeutic or beneficial.
However, there are other instances where emotion contagion can lead to

tragedy. A demagogue may shout his biases to the crowd and create or reinforce prejudices, and a mob can be whipped into a frenzy that results in violence. Any leader with charisma can make use of the principle of emotion contagion. It can be used for constructive as well as destructive purposes.

The Principle of Self-Regulation and Utilization of Emotions

According to the principle of self-regulation of emotions the individual can regulate or control his emotion states through his own effort. Since the components of emotion operate in an interactive fashion, or as a feedback loop, any component of emotion is potentially a vehicle for controlling or regulating the emotion process. One component of emotion, facial expression, is actualized by muscles that are entirely under the voluntary control of the individual. Although there is the possibility that different neural pathways are involved in voluntary and involuntary expression, voluntarily performed facial expressions combined with appropriate cognition and action can activate emotions. The work of Schwartz *et al.* showed that emotion-specific imagery produces emotion-specific EMG activity in the expressive muscles of the face. Rusolova, Izard, and Simonov (1975) found EMG changes and increased heart rate in Stanislavski-trained actors and actresses who were asked to create emotion voluntarily, through imagery and cognition.

Feedback from the facial muscles allows a person not only to "turn off" facial expressions of experienced emotions but to simulate, perhaps convincingly, emotions not felt. Recent research has shown that untrained individuals can deceive others by managing and masking their facial expression (Ekman & Friesen, 1969, 1975).

Leeper and his colleagues (1948, 1965; Leeper & Madison, 1959) have marshaled evidence in support of their hypothesis that emotion has an organizing rather than a disorganizing effect on thought and behavior. Emotion may narrow the field of perception (reduce the number of things the person attends to) and hence momentarily reduce cognitive and behavioral alternatives. Nevertheless, the individual may be very well-organized to perform within the sphere circumscribed by the emotion. A number of different theoretical approaches recognize that emotion has motivational value. It is also generally recognized that emotion mobilizes energy. If an emotion mobilizes energy, has an organizing effect on behavior, and motivates thought and action, it seems reasonable to assume that the emotions are important human resources. According to the general principle of emotion utilization, capitalizing on the inherently adaptive functions of the emotions is a prerequisite for a healthy, integrated personality and effective functioning.

In general, people utilize their emotions in more or less constructive fashion. For example, people differ in the degree to which they effectively "harness" their interest. Some students seek subjects which are attractive and interesting and upon graduation they try to find careers that will be interesting and enjoyable through the years. Insofar as they succeed, they will be able to utilize the organizing and motivating value of the positive emotions of interest and joy in their study and work.

Optimal utilization of emotion experience often requires the individual to allow his emotion to influence his thought and action immediately, in a spontaneous, natural way. Yet, in certain situations it is most appropriate not to exhibit strong emotion or "act it out." The challenge for the individual is to be able to modulate emotions when necessary or desirable and still be capable of thinking and acting spontaneously in harmony with one's emotions when such freedom is feasible.

Although much remains to be learned about the application of the principles of emotion to human problems, Singer (1974) and Izard (1971) have described a number of techniques that have proved useful in psychotherapy and other behavior-change procedures. For example, Singer presents clinical case material showing how imagery-induced positive emotion can be used to increase the sense of self-control and help alleviate the burden of debilitating negative emotions.

Methods of Studying the Emotions

The concepts and evidence presented in the preceding pages emphasize the idea that emotions are complex phenomena with neural, expressive, and experiential components. Thus, the study of emotion may take place at any of the three levels, each level corresponding to one of the basic components of the emotion process. Methods and techniques of investigation are dictated in large measure by the components being studied.

Research on the Neurophysiological Level

Studies of the role of the brain and the central nervous system in emotion are basic to the advancement of the science of emotions. Although considerable progress is being made in the general area of brain and behavior (e.g., see Fox & Rudell, 1968; Kinsbourne, 1971; Magoun, 1958; Olds, 1963; Luria, 1966, 1973), relatively less research has been conducted in the study of brain and emotion. Some of the major methods and techniques used in the study of emotion at the neurophysiological level will be briefly described below, together with some illustrative summaries of experiments.

Surgical Ablations and Lesions. Systematic research with surgical ablations and lesions has been conducted only on nonhumans for ethical reasons that are quite obvious. This may limit the generalizability of some of the findings, particularly if the experimental subjects are lower animals (e.g., mice, rats, gerbils), but some of the findings apparently have validity across species (including human beings), and research of this type continues to contribute to the fund of knowledge on the basic functions of the brain mechanisms of emotion and emotion-related behavior. The investigator hypothesizes about the role of a particular brain mechanism in emotion, then proceeds to remove or incapacitate this brain area. Researchers usually render the brain area or mechanism nonfunctional either by neural surgery or by use of carefully dosed electrical current administered via microelectrodes implanted in the selected brain tissue. Following the operation or treatment the investigator observes the effects of the ablation or lesion on various types of behavior. After many years of investigations of this sort, a number of investigators have pointed out various limitations of this approach. One of the most serious problems has been the relative imprecision of the ablations or lesions. The greater the imprecision, the more difficult it is to draw conclusions regarding relationships of particular brain areas to specific emotional responses, or the lack of them. Sometimes a very small area of the brain has different and complex functions.

Simonov's (1972) integrative review of studies of the functions of the hippocampus affords a good example of the experimental contributions from this approach. Douglas and Pribram (1966) had advanced the notion that the hippocampus registers the fact of nonreinforcement of external stimuli as a biologically meaningful event. They also concluded that the hippocampus contributes to the concentration of attention by blocking the effect of extraneous stimuli (Douglas, 1967). However, other investigations (Hendrichsen, Kimball, & Kimball, 1969; Morell, Barlow, & Brazier, 1960) showed that rats with damaged hippocampus are distracted much less than control animals. The work of Vinogrado (1970) showed that the hippocampus was not a recorder of nonreinforcing events but a detector of novelty (which activates interest) capable of abstracting meaning from a stimulus that has been appraised by other brain mechanisms. Pigareva (1969, 1970) performed additional experiments on hippocampal functions using the technique of training the animal to display different types of conditioned reflexes to the same stimulus, a method first described by Asratyan (1938). An example of Asratyan's method is as follows: in the morning an animal is trained to press a lever at the onset of a light in order to obtain food (elementary conditioned response or CR), and during the same period the animal is taught to respond to a bell by pressing a lever that avoids electrical shock (defensive CR). In the evening the stimuli are given opposite meanings. Now when the light comes on the animal has to press the bar that avoids shock, and when the bell comes on he has to press the bar that provides food. When the meaning of the stimuli are switched, rats have great difficulty in learning the new meaning of the stimuli, and continued training to bring about "switching" can "lead to severe disorders of higher nervous activity with marked autonomic components of emotional stress" (Simonov, 1972, p. 35). However, when the hippocampus of rats was destroyed bilaterally, they were able to attain consistent switching (respond appropriately to each signal despite the fact that its significance had been switched) in a relatively short number of conditioning sessions. These rats retained both of the CRs to light and both of the CRs to bell. Hence the change in switching ability could not be explained in terms of a memory defect brought about by the destruction of the hippocampus. Simonov concluded "that the behavior of rats with damaged hippocampus is selectively oriented to signals of highly probable events" (Simonov, 1972, p. 135).

In another study Pigareva (1970) established elementary CRs with partial (probabilistic) reinforcement. Hippocampectomized rats conditioned as readily as intact animals when random reinforcement of the CS presentations occurred 50 to 100% of the time. However, when the frequency of the reinforcement was reduced to a range of 33–25%, hippocampectomized rats were unable to form the CR over a period of ten experimental days while intact rats attained high CR levels by the eighth to ninth day.

Simonov interpreted this series of experiments to be consistent with his information theory of emotion (see Chapter 2, p. 37). His theory postulates that the degree of emotional stress is a function of the magnitude of the need (motivation) and the assessment of the probability of its satisfaction at a given moment. "From this viewpoint, the hippocampus is associated neither with motivational excitation (which forms in other structures, primarily the hypothalamus) or with the assessment of reinforcement probability which is performed by neocortical mechanisms. The hippocampus pertains to that system in which motivational and informational excitation are integrated and serves as an intermediate station through which these two streams of excitation exert a modulating effect on the neural substrate of emotions" (Simonov, 1972, p. 39). Regardless of whether Simonov's conclusion is entirely correct, his work and that of the investigators he reviewed showed that the method of ablation and lesion can contribute to the understanding of brain mechanisms involved in the emotions.

Surgical ablations and lesions have been used as medical and psychiatric treatment techniques for intractable pain (e.g., cancer) and for various psychiatric and psychological problems. Chronic psychotics considered incurable by other methods have been subjected to lobotomies or topectomies, radical brain surgeries. They involve the sectioning of many of the tracts connecting the frontal lobe to the rest of the cortex or removing sections of cortical tissue. With the development of the technology for microelectrode implantation, surgical treatment of psychiatric patients has become considerably more delicate and precise. For example, Walter (1966) implanted electrodes in the frontal lobes and effected carefully dosed coagulations. He claimed that 85% of these patients who had been suffering from anxiety and obsessions realized complete recovery and began functioning in their social environment in a normal fashion. Bechtereva and her colleagues (1974) have treated patients suffering from severe Parkinsonian disease, a neurological condition that appears to render the patient incapable of normal emotional responsiveness and which also causes tremors of the extremities, by administering electric stimulation via microelectrodes implanted in the thalamus. They have maintained that stimulation of particular areas of the thalamus elicit positive emotional responses and that continued treatment has a therapuetic effect on the patients. Speigel and Wycis (1961) claimed to have successfully treated anxiety and obsessive–compulsive neurosis by destruction of discrete parts of the thalamus. One problem with these studies is that they seldom give a careful account of the side effects of these treatments. It is difficult to ascertain short-term and long-term effects on the total lives of the patients, although the evidence that they obtained some relief from their psychiatric condition appears convincing.

Microelectrode Implantations for Direct Stimulation of the Brain. This technique was made possible by technological advances that enabled the experimenter to place tiny needle electrodes into specific areas of the brain. The introduction of the very small electrode causes minimal damage, and thus this technique offers the possiblity of studying response to stimulation of healthy, intact brain. In the direct brain-stimulation studies the aim is not to damage or destroy a particular area or mechanism in order to study subsequent deficits and changes; rather, studies using microelectrodes for electrical stimulation of the brain attempt to ascertain the effects of stimulating highly specific sites in the brain. Since microelectrodes can be implanted with considerable precision, conclusions regarding the role of particular brain areas in motor, cognitive, and emotion responses can be made with considerably more confidence than is the case for ablations and lesions.

Studies involving the electrical stimulation of the brain (ESB) is a part of a new area of science (neuroscience) that is still rapidly developing. Findings from early studies may well be modified as more laboratories become equipped to conduct these studies and as science and techology in this area continue to improve. One problem that makes these studies complex and their findings difficult to interpret is the fact that even minute stimulation of a very small area may produce highly complex effects.

Nevertheless some of the results of these studies are not only interesting and provocative, they appear to point clearly to some reliable relationships between stimulation of specific brain sites and particular emotion-related responses.

The work of Delgado (1971) has provided some exciting and controversial findings. He credited W. R. Hess (1927) with the first demonstration that ESB could produce threat and attack behavior in the cat. When he stimulated the periventricular gray matter, the cat showed piloerection (hair standing on end on back and tail) spat, hissed, growled, unsheathed its claws and struck out with them. At the same time the cat's pupils widened and the ears lay back or moved back and forth.

Delgado suggested that ESB can be used to obtain two types of responses that may be classified as emotional. First, he maintained, stimulation of the anterior hypothalamus produces "false rage"—a threatening display with hissing and growling that is not directed against other animals in the social environment. Even when attacked by other cats the stimulated animal did not retaliate or try to escape. It simply flattened its ears and lowered its head. In contrast, stimulation of the cat's lateral hypothalamus produced "an aggressive display clearly directed toward a control animal which reacted properly in facing the threat" (Delgado, 1971, pp. 125–127). Delgado maintained that the cat directed its hostility "intelligently, choosing the enemy and the moment of attack, changing tactics and adapting its movements to the motor reaction of its opponent" (Delgado, 1971, p. 128). The stimulated cat would attack only subordinate animals, always being careful to avoid attacking the most powerful cat in the group.

Delgado performed another series of studies to see if the effects obtained with cats would generalize to higher primates. He used rhesus macaque monkeys who, like many other primates, live in social groups and form a social dominance heirarchy which remains relatively stable. Delgado selected a female monkey named Lina and then for purposes of testing divided her colony into three groups. In the first group of four animals, she ranked lowest in dominance heirarchy, in the second group she ranked third, and in the third group she was next to the top in rank. Delgado implanted electrodes in the nucleus posterolateralis of the thalamus and used a remote control radio signal to stimulate Lina for five seconds each minute for an hour on two successive mornings in each of three groups separately. In each group the stimulation produced some common effects—running and climbing, licking, and vocalizing. However, her aggressive behavior varied according to her status in the group. In the group where she was of the lowest rank she attempted to attack another monkey only once but was herself threatened and attacked 24 times. In the second group where she ranked third in the group of four she made 24 aggressive attacks and was attacked only three times. In group 3 where

Lina was second to top rank, she attacked other monkeys 79 times and was never threatened (for illustrative photographs, see Delgado, 1971, pp. 124–127, 130–131).

The use of ESB as a treatment technique for neurological and psychiatric disorders has produced some provocative though not always consistent findings regarding brain–emotion relationships. Van Buren (1961) reported that ESB in the temporal lobe resulted in the sensation of fear. Delgado reported that stimulation of the right amygdala (an anatomical area of the limbic lobe) produced "a fit of rage" in a psychiatric patient who was playing a guitar and singing when she was stimulated by remote control radio signal. King (1961) has also reported anger expression and verbal aggression as a result of amygdaloid stimulation. Delgado has maintained that it is also possible to elicit positive emotion through ESB. He reported the case of a depressed patient who changed a very sad expression to a smile following brief stimulation of the rostral part of the brain.

Psychophysiological Studies. Until recently most of the human psychophysiological research in the area of emotions involved the measurement of the activity of various organs or systems innervated by the autonomic nervous system. Experimental studies often involved the experimental induction of stress and the measurement of such functions as heart rate (HR), galvanic skin response (GSR), or respiration rate (RR). Through use of this research method a great deal of information has been accumulated on the influence of various types of stress conditions on visceral functions (e.g., see Appley & Trumbull, 1967; Gasonov, 1974).

One line of research using psychophysiological techniques has attempted to show that anxiety is associated with increase in activity of the organs innervated by the sympathetic branch of the autonomic nervous system. Levitt (1967), who defined anxiety as fear, reviewed a number of psychophysiological studies and concluded that anxiety or fear involves primarily sympathetic reactions. These studies showed that fear or anxiety increased systolic (central) blood pressure and heart rate (Martin, 1961). A number of other investigations have supported this conclusion. Zimmerman (1968) showed that light sleepers scored higher on trait anxiety than sound sleepers. He then demonstrated that light sleepers (subjects who also score higher on anxiety and conflict subscales of personality tests) showed higher HR, RR, and GSR than did sound sleepers (subjects who scored lower on anxiety and conflict subscales of personality tests).

Bauman and Straughon (1969) studied the relationship between trait anxiety (IPAT anxiety scale scores) and GSR during conditions of stress and nonstress. Anxiety was induced by electric shock. A psychogalvanometer recorded GSR. The examiners concluded that the GSR was not related to trait anxiety but was a good index of state anxiety induced by the experimental stress (electrical shock). The GSR, measured in terms of basal skin resistance, was lowest during the experimental stress condition and highest during nonstress.

Fenz and Epstein (1965) developed an autonomic arousal self-report scale from items of the Taylor Manifest Anxiety Scale, and Brandt and Fenz (1969) used this scale to study responses under stress. They showed that a group who scored higher on the autonomic arousal scale (self-report measure) showed greater changes in GSR and heart rate than did a group scoring lower on the autonomic arousal scale.

These studies tend to show that experimentally induced stress or anxiety tends to be associated with increased activity in the sympathetic branch of the autonomic nervous system. However, this approach to the study of anxiety or stress has been criticized (e.g., Buss, 1961) on the grounds that it tends to oversimplify the physiology of anxiety. Another problem with this line of research is the fact that researchers have not all used the same definition of anxiety. Some equated anxiety with fear while others explicitly or tacitly assumed that anxiety was a combination of emotions and feeling states.

Although Gellhorn (1965, 1967) distinguished between acute fear and chronic fear and equated the latter with anxiety, he maintained that chronic fear (anxiety) was not associated simply with arousal of the sympathetic nervous system. He thought that chronic fear or anxiety involved both the ergotropic system (sympathetic system plus related neural structures) and the trophotropic system (parasympathetic systems plus related neural structures) functioning in an antagonistic fashion.

Whether there is only sympathetic or both sympathetic and parasympathetic activity in anxiety there is yet one additional problem in using autonomic nervous system functions as indexes of emotion. Activities other than emotion (physical exercise) can activate the autonomic nervous system. Thus when an investigator uses peripheral measures of autonomic nervous system activity without supplementary emotion-validating techniques he has the burden of demonstrating that his experimental stimuli or conditions activate emotion rather than simply undifferentiated arousal. The adequacy of autonomic indexes as measures of emotion has been seriously questioned since the work of Cannon and Bard in the thirties and forties showed that organs innervated by the autonomic nervous system were not essential in emotion or at least in the expressive component of emotion. They showed that after all of the autonomic nerve pathways to the viscera had been sectioned it was still possible to elicit emotion expression in cats.

Nevertheless, in the normal organism genuine emotion is typically accompanied by increased activity in the autonomic nervous system and many contemporary investigators now view the autonomic nervous system as an auxiliary system in the emotion process. When research utilizes emotion-specific measures (e.g., electromyography, self-report emotion scales), measures of autonomic nervous system activity can add significant data for the study of the overall emotion process and emotion-related functioning. Some studies using measures of autonomic and somatic nervous system activities and self-report measures will be summarized later.

An example of a study combining peripheral measures of somatic-system functioning and self-report of subjectively felt emotion is that of Schwartz, Fair, Greenberg, Freedman, and Klerman (1974). They used electromyography (EMG) as an approach to quantifying the expressive component of emotion. They were interested not only in readily observable facial patterns but in "covert" expressions as well. As shown in Figure 5-2, they demonstrated that it was possible to make clear discriminations between EMG profiles (based on neuromuscular activity) of subjects who were instructed to think about or image a happy situation, a sad situation, and an angry situation.

Studies of the Expressive Component of Emotion

The term expressive is used to describe the component of emotion which is observable primarily in facial patterns and secondarily in postural and vocal behavior. The term does not refer to instrumental, motor, or locomotor responses subsequent to the intraperson emotion process. The number of studies using research techniques focusing on expressive behavior has been increasing rapidly over the past decade. Confidence in the validity and usefulness of such techniques has been substantially increased by recent robust evidence from studies in numerous literate and preliterate cultures supporting Darwin's century-old proposition that certain fundamental emotion expressions are innate and universal (Ekman, 1972; Izard, 1971).

A number of studies of the expressive component of emotion will be summarized in later chapters of this text. In the present survey of methods, two types of emotion-expression studies will be briefly discussed and illustrated: studies of emotion expression (encoding emotions), and studies of the recognition (decoding) of the cues or signals of emotion expression.

Techniques for Studying Emotion Expression. Studies of this type fall into two groups: studies of (a) voluntary expression and (b) involuntary or spontaneous expression. Very little research has been done on voluntary expression, the ability to produce a particular facial expression of an emotion on request. Although Goodenough (1932) and Thompson (1941) showed that facial expressions develop in congenitally blind children in near-normal fashion, Dumas (1932, 1948) indicated that the voluntary expressions of the congenitally blind were considerably inferior to the voluntary expressions of normals. Kwint (1934) tested children's ability to

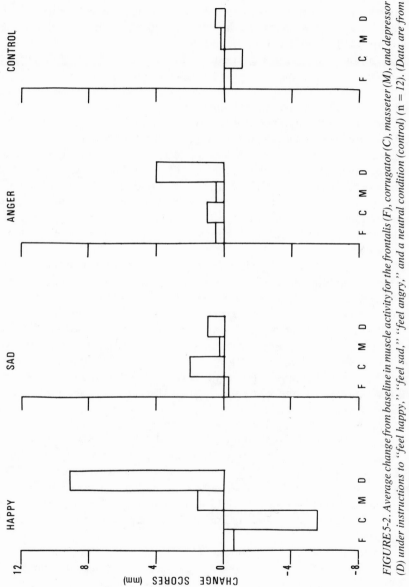

FIGURE 5-2. Average change from baseline in muscle activity for the frontalis (F), corrugator (C), masseter (M), and depressor (D) under instructions to "feel happy," "feel sad," "feel angry," and a neutral condition (control) (n = 12). (Data are from Schwartz et al., 1973.)

execute a number of facial movements. He described each movement requested of the child both verbally and by modeling it on his own face. He showed that children's ability to execute voluntarily the requested facial movements (many of which were components of discrete emotions) developed in a rather regular fashion from age four through fourteen. Kwint did not attempt his test with younger children.

The problem of capturing spontaneous expressions in a variety of situations has been an obstacle in the study of voluntary expressions. Some of the more important contributions to the study of children's spontaneous behavior, including facial expressions, head movements, and emotion-related gestures and manipulations, have been made by ethologists. An example of this type of study will be given in a later section.

Observers of expressive behavior have used three techniques: direct observation using a behavior checklist, still photographs, and videotape recording or filming. Each of these methods has advantages and disadvantages. Neither the method of direct observation or the method of still photographs are as comprehensive as videotaping or filming. However, when using a videotape recorder or movie camera it is not always possible to focus on the face.

Ekman, Liebert, Friesen, Harrison, Zlatchin, Malmstrom, and Baron (1971) videotaped the facial expressions of five- and six-year-old boys while they were watching violence on television. They obtained judges' estimates of the degree to which each child expressed interest, joy, surprise, sadness, anger, disgust, fear, and pain during the TV show. Following the TV watching the children were given an opportunity to press one of two buttons that would "help" or "hurt" a child playing a game in the next room. They found highly significant correlations between the type of emotions expressed while watching TV and the type of behavior (aggressive, altruistic) exhibited afterwards. Those boys who showed the most joy while watching violence later showed more aggression, and those who looked disinterested and pained gave more helping responses.

Singer and Singer (1976) studied the effects of a "happy" TV show (Mister Rogers) on imaginative play and emotion responses of nursery school children. They found that children who watched the show with an adult who occasionally interpreted or reiterated material and encouraged mimicry showed significant gains in imaginative play and positive emotion expressions.

Ekman, Friesen, and Tomkins (1971) have developed a detailed method for measuring facial behavior, the Facial Affect Scoring Technique (FAST). FAST can be applied to still photographs, videotape, and movies. FAST provides a means of scoring each observable facial movement in each of three areas of the face: (a) brows–forehead area, (b) eyes–lids; (c) lower face, including cheeks, nose, mouth, chin. FAST uses photographic examples to define each of the movements within each area of the face. The investigators assumed that photographic examples offered greater objectivity and reliability of scoring than verbal description of facial movements. For examples, instead of describing a particular facial movement as a frown brought about by action of the corrugator muscles, FAST presents a picture of this portion of the face showing the particular movements. An example of the types of picture models used for scoring the emotion of anger are presented in Figure 5-3.

In order to use the FAST a coder views a given facial expression one part at a time with the other parts of the face blocked from view. The coder then matches this area of the face with a model from the FAST atlas of expression photographs. The coder does not judge what emotion is shown on the face, rather he simply classifies the movement in each area of the face according to the standard of photographs in the FAST atlas. The type of emotion present in a given photograph or section of videotape is determined by applying a formula to the ratings made by the coder. The formula can take into account the scoring of more than one independent coder. In scoring filmed records the FAST technique yields measures both of duration of facial movements and of frequency of occurrence of each component of emotion expression within each facial area.

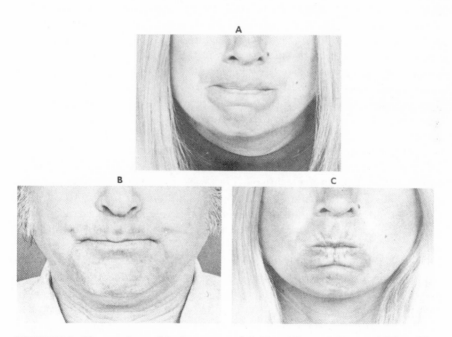

FIGURE 5-3. Three variants of the "anger mouth." (From Ekman & Friesen, 1975, p. 172.)

The FAST yields scores for six emotions: joy (happiness), surprise, distress (sadness), anger, disgust, and fear. Ekman and his colleagues have completed a number of validity studies for the FAST. In one of these studies the investigators made videotaped records of subjects' faces while they watched a film of autumn leaves and then a stress-inducing film of sinus surgery. The FAST scoring system was applied to every observable movement in each of three areas of the face for approximately three minutes of facial behavior during the neutral film and three minutes during the stress film. The results revealed large differences in facial behavior of the subjects while watching the film of fall leaves and the stress film of sinus surgery. Both the FAST frequency scores and FAST duration scores indicated that there was more facial behavior which FAST identified as surprise, sadness, anger, and disgust while watching the stress film and more behavior which FAST measured as joy or happiness during the film about fall leaves (Ekman, 1972, pp. 116–117).

Recognition or Discrimination of Emotion Expressions. The study by Ekman, Friesen, and Tomkins summarized in the preceding section was a study using an objective scoring technique to analyze facial expressions in terms of emotion categories. The scoring technique was applied by observers who could watch the videotaped records as many times as necessary to match the various facial movements seen in the data records with the model of movements in the photograph atlas of the FAST. Another type of study at the expressive level is the study of people's ability to recognize or discriminate among the expressions characteristic of different emotion categories. Two series of basic studies in this area are those described by Ekman, Friesen, and Ellsworth (1972) and Izard (1971). As already indicated these studies showed that certain fundamental emotion expressions were reliably identified by samples of individuals in many different cultures, including both literate and preliterate cultures.

A number of different kinds of studies have been conducted that focus on emotion-recognition scores or attention to emotion expression. Lévy-Schoen (1964) conducted a series of studies aimed at comparing the role of facial expressions and clothing accessories in children's perceptions of others. She tested 30 children at each age from four through thirteen years. Her photographs contained three expression categories: Pleasant or happy (smiling), neutral, and unpleasant (frowning). She presented children the task of deciding which two pictures in a set of four were the most similar. The child could choose on the basis of accessories (e.g., the two persons with the earrings) or expressions (e.g., the two with smiles). She found that most children made their choice on the basis of accessories until about age eight. From eight to ten years they made about half their choices on each basis, and from eleven years on most made their choices on the basis of expression.

Savitsky and Izard (1970) did a follow-up study similar to that of Lévy-Schoen but they used stronger and clearer (cross-culturally standardized) expressions of four emotions: joy, distress, fear, and anger. They developed a series of 96 triads (groups of three photographs) in which two of the three photographs contained either the common elements of hats or facial expressions. In some triads the only possible correct answer was to point to the two with hats, in others the only possible correct answer was to point to the two faces that showed the same emotion expression. In other triads it was possible to point either to two faces in which the photographs showed the people wearing hats or to two faces that had the same emotion expression but different headdress (hat and no-hat). The latter was considered the critical choice for determining when the child used emotion expression as a basis for pairing or deciding which pair was most similar. In the series of triads in which the child could pair either on the basis of hats or on the basis that both people showed the same emotion expression, only the four-year-old children paired most frequently on the basis of hats. Children ages five through eight answered the question as to which of the two were most similar by pointing to the two people with the same emotion expression, even though one of them was bareheaded and one wore a hat. The children paired the expressions of the four different emotions (joy, distress, anger, fear) equally well. The results of this study suggest that emotion recognition is an important aspect of person perception (how we see others) as early as the age of five years.

A study by Odom and Lemond (1972) used both emotion recognition and emotion expression techniques. They studied the relationship between children's ability to discriminate among emotion expressions and their ability to produce emotion expressions on request. They used two different tasks to measure emotion discrimination: a matching-discrimination task in which the child had to match one of the four photographs with a model held by the examiner and a situation-discrimination task in which the child had to point to the photograph that matched a situation verbally described by the examiner (e.g., "show me the one being chased by a mean dog"). They also used two means of obtaining voluntary expressions: an imitation-production task in which the subject attempted to "make a face like you would if you felt like these people do," the stimuli being two photographs of different people showing the same expression. The second technique was a situation-production task in which the experimenter read the same situations as used in the imitation task and asked the subject to make a face like he would if he were in that specific situation. The experimenters used the series of photographs developed by Izard (1971). Their subjects were 32 kindergarten and 32 fifth-grade children from schools in middle-class neighborhoods.

Their results showed that the older children made more correct responses on both tasks than the younger children and that more correct responses were made in the discrimination tasks than in the production tasks. Further, more correct responses were made to some expressions than to others. Subjects who had a discrimination task first made more correct responses across both tasks than did subjects who had a production task first. The results also showed that subjects obtained higher scores on the discrimination tasks than on the production tasks. The discrepancy between discrimination and production was significant ($p < .01$) for all expressions except interest and joy. The authors thought that the improvement in production (voluntary expression) with age might reflect greater refinement in the stored representations of expressions (Gibson, 1969), but that the level of production accuracy might be lowered by the inhibiting effects of socialization factors as well as other unidentifiable influences (Izard, 1971).

Naturalistic Observation of Emotion Expression. There are two procedures for implementing the method of naturalistic observation. One is to train observers to use a standardized behavior observation scale for recording the appearance and sequences of various emotions as they occur in the different children being studied. This method has certain limitations. Haggard and Issacs (1966) showed that discriminable micromomentary emotion expressions occurred within a period of approximately one-eighth of a second and went unnoticed by experienced psychiatrists who were acting as observers. In addition to the possibility of missing a certain amount of data, a live observer is limited in the number of children or number of possible behaviors that can be covered in a session. The number of children which may be reliably observed will depend on the comprehensiveness of the observation scale.

The second procedure for implementing naturalistic observations is by use of videotape recording or filming. Videotape recording of children's facial expressions, head movements, gestures, and other emotion-related activities in various situations and conditions (playroom or playground, classroom, study hall) can provide a comprehensive and accurate record of these events. Trained observers can then play and replay the tapes in order to classify the children's responses or code them on standardized observation scales and demonstrate observer or rater reliability. A number of techniques such as FAST can be used to score the facial expressions recorded by videotape or film. The great advantage of naturalistic observation is that the emotion expressions can be placed in the context of larger sequences of behavior showing both the antecedents and consequences of the emotion expressions.

Another significant approach to the study of children's behavior in ordinary life situations is that of ethology (e.g., see Tinbergen, 1972; McGrew, 1972, and Blurton Jones, 1972; Blurton Jones and Konnor,

1973). Ethologists are zoologists who study the behavior of animals in their natural habitat. Recently a number of them have turned their attention to the study of human beings. One rather comprehensive study of the ethology of children in nursery schools was conducted by McGrew. McGrew and other contemporary ethologists simply record and classify small or esaily observed units of behavior according to standard verbal descriptions. They do not infer from a particular set of expressive movements, gestures, or manipulations that the subject felt a particular emotion. They describe expressions and movements without any inference with respect to subjective experience. They feel that this is the most objective approach to the task of classifying and analyzing sequences of movements and activities in relation to the social environment or ecological conditions.

McGrew's (1972) studies led to the development of an "ethogram" for nursery school schildren, ages three to five. The responses described by McGrew using the ethological approach and the expressive movements described by emotion-expression scoring techniques such as the FAST show considerable overlap, especially with respect to the responses and activities of facial muscles. Although the two approaches have different aims they produce overlapping data, and one of the challenges for future research will be to show the relationship between various scores derived from the two techniques and the relationship between these scores and other psychobiological phenomena. Listed in Table 5-1 are the facial and head movements described by McGrew. Some of these movements are associated with two or more different discrete emotions (e.g., mouth open, wide eyes), some primarily with one emotion (e.g., pucker face, laugh), and some with no emotion in particular (e.g., glance, vocalize).

Methods of Studying Emotion Experience (The Phenomenology of the Emotions)

Usually when one studies emotion at either the neurophysiological or expressive level one studies an emotion process that includes "felt-emotion" or emotion experience. Certainly when a researcher observes the spontaneous expression of emotions in children in day-to-day life or in school situations the investigator is also obtaining indexes of their inner experiences. Nevertheless it is appropriate to distinctly categorize certain techniques for more direct analysis of the subjective experience of emotion.

Several adjective checklists or scales have been used to get immediate self-reports of emotion experience (see Izard, 1972; Izard, Dougherty, Bloxom, & Kotsch, 1974; Nowlis, 1965; Zuckerman, 1960). These scales have most frequently been used with college students though some of them have been used in research in the high school.

The Differential Emotions Scale (DES) is a self-report instrument

TABLE 5-1
Repertory of Preschool Children's Facial and
Head Movements[a]

Facial movements	Head movements
1. Bared teeth	1. Bite
2. Blink	2. Blow
3. Eyebrow flash	3. Chew lips
4. Eyes closed	4. Chin in
5. Grin face	5. Face thrust
6. Low frown	6. Gaze fixate
7. Mouth open	7. Glance
8. Narrow eyes	8. Grind teeth
9. Normal face	9. Head nod
10. Nose wrinkle	10. Head shake
11. Play face	11. Head tilt
12. Pout	12. Kiss
13. Pucker face	13. Laugh
14. Red face	14. Lick
15. Smile	15. Look
16. Wide eyes	16. Mouth
	17. Spit
	18. Swallow
	19. Tongue out
	20. Verbalize
	21. Vocalize
	22. Weep
	23. Yawn

[a]Adapted from McGrew (1972).

designed for use in the assessment of an individual's experience of fundamental emotions or combinations (patterns) of emotions. The DES represents a new development in adjective checklists currently in use in that it is
a standardized instrument that reliably divides the individual's description
of emotion experience into validated, discrete categories of emotion. The
DES has the potential to assess the entire range of human emotions. It has
proved useful in the measurement and analysis of the several emotions that
characterize a given situation or condition when instruments designed to
yield a single score for a complex pattern of emotions (such as "anxiety")
prove too simplistic for the purpose.

The DES was originally conceived as a "state" measure of one's
emotions, but variations in the instructions allow the same set of scales to
be used in the assessment of emotion experiences as they are perceived
over an extended period of time. (The frequency with which an emotion is
experienced over time may be viewed as an "emotion trait.") This varia-

tion of the DES is labeled the Differential Emotions Scale II. The DES and DES II both consist of thirty adjectives (items), three for each of the ten fundamental emotions described in Chapter 4. The usual DES instructions ask an individual to rate on a single five-point intensity scale the extent to which each word describes the way he feels at the present time. The DES II, on the other hand, is composed of a five-point frequency scale. The DES II instructions ask the individual to consider a specified time period or his day-to-day life and to rate the *frequency* with which he experiences each emotion during the time considered. The time period to be considered by the individual completing the DES II can be varied to suit the purpose. This period may be a specified block of time in the past (i.e., the past week, month, experiment, therapy hour) or may refer generally to the individual's entire life (i.e., "How often do you have these feelings in your day-to-day living?"). The purpose of the DES II frequency scale is to determine how *often* one experiences each of the fundamental emotions, with frequency of experiencing a given emotion being considered an index of an "emotion trait." The DES and some reliability statistics are presented in Table 5-2.

A rather extensive study of the subjective experience of emotion was conducted by Bartlett and Izard (1972). They asked subjects to imagine or visualize situations in which they felt a particular discrete emotion very strongly. While visualizing or imaging the emotion situation they were asked to describe their subjective experience by completing two self-report rating scales. On one scale the subject indicated the degree to which he or she felt pleasant, tense, self-assured, active, deliberate impulsive, controlled, and extraverted (the Dimensions Rating Scale, DRS). The subjects also described their experiences by completing the Differential Emotions Scale (DES) which contained descriptive adjective scales for eight fundamental emotions. Both instruments made good discriminations between the various imaged or visualized emotion situations. In addition, each particular emotion situation yielded extremely high scores on the adjective scales representing that discrete emotion and tended to have high scores on particular dimensions of the DRS. For example, when subjects visualized the joy situation they scored very high on the DES joy scale, and on the DRS they had higher pleasantness scores and lower tension scores than was the case for any other emotion. Similarly, subjects visualizing the fear situation had very high DES fear scores, and on the DRS they had higher scores on tension than was the case for any other emotion situation; they also had very low pleasantness scores. Interestingly, subjects reported feeling greatest self-assurance in the joy and interest situations, but they also showed relatively high self-assurance in the anger situation. The DRS self-assurance score in the anger situation was much higher than the self-assurance score in any of the other negative emotion situations. Another interesting finding was the fact that the shyness situation received signifi-

TABLE 5-2
The Differential Emotions Scale[a]

Factor	Item	Item–factor correlation	Factor	Item	Item–factor correlation
I. Interest (.76)	Attentive	.88	VI. Disgust (.73)	Feeling of distate	.86
	Concentrating	.79		Disgusted	.85
	Alert	.87		Feeling of revulsion	.78
II. Enjoyment (.87)	Delighted	.81	VII. Contempt (.78)	Contemptuous	.89
	Happy	.87		Scornful	.90
	Joyful	.86		Disdainful	.84
III. Surprise (.75)	Surprise	.83	VIII. Fear (.68)	Scared	.88
	Amazed	.85		Fearful	.90
	Astonished	.87		Afraid	.89
IV. Distress (.85)	Downhearted	.86	IX. Shame/ shyness (.83)	Sheepish	.73
	Sad	.79		Bashful	.87
	Discouraged	.82		Shy	.88
V. Anger (.68)	Enraged	.74	X. Guilt (.77)	Repentant	.78
	Angry	.84		Guilty	.83
	Mad	.86		Blameworthy	.80

[a]Item factor correlations for "state" instructions, $N = 259$; test–retest reliabilities for trait instructions given in parentheses, $N = 63$.

cantly higher ratings on pleasantness than any of the other negative emotions. More of the findings of this study will be presented in the chapters devoted to the fundamental emotions.

In another study, Bartlett and Izard administered both the DES and the DRS to students prior to a midterm examination. The subjects had previously received a standard anxiety scale (Spielberger–Lushene–Gorsuch State–Trait Anxiety Scale, STAI) and had been divided into high-anxiety and low-anxiety groups according to their scores on STAI. Both the DES and DRS clearly distinguished between high-anxiety and low-anxiety subjects in the test-anxiety situation. The pattern of scores on the DES and DRS in an imagined anxiety situation, obtained in an earlier occasion, were very similar to the DES and DRS scores obtained in the test-anxiety situation, especially for the subjects who showed high STAI anxiety scores prior to the examination. This finding supported other studies by Izard (1972) showing that anxiety is a complex (multivariate) phenomenon consisting of a combination or pattern of emotions and feelings.

Various inventories have been used in studies of anxiety in children. Prominent examples are the anxiety tests used by Sarason and his colleagues (Sarason, Davidson, Lighthall, Waite, & Ruebush, 1960). The advantage of these scales is that they have proved useful with elementary-school-age children. A disadvantage is the fact that the scales deal with anxiety as an entity rather than as a pattern of discrete emotions. An inventory used by Izard (1971) attempts to measure the extent to which each of several discrete emotions occur in different social situations. This instrument was standardized on college students but has been adapted in experimental form for children of third grade level and higher.

A very promising approach to the study of emotion experience in preschool children has been presented by Singer (1973). He and his associates (see chapters in Singer, 1973, by Biblow, Freyberg, Gottlieb, & Pulaski) have devised ingenious techniques for measuring predisposition to play, play content, and the differentiated emotions associated with spontaneous play and fantasy. They have studied children's fantasies and imaginative play in relation to such discrete emotions as interest, joy, anger, distress, fear, and shame. The work of Singer and his colleagues represents a pioneering effort to analyze some of the relationships between emotion and cognitive processes.

Allen and Hamsher (1974) have developed a test of "emotional styles" that measures (a) responsiveness (affect intensity), (b) expressiveness (interpersonal communication of affect), and (c) orientation (attitudes toward emotion). Construct validity has been established with experimentally induced affect, peer ratings of emotionality, and a number of emotion measures such as the Mosher Forced-Choice Guilt Scale. Females score significantly higher than males on all three factors. The test seems promising as a measure of some general dimensions of emotion or affective–cognitive orientations, but it provides no information about specific emotions.

Summary

An increasing number of theorists and investigators support the basic concept of differentiated emotions or affects despite some differences in conceptualizations of emotions and their relationships to other personality subsystems. Many of them would agree with the principles discussed in this chapter.

According to the principle of differential emotions a number of discrete emotions can be differentiated in terms of their neurophysiological underpinnings, their facial patterns, and their experiential–motivational characteristics. Each of these emotions affects people, their perceptions, thoughts, and actions in a different way. The principle of interacting emotion components assumes that the neural, expressive, and experiential components of emotion have a degree of independence but are basically interactive. It cautions against considering any one component as a complete index for a description of emotion. The principle of emotion patterning indicates that one emotion can elicit another and that emotions often occur in patterns or combinations.

The principle of emotion communication holds that the expressive component of emotion is a source of signals of considerable importance in social interactions. Many emotion signals have specific and reliably interpretable meanings, but many are complex and difficult to understand. The principle of emotion-facilitated personal growth and emotional attachment states that emotion experiences influence individual and social development and play a critical role in the formation of interpersonal ties. Lack of positive emotion interactions in early infancy can result in serious psychological problems. The principle of inherently adaptive functions maintains that each discrete emotion has the capacity to facilitate adaptive action.

The principle of interactive systems holds that the emotion system interacts with and influences the functions of the homeostatic drive, perceptual, cognitive, and action systems. Harmonious interaction of subsystems facilitates healthy development and effective functioning. The principle of emotion contagion indicates that in many situations emotion is transmitted from one person to another. This principle operates in personal empathy as well as in riots and war. The principle of self-regulation and utilization of emotions draws attention to the possibility that any emotion component or any subsystem that interacts with emotion is potentially a vehicle for emotion control. Experiments have shown that at least some people can self-generate emotion by means of affective imagery and expressive movements.

There are methods for studying each of the components of emotions though few techniques yield hard data on all components at once or on emotion as a whole. The method of surgical ablations and lesions is decreasing in popularity, since advances in technology have made possible microelectrode implantations and similar refined techniques. In the realm of psychophysiology facial electromyography of various affective states seems to hold considerable promise.

The expressive component of emotion is studied both in terms of voluntary and involuntary expressions. Ekman, Friesen, and Tomkins have developed a detailed method for measuring facial behavior and, though this technique has already been found useful, it is still being refined. Standardized emotion expressions were used in cross-cultural studies that support the hypothesis of universality, and they are currently being used to study emotion recognition or discrimination in infants and young children. The naturalistic observation of emotion expressions in normal life-situations holds great promise for the understanding of the antecedents and consequences of expressing various discrete emotions in social situations.

A number of techniques have been developed for the study of emotion experience or the phenomenology of the emotions. These measures necessarily rely upon self-report, and the interest and cooperation of the participant is a necessity. Given the participant's interest and cooperation self-report measures remain the only devices for studying the subjective experience of emotion, and hence they are potentially quite useful.

6

EMOTIONS AND CONSCIOUSNESS

> No longer is it possible to throw the question out as meaningless, though it is stranger than science has ever met before: Has the universe had to adapt itself from its earliest days to the future requirements for life and mind? Until we understand which way truth lies in this domain, we can very well agree that we do not know the first thing about the universe.
>
> One view holds that as we keep on investigating matter, we will work down from crystals to molecules, from molecules to atoms, from atoms to particles, from particles to quarks—and mine to forever greater depths. A very different concept might be called the "Leibniz logic loop." According to this view the analysis of the physical world, pursued to sufficient depth, will lead back in some now-hidden way to man himself, to conscious mind, tied unexpectedly through the very acts of observation and participation to partnership in the foundation of the universe. To write off the power of observation and reason to make headway with this question would seem to fly against experience. (Wheeler, 1974, 688–689)

Although a number of scientists have always considered consciousness to be the primary subject matter of psychology, it has received a disproportionately small amount of attention from theorists and investigators. In some respects consciousness has been taken for granted. It has been considered as the background or the "given" underlying the more restricted discrete variables that are manipulated and measured in scientific psychology. There is no widely accepted definition of consciousness, and clear and concise definition is difficult. Scientists often talk about consciousness without attempting a definition and without delineating it from the related concepts of mind (mental structures) and subjective experience. This chapter cannot solve all of these problems but it will attempt to bring some of them into clearer focus. It will present some definitional statements about consciousness and a tentative delineation of consciousness from related and overlapping concepts. This will be followed by a discussion of the emotions as organizing factors in active representational consciousness, modes of consciousness, and brain–emotion–consciousness relationships.

Conceptualizations of Consciousness

Everyday language distinguishes between consciousness and unconsciousness, wakefulness and sleep. Although we do not distinguish between consciousness and wakefulness, we customarily think of sleep and unconsciousness as different things. Sleep is now described as an active process. It seems reasonable to consider it as a state of consciousness in which the thresholds of sensory receptors are increased over thresholds during wakefulness. We have always known that we dream during sleep and dreaming is an affective–cognitive process that serves a useful purpose in human life. Our own experience, as well as laboratory research, tells us that it can be very disturbing to be deprived of our dreaming.

One way in which sleep can be considered a state of consciousness and distinguished from unconsciousness is the fact that dreams occur, and we can report our dreams when we awake. Apparently some kind of affective–cognitive process occurs in sleep by means of dreaming. No one knows the exact nature of these affective–cognitive processes, but they occur with little or no input from the environment and depend in large measure, if not entirely, upon imagery originally created by the individual during a waking state. Novel images or image sequences occur in dreams by virtue of some kind by recombination of past images.

No one can seriously question the occurrence of emotion during sleep; the proof is in the dream process. Who at one time or another has not awakened in terror by the events in a dream? Apparently such waking occurs when the emotion reaches such an intensity that it changes the threshold of receptors; in other words, the emotion by its own intensity created wakeful consciousness.

In a state of unconsciousness there are apparently no perceptual or cognitive processes, no emotions, no dreaming. We cannot make reports on what happened during moments of unconsciousness. We not only lose awareness of the world around us, we lose awareness of time and place. We are for the moment no different sensibly from a rose or a tree. We are alive but have no awareness of being alive. The Freudian unconscious is a different matter. In it, Freud assumed, cognitive processes operate outside the realm of awareness. It is now generally accepted that some kinds of "mind processes" operate at a preconscious or unconscious level (or at a low level of awareness, out of focal awareness) and influence consciousness and conscious processes. The latter, however, are the primary concern of this chapter.

Consciousness as Stream of Thought

Since a clear and succinct definition of consciousness has not been presented in the literature, it is necessary to begin with partial definitions, descriptive statements, or ideas about consciousness. Many of our current ideas about consciousness stem from the pioneering writings of William James, whose work remains a rich resource for the student of consciousness, although it does not provide a singular definition. In speaking of "personal consciousness," James said: "Its meaning we know so long as no one asks us how to define it, but to give an accurate account of it is the most difficult of philosophic tasks . . ." (1890, p. 225). Here, at least, James indicated his belief in the personal nature of consciousness. In his view consciousness is identified with a single individual. Beyond this point James failed to distinguish between consciousness and the contents of consciousness, and, in fact, most of his writing on the topic focused on the cognitive processes of consciousness. In his famous description of the continuity of consciousness he equated stream of consciousness with stream of thought. It is not unusual to find contemporary scientists who do not draw any clear distinctions between stream of thought and consciousness, thus de-emphasizing the role of affects.

James's failure to distinguish thought and consciousness created one of the problems in devising a definition or even a set of characteristic statements about consciousness. It is clear that James did not actually exclude emotions, since he used the term thought in a very general sense, meaning everything that goes on in the mind. He spoke of recognizably different classes of conscious states: seeing, hearing, reasoning, willing, recollecting, expecting, loving, hating, "and the hundred ways we know our mind to be alternately engaged" (p. 230). Nevertheless, neither in James's work nor in that of many contemporary scientists can we find clear distinctions between consciousness (as sensibility/awareness/attention) and the contents and operations of consciousness, although Cantril (1962), Deikman (1971), Mandler (1975), and Tart (1976) have given some attention to this problem.

Thus James's ideas seem to apply mainly to the content and operations of consciousness rather than to the sensibility/awareness that characterizes the mind. We have already noted that James characterized thought or mind-stuff as personal in nature. He noted that the breaches between the thoughts and feelings of individuals were the most absolute breaches in nature. He also felt that it is very important to recognize that the content of consciousness is in constant change. He held that even sensations change and that the same bodily sensation is never experienced twice by the individual. "Experience is remolding us every moment and our mental reaction on every given thing is really a resultant of our experience of the world up to that date" (p. 234).

James noted that the contents of consciousness are "sensibly continuous." Even when there is some kind of time gap in consciousness the consciousness before the time gap seems to belong to the consciousness that comes after it. In this respect consciousness *feels* unbroken. In addition, to the continuity in the time sense (continuity over time), there is also continuity in the sense that the parts of consciousness seem inwardly connected, belonging together as parts of a common whole. According to James the natural name for this common whole is *myself, I,* or *me*. Toward the end of his writings on consciousness James said: "Looking back, then, over this review we see that mind is at every stage a theatre of simultaneous possibilities. Consciousness consists in the comparison of these with each other, the selection of some, and the suppression of the rest by the reinforcing and inhibiting agency of attention" (p. 288). It is clear that James here is talking about the contents and operations of consciousness and about these he has provided useful insights. Other of James's observations on consciousness will be noted in later sections.

An Experimental Approach to the Stream of Consciousness

Singer and his colleagues (Singer, 1974, 1975; Singer & Antrobus, 1963; Antrobus, Singer, & Greenberg, 1966; Pope & Singer, 1976; Rodin & Singer, 1974; Pope, 1977) are conducting a series of important studies on problems of consciousness and inner experience. Theoretically they are in the tradition of James and Tomkins, but they have added contemporary concepts and rigorous scientific method in an area often thought to be scientifically unmanageable.

Their studies have focused on separate aspects or functions of consciousness such as daydreaming, imagery, and fantasy. For example, Singer has proposed that such internal processes compete with external stimuli for focal attention or dominance of consciousness. A study by Antrobus, Singer, and Greenberg (1966) supported this idea. They showed that task complexity significantly reduced the frequency of stimulus- or task-independent thoughts. They measured the latter by interrupting subjects during task performance and asking them whether they were aware of task-unrelated thoughts just prior to the interruption. In another study, they showed that subjects who heard about a serious escalation of the Vietnam war just prior to participating in a signal-detection experiment showed a significant increase in stimulus-independent thought.

Personality characteristics, richness of environment, and a number of other factors apparently influence the balance in the processing of internal events and external stimulation. Singer and Antrobus (1963) and a number of other investigators have factor analyzed the contents of daydreams and found evidence for three fairly stable patterns or styles of daydreaming.

One is a guilty-dysphoric style involving self-recrimination, hostile wishes, and concern over achievement striving and failure. The second style is characterized by distractibility, mind-wandering, and underlying fear. The third is associated with positive affects and includes future-oriented, planful fantasies.

Rodin and Singer (1974) found that obese individuals were more sensitive to external cues than others. Thus sensory data from the environment, including food and food symbols, have a greater impact on the stream of thought in overweight people. Pope (1977) found that verbalization tended to slow down the stream of thought or otherwise to alter self-report of ongoing mental processes.

Singer and his colleagues (Pope and Singer, 1976) have discussed eleven determinants of the stream of consciousness: The mind as activity, sensory input, a continuum of awareness, attention, a bias favoring sensory input, predictability of the environment, the matching function (how input is assessed), affect, current concerns, the set toward internal processing, and structural characteristics of the stimuli. Schachtel (1959) and Tomkins (1962) influenced their treatment of affect, to which they attributed considerable importance as a determinant of consciousness and as a regulator of schema development and the matching function.

Consciousness as a Paradigm

In Tart's (1973) view an ordinary state of consciousness, like a paradigm in science, constitutes a set of rules and theories that facilitates person–environment interactions and interpretations of experiences. The rules are mainly implicit and operate automatically, and in following them people feel they are doing the natural thing. In keeping with his concept of consciousness Tart defined knowledge as an immediately given "feeling of congruence between two different kinds of experience, a matching. One set of experiences may be regarded as perceptions of the external world, of others, of oneself; the second set may be regarded as a theory, a scheme, a system of understanding" (p. 45). The scheme or system of understanding in Tart's framework would be the personal paradigm or consciousness.

Tart (1976) postulates a basic awareness, an awareness of being aware or self-awareness, and attention/awareness, the focusing of which is partially volitional. He distinguishes between discrete states of consciousness (d-SoCs—unique, dynamic patterns of psychological structures) and discrete altered states of consciousness (d-ASCs—a departure from some baseline d-SoC). A d-SoC is stabilized by volitional focusing of "attention/awareness energy" and by positive and negative feedback processes. A d-ASC is induced by disrupting forces that push various structure subsystems beyond their limits of stable functioning and by patterning forces that organize a new system of structure subsystems. The ten major subsystems that play varying roles in known d-ASCs are: exteroceptors, interoceptors, input processing, memory, the subconscious, emotions, evaluation and decision making, time sense, sense of identity, and motor output. Thus, Tart recognizes emotions as one of the subsystems of consciousness (or d-ASCs), but he does not elaborate on the significant interactions that can occur between emotions and the other postulated subsystems.

Tart's analysis seems to allow for the possibility of studying consciousness as sensibility/awareness/attention apart from its contents and operations. The difficulties that most Western scientists and philosophers have in thinking of consciousness or any aspect of consciousness as distinct from its contents was well illustrated by Scher (1962), when he wrote: "In the absence of 'sensory flux', consciousness cannot be maintained (Hebb, 1961); but sensory flux alone is not consciousness. Novelty (Vernon *et al.,* 1961), order and meaning (Freedman *et al.,* 1961), differential responsiveness (Lindsley, 1961), amplitude and rate of change (Kubie, 1961) all help to shape the participating mind. Isolated man, or nonparticipant man, is by these studies almost the antithesis of man as a human entity" (p. 356). Despite his rather detailed theoretical framework, Tart's approach has not generated much empirical research.

Consciousness as the Complement of Biological Organization

Deikman (1973), unlike most other Western theorists, has emphasized the importance of the distinction between consciousness and the contents of consciousness. As evidence of the validity of this distinction, he pointed out that in disciplined meditation one heightens consciousness or awareness by subduing the conventional operations of the mind (perceptions, thought, memory). Thus, to expand consciousness is to expand its sensitivities, not its contents. In Deikman's view thoughts, images, and memories are chief examples of the contents of consciousness. He believes that it is possible for thoughts, sensations, images, or other mental phenomena to disappear while consciousness or awareness remains. The contents of consciousness are functions of neurological systems consisting of receptor organs and brain mechanisms. Deikman believes that this is not the case for awareness or consciousness. Awareness is viewed as the *organization* of the biosystem, not the product of a particular neural circuit. More particularly, "awareness is the *complementary* aspect of that organization, its psychological equivalent" (p. 319). He sees consciousness and neuromechanisms as complementary aspects of the biological system that constitutes an individual. On the biological side the organization of certain chemical entities constitute life, while on the psychological side this organization constitutes awareness. He likens the electrochemical and psychological aspects of the biological system to the apparent duality that obtains when physicists observe the wave-like characteristics of light under one set of conditions and the particle-like characteristics under another. Deikman does not mean that there is a separate system that senses consciousness in the way that the eye senses light or the ear senses sound. Rather, he means that "awareness is the complementary aspect of organization—it is organization, itself, in its mental dimension." He maintains that the contents of consciousness (e.g., sensations, thoughts) are individual-bound or personal while awareness itself is universal.

It may prove useful both for science and for the student's understanding of the area to distinguish between consciousness on the one hand and the operations and structures of consciousness on the other. Without making these distinctions the concept of consciousness might be so broad that it would be meaningless. If consciousness is defined as the total array of sensations, perceptions, cognitions, and affects that characterize the individual, then the study of consciousness becomes the study of everything mental or psychological, and the organization of these things may be equated with personality. The structures and operations of the mind may give consciousness its "character," but it is not at all clear that they adequately define it. If we do assume that consciousness is distinct from or more than its contents, then perhaps it is more accurate to think of special states as changes in structures and operations of consciousness (e.g., emotion, perception, cognition) rather than as altered consciousness.

While Deikman's treatment has intuitive appeal, it may be subject to the criticisms that apply to any philosophic dualism. In one sense it is nothing more than a contemporary resolution of the ancient mind–body problem. There are several ways of responding to this criticism. First, the fact there is a dualistic conception of life may simple indicate the current limits of mind attempting to understand itself. Second, such limitations do not apply only to the chemical-organization–consciousness duality, but a dualistic conception also yields the most workable characterization of a number of phenomena of nature, such as light. Third, instead of considering Deikman's concept a duality it may be described as two levels of conceptualization. Finally, we simply may be epistemologically unwilling to accept as fact that a certain complex organization of a particular origin is a singular whole that can be conceptualized equally well as an electrochemical complex or as consciousness. In any case, Deikman's views do not readily lend themselves to empirical test, and they have generated little or no systematic experimentation.

Consciousness Derived from Experiencing Biological Processes as Emotions

Sinnott (1966), approaching the problem from the standpoint of a geneticist, claims that his conception of psychical life and consciousness avoids the pitfalls of philosophic dualism. He argued that the steps from physical materials to life to mind were a natural progression in evolution and that consciousness was a logical outcome of biological processes. In short he maintains that consciousness is simply the "felt" or "experienced" electrochemical activities of the body, mainly the brain. This position is similar to that of Feigl (1962), who proposed an identity theory to resolve the mind–body problem. In this theory the mental and physical are the same in the sense that certain phenomenal terms refer to the same events as those referred to by certain neurophysiological terms. Thus neurophysiological and phenomenal terms have identical referents and these referents are "the immediately experienced qualities, or their configurations, in the various phenomenal fields" (p. 577). Perhaps Bertrand Russell (1918) came as close to a succinct resolution of the mind–body problem as anyone when he said that the difference between matter and mind is merely one of arrangement.

Sinnott interprets consciousness and mind in terms of biological organization and biological processes. Fundamental to his argument is the proposition that there is a genuine similarity between the processes of bodily development and the functions of mind. He pointed out that bodily development is a controlled progression, regulated at every step so as to produce a precise end, and this same *regulation to ends* is evident in behavior. Biological development toward a precise end is similar to the more complex goal-seeking evident in behavior. Biological development conforms to norms (or innate neural programs) that are imbedded in the organism in such a way that growth is "set" for a particular course toward a precise end. According to Sinnott behavorial norms, like biological-developmental ones, are represented by protoplasmic patterns, chiefly in brain cells. In making his point Sinnott raised the provocative question as to when embryological development ends and behavior begins. "Where, in the hatching egg, does embryology end and behavior begin? When the chick, with a peck of its beak, breaks the shell, we call this behavior, an instinctive act; but how does it differ, in essence, from earlier movements of the growing embryo that lead up to it?" (p. 148). Sinnott further illustrated the morphogenetic nature of behavior by pointing out that a naturalist can identify a species of bird by the nest it builds and an arachnologist the species of spider by its web alone.

A vital link in Sinnott's argument is that the biological directedness toward ends that characterizes living things is *experienced as desire and purpose* and that "psychical life is the sense of being consciously oriented toward ends" (p. 153). [Sinnott does not use the word "purpose" in a teleological sense, but simply to recognize "the presence in a system of something that guides the activity of that system in conformity to a particular norm set up in it as in a feedback mechanism" (p. 154).] Sinnott does not attempt to explain how the all-important phenomenon of *experiencing* comes about; he simply states that in any living system where there is a brain pattern or norm which directs behavior toward specific ends that it is logical to expect such directiveness to be *felt*. The feeling of being oriented or drawn toward a particular end produces desire or want. "Desire, at bottom, is that same sort of biological orientation evident in the far simpler directiveness of bodily development, but it is subjectively *experienced*. Wanting, desiring, craving (and their opposites) are emotions" (p. 153).

Sinnott maintained that consciousness as such is more than a general awareness of the environment, and that it includes an element of directiveness and an involvement of the organism with the environment. He maintained that human consciousness is always accompanied by at least some degree of wanting or desiring (emotion), and thus consciousness is an active condition of a clearly biological nature. It is awareness of being alive and actively involved with the surround, and in Sinnott's conception this means experiencing desire, want, or emotion. Whether emotion-experiencing is consciousness or a structure/operation of consciousness that tends always to be present, the position of the present author is congruent with that of Sinnott's in seeing the emotions as the chief determinants of the quality of life and as the main provider of blueprints for cognition and action.

The Emotions as Organizing Factors in Consciousness

Although it is considered useful to distinguish between consciousness as sensibility/awareness and the contents of consciousness, it is recognized that consciousness is typically conceived as a set of structures and operations. The conscious mind has a strong tendency to be active and its activity typically involves images, thoughts, emotions, and affective–cognitive orientations—the latter being the most common structures in consciousness. While disciplined meditations deriving mainly from the philosophies and religions of the Orient have taught us that consciousness can exist seemingly without content and apparently with a minimum of activity, this absence of content is a special (unique) state of consciousness. In contrast, ordinary states of consciousness and most other special states are characterized by contents. The position taken here is that the most fundamental contents of consciousness and the ones that provide it with its essential organization and directiveness are the affects and affective–cognitive orientations.

Anshen (1966), editor of *Credo Perspectives,* a series of intellectual autobiographies by some of the outstanding minds of our times, wrote: "Personality itself is an emotional, not an intellectual experience; and the greatest achievement of knowledge is to combine the personal within a larger unity, just as in the higher states of development the parts that make up the whole require greater and greater independence and individuality within the context of the whole'' (p. 9). She went on to point out the critical role of emotion in life and in creative endeavor: "Refusing to divorce work from life or love from knowledge, it is action, it is passion that enhances our being" (p. 17).

Many scientists, philosophers, and artists have recognized the ultimate importance of the emotions in human consciousness and behavior. Himwich (1962) coined a new term, thymencephalon, to designate the parts of the brain especially involved in feeling and emotion. The prefix of his term is from the Greek word *thymos* which has as one of its meanings "strong feeling and passion." Himwich considered emotion a chief aspect of consciousness and maintained that the thymencephalon contributed to consciousness a crude awareness of emotion. John (1962) defined consciousness as the totality of endogenous and exogenous sensations and maintained that consciousness is "ordered and colored by affect and evaluation unique to, and a characteristic of, the experiencing organism" (p. 81). Shagass (1962) defined emotion as the aspect of behavior that is subjectively felt and indicated that emotion may be an aspect of all behavior.

As we have noted earlier, Freud and the mainstream of psychoanalytic theory did not deal extensively with concepts of discrete emotions. However, Freud was quite specific in his conceptualization of the relationship between emotion and consciousness. "It is surely of the essence of an emotion that we should feel it, i.e. that it should enter consciousness. So for emotions, feelings, and affects to be unconscious would be quite out of the question" (Freud, 1959, p. 109). Freud went on to point out that it is possible for the ideational representation of an emotion to be repressed and thus "unconscious." He also suggested that an affect or emotion may be perceived and present in consciousness but misconstrued. Both in the cases of misconception and repression of the emotion-relevant cognition, the motivational impact of the emotion may result in ego-defensive maneuvers or in ineffective or maladaptive behavior.

As already indicated, Sinnott (1966) believes that the sensing or experiencing of the biological directiveness of organic processes forms the wants and desires that constitute the emotions and bridge the gap from matter to life (consciousness). "Human beings are material systems, to be sure, and subject to the laws of nature, but they are *alive*. With them comes into the material world a breath of uncertainty and of excitement. They are not automata, but creatures who think and feel; whose problems center around mind, soul, and spirit—the emotions, purposes, values, and ideals of men" (p. 88). Sinnott remarked that the biologist studying life objectively from an external standpoint may never understand it as well as the poet who can *feel* what it is like. Here Sinnott was emphasizing the importance of affective experience even in the business of achieving understanding and knowledge.

In the following sections various structures and operations of consciousness will be considered in their relationship to the emotions. In the framework of differential emotions theory the affects, primarily the fundamental emotions, constitute the basic structures of consciousness. Affect is so constant and pervasive in consciounsness that it is difficult to separate emotion as structure from consciousness itself, and whether this (or any) aspect of the distinction between consciousness and its contents proves valid and fruitful is a crucial problem for future research.

Sensation, Emotion, and Consciousness

In our present state of knowledge, sensation has to be considered as the most elementary aspect of consciousness. At the neurophysiological level sensation is the electrochemical response of the organism to any stimulation whether external or internal. In consciousness sensation is the experiencing of this electrochemical response. When we ask the question "How is sensation experienced?" we are back to the basic problem of the transition from matter to mind.

The tendency among Western thinkers is to rule out the possibility of experiencing "pure" sensation (James, 1890; Nathan, 1969). According to this line of thought, when sensation achieves consciousness we have perception. In other words, perception is defined as sensation plus meaning and sensation typically acquires meaning immediately. "We hear music not sound; we see objects, not light reflected from edges and angles" (Nathan, 1969, p. 260). However, Nathan did allow for the possibility that sensation was separable from perception and suggested that sensation without meaning was a spur to further investigation.

Sensation, Meaning, and Emotion. The position taken here is that while sensation is a separable phenomenon, consciousness has a strong tendency to transform sensation or sensory data into affect, perception, and cognition. Sensory data are transformed first into affect, which in turn organizes ongoing sensory messages into perception and cognition. In keeping with the principles of affect activation already discussed, the type of affect elicited by the sensory message would be a function of the gradient of stimulation and of the selective sensitivity and organizing functions of the receptors. (In Singer's terms it would be the assimilability of the sensory data or information.)

The sensory data of day-to-day life are most frequently transformed first into the emotion of interest, the topic of Chapter 8. The postulate that some degree of emotion characterizes ordinary states of consciousness and precedes perception and cognition is also affirmed by Spitz (1965). Based on his analysis of the continual workings of emotion in consciousness, Leeper (1965) made a strong case for considering emotion as an actual part of the perceptual process.

When Western scientists and philosophers indicate that perception is sensation that has acquired meaning they may be interpreted as being in agreement with the position of differential emotions theory if it is conceded that meaning involves some emotion—e.g., interest, joy, distress, anger— at some level of intensity. The intensity of emotion in consciousness may be minimal and its effects very subtle. But it is emotion and its effects upon neurohumors and hormones that causes the meaning of things to change with time and season. When feeling fatigued and annoyed by the sounds and labor of operating a lawn mower, grass may be perceived as vexatious or noxious, but while experiencing sexual attraction and affection grass may be perceived as a beautiful carpet to make love on.

The way in which sensory data are transformed into emotion was discussed in Chapter 3. To recapitulate, changes in gradients of stimulation coordinated with the selectivity and organizing functions of receptors trigger, via limbic–hypothalamic structures, a particular set of facial movements. The sensory data (feedback) from these movements are integrated in the cortex as felt or experiential emotion. Differential emotions theory holds that some emotion is always present in ordinary states of consciousness. Its emotion-activation model explains how a new or different emotion achieves consciousness.

Affects and Levels of Consciousness. Differential emotions theory and psychoanalytic theory agree that emotion is by its very nature a phenomenon of consciousness, and the former theory postulates the subjective experiencing of emotions as the principal organizing factor in consciousness and the basis of the selectivity and directiveness that characterize the human mind. While emotion is always conscious, it is not always cognized or symbolized. Undifferentiated arousal may be neither conscious nor cognized. The relatively greater specificity of cues or information from emotions makes them of greater value for adaptation and effective behavior than is the case for undifferentiated arousal states. The emotion of interest provides much of the selectivity and focusing of attention that characterizes ordinary states of consciousness.

There seems to be no useful distinction between the concepts of subjective experience, consciousness, and awareness, and all these terms seem to imply an existential dichotomy—experiencing–not-experiencing, conscious–unconscious, aware–unaware. However, such dichotomizing may not be the most accurate way of describing the processes of the mind. A wide array of things can exist in consciousness at different *levels of awareness* (Snygg & Combs, 1949). At present I am most keenly aware of my *interest*-sustained effort to write clearly and make a valid point. I know that I am sometimes *distressed* by the difficulty of the work or the thought of failing to do a good job. I am less aware of the pressure on my bottom from the pull of gravity, and even less (only sporadically) aware of the sounds in my office or on the campus outside. These things affect my thought and action (interest or annoy me) in relation to their status in my consciousness. As a rule the level of awareness of a phenomenon is an index of its motivational value for ongoing behavior.

Emotion and Perception

Classical studies of perception (e.g., Ittelson & Kilpatrick, 1951) show that the perceptual process as we know it in adulthood is almost never a simple transformation of sensory input. The observer tends to add something to the sensations resulting from the stimulus pattern. The "something" added has typically been explained as a function of the observer's past experience. After reviewing a number of studies that show how misperceptions can be caused by unusual and unexpected arrangements of stimulus configurations, Ittleson and Kilpatrick concluded: "All these experiments, and many more that have been made, suggest strongly that perception is never a sure thing, never an absolute revelation of 'what is.' Rather, what we see is a prediction—our own personal construction designed to give us the best possible bet for carrying out our purposes in action. We make these bets on the basis of our past experience" (p. 184). It seems quite reasonable to restate their conclusion: We perceive in terms of our wants, desires, and purposes and our wants, desires, and purposes are our emotions or functions of them.

We perceive and attend to the stimulus patterns surrounding us in a highly selective fashion. This selectivity can best be explained as a function of affect. The affect that operates most frequently in guiding perception and attention in ordinary consciousness is the emotion of interest. We are always interested in something, but interest can operate at low levels of intensity and in its milder form it can operate very subtly and seemingly automatically.

Since some degree of emotion characterizes ordinary states of consciousness at all times, emotion may be said to precede the perception of objects, events, and people that parade through our field of awareness. The emotion or combination of emotions present in consciousness influence the perceptual process and, in effect, filter or otherwise modify the raw sensory data transmitted by the receptors. It is the interaction of emotion with sensory input that usually prevents "pure" sensation from registering in ordinary states of consciousness. Visual, auditory, somesthetic, and even gustatory and olfactory sensation can be altered by emotion. Rafe, joyous over a good test grade he just received, will see the instructor and hear the lecture and discussion that day in a quite different way than a dejected or disgusted student just having received a disappointing grade on the test. Poor or highly difficult items might be seen by the former student as an unfortunate error on the part of the instructor but as unfair or even unethical by the latter.

Each of the affects—drives, emotions—and each of an almost endless variety of affect combinations influence perception in a different way. In a state of joy we perceive the world through rose-colored glasses and we see joy and harmony everywhere. In distress we perceive the world through dark glasses and things appear to be dull and gloomy. In anger we have a greater tendency to perceive obstacles and barriers, and when disgust mixes with incoming sensations, what we perceive tends to be distasteful and ugly. In contempt we perceive others as in some way inferior or defective. In fear our perceptual field narrows and more things seem to be threatening. At the height of shame we seem to perceive only the self-in-error, and consciousness of self is sharply heightened. In guilt we perceive others in a different light as a result of the breakdown in interpersonal relations. To paraphrase Sinsheimer (1971), so much of what we perceive is in truth what we conceive and what we conceive is born of an affair with our emotions and feelings.

Emotion–Cognition Interactions and Consciousness

Most operations of consciousness involve some kind of representational process. To be conscious of an object is to represent that object (as an image) in the mind. The representation formed by the receptors (e.g., proprioceptors and cutaneous receptors of the face) is transmitted by the sensory nerves as a message to the brain (e.g., facial feedback). By a process still unknown, the sensory cortex transmutes this message into a report or representation of which we are aware (e.g., subjective experience of emotion). Thus the usual contents of consciousness result from a unique type of representation by which one re-presents (duplicates, imitates) to one's self some other aspect of the world. In the example of the emotion process, consciousness represents the "face of emotion" by integrating the pattern of proprioceptive and cutaneous impulses from the facial expression. It is partly because of the finely differentiated facial muscles of human beings and the sensory data from the patterns they form that emotions can exist in consciousness or awareness separate and apart from cognition. Emotion can be autochthonous or spontaneous in consciousness.

Conditioning Emotion Activators. Emotion can also exist in consciousness as a result of a conditioned stimulus (CS), via classical conditioning. In "traumatic conditioning" in animals, the response is most often described as "emotional excitement . . . manifested by behavioral signs of physiological arousal . . ." (Janis, Kagan, Mahl, & Holt, 1969, p. 42). Some studies of animal learning have inferred that traumatic conditioning also works in the case of the discrete emotion of fear (e.g., Miller, 1948; Liddell, 1962) and hence that fear can be learned as a conditioned response (CR).

Classical conditioning can also be viewed as a source of information randomly acquired (Fair, 1969). The conditioned stimulus (a) may be unattended or at low level of awareness, or (b) it may be a random sight or sound or other stimulus having no logical relationship to the unconditioned stimulus (US) or the unconditioned response (UR). Thus the CS–UR connection may be inaccessible (unavailable) in a logical sense. When the UR is an emotion or undifferentiated arousal there may be important consequences following from a "random" or "unattended" stimulus.

Liddell's (1962) studies of classical conditioning in the sheep provide an excellent illustration of an association between a conditioned stimulus and an unconditioned response (emotion) and demonstrates the potential hazards of this type of learning. Liddell observed that a brief electric current that would hardly be noticed by a human being would produce in the laboratory-accommodated sheep vehement struggling, suggesting fear at the level of panic. After about twenty repetitions of the shock the sheep appeared to regain composure and to react with a brisk energetic flexation of the stimulated forelimb followed by nose licking, teeth grinding, and yawning. After associating a metronome clicking once per second (CS) with the electric shock (US) on ten occasions a CR was formed. Now simply the sound of the metronome clicks would produce the fear and panicky behavior. After one hundred simultaneous presentations of the metronome beats and the electric shock, the conditioned fear response was established for the life of the animal. "Over thirty-five years of experimental work in our laboratory confirmed this seemingly dogmatic statement. The animal can never again listen to the metronome with equanimity. Indeed, the clicking of a typewriter visibly disturbs her" (p. 204). According to Liddell many of our emotion experiences arise from such "seemingly innocuous coincidences." In the case of most conditioned emotional responses the individual "is compelled to behave ineffectually in response to the inevitable" (p. 204). Liddell argued, further, that as such conditioned reflexes are ineffectual in adjusting to actual situations. Because these conditioned emotions and emotion-related responses result from a misperception or misconception of a stimulus situation and are ineffectual in adapting or coping, they may be considered as neurotic traits (Liddell, 1960).

Organismic Complexity and the Complexity of the Structures and Operations of Consciousness. Some distinctions can be made between consciousness and unconsciousness, but what can we say about differences in the contents and structures of consciousness among the different species of the animal kingdom? What is the difference in the structures of consciousness in cats, apes, and human beings? We know that human beings have the most complex conscious operations of any animal, but it was not evolutionary changes in our basic cells or gene structure that brought about changes in the complexity of life and the contents of consciousness. The haploid DNA content of the human and the monkey are identical, within the precision of measurement. The alpha hemoglobin in the gorilla differs from man by only one amino acid. In the chimpanzee it is identical with that of man (Sinsheimer, 1971). However, there are obvious differences between apes and humans in the structures and operations of consciousness.

What distinguishes humans from nonhuman animals in the operations of consciousness? The heart of the difference lies in the management of emotions and feelings and their role in learning and thinking.

Emotions are organizing forces in consciousness and they continually organize sensory input and reorganize information in creative ways. And the human being has the greatest array of differentiated affects of any animal.

As Sinsheimer (1971) observed, the quality of the contents of consciousness in animals (at least imaginary ones) contrasts to that of humans. He illustrated the point with one of the experiences of Edward Bear.

> Here is Edward Bear, coming downstairs now, bump, bump, on the back of his head, behind Christopher Robin. It is, as far as he knows, the only way of coming downstairs, but sometimes he feels that there really is another way, if only he could stop bumping for a moment and think of it.
>
> " . . . what I like doing best is Nothing," said Christopher Robin.
>
> "How do you do Nothing?" asked Pooh, after he had wondered for a long time.
>
> "Well, it's when people call out at you just as you're going off to do it, What are you going to do, Christopher Robin, and you say, Oh, nothing, and then you go and do it."
>
> "Oh, I see," said Pooh.
>
> "This is a nothing sort of thing that we're doing now."
>
> "Oh, I see," said Pooh again.
>
> "What do you like doing best in the world, Pooh?"
>
> "Well," said Pooh, "what I like best—" and then he had to stop and think. Because although Eating Honey was a very good thing to do, there was a moment just before you began to eat it which was better than when you were, but he didn't know what it was called."

What Pooh liked best in the world was the excitement of the imminent act of eating honey. Human beings can achieve a higher quality of consciousness than Pooh by binding their excitement not simply to the limited array of sensory pleasures but to experiences and actions that lead to personal growth, creative endeavor, and human welfare. The emotion that plays the most crucial role in determining the complexity and quality of consciousness and life itself, is interest–excitement. For what you are, and what you are most conscious of, is what excites you.

Emotions, Consciousness, Cognition, and Action. Since emotion can exist in consciousness independent of cognition, it is not unusual for a person to respond in terms of an emotion without cognizing it, without labeling it as such. To experience anger and to cognize anger are two different phenomena, although they can and frequently do influence each other via emotion–cognition interactions. Experiencing anger tends to elicit anger-related ("angry") thoughts and actions (see Figure 6-1), but cognizing or reflecting on one's anger tends to alter the anger experience.

Thus, cognition can exercise a certain amount of control over the emotion process, as in the case when an individual deliberately decides to inhibit the facial expression of an emotion. This decision and the lack (or minimizing) of expression may serve to decrease the intensity of the subjective experience of a discrete emotion (of, say, anger) while increasing autonomic activity that may be experienced as "stress," "strain," or even a more vague sort of discomfort. As already indicated, a person can initiate and sustain cognitive and motor activities that inhibit the facial-expression component of emotion; and it is also possible for such inhibitory processes

FIGURE 6-1. An angry Nepalese mother whacks her son on the head in a square in Katmandu.

to influence the feedback from a facial expression in such a way that the subjective experience of the discrete emotion does not occur. When the energy generated by an emotion activator is not channeled into facial expression and the subjective experiencing of emotion, unexpended energy exists in the nervous system. This energy may be directed to the brain stem reticular formation, resulting in an increase in nonspecific activation or undifferentiated arousal. In this case the internal (arousal) cues for thought and action are vague. Action may become ineffective or maladaptive; inaction may lead to psychosomatic symptoms.

The "relationship between emotions, their activators, and consciousness must specify both density of the emotion activator and the density of the activated emotion" (Tomkins, 1962, p. 274). Specific hypotheses concerning the relationships between emotions, consciousness, and cognition have been detailed by Tomkins (1962, pp. 282–304). The hypotheses given below are based mainly on Tomkins's ideas.

(a) In the case of competing emotion activators, the one that produces an emotion in consciousness is the one that generates the greatest density of neural firing. In some cases, however, the impact of the density of stimulation triggered by an activator may be modified or offset by the selectivity and organizing functions of receptors.

(b) The gradient of stimulation density is highly correlated with the intensity of the emotion; hence, the emotion experience is similar in profile to its activator; e.g., the experience of startle is as peaked, sudden, and brief as its characteristic activator.

(c) Emotion activators that produce peak stimulation will cause an emotion to achieve consciousness in competition with emotions activated by absolute density levels. This is true at least during the moment of the peak stimulation. However, emotions associated with absolute density level (distress, anger) will override the emotion associated with peak stimulation whenever there is a lapse of peak stimulation.

(d) Continuing novelty will support the continuing operation in consciousness of a stimulation-increase emotion (e.g., interest) and inhibit density-reduction emotions (joy, shame). This is the principle that enables the human being to experience substantial periods of excitement in relation to anything having sufficient complexity, novelty, or uncertainty.

(e) The emotion system is the primary provider of blueprints for cognition, decision, and action. The human being's representational powers and adaptive abilities are guaranteed not only by a responsiveness to drive signals but by a responsiveness to whatever circumstances activate positive and negative emotion. Some of the triggers of interest, joy, distress, startle, disgust, anger, fear, and shame are unlearned. At the same time, the emotion system is also capable of being instigated by learned stimuli. In this way the human being is born biased toward and away from a limited set of circumstances, and he is also capable of learning to become interested in a limitless variety of objects.

The ultimate combinations (in the human being) of emotion with the analyzer and storage mechanisms of the cognitive system produces a much more complex set of motivation–action sequences than could be generated by the emotion system alone. The gain in organismic flexibility and adaptability from the interaction of the emotion, cognition, and motor systems within the organism are likened to the gain in information from a set of semantic elements when they are combined according to the rules of a language. Indeed, it is the individual's capacity to integrate in the cortex the vast possible array of affective, cognitive, and motor elements that guarantees the basic freedom of the human being.

The Emotions and Consciousness of Self: Self-Awareness. A number of theorists have argued that the emotions play a critical role in the development of self-awareness and self-identity and in the development and functioning of the self-concept (Lynd, 1961; Lewis, 1971; Tomkins, 1963). Duval and Wicklund (1972) presented a theory of self-awareness in which they drew a distinction between "objective" and "subjective" self-awareness. They assume that the "components or elements of self-consciousness are indigenous to the person's original psychological structure" (p. 31). They maintain that there is only one consciousness and that subjective and objective self-awareness are merely two different foci of attention. Similarly, according to their theory there is only one self, termed a "causal agent self," that is equated with perception, thinking, and action. Thus subjective self-awareness obtains when the causal agent self is not the focus of consciousness, and objective self-awareness exists when the causal agent self is the object of consciousness. In a state of objective self-awareness the individual focuses attention on the self (on consciousness, personal history), but the person in subjective self-awareness is aware of the self only as a source of forces that are exerted on the environment.

The Duval–Wicklund theory focuses on the motivational consequences of objective self-awareness. Their central assumption is that "negative affect results to the degree that a person is objectively self-aware and is focused on a sizeable intraself discrepancy" (1972). Although Duval and Wicklund never specified the negative affect, their description of it and its consequences fit very nicely with the concept of shame (see Chapter 15). As we examine the other discrete emotions in later chapters it will be seen that each discrete emotion has a particular influence on the structures and operations of consciousness. For example, while intense shame tends to heighten self-consciousness and decrease the logical–intellective operations of consciousness, guilt tends to be associated with increased cognition as the individual ruminates over the feeling that all is not right with others or with God.

Hemispheric Functions of the Brain, Emotions, and States of Consciousness

The possibility of experiencing altered or special states of consciousness that differ remarkably from ordinary states of consciousness is commonly accepted by a large percentage of the youth of our day. The notion is apparently as old as recorded human history. It is certainly evident in Eastern thought, and at least since the middle of the 19th century (Taylor, 1958) biological scientists have presented some evidence for the possibility that each of the separate hemispheres of the brain controls a completely separate consciousness. A contemporary neurologist (Gazzaniga, 1967) concluded: "All the evidence indicates that separation of the hemispheres creates two independent spheres of consciousness within a single cranium, that is to say, within a single organism" (p. 100). He recognized that this conclusion, a conclusion supported by Sperry (1968) and Galin (1976), would be disturbing to people who view consciousness as an indivisible property of the human brain.

Hemispheric Functions, Modes of Knowing, and the Organization of Consciousness

Related to the notion that there may be more than one type or state of consciousness is the long-standing idea that there are different ways of knowing. In the 13th century Roger Bacon spoke of two modes of knowledge, one gained through argument, the other through experience. A number of contemporary scientists and philosophers (e.g., Ornstein, 1973; Tart, 1969; Polanyi, 1958; Galin, 1976) also speak of these different ways of knowing, cognitive styles, or of distinct types of knowledge. The kind of knowing that dominates in modern thought is typically described as logical and rational. The other type of knowing is described as intuitive, tacit knowing, or the receptive mode.

Chapter 1 presented a brief discussion of the possibility that different modes of knowing or experiencing may be related to different and potentially independent spheres of consciousness, each under control of a different hemisphere of the brain. The clinical and experimental evidence that led some neurologists to this conclusion also shows that the two hemispheres have some distinct functions. For example, it is generally thought that the dominant (usually left) brain hemisphere controls speech and most linguistic or verbal functions. In contrast a number of clinical investigations have suggested that the emotions are largely under the control of the right hemisphere.

The assumption that all verbal (e.g., linguistic, cognitive) and nonverbal (e.g., spatial, musical) functions occur in the left and right (or dominant and nondominant) hemispheres respectively has been seriously questioned (e.g., Galin, 1976). While the dominant hemisphere has been shown to be superior in controlling verbal functions, the nondominant hemisphere apparently plays a significant part in some verbal and cognitive processes. (It is important to remember that verbal or linguistic abilities cannot be equated with cognitive abilities.) Bogen (1969) cited a number of investigators who have maintained that the intellect remains intact after dominant-hemisphere damage produced severe speech disorders such as aphasia.

Bogen (1969) has pointed out that injuries to the nondominant hemisphere can result in defects in linguistic or verbal abilities, and that gross speech defects usually involve damage in both dominant and nondominant hemispheres. He also reported that stimulation of the nondominant hemisphere has produced vocalization and that the nondominant hemisphere of split-brain patients (patients with hemispheres divided by sectioning the corpus callosum) can read many words and understand spoken sentences. In concluding his review, Bogen argued for considering the dominant hemisphere as the seat of "propositional" capacities, the abilities to relate words (or symbols) to each other in meaningful sequences and to assume an "as if" stance while thinking. This would include analytical, assumptional, and inferential thought processes.

Bogen characterized the nondominant hemisphere as "appositional."

> This term implies a capacity for apposing or comparing of perceptions, schemas, engrams, etc., but has in addition the virtue that it implies very little else. If it is correct that the right hemisphere excels in capacities as yet unknown to us, the full meaning of "appositional" will emerge as these capacities are further studied and understood. The word appositional has the essential virtue of suggesting a capacity as important as "propositional," reflecting a belief in the importance of right hemisphere function. (Bogen, 1973, p. 111)

The division of hemispheric functions that Bogen has proposed seems consistent with the idea that there are different modes of consciousness and of information processing. Some examples of empirical investigations of differential hemispheric functions can be found in Ornstein and Galin (1976). The division of labor between the propositional and appositional hemispheres might be considered as the basis for Blackburn's (1971) concept of intellectual–sensous complementarity, Deikman's (1971) idea of bimodal consciousness, and Polanyi's (1958) notion of explicit and tacit knowing.

Blackburn used the term "sensuous" not to refer to sexuality but to a responsiveness "of the whole body, including the senses." He also characterized sensuous knowing as dependent on subjective factors such as mood and attention. Sensuous knowledge is direct and intuitive, qualitative rather than quantitative. He proposed that scientists should be trained to become more aware of sensuous clues in nature and made to understand that sensuous knowledge is a part of the intellectual structure of science.

Deikman has argued that consciousness is characterized by two primary modes of organization: an action mode and a receptive mode. In his view the principal biological agencies of the action mode, the sympathetic nervous system and the striate muscle system, serve as a means for the organism to manipulate his environment. The parasympathetic nervous system and the sensory–perceptual system are the principal agencies of the receptive mode, which aims at maximizing intake from the environment. Deikman thinks that the receptive mode originates and functions maximally during infancy. Of course, it is during the prelingual stage of life that the emotions and emotion communication dominate organism–environment interactions.

Polanyi defines explicit knowledge or knowing as something that can be reflected upon critically and tacit knowledge or awareness as an experience that cannot be the subject of reflection. One is reminded here of the fact that a successful effort to reflect on and analyze an emotion experience inevitably changes the experience. Tacit knowledge, like emotion while it is being experienced, is not subject to critical analysis by the person experiencing it. Polanyi believes strongly that we should learn to accept "acritically the unreasoned conclusions of our senses."

Hemispheric Functions and Emotions

Most of the evidence relating to the role of the two brain hemispheres in emotion has come from observations and investigations of clinical cases of brain-damaged individuals. The most widely held opinion is that emotion processes are primarily nondominant (right) hemisphere functions, while cognitive processes are primarily dominant (left) hemisphere functions. For example, Galin (1976) believes that verbal and nonverbal (e.g., facial) types of information are processed by the left and right hemispheres, respectively, and that difficulties in coping with messages containing conflicting verbal and nonverbal cues can be understood at the neurological level in terms of conflict between hemispheres. The scant evidence on emotions and hemispheric functions is divided.

Schwartz, Davidson, Maer, and Bromfield (1973) studied patterns of hemispheric dominance in musical, emotional, verbal, and spatial tasks while recording EEG activity from both left and right hemispheres. From their review of the literature they had concluded that for right-handed subjects, cognitive processes such as verbal activity and sequential logic occurred in the left hemisphere, while musical and visual–spatial activities were processed in the right hemisphere. Mainly on the basis of the clinical studies of various investigators, they hypothesized that emotion, like visual and spatial matters, was primarily a right-hemisphere function. In their experiment, Schwartz *et al.* had subjects whistle songs (right-hemisphere task), recite lyrics (left-hemisphere task), and sing a familiar song (a dual-hemisphere task). They used degree of alpha (brain-wave) blocking as a index of hemispheric dominance (alpha blocking is highest in the hemisphere that is dominant at any given time). They found that whistling produced relative right dominance, talking, relative left dominance, and singing resulted in comparable alpha blocking in both hemispheres. In a second experiment, they used right or left lateral eye movement as an index of hemispheric dominance, while subjects answered questions of a verbal, spatial, or emotional nature or some combination of these. Spatial questions resulted in significantly more frequent left lateral eye movements (indicating right-hemisphere dominance), and emotional questions had a similar effect. The data suggested that while important cognitive processes are primarily left-hemisphere functions, emotion processes are primarily right-hemisphere functions. This conclusion was also supported by Safer and Leventhal (1976), who showed that for most subjects emotionally toned monaural vocal cues were more salient for those who listened with the left ear (indicating right-hemisphere processing).

A series of studies conducted at the Institute of Evolutionary Physiology and Biochemistry in Leningrad (e.g., Deglin, 1973) yielded data inconsistent with the conclusion of Schwartz *et al.* (1973) and Safer and Leventhal. These studies compared the effects on depressed patients of electroconvulsive seizures in either the right or left hemispheres of the brain. Instead of administering shock in the traditional manner (bilaterally to both hemispheres), they administered shock either to the right or left hemisphere, the shock being sufficient to block or impair functions in the shocked hemisphere for a brief period of time. They found that certain basic sensory functions were about equally impaired regardless of which brain hemisphere had been paralyzed by electric shock. After finding that the shock to the right hemisphere not only failed to produce asphasia but made the patient more talkative, they concluded that the right hemisphere has a suppressive effect on talking or verbalization. They inferred the possibility that the mutism sometimes observed in depression may be a result of right hemisphere suppression of the left hemisphere.

A number of findings led them to a different conclusion than Schwartz *et al.* regarding hemispheric dominance and emotion. After administration of shock to the right hemisphere, patients showed a significant decrease in their ability to recognize vocal intonations indicative of discrete emotions such as joy, sadness, and anger. More importantly, they found that after administering shock to the right side, the patient showed very definite changes in facial expression and emotion as he recovered from shock. The patient's face gradually changed from a silly smile to what appeared to be a real smile of joy. In keeping with the apparent joyful facial expression, the patient's vocal intonations, verbalizations, gestures, and posture appeared commensurate with that of a happy person. In contrast, after the left hemisphere had been paralyzed by electric shock the patient displayed distressful and fearful facial expressions and consonant verbalizations, intonations, gestures, and posture.

Differentiated Affects and Consciousness

Current knowledge of the nature of consciousness and its structures and operations has not really taken us much beyond the seminal ideas of Spencer (1855). He anticipated aspects of contemporary theory in pointing out the close relationship between perception, cognition, and emotion. Some of his ideas are supportive of the position of differential emotions theory. He drew distinctions between sensation and perception and between emotion and cognition. In particular, his idea that emotion is an integration of sensations is a fundamental thesis of differential emotions theory.

Spencer and other life scientists of his and the following generation considered the operations of consciousness to be of two types of processes. The simplest type of intellectual or cognitive function was thought to be perception, while the simplest type of feeling was considered to be sensation. Anticipating some future formulations in psychology, Spencer rejected the idea that perception and sensation were strictly dichotomous. "Every sensation, to be known as one, must be perceived: and must so be in one respect a perception. Every perception must be made up of combined sensations; and must so be in one respect sensational" (Spencer, 1890, p. 475). Nevertheless, he went on to point out distinctions between sensation and perception, the elementary processes underlying feeling and cognition. "In sensation, consciousness is occupied with the relations among those affections" (Spencer, 1890, p. 475). He described cognition and feeling as "at once antithetical and inseparable . . . only in those rare cases in which both its terms and its remote associations are cognitions *absolutely* free from emotion" (Spencer, 1890, p. 478). Thus while Spencer believed it was virtually impossible to disentangle completely emotion from cognition, he recognized some distinctive features of sensation and emotion on the one hand and of perception and cognition on the other. He also believed that cognition was always joined or influenced by emotion. We have to consider Spencer as one of the early scientists to conceptualize emotions or feelings as dimensions (or states) of consciousness, and hence dimensions of personality and behavior.

Wundt (1896) extended the Spencerian tradition and proposed that the sphere of consciousness described by emotion or feeling could be accounted for by three dimensions: pleasantness–unpleasantness, relaxation–tension, and calm–excitement. Wundt's dimensions were revived by Woodworth (1938), Schlosberg (1941), and their colleagues in a long line of successful research on the dimensions of emotion expression.

Borrowing from the Spencerian tradition, Bartlett and Izard (1972) did a dimensional analysis of the subjective experience of eight fundamental emotions. They found that each emotion tended to be characterized by a particular profile (different intensities) of dimensions such as pleasantness, tension, and impulsiveness. The details of the Bartlett–Izard study of dimensions of experiential emotion will be presented in the later chapters on discrete emotions.

Affects and the Organization of Consciousness. Differential emotions theory proposes that the affects, particularly the emotions, are the principal organizing and controlling forces in consciousness, self-awareness, and the ego or self-concept. The affects exert their control or influence by means of an intraindividual communication system consisting of feedback loops and interactive systems. According to this theory, the organization of consciousness is as follows. Sensations from both interocepters and exterocepters provide the basis for consciousness. Consciousness at its most basic level is awareness of sensation. Emotion is the most fundamental organization of sensation that has significance or meaning (and that has specific experiential, motivational properties). The very basic sensory–cortical process that produces affect lays the groundwork for perception, cognition, and all other operations of consciousness. Consciousness that consists of awareness of "pure sensation" or of sensation that is only loosely organized by the usual perceptual–cognitive processes is attained by adults only under unusual conditions. Ordinary states of consciousness are characterized by affect and, most importantly, in human beings, by emotion; and the emotions in consciousness influence all perception, cognition, and behavior.

Gray (1973) has proposed a theory of mind that bears considerable similarity to differential emotions theory. He maintains that all cognition is coded by emotion. Thus emotions in nuance form "pick up and organize cognitive elements into . . . an emotional–cognitive structure, and it is the repetition of this process, aided by the development of hierarchical levels of organization that constitute the development of mind" (pp. 1–8, 1–9). Gray's conception of "emotion in nuance form" is similar to Plutchik's (1962) emotion mixture and Izard's (1972) patterns of emotions. There can be a great variety of nuances (mixtures, patterns), and hence a virtually infinite set of "emotional–cognitive" structures.

A number of social psychologists have reported evidence for affect and cognition as separable but interacting variables in attitudes. For example, Kilty (1969) correlated scores on a cognitive measure of attitude (the implicative meaning procedure) with an independent measure of affect (as it related to the attitude objects). He interpreted the relatively low correlations as support for a conceptualization of attitude which distinguishes affect and cognition as relatively independent components. In a later study Kilty showed that the relationship of attitudinal affect and cognition was a complex one. He found that the strength of the affect–cognition relationship depended on such variables as type of concept and source of beliefs involved in the attitude. Attitude as studied by Kilty is quite similar to the concept of affective–cognitive orientation which allows for a great variety of affect–cognition relationships, not only in terms of the concept, but also in terms of the quality and intensity of the affect.

In his analysis of "natural cognitions" Scott (1969) gave a significant role to affect, although he dealt with affect only in terms of the broad classes of like–dislike or desirable–undesirable. He maintained that objects as conceived by persons have an affective attribute that is closely related to evaluative attributes but orthogonal to purely descriptive attributes. This suggests that his concept of natural cognition has some similarity to the notion of affective–cognitive orientation. He defined affective balance as a mode of integrating attributes so that objects (concepts, images) are grouped cognitively in a fashion consistent with their *affective relevance* to the individual. He concluded that affective balance is incompatible with the ambivalence toward objects that is found in schizophrenia and other types of maladjustment.

Bugelski (1970) suggested that a study of images and meaning may require a return to the tripartite analysis of behavior into cognitive, affective, and conative factors, systemic divisions similar to those postulated in differential emotions theory. One of the practical implications of such a differentiation was demonstrated by Bostrom (1970). In a study of attitudes toward public speaking he found that the affective component of attitude was much more strongly related to the actual behavior of making a speech than was the cognitive component. An increasing number of investigators representing a variety of theoretical orientations have begun studying the role of affect in attitude formation (Wachtel & Schimck, 1970) self-concept and values (Carlson & Levy, 1970), interpersonal perception (Danish & Kagan, 1971), nonverbal communication (e.g., Mehrabian, 1972), memory (Holmes, 1970), creativity (Simonov, 1970), and other cognitive processes (Pecjak, 1970; Kuusinsen, 1969; Harrison & Zajonc, 1970).

Affects and Special States of Consciousness. Any radical shift in the affective–perceptual–cognitive processes that characterize the chief contents of consciousness may result in a special or altered state. In terms of differential emotions theory an altered state of consciousness most frequently results from a radical shift of interest and a breakdown of strong and early learned affective–cognitive processing patterns. In his own experience with mescalin, A. Huxley (1954) observed that his interest in space diminished and his interest in time fell almost to zero. With interest shifted drastically out of its usual channels—away from ordinary space–time object relations—a new state of consciousness emerges.

Special states of consciousness characterized mainly by the emotions (especially certain combinations of interest and joy) have the capacity to facilitate the phenomena of intuition, tacit knowing, and the receptive mode. Operations of consciousness such as analytical, critical, logical, and rational processes may involve interest in interaction with a negative emotion such as distress.

An emotion provides certain "information" to the organism, but this information (e.g., a certain pattern of pleasantness, tension, impulsiveness, and other experiential phenomena), unlike the abstractions of cognitive processes, has a direct relationship to sensory events. The information contained in emotion is nonlinear and nonrational, and emotion cues foster intuitive knowing as well as analytical–intellective processes. Thus emotion and cognition are sometimes contrapuntal—they may be in opposition or in harmony. In either case emotion alters perception and cognition. It is proposed that certain emotion states deautomatize or otherwise alter the structures and contents of consciousness in such a way as to preclude cognitive processes as they usually operate.

Special states of consciousness may emerge as a result of an extraordinarily strong drive—as when the person thirsting for water has a mirage, an optical illusion of an oasis. A special state may also derive from the intense sensory pleasure that comes with combining excitement and sexual stimulation. An altered state may also result from the interest–excitement and perceptual–cognitive processes that characterize creativity. The emotion of interest at once restricts or focuses perception and cognition so as to immerse the individual in the subject and free the mind of interfering operations. The net effect of the emotion under these conditions is to foster the intuitive mode of knowing.

Ordinary states of consciousness are characterized mainly by combinations or integrations of emotion, perception, and cognition, or what was described in Chapter 4 as affective–cognitive orientations. In adulthood much of the cortical-integrative activity in consciousness is seemingly automatic. The integration of sensory data seems automatic, partly because it is influenced by innate neural programs that interrelate affective and perceptual–cognitive processes and partly because much of the framework for interpreting the world as we sense it has resulted from strong and early-learned affective–cognitive structures. Therefore, the difficulty experienced by adults in achieving an altered state of consciousness, without the use of psychoactive drugs, is due to the fact that most of the structures and operations of ordinary consciousness are firmly entrenched.

The strength of the bond between the affects and the cognitive structures and operations of consciousness is a function of the quality and intensity of the affective component. When the affect is strong we have something similar to the traditional concept of attitudes or personal values that are expressed in the form of prejudice (cf. Liddell, 1962), dogmatism, and authoritarianism, or as ambitions, goals, and ego-ideals. Since bonds between affect and cognition provide the principal structures of ordinary consciousness, it follows that special states of consciousness will result only if the individual can alter or temporarily break these bonds or interrupt the seemingly automatic bonding processes. The individual has to be able to sense things without the affect usually activated by them. Some of the ancient Eastern philosophers had similar ideas. In attempting to describe the path to "universal consciousness," or the feeling of "oneness with the universe," Huang Po (c. 900 A.D.) advised his disciples to get rid of "all thought and cognition." A central theme running through much of the Eastern thought on the problem of achieving universal consciousness is that of a need for radical departure from self-hood (the self-awareness structure in consciousness) as conceived in the West. A second theme focuses on the matter of sensing (processing sense data) without "desire," suggesting at least temporary abandonment of emotion attachments.

My position is that a special state of consciousness is obtained by altering the structures and processes that are the contents of ordinary states of conscousness. Without drugs or cerebral accidents, this cannot be done easily or summarily. It has to begin with efforts to rechannel ordinary emotion and perceptual–cognitive processes. The ubiquitous emotion of interest has to be narrowly channeled into sharply focused attention on some simple object or process. As one maintains focal attention toward simpler and simpler phenomena, the seemingly automatic affective–perceptual–cognitive processing of sensory input is slowed and interrupted, and things are sensed differently. The emotion of interest begins to operate in a different way, with less of its usual focusing, structuring, and organizing functions, and sense data from images or external objects can be processed in extraordinary fashions. If percepts result from the sense data they may lack structure but be unusually rich in color, texture, or tone. If an affect other than interest emerges in the altered state, it will be experienced in an extraordinary way. A rare moment of receptive joy or joy combined with tranquility may be the closest we usually come to a special state of consciousness characterized by emotion. Perhaps excitement simply over being alive is another example. Giving up or restricting the automatic affective–perceptual–cognitive operations of consciousness frees our sensibilities for dramatically new experiences.

Summary

There is renewed and vigorous interest in the study of consciousness, a concept largely neglected in the first half of this century. Theoretical developments, changes in the current of belief, and advances in the methodologies and the technology of the human sciences have brought consciousness to the forefront of inquiry. Although it is widely accepted that some kinds of "mind processes" operate in the preconscious, unconscious or out of focal awareness, the concern here is with consciousness, its structures and operations. James emphasized that consciousness is personal in nature, sensibly continuous, the source of self-identity, and highly selective with respect to what is processed.

Although it appears heuristically profitable to distinguish between consciousness as sensibility/awareness and the structures and operations of consciousness, few theorists and investigators have given this division much attention. Tart is at least a partial exception since he postulates a basic awareness, a kind of self-awareness, and attention/awareness as phenomena that are distinguishable from structures or structure subsystems such as input processing, memory, and emotions.

Deikman also argues for a distinction between consciousness and its contents. He defines consciousness or awareness as the *complementary* aspect of the organized biosystem. Deikman notes that the great challenge for the investigators in this realm is to elucidate the processes whereby neurochemical events are transformed into perceptions, cognitions, and affects.

Singer and his colleagues, unlike Tart and Deikman, have extended the theorizing of James and Tomkins and developed rigorous empirical tests for their ideas. Their studies support the notion that consciousness can be considered an alternative stimulus field to externally derived sensory information and that it is possible to change the balance between internal (imagery, fantasy) and external sources of stimulation (information) by manipulating environmental input.

Sinnott argues for continuity between embryological development on the one hand and the development of consciousness, feeling, thought, and action on the other. He believes that all living organisms are characterized by a biological directiveness that is experienced as desire and purpose. Thus, basic consciousness is simply the felt or experienced electrochemical activities of the brain and body. In Sinnott's view consciousness includes not only directiveness but the kind of involvement of the organism with the environment that comes from wants and desires, which Sinnott equates with emotions.

In differential emotions theory the affects, primarily the fundamental emotions, constitute the basic structures of consciousness. The interactions of affects and patterns of affects with perception and cognition make possible an infinite variety of affective–cognitive structures and orientations that influence perception, thought, and action (input and output processing). It is argued that emotion can exist in consciousness independent of cognition and that this helps explain why a person may respond in terms of an emotion without cognizing it or labeling it as such. Experiencing anger and cognizing anger are different phenomena, although such emotion experiencing and related cognition are typically intertwined in affective–cognitive interactions. Although emotions are the most fundamental of the motivational phenomena, cognition can play a significant role in the activation and regulation of emotion processes.

The emotions play a critical role in the self-awareness and self-identity aspects of consciousness. For example, there is both theoretical and empirical support for the role of shame in the development of self-awareness and self-identity.

There is some evidence that the dominant and nondominant hemispheres of the brain play differential roles in the processing of emotion- and cognition-related phenomena. The scant evidence relating to emotions and hemispheric functions is divided and future research in this area has an important challenge.

Differential emotions theory proposes that emotion is the most fundamental organization of sensation that has meaning or experiential/motivational significance. The basic sensory-cortical process that produces affect lays the groundwork for all other operations of consciousness. The affect that is most typically present in consciousness and active in perceptual selectivity and cognitive processes is the emotion of interest–excitement. Special states of consciousness characterized by certain combinations of interest and joy facilitate intuition, tacit knowing, and the receptive mode. Analytical–critical processes may involve interest in interaction with a negative emotion such as distress. Altered states of consciousness result from a radical shift of interest and a breakdown of strong and early-learned affective–cognitive processing patterns.

7

EMOTIONS, DRIVES, AND BEHAVIOR

This chapter will be concerned primarily with the relationships between emotions and drives. The drive concept will be illustrated mainly by the commonly experienced but complex phenomenon of pain and the equally complex but highly pleasurable experiences associated with sexual intercourse. The chapter will also discuss emotion–drive interactions, particularly the interactions of emotions with pain and with the sex drive.

The concept of drive, already briefly defined in Chapter 3, will be further elaborated in this and following sections. The term behavior as used in this chapter refers to any activity of the organism as a whole that follows or is influenced by one of the major classes of motivation—emotions, drives, affect interactions, affective–cognitive structures.

The concept of drive has a complex history and the controversy over the meaning and significance of drives has not yet been fully resolved. In retrospect, it appears that much of the controversy and misunderstanding surrounding the concept of drive resulted from attributing too much to the concept. In the 1930s and 1940s highly influential theorists proposed that drives could be used to explain the motivational aspect or the "why" of all behavior. Behavior not readily accounted for by the primary drives (e.g., hunger, thirst) was presumably accounted for by secondary drives, learned or acquired as a function of the association of the primary drive with a previously neutral stimulus.

One of the early conceptions of drive was that it consisted of internal stimuli arising from an organ that was undergoing tissue change or deprivation; for example, hunger was thought to consist of contractions in the empty stomach. A number of studies reviewed by Cofer (1972) and Cofer and Appley (1964) presented evidence that hunger and hunger-related behavior could be found even after the stomach was removed. Similarly, simply moistening the mouth and throat or even passing water through the mouth and throat does not necessarily quench thirst and inhibit thirst-related behavior. Further, sexual arousal and sex behavior may continue after sex organs have been removed or denervated. This kind of evidence against the local or peripheral theory (drives cues emanate from peripheral organs like the stomach and genitals) led to the concept of drive as a central state. The central-state concept defined drive as a single state that could be contributed to by any or all or the specific deprivations such as hunger and thirst. This highly influential conceptualization (Hull, 1943) continued to use concepts like deprivation and consummatory behavior and continued to present drive as a homeostatic process; i.e., the drive state represented an imbalance brought about by deprivation and restored by consummatory behavior.

For a while it appeared that the best evidence for a central drive state was an apparent relationship between the quantity of general activity and the amount (or time) of deprivation. However, an experiment by Sheffield and Campbell (1954) showed that activity patterns were subject to learning and suggested that activity may be as much related to environmental cues as to a central drive state. In Cofer's (1972) view this was another serious blow to drive theory.

Most of the evidence against drive theory applied more to the so-called primary drives than to secondary or acquired drives, and research on the latter began to flourish. When Miller (1948) demonstrated that shock-induced pain and fear associated with a tone led an animal to fear the tone and to perform in a certain way to avoid the shock, the potential explanatory power of a wide variety of acquired drives seemed vast indeed. After a review of the research in this sphere, however, Cofer (1972) concluded that there had been very little success in demonstrating the acquisition of secondary drives from primary drives such as hunger and thirst. He thought that the only success in this area was the demonstration of acquired drives based on fear.

As Cofer (1972) pointed out, most of the findings from the research conducted within the framework proposed by Hull and similar drive theorists were subject to alternative explanations. In addition, a number of investigations showed that some quite important types of behavior simply did not fit the homeostatic model required by drive theory. The studies showed, for example, that preferences could be learned when the consequences of the behavior brought about an increase in stimulation rather than a decrease. Sheffield and his associates (Sheffield, Wulff, & Bacher, 1951; Sheffield & Roby, 1950) showed that animals would learn when the "reward" (incomplete copulation, saccharine) did not result in drive reduction or the decrease in tension or stimulation associated with drive satisfaction. Harlow (1950) showed that monkeys would learn to disassemble objects and solve puzzles with no apparent drive or reinforcement except that provided by the objects and the activities themselves. Experiments such as those of Sheffield *et al.,* Harlow, and many similar ones conducted in the 50s and 60s led to a number of theoretical concepts intended to replace drive-reduction explanations of behavior, especially human behavior such as play, exploration, higher order intellectual activities, and creativity. This line of research and theorizing will be discussed in Chapter 8.

The mounting evidence against various forms of drive theory and the emergence of viable competing theories led to a conceptualization of motivation that combines certain aspects of the notion of a central drive state and the idea of incentive (objects, conditions, or stimuli which tend to elicit either approach or avoidance responses). In human beings incentives may consist of internal states such as images or cognitions about positive or negative objects, conditions, and stimulus situations. Incentives not only tend to elicit approach or avoidance responses, they evoke a state of arousal which, in effect, motivates the approach or withdrawal behavior.

Bindra (1969) defined a "central motive state" as a combination of physiological arousal and incentive stimulation. The physiological condition in the central motive state is considered to be general in nature, such as the state of wakefulness, while incentive stimulation is considered to be more related to specific stimuli that have positive or negative valence for the organism. Apparently Bindra accepts the possibility that his concept of central motive state can incorporate emotion concepts as well as other phenomena considered to be motivational in nature. Thus, in Bindra's theory the central motive state could be an emotion and the incentive could be an object, condition, or situation that tends to elicit or in some way influence the emotion.

The foregoing summary of Bindra's conceptualization of motivation suggests that there is substantial similarity between his position and some of the cognitive theories of emotion. Bindra emphasizes the importance of the joint functioning of a general physiological arousal state and the incentive value of environmental or contextual cues. This sounds a lot like Schachter's definition of emotion as physiological arousal plus cognition, the cognition consisting mainly of an evaluation of situational cues.

Bindra's formulation differs from differential emotions theory in that the latter conceives of emotion as involving a central state or process (sometimes activated and otherwise influenced by peripheral processes) that has a relatively high degree of specificity and hence the capacity to generate its own cues for the guidance of behavior. While environmental cues and peripheral sensation are recognized as potentially salient and important for the organism and its behavior, they are considered to be clearly secondary to the central emotion process which has an important regulatory influence on the perceptual–cognitive evaluation of the cues in the environment.

In the remainder of this chapter, the term drive will be used to refer primarily to physiological processes that normally relate to changes or deficits in the cells or tissues that relate to the survival and physical well-being of the organism and the species. The physiological processes consist both of central nervous system (brain) processes and of activities in the peripheral organs (e.g., mouth, throat, free nerve endings, genitals). The term "drive cue" or "drive signal" will refer to neural messages or information emanating either from the peripheral organs or from the central physiological arousal state.

The basic proposition of this chapter, similar to one enunciated by Tomkins (1962), is that the drives constitute a motivational system of definitely limited functions—the maintenance of the body and the propagation of the species. Even the body maintenance drives are influenced by accompanying emotions. The accompanying emotion interacts with the drive and regulates it in any of three ways: (a) by amplification, (b) by attenuation, or (c) by inhibition. For example, an exciting dinner companion plus enjoyable music and aesthetic surroundings can enhance the hunger drive, while disgust elicited by bones in a mouthful of wine and fish or chips of shell in a mouthful of crab meat can greatly attenuate or inhibit the hunger drive. Similarly, the emotion of interest–excitement can greatly enhance and amplify the sex drive, and fear can completely inhibit it.

Functions and Characteristics of Drives

Emotions and drives are characterized primarily by their motivational properties. Although behavior or action of some kind may have motivational value, it is characterized mainly as what results from a motivational experience. The most readily identifiable behavior consists of the actions executed by the striate muscle system. As the term behavior is used here, however, it may also mean imaging, remembering, planning, or anticipating.

The functions and characteristics of drive states as distinguished from those of the emotions were originally presented in detail by Tomkins (1962). The following synopsis draws heavily from his material, to which the reader is referred for a brilliant and interesting elaboration of the points summarized below.

Differences between Emotions and Drives

1. In contrast to the limited functions and specificity of the drive system, the emotion system has the independent motivational power and those more general properties which make it the primary motivational system for human beings. Drives unamplified by emotion will not motivate

learning or sustain behavior, but emotions are sufficient motivators in the absence of drives. For example, fear can motivate escape behavior without the participation of any drive state.

2. Emotions can amplify, attenuate, or inhibit drive states. During periods of intense emotion, drive signals may go unnoticed, as in the case when excitement over work inhibits or attenuates hunger pangs, or when the athlete does not discover a fracture or sprain until after the game. Much of the apparent urgency of a drive is an artifact of the combined strength of both emotion and drive. Thus, if Rafe is in pain and at the same time afraid of greater pain, he may panic. If he is excited and sexually aroused, the excitement (which is felt in the chest and face, not in the genitals) will sustain his potency and greatly enhance his sensory (drive) pleasure; but if he is guilty or afraid about sexuality, he may lose his potency entirely.

3. Drive–behavior sequences have characteristics distinct from those of emotion–behavior sequences. While the notion of a drive–response–reward sequence may in some cases be defensible, the concept of emotion–response–reward is not. In the case of the drive–reward sequence there is typically a cyclical, fixed pattern: increasing drive → increasing goal-directed activity → consummatory response → drive reduction → period of cessation or decrease of drive-related activity → increasing drive → repetition of cycle. The case of emotion activation and increase and decrease in emotion intensity is different. Emotion activation is *not* followed by a fixed and irreversible pattern of events; there is no consummatory response followed by emotion reduction and decrease in emotion-related activity. For the emotions the sequence is this: emotion-activation → motivating/cue-producing experience → emotion instigated/sustained/cue-producing activity → 1 . . . *n* possible events. (For further elaboration of this point, see Izard & Tomkins, 1966.)

Other Functions and Characteristics of Drives

The drives play a critical role in the maintenance of the body and in the survival of the species. Their primary function in the individual is to provide particular types of information.

1. Drive information relates to time, place, response, and hedonic quality. A drive lets us know when we need to start or stop some activity that will satisfy the drive. It is quite adaptive that we feel hunger pains long before there is any extreme deficiency of nourishment and before the cells of our bodies are depleted.

Drive signals tell us *where* something needs to be done. The hunger signal tells us that we have a problem in the mouth and stomach and the pain signal lets us know that the problem is in the finger or the foot or wherever the injury or inflammation may be.

Finally, the drive tells us *what* to be responsive to. The hunger drive tells us that we need to be responsive to food; so we eat, rather than seek comfort by relaxing.

In contrast to the various messages generated by the emotions, drive information falls into one of two broad hedonic classes. That is, drives signal only pleasure or pain.

2. Drive signals differ from the signals of the homeostatic system. The homeostatic system is silent and automatic. The signals it sends, usually chemical or electrochemical in nature, do not need to be represented in consciousness, and indeed they are not.

The person is born with built-in information sufficient to circulate the blood, to breathe, and to do numerous other things which are controlled by homeostatic mechanisms. Emotion interacts with homeostatic processes in emergencies such as when we breathe too much smoke or start to breathe water. In this case the pain drive steps in and signals danger and breathing is postponed for a while or action is instigated to bring the individual into an atmosphere where breathing can be resumed at its normal automatic rate.

3. Drive signals differ from emotion signals. Emotion information, unlike drive information, is very general. For example, the prototypic expression of the emotion of distress is crying, and crying may be elicited in relation to a number of different conditions. The baby Rafe feels distressed and cries when he is hungry or when feeding is interrupted; he cries when he is in pain from a hypodermic needle, or from the discomfort of a cold, wet diaper; and he cries if he is suffering from fatigue or sleepiness or if his sleep is interrupted; and when he is a little older he will cry when separated from his mother.

4. Drive signals are more time-bound than emotion signals. Drive information is effective as a motivator only within the time that the drive is strong enough to be operating and sending signals. The drive, therefore, is specific with respect to time, whereas emotion has generality with respect to time (Tomkins, 1962). What this amounts to is that the memory of hunger does not motivate eating. Rafe wouldn't go to much trouble at all to get to a very fine meal, even in the presence of the keenest memory of eating, if he had eaten only an hour previously.

Likewise, memory of pain probably is not capable of teaching us to avoid the stimulus that elicited the pain. However, pain typically recruits distress in the neonate and distress and/or fear in the older infant and the emotions of distress and fear are motivating. It is the possibility or anticipation of pain that later comes to elicit distress or fear, and it is the emotion or anticipation of it that in turn motivates and sustains avoidance behavior. (For further discussion of this point see Tomkins, 1963, or Izard & Tomkins, 1966.)

Pain and Sex and Their Interactions with Emotions

The phenomena of pain and sex have been selected for more detailed discussion for several reasons. They have greater complexity than other drive-arousal states, they typically recruit and interact with a number of different emotions, and their importance for the individual and for society is relatively independent of the factors (e.g., economic conditions) that determine the importance of survival drives like hunger and thirst. The latter drives must be satisfied periodically to sustain life, but an individual may go indefinitely without experiencing pain and pain relief. One can also survive without sexual arousal and sexual gratification, although the effects of prolonged abstinence on personality and psychobiological well-being are not fully known.

Intractable or chronic pain can affect the individual adversely, but it has no certain and inevitable consequences for personality and behavior. Adjustment to chronic pain is a highly individual matter. Some people may become pessimistic and bitter, and pain may induce anger that leads them to be inconsiderate or cruel to other people. Other individuals may become more tender and compassionate, and their pain may induce distress that results in generosity and concern for others. The same kind of reasoning can be applied to abstinence from sexual pleasure. Although indefinite periods of abstinence have no specific known effects, such abstinence in an environment in which the individual is continually bombarded by sexually arousing stimuli may lead to psychological and medical (e.g., psychosomatic) problems.

As already noted, neither pain nor sex is a drive that demands consummatory or reparatory behavior for individual survival. As we shall see later, pain and sex have some of the characteristics of drives and some of the characteristics of emotions. Ordinarily, they are more likely to be accompanied by emotion, particularly strong emotion, than the body maintenance drives. One can eat or drink with relatively little emotion other than that which is characteristic of one's day-to-day life, but the feelings of pain and the feelings of sexual arousal almost immediately and inevitably recruit and continually interact with strong emotions.

Characteristics of Pain

Except for a few rare and abnormal cases, everyone experiences pain, and, though it is difficult to describe precisely, everyone knows what it feels like to be in pain. Pain typically accompanies birth and death, and it can even result from certain processes of growth. Rank (1929) considered the pain experienced at birth as a critical part of individuation. In discussing the significance of pain, Bakan said: "It is among the most salient of human experiences; and it often precipitates questioning the meaning of life itself . . . No experience demands and insists upon interpretation in the same way . . ." (Bakan, 1968, p. 57).

Pain is a physical discomfort or hurt, a hurt of which we are aware, conscious. There is no pain in unconsciousness. Pain is a unique and completely personal experience: No one can suffer your physical pain with you (though one may feel distress with you or for you).

Pain, like emotion, is essentially an intraindividual phenomenon. Also like emotion, pain may result from either internal or external stimulation. Due in part to the fact that the understanding and explanation of pain is so closely linked to inner experience, behaviorism has no way of conceptualizing and dealing with pain. Behaviorists have to either define pain as stimulus or response. Pain is literally in between stimulus and response, and it has some of the properties of both. It can be described in several ways or at several levels. A full understanding of pain must necessarily take into account the data from all of these levels.

Cellular Level. At the cellular level pain has been defined as the release of some form of potassium in the cells. At this level pain is cell or tissue damage. However, "Tissue injury is not an adequate explanation of pain. There are instances in which there is pain without tissue injury, and instances in which there is tissue injury without pain" (Bakan, 1968, p. 82). For explanation of such phenomena it will be necessary to turn to data from other levels and other approaches.

Neural Level. At the neural level pain is the stimulation of certain kinds of receptors and nerve fibers. We have many kinds of receptors (e.g., merkel discs, Ruffin's cylinders, etc.), but it is generally believed that the pain receptors are the free, undifferentiated nerve endings. Pain impulses are carried by the A-delta and unmyelinated fibers. The thalamus and the sensory cortex are not required for the experience of pain, but these structures are necessary for the interpretation of pain (Sternbach, 1968). An example from neurosurgery illustrates the role of the sensory cortex in the interpretation of pain. Intractable pain and certain types of chronic psychoses have been treated by lobotomy, which severs the sensory fibers connecting the temporal and frontal lobes of the brain. After this operation, patients may be conscious of pain at one level of awareness but express no great discomfort or concern about it.

Physiological Level. At the physiological level pain has been considered in terms of changes in the functioning of organs innervated by the autonomic nervous system. Indicators such as heart rate, respiration, and basal skin resistance have been used. The problem in using these indicators of pain are similar to the problems in using them as indicators of emotion. Changes in functions of the autonomic nervous system can result from physical exercise, pain, emotion, or combinations of these. When using these indicators it is necessary to have other evidence of the existence of pain, for example, the nature of the stimulus conditions and self-report data.

Experiential Level. At the experiential level pain can be described simply as the hurt one feels when there is an injury to the body, but this is not a very satisfying description of the experience of pain. It is difficult to give pain a clear and understandable phenomenological description. This is true partly because pure pain unmixed with emotion is fairly rare. What we often find in the literature are descriptions of pain mixed with distress, pain mixed with fear, pain mixed with anger, or pain with some combination of these or other emotions. Pain is sometimes described as sharp or cutting, and it may be that when these adjectives are applied to pain it is not simply a reflection of the physical characteristics of pain but those of pain plus fear. Pain is sometimes described as deep or dull and such expressions may reflect the mixture of pain with distress. Pain is also described as gnawing or irritating, and such descriptions may reflect the mixture of pain and anger. Further discussion of pain–emotion interactions will be presented in the following section.

Szasz (1957) has pointed out that in pain the body is reacted to in a fashion similar to the way an individual may respond to another person. What is implied here is that pain increases our awareness of the body and tends to give the individual a keener awareness of the relationship (or oneness) of body and mind. When an individual's body is in pain, it is immediately evident to him that a part of himself is hurting, and that pain or hurt greatly influences his perception, thought, and affective functioning. In a similar vein the studies of Hardy, Wolff and Goodell (1952) led them to conclude that " . . . recent evidence supports the old view that the feeling state may perchance be the most relevant aspect of pain to the one who suffers" (p. 24).

Whatever its phenomenological characteristics, pain is almost always accompanied by efforts to obtain relief and to avoid or prevent its further occurrence. Pain is almost universally dreaded but it is fruitless and vain to seek a life totally without pain. Pain is apparently an inevitable part of life, and even with the greatest care some accident, disease, and ultimately death is virtually certain to bring a measure of pain into every life. A better understanding of the role of emotion in pain and of the principles of emotion control may enable the individual to develop a suitable philosophy of pain that will enable her or him to learn to manage it without undue disruption of thought and action.

The Social Communication of Pain. Pain is a highly individual and personal experience, but the expression of pain on the face and the cry of pain in the voice are signals for sympathy and help. Wolff's (1969) observational study of mothers and young infants led him to conclude that mothers could distinguish between the pain cry of their infants and the crying that results from other stimulus conditions. Mothers came more quickly to the aid of infants who were crying in pain. These data suggest that the pain cry (as well as possibly other pain-expression signals) are releasers of environmentally stable helping behavior, at least among family members and friends.

The Functions of Pain: A Paradox

There are many paradoxes associated with pain, but the most important is the fact that pain can be both harmful and helpful. Pain may be helpful by serving as a signal that the body has sustained an injury that requires attention. Pain may also serve to warn the individual that damage to tissues or cells is imminent (Bakan, 1968; White & Sweet, 1965). However, it is misleading to consider pain simply as beneficial. A moderately high level of persistent pain can impair sleep and appetite and, more importantly, the person's ability to think clearly and to maintain an appropriate affective–cognitive orientation toward life and work. In some cases long-endured chronic pain can destroy people's desire to help themselves and even the desire to live.

Despite the variety of problems that pain can cause the individual there are certain benefits even beyond the function of pain as a warning signal. For example, when a person sustains an injury to a part of his body, the area around the injury usually becomes more sensitive to pain. This lowered pain threshold in the area of the injury increases the individual's motivation to avoid further damage to the injured area. Protection of the injury increases the opportunity for it to heal properly. In some cases a severe injury will decrease the organism's mobility and hence lessen the chances of further injury.

The effect of injury on pain threshold and mobility may present another paradox. Certain types of injuries apparently heal better when the muscles, joints, and tendons around the injured area are given a certain amount of exercise. Although exercising the bruised or strained muscle or ligament is virtually certain to bring on more pain, the exercise helps heal the injury. To endure such exercise one must be motivated by an emotion or affective–cognitive orientation that affects the pain.

Pain–Emotion Interactions and Relationships

The experience of "pure" pain and pain alone is so unusual that some students of pain have considered it an emotional response (e.g., Sternbach, 1968). Differential emotions theory maintains that while pain has a number of the characteristics of emotion it is useful for the investigator of pain to consider it as a special type of drive or quasi-drive arousal state. In this way it is possible to reconcile the great variation that is found in different self-reports of pain. The phenomenology of pain varies from situation to situation due to the fact that under different conditions and for different individuals pain activates different emotions or combinations of emotions. A given pain condition can activate more than one emotion, including emotions that tend to set up conflicting tendencies within the individual.

Pain and Fear. For most people acute and unexpected pain is likely to elicit fear, or startle followed by fear. The suddenness of the stimulus and the steep gradient of stimulation are sufficient to account for surprise or startle. In the wake of the startle and perhaps before the individual can fully assess the damage that gave rise to the pain, fear may be activated. From an evolutionary perspective the ability of acute unexpected pain to recruit fear has adaptive value. Fear increases the individual's vigilance and readiness to escape the object or condition that caused the pain. The likelihood and intensity of pain-induced fear are related to the environmental conditions surrounding the event. A cut finger while slicing vegetables in the relative safety of one's own kitchen would not be as frightening as the sting of an unseen hornet while trekking in the woods. The high probability that acute unexpected pain will activate some level of fear suggests that such pain is an innate releaser of fear or that the relationship between acute unexpected pain and fear is environmentally stable.

Bakan (1968) has argued that every experience of pain evokes in the mind of the individual the possibility of annihilation or death. Contemplation of such a possibility would certainly be expected to be an effective stimulus for fear. This idea of a possibility of annihilation constitutes what Bakan calls the attitudinal factor in pain, and he maintains that the importance of this factor depends upon the extent to which the individual has differentiated an apprehension of annihilation from the actual sensation of pain. Bakan surveyed a large number of studies which showed that a placebo was effective for those patients who had differentiated the apprehension of annihilation from actual pain stimulation and that such differentiation was more likely in a context where the patient sensed that he was being well cared for and that his life was not in danger.

Pain and Distress. Pain that persists for an extended period of time or even pain that is intermittent over a period of hours or days tends to elicit distress. Even though acute pain may first elicit fear, if it continues for a long enough time the fear is likely to give way to distress. Unrelieved pain can discourage the individual, and chronic pain for which little or no relief can be found may lead to despair. Chronic pain, pain-induced distress, and the continuing lack of a feeling of well-being can lead to a sense of hopelessness and ultimately to severe depression. As long as the distress does not become severe it can serve an adaptive function by increasing the individual's concern and effort to remove the cause of the pain. Pain and pain-induced distress can also aid in the development of sympathy and compassion for other people who suffer. Feelings and thoughts associated with the pain–distress experience can also serve to remind the individual of the vulnerability and mortality of the body, and foster a keener appreciation of life and well-being.

Pain, Anger, and Aggression. Unrelieved pain, particularly when accompanied by distress, can lead to anger. As already noted, Tomkins (1963) hypothesized that extended distress is an innate activator of anger. Tomkins maintained that both anger and distress are "density-level" emotions that are activated by a sustained level of neural stimulation, a level that is a little higher than the person's characteristic level in the case of distress and considerably higher in the case of anger. The level of stimulation brought about by pain combined with that of distress could easily increase the stimulation level beyond the threshold for anger. Environmental conditions can also influence the probability of anger arousal. If one's pain was caused by the careless and needless act of another, anger is more likely than in the case where pain occurred as the result of an effort to help someone else. Under certain circumstances anger alone can lower the threshold for aggression. When there is pain arousal plus anger arousal the threshold for aggression may be even lower. This may be particularly true if there is someone or something to strike out against. Under certain conditions striking out in pain and anger may be an environmentally stable behavior pattern that functioned in the evolutionary process as a defensive reaction. Research with nonhumans (Ulrich, Hutchinson, & Azrin, 1965) has shown that in certain species pain can function as an unconditional stimulus for aggressive behavior. These investigators did not consider the possible role of discrete emotions such as anger in these instances of pain-related aggression, but they did speculate that the relationship they found between pain and aggression might also hold for human beings.

Pain and Guilt. Pain may only rarely induce guilt, but under certain circumstances it can directly or indirectly relieve guilt. If an individual suffers pain as a result of actions in violation of his religious, moral, or ethical code, the guilt brought about by his actions may be relieved by his suffering. He may feel that the pain is a way of making recompense and that the pain will lead to contrition and help remind him to avoid such behavior in the future. If a person contracts venereal disease as a result of sexual behavior that violates his or her beliefs, the pain and suffering that follow may in some way expiate the guilt. Beecher (1966) described the reactions of soldiers wounded on Anzio Beachhead in World War II. Two-thirds of these soldiers declined analgesics when they were offered, while only twenty percent of a group of civilians preferred their pain to medical relief. Beecher reasoned that the soldiers refused the pain-relieving medication because their wound increased their sense of being alive and safe and reduced the threat of annihilation. However, these soldiers may also have felt some guilt over having to leave their post and "abandon their buddies." In this case the pain would remind them that they had no option and were no longer able to carry out their responsibilities in the combat area.

Pain–Emotion–Cognition Interactions. Just as pain typically elicits one or more fundamental emotions, it also sets off and influences a chain of perceptual–cognitive processes. Affective–cognitive structures involving pain have a very decisive effect on one's pain tolerance and one's tendency to complain of pain. As in the case of socialization of the emotions, parental attitudes toward pain and parental responses to the child in pain have a strong influence on shaping the individual's personal attitude toward pain. If the child's screams of pain create alarm and panic in a parent, the parent's fear is likely to be contagious and the child may develop a pain–fear bind. The pain–fear bind makes it more likely that the individual will be handicapped by unnecessary dread of pain (even that which comes routinely with medical examinations, vaccinations, etc.) and in the pain situation the fear may serve to amplify the pain experience.

Certain attitudes and personality characteristics have been found to relate to pain, and these cannot readily be judged as desirable or undesirable. For example, Sternbach (1968) has found that the people who are most tolerant of pain tend to be extraverted and field-dependent. The behavior of a field-dependent person is governed more by environmental cues (including social cues from other persons) than is that of field-independent individuals. Field-dependence, which characterizes women more often than men, may also be associated with increased emotion sensitivity, and most people would agree that a certain amount of emotion sensitivity can be a highly desirable personality characteristic.

Neurotics, as well as individuals who have a tendency to direct hostility inward (intropunitive), are more likely to complain of pain. Sternbach (1968) has also pointed out certain non-personality-factors associated with tendency to complain of pain. Older people, people who have had more pain experiences, people with more siblings, those from lower socioeconomic classes, and people in certain ethnic groups have a greater tendency to complain of pain.

Tomkins (1963) discussed several ways in which emotion and cognition interact with pain:

1. Pain-inducing stimulation that goes unattended and holds no interest for the individual may be entirely painless.
2. Pain may take on a completely different meaning when it occurs in an overall positive context of sexual pleasure and excitement as in the case of sexual masochism.
3. Pain may be attenuated by being combined with positive emotion.

4. Pain may be attenuated by a change in affective–cognitive orientation (belief or attitude) about what is happening. Examples of this are the placebo effect, the frontal lobotomy, and hypnosis.
5. Pain may be attenuated by a strong competing emotion, whether positive or negative.
6. Pain need not be amplified by fear if the fear is not fear of pain, but fear of pain acts as an amplifier.
7. Pain typically elicits an accompanying emotion; it may be fear, distress, anger, or some combination of these, and the pain–emotion interaction tends to generate perceptual–cognitive processes consonant with these affects and the individual's experiences.

The Sex Drive

The word sex conjures up a multiplicity of meanings and the meanings vary widely from individual to individual and from culture to culture. Every individual and every society, both past and present, has had problems with sex. Expert opinion (May, 1973; Masters & Johnson, 1970; McCary, 1973) indicates that the present "sexually liberated" generation, the educated young people of the affluent countries of the world, represent no exception. The perennial problem with sex has many sources.

Some Complicating Problems. Except under unusual circumstances sexual intercourse between man and woman is a physically and emotionally involving intimate encounter. It always involves emotions, which vary in quality and intensity according to the relationship of the two people. Many different meanings can be attributed to such an intimate emotional encounter, and difficulties may arise when the man and woman make conflicting attributions or misattributions. Further, the consequences or possible consequences of the sex act are complicated. Even with modern contraceptive devices, there is always the possibility of pregnancy with its vast implications. Current statistics show that in premarital sex the likelihood of pregnancy is greatly reduced with an appropriate contraceptive, but the risk of venereal disease is substantial and increasing.

Some behavioral scientists (Eibl-Eibesfeldt, 1972; Morris, 1968) maintain that sexual intercourse constitutes a significant force in binding people together as mates and in maintaining the pair bond, whether or not pregnancy results. These biologists hold that the pair-bonding and pair-maintenance function of sex has evolutionary-biological roots, and they imply that attitudes and practices that disregard these roots run the risk of developing individual behavior and customs contrary to nature. Finally, there are the seemingly inevitable religious–moral–ethical questions as to which sexual practices are right and good for the individuals involved, and which are wrong and bad for them. The behavioral scientists referred to in this section, including ethologists, sexologists, marriage counselors, and psychotherapists, have significant disagreements even on such seemingly basic matters as to whether "love makes it right."

Some of the issues raised here will be dealt with as specifically as possible, but it is the central thesis of the present and following sections of this chapter that the best contribution that can be made in this volume is an attempt to place the sex drive and sexual behavior in the context of the whole person, particularly as seen in terms of the emotions and the interactions of emotions with the sex drive, cognition, and sexual behavior. Hopefully this will give a new perspective on the sex drive as such and on the complexity and intricacy of sexual intercourse and the sexual relationship as they involve the emotions and the other subsystems of the personality.

Characteristics of the Sex Drive. As was the case with hunger and thirst, the sexual drive cannot be accounted for in terms of peripheral organs; i.e., the genitals and erogenous zones of the body. Castration in the adult male and ovariectomy in the adult female do not necessarily destroy the sex drive. However, there can be no doubt that the genitals and other erogenous zones of the body play a significant role in sexual arousal and sexual behavior. At the same time there is quite sufficient evidence to conclude that central (brain) mechanisms and hormonal conditions have an important part in the control and regulation of the sexual drive and sexual behavior. Currently available evidence suggests that sexual arousal and activity result from an interaction of brain processes, hormonal conditions, external stimulation, and experiential phenomena such as imagery (visual, auditory, somesthetic) and thought processes. The cognitive determinants may function in the absence of external stimulation.

The neural control of sexual behavior is complex but current evidence suggests that the hypothalamus, particularly the anterior portion, is an important brain mechanism in sexual functioning. The hypothalamus has numerous interconnections and relationships with the pituitary (master) gland, and therefore, the controlling functions of the hypothalamus may be either direct or by way of its influence on the pituitary gland, which in turn influences the activities of the sex glands. As indicated earlier, the hypothalamus is considered a highly important brain mechanism in emotion, and the glandular system is an auxilary system in the emotion process.

Masters and Johnson (1966) have presented a detailed analysis of the physiology of sexual stimulation and orgasm. They showed that successful sexual intercourse leads to a predictable but complex course of changes in the cardiovascular and hormonal systems. These changes are essential to healthy and fully gratifying sexual intercourse. For example, variations in hormones and circulation govern the delicate responses of the vagina that make sex so pleasurable for the man. They showed that clitoral stimulation

was the primary basis for the female's orgasm, and Sherfey (1966) and
Bardwick (1971) have suggested that the relatively nerve-free vagina is
mainly of psychological importance in the woman's gratification. Equally
complex changes occur in the clitoris in order to maximize responsiveness
and receptivity to stimulation. All the physiological mechanisms involved
in sexual stimulation and orgasm are highly sensitive to the effects of
negative emotion arousal.

While neural mechanisms and hormonal conditions have important
influences on the development and functioning of the sexual organs, some
studies suggest that effective sexual behavior depends to a significant
degree on learning and experience. Harlow (1962) showed that monkeys
reared in isolation were awkward and ineffective in attempts to copulate. If
the social isolation was continued for a long enough period, successful
mating never occurred. However, before concluding that effective sexual
performance depends heavily on teaching and learning processes, some
other facts need to be considered. Rearing an animal in isolation is very
severe treatment that has a devastating effect on the organism and the
whole of its social life. Rearing monkeys in an all-male but otherwise
normal environment might provide a much better test of the questions of
the relative importance of innate and learned factors in sexual performance.
While such a colony might never arise in nature, the weight of biological
evidence suggests that a male from such a colony would mate effectively
with a receptive female with no more practice than he would be able to
obtain on his own. The point here may be important in considering programs of sex education. In our society and probably many others, effective
sexual performance for many people may depend far less on learning than
"unlearning"; that is, finding ways to remove the overlay of inappropriate
attitudes and habits laid down by socialization and culture. Of course, some
of the restraint and regulation of sexual activities accomplished during
socialization are necessary for social organization.

The Functions of the Sex Drive

The purposes served by the sex drive and sexual behavior are highly
influenced by individual value systems and cultural norms. The sexual
drive and sexual behavior have the fundamental function of reproduction.
While this is an unquestionable requirement for the species, even the
reproductive function of sex has in many societies come more and more
under the control of individual value systems and sociolegal codes.

As already noted, a number of behavioral scientists believe that one of
the important functions of sexual behavior is to facilitate the mating process
by establishing and maintaining bonds between people. The emotions,
drive–emotion interactions, affective–cognitive orientations, and unique

sensory pleasure all contribute to the bonding power of sexual intercourse. The male–female pair, once it has been formed as a social unit, may serve many functions seemingly unrelated to sexual stimulation and gratification; for example, mutual protection, security, and affection. If the pair-bonding hypothesis is correct, it may be some indication of the importance of the male–female pair and the family unit in the origin and development of the human species. A male–female pair, dividing the many and varied responsibilities of a social unit, especially child rearing, may provide the optimal conditions for the survival, growth, and development of the individual.

Another possible function of the sex drive, and more particularly of sexual activity, may be the facilitation of sexual and personal identity. Assuming that over the life span the sexual drive and sexual activity are equally important for men and women, it would follow that it is heterosexual activity rather than sexual drive that serves the identity and selfhood functions. Successful heterosexual relationships, including satisfying sexual intercourse, can contribute to selfhood and personality in a number of ways. They can enhance masculinity and femininity, mutual respect, and confidence. They may also contribute significantly to the development of sexual identity (maleness, femaleness), but this feature can probably be easily overemphasized. To have confidence in the knowledge that one is truly male or female and can perform appropriate gender functions effectively has some psychological value, but its importance is probably directly related to the amount of self-doubt that has been generated by sociocultural forces.

Any complete description of the sex drive must take into account its variation with age. The male achieves peak sexual capability in his teens, when, depending upon the circumstances, he may be either proud and delighted or ashamed and frightened by a virtually instant erection. During these years, the male is capable of four to eight orgasms a day and the refractory period between orgasms may be only a matter of seconds. The sexual drive continues at a high level through the twenties, though some decline occurs. In the thirties the sexual urge becomes less acute, more sexual stimulation is necessary to produce an erection, and the frequency of orgasms decreases. By the late thirties, the refractory period may be as much as thirty minutes. The sexual drive continues to diminish through the forties, and by age fifty the average man feels he is enjoying a satisfactory sexual life with about two orgasms a week. The refractory period has now increased to 8 to 24 hours, and sexual pleasure has become more diffuse and less genitally centered.

The evidence suggests that the relationship between age and sexual drive is less strong for women and subject to a good deal more individual variation. Nevertheless, research indicates that the growth of a woman's enjoyment of the sensory pleasure of sex is slower than for men and that women typically reach their peak orgasmic capability in the late thirties or early forties. Women remain quite capable of multiple orgasms through their fifties and sixties, experiencing only a slight decline in sexual drive during these decades. McCary (1973) agreed with the findings from some investigations that suggest that female sexuality is more a function of learning and experience than is the case for male sexuality. However, it may simply be the case that the overlay of taboos and restrictions laid down during socialization and adolescence are greater for women than for men and therefore more "unlearning" is necessary.

Sex and Emotions

All authorities in the field of sexual behavior agree that the sexual drive and sexual behavior inevitably involve emotion. Bardwick (1971) reviewed a number of studies that suggest that some of the sex–emotion relationships have their roots in biological processes. The results of these studies suggest that certain emotion states in women may vary to some extent with change in estrogen and progesterone levels during the different phases of the menstrual cycle. Although the relationship between emotion and hormonal level is biologically based, the effects on emotion of hormonal changes apparently affect some individuals more than others and the effects vary considerably from culture to culture, particularly when moving from more complex to simpler cultures.

The importance of hormonal changes can be illustrated by the example of estrogen. Estrogen changes from a low level during and immediately following menstruation to a peak level at about the time of ovulation, followed by a decrease for a few days, and then another increase to a high level on or about the twenty-second day of the period. A number of investigators have shown the low-estrogen and low-progestrone premenstrual period to be characterized by the emotions of distress and anger (often described as depression, irritability, hostility). On the other hand, women tend to show a high level of self-esteem and a low level of negative affects during the high-estrogen phase of ovulation. Some authorities have suggested that the positive emotions and affects of the menstrual cycle increase the sociability and heterosexual tendencies of the female and have copulation as their underlying biological aim.

The distress often associated with the phase of the menstrual cycle just prior to menstruation may stem in part from pain and discomfort and a pain–distress combination may elicit anger. Variations among individuals and cultures suggest that the amount of discomfort, distress, and anger has a psychological as well as biological base. However, Bardwick's review of the literature and her own studies led her to conclude that even in normal subjects changes in emotion states were predictable on the basis of physiological changes alone.

The question as to whether men also experience a cycle of endocrine changes and an associated cycle of affective changes has not been as frequently and thoroughly investigated. There are some indications that men experience some cyclic changes, though probably less pronounced than those experienced by women.

In addition to the sex–emotion interactions related to physiological processes, there are a number of sex–emotion interactions and relationships that stem more from experiential factors than biological ones. Individual differences of a biological, sociocultural, and experiential nature determine the presence and intensity of these affective patterns in the individual.

Sex–Interest Interactions. The sex drive, especially in the age period when it is strongest, often becomes so compelling and urgent that it dominates cognition and greatly influences actions. However, as already noted, the sex drive, like any other drive, receives its amplification from emotion. In the case of the sex drive it is interest–excitement or the sex–excitement interaction that creates the sense of urgency. Sex symbols and all sorts of sexually attractive paraphernalia are designed to capture interest at the same time that they activate sexual arousal. Interest not only amplifies the power of the sex drive it also contributes to the overall heterosexual relationship. Other things being relatively equal, the interesting person is the sexually attractive person. More particularly, the interesting individual is more likely to sustain a satisfying affectional relationship that provides the context for exciting sexual activity. When interest combines with joy and certain affective–cognitive structures, the result is love and the best possible context for sexual relations.

Aberrations in sex–interest interactions can produce maladjustment and even serious psychopathology. For example, the misplacement of sexual interest in sex-associated objects or symbols is the source of sexual fetishism. Further, imbalance in interest–fear reactions toward males and females in the context of sexual arousal can contribute to the development of homosexuality.

Sex–Fear Interactions. As already noted, fear and sexual behavior are incompatible and at least in the male the interaction of fear with the sex drive prevents sexual arousal and makes it impossible to obtain an erection and engage in sexual intercourse. Any substantial increase in fear during sexual intimacy can result in premature ejaculation, either prior to or immediately after intromission. If sexual arousal precedes emotion activation, mounting fear can cause the immediate collapse of an erection. While the effects of fear on the female may not be as dramatically visible to the partner, it may be equally devastating. A women's fear of intromission of the penis, pregnancy, or sexual inadequacy can inhibit the production of vaginal lubrication (Masters & Johnson, 1970). Insufficient vaginal lubrication can make intromission acutely painful, and the resulting pain will likely amplify the fear and set off a vicious cycle of pain and fear.

Many of the sex-related fears experienced by men and women are learned or certainly heavily influenced by experiential factors. The "object" of the fear varies with individual personality and with gender. Changes in personal and sociocultural values have also had significant influences on the nature of sex-related fears. For example, contraceptives may decrease a young woman's fear of pregnancy, but the positive correlation between the growth in use of contraceptives among unmarried people and the increase in venereal disease may lead to fear of infection.

One type of fear that may well have increased as a function of the increase in sex information and the increasing number of people engaging in premarital and extramarital sexual relations is that of fear of failure in sexual performance. The knowledge that women are the equal or superior of men in capacity for sexual pleasure and orgasm may make the ambitious, achievement-oriented young male perceive the lack of orgasm or even multiple orgasms in the female as a sign of his inadequate sexual performance. The female may feel equally responsible for displaying the "authentic" signs of orgasmic pleasure and for exacting from the male some telltale evidence of his total loss of control in a flood of ecstatic sensation. Such an affective–cognitive orientation can be inhibiting and self-defeating. Masters and Johnson (1970) have reported that fears associated with sexual performance are a major factor in sexual inadequacy. Fear that one will not achieve an erection or that he will not be able to maintain the erection and perform like a "normal" man can result in impotence. The nonorgasmic female may fear that something is basically wrong with her, that she is not a "real woman." Such self-doubts may turn into fears of performance. "It should be restated that fear of inadequacy is the greatest known deterrent to effective sexual functioning, simply because it so completely distracts the fearful individual from his or her natural responsibility by blocking reception of sexual stimuli either created by or reflected from the sexual partner" (Masters & Johnson, 1970, p. 12–13). Masters and Johnson go on to point out that one of the most effective ways of avoiding fear of sexual performance is to take sex out of an achievement-oriented or goal-oriented context. (It should be noted that the clinical evidence supporting Masters and Johnson's conclusion was obtained from their treatment of married couples, where sex-related negative emotions should be minimal.)

The association between sexual intercourse and the emotion of fear may not be entirely the result of socialization and learning, as many have proposed. A woman's fear of sex with a stranger or a noncommitted male may have served an adaptive function during evolution. Pregnancy increases a woman's vulnerability, if one considers the survival problems associated with childbirth and the care of an infant. A male's fear of sexual intercourse with a strange or noncommitted female may also have evolutionary-biological roots. The male is highly vulnerable physically during sexual intercourse and orgasm, and a female who has no affection for him (possibly even hostility toward him) would have little or no motivation to be protective.

Sex and Guilt. Sexual attitudes and sexual behavior apparently have liberalized rapidly in the last few years. Yet, in 1970 Masters and Johnson concluded that the notion that sensate pleasure in sex is sin "still permeates society sufficiently to influence the affectional, sexual patterns of many marital relationships, although most marital partners would intellectually deny conformation to such a concept" (p. 75). The fact that people can and do intellectually deny or rationalize guilt makes it difficult to assess its role in sexual relationships. The effects of guilt, while quite damaging, are not as severe or observable as those of fear. McCary (1973) agrees with Masters and Johnson that even the marriage ceremony far too frequently fails to eradicate the sex-is-sinful attitude handed down by parents and society. The Judeo-Christian tradition as well as a number of other religions and philosophies have generally been considered as a source of negative attitudes toward sex, or more generally toward any form of pleasure-seeking.

As was the case with fear, the sex–guilt interaction may not be solely a function of learning and experience. As soon as evolving men and women became aware that sexual intercourse leads to conception, pregnancy, and childbirth, sexual intercourse could have easily become associated with some degree of commitment and responsibility and hence with guilt. A lack of feeling of commitment and responsibility on the part of either or both partners could prove disadaptive, if what has already been said about pair bonding and family formation is true. An infant without the benefit of the protective and nurturing environment provided by affectional parents and family may be less likely to survive. Guilt or anticipation of guilt about sexual intercourse may still serve an adaptive function. Guilt avoidance may foster a more considerate and responsible attitude on the part of both partners.

Since guilt is not as strong as fear, it need not necessarily inhibit sexual behavior. It may simple serve to dose or regulate the rate at which a couple can become fully intimate. Many young couples find that a certain level of intimate sexual behavior that once produced feelings of guilt loses its guilt-inducing power if the behavior is repeated under favorable circumstances. Reiss (1967) has reported that about 60% of men and about 90% of women eventually come to accept sexual behavior that once elicited guilt feelings.

Some clinicians and sexologists believe that men are generally more troubled by guilt in relation to sexual behavior than are women. They suggest that one cause of this is the typical conception of the male as the instigator or "seducer," and as such the one who is responsible for the woman's participation.

Guilt-free sex for a couple who enjoys feelings of mutual respect, mutual responsibility, and love is undoubtedly highly desirable, but guilt-free sex under all conditions may be disadaptive for the individual and for society. The emotion system of human beings may not be capable of an indefinite series of intimate physical relationships without emotional attachment and consequent feelings of commitment and responsibility. The sexual drive, particularly of young men in their teens and twenties, completely unrestrained by guilt, guilt-avoidance, and other forces might prove a highly disruptive factor in social organization.

Sex and Distress. The relationship of changes in endocrine (e.g., estrogen) levels has already been cited as a possible source of distress and depression. A number of other factors contribute to the association of sex and distress. Either male or female may have become distressed and downhearted over his or her failures or seeming failures to be sexually attractive and to enjoy satisfying heterosocial relationships.

Unlike fear and guilt, distress may increase as well as decrease sexual arousal and receptivity to sexual stimulation. It will be recalled that the prototypical distress response is crying, and crying is a social signal calling for comforting and reassuring gestures. The sexual embrace has great power to reassure and comfort.

Physiological changes during menopause, like those of the menstrual cycle, may contribute to feelings of distress and even depression. Some people believe that men experience a physiological change somewhat similar to that of menopause in women, with similar effects on emotion states.

While there is not adequate evidence to describe possible hormone-related emotions in the male, there can be little doubt but that certain sex-related physiological processes in the male are cyclic (or periodic) and these processes are influenced by sexual stimulation and sexual behavior. For example, the prostate gland of a healthy male normally secretes between 1/10 and 4/10 of a teaspoonful of prostate fluid daily, and this fluid dribbles into the urethra and is expelled with the urine. Under conditions of sexual arousal the prostate gland secretes from 4 to 10 times the usual amount. Some urologists maintain that orgasmic ejaculation is necessary in order to get rid of this amount of prostatic fluid and that repeated sexual arousal without ejaculation may result in enough backed-up fluid to cause congestion and possible inflammation of the prostate gland. The resulting prostatitis or prostatosis can be a nagging and persistent problem that could reasonably be expected to elicit distress and anger (the same irritability, hostility, and depression as found in the female cycle). Whether from sexual abstinence in the face of frequent sexual arousal or one of many other possible causes, authorities have estimated that 60% of North American men over age 60 suffer from prostate enlargement and the percentage may rise as high as 95% by age 80. Though the problem more typically arises in middle years it can begin in youth as a result of gonorrhea or even from very common bacteria that live in apparently healthy genitalia.

Whether or not there is a male counterpart to menopause, there is a strong likelihood that at sometime during middle age the male becomes increasingly conscious of his waning sexual powers and such awareness may well contribute to periods of distress and depression. The 40- to 60-year-old man's awareness of his wife's relatively greater capacity for orgasm may increase his distress over decreasing potency.

Sex in Interaction with Anger, Disgust, and Contempt. In a number of species, there is an apparent correlation between sexual and aggressive activity. In nonhuman primates the receptive phase of the female sexual cycle is often accompanied by a general increase in activity in the social colony and an increase in agonistic behavior. In some lower animals it is difficult to differentiate between mating behavior and aggressive behavior, and mating behavior in these animals often results in physical injury to one or both partners. The apparently "aggressive" aspect of such mating behavior does not necessarily mean that this behavior is accompanied by anger or other negative emotion arousal. In the evolution of some species the aggression stemming from the female's resistance to copulation may have served to ward off mates who were physically unfit or to prevent mating prior to the optimal time for conception. In the male the seemingly "aggressive" behavior is apparently in the service of the sexual drive (part of the effort to effect copulation) and thus distinguishable from aggression associated with such phenomena as protection of young and territorial defense. Although the meaning of this apparent similarity between some aspects of mating behavior and aggressive behavior in lower animals has not been fully explained, it has called attention to the fact that some of the brain mechanisms involved in sex and aggression are in close proximity.

Perhaps as part of a carryover from our evolutionary ancestry, heated arguments among young married couples often end in passionate lovemaking. It may not be altogether accidental that the parasympathetic discharges in anger increase the blood flow to the vagina, a phenomena also characteristic of some phases of sexual excitement and orgasm in the female. While evidence is not sufficiently clear to warrant the assumption of a biological basis for a sex–aggression or sex–anger interaction, the possibility of its existence may help sound a cautionary note. Any potential danger from such a relationship would be much more likely to materialize in sexual relationships characterized by the lack of mutual affection, respect, and love. Prostitution has frequently been cited as a contributor to crimes of violence.

If disgust is strong enough it may lead to avoidance of sexual contact altogether. In lesser intensities it may diminish the pleasure of sex and result in some psychological or physical abuse of the partner. Undoubtedly one of the more important contributors to the sex–disgust interaction is the attitude that sex is dirty, an idea that probably generalized from the sex-is-sinful idea. However, it should not be completely overlooked that certain body odors associated with the genitalia can, without proper body hygiene, become quite distasteful. Thus disgust–avoidance behavior may serve an adaptive function, both biologically and socially.

A sex–contempt interaction can result in quite harmful behavior. For example, if a man has contempt for a woman he is much more likely to view her as a sexual object and to feel justified in attempts to seduce and manipulate her. Contempt is the cool and subtle emotion in the hostility triad and its presence in consciousness may go relatively unnoticed by either parties. If either of the sexual partners look upon the other as inferior in any respect there is a basis for suspecting contempt. The man who can find sexual satisfaction only with prostitutes or with women who have fewer status symbols than he undoubtedly suffers from a strong sex–contempt bind. Sexual crimes, including rape, probably are motivated in part by interactions of the sex drive with some combination of anger, disgust, or contempt.

Affective–Cognitive Structures Involving the Sex Drive. In recent years a sizeable body of literature has developed around the concept of sexual attitudes. The term attitude as used in many of these studies is roughly equivalent to the concept of affective–cognitive structure or orientation. The principal difference is that most studies of sexual attitudes have made no effort to delineate discrete emotions and affects. Nevertheless, these studies have made a significant contribution to our understanding of thoughts and feelings associated with the sex drive and sexual behavior.

In any attempt to understand sexual attitudes, it is very important to keep in mind that attitudes toward sexual behavior vary with age, perhaps much in the same fashion as does the sexual drive. Thoughts and feeling about sex are generally quite different in adolescence and in middle age. One adolescent might be all fired up to campaign for sexual freedom and another for abstinence and asceticism, but in middle age both are fairly likely to accept the fact that sexual behavior of one form or another plays an important role in the life of the individual.

Sexual attitudes, or the way we have linked affects and cognition related to sex, play an important role in our sex life. Sexual attitudes are in large measure a product of socialization and the attitudes and behavior modeled by parents. But sexual attitudes are subject to change as a result of the influence of peers, counselors, and accurate sex information.

Some experts (see McCary, 1973) maintain that while there is still no evidence of a true sexual revolution (dramatic change in attitudes and ethics governing sexual behavior), there are a number of indications that there has been a growing liberalization of sexual attitudes. The evidence suggests that women have profited more from this liberalization than men. The recognition and acceptance of female sexuality has increased greatly among men and women. McCary cited anthropological studies which suggested that cultures that disapprove of women having orgasms produce women who fail to have orgasms, and vice versa. Particularly among educated people, it is becoming much easier for women to accept their sexuality, to have a clear consciousness of their sexual urges, and to anticipate their full satisfaction. One interesting aspect of the current changes in sexual attitudes and sexual behavior is the fact that the young men and women who are undergoing the greatest change may be engaging in less casual sex than was the case a decade or so ago (at least in the case of men). There is pretty good evidence (Davis, 1971) that most college women who participate in premarital intercourse (and there are considerably more now than in decades past) are doing so in the context of a meaningful affectional relationship that tends to have considerable stability over time. This suggests that the style of premarital sexual relationships today are more in keeping with the natural emotion makeup of men and women and with the emotional climate necessary for optimal sexual relations.

Authorities on psychosexual adjustment disagree regarding the value of the current changes in sexual attitudes and on their ultimate effects on sexual behavior and society. Albert Ellis (1973) has made a case for sex without love, thus going a step or two beyond the norms of many of today's youth. He argues that while sex with love is important, the biological aspect of sex is essentially nonaffectional. In his view all efforts to civilize the sex drive, which he recognizes as worthwhile and useful efforts, will not succeed in eliminating highly pleasurable sexual relationships that occur apart from the bonds of love and affection.

In contrast to Ellis, Rollo May (1973) has argued that the present changes in sexual attitudes and sexual behavior can lead to substantial individual and social problems. According to May, our highly vaunted sexual freedom is simply a new form of puritanism. Like the old form of moralistic puritanism of Victorian times, the new puritanism also results in alienation from the body and from feeling, the conception of the body as a machine (sexual machine), and separation of emotion from reason. In an impressionistic word picture of the "new intellectual," May said: "He is deathly afraid of his passions, unless they are kept under leash, and the theory of total expression is precisely his leash . . . The first Puritans repressed sex and were passionate; our new man represses passion and is sexual . . . The modern man's rigid principle of full freedom is not freedom at all but a new straightjacket as compulsive as the old . . . And you gain power over sexuality (like working the slave until all zest for revolt is squeezed out of him) precisely by the role of full expression" (pp. 373–374).

Attitudes toward sexual drive and sexual behavior are not only a function of socialization and age but of the sex of the individual as well. Some recent studies have pointed out differences between males and females in emotion responses to erotic literature and to imaging or visualizing sexual intercourse (e.g., Izard & Caplan, 1974). These studies have also shown that factors such as moral–ethical standards and sexual experience significantly affect emotion responses to sexually arousing stimuli and to imaging sexually intimate relationships. These studies are discussed in greater detail in Chapters 15 and 16.

Summary

The concept of drive occupied an important place in psychology for more than half of this century, but some of the scientists responsible for its development have been instrumental in loosening its grip on theory and research. Some of the more liberalized conceptions of drive as a central motive state can encompass the notion of emotion-as-motivation, but none of these deal effectively with the discrete emotions nor with the distinction between emotions and other motivational phenomena.

In differential emotions theory the concept of drive is defined mainly in terms of tissue needs that relate to individual survival and body maintenance. In this view the drives are significant factors in individual thought and action only when biological well-being is jeopardized, something that happens rarely in affluent societies. Drives may become important depending upon how they interact with emotions. Drive signals do have informational value in that they signal pain or pleasure, and indicate when, where, and what needs to be done in relation to the drive.

Emotion information, unlike drive information, is very general and therefore can have motivational significance for an infinitely greater array of phenomena.

The pain and sex drives were selected for discussion since they are drive-arousal states that typically recruit and interact with a number of different emotions and since their importance for the individual and for society is relatively independent of cultural and economic conditions. Further, pain and sex differ in certain respects from body maintenance drives.

Pain can be defined at the cellular, neural, and physiological levels, but it is the experiential aspect of pain that has special psychological significance. The drive function of pain signals an injury or malfunction that requires attention. In this role it is beneficial, but chronic pain can destroy people's desire to help themselves and even the desire to live.

Acute and unexpected pain typically recruits the emotion of fear that increases the individual's vigilance and facilitates escape from the object or condition that causes the pain. Depending upon the circumstances, fear may amplify or attenuate the pain.

Extended periods of pain are likely to elicit distress, and chronic pain combined with pain-induced distress can lead to the sense of hopelessness and helplessness that characterizes depression. The pain–distress experience, however, can also remind the individual of the vulnerability and mortality of the body and foster a keener appreciation of life and well-being.

Pain, especially when combined with distress, can lead to anger. The likelihood of aggression may be increased in such circumstances.

Under unusual circumstances pain may induce or be associated with the emotion of guilt. Thus pain can remind or relieve the individual of the sense of personal responsibility.

Pain–emotion–cognition interactions can develop into affective–cognitive structures that can influence pain tolerance and the tendency to complain of pain. Pain tolerance and pain complaints vary with certain personality characteristics and psychopathological conditions. Different affective–cognitive orientations can either amplify or attenuate pain.

Consideration of the sex drive and sexual relations is complicated by a host of affective–cognitive structures or attitudes, many of which stem from the fact that sexual intercourse is a physically and emotionally involving encounter. Further, contemporary ethologists maintain that sexual intercourse has a significant pair-bonding effect on the participants.

The sex drive does not fit the homeostatic model; successful heterosexual activity is essential for the survival of the species, but not for the individual. The functions of the sex drive are greatly influenced by individual value systems and cultural norms. The sex drive and heterosexual activity may play a role in sex- and self-identity, but their importance in this respect is probably related to the amount of self-doubt that has been generated by sociocultural forces.

Sex and emotions interact in important ways, and some of these interactions may be gender-linked. For example, a pain–distress experience is often associated with phases of the menstrual cycle.

The sex drive is greatly amplified by the emotion of interest–excitement, and mutually experienced sex–interest–joy interactions provide the optimal conditions for sexual pleasure and love relationships. Fear and guilt interacting with the sex drive can destroy or greatly distort the sexual experience. Sex in interaction with anger, disgust, and contempt can lead to rape and murder or to irresponsible sexual activity that can have serious consequences for the participants.

The sex drive can form a part of numerous affective–cognitive structures that have considerable importance, especially during the formative years of life. Adolescents and young adults, and to a lesser extent people of all ages, face a difficult task in sifting through widely differing opinions and other forces and counterforces as they try to develop and maintain a moral–ethical framework for happy and healthy sexual relationships.

8

INTEREST–EXCITEMENT
AND INTRINSIC MOTIVATION

Chapter 7 presented a discussion of the shift away from drive reduction theory to more comprehensive and complex conceptualizations of motivation. Much of the theorizing and empirical research involved in this movement aimed at explaining why people do things in the absence of any drive state and why they sometimes seek stimulation increase rather than stimulation decrease (drive reduction). James's (1890) concept of selective attention, Freud's (1938) term cathexis, and McDougall's (1908) idea of an instinct of curiosity provided a conceptual background for a number of theoretical formulations.

A central problem was the explanation of behavior related to novelty and curiosity, which Berlyne (1950) suggested were important topics for the understanding of complex levels of motivation. All animals tend to respond to novelty and change, phenomena that are particularly effective in capturing the receptors of all sense modalities and in eliciting action in the absence of drives as traditionally conceived. If stimulation from novelty and change is not present in the environment, the organism—whether protozoa, rodent, monkey, or human being—tends to seek it. In a recent volume edited by Lester (1969), a number of authors have described and documented the tendency of a wide variety of species to respond to novelty and change, explore their environment, and seek stimulation.

This chapter will review a number of theories or models that have been proposed to account for "drive-free," "stimulation-seeking" behavior. It will attempt to relate these approaches to the emotion concept of interest–excitement, the motivational construct proposed by differential emotions theory to account for exploration, adventure, problem solving, creativity, and the acquisition of skills and competencies in the absence of (or despite) drives and negative emotions. The emotion of interest will be discussed more fully in Chapter 9.

Some of the early investigators who showed that organisms would explore novel objects or places in the absence of any known drives suggested that they had discovered a new drive, the "exploratory drive" (Montgomery, 1952, 1953, 1954, 1955; Butler, 1953, 1954, 1957, 1958). Others explained similar behavior in terms of a "boredom drive" (Myers & Miller, 1954; Zimbardo & Miller, 1958; Issac, 1962). In a series of experiments Harlow and his associates (e.g., Harlow, 1950, 1953; Davis, Setledge, & Harlow, 1950) showed that monkeys would repeatedly manipulate and eventually solve complex mechanical puzzles on the basis of what they termed a "manipulatory drive." Nevertheless, as a number of theorists have argued (e.g., Berlyne, 1971, and Deci, 1975), "drive naming" does not resolve the underlying theoretical issues but only tends to simplify and suppress important problems involved in explaining behavior unrelated to drives or drive-reduction.

A number of theorists abandoned drive concepts of all kinds in developing either general motivational theories or in explaining what is now frequently termed intrinsic motivation—why people perceive, think, and act in ways and for reasons that cannot be explained in terms of tissue deficits or physiological needs. Koch (1956) suggested that intrinsic motivation may be the primary and normal form of human motivation.

McClelland, Atkinson, Clark, and Lowell (1953) proposed an affective–arousal theory in which all motivation has a physiological basis, but not underpinnings related to specific drive states. In their theory all motives are learned through pairing of cues with affective states, and behavior is motivated when cues associated with these affective states redintegrate them. Cues associated with mild incongruity or slight departure from characteristic level of affective arousal redintegrate positive affect and motivate approach behavior. Cues associated with large descrepancies redintegrate negative affect and motivate avoidance behavior. An individual is intrinsically motivated (i.e., not motivated by drives) when a cue redintegrates a positive affective state and leads to behavior for which there is no extrinsic reward.

Dember and Earl (1957) have proposed that intrinsic motivation is a function of a need for an optimal discrepancy between input and expectation. A number of theories have proposed that intrinsically motivated behavior can be accounted for on the basis of a need to reduce cognitive dissonance (e.g., Festinger, 1957) or uncertainty (e.g., Kagan, 1972). In keeping with the notion that such a need or tension does not represent a traditional drive state or any form of arousal, Driscoll and Lanzetta (1964) and Hawkins and Lanzetta (1965) have shown that experimentally induced uncertainty is unrelated to certain indexes of physiological arousal.

Piaget (1952, 1967) has explained intrinsically motivated behavior in terms of cognitive structures, but as Mischel (1971) has pointed out, Piaget places a strong emphasis on the interrelationship between cognition and affect. In his view, affect can explain intrinsic motivation in that affectivity gives psychological value to activities and provides energy for them.

As discussed in Chapter 3, differential emotions theory holds that there are three major types of stable motivational variables: drives, emotions, and affective–cognitive orientations. Thus, what other theories explain in terms of some variant of the concept of intrinsic motivation, differential emotions theory explains in terms of the motivational properties of the two positive emotions and their interactions with other affects and cognition. It maintains that much of the behavior explained in terms of intrinsic motivation is a function of the emotion of interest–excitement and its interactions with perceptual and cognitive processes. The emotion of enjoyment–joy also helps account for some intrinsically motivated behavior, as does, of course, interest–joy interactions.

An effort will be made to point up important similarities and differences between differential emotions theory and the other theoretical formulations, most of which are in the framework of cognitive psychology. There are certainly some important similarities. As Deci reported, one cognitive approach "notes that intrinsically motivated behaviors are ones which are supposedly *interesting* and *enjoyable* to the actor . . ." (Deci, 1975, p. 149).

Selectivity of Perception and Attention

William James called attention to the fact that some kind of selection process constantly guides perception and attention and thus keeps the brain from treating with equal importance the multitude of stimuli that impinge upon our sensory receptors at all times (see Figure 8-1). "Accentuation and emphasis are present in every perception we have. We find it quite impossible to disperse our attention impartially over a number of impressions" (James, 1890, p. 163). James actually used the term interest, but not systematically and not, strictly speaking, as an explanatory concept. For example, he stated that "thought is always *interested*" and in explaining the different impressions that four different individuals would bring home from a tour of Europe, he said: "Each has selected, out of the same mass of presented objects, those which suited his private *interest* . . ." (James, 1890, p. 165, italics added). It seems quite compatible with James's theorizing to recognize something like an innate emotion of interest that provides the motivational support for the mechanism that executes perceptual and attentional selectivity and brings order as well as excitement to the individual's world.

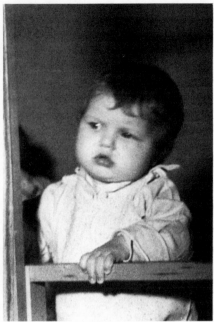

FIGURE 8-1. Russian infants attending selectively to the variety of sights and sounds in their environment.

A number of investigators have documented the fact that selective attention operates in infants from birth (see, for example, Stone, Smith, & Murphy, 1973). From the first hours of life, certain visual patterns are preferred over others (Fantz, 1965), and in early infancy perception and attention guide behavior even in situations where little or no learning has occurred (Gibson, 1969, 1970). "The young infant appears to see things because he explores his surroundings with his eyes, gazing in the direction of various objects or parts of the room and on occasion looking for a longer period in a particular direction as if something of particular interest has caught his attention" (Fantz, 1973, p. 622). Saayman, Ames, and Moppett (1964) have shown that infants as young as twelve weeks can discriminate geometric forms and that the discrimination is in part a function of the increased visual attention elicited by novel stimuli.

Novelty and complexity, two of the principal activators of interest, bear definite though complex relationships to patterns of attention. Chapter 4 discussed infants' selective attention to faces and facelike configurations at various stages of their development and the importance of this phenomenon for social development. A number of investigators of perceptual development and attention in infants have used the term interest to help explain their observations and findings, although they did not define interest as an emotion. For example, Fantz concluded that the infant's "visual *interest* in those configurations which accompany social objects or in those which will later aid in object recognition and spacial orientation, is seen as a type of primitive knowledge of the environment which 'provides a foundation for the vast accumulation of knowledge through experience'" (Fantz, 1973, p. 628, italics added). Gibson (1969, 1970) reached a similar conclusion.

Charlesworth (1968) suggested that more attention to emotions and their facial expressions might facilitate the study of perceptual and cognitive development. He leaned toward accepting the notion that innate mechanisms such as those underlying surprise and interest may help explain adaptive functioning in early infancy. He proposed that further study of these mechanisms and the preprogrammed behavior related to them should balance our study of the role of learning in the ontogenesis of cognition and action.

Cathexis

Brill (1938) introduced the term cathexis (from the Greek "kathexo," to occupy) into the psychoanalytic literature as a translation of Freud's term "besetzung," which connotes a charge or investment of energy.

Freud never gave an unequivocal or operational definition of cathexis, although the concept is central to an understanding of personality dynamics in terms of classical psychoanalytic theory. He explained cathexis as "a sum of psychic energy, which occupies or invests objects or some particular channels" (Freud, 1938, p. 734). Freud elaborated this definition, not so much by further conceptual analysis as by showing how cathexes and the process of cathecting play a role in the distribution and utilization of psychic energy in the id, ego, and superego. Apparently it is possible for an individual to cathect any person, object, idea, or image. Of considerable importance to a possible analogy between cathexis and the emotion of interest, is Freud's notion that an individual can cathect thought or thinking as well as attention and perception. In summary, Freud used the term cathexis to explain how psychic energy is channeled and utilized.

Freud maintained that the development and direction of cathexes were a function of the affective quality of the objects or processes involved. The perception of objects and processes is transposed in the psychic apparatus as either pleasure or pain and "these releases of pleasure and pain automatically regulate the course of the cathectic processes" (Freud, 1938, p. 515). The id, ego, and superego, can cathect objects; the id may cathect images or objects indiscriminately, and it makes no distinction between perceptions and halucinations. The basic aim of the id is instinctual gratification and its cathexes serve this aim. The ego has to come into play in order to cathect cognitive processes and to bring reasoning and judgment to a higher level of development. The ego must also cathect inhibitory processes, that is, form anticathexes in order to restrain the unacceptable sexual and aggressive forces or cathexes of the id. These anticathexes appear as defense mechanisms, which can be analyzed in terms of special interests (or cathexes) that guide thought and action in defense of the ego.

Typically, parents become the first important objects cathected by the infant. Freud thought this was the case because of the infant's dependence upon the parents for the satisfaction of needs. "Later the infant cathects parents' ideals and these become his ego ideals; he cathects their prohibitions and these become his conscience" (Hall and Lindzey, 1970, p. 42).

One of the principal functions of the superego is to form anticathexes to control and restrain the cathexes and instinctual aims of the id. With the formation of the superego, personality dynamics become complicated by interplay of a large number of driving and restraining forces. "In the final analysis the dynamics of personality consist of the interplay of the driving forces, cathexes, and the restraining forces, anticathexes. All of the conflicts within the personality may be reduced to the opposition of these two sets of forces. All prolonged tension is due to the counteraction of a driving force by a restraining force. Whether it would be an anticathexis of the ego as opposed to a cathexis of the id or an anticathexis of the superego as opposed to the cathexis of the ego, the result in terms of tension is the same" (Hall and Lindzey, 1970, p. 43).

There are a number of parallels between the concepts of cathexis and interest–excitement, but there are also some important distinctions between the terms and their implications for personality dynamics, thought, and action. One can cathect virtually anything and one can be interested in virtually anything. A cathected object attracts and holds attention; an object of interest does the same things. The relative inclusiveness of the two terms, however, distinguishes sharply between them. Cathexes may be positive or negative and act either as driving (cathectic) or restraining (anticathectic) forces. On the other hand, interest is a positive emotion that motivates approach, exploration, and creative encounter. Instead of a global concept of "negative interest," differential emotions theory posits the various discrete negative emotions to account for restraining forces, avoidance behavior, and a number of other kinds of thought and action. While in psychoanalysis all personality dynamics can be explained in terms of the interplay of cathexes and anticathexes, interest–excitement is conceived as motivating only that perception, thought, and action not instigated by the biological drives, the other positive affect of joy, and the negative emotions. Nevertheless, interest is considered by far the most prevalent of the two positive emotions and in the normal, healthy person more prevalent than all the negative emotions combined. Except when drive-related behavior becomes critical to survival, interest motivates most of the effort expended in learning, working, exploring, creative endeavor, and recreational activities. Actually, the breadth of the positive motivational functions of the emotion of interest points to another difference between classical psychoanalysis and differential emotions theory, since the former attributes far more pervasiveness and importance to negative motivational conditions than does the latter.

Functional Autonomy, Propriate Striving, and Ego Involvement

G. W. Allport (1937, 1955, 1961) discussed three motivational concepts that relate to intrinsic motivation and bear some similarity to the emotion of interest–excitement. He introduced the principle of functional autonomy to explain how an activity can become an end or goal in itself, even though it may have been engaged in originally for some other reason. For example, a fisherman may first go to sea in order to satisfy survival needs (to make a living), but he later finds that whether or not he needs to continue work simply to find food or earn money, he now likes to go to sea. The fisherman likes the sea because he has developed an interest in it and now finds it continually exciting. Allport introduced the term during his struggle to free psychology from dependence on primary drive concepts and their derivatives as the sole explanatory constructs in learning and personality. Recognizing emotions as motivational concepts is in keeping with Allport's main intent.

The concept of propriate striving also contrasts with the tension-reduction model of motivation that was dominant at the time of Allport's writing. Activities motivated by propriate striving resist equilibrium and tension is maintained rather than reduced. In this concept Allport anticipated many later motivational constructs such as drive-induction (e.g., Sheffield, Roby, & Campbell, 1954), stimulation-seeking (e.g., Hebb, 1955; Zuckerman, 1974), and motivation inherent in information processing (e.g., Hunt, 1965). In illustrating his concept, Allport described the behavior of great explorers such as Amundsen, who had an "insatiable" urge to discover the South Pole. In further elaborating the concept Allport actually used the term interest as a partial synonym: "Along with *striving* we may mention *interest, tendency, disposition, expectation, planning, problem solving,* and *intention*" (1955, p. 51).

In discussing the principles of learning Allport gave great emphasis to the concept of participation. At one level of participation the individual is *task involved,* actively doing something about the object of his attention. One takes an active role in the learning situation and thus acquires information or skills more rapidly and efficiently. At the second and deeper level of participation the individual is *ego involved*. One who is task involved may or may not care very much about what one is doing. The individual who is ego involved cares a great deal; one's actions are at the center of one's attention and effort. In explaining this concept, Allport again made direct use of a concept of interest: "We are obviously speaking now of *interest*. In this chapter we have encountered various principles that claim to be 'the most important' law of learning; but the case of interest is strongest of all. Interest is participation with the deepest levels of motivation" (Allport, 1961, p. 106). Although Allport never discussed interest as an emotion, his use of the term in defining the concepts of functional autonomy, propriate striving, and ego-involved participation clearly gave the concept of interest motivational status and an affective connotation.

Curiosity and the Urge to Explore

The first psychologist to treat curiosity as a major psychological construct was William McDougall. He conceptualized curiosity as an instinct, and in order to appreciate his contribution to the topic it is necessary to consider his view of instincts and their role in human activities. McDougall's concept of instinct is closer to the meaning of this term in contemporary ethology than one might expect. Indeed some biologically oriented behaviorial scientists might consider McDougall's statement of nearly three quarters of a century ago as an accurate prediction: "the recognition of the full scope and function of the human instincts . . . will, I feel sure, appear to those who come after us as the most important advance made by psychology" (1908, p. 24). McDougall defined an instinct "as an inherited or innate psycho-physical disposition which determines its possesser to perceive, and to pay attention to, objects of a certain class, to experience an emotional excitement of a particular quality upon perceiving such an object, and to act in regard to it in a particular manner or at least to experience an impulse to such action" (McDougall, 1908, p. 29). He stressed the importance of the "psychical side of instinctive processes," their affective and cognitive aspects. He recognized the modifiability of instincts through learning and experience, but differed from the contemporary ethologists in his emphasis on the affective component of instinct and in his linking of each principal instinct with a primary emotion.

McDougall considered the emotion component of instincts to be the nucleus of motivation. He defined the instinct of curiosity and the associated emotion of "wonder" as one of the principal instinctive processes in human beings. McDougall thought that curiosity was relatively weak in higher animals, however, due to the pressure of natural selection to restrain an exploratory urge that might needlessly lead the organism into dangerous situations. Apparently McDougall did not weigh the need for restraint against the possible benefits of exploration and beneficial discoveries.

McDougall originated several ideas about curiosity that have been adopted by contemporary theorists and investigators. First, he recognized the role of novelty in instigating curiosity: "The native excitant of the instinct would seem to be any object similar to, yet perceptably different from, familiar objects habitually noticed" (p. 57). Second, he recognized, as have Berlyne (1950) and Tomkins (1962), the close and unstable equilibrium that exists between curiosity (or interest) and fear and the similarity between "excitants" of the two states. His belief that lesser degrees of strangeness or unusualness elicited curiosity and greater degrees fear, presages Tomkins's notion that the activation of interest and fear differs only in terms of the steepness of the gradient of stimulation.

McDougall's work also contains precursors of Tomkins's (1962) ideas about the role of interest in intellectual development and cultural evolution and of Murphy's (1958) notions about the importance for humanity of the urge to discover. "The instinct of curiosity is at the base of man's most splendid achievements, for rooted in it are his speculative and scientific tendencies." McDougall thought that the place of a society in the scale of civilization could be judged by the prevalence of curiosity among its people and that the rise and fall of civilizations were correlated with the degree to which the great minds of the time were following the urge to be speculative and adventuresome rather than brood over the achievements of the past. He thought that curiosity made its greatest contribution by leading to improvements in the conception of causation, which he saw as the fundamental factor in increasing the level of civilization. McDougall argued that continued progress was possible only in a culture where the stabilizing and conservative functions of religious sentiment balanced the actions stimulated by curiosity and the spirit of inquiry.

Berlyne probably ranks first among contemporary contributors to theory and research on curiosity. His definition of curiosity does not differ much in substance from that of McDougall and even less from a definition by Shand (1914). Shand (cited in Berlyne, 1950) defined curiosity as a "primary emotion" consisting of a "simple impulse to know, instinctively governing and sustaining the attention, and evoking those bodily movements which will enable us to gain fuller aquaintance with the object" (Shand, 1914, pp. 438ff.; Berlyne, 1950, p. 69). In his early writings, Berlyne considered interest as more or less synonymous with curiosity. In refuting Freud's notion that curiosity is first awakened by sexual problems Berlyne noted that Piaget and many other observers of early childhood had reported intensive curiosity and investigatory activity in children long before the advent of speech.

Berlyne's early theory of curiosity consisted of two main ideas. First, a novel stimulus elicits a drive-stimulus-producing response (curiosity) which diminishes with continued exposure to the stimulus. Second, an organism will act in relation to a curiosity-arousing stimulus so as to increase stimulation.

Berlyne has found some support for his hypotheses in experiments with lower species and with human beings (see Berlyne, 1960). Although he conceptualized curiosity as a response, he attributed to it a stimulus-producing characteristic and thus gave it motivational status. He assumed that curiosity was innate, but that it could also be acquired.

Arousal and Intrinsic Motivation

In later work Berlyne (1960, 1967) elaborated and extended his early theory of curiosity in an effort to explain the stimulus selection process in perceptual and intellectual activities that occur "in the absence of the more obvious sources of motivation" (1960, p. 6). Novelty continued to be a central concept but he recognized three supplementary variables: change, surprisingness and incongruity. He proposed novelty, uncertainty, complexity, and conflict (defined broadly as a need to choose between alternatives) as the major collative variables in explaining stimulus selection, and attention and exploratory behavior as the main process variables. He considered activity of the brain stem reticular formation as the neurological underpinning of attention; hence, anything that elicits arousal also elicits attention. He suggested that the two processes that subserve selective attention were central processes like gating or filtering. Exploratory behavior, like attention, is determined by the variables of novelty, uncertainty, complexity, and conflict. Since the late 1950s Berlyne has made the concept of arousal more and more central in his general theory of motivation and in explaining the motivation involved in high-order human functions such as symbolic thought and creativity.

Types of Arousal and Their Relationships to Drive Feelings and Emotion

Berlyne dismissed the early notion of arousal as a clear-cut unitary variable and recognized different types of arousal. He noted that Lacey had specified three types—autonomic, electrocortical, and behavioral—each functionally and anatomically separable. Different types of arousal are made possible by considerable differentiation of structure and formation within the reticular formation (Anokhin, 1958; Olds & Peretz, 1960) and by contributions to arousal from the hypothalamus (Gellhorn, 1961), the limbic system (MacLean, 1949), and the specific lemniscal sensory pathways

(Sprague, Chambers, & Stellar, 1961). The findings of the foregoing investigations are also consistent with the differential emotions theory position that each of the emotions has a unique arousal pattern or neurophysiological basis; the evidence for discrete and universal facial expression indicates that the face–brain feedback (and hence cortical activity) is different for each of the fundamental emotions.

Although he did not treat it in any great detail, Berlyne recognized the possibility that different types of arousal may correspond to different feelings and emotions ("psychological states"). He suggested that specific drives such as hunger and pain and specific emotions such as fear and anger have some common effect on certain indexes of arousal. "But each of them can be expected to implement its characteristic modulation of the arousal pattern, heightening certain component indexes and dampening others, as well as producing specialized psychophysiological effects that are not included among the widely used indexes of overall arousal" (1967, p. 15). Berlyne has not yet elaborated on this seminal idea, but he did note that specific drive conditions have been shown to increase arousal (see Berlyne, 1960). The evidence he cited did not clearly indicate whether the drive condition is increasing some undifferentiated arousal state or undifferentiated arousal is amplifying the drive. Differential emotions theory holds that the latter is more likely to be the case, though it allows for the possibility that there can be a reciprocal relationship between a specific drive or a specific emotion on the one hand and undifferentiated arousal on the other.

Determinants of Arousal

Berlyne recognized three types of determinants of arousal. First, there are psychophysical variables that depend primarily on the quantity or quality of stimulation and to some extent perhaps on other physical and chemical properties of stimulus objects. Second, there are the "ethological variables," those related to specific requirements of survival; and these include specific drive states such as thirst and sexual appetite and specific emotions such as fear and anger. Here Berlyne seems to acknowledge specific drives and emotions as activators (or amplifiers) of arousal. Third, there are the collative variables that influence stimulus selection, curiosity, and exploratory behavior—novelty, change, complexity, and incongruity, uncertainty, and conflict. It is this class of variables that relates the concept of arousal to curiosity (interest), exploratory activity, and investigatory activity.

Berlyne affirms that all forms of motivation and reinforcement operate through some type of neurophysiological arousal. A motivating or reinforcing state may derive from either an increase or a decrease in arousal, but curiosity and exploratory-investigatory activities are considered functions of stimulation (arousal) increase.

Nunnally and his co-workers carried out a series of experiments on the effects of novelty and complexity on visual exploration. Their results led them to question the emphasis of Berlyne and others on the role of arousal or changes in arousal in intrinsic motivation. They thought the results of their experiments in visual exploration could "be explained by a simple principle: information conflict and other types of novelty elicit and hold attention" (Nunnally & Lemond, 1973, p. 105). Rather than viewing the response to novelty or information conflict as a result of a change in arousal or some other internal bodily state, Nunnally made a case for explaining such responses in terms of a human tropism for attending to and trying to make sense of novel objects and events (Nunnally, 1972). Kagan's (1972) position and the Driscoll–Lanzetta and Hawkins–Lanzetta findings are congruent with Nunnally's de-emphasis of arousal. The apparent conflict, however, may be a result of an inadequate psychophysiological technology or in the choice of arousal indexes.

Arousal, Epistemic Behavior, and Learning

Berlyne believes, as do Hebb and Thompson (1954) and others, that over the long haul organisms strive for an optimal level of arousal. What is optimal at any given time seems to be variable, but for the most part it is intermediate between high and low states of arousal. Stimuli, depending upon their arousal potential (a function of the collative variables), attract and hold attention, and organisms respond to the stimuli in such a way as to regulate arousal and keep it in the vicinity of the optimal level. Perceptual curiosity is considered a high arousal state that is relieved by specific exploration. The exploration leads to stimulation decrease and habituation. In a low state of arousal (boredom), organisms may respond to stimuli with high arousal potentials in order to increase arousal toward the higher levels. Epistemic behavior, that which augments knowledge, is seen as a function of epistemic curiosity resulting from conceptual conflict. Berlyne elaborates his notion of conceptual conflict by delineating several types: doubt, perplexity, contradiction, incongruity, confusion, irrelevance. Any one of these types of conceptual conflict will increase perceptual curiosity (and arousal) which is reduced by the acquisition of knowledge. Berlyne's idea of conceptual conflict might correspond to the differential emotions theory notion of an affective–cognitive interaction which involves affect incongruent with the related cognition or two opposing affects.

Berlyne reviewed a number of studies consistent with his notion that the relationship between learning and arousal is best described by an inverted U-curve. Some of his data, however, were not completely consistent with this idea. In some experiments he found an increasing monotonic relationship between judged "interestingness" and exploratory behavior. Consistent with differential emotions theory, no data support the idea that anything can be too interesting to explore. There is the possibility that excitement, the most intense form of interest, can reach a point where learning, exploration, or performance might become less efficient.

The Effectance Urge: The Motivational Aspect of Competence

In a cogent integrative paper on motivation, White (1959) discussed the shortcomings of drive theories (mainly those following the tradition of Hull and Freud) and pointed up several weaknesses, particularly in relation to the achievement of competence. His carefully documented article will undoubtedly be counted as one of the significant contributions to the trend away from drive reduction theory toward more complex conceptualizations of motivation.

White's effort continued the Allport tradition of seeking motivational variables in addition to those that are rooted in tissue deficit. He cited the early work of Berlyne (1950, 1955) and Butler (1953) which showed that animals would respond (discriminate, perform) in the absence of any known drive or tissue deficit. He also cited evidence in support of Woodworth's (1958) notion that "the exploratory tendency" does not become extinguished, although exploration of a specific object decreases as familiarity increases. White also reviewed the evidence in support of the notion that even without the presence of novel objects that instigate exploration, organisms will manipulate objects (Harlow, 1953) or even learn an instrumental response in order to gain access to an activity wheel where they can run (Kagan & Berkun, 1954). He related these findings on the "exploratory" ("manipulatory, activity") drive to investigations which suggest that reinforcement or reward is not necessarily identifiable with drive or need reduction (see Chapter 7).

In tracing the history of his concept of effectance motivation, White considered as related ideas the "instinct to master" (Hendrick, 1942), the "pleasure of enjoying one's abilities" (Fenichel, 1945), the "autonomous factor in ego development" (Hartman, 1950), "functional autonomy" (Allport, 1937), and the "sense of initiative" (Erickson, 1956). While theorists such as Hartman were giving more importance to an active autonomous ego, "general psychology began more frequently to acknowledge that such things as solving problems and running mild risks are inherently rewarding . . ." (Hebb & Thompson, 1954, p. 551). Hebb (1949) attempted to explain the organism's sustained interest in an object as a neurological state in which "phase sequences" are relatively complex and increasing in complexity through the establishing of new internal relations. Hebb's reasoning harked back to McDougall when he argued that this neurological state and the accompanying psychological state of continuing interest results from "differences-in-sameness" in the stimulus field.

In conclusion, White argued that the "neo-drives" or motives termed exploration, curiosity, manipulation, and mastery should be combined into the single concept of effectance—a motivation for competence. He assumed that effectance motivation is neurogenic: "its 'energies' being simply those of the living cells that make up the nervous system . . . the effectance urge represents what the neuromuscular system wants to do when it is otherwise unoccupied or is gently stimulated by the environment" (White, 1961, p. 315). Although he favored the general concept of effectance motivation, he thought that this type of motivation, while undifferentiated in infancy and childhood, becomes distinguishable in adulthood as various motives such as cognizance, mastery, and achievement. White's definition of effectance motivation has much in common with Tomkins's (1962) original elaboration of the concept of interest–excitement as the motivational condition that sustains exploration and constructive endeavor. White noted that "effectance motivation may lead to continuing exploratory *interests* or active adventures" and contribute "significantly to those feelings of *interest* which often sustain us so well in day-to-day actions . . ." (White, 1961, pp. 316–317, italics added).

The Yen to Discovery

Murphy (1958) conceptualized the affective tendency to explore as the "urge toward discovery." Taking an evolutionary-biosocial perspective Murphy explained his concept in the context of long term changes in the biosocial nature of human beings. He described three kinds of human nature that are correlated with biosocial evolution. The first human nature is defined by two broad principles, one that relates to a general biochemical and nervous organization that gives human beings a certain peculiar capacity for knowing, feeling, and acting and another that relates the processes that insure some individuality. Even the first human nature had, as part of its distinctiveness or humanness, keener exploratory functions than those of other animals. The second human nature came with the emergence of culture. It is characterized by those largely acquired phenomena relating to language, physical invention, religion, ethics, scientific, and mathematical reasoning, and other information, values, and norms that are transmitted from generation to generation. The third human nature is linked to the urge toward discovery. Murphy described this urge toward discovery as a "living curiosity beginning with a sort of 'freeing of intelligence' from cultural clamps and moving forward in a positive way activated by thirst for contact with the world and for understanding and making sense of it . . . (p. 19)." Murphy spoke of the yen to discovery as a function of deep forces within us that strive to break through the mold of culture, as the creative thrust of understanding.

In discussing the nature of the impulse toward discovery, Murphy rejected the temptation to label it as a curiosity drive. He thought such a name might suppress the need to analyze and understand its many unknown aspects. However, by defining it as a "craving to know and understand" (p. 179), it is congruent with Berlyne's concept of epistemic curiosity.

Murphy maintained that there was a threefold basis for the yen to discovery: "(1) the visceral drives; (2) the love of order; (3) resonance to the nature and structure of that which surrounds us" (p. 179). All these components were present in the first human nature, were reworked and enriched by culture in the second human nature, and finally began to transform the first two human natures into the third. In support of the idea of a connection between the visceral drives and the impulse toward discovery, Murphy pointed to the clinical data of psychoanalysis and ethology which "underscore the reality of veiled instinctual satisfaction from the rhythms of wind and water . . ." (p. 179). In linking the visceral drives to the love of order he pointed out the "goodness of form" and the beautiful rhythms of courtship behavior in birds and insects. Regarding the third basis for the yen to discovery he noted: "the more complex the central nervous system as we go from simpler to higher animals, the more there is of the response to anything and everything as *exciting* and *interesting*. . ." (p. 180, italics added).

Throughout his discussion of the urge toward discovery Murphy used the terms interest and excitement to help define and delineate his concept. He looked upon the yen to discovery as the apex of human development, the third human nature, "the craving for sensory and motor contact and for understanding and manipulating the world . . ." (p. 180). At one point he described this yen to discovery as a "nonspecific definition of human *interest* which makes the human constitution capable of almost unlimited resonance . . ." (p. 179, italics added).

Expectation and Hope

The emotion of interest bears a relationship to the concepts of expectation and hope; however, the interrelationships of these concepts cannot presently be stated precisely. The concept of expectancy has not yet

enjoyed wide acceptance as a theoretical construct, although some theorists have attempted to treat it systematically. For example, Epstein (1972)
sees expectancy as a parameter of arousal. "The violation of expectancy is
a sufficient, although not a necessary, condition for producing an increase
in arousal, and this applies to both the small increases in arousal associated
with orienting responses, and to the larger increases associated with anxiety" (p. 314). According to Epstein, expectancies are not only involved in
changes in arousal but also in the control or inhibition of the arousal state.

One of the problems in developing a systematic definition of expectancy is the fact that one can "expect" the best or the worst or anything in
between, and what is expected may be associated with or connote any of
the positive or negative emotions. Thus in terms of differential emotions
theory expectancy may be defined as a type of interest–cognition interaction. If this affective–cognitive interaction is negative in nature it may
produce fear. On the other hand, if the affective–cognitive interaction is
positive it may result in hope.

Although hope as generally understood by people is of vital importance in human life, it has received very little attention from scientists.
Again, part of the problem has been that of capturing this concept in a
definition that lends itself to systematic investigation. Stotland (1969) has
devoted an entire volume to the psychology of hope. He defined hope in
terms of expectation about goal attainment. One has hope when one has an
expectation greater than zero about achieving a goal. One of his basic
propositions is that organisms are goal oriented, and motivation to achieve
a goal is a joint function of the perceived possibility of attaining it and the
perceived importance of it. Important goals with high possibilities of attainment (high hope) generate positive affect (joy, pleasure); important goals
with a low probability of attainment (little hope) generate anxiety or
depression. Stotland's theory, like differential emotions theory, links affect
and cognition in defining the concept of hope. In applying his psychology of
hope to psychopathology, Stotland argued that a schizophrenic is one who
has lost hope of goal achievement in the real world and one who, as a
consequence, has created his own unreal world. Depression is seen as
another form of hopelessness.

Mowrer (1960a) sees hope as one of the four basic emotions that
instigate and direct behavior. Mowrer interprets emotions as conditionable
responses and he sees hope as the response to a type of secondary
reinforcement. He distinguished two types of secondary reinforcement.
Type one is the reward or satisfaction experienced when a danger signal
terminates (relief is implied). Type two is the reward or satisfaction experienced when a stimulus signals the imminent occurrence of a *desired* event
(hope is implied). Thus Mowrer, too, has defined hope in terms of some
kind of affective–cognitive interaction. The usefulness of Mowrer's defini-

tion of hope depends upon how broadly one wishes to apply the concept of secondary reinforcement. Mowrer sees secondary reinforcement as providing stimulation (rather than reduction in stimulation); differential emotions theory holds that the affective component of hope (interest) provides stimulation.

In one respect Mowrer's formulation of the affective component of hope is similar to the concept of interest–excitement. In emotion theory interest and fear are dynamically related in several ways. At the neurophysiological level the activation of interest and fear is differentiated in terms of the steepness of the gradient of stimulation, and fear reduction may result in excitement. In a somewhat similar fashion Mowrer reasoned as follows: "The present analysis assumes that type-two secondary reinforcement (hope) consists of a reduction in drive fear, cued off by some stimulus or situation which has commonly been associated with the primary-drive reduction, whereas common observation suggests that the appearance of such a stimulus or situation often produces in the subject, not a relaxation (as the notion of drive-fear reduction would seem to require), but a state of excitement and heightened activity" (Mowrer 1960a, p. 196). He recognizes the similarity between his ideas and those of Tolman, who defined such internal (affective) events as "fear cognitions." By adding an affective or emotional connotation, Mowrer thought he was conceptualizing such internal events (e.g., hopes and fears) more dynamically. The concept of hope as an affective–cognitive interaction would probably be acceptable to Mowrer.

Motivation Inherent in Information Processing

J. McV. Hunt (1965) was one of the first to treat the concept of intrinsic motivation in a systematic and detailed fashion. Hunt defined it as the motivation inherent in information processing. He attempted to apply this concept in answering questions of how behavior is instigated, energized, and directed, and in accounting for choice of response, choice of goals, and behavioral change (or learning), and the persistence of goal-seeking behavior. His answers as they relate primarily to activities such as play and exploration and manipulation will be summarized briefly. Behavior is instigated by incongruity between the input (sensory data, information) and an internal norm or standard. The standard may be genetically or experientially determined. Behavior is energized by arousal that results from the incongruity. This is an emotional arousal that is "inherent within organisms' informational interaction with their circumstances" (Hunt, 1965, p. 212). Behavior is directed toward or away from the object or situation depending upon the hedonic value (positiveness or negativeness) of the emotional arousal. Choice of response is the function of such factors as change or novelty or, in other words, by the attention value and arousal potential of the stimulus. In summary, choices are based on informational interaction of the organism with its circumstances, and behavior change and learning are motivated by "an optimal standard of incongruity." In adopting this latter explanatory construct, Hunt was rejecting the concept of optimum level of arousal (e.g., Hebb, 1955; Berlyne, 1967; McClelland et al., 1953). Hunt's formulation of intrinsic motivation is more forthright cognitive formulation. For him it is cognitive incongruity or uncertainty that motivates behavior, not the quantitative level of some physiological state such as activation or arousal. He conceives the latter as effects rather than causes.

Affect-Determined Intrinsic Motivation

Deci (1975) outlined a general theory of motivation that he preferred to describe as a cognitive approach. Close examination of his concepts and principles, however, suggests that the theory is more fundamentally affective than cognitive. Deci's theory is a comprehensive analysis of intrinsic motivation and it either incorporates or offers alternative explanations for many of the features of the theories previously discussed in this chapter.

Deci summarized his model as follows. Stimulus inputs create an "awareness of potential satisfaction which instigates and energizes a goal-directed sequence" (Deci, 1975, p. 123). "Awareness of potential satisfaction" is the basic motivational condition. This awareness can be instigated by stimulus inputs (cues, information from the environment), (a) drives (tissue deficit), (b) affects (a term Deci equates with emotion), or (c) "the intrinsic need for feelings of competence and self-determination." Awareness of potential satisfaction "causes the person to establish goals which he expects will lead to the reward, and hence the satisfaction, which he became aware of in the previous step" (p. 123). Goals provide direction for the behavior which is terminated upon achievement of the goal. Behavior may be followed by rewards: extrinsic rewards in the case of drives, affective rewards in the case of underlying emotion, or intrinsic rewards in the case of desire for competence or self-determination. Rewards lead to satisfaction.

Conditions That Influence Intrinsic Motivation

Deci extended his theory of intrinsic motivation with three propositions (cognitive evaluation theory) that indicate what conditions or situations influence intrinsic motivation. The first proposition suggests that intrinsic motivation is decreased when an individual perceives a change in the locus of causality from internal to external. The second maintains that intrinsic motivation increases as a person's feelings of competence and self-determination are increased. The third proposition assumes that every reward has both a "controlling aspect" and an "informational aspect." The greater the salience of the controlling aspect the more likely the individual will change his perception of the locus of causality which in turn affects intrinsic motivation. Greater salience of the informational aspect leads to changes in feelings of competence and self-determination, which also affect intrinsic motivation. Deci reviewed a number of empirical studies in support of each of these propositions. In studies relating to proposition 3 he found a sex difference. Positive feedback (verbal encouragement or praise) enhanced intrinsic motivation in men but decreased it in women. He explained the difference largely in terms of the greater field dependence of females, which he attributed to the socialization process. In his words, the controlling aspect of positive feedback was more salient for women than for men, and thus for women it shifted the perceived locus of causality from internal to external and decreased their intrinsic motivation.

The Primacy of Affect

The notion that Deci's theory gives affect primacy over cognition is supported by his contention that "awareness of potential satisfaction" is a function of the cues or information derived from "drives, intrinsic motivation, and affective states" (p. 99). All three of these are affective in nature; they are motivational conditions, and they stand in contrast to perceptual or cognitive phenomena. Even intrinsic motivation is defined by Deci in terms of a *need* (want, desire) for a *feeling* of competence and self-determination. The concepts of need, want, and desire are generally considered as affective in nature, or at least as having an affective component.

In addition to the fact that his "prime movers" of behavior can be classified as affective in nature, Deci, in contrast to the other theorists reviewed in this chapter, gives a rather prominent place to emotions in his theory of motivation. His position is similar to differential emotions theory in recognizing emotions as motivational and in recognizing the interactive nature of emotion, cognition, and action: "Emotions are both antecedents and consequences of behaviors" (p. 102).

Although not acknowledged by Deci, his classification of motivational concepts is quite similar to that of differential emotions theory as detailed in Chapter 3 and elsewhere (Tomkins, 1962; Izard, 1971). Both theories recognize the motivational properties of drives and emotions. Deci's use of the term affect is similar in connotation to the broad categories of positive and negative emotion in differential emotions theory, but

Deci does not deal explicitly with specific emotions. Finally, Deci's concept of "awareness of potential satisfaction" is similar to the differential emotions theory concept of affective–cognitive interactions.

Perhaps the thing that keeps Deci's theory within a cognitive framework is his emphasis on cognition in his key motivational construct. Although he indicates that the "awareness of potential satisfaction" is generated by affects (drives, feelings, emotions), he thinks their *cognitive representation* is the most significant aspect of motivation. Differential emotions theory also recognizes the great importance of cognition, but it stresses the importance of interaction between affect and cognition in the development of the many motives that characterize human behavior.

Deci's emphasis on the future aspect of motivation (awareness of *potential* satisfaction) also helps bring his formulation within the cognitive camp. The phrase suggests cognitive processes (anticipation or expectation), but it is similar to the differential emotions theory idea of emotion anticipation (an affect–cognition interaction) as a motivational condition.

Some Similarities and Differences between Deci's Approach and Differential Emotions Theory

One might argue that the main difference between Deci's position and differential emotions theory is partly a matter of what to call most basic, affective states or cognitive representation of affective states. But even if this were true a significant difference remains. Deci's system focuses only on accounting for the behavior which differential emotions theory accounts for largely in terms of a single emotion, interest–excitement, and its interaction with cognition and action. Differential emotions theory goes on to consider each of the discrete emotions as having motivational significance for particular realms of behavior. Further, Deci, like some affective theorists (e.g., McClelland *et al.*, 1953), admittedly takes a frankly hedonistic position, while differential emotions theory does not.

In the latter framework, day-to-day perception, cognition, and action is explained by a multiplicity of affects and affect–cognition interactions, only some of which can be organized in terms of hedonism. To say that the neonate's visual exploration of his environment is a search for pleasure or comfort or pain avoidance is hardly convincing. Equally weak is an explanation of the day-to-day activities involved in extended adventures in the face of painful, frightening, and distressing hardships in terms of a hedonic end-state or its anticipation. To invoke a pleasurable or hedonic end-state as the ultimate human goal seems to fly in the face of much of the evidence for a motivational concept like intrinsic motivation or interest–excitement, and it does not fit well into an evolutionary account of human development. In evolutionary perspective there were undoubtedly many occasions when adaptive behavior was totally unrelated to positive or negative hedonic tone or their anticipation. The possible maladaptive consequences of continual or extended states of joy will be discussed in Chapter 9.

Summary

A series of excellent experiments by Harlow, Montgomery, Butler, Berlyne, and others started a shift away from drive reduction theory to more complex conceptualizations of motivation. These experiments showed that a number of different types of behavior, especially exploratory or investigatory activity, occurred in the absence of any known drive and would reoccur without apparent relationship to drive or tension reduction. The trend begun by these pivotal studies produced a number of important new models for linking motivation and behavior. Most of these formulations have been subsumed under the rubric of intrinsic motivation. They have in common an aim to explain exploration, investigation, and creative thought and action that occur not only in the absence of known drives and without the contingency of drive or tension reduction, but sometimes in harmony with, or in search of, an increase in stimulation.

William James paved the way for new formulations with his idea that perception and attention operate selectively. It is easy to infer from James's writing that it is one's interest that guides one's perception and thought and focuses one's attention. In the past decade numerous studies have shown that selective attention operates in infants from the very beginning of life. One of these investigators (Charlesworth, 1968) suggested that more attention to emotions and their facial expressions might facilitate the study of perceptual and cognitive development.

Some analogies can be drawn between Freud's concept of positive cathectic processes and the development of interest–cognition interactions. Allport's concepts of functional autonomy, propriate striving, and ego-involving participation provide substance for theories of intrinsic motivation and have some of the characteristics of the emotion of interest–excitement. Allport's ideas contributed to our understanding of the behavior that occurs in the absence of drive, in the presence of increased stimulation, and that continues in spite of high drive states and other negative affects.

Building on the pioneering and insightful observations of McDougall, Berlyne gave impetus to the study of curiosity and novelty and their relationship to exploratory and investigatory behavior. He established the case for placing these phenomena at the center of drive-free, constructive, creative activities.

In later works Berlyne made the concept of arousal central to his theory of a motivation. His trenchant analysis of arousal allowed for the possibility of different types of arousal, including emotion-specific arousal states. Berlyne recognized incongruity or conceptual conflict as one of the important determinants of arousal; he also noted a relationship between the arousal potential of an object or situation and its judged "interestingness."

White made a strong case for the inadequacies of drive reduction theory and introduced the concept of competence or effectance motivation. His definition of this concept links various concepts of intrinsic motivation and the differential emotions theory concept of interest–excitement. Murphy introduced a similar idea, the "urge toward discovery." He put his notion in an evolutionary-biological perspective, saw it as the apex of human development, and described it as a nonspecific definition of human interest that resonates to an infinite variety of things and supports constructive endeavor. Working within quite different theoretical frameworks, Stotland and Mowrer presented concepts of hope that bear some similarity to concepts of intrinsic motivation and the affect of interest.

J. McV. Hunt defines intrinsic motivation as the motivation inherent in information processing. He sees incongruity as the source of an emotional arousal which brings about efforts to reduce the incongruity or to bring it in line with some optimal standard. Hunt made an excellent analysis of the processes involved in the development of intrinsic motivation in infants.

Deci presented a very good review of intrinsic motivational concepts and research and then proposed his own theory in which awareness of potential satisfaction is the basic motivational condition. Unlike other intrinsic motivation theorists, Deci gives emotions and other affective states a prominent place in his theory and assumes that they are among the basic determinants of his key motivational condition—awareness of potential satisfaction. It appears to me that Deci's concept of awareness of potential satisfaction is similar to the differential emotions theory concept of affective–cognitive interaction.

A review of the concepts related to intrinsic motivation revealed a number of ideas that overlap with the substance of differential emotions theory, particularly with respect to the role of interest–excitement in intellectual, artistic, and creative thought and action. The delineation of the concept of interest–excitement in Chapter 9 will attempt to provide a comprehensive model for explaining much of what intrinsic motivation theorists try to explain.

9

INTEREST–EXCITEMENT AS FUNDAMENTAL MOTIVATION

Chapter 6 presented the case for the postulate that some affect or combination of affects exist in ordinary states of consciousness at all times and that the most frequently involved affect is interest. Among the theories that support this assumption, G. W. Allport's (1955, 1961) is particularly relevant here. He maintained that human activities that lead to personal growth and creativity are accompanied by a type of tension or excitement. "It is only through risk taking and variation that growth can occur. But risk taking and variation are fraught with new and often avoidable tensions which, however, we scorn to avoid" (1955, p. 6). Allport was describing human beings' penchant for investigatory and exploratory activity and his well-chosen illustrative material helped document his point that growth motives are characterized by a tension that sustains behavior directed toward distant and sometimes unattainable goals. His description of the key motivational condition involved in personal growth, exploration, and creative endeavor seems quite similar to the Tomkins–Izard definition of the emotion of interest–excitement.

In addition to the theoretical arguments for the continual presence of affect in ordinary states of consciousness, studies with affect and mood scales lend empirical support (Nowlis, 1965; Wessman & Ricks, 1966). In administering the Differential Emotions Scale to several large samples of high school and college students under instructions simply to rate their emotions and feelings at the present time, no individual ever failed to indicate the presence of one or more emotions, and interest was typically elevated (Izard, Dougherty, Bloxom, & Kotsch, 1974).

Differential emotions theory assumes that interest is the most prevalent motivational condition for the day-to-day functioning of normal human beings. It is often in combination, and sometimes in conflict, with one or more of the other affects and it continually interacts with perceptual–cognitive processes. Interest–cognition interactions that frequently recur form the affective–cognitive orientations or structures that characterize the constructive and creative activities of the healthy individual. To the extent that one is free of survival needs and negative emotions, one is free to act in relation to the positive motivational thrust of interest–excitement and interest-dominated affective–cognitive structures. Joy, the other positive emotion, plays only a secondary role in supporting constructive, creative endeavor (see Chapter 10).

The emotion of interest has motivational properties similar to those of the concepts of intrinsic motivation discussed in the preceding chapter. The emotion–cognition model differs from most of the intrinsic motivation formulations in one important respect—it holds that emotions are the primal and fundamental motivational variables and that they are present in consciousness prior to "input," "information," or "information processing." Affect not only precedes input, but it selects and influences (regulates) input via its relationship with perceptual processes. The information processing or cognitive awareness stressed in the intrinsic motivation models are similar in effect to the differential emotions theory concept of affective–cognitive interactions, some of which will recur frequently and become affective–cognitive orientations or traitlike structures of the personality. Despite theoretical differences, much of the empirical support for intrinsic motivation formulations is congruent with the affect–cognition interaction model.

Actually, as indicated in the preceding section, several of the intrinsic motivation models make explicit their reliance, in some degree, on an emotion or affect concept (e.g., McDougall, 1908; Hunt, 1965; Deci, 1975). Emotion as a component of intrinsic motivation is implicit in the ideas of most of the other theorists (especially Allport, 1937; White, 1959; Murphy, 1958). Theorists who depend on a concept of arousal in explaining intrinsic motivation (e.g., Berlyne, 1967) are at least dealing with a condition that could be determined or influenced by emotion.

The Characteristics of Interest–Excitement

Interest is the most frequently experienced positive emotion. It is an extremely important motivation in the development of skills, competencies, and intelligence. Interest is the only motivation that can sustain day-to-day work in a healthy fashion. It is essential for creativity.

The emotion of interest should not be confused with the orientation reflex. If a hungry infant's cheek is touched by the nipple it will reflexively orient the mouth toward the nipple. Auditory stimulation will activate orienting reactions in one- to five-day-old infants (Sameroff, 1971). In the visual system a bright object will usually cause the infant or adult to orient in the direction of the bright object. There are also involuntary orienting reflexes that operate for the senses of hearing and touch. These motor reflexes may subserve and support interest. Interest combined with these orienting reflexes "enables the individual to sustain attention to complex objects" (Tomkins, 1962, p. 338).

In some cases the emotion of interest may initiate the orientation reflex, and the role of the orientation reflex, then, is to direct the head and eyes toward the object of interest. Interest is distinguishable from the orientation reflex since it can be activated by imagery and memory, both of which can occur without external stimulation. Further, shifting of the eyes away from the external object may be indicative of a high degree of interest in the object, since shifting away gives time for rehearsal and reflection on information about the object (Meskin & Singer, 1974). Finally, interest in ideas requires no particular orientation of the head in space.

Interest should not be confused with surprise or startle, although surprise also tends to give the individual the appearance of being grossly absorbed by the object and of rapid orientation toward the object for increased input from the object.

The emotion of interest, like all of the fundamental emotions, is receptive to nonspecific amplification by the brain stem reticular activating system. It is very important in the understanding of interest (or any fundamental emotion) to see the emotion as separate and distinct from its amplification, and thus distinct from what is usually termed activation or arousal.

When the emotion of interest is using the visual system, the eyes tend to fixate on the object and quickly explore it. While the eyes are fixated the interested person is caught and fascinated. When the eyes are exploring, the individual is actively working to increase his knowledge and experience with the object (Tomkins, 1962, p. 340). In principle, interest uses the other sensory systems in a similar fashion.

The Activation of Interest

A detailed discussion of the activation of emotions and the causes of emotions was presented in Chapter 3. This section briefly describes the activation and causes of the emotion of interest–excitement. The activation of an emotion at the neurological level results from the selective activity of receptor organs, coordinated changes in the level or gradient of neural stimulation, and subsequent activity in certain neural pathways and brain mechanisms. The causes of emotion activation typically (though not necessarily) involve perceptual–cognitive processes, person–environment interactions, or both. Such causes, as well as other affects and a limited number of innate releasers, lead to changes in the nervous system that actually activate the emotion process.

The activation of interest (at the neurological level) involves a moderate increase in the density of neural firing. This is best understood if we picture the individual in a relatively relaxed state or even in a state of enjoyment. In order for the individual to experience the emotion of interest something has to happen which brings about an increase in neural activity. Tomkins (1962) defines density of neural firing as the number of neural impulses per unit of time and maintains that the number has to increase in order for interest in a specific object to be activated. However, he also suggests that a shift downward from the steeper gradients of neural firing in fear or startle can also activate interest. Since interest is frequently present in consciousness to some degree, the principles of activation apply most often to shifts in interest from one thing to another.

The Conscious Causes of Interest

It is important to distinguish between neural activation of emotion and the causes or antecedents of emotion activation. For example, perception (or appraisal) of a novel situation may lead to a moderate increase in neural stimulation. The appraisal may be considered a cause, but the change in gradient of stimulation is the interest activator. As explained in Chapter 3, such a perceptual or appraisal process is only one of the many antecedents or causes of emotion activation.

At the conscious level perception of change and novelty is a key determinant of interest. One becomes interested in what is new and different. One is also interested by the conception of possibility. The change or novelty may relate to something outside one's self or may emerge from within by way of imaging, memory, and thinking.

A subtle and pervasive cause or amplifier of interest is self-generated imagery (including fantasy, daydreaming) that is often related to novelty or change but which is more particularly related to goals (Singer, 1966), or as Tomkins (1962) put it, to what is possible. The term goal in this case implies a goal-concept or goal-image that is constantly subject to change—hence its power as cause of interest. Over time, individuals entertain numerous goal-images that are vested with interest and interest-arousal potential and that change as the person works toward goal realization. Achievement of a goal-object that approximately matches the goal-image usually results in shifts of interest toward other goal images. Activity in pursuit of a goal-image may appear as stimulation-seeking behavior (see Zuckerman, 1973), since a low level of interest may increase to excitement as the individual becomes immersed in the relevant actions.

What It Looks Like to Be Interested

At the expressive level interest is difficult to define precisely because the facial patterns in interest are not as distinct as they are in many of the other emotions. The innate expression probably involves a slight raising (or lowering) of the eyebrows and a slight widening (or narrowing) of the eyelid opening as though to increase the field of vision (or sharpen the focus of the eyes). Some of the facial activity in interest consists of increased muscle tone, without readily observable movement. In general the interested person takes on the countenance of a person who is tracking, looking, listening, and maintaining a high degree of attention and alertness. The person shows signs of curiosity or fascination. A partial exception to this is the case of interest in inner experience (fantasies, daydreams) which may sometimes occur when the eyes are closed. Figure 9-1 shows several examples of the expression of interest.

Hass (1970) made observations on the expression of interest in a number of complex and simple cultures. His description of interest expression has elements in common with the earlier description of Tomkins (1962).

> Our films showed that the different races express interest, for example, in a very similar manner, employing various movements which additionally convey intensity of interest. The face may at first remain immobile, interest being expressed merely by the direction of the eyes. Then mounting interest manifests itself in an opening of the sensory orifices designed to admit as many messages to the brain as possible. There is a widening of the eyes—the most important of such orifices—and the head turns in the appropriate direction.

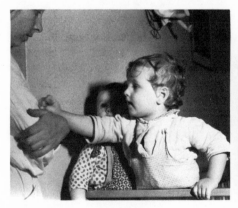

FIGURE 9-1. A partially hidden object elicits heightened interest (and action) from Russian toddlers (left), and movement in the brush captivates a teenager in the hill country of northern India (right).

A further sign of interest, as Darwin himself noted, is the opening of the mouth. It is still debatable whether this stems from the relaxing of the jaw muscles—in consequence of heightened attention—or whether it is an aid to keener hearing. Darwin inclined to the second alternative but pointed out that man breathes more quietly through the mouth, which can certainly be an advantage when listening intently.

Another natural sign of interest or curiosity is the inclination of the head, which frequently cocks itself on one side and describes lateral or circular movements. Inclining the head brings not only the eyes and ears but also the nose closer to the object of interest, and there may be an associated intake of breath designed to improve the perception of smells. The oblique posture is probably an aid to acoustic localization, while lateral or circular motions help improve spatial vision and enable one to investigate the object in question from various angles. (Hass, 1970, p. 113–114)

What It Feels Like to Be Interested

At the experiential level interest–excitement is the feeling of being engaged, caught-up, fascinated, curious. There is a feeling of wanting to investigate, become involved, or extend or expand the self by incorporating new information and having new experiences with the person or object that has stimulated the interest. In intense interest or excitement the person feels animated and enlivened. It is this enlivenment that guarantees the association between interest and cognitive or motor activity. Even when relatively immobile the interested or excited person has the feeling that he is "alive and active." Further analysis of the phenomenology of interest will be presented in the following section, which summarizes two approaches to the study of subjective experience and a study that provides data on the experience of interest and seven of the other emotions discussed in subsequent chapters.

Two Approaches to the Study of Subjective Experience

The dimensional approach to the study of subjective experience requires the individual to rate his feelings on a number of general scales on which affective states vary quantitatively. Affective states are differentiated by analysis of the pattern of scores on the relevant dimensions. The discrete emotions approach relies on emotion-specific self-report. The theory and research underlying these two approaches has been detailed elsewhere (Izard, 1971; Bartlett & Izard, 1972), so a brief summary will suffice here.

The Dimensional Approach and a Dimensional Rating Scale. The dimensional approach to the description of feelings has roots in Spencer's concept of a pleasantness–unpleasantness (P–U) continuum and in his early enunciation of the concepts of activation and adaptation level (Spencer, 1890). In an extension of this line of thinking, Wundt (1896) proposed that emotion experience varied along the dimensions of pleasantness–unpleasantness, excitement–quiet, tension–relaxation. Woodworth (1938) modified the meaning of these dimensions when he concluded that "pleasantness and unpleasantness correspond to the attitudes of acceptance and rejection, excitement and depression to the momentary level of muscular activity or readiness for activity, tension and relaxation to the degree of muscular tension" (p. 241). Woodworth's concept of emotion experience as a function of attitudinal and neuromuscular processes anticipated elements of both cognitive theory and differential emotions theory. The Spencer–Wundt–Woodworth tradition has a number of other contemporary offshoots. Duffy (1941, 1957, 1962) and Lindsley (1951, 1957) used a concept of neurophysiological activation in an attempt to explain emotion and behavior in general. Schlosberg (1941, 1952, 1954), Triandis and Lambert (1958), Frijda (1970), Frijda and Phillipszoon (1963), and Abelson and Sermat (1962) delineated dimensions of facial expression and considered these as dimensions of emotion. Osgood (1966, 1969), Block (1957), Davitz (1970), and Nowlis (1970) developed dimensions of verbal expression and treated them as indexes of emotion or emotion expression.

In the Bartlett–Izard study of the subjective experience of fundamental emotion (partially described in Chapter 5, pp. 125ff.), the investigators assumed that the assessment of subjective experience in terms of dimensions was a complex process in which the essential measurement technique, self-report, reflects aspects of feeling, cognition, and behavior. For this reason, each general scale on their Dimensional Rating Scale (DRS) was represented by three subscales, one for each of these three levels of functioning. The instructions defined the feeling level as bodily cues, such as breathing, heart rate, respiration, and muscle tension. The behavior level was defined as primarily facial–postural expression. The thought level subscale permitted a subject to evaluate the way in which he was cognitively appraising (Arnold, 1960a, 1968) the emotion situation. The intention was to give additional specificity to the dimension as well as flexibility to the communicator. The DRS is presented in Table 9-1.

Dimensions were selected on the basis of their apparent salience for assessing subjective experience in a specifically defined emotion situation. Since the results of the study showed that most of the information from the DRS was represented by four of the eight dimensions, only these will be considered here. The rationale for selecting these dimensions for the DRS was as follows.

Pleasantness was unequivocally the first dimension to be chosen because of its wide empirical support and obvious salience for assessing the hedonic tone of subjective experience. Tension was chosen as a dimension

TABLE 9-1
Dimensions Rating Scale (DRS)

Directions: A number of questions are given below that ask people to describe themselves. As you recall and visualize the emotion situation, please try to answer each question by taking a moment to evaluate thought patterns, behavior (e.g., facial expressions) and inner bodily feelings (e.g., breathing, heart rate, perspiration, muscle tone, etc.). Give your answer by circling the appropriate number to the right of each question.

There are no right or wrong answers. Do not spend too much time on any one question.

	Not at all	Moderately	Extremely
1			
a. How active do you feel?	0 1	2 3	4 5 6
b. How active are your thoughts?	0 1	2 3	4 5 6
c. How active is your behavior?	0 1	2 3	4 5 6
2			
a. How deliberate do you feel?	0 1	2 3	4 5 6
b. How deliberate are your thoughts?	0 1	2 3	4 5 6
c. How deliberate is your behavior?	0 1	2 3	4 5 6
3			
a. How tense do you feel?	0 1	2 3	4 5 6
b. How tense are your thoughts?	0 1	2 3	4 5 6
c. How tense is your behavior?	0 1	2 3	4 5 6
4			
a. How impulsive do you feel?	0 1	2 3	4 5 6
b. How impulsive are your thoughts?	0 1	2 3	4 5 6
c. How impulsive is your behavior?	0 1	2 3	4 5 6
5			
a. How controlled do you feel?	0 1	2 3	4 5 6
b. How controlled are your thoughts?	0 1	2 3	4 5 6
c. How controlled is your behavior?	0 1	2 3	4 5 6
6			
a. How self-assured do you feel?	0 1	2 3	4 5 6
b. How self-assured are your thoughts?	0 1	2 3	4 5 6
c. How self-assured is your behavior?	0 1	2 3	4 5 6
7			
a. How extraverted do you feel?	0 1	2 3	4 5 6
b. How extraverted are your thoughts?	0 1	2 3	4 5 6
c. How extraverted is your behavior?	0 1	2 3	4 5 6
8			
a. How pleasant do you feel?	0 1	2 3	4 5 6
b. How pleasant are your thoughts?	0 1	2 3	4 5 6
c. How pleasant is your behavior?	0 1	2 3	4 5 6

to represent neurophysiological activation which has both theoretical and empirical support as an amplifier of emotion. The tension dimension was thought to relate to activation and to reflect phenomena such as increased muscle tone and inhibition in the expression of emotion semantically and behaviorally. The hedonic and activation dimensions were expected to be the necessary but not sufficient dimensions for distinguishing between discrete emotion experiences.

Following Osgood's (1966) suggestion, the dimension of impulsiveness was selected. The degree of reported impulsiveness communicates a lack of anticipation or preparedness for the given emotion situation. The impulsiveness scale also carries the connotation of spontaneity, which characterizes the suddenness with which an emotion is experienced. Spontaneity also implies a personal mode of expression.

The final dimension was the positive pole of Frijda's (1970) self-assured–insecure dimension. The self-assurance dimension enables a person to communicate feelings of competence and adequacy. On the cognitive level one can report the degree to which one understands the dynamics of the emotion-eliciting situation. At the behavioral level one can report the degree to which he thinks his actions are appropriate for the emotion situation.

The Discrete Emotions Approach and the Differential Emotions Scale. Differential emotions theory provides the rationale for the measurement of subjective experience in terms of discrete emotions, affects, and affective–cognitive structures. In particular this position maintains that the fundamental emotions and certain other affective states are qualitatively distinct and differentiable by self-report in terms of affect-specific descriptors. An earlier work (Izard, 1972) presented a number of studies with early versions of the Differential Emotions Scale (DES) and the DES Manual (Izard, Dougherty, Bloxom, & Kotsch, 1974) reported studies of its reliability, validity, and standardization. In brief, each of ten fundamental emotions and eight other affects or affective–cognitive structures are represented by three substantive items on five-point scales. The item content of the emotion scales was presented in Table 5-2, p. 126.

The Bartlett–Izard DES–DRS Study. Two hundred twenty-nine subjects participated in this study. They were volunteers from the Vanderbilt University classes in general psychology. Each subject received 2 hours of credit toward his 4-hour minimum requirement for research participation. This population of subjects had an approximately uniform socioeconomic status, intelligence, and level of academic achievement.

Each subject received a packet containing a statement of purpose, formal instructions, and eight sets of DES and DRS (stapled together), one for each of eight discrete emotion situations.

1. The subjects were given the name of a fundamental emotion and were asked to recall a situation or event in their lives in which that emotion was strongly experienced.
2. They were asked to give a brief description of the event.
3. They were asked to recall and visualize or imagine the event as vividly as possible while filling out the DES and DRS scales. The order of presenting the DES and DRS was randomized for each emotion situation.

The order in which the emotion situations were visualized was left to each subject's preference. However, since the completion of two or more situations at one sitting might attenuate the intensity with which the latter

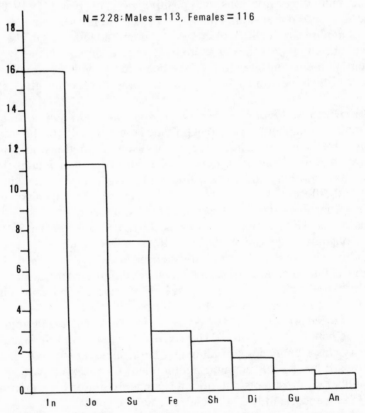

FIGURE 9-2. *The profile of emotions in the interest situation. The emotion (DES) scales are abbreviated: (In) interest, (Jo) joy, (Su) surprise, (Di) distress, (An) anger, (Gu) guilt, (Sh) shyness, and (Fe) fear. (DES score range, 0–18, as shown on ordinate.)*

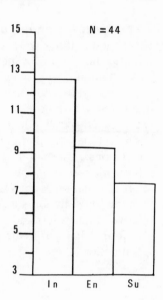

15 ___   N = 44

13 ___

11 ___

9 ___

7 ___

5 ___

FIGURE 9-3. The profile of emotions in the interest   3 ___
situation. (Adapted from Izard, 1972.)   I n   E n   S u

situations were recalled or experienced, subjects were asked to visualize and rate only one situation per day. They were requested to average at least three a week.

An analysis of variance of the DES and DRS showed that both instruments discriminated among the emotion situations. The DES and DRS profiles for interest will be considered in this chapter. The data on the other emotions will be discussed in subsequent chapters.

When a person visualizes a particular emotion situation a pattern of emotions emerges, with the target emotion showing the highest mean and with other dynamically related emotions means also elevated. The profile of emotions in the imaged interest situation, as measured by a modified DES, is presented in Figure 9-2. The profile of substantially elevated emotions consists of interest, joy, and surprise. No other emotions means were remarkably elevated. It is reasonable that, on the average, the positive emotion of joy would be the second most prominent emotion in an interest-eliciting situation. If the second highest mean had been on the emotion of disgust, one would have grounds for suspecting the validity of the DES.

Results very similar to those shown in Figure 9-2 have been obtained in other studies using the standard DES. (The Bartlett–Izard study used a modified DES representing eight emotions on 6-point scales, score range 0–18, while the standard DES represents ten emotions by three 5-point scales, score range 3–15.) The profile for interest using the standard DES is presented in Figure 9-3. In this study (Izard, 1972), the positive emotions were elevated as in the Bartlett–Izard study, and none of the means for negative emotions were above 5.50, the level arbitrarily adopted as the intensity necessary for inclusion in the discussion of the emotion dynamics of a situation.

The results shown in Figure 9-4 describes subjective experience in an interest situation in terms of the general affective dimensions of the DRS. On the average the individual in the interest situation experiences a positive hedonic tone, the pleasantness scale mean being the highest of the four dimensions. The individual experiences greater pleasantness in only two other emotion situations—those for joy and surprise. The fact that the interest situation is characterized by less pleasantness and more tension than the joy situation suggests that in the interest situation the individual is relatively more alert and prone to person–environment interactions. It was also found that self-assurance is lower in the interest situation than in the joy situation.

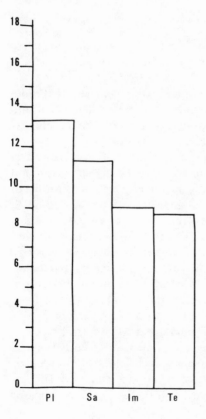

FIGURE 9-4. Profile of dimensions in the interest situation. The (DRS) dimensions are abbreviated: (Pl) pleasantness, (Sa) self-assurance, (Im) impulsiveness, and (Te) tension. (Adapted from Bartlett & Izard, 1972.)

The Significance of Interest–Excitement

The significance of the emotion of interest–excitement in individual development, personality, and human relations can hardly be overestimated. This section will consider its significance in the evolutionary, biological, and psychological realms.

Evolutionary Significance

Interest played an important role in the evolution of human beings. Although it is difficult to present hard data for this conclusion the arguments seem quite convincing, especially if we accept the definition of interest that we have discussed. Hass argued:

> Among primitive men, this simple procedure (widening of eyes and head turning in appropriate direction) no doubt possessed importance as a signal to the young and to other members of the clan, who could deduce from it where the center of interest lay—a potentially important piece of information to those out hunting or in danger. If the clan leader, normally the most experienced individual, had noticed something, the ability to indicate its position silently might well be crucial in the next few moments. (1970, p. 113)

Interest and the Evolution of Social Life. People obtain and remain in relationship with each other in large part because the human being holds greater interest for people than any other being, object, or situation. People are the most complex units in our world and interest thrives on complexity. People are the most changing and unpredictable aspects of our world and interest is activated and sustained by change and novelty. In nonhuman and human primates the activities described as play are initiated and sustained in large measure by interest, and play provides a vehicle for the formation and maintenance of social units (Jolly, 1966). It keeps the young together and engaged in play, exploratory, and venturesome activities and keeps the parents together maintaining a watchful eye.

Interest in the Support of Sustained Sexual Relationships and the Family Unit. Emotions and sex were discussed in Chapter 7, but in considering the evolutionary significance of interest, it should be noted again that interest plays an important part not only in heightening sexual pleasure but in the maintenance of a long-term sexual relationship. Sexual partners or the married couple who continue to interest each other as human beings are the ones who stay happily married and enjoy each other's presence.

Interest and the Development of Competencies and Intelligence. This topic will be developed further when we consider emotions and creativity, but in the evolutionary perspective it is necessary to note that it is the emotion of interest that keeps the individual engaged in an activity or skill until he or she has competence with it (see Figure 9-5). Competencies add up to functional intelligence. It is interest that sustains Rebecca's effort to differentiate and delineate the aspects of her world and that gives her the feeling of wanting to know and to experience.

Biological Significance of Interest

It is essential that people be sufficiently motivated to obtain what is necessary for their survival. Interest can be an important source of motivation in this regard. Interest can amplify any of the drives including the survival needs. It is not too often that we see dramatic instances of the need for the emotion of interest to amplify a drive but there are such occasions. There are instances when one is so depressed or so sick physically that one loses interest in eating. It is interest in some other activity, person, or in life and the self as a whole that has to be marshaled in order to amplify the hunger drive sufficiently to sustain the body. Tomkins (1962) has argued that interest is necessary for the physiological support of any long-term effort, since it provides the amplification of the physiological functions required for prolonged and fatiguing work or play.

FIGURE 9-5. Interest sustains this young Nepalese boy's efforts to master the ancient wheel-and-stick game with only a crude circle of stiff wire and a twig for props.

Psychological Significance of Interest

In a very general sense the psychological significance of this emotion is to engage the person in what is possible, in investigation, exploration, and constructive activity. If people lived in a world that was stable and unchanging forever, then perhaps there would be no need for the emotion of interest. But the fact is that we are in an ever-changing world and have the capacity for the emotion of interest, and our interest will not permit the change and flux to go unnoticed. Our interest makes us want to turn things around, upside down, over, and about. This is because we see some possibility in the object or person or condition that is not immediately manifest to the senses. The possibility may be inconsequential or vitally important and its realization may lead to positive or negative consequences. Pursuit of goals of interest may lead to destructive changes in the environment and ecology or to improvements in human welfare and advances in civilization. Tomkins (1962) noted that interest can be invested in things that prove to be sources of distress or fear and that chronic excitement or the continual pursuit of ever more exciting things can destroy a person.

The Early Development and Socialization of Interest

Interest characterizes the infant's functioning from the beginning of life. Except when the infant is experiencing the discomfort of a strong drive state or a negative emotion, its looking, listening, vocalizing and motor movements are motivated and guided by the emotion of interest. Interest also facilitates intersensory and sensorimotor coordination and skill development (B. White, 1975). Interest-motivated activities and interactions build the foundations for growth and development in all spheres, and their absence can result in gross developmental retardation (Dennis, 1960). Hunt (1965) has cited evidence to support the contention that lack of interactions that result in positive involvement of the infant produces apathy. He wrote, "Although hunger and thirst are of the essence for survival, opportunities for such informational interaction are very likely of the essence for *interest* in objects, persons, and places" (p. 234, italics added).

The infant's interest in the human face results in its ability to discriminate its mother from other people. Interest in mother's face also leads the infant to track it through space and to begin to learn something about distance and spatial relations between objects. Interest in space and movement is necessary in order for the infant to learn to walk. In order for the infant Rafe to learn to deal with objects, his interest must support his efforts to learn about forms and spatial relations among objects. To judge distance he must be interested in the size and brightness of objects. What seems in adulthood to be an automatic perceptual process is actually the product of perceptual learning originally motivated and sustained by the organism's interest in adapting and exploring. As Huxley (1954) suggested, sense data are only gradually "subordinated to the concept" (p. 25).

The Development of Interest and Interest Interactions

Some of Piaget's notions about intellectual development and Hunt's ideas on the development of intrinsic motivation have some implications for the emotion–cognition interaction model, a model concerned with the development of the emotion of interest and the interactions of interest with perceptual, cognitive, and motor activity. Hunt (1965) gave a detailed description of the development of intrinsic motivation and compared some of his ideas with some of Piaget's observations.

Hunt divided the development of intrinsic motivation (motivation inherent in processing information) into three stages. Stage 1 is character-ized by an innate responsiveness to changes (incongruities) in ongoing input. At this stage the standard or norm by which new inputs become incongruous (and hence instigate processes that have motivational proper-ties) is the ongoing input and, thus, outside the organism. Hunt agreed with Piaget's observation that the motivational basis for the responsiveness in stage 1 is comparable to the Russian concept of orienting reflexes. How-ever, an orienting reflex can account only for the initial sensory contact with the object, and the concept of an innate interest affect can better account for the infant's continuing responsiveness. Further, the affective–cognitive model maintains that the infant is never merely responsive, as Hunt suggests, but is also an active participant in person–environment interactions. Even in the first three or four months of life that Hunt claimed to be the period of responsiveness (stage 1), the innate emotion of interest generates perceptual and sensorimotor activities.

According to Hunt the second stage (age four to nine months) in the development of intrinsic motivation emerges when the infant begins acting to regain perceptual contact with various kinds of receptor input (p. 236). As Piaget (1936) observed, the infant now carries on activities "to make interesting spectacles last." Hunt deduced from this that in stage 2 specta-cles are interesting because they have been encountered repeatedly. He developed the hypothesis that the effects of such "emerging recognitive familiarity is a basis for cathexis or emotional attachment" (p. 237). Hunt believes that during this stage of development objects acquire their attrac-tiveness through repeated encounters and become interesting because of their recognitive familiarity.

In terms of differential emotions theory what is being observed in this stage is the emergence of joy responses to one's own activity, and an interaction of interest and joy sustains repetitive activity. Familiar persons, places, and objects are more a stimulus for joy than for interest–excitement. It is the interaction of interest with the joy derived from recognitive familiarity that supports efforts to obtain or regain perceptual contact with the familiar.

It is only in stage 3 (at about age nine months), according to Hunt, that the infant becomes interested in things that are novel. This is not consistent with the affective–cognitive model, which sees novelty as an interest activator from the beginning of life; nor does it seem consistent with the previously reviewed studies that demonstrated the effects of novelty and complexity on infant perception and attention. Despite some differences between Hunt's formulation and the emotion–cognition interaction model, both are agreed on the importance of interest in novelty. Its impact on development in the last quarter of the first year of life and throughout the second was cogently delineated by Hunt. He pointed out three developmental consequences of interest in novelty during this period. First, interest in novelty provides the motivation for "the shift of attention from spectacles and action schemas *per se* to objects and what objects do as the infant drops them, throws them, and manipulates them" (pp. 248–249). An interest in the action schema of "letting go" (for the joy of it) changes from a seemingly passive dropping to an action schema that consists of intentional throwing and attention to the trajectory of the object and other subsequent events. Second, interest in the novel motivates "what Piaget calls 'discovery of new means through active experimentation'" (p. 250). Action schemas are no longer merely repetitive but are now modified in order to influence the environment in some new or different way. Third, the infant's interest in novelty motivates imitations of the actions, gestures, and vocalization that are so important in development and in socialization. These ideas of Hunt are essentially congruent with the affective–cognitive model, except for the following differences. First, differential emotions theory postulates that the emotion of interest is innate and that novelty is an innate activator of interest. Second, developments like those summarized by Hunt have their beginnings in the neonate rather than in the nine-month-old infant.

The Socialization of Interest

Some of the important factors that influence the socialization of interest are very general and pervasive. Among these are socioeconomic conditions, the amount and variety of stimulation provided in the neighborhood, and the complexity of the family in terms of the occupations, hobbies, and other activities of its members. Poverty tends to restrict the variety of constructive activities available to individuals and thus to limit the possibilities for the development of strong and varied investments of interest. Poverty also leaves less time to pursue intellectual and artistic endeavors and other activities that are relatively free of drives.

Regardless of socioeconomic conditions, however, the happy infant, toddler, and growing child has a low threshold for interest–excitement and a healthy interest affect can develop if parents permit and encourage play, exploration, and investigation. If the parents' preoccupation with their own needs or frustrations make them intolerant of the child's interest-motivated ventures, the child's curiosity and exploratory urges will be punished and hence inhibited.

Curious, adventuresome parents are much more likely to nourish strong interest–cognition orientations in their children than are parents who are disturbed by change and novelty and prefer to live by established opinions and dogmas. Parents, by their actions and words, can either encourage or discourage the curiosity and exploratory activity of their children. Parents who are themselves open and receptive to new experiences are much more likely to transmit to children similar attitudes and to foster the development of a low threshold for interest-motivated constructive activities.

Giving a child freedom to play, to enjoy make-believe and fantasy, and to move freely from the real to the imaginary world has a strong and lasting influence (Singer, 1966). Such activities have a decisive effect upon the development of the child's capacity for excitement and interest. Even when socioeconomic or other cultural–familial conditions restrict the variety of stimulation and the possibilities for novelty and change, the child with proper encouragement and help can find a never-ending variety of people, places, objects, and events in the make-believe worlds created by his or her own imagination. The work of Singer and his colleagues (Singer, 1973) and Klinger (1971) testifies to the importance of imaginative play and fantasy in the life of the growing child. The research of Smilansky (1968) suggests that certain types of deprived children may be deficient in imaginative play and make-believe and that such children may require special help in developing these important aspects of childhood.

Interest–Drive Interactions

Chapter 7 discussed emotion–drive interactions, including the interactions of interest with the pain and sex drives. Of all the emotions, interest is the most important as a source of drive amplification, and it can influence or regulate any of the drives.

The Development of Interest—Cognition Interactions

The discussion of the interactions of interest with perception and cognition should be considered as an extension of the preceding ideas on the early development and socialization of interest. Whether interest interacts with perceptual–cognitive processes and the action system to produce constructive, intellectual, artistic, or creative activities on the one hand or nonconstructive or psychopathological behavior on the other is largely a matter of how interest is experienced and socialized in the early years.

In discussing the psychological significance of interest, it was pointed out that interest is the primary motivational accompaniment and underpinning of perception, attention, and the cognitive processes. Even the very fundamental process of perceptual learning in the infant requires the sustaining motivation of interest.

Interest and Perceptual–Cognitive Development

Interest plays a significant role in the development of competencies and skills and in the development of intelligence. The relationship between interest and the development of cognitive functions has been aptly described by Tomkins:

> Interest is not only a necessary support of perception but of the state of wakefulness. Indeed insomnia may be produced not only by disturbing negative affect but also by sustained intense excitement. Again, without interest the development of thinking and the conceptual apparatus would be seriously impaired.
>
> The interrelationships between the affect of interest and the functions of thought and memory are so extensive that absence of the affective support of interest would jeopardize intellectual development no less than destruction of brain tissue. To think, as to engage in any other human activity, one must care, one must be excited, must be continually rewarded. There is no human competence which can be achieved in the absence of a sustaining interest . . . (Tomkins, 1962, p. 343).

In order for the infant Rebecca to perceive any object, she must attend to it over a period of time. Almost any object is too complex for her to perceive instantaneously. It is necessary for her to attend to the various features of the object, yet she must perceive it as a whole; she must perceive its diversity as well as its unity. Her interest must hold her attention on a given feature until it has been grasped and then move her attention to another aspect of the object. Only sufficient interest can keep attention moving from one feature of the object to another long enough to see its diversity and unity, without destruction of attention by the multiplicity of other stimuli in the environment. Without this kind of focusing of interest on particular objects in the environment, the infant's attention might bounce around randomly to the great detriment of perceptual development. Tomkins has summarized the role of interest in perceptual development as follows:

> In order to shift from one perceptual perspective to another, from the perceptual to the motor orientation and back again, from both the perceptual and the motor to the conceptual level and back again, and from one memory to another, one must at the very least maintain a continuing interest in all of these varying transactions with what is the same object. Without such an underlying continuity of motivational support there could indeed be no creation of a single object with complex perspectives and with some unity in its variety (Tomkins, 1962, p. 348).

In the discussion of the psychological significance of interest, it was pointed out that interest plays a highly significant role in an individual's cognitive development and intellectual functioning. Rafe's intellectual activity is guided and sustained by his interest. He cannot become immersed in a subject in which he has no interest. He can memorize facts out of fear of failure or to avoid the shame of defeat, but such learning will have limited life and limited value. For Rafe to be imaginative and creative in a given field, he must have the kind of investment and involvement that only strong interest can sustain. If adventure into the depths of a subject becomes a way of life for Rafe, sustained effort to go beyond existing knowledge will become exciting adventure for him. The work of Singer (1966, 1973) suggests that it is the interaction of interest and joy that form the motivational basis for the very origins of imaginative–creative endeavor.

Interest, Art, and Intellectual–Creative Activity

Interest also plays a significant part in the development of artistic and aesthetic activities. In order to become an artist, the individual from early childhood must develop strong interest in the requisite skills of artistry. For example, to be a ballerina, one must not simply have sufficient interest to learn the necessary skills and techniques, although this in itself requires a great deal of motivation and energy, but one must also have a keen appreciation of the human body and its capacities. One must have an intuitive appreciation for the role of emotions and other affects in body movements. One's interest in the body and its capacity for rhythmical and patterned movements must lead to a continuing appreciation of kinesthesia and proprioception. Similar processes are involved in the development of a devoted scholar or scientist. Expanding on the pioneering ideas of Perry (1926, 1954), Schachtel (1959), and Tomkins (1962), Wessman and Ricks

(1966) gave the following insightful description of the role of interest in aesthetic and intellectual activity.

> This is a feeling or experiential quality that is seldom violent, dramatic, or disruptive, but it attends every event or proceeding of any significance to the individual. It is an affective accompaniment of any degree of conscious awareness and attention. It is an affect that would seem a necessary part of any object-cathexis made by the individual—some "object" (thing, person, symbol, idea) has become affectively important to him or sufficiently salient to occupy his attention and mental processes. Interest will often appear prior to the arousal of other affects, and seems to be a constituent of any experience or thought important enough to be registered in conscious awareness. Its "purest" and most vivid state is found in completely absorbing and sustained intellectual or esthetic activity. When this affect is fully developed, experience becomes immediate and real, competing distractions and disruptions are suspended in the pursuit of some goal of complete understanding or participation (p. 5).

In his discussion of the creative attitude, Maslow (1971) has given the emotion of interest a central role without conceptualizing it as such. He said " . . . the creative person, in the inspirational phase of the creative furor, loses his past and his future and lives only in the moment. He is all there, totally immersed, fascinated and absorbed in the present, in the current situation, in the here and now, with the matter in hand" (Maslow, 1971, p. 61). This kind of total immersion, fascination, and absorption is precisely what follows from intense interest or excitement.

Maslow speaks of two phases of creativeness, primary creativeness and secondary creativeness. The primary phase is characterized by improvisation and high inspiration. In this phase the individual is undoubtedly motivated by intense interest or excitement. Secondary creativeness is the working out or the development of the original inspirations spawned in a moment of high excitement. The secondary phase requires a continued creative attitude but also a lot of discipline and plain hard work. Many more people are capable of primary creativeness (the inspiration) than of primary plus secondary creativeness. "Inspirations are a dime-a-dozen. The difference between the inspiration and the final product, for example, Tolstoy's *War and Peace,* is an awful lot of hard work, an awful lot of discipline, an awful lot of training, an awful lot of finger exercises and practices and rehearsals . . . and so on" (Maslow, 1971, p. 59). If primary creativeness— the improvisational phase—is characterized by excitement, the secondary creativeness or the working out and development of the creation has to be characterized by a moderately high level of interest. The interest may fluctuate, but it must be strong and continuous enough to counteract fatigue and negative emotions. The plain hard work of developing the final product of creative endeavor inevitably results in periods of distress and fear— discouragement, dejection, loneliness, isolation—and in the weariness of fatigue and negative emotion states, the motivational power of sustained interest is essential to overcoming the hurdles to creativity.

Kierkegaard's (1844) provocative and insightful analysis of anxiety is a precursor of the Tomkins–Izard idea of the relationship between interest–excitement, fear, and creative endeavor. Kierkegaard maintained that anxiety was the possibility of freedom, the result of man confronting choice or possibilities. Such possibilities involve unknowns, uncertainties, and hence anxiety. According to Kierkegaard, the more "possibility" one has, the more creativity one is capable of and the more likely one will experience fear or anxiety. In linking anxiety with freedom and creativity, Kierkegaard was laying the groundwork for differentiating the positive emotion of interest–excitement and the pattern of emotions called anxiety (see Izard, 1972, and Chapter 14 of this volume). He came very close to making the differentiation when he distinguished between fear as the emotion that supports avoidance or retreat from the object and anxiety as the basis of an ambivalent relation to the object. This ambivalence is what Tomkins (1962) and Izard and Tomkins (1966) have described as an oscillation between fear and excitement. The fear may result from the unknown, uncertain qualities or possibilities in the object or choice; the excitement from the novelty and possibility as such and from investigatory activity that reduces the uncertainty and fear and permits interest to operate. Fear places limits on a person's thrust into the unknown; interest–excitement sustains the exploration.

Interest–Cognition Orientations

The interaction of innate individual differences in emotion thresholds and life circumstances leads to a great variety of interest–cognition structures and orientations. Rebecca may become primarily interested in (oriented toward) objects (object oriented), ideas (intellectually oriented), or people (socially oriented), and within each of these broad orientations her interest and activities can take one of many different forms. Further, on any of the possible interest–cognition orientations relating to objects or people she may superimpose one that makes her mainly a thinker, a "doer," or one that places more emphasis on affective experiencing than on thought and action.

Adler's (1964) concept of "social interest" or "social feeling" may be considered a type of interest–cognition orientation—one characterized by interest in human beings and their welfare. He wrote:

> The surface of the earth on which we live makes labour and the division of labour a necessity for humanity. Social feeling takes the imprint here of co-operative work for the benefit of others. The socially minded man can never

> doubt that every one is entitled to the reward of his labour, and that the exploitation of the lives and the toil of others cannot in any way further the welfare of humanity (p. 58).

Adler thought that only people with an adequate endowment of social feeling could be expected to solve the great problems confronting human beings.

Spranger's (1928) types of value orientation and Jung's (1933) psychological functions or types of personality organization may be understood in terms of the differential investment of interest in different objects and types of activity. For example, a person in whom the thinking function is dominant is one who is excited by thinking, and one in whom the feeling function is superior is a person who is interested mainly in affective experiences. A "doer" is one who is interested in action and excited by the results of his or her activities. The myriad individual variations in human personalities are created by the innate differences in emotion thresholds and capacities and the differential investment of all the affects, but the investment of interest–excitement is the crucial one for attracting and holding the individual to a particular way of life. In the poetic language of Tomkins (1962), "I am, above all, what excites me" (p. 347).

Interest–Excitement and Psychopathology

As noted in an earlier chapter, Zuckerman's (1974) definition of the sensation-seeking motive overlaps substantially with the concept of interest–excitement as an emotion. Zuckerman's treatment of the sensation-seeking motive differs from differential emotions theory in isolating the cortex as the sole site of the sensation-seeking motive and optimal level of arousal as its source. Despite this difference in definition at the neural level, much of Zuckerman's work continues to suggest similarities between the two concepts at the experiential level.

It is conceivable that extremely low or high levels of sensation seeking may represent pathological states (or thresholds) of interest–excitement. Zuckerman reviewed theory and evidence suggesting that high or low levels of sensation seeking are associated with various problems of adjustment. Brownfield (1966) and Kish (1970) used Zuckerman's sensation-seeking scale and showed that chronic schizophrenics tended to score lower than normals and certain other psychiatric groups. This was considered to be consistent with several theoretical formulations of schizophrenia that suggest that schizophrenics have difficulty screening out irrelevant stimuli and focusing attention. Thus, since they already suffer from a sensory overload, they would tend to avoid rather than seek stimulation. Differential emotions theory postulates that a properly functioning emotion of interest provides the screening of stimuli and focusing of attention that is lacking in schizophrenia.

Zuckerman also reviewed studies which suggest a relationship between sensation seeking and sociopathy. In one study, female delinquents and felons scored significantly higher on sensation-seeking scales than did a sample of psychiatric patients. Marshall and Izard (1972a) found that interest as measured on the Differential Emotions Scale was extremely low in both normal and psychotic depressives. Chapter 7 noted that maldevelopment of interest–sex-drive interactions could lead to sexual fetishism and imbalance in interest–fear reactions toward the opposite sex to homosexuality.

An Empirical Study of Antecedents and Consequences of Interest–Excitement

Interest is indeed the most general and pervasive of the positive affects. It accompanies and sustains virtually every significant transaction of the individual except those where a negative emotion dominates. Even in situations where a negative emotion is dominant, some degree of interest ordinarily obtains and helps motivate the coping behavior that eliminates or attenuates the negative emotion. Interest is lowest in the distress situation and this probably helps account for the fact that distress, particularly the severe and prolonged distress that shades into depression, is one of the most difficult affective patterns to change.

In the studies of the various emotion situations (Izard, 1972), the participating individuals were asked to write a brief description of the situations they visualized for each of the various emotions. The kinds of situations which were visualized in the interest–excitement condition ranged from reading, listening to lectures, and participating in intellectually stimulating discussions on the one hand, to new or unusual experiences, including sex and drug experiences, on the other. A number of situations also involved sports (e.g., water skiing without skis, learning a new sport) and numerous activities involving friends or acquaintances (planning an upcoming social event, going to see someone in his home).

In order to study emotion-related behavior sequences more systematically Izard adapted Triandis's (1972) idea and developed a measure called "Antecedents and Consequences of the Emotions." The test shows a photograph representing each of the fundamental emotions, and for each emotion the participant writes a brief statement about the thoughts, feelings, and actions that lead to a given emotion and the thoughts, feelings, and actions that follow from experiencing that particular emotion. The antecedents and consequences of interest are summarized in Table 9-2.

TABLE 9-2
Antecedents and Consequences of Interest
(N = Approximately 130 College Students)

Responses	Percentage of subjects giving responses
Antecedents of interest	
Feelings	
1. Personal involvement, concern, feeling that you can gain something	38.1
2. Desire to learn, gain knowledge	26.7
3. Curiosity, etc. (interest itself)	10.7
4. Feeling active, energetic	9.2
5. Feeling accepted, needed	6.1
6. Enjoyment of something	3.0
7. Other	6.1
Thoughts	
1. Thinking was clear, efficient, logical	29.8
2. About desire to learn, gain knowledge	16.8
3. Of some specific person or activity	11.4
4. About enjoyable people, activities	9.2
5. About life and future	7.6
6. Of personal gains or benefits	6.1
7. Of being accepted, needed	4.6
8. About a subject, related topics	3.0
9. Other	11.4
Actions	
1. Something with a specific person, or did something I like	22.9
2. Something enjoyable	21.4
3. Did something very well, did my best	14.5
4. Something different, creative, original, discovering something	12.2
5. Interesting things	6.9
6. Something challenging	5.3
7. Worked enthusiastically	3.0
8. Other	13.7
Consequences of interest	
Feelings	
1. Desire to learn, gain knowledge	26.8
2. Personal involvement, concern	23.2
3. Interest–excitement itself	15.2

Continued

TABLE 9-2 (continued)
Antecedents and Consequences of Interest
(N = Approximately 130 College Students)

Responses	Percentage of subjects giving responses
Feelings	
4. Alert, active, energetic	13.8
5. Self-confident, happy with self	11.6
6. Involved in thought, inspired	5.8
7. Other	3.6
Thoughts	
1. Clear, quick, logical thinking	35.5
2. About particular subject, new things	31.1
3. About desire to learn, gain knowledge	15.9
4. Of possible gain or benefit	8.7
5. Of enjoyable and pleasant things	2.9
6. Other	5.8
Actions	
1. Learns, gains knowledge, participates, and accomplishes something	58.7
2. Did something well, my best	26.8
3. Enjoys self	3.6
4. Something meaningful, reflects interest	2.9
5. Other	7.2

Since differential emotions theory assumes that interest is very frequently in consciousness, it follows that the foregoing list of antecedents may be either activators of interest or conditions that change the limit or direction of ongoing interest. This explains why individuals often listed interest synonyms as antecedents of interest.

Summary

Interest is assumed to be one of the innate fundamental emotions and it is considered the most prevalent of all emotions in normal, healthy human beings. It is assumed that some emotion is present in ordinary consciousness at all times and that it is the emotion of interest together with interest–cognition structures and orientations that guide perception, cognition, and action most of the time. The only exceptions occur when high drive states (survival needs) or negative emotions dominate consciousness. Of all the theoretical formulations considered, the emotion–cognition model of intrinsic motivation (and related motivational states) is the only one that holds emotion, not information input, or information processing, to be the primal and fundamental motivational variable. Sensory input is of great importance, but it cannot be primal since it is selected and influenced by affect.

At the neurological level interest is activated by an increase in the gradient of neural stimulation. At the conscious level, change and novelty are the key determinants of interest. The change or novelty may relate to something outside ourselves or may emerge from imaging, memory, or thinking. When one is interested, one takes on the countenance of a person who is captivated and alert, of one who is looking and listening or attending intensely. One feels engaged, caught up, fascinated, curious; the phenomenology of interest is also characterized by a relatively high degree of pleasantness, self-assurance, and a moderate degree of impulsiveness and tension. The emotion of joy is often an accompaniment of the interest affect.

Interest played a significant role in the development of primate social life and continues to play a role in maintaining significant interpersonal relationships. Interest also helps support and sustain sexual relationships and the family unit. It is important in the development of competences and intelligence. It may, on occasion, be a necessary amplifier of survival drives.

The emotion of interest can be invested in possibility and thus support investigation, exploration, and constructive activity. It is a necessary support for perceptual and cognitive development.

Interest characterizes the infant's functioning from the beginning of life. It is the focusing power of interest that makes possible perceptual learning and cognitive development. Differential emotions theory postulates that novelty is an innate activator of interest and that interest-sustained development of perceptual–cognitive and motor activities begins in the neonate.

Although interest is innate, its socialization plays a great role in its development and hence in the shaping of the human personality. Socioeconomic conditions can affect the development of interest adversely, while tolerant and encouraging parents can nourish the development of this all-important emotion.

Emotions regulate drives and the emotion of interest is perhaps the most important of all the emotions as a source of drive amplification.

The interaction of an innate capacity for interest with forces of socialization determine the type of interest–cognition interactions and orientations that develop. Interest may be focused an anything, but of most importance for human welfare it can be invested in intellectual, artistic, and other creative and constructive activities. A person may become primarily interested in objects, ideas, or people. An interest–cognition–action relationship may determine whether a person is primarily a thinker, a doer, or one who places more emphasis on affective experiencing.

Interest–excitement gone awry can result in psychological problems and even psychopathology. For example, the attachment of interest to sex-related paraphanelia can result in fetishism.

An empirical study of the antecedents and consequences of interest yielded results quite congruent with the theoretical description of the emotion and its relationships to thought and action. For example, people see the possibility of learning and personal involvement as an antecedent of interest, and efficient thinking, learning, and accomplishment as its consequences.

10

JOY

Observations of doting parents, as well as some experimental data (Emde & Koenig, 1969; Wolff, 1963) indicate that infants smile—and perhaps experience joy—during the first days of life. These early smiles typically occur during drowsiness or light sleep, raising the fascinating question as to whether an emotion mechanism is operating spontaneously or the infant is responding to inborn images.

The individual's first social smile occurs in response to the presence of another human being. An infant may smile at the sound of a high-pitched voice in the first week of life and at the sight of a face by the fifth week. The infant is born with a particular capacity or threshold for joy, but the manner in which the mother responds to the infant's smile will play a significant role in the development of his or her affective disposition.

Although the experience of joy seems simple enough and relatively easy to understand, eliciting or obtaining joy and the significance of joy and its relationship to other affects present a challenge for scientist and student alike. Most scholars and researchers who have attempted to study joy agree that one cannot obtain it by one's own effort. It is not an experience that can be chased and caught, and it is not necessarily won by success or achievement. Success and achievement may increase your distress or your fear of increased responsibility or failure. You may pursue your interest, what excites you, and in some instances the pursuit will heighten the excitement. On the other hand, joy seems to be more of a by-product of efforts that have other aims. It seems that in most cases joy just happens, and some of the greatest moments of joy are unplanned and quite unexpected.

Joy and Its Significance

Let us say first what joy is not. Joy is not eating, drinking, or copulating. Nor is it a secondary drive based on these processes. It may or may not follow from any of the foregoing activities. Joy is not the same as a sensation of pleasantness. It is not drive pleasure or sensory pleasure (Schachtel, 1959; Tomkins, 1962). Drive pleasure or sensory pleasure may be exemplified by a warm bath, a back rub, wine tasting, or kissing. Although these events may precede or accompany an experience of joy, they do not exemplify it. Joy often follows personal achievement or creation, but hard work or even creative endeavor does not guarantee a joyful experience. Joy is not the same as having fun. Joy may be involved in fun and games, but the experience of having fun probably includes interest–excitement as a principal ingredient. Similarly, being amused or entertained is not equivalent to the joy experience. Amusement often involves interest and sexual arousal, and it may include fear in the case of the thrill-seeker (Zuckerman, 1974), aggression in the case of the sadist, or pain in the case of the masochist. Perhaps in its purest and most meaningful form, joy is what obtains after some creative or socially beneficial act that was not done for the express purpose of obtaining joy or doing good.

The Feeling of Joy

Joy is characterized by a sense of confidence and significance, a feeling of being loved or being loveable. The confidence and personal significance that obtains in joy gives you the feeling that you are capable of coping with the problems and pleasures of living. Joy is accompanied by at least momentary self-contentment, contentment with others and with the world. In view of this characteristic of joy it is easy to understand that as long as there are problems in the world, matters that create stress and call for discontent, people can ill afford to remain permanently in a state of joy. The needs of the world that require other emotions help explain why human beings cannot simply turn on joy and keep it by some particular act.

Joy is characterized not only by acceptance of self but by acceptance of and good relations with other people and the world in general, especially with the source of joy. Joy with others leads to trust in others.

Some emotion theorists have distinguished between active and passive joy (Buytendijk, 1950; Dumas, 1948). One basis for this distinction may be different levels of intensity of the joy experience. Intense joy may give forth with such exuberant expressions that it may appear to be active, and mild joy may be characterized by so much contentment that it may appear to be passive. Since joy is an emotion experience, it is never completely passive or completely active. It is never passive because there is always some neural activation and a degree of alertness. What has been termed active joy may actually be a combination of excitement and joy in interaction with the cognitive and motor systems. Perhaps a better way of distinguishing among varieties of joy experiences would be to consider them along a continuum represented by the concepts of active and receptive.

The Expression and Recognition of Joy

The joyful face readily signifies joy to all observers. The facial expression of joy is universal and easily recognized by all peoples. Joy is the expression that pulls the lips back and curves them gently upward like a crescent moon and puts a twinkle in the eyes. (See Figure 10-1.) The smile of joy is expressed and recognized even by very young infants.

La Barbera, Izard, Parisi, and Vietze (1976) studied the visual responses of four- and six-month-old infants to joy, anger, and neutral expressions. Their subjects were twelve four-month-old and twelve six-month-old infants. They selected slides of facial expressions that were correctly categorized as joy, anger, or neutral slides by 85% or more of adult observers. In the experiment the infants were held approximately 60 cm in front of a 31.7 × 32.0 cm translucent projection screen. They used a rear projection technique to show the infants the three different facial expressions, each repeated six times in random order. For each projected expression they measured the amount of time the infant fixated on the photograph. Their results showed that both four- and six-month-old infants looked significantly longer at the joy expression than at either the anger or neutral expressions. They interpreted their results as consistent with the hypothesis that biological mechanisms underlying a particular discrete emotion become functional as that emotion becomes adaptive in the life of the infant (Izard, 1971). Recognition of anger by the four- or six-month-old infant might not prove to be adaptive, in view of the inability of the infant to

FIGURE 10-1. The joy expression.

cope with "an angry look." On the other hand, recognition of joy can provide rewarding and self-enhancing experiences for the infant and strengthen the mother–infant bond that facilitates mutually rewarding experiences.

Joy Activation and Joy Determinants

In preceding chapters a distinction was made between the neural activation of an emotion and the determinants or causes (antecedents) of an emotion. The former refers to changes in the brain and nervous system, and at present we can only speculate as to the specifics of these processes. Some of the determinants of the emotion of joy have been studied empirically, but sometimes the antecedents of joy or any emotion appear indeterminant and in these instances we may speak of spontaneous or "objectless" emotion (Izard, 1971). Mandler (1975) has also reasoned that an emotion (fundamental distress in the infant) can occur without a specific antecedent event (pp. 193–195).

The Neural Activation of Joy. According to Tomkins's theory of emotion activation, joy is one of the emotions that is activated by a fairly sharp reduction in the gradient of neural stimulation. Whatever emotion or feeling characterizes your ongoing experience, according to this principle, there has to be a decrease in the density of neural firing in order to experience joy. The baby's excitement on being tossed into the air and his joy on coming to rest securely in his father's hands (Figure 10-2) illustrates the activation of joy through increasing then decreasing stimulation.

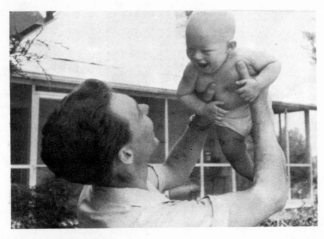

FIGURE 10-2. Joy in a six-month-old boy following the excitement of being tossed in the air.

In their opponent process theory of motivation, Solomon and Corbit (1974) hold that the activation of positive affect indirectly activates a subsequent opposing negative affect. Conversely, they propose that positive affect (including the emotion of joy) is activated indirectly by the activation of negative affect. In this case, joy is a function of an immediately prior experience of an "opposite" (negative) state such as pain, distress, or fear. If this is interpreted as joy following from a decrease in negative affect, they may be said to be in agreement with Tomkins's position, indicating that joy follows from a reduction of the gradient of stimulation. In Tomkins's view, however, joy also results from a marked decrease in the positive affect of interest–excitement, and therefore there is no necessary economic or cost relationship between positive and negative affective experiences as Solomon and Corbit maintain.

There is some evidence that selective sensitivity of receptors and neural mechanisms (Izard, 1971) may play a role in the activation of joy. Lorenz (1966) and Eibl-Eibesfeldt (1972) have suggested that the shape of a baby's head and face is an innate activator of joy or positive affect. It is no accident that doll manufacturers take care to give their products genuine baby features: disproportionately large head and eyes, chubby cheeks, and smooth textures.

Phenomenological Determinants of Joy. It is very difficult to speak of the causes of joy at the experiential level since the experience of joy does not necessarily follow from a specific situation or action. It is more a by-product of a perception, thought, or action. Joy may follow from various stages of creative endeavor, from discovery, from the final creative accomplishment, or from triumph. Joy may follow from exercise that keeps the body fit, from eating and drinking that bring relief from hunger or thirst, or from anything that reduces the stress, anger, disgust, contempt, fear, or shame that invade our daily life.

Joy may also follow the recognition of the familiar, particularly after a long absence or separation from the familiar person or object. Common examples are the student returning to his or her hometown after a semester or year at college and recognizing a friendly face in a crowd of strangers. Such instances suggest that familiarity is to joy as novelty is to interest. This principle explains how interest-sustained exploration of an unfamiliar nature spot or continued interaction with a new group of people may lead to joy. Becoming "comfortable" or "familiar" may simply mean that a reduction in interest–excitement with the novel aspects of the place or persons triggers joy. Acquaintances or friends renew your interest by revealing new aspects of themselves and the resulting increase in familiarity (deeper knowledge of a person) brings joy. In lasting friendships or love relationships this cycle is repeated endlessly.

The experience of joy sometimes occurs during reverie, daydreaming, or other types of imaging and cognition (Singer, 1966). It is even possible to experience joy during sleep, and such joy may recur as the happy dream is recounted. Virtually every parent has seen evidence of joy in sleep, the smile on the face of the sleeping child. Finally, joy, like other emotions, can occur spontaneously or without any specific antecedent event. More about perceived causes of joy will be presented in a later section.

The Significance of Joy

Joy has great significance for life, significance beyond the contentment or ecstasy of the experience itself. Joy plays a role in many aspects of thought and action. We shall consider the significance of joy in the evolutionary, biological, psychological, and social spheres.

Evolutionary Significance. Enjoyment complements the emotion of interest in guaranteeing that human beings will be social creatures. The smile of joy on the human face is the most ubiquitous and effective social stimulus in existence. It is at once personally and interpersonally fulfilling. One's smile tends to evoke a smile on the face of the other person and vice versa. This is virtually automatic in the beginning—with the infant and its mother—and people have to use learned inhibitions if they want to prevent smiling in response to the warm smile of another human being. Just as people are the most interesting things around, so also are they the greatest sources of joy.

There can be little doubt that the smile of the infant brings joy to the mother, increases the strength of the mother–infant attachment, and increases the infant's chances of survival.

The Biological Significance of Joy. Joy has several biologically significant effects on the person and his or her functioning. First, joy facilitates and increases social responsiveness, and for many reasons it is of evolutionary and biological value for human beings to exist in social groups. Second, joy offers relief from the negative stimulation of drives and negative emotions. Third, since joy may follow from the reduction of pain, high drive states, and negative emotions, it may facilitate attachment, commitment, or addiction to objects that have helped reduce drives or negative emotions. Finally, joy's facilitation of attachment and social responsiveness helps provide the social framework within which the infant can learn how to become a fully functioning human being.

The Psychological and Social Significance of Joy. Philosophers and psychologists who have written about joy have differed in their interpretation of its psychological and social significance. Sartre (1948) explains joy as a magical attempt to completely and instantaneously possess the desired object. Bull (1951) holds that joy is often mixed with triumph and maintains that the two concepts are overlapping. The feeling of triumph associated with joy probably accounts for the fact that the phenomenological descriptions of joy often include feelings of power, vitality, and confidence. In contrast to writers who speak of the momentary and precarious nature of joy, Goldstein (1939) suggests that joy functions as a kind of "productive disequilibrium leading to self realization." The idea that joy is somehow a motivational force facilitating personal growth or self-actualization is quite different from the notion that joy is distinguishable from the feeling of triumph only in terms of orientation in time and space (Bull, 1951).

Schachtel (1959) distinguishes two types of joy. He calls the first type magic joy, an experience based on the anticipation of the fulfillment of a drive or wish. During this short-lived experience the person feels that his or her anticipated or present fulfillment will suddenly change the "whole character of life and of the world. Everything seems or promises to be perfect—it is indeed a magic transformation of the world" (p. 41). There is some "unreality" in this experience, since no single event can possibly change the whole world so completely. According to Schachtel the person experiencing magic joy expects the fulfillment of the drive or wish to result not from effort but as a gift of luck or fate. Schachtel sees some overlap between his concept of magic joy and the feeling of triumph. In both there is a feeling of being singled out and favored above others. However, by virtue of having been singled out as the favorite, magic joy may elicit the "*fear of envy,* or the feeling of the precariousness and perilousness of the state brought about by or expected from the joyful event. This fear of envy may be a fear that other people, or the gods, or fate will envy one, or this fear may have a more impersonal character, expressed in such superstitions as having to knock on wood lest the good fortune turn into something bad" (p. 42). Magic joy does not necessarily bring people closer together; the feeling of having been favored above others may tend to bring on feelings of isolation. Even if Rafe wants to tell others of his good fortune, he may do it with such egocentricity and lack of sensitivity for others (as might be the case in a hypomanic state) that social isolation might become serious.

The second kind of joy discussed by Schachtel is "real" joy. This joy is not associated with any feeling of impatience, nor is it linked with feelings of triumph or fear of envy. It is not dependent upon unexpected or unanticipated fulfillment. Real joy can be found in any ongoing activity which brings the individual into physical contact with some aspect of the surrounding world. It can occur when a child plays with a toy or when a grown-up works in the garden or does something to improve the house or neighborhood. Real joy is distinguished from the first type in that it is not based on magic or passive anticipation, but on ongoing activity and the reality of the moment.

It has already been noted that joy (Schachtel's real joy) tends to facilitate social interaction and increase social responsiveness. The perception of the smile of joy on the face of another can amplify the perceiver's own enjoyment. Tomkins (1962) has pointed out that joy provides for social interaction that is not dependent upon the drives or drive satisfaction. Thus people can experience joy together without eating and drinking and sleeping together. This makes the contribution of joy to interpersonal relationships and to interpersonal affective ties quite different from the contribution of drives or sensory pleasure. This is beautifully exemplified in a study by Kistiakovskaia (1965). She showed that institutionalized infants were responsive and attached to the pediatrician who took time to engage the infant in face-to-face activity and other forms of play but not to the caretaker who simply performed the duties necessary for satisfying all of the infant's drives or biological needs.

Another function of joy is to make life more tolerable and to facilitate the work of everyday life. Intermittent joy increases frustration tolerance and thus the ability to cope with pain and pursue difficult goals. Joy promotes confidence and courage.

Finally, joy serves as an antidote for the "rat-race" or "success-or-death" syndrome. Intense interest or excitement in the pursuit of a goal tends to keep the individual moving at a fast pace. The inevitable problems and barriers add distress, anger, or fear to the picture. Occasional failures may bring shame, and cheating a little along the way to insure a victory can lead to guilt. When the success-or-death syndrome has the individual in its grip, receptive joy can effect the slowing down and tranquility that is necessary to bring ambition in balance with grace and beauty.

The Development of Joy in the Child

Since joy is not a direct product of human effort, a goal that can be pursued for its own sake, the development of joy in the child proceeds in a somewhat different fashion than is the case for interest–excitement. Parents cannot teach or train the child to be happy, nor can they model ways of pursuing joy directly. It is possible to entertain the child and to engage the child in fun and games, and though joy so derived is important for healthy development, it is short-lived and dependent on the generosity of others. Parents can and should share their joy with the child and the child may experience joy empathetically, but in the long run each individual must find joy as a part of his or her own life-style.

Biogenetic Factors

As is the case with interest, intelligence, motor agility, and musical aptitude, the capacity for joy varies from individual to individual depending upon genetic makeup. Some people are born with a high threshold for joy and this affects them directly—their happiness, sense of well-being, and confidence. It also affects others' responses to them, since the frequency with which people express joy plays a significant role in others' responses to them and in the development of what Fitts (1971) has called the social self-concept—one's ideas about others' perceptions of one's self. Some people are born with greater capacities for sustaining joy, and this may be negatively related to their threshold for excitement. Studies of emotion expression in infants (Parisi & Izard, 1977) and toddlers (Izard, Izard, & Makarenko, 1977) lend support to the hypothesis of biogenetic determinants of joy (and other fundamental emotions). Frequency of smiling and laughing varied significantly among Soviet toddlers institutionalized since birth, despite a communal living and care system in which infants shared equally the attention and affection of the same caregivers.

In her early study of laughter, Washburn (1929) observed wide individual differences between her subjects, noting that in response to her stimuli four children laughed as early as twelve weeks and one child did not laugh at any stimulus until 52 weeks of age. McGrade (1968) found that "stress reactions" to removal of a nipple between three and four days of life were associated with stress reactions during developmental testing at eight months of age. She also found that infants at three and four days of age who showed relatively little activity after nipple withdrawal were rated as happier, more active, and less tense at eight months of age.

Socioeconomic and Cultural Factors

Cultures and subcultures vary immensely in the opportunities they afford for experiencing joy. Some of the specific obstacles to joy will be discussed later. For the moment let us note that economic, social, and cultural conditions that create fatigue and boredom and in which people literally must struggle for survival produce frequent negative emotion experiences and militate against the experiencing of joy (Davis & Dollard, 1940; Coles, 1971). Despite these limitations one might argue that an impoverished environment affects the development of interest more than it influences the development of joy; at least this would be true for restricting conditions which are not painful or that do not create high drive states. Children have an amazing capacity to create their own fun and games out of whatever resources are available to them, but if the material at hand offers little challenge to the growing mind the expansion of interest, skills, and competencies will be deficient.

The Socialization of Joy

Just as joy as an experience is more a by-product of the pursuit of some other goal, so very probably is the socialization of joy. You can facilitate the development of interest at least within limits, by exposing the child to a variety of objects, places, and people, and by pointing out new facets of a thing or how to see it in different perspectives. Everyone will agree that a child may readily learn what to be afraid of and what to be angry or disgusted or contemptuous about, but it is unlikely that you can teach a person what to be joyful about.

In all cases it may be necessary to elicit some of the emotion in question in order to teach a person something about one of the activators of that emotion. This seems to hold especially true for joy. Creating or eliciting joy in the infant and child is probably the best way to see that joy develops in the child's life and that his or her life has an appropriate quantity and quality of joyful experiences. If parents can elicit joy in a wide variety of situations and in relation to a wide variety of persons, events, and situations, then the infant and child through social learning can enjoy a broader spectrum of people, activities, and objects.

The Development of Smiling and Laughing

Charlesworth and Kruetzer (1973) and Vine (1973) have presented extensive reviews of the literature on the development of smiling in the infant. Sroufe and Wunsch (1972) and Rothbart (1973) have reviewed the literature on the development of laughter in infants and children. These' reviews make it clear that there is still much to be learned about the development of the expressions of joy in infancy and childhood, but the major hypotheses and findings regarding these developmental processes are well worth summarizing here.

The Development of Smiling in Infants. It is now generally accepted that the smiling response is innate and universal (Darwin, 1877; Goodenough, 1932; Thompson, 1941; Tomkins, 1962; Wolff, 1963; Eibl-Eibsfeldt, 1972). Wolff (1963) made a detailed study of smiling in newborn infants. He observed them for four hours a day five days a week and for ten hours on the sixth day. He reported facial movements which morphologically resembled smiling in two to twelve hours after delivery. This occurred during irregular sleep or drowsiness and was considered as a spontaneous unlearned discharge of a reflex nature. He found a recognizable smile to be elicited in the first week of life by a variety of sounds including a high-pitched human voice. The broad clear-cut smile appears about the third week in response to the high-pitched human voice. By the fifth week the voice alone loses its efficiency in evoking a smile and the infant begins to respond to vocalization with a vocal reply. By the fifth week of age a number of visual stimuli including variations on the human face elicit the smiling response. In the second and third month the baby smiles spontaneously without seeing or hearing anyone. Wolff concluded that the most effective single stimulus for eliciting the smile is the normal human face.

In a series of studies at the Academy of Medical Sciences in Moscow, Kistiakovskaia (1965) reported that healthy infants began to exhibit the animation complex (positive emotional reaction including smiling) toward the end of the first and beginning of the second month of life. In addition to smiling, the animation complex includes quick and generalized animated movements with repeated straightening and bending of hands and feet, rapid breathing, vocal reactions, and eyeblink. Several of Kistiakovskaia'a conclusions have important implications for parents or caregivers: (a) an adult may become a principal source of positive emotions in an infant only by supplying the infant with auditory and visual sensations for a sufficiently extended period of time to enable the infant to practice and master the actions of visual concentration; (b) the satisfaction of an infant's organic needs may best be conceived as a method of eliminating the causes of negative emotions, thereby creating the condition for positive emotion experiences; (c) positive emotions tend to sustain the duration and enhance the stability of visual concentration.

The classical study of Spitz and Wolf (1946) suggested that between the ages of about two to five months the social smile is elicited more or less indiscriminately by any human face. At about four to five months of age the infant begins to discriminate mother from others and after this age the infant is less likely to smile at strangers than at mother or at other familiar faces. After their intensive study of the smiling response, Spitz and Wolf concluded that the emotions play a pioneering role in the general development of the infant and in "every human activity, be it perception, physical proficiency, memory, inventiveness, or understanding" (p. 94).

Observations of the effect of infant smiling on the mother tend to support the hypothesis that emotion and emotion expression is motivating. Smiles produce smiles and facilitate attachment, interpersonal bonds, and the exchange of warmth and affection.

Emde and Koenig (1969) investigated the relationship of neonatal smiling and the organismic states characterized by crying, fussiness, alert activity, and the various stages of drowsiness and sleep. Their 30 infant subjects met several criteria for normality and were observed during the days while the mother and infant were still in the hospital following the delivery. During 45 different observation sessions they observed 194 smiles, all but four of which occurred in the state of sleep characterized by rapid eye movement (REM). So little smiling was observed in other organismic states that the authors concluded that smiling during the first days of life occurs predominantly, if not exclusively, during the state of REM drowsiness and REM sleep.

Infants of the sixteen mothers who received depressant medication within eight hours of delivery smiled significantly less than infants of mothers not receiving such medication. They considered this finding consistent with those of earlier researchers who had shown that medication given during the mother's labor decreased sucking efficiency (Kron, Stein, & Goddard, 1956) and had an adverse affect on visual fixation (Stechler, 1964) during the first days of postuterine life.

In the course of their investigations, Emde and Koenig obtained substantial evidence that neonatal smiling is unrelated to gas in the gastrointestinal system. They designated burps, regurgitation, and flatus as indicators of gas and then showed that of the observed 138 "gas behaviors," only one percent occurred within one minute of a smile. Seventy-six percent of the gas behaviors occurred during feeding, but only 13% of the smiles occurred during this time.

The authors suggested that it is not appropriate to assume that neonatal smiling has the same "meaning" as social smiling. For one thing, neonatal smiling is essentially spontaneous and linked to an internal state, while social smiling is typically elicited by another person. However, the authors thought that neonatal smiling and social smiling might well be similar at the neurophysiological level. They cited an earlier study (Hernandez-Peon, 1966) which showed that REM sleep "is associated with a release of limbic system activity which in human adults may trigger the recent memories and affective state of dreaming" (p. 289). The authors concluded that the smiling and frowning seen during the neonate's REM sleep are associated with activity of the limbic system, an area of the brain that has generally been accepted as involved in human emotions.

In summary, it appears that the smile is an innate expression, preprogrammed in the human infant to elicit and assure a strong bond with the mother and to facilitate positive social interactions with other human beings. A morphological facsimile appears in the first hours of life and a readily recognizable smile enlivens the face by the end of the third week postpartum. The fact that the infant smiles indiscriminately at all human faces from approximately three to five months of age probably testifies to the importance of smile-elicited affectionate behavior for the infant's welfare and healthy development. The effect of mutual smiling on the mother–infant relationship and infant development probably shows more clearly than any other situation the importance of emotion and emotion expression as motivational variables in human affairs.

The Development of Laughing. A number of observers have reported laughter in infants as early as five to nine weeks of age (Church, 1966; Darwin, 1877; Major, 1906). Wolff (1966) recorded vocal responses of five-week-old infants to a patty-cake game and these responses were later judged by adults to be laughter. Laughter is typically associated with joyful experiences as distinct from simple sensory events, for as Rothbart (1973) observed, the sensory pleasure of sucking does not produce laughter.

Washburn (1929) conducted the first empirical study of laughing in infancy. She used several different stimulus situations in an effort to elicit laughter, but most of the stimuli involved both intense auditory and tactile stimulation (e.g., "threatening head," "rhymic hand clapping"). Using this restricted range of stimuli, she found no developmental changes in amount of laughter for the different stimulations and no relationship between frequency of laughter and developmental status.

Sroufe and Wunsch (1972) have conducted much more extensive research on the ontogenesis of laughing. Building on the work of Washburn and following suggestions of Bergson (1911), Darwin (1872), Koestler (1964), and Hebb (1949), they developed a much more heterogeneous set of stimuli than that used by Washburn and proceeded to conduct a number of systematic studies with large samples of infants. In their first study they tested 70 healthy white babies (29 males and 41 females), ages four months through twelve months. They used 24 test items grouped into four categories: auditory (e.g., speaking to the infant in a high-pitched squeaky voice), tactile (e.g., kissing stomach), social (e.g., peek-a-boo), and visual (e.g., mother crawling on floor). In all instances the mother administered the test items in the home. The investigators hypothesized that items making the greatest cognitive demands on the baby (visual and social items) would tend to elicit laughter later in development than cognitively less demanding items (tactile and auditory stimuli). Mother's judgment and independent raters determined whether the baby laughed or not.

With their more heterogeneous test items these investigators, in contrast to Washburn, found a substantial increase in the amount of laughter with age. They also found a developmental trend in the type of items eliciting laughter, especially in the comparisons of 7–9 and 10–12-month-olds. The older of these two groups laughed significantly more in response to the visual and social items while the younger of these two groups laughed significantly more at the auditory and tactile items. For the 4–6-month-olds, nine of the eleven items that produced laughter involved auditory or tactile stimulation. The most effective social item for the 4–6-month-olds ("gonna get you") included both auditory and tactile stimulation.

Another study using more standardized and less animated procedure for presentation of test items resulted in considerably less laughter than was the case in study 1, but the overall pattern of results were the same for both experiments. The modal ages for the four categories of stimuli were as follows: tactile 6.5; auditory, 7.0; social, 8.0; visual, 10.5. The median modal age at which the most "cognitively sophisticated" items elicited laughter was 11.5 months, tending to support the investigators' hypothesis that items making the greatest cognitive demand on the infants would elicit laughter only in the older infants. The investigators also found some evidence for the relationship between the development of laughter and motor development. They found a statistically significant relationship ($r =$ .69, $p < .05$) between the age of crawling and the age of first laughter to mother crawling on floor.

Sroufe and Wunsch thought that the laughter response to a few of their items (e.g., the mock attack of "gonna get you") could be well explained by the ambivalence hypothesis of Ambrose (1963). To this test item infants often seem to waver between expressing distress or fear on the one hand and laughter on the other. However, many of their observations were not consistent with the ambivalence hypothesis. For example, in the case where the mother put on a mask, a clear majority of the infants leaned forward toward her and strived to reach the mask, smiling or laughing as they made the effort.

Sroufe and Wunsch thought their data were generally consistent with Zigler, Levine, and Gould's (1967) cognitive congruency principle or cognitive challenge hypothesis—children are more likely to laugh at jokes (incongruities) neither too obvious nor beyond their comprehension, things that lie at the growing edge of their capacities. McGhee (1971a,b) refined this idea and verified the role of cognitive challenge in relation to cognitive mastery by measuring the specific developmental cognitive acquisitions of his subjects. In a later study, however, McGhee (1974a) suggested that with increasing age cognitive challenge plays a lesser role, and emotional factors such as the type of affect involved in the incongruity and affective state (or mood) of the subject play an increasingly important role.

Sroufe and Wunsch's extensive studies of the development of laughter also offered further support for the differential emotions theory hypothesis that emotion is motivational and plays a role in guiding behavior. They concluded: "We have observed repeatedly that when an infant cries he pulls back in the high chair and turns from the stimulus, whereas when laughter occurs the baby maintains an orientation towards the agent, reaches for the object, and seeks to reproduce the situation" (p. 1341). If the motivation for the behavior described here was solely a function of information processing or other cognitive activity then the resulting positive or negative emotion would seem to be superfluous. However, the emotion is clearly related to the direction and intensity of the behavior of the infant. Further, as already suggested in the discussion of the smiling response, the infant's laughter (positive emotion expression) tends to motivate laughter (joy and joy-related responses) from the mother or caretaker.

Rothbart's arousal–safety model of laughter seems generally consistent with the Spencer–Tomkins position. Simply stated, her model explains laughter as the expressive consequence of arousal resulting from unexpected, sudden, intense stimulation, or stimuli that do not fit into the infant's present knowledge or schema. If the arousing stimulus is judged to be not dangerous (trivial, inconsequential), smiling or laughter are likely to result. In expanding this model Rothbart again came rather close to Tomkins's ideas of emotion activation. She noted that if a person's initial arousal to a stimulus is very high the response would likely be avoidance (fear or distress), while if the arousal is only moderate, curiosity and attempts at problem solving or exploration may follow rather than laughter. It is only when the stimulus is judged as not dangerous (fear-eliciting) or challenging (curiosity-, interest-eliciting) but rather trivial or inconsequential that laughter results. This conceptualization follows rather closely Tomkins's idea that the steepest gradient of stimulation evokes startle, the next steepest fear, the next steepest (a more moderate increase) interest, and that it is actually a decrease in stimulation (conceivably brought about by assessment of the stimulus situation as trivial and inconsequential) that activates joy.

In discussing the functions of laughter, Rothbart made a cogent argument for a function of laughter other than that of dissipating tension in the individual. She maintained that if arousal due to discrepant or strange stimuli always elicited negative responses (distress, fear), the infant would very likely be comforted by the caretaker and removed from the disturbing stimulus. However, when the infant responds to such stimuli with laughter the mother or caretaker is inclined to reproduce the disturbing stimulus, giving the infant the opportunity to experience and explore the situation. She also suggested that early laughter games may foster two kinds of learning: (a) the development of general expectations and (b) the social experience of learning that one's actions (in this case expressive behavior) influence the activities of other people. The observations of other theorists and investigators, together with those of Rothbart, make a good case for the adaptive value of laughing.

Rothbart correctly pointed out that it is the infant or child who initiates the behavior sequence involved in mother–infant interactions surrounding distress and laughter. The child's crying in distress initiates the mother's efforts to comfort and care for the child; and in the laughter game, although the mother may present the initial stimulus for arousal, if the child does not laugh the sequence is terminated and the game does not begin.

Humor Appreciation. Humor at its best involves the positive affect of joy, but when humor occurs at other people's expense it may be associated with anger, contempt (as in derisive laughter), and subsequent guilt. Humor appreciation is a function of both affect and cognition, and in differential emotions theory it is considered a special kind of affective–cognitive interaction. Laughter games in infancy set the stage for the development of humor appreciation, and one's ultimate sense of humor depends on one's freedom during developmental years to express vocally the sudden bursts of joy that accompany certain cognitive–affective processes.

An excellent series of studies on the psychology of humor has been conducted by Levine and his colleagues (e.g., Levine, 1956, 1968a,b; Levine and Rakusin, 1959; Levine and Redlich, 1960; Levine and Zigler, 1976). Levine has worked mainly with adults, normals and psychiatric patients. He discusses three theoretical models for the study of humor: (a) perceptual–cognitive theory which emphasizes successful and surprising resolution of incongruity, (b) drive- or tension-reduction theory, and (c) psychoanalytic theory that emphasizes release or gratification of unconscious sexual or aggressive urges in conjunction with cognitive activity which may include resolution of incongruity. He has shown how psychiatric conditions and certain affective states can inhibit or enhance the appreciation of humor.

An equally fine series of studies on the development of humor in children has been done by McGhee (e.g., 1974b,c). He has found considerable support for the perceptual–cognitive model, particularly for the role of cognitive mastery and the resolution of incongruity. As already noted, however, he suggested the idea that with increasing age affective content of the material and affective state of the child may increase in importance as factors in humor appreciation. His conclusions are similar to those of Levine's, although McGhee does not relate his ideas and findings to certain of the psychoanalytic concepts employed by Levine.

Zillman and his colleagues (Cantor, Bryant, & Zillman, 1974) studied the effects of prior arousal or "excitation transfer" (Zillman, 1971) on humor appreciation. They found that residual excitation from both positive (sexual) and negative (distressing, fearsome) stimuli enhanced subsequent appreciation of cartoons and jokes. Their position is that residual excitation enhances emotion responses only when it is not attributed to its actual source (Cantor, Zillman, & Bryant, 1975). However, their finding on humor appreciation may be explicable in terms of Tomkins's hypothesis that joy results from a decrease in neural stimulation. The subjects were presented the humorous stimuli during a period when their arousal level from prior stimulation was decreasing but not yet at baseline. Since Cantor, Bryant and Zillman (1974) found that both positive and negative arousal subsequently enhanced humor appreciation (and presumably an accompanying positive affective state) their data seem to run counter to the Solomon–Corbit opponent process theory.

Leventhal and his colleagues describe an information-processing model of humor appreciation. The steps in the process consist of perception, interpretation, information integration, and overt judgment. They assume that each step represents different processes and that sex differences may occur at any one of them.

Leventhal and Mace (1970) showed children a humorous film under an inhibition condition ("restrain from laughter") and a facilitation condition ("laugh as much as you like"). They confirmed their hypothesis that expressive behavior (laughter) would increase the strength of subjective feeling, a finding consistent with differential emotions theory and other theories linking facial expression and experiential emotion.

Cupchik and Leventhal (1974) showed that audience (canned) laughter and self-observation of one's own expressiveness affected males and females differently. Audience laughter caused females to be more expressive and to give higher funniness ratings to cartoons, but self-observation of their expressiveness produced significantly lower funniness ratings. When males heard audience laughter and observed (rated) their own expressiveness, they did not show the same pattern of responses as females but differentiated more sharply between good and poor cartoons. The authors inferred that women are more susceptible to expressive reactions as such, while males are more susceptible to informational influence. They found support for this inference in a later study that showed that females were more influenced by "canned laughter from a party" while males were more influenced by "canned laughter from a classroom" (Leventhal & Cupchik, 1975).

Another study (Leventhal & Cupchik, 1977) further confirmed the foregoing assumptions and empirical findings. They concluded that, as compared to males, females base their humor judgments more on feelings and that feelings vary as a function of the level of spontaneous expressive behavior.

Joy Interactions with Other Affects, Cognition, and Action

Joy, at least temporarily, can attenuate or inhibit the drives. The fulfillment of drives or the satisfaction of drives does not necessarily lead to joy, but drive satisfaction often lowers the joy threshold or creates a state conducive to joy. In any case, we know that joy often follows a good meal or exciting sexual relations with one who is loved. Joy can also influence other emotions, cognition, and action.

The Interactions of Joy with Other Emotions

Joy, like any emotion, can amplify, attenuate, mask, or inhibit another emotion. In day-to-day living, joy probably attenuates, masks, and inhibits emotions more frequently than it amplifies them. However, there are occasions in which joy does amplify another emotion; an example of this will be discussed later.

Joy and Interest. The interaction or combination of interest and joy supports the development of play and social activity (Figure 10-3), and probably constitutes the cornerstone of love and affectional relationships. A person who is a continuing source of excitement and joy is likely to be one for whom there is strong and enduring affection. This combination of emotions makes up most of the positive emotion aspects of romantic, sexual relationships. As is evident to anyone who reflects on the emotions

FIGURE 10-3. Interest–joy interaction in six- to ten-month infants at play.

in relation to love, virtually every emotion comes into play in a continuing intimate relationship, but joy and interest form its foundation.

Joy and Shame. When the person who excites and brings joy fails to show interest or enjoyment in your presence, that person may become a stimulus for shame. The prototype of this negative interpersonal interaction is the unrequited smile.

Joy and Guilt. Whenever we experience joy or fun at somebody else's expense we may, in retrospect, experience guilt. When we enjoy forbidden things we may subsequently experience guilt. If our enjoyment of the "forbidden" has violated our conscience or moral–ethical standards, guilt is pretty sure to follow. This sequence can occur either as a result of actual performance in real life situations or equally as well as a result of fantasy.

Joy and Contempt. When joy and contempt combine, the result may be cruelty. When this combination of emotions occurs with such regularity that it forms a personality trait the result may be a sadistic character formation.

The prototype of the joy–contempt response may be a smile of triumph when the triumph is at the expense of a defeated opponent. The joy–contempt pattern occurs when you enjoy a victory that you think occurred because you are a better person than the one you defeated.

Interactions of Joy with Perception, Cognition, and Action

The interaction of joy with the perceptual system has marked and readily observable effects. All sensory input seems relatively more pleasant than when you are distressed or experiencing some other negative emotion. Roses are redder, violets are bluer, and the sunshine is brighter; even rain that might be a pesky nuisance on other occasions is now refreshing or soothing. It is while experiencing joy that one "sees the world through

rose-colored glasses." The apparent change that joy effects on the perceptual system (thus increasing thresholds for negative emotions) makes the
recipient seem imbued with patience, tolerance, and generosity. Joy tends
to have the same kind of salubrious effect on cognition that it has on
perception. Problems melt and float away—they are either solved or
become of less concern.

Depending upon the cognitive tasks at hand, joy may bring about a
decrease in productive thinking. If the kind of problem at hand requires a
great deal of persistence and hard work, joy may put the problem aside
before it is solved. In some situations then the interaction of joy and
cognition may be paradoxical. If your intellectual performance, whatever it
may be, leads to joy, the joy will have the effect of slowing down performance and removing some of the concern for problem solving. This change
in pace and concern may postpone or in some cases eliminate the possibility of an intellectual or creative achievement. In some cases the paradox
can be effectively resolved. If excitement causes the "rushing" or "forc-
ing" of intellectual activity, a joy-elicited slowing down may be exactly
what is needed to improve intellectual performance and creative endeavor.

Joy and Styles of Life. Some people have invested the emotion of joy
in the process of living. This doesn't necessarily mean that they have
invested it in specific thoughts, actions, competencies, or skills. It simply
means that they enjoy being alive. Such a person may appear to move
through life more slowly as well as more tranquilly. Insight into the kind of
conflict that seems to exist between a life of joy and one of excitement was
captured by one of George Bernard Shaw's characters when he said, "I
don't want to be happy; I want to be alive and active."

Shaw's very clever line seems to pit "aliveness and action" against
happiness or joy as though they are mutually exclusive. The playwright's
thought inspires some reflection on the life process. Some will undoubtedly
say: "I am happy only when I am active. Shaw's line does not make
sense." Two things may be causing a person to make such a statement.
First, the person may be confusing excitement and joy. Interest–excitement is the positive emotion that is associated with constructive activity
and adventure. Excitement tends to call for action and in turn action tends
to amplify the excitement. This is particularly true if the activities in which
one is engaging are meeting with success. Second, the people who link
activity with joy may be saying that they can experience joy only after they
have "earned it," only after action, hard work, vigorous effort. Undoubtedly joy is interspersed in the lives of some as they engage in work or
strenuous activities. But hard work does not guarantee joy, and whatever
joy is sandwiched between projects or responsibilities may not have the
same enriching and enhancing effect as joy accompanied by calmness and
tranquility of mind and body. We are left with some challenging questions.

Do people need to set aside more time to allow for joy to occur with calmness and tranquility? Would a significant increase in "tranquil joy" represent a genuine improvement in our life-styles, or would it be a cop out?

Joy and Development of "Emotional Needs." The concept of "emotional needs" is typically treated in psychology in a rather general and vague fashion. A more precise definition can be developed from differential emotions theory. An emotional need is a kind of dependency on a person, object, or situation for the realization of positive emotion or for the prevention of negative emotion. The greater the dependency the greater the need and the more likely will be a general restriction on the emotion experiences or "emotional life" of the individual. In infancy everyone has an emotional need for the mother (or mother-substitute). Generally the infant is quite dependent on the mother for excitement and joy. It is the mother or caretaker who is responsible for presenting the infant with new objects and novel situations, and the mother is the most significant and continual source of comfort and joy. At the same time the infant is dependent upon the mother for the prevention of negative emotion. The mother's presence often prevents distress and fear, and the mother's helping hand prevents frustration and anger. The more a mother is the sole agent for bringing excitement and joy and preventing distress, anger, fear, and shame, the greater will be the infant's emotional need for her. Too great a dependency is prevented only by the careful work of the mother in introducing the infant and child to an ever increasing variety of sources of excitement and joy and by helping the child develop the skills and competencies for keeping negative emotions from becoming overwhelming.

Maladaptive Interactions of Joy, Cognition, and Action. The possible maladaptive effects of certain joy–cognition interactions can be illustrated by a description of the role of joy in the formation of addictions (Tomkins, 1962). An addiction is similar to an emotional need, except that in addiction a particular object becomes the *only* or *primary* means by which an individual obtains positive emotion and/or prevents negative emotion. An addiction is also somewhat similar to the bond that exists between a person and the familiar objects in the environment. Such familiar objects as one's room, a favorite chair, a pet, a tennis racquet, school books, blue jeans, or a picture represent a variety of commitments. An addiction represents an extreme and virtually irreversible commitment.

The emotions of joy and interest play a part in the development of psychological addictions. According to Tomkins, addiction to an object results when it elicits two kinds of emotion responses. First, the object by its presence physically, or by its place in our imagery or reverie, evokes intense joy or excitement. Second, the absence of the object or an awareness of the possibility of its absence in the future, creates intense negative emotion. When this complex of emotion–cognition responses characterize our relationship to an object, the relationship may be described as a psychological addiction.

Habitual marijuana smoking may be a good example of this type of addiction. This would be the case if the smoking of marijuana or its anticipation is the primary source of excitement or joy, and if the absence of marijuana or the absence of the possibility of smoking it elicits negative emotion. Apart from the possibility of physiological effects, the potential psychological harm from marijuana addiction would have to be judged in each individual case. To the extent that the individual can find joy and excitement *only* in marijuana smoking, and to the extent that the absence of smoking or of the possibility of smoking creates intense negative affect, the addiction may have very serious psychological effects.

Careful examination of the conditions described for addiction shows that the addicted individual's motivational system tends to be dominated by the object of addiction. Thus, other objects, whether they be books or pinball machines, lose much of their excitement, and even interpersonal affective ties, including love relationships, tend to deteriorate.

Tomkins (1962) has pointed out how a tight reciprocal and enduring two-way interaction can be established between the presence or absence of the object of addiction on the one hand and intense positive or negative affect on the other. If, after the addiction has just formed, the absence of the object coincides with a situation that elicits a strong negative emotion, such as fear, and if the fear is later reduced by the object (smoking marijuana), then the absence of marijuana may begin to be experienced as the absence of a protector, the absence of something that can reduce the fear. Thus marijuana may become a kind of security blanket as well as a source of excitement and joy.

All addictions are by no means altogether negative. We can become addicted to learning, to creating. Many people in Western civilization become addicted to achievement and success and for them the presence or absence of the currently desired sign of success (status symbol) is no less powerful as a stimulus for positive or negative emotion than is marijuana for the dope smoker. Some people, especially members of the younger generation, have raised the question as to whether the addiction to success is positive or negative, and even some members of the older generation admit that it has both positive and negative components.

Empirical Studies of Joy in Adults

As was the case with the emotion of interest, the emotion of joy has been the subject of only a few empirical studies. Even among these few there is no consistent definition of the concept of joy.

Antecedents and Consequences of Joy

In the study of the patterns of emotions in the joy situation (Izard, 1972), the participants in the study listed a wide variety of phenomena that were imaged or visualized as joy situations. A large proportion of these situations related to loved ones. Three types of situations involving loved ones led to joy: (a) making someone you love happy; (b) someone who loves you goes out of his or her way to please you, and (c) simply sharing experiences with someone you love. The category of "making others happy" included doing something out of the ordinary with someone you love, seeing gratitude in the face of a loved one for something you did, and feeling that you are making someone joyful simply by being with him or her.

Companionship with friends was also a frequently mentioned joy situation. Such situations included things such as meeting a friend after a long absence and being with friends in a "nature setting."

Although it has been suggested that joy is not earned or gained through direct effort, some people seem to remember it as resulting from their actions. A number of individuals indicated that joy resulted from various activities ranging from "creative nonrational thinking" to completing a difficult project after much personal involvement. However, they did not say that they undertook these tasks in order to experience joy.

It has also been suggested that joy is distinguished from drive pleasure, though it has been recognized that drive pleasure may lower the threshold for joy experience. Perhaps because of the latter phenomenon, a number of individuals describe joy situations associated with drive pleasures. Such situations included an intimate dinner with a member of the opposite sex and sexual intercourse.

The study of the antecedents and consequences of the fundamental emotions was described in Chapter 9. The results of the study for the emotion of joy are presented in Table 10-1. This effort to summarize the antecedents and consequences of joy is intended only to give the reader an appreciation of the variety of phenomena that lead to joy and that follow from it. As is the case with every emotion, the specific things that lead to joy and that follow from it are in some measure idiosyncratic.

The Pattern of Emotions and Experiential Dimensions in the Joy Situation

The Bartlett–Izard study, described in detail in Chapter 9, showed that the profile of emotions and dimensions in the imaged joy situation are more like those in the interest situation than in any other emotion situation. The profile of emotions in the joy situation are presented in Figure 10-4. As expected, the joy situation was characterized by a very high level of joy and

TABLE 10-1

Antecedents and Consequences of Joy

(N = Approximately 130 College Students)

Responses	Percentage of subjects giving response
Antecedents of joy	
Feelings	
1. Enjoyment	31.5
2. Relieved, problemless, relaxed, comfortable	26.9
3. Self-confident, successful	25.4
4. Accepted and needed, have something to offer	11.5
5. Other	4.6
Thoughts	
1. Of pleasant, happy times	26.9
2. Of a particular person, or activity	23.8
3. Of people, special activities	21.5
4. About own capability, success	12.3
5. About goodness of life and future	6.2
6. Of being accepted and needed, having something to offer	3.8
7. Other	5.4
Actions	
1. Doing one's favorite thing	32.3
2. Doing well, one's best	28.5
3. Helping others	14.6
4. Doing something with a particular person	11.5
5. One's duty	6.9
6. Being involved in something stimulating	4.6
7. Other	1.5
Consequences of joy	
Feelings	
1. Enjoyment–joy	51.1
2. Feel relieved, relaxed, good, carefree	27.7
3. Self-confident, successful	5.8
4. Interest–excitement	5.1
5. Desire to share joy with others	2.9
6. Healthy, active, energetic	2.9
7. About specific person, activity	1.4
8. Other	2.9
Thoughts	
1. Pleasant, happy thoughts	40.9
2. How great life is	16.8

Continued

TABLE 10-1 (continued)
Antecedents and Consequences of Joy
(N = Approximately 130 College Students)

Responses	Percentage of subjects giving response
3. About one's favorite things, good times	13.9
4. About event that caused joy	9.5
5. Of self-confidence, success	4.4
6. About sharing joy with others	4.4
7. Gratitude for joy	3.6
8. About one's achievements	2.9
9. Names specific person, activity	1.4
10. Other	2.2
Actions	
1. Favorite things	27.7
2. Expresses joy, verbally or physically	19.0
3. Shares joy with others, friendly acts	13.1
4. Does something to continue joy	9.5
5. Becomes carefree and happy	6.6
6. Does well, one's best	4.4
7. Contemplates joy inwardly	2.9
8. Other	11.6

a moderately high level of interest. The interaction of joy and interest probably characterize the subjective experience of most individuals in a joy situation. The mean of surprise is also moderately high in the joy situation. This is consistent with data from other studies suggesting that in the American culture a surprise is more often associated with positive emotion situations than with negative emotion situations. No negative emotion registers to any appreciable degree in the joy situation and only shyness showed a mean exceeding the arbitrary cutoff point of 2.5. A joy–shyness interaction is observed whenever one is seen laughing in joy and at the same time lowering the face and averting the gaze in shame or shyness.

The profile of experiential dimensions, as measured by the DRS, are presented in Figure 10-5 (Bartlett & Izard, 1972). The gaps between all the means in the joy situation were highly significant ($p < .01$). As expected, pleasantness had by far the highest mean of any of the dimensions, and self-assurance had the next highest mean. Students' descriptions of the phenomenology of joy led to the expectation of high scores on the dimension of self-assurance, and the self-assurance mean in the joy situation was substantially higher than in any other emotion situation. The self-assurance means closest to that in the joy situation were those in the surprise and interest situations.

The high mean on impulsiveness is also consistent with the phenomenological description of joy. The pleasant, self-assured, and carefree nature
of the joy experience undoubtedly plays a role in lowering the threshold for
impulsiveness. The mean for impulsiveness was higher in the joy situation
than in any other emotion situation except for anger. Judging from the data
from the study of antecedents and consequences, it is reasonable to assume
that the nature of impulsive thoughts and actions in joy are quite different
from those in anger.

Cognitively Induced Joy and Altruism

Moore, Underwood, and Rosenhan (1973) studied the effects of happy
thoughts and imagery on altruistic behavior in seven- and eight-year-old
middle class white children. The experimenter told the children that they

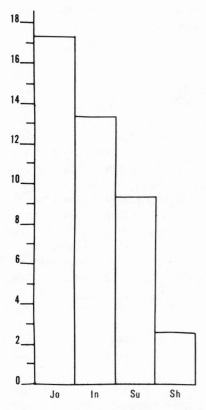 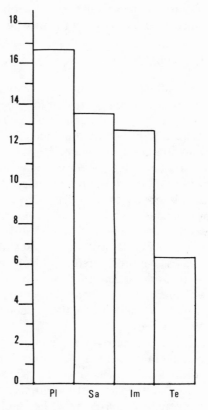

FIGURE 10-4. Profile of emotions in the joy situation. The emotion (DES) scales are abbreviated: (Jo) joy, (In) interest, (Sr) surprise, and (Sh) shyness.

FIGURE 10-5. Profile of dimensions in the joy situation. The DRS dimensions are abbreviated: (Pl) pleasantness, (Sa) self-assurance, (Im) impulsiveness, (Te) tension.

were helping test some new hearing equipment by taking a brief hearing test. The experimenter administered the hearing test individually to the children, gave each 25 pennies for participating, explained that some money would be given to the students who did not get a chance to participate, and then told them that if they so desired they could contribute some of their pennies for the nonparticipants by putting them in a nearby container. The experimenter then left the room so the child could donate, or not, in privacy. Before the 25 pennies were given to the children they were asked either to think about things that made them happy or things that made them sad, or were assigned to a neutral condition. As the experimenters predicted, the children who thought about happy occasions contributed significantly more of their pennies than those in the neutral condition, and those who thought about sad occasions contributed significantly less than those in the neutral condition. The experiment demonstrates very clearly that that type of affective–cognitive interaction is a significant determinant of action and, specifically, that on the average a cognitively induced joy experience increases altruism while sadness decreases it.

An Empirical Analysis of the Phenomenology of Joy

Following his exhaustive review of the literature on joy, Meadows (1975) developed a 61-item joy inventory with items representing each of six aspects of joy phenomenology. He reasoned that joy could be adequately described by the dimensions of activeness–passiveness, individuation–affiliation, and excitement–serenity. Activeness was seen as an aspect of joy that is felt when one plays an active role in the events that brought about the joy or when one feels active during the joy experience. Passiveness is similar to what has been discussed as receptiveness. Individuation was defined as a feeling of "centeredness" of self, a feeling that the self is distinct and separate from the surrounding world. Affiliation was described as that aspect of joy which arises from communal participation, a sense of oneness with the persons, objects, or events in the surrounding world. The excitement aspect of joy was characterized as a feeling of vigor (associated with alertness). Serenity was defined as a relaxed peacefulness, an absence of muscular tension, and a tendency to savor the world and experience a sense of harmony.

Five of these six aspects of joy emerged as distinct factors in a factor analytic investigation of the data from the administration of Meadows's Joy Scale to 333 college students. The sixth factor, activeness, emerged as one end of a bipolar factor with passiveness at the other end. The alpha coefficients (internal reliability indexes) were somewhat low for certain purposes. Nevertheless, the alpha coefficients for individuation, excitement, serenity, and activeness ranged from .70 to .62, and these are sufficiently high to suggest that Meadows's ideas about joy phenomenology are worthy of further investigation. One important question is whether all these factors represent aspects of joy or both joy and other affects.

An Empirical Study of Happiness and Personality Development

Although happiness is not necessarily synonymous with joy, the two concepts are certainly related and most would readily agree that a happy person experiences more joy or experiences joy more frequently than does an unhappy person. Constantinople (1970) did a relatively large scale cross-sectional study of four college classes (freshman through senior year) to test the relationships among level of happiness, personality development, and attitudes toward goal attainment in the college environment.

She found that males began college life at a lower average level of happiness than did females. However, college males increased in average level of happiness significantly from freshman to senior year while college females decreased in level of happiness. The decrease for females was not statistically significant, but it should be noted that the direction of change was opposite for men and women. Means for males and females decreased significantly on shame and guilt and increased significantly on autonomy and identity from freshman to senior year. For all participants level of happiness was positively correlated with basic trust, initiative, and identity, and negatively with basic mistrust, guilt, and isolation.

An important question raised by Constantinople's study was why the women showed a decrease in relative level of happiness as they progressed through college despite the fact that men showed an increase. Constantinople suggested a possible answer. She pointed out that although the development of social competence may be an indirect goal of some residential colleges, it is rarely deliberately fostered. This may be the crux of the problem, at least for those women who judge their social competence in terms of their romantic relationships and place high priority on life goals of marriage and motherhood. Pressures to attain such goals become greater as the senior year passes. Social competence judged by the senior woman in terms of progress toward the goals of marriage may be as important an ingredient of her identity as vocational competence for men. However, contrary to her needs, her sphere of social influence seems to decrease through the college years, as indicated by the significant increase in the women's average score on isolation.

Constantinople's study was conducted in the late '60s. It would be interesting to see the extent to which changes in women's attitudes and values relative to sex, marriage, and family on the one hand and autonomy, competence, and career on the other would result in different findings if this study were repeated today.

An In-Depth Study of Elation–Happiness and Personality

By far the most extensive longitudinal study of affective states and personality is that of Wessman and Ricks (1966). Working in the tradition of Gordon Allport and Henry Murray, Wessman and Ricks developed a set of 16 ten-item affective scales (Personal Feeling Scales) and applied them in the study of a small sample of college men and women who were given intensive personality assessment. Although most of Wessman and Ricks's scales do not correspond to discrete emotions or single affects, the one scale (elation–depression) that proved most important in terms of a number of criteria appears to involve the fundamental emotions of joy and distress. In particular the items at the positive pole appear to be rather straightforward joy items.

Their studies led them to conclude that for both men and women the most frequent and reliable element of happiness was the feeling that life was full and abundant. Wessman and Ricks also found that elated states were often characterized by high levels of energy and self-confidence, tranquility, love, sociability, companionship, and receptivity. This characterization of elation is quite similar to Meadows's findings on the phenomenology of joy.

Wessman and Ricks administered their Personal Feelings Scale to 25 Radcliff women and to 18 Harvard men. The group of Harvard men were intensively studied by means of a number of projective and objective personality tests, as well as through interview. They found that happy men and women exhibited zestfulness, high energy, and relatedness to others during their zest phase.

Wessman and Ricks considered their Personal Feelings Scales as a means of measuring moods. In a fashion similar to that of Nowlis (1965), they defined mood as a basic expression of the individual's continuing total life condition, as a characteristic of the individual that is intimately related to feelings and behavior. Mood as defined by Nowlis, as well as by Wessman and Ricks, seems rather similar to the concept of emotion trait in differential emotions theory.

On the basis of their Personal Feeling Scales they delineated four types of people: happy, unhappy, variable (in mood), and stable. They concluded that these four types experienced elation or their "highest mood" in somewhat different fashion. Happy people experience elation as zest, a feeling characterized by intense energetic, open, and receptive interest in a full and abundant world, a world in which they actively engage themselves. Unhappy men and women tend to experience their highest mood as sense of relief, a kind of temporary or transient peace in an otherwise turbulent world. Stable men and women experience their peaks of elation as contentment, feelings of harmony with others, tranquility, love, and sexual tenderness. People who are variable in mood tend to experience their peaks of elation as joy, an intense inner feeling of satisfaction in a full and abundant world. This state is distinguished from zest by less active engagement in the world and greater involvement with inner feelings such as self-assurance and freedom from care.

Wessman and Ricks used a number of self-description inventories (Q-sorts), projective techniques (including the Thematic Apperception Test and the Rorschach), and interviews in their intensive study of the personalities of their subjects. They found that happy men were more self-confident, more optimistic, and actually more genuinely successful. They enjoyed intimate and mutually rewarding relationships. Their work showed continuity, purpose, and meaningfulness. They had a rewarding sense of identity and the necessary skills and mastery to achieve their goals and receive a great deal of satisfaction in the process of doing so. The less happy men were more unsure and more pessimistic. Fear, anger, and guilt tended to characterize their interpersonal relationships, and they showed a certain tendency to withdraw and isolate themselves from others. Their work proved more burdensome, less satisfying, and a sense of failure led them to be self-critical and less effective. Their lower sense of ego-identity and poor ego-integration left them less well-equipped to meet the challenges of day-to-day life and to experience personal growth.

Wessman and Ricks's studies led them to some inferences about the sources of happiness and unhappiness. Happy men apparently enjoy frequent success experiences during childhood, enabling them to develop a strong sense of competence. The nature of their relationships enables them to achieve trust and intimacy and to enjoy initiative and industry. Happy men typically appear well-adjusted social extraverts who obtain a great deal of satisfaction from their work and their personal relationships. Unhappy men on the other hand show little zestful commitment to their studies and do not achieve regular satisfaction from their academic work. Happy men are apparently more capable of achieving what Freud thought the normal person should be able to do well: to love and to work.

Psychophysiological Studies of Joy

Most psychophysiological studies of affective phenomena have investigated various physiological responses to laboratory-induced arousal, activation, or complex affective states such as anxiety. A few psychophysiological studies have focused on discrete emotions, including the emotion of joy.

One of the problems in conducting psychophysiological studies of discrete emotions is that of inducing the emotion in the laboratory. Two techniques for eliciting joy, as well as other emotions, are self-induction through imagery and the use of films especially selected for their ability to elicit a particular emotion. In the imaging technique participants are requested to recall, visualize, and/or imagine a situation in which they experience the desired emotion. They are asked to take time to get into the scene as completely as possible and to picture the situation as vividly and clearly as they can. This is the technique used in obtaining the emotion profiles and the profiles of dimensions in emotion discussed in Chapter 9 and the preceeding sections of this chapter. In those studies, however, the only evidence for the presence of emotion was the participants' self-report (e.g., on the Differential Emotions Scale). The effectiveness of the imaging technique has now been substantiated by means of other ("objective") indexes of emotion or arousal. Rusalova, Izard, and Simonov (1975) had subjects image a joy situation and measured heart rate, changes in muscle potential in the expressive musculature of the face (EMG), as well as self-report. In the condition in which the subjects imaged a joy situation and consequently reported joy experience, they showed a substantial increase in heart rate and in facial muscle activity. The changes in the facial muscles were in those that were predicted to be the ones involved in the expressions of joy.

Schwartz, Fair, Greenberg, Freedman, and Klerman (1974) compared the EMG profiles of subjects who were instructed to self-generate happy, sad, and angry imagery so as to feel the target emotion. They also recorded EMG activity while the subjects thought about "a typical day." They recorded from the frontalis, corrugator, depressor, and masseter muscles and showed that the changes in muscle potential in these selected muscles varied significantly from one emotion to another. They also showed that the profile of muscle activity from happy imagery and from thinking about a typical day were more similar for normals than for depressives. In the normal subjects the typical day looked relatively similar to the profile during happy imagery.

Figure 10-6 shows the profile of EMG activity for self-generated happiness and for subjects who were told to make an exaggerated smile and hold it for 30 seconds. Although the muscle activity in the smile condition is greater, the profiles for the happy imagery and smile conditions are quite similar.

Averill (1969) studied autonomic response patterns during joy (mirth) and sadness. He used movies as stimuli to induce the desired emotions. For the mirth condition he used an adaptation of Mack Sennett's silent film "Good Old Corn" (Warner Brothers) with music and commentary added. For the sadness condition he used the film "John F. Kennedy 1917–1963" (Twentieth Century Fox), edited to give prominence to the assassination, funeral, and burial of the president. He found four physiological measures which distinguished sadness from mirth, but only one of these also distin-

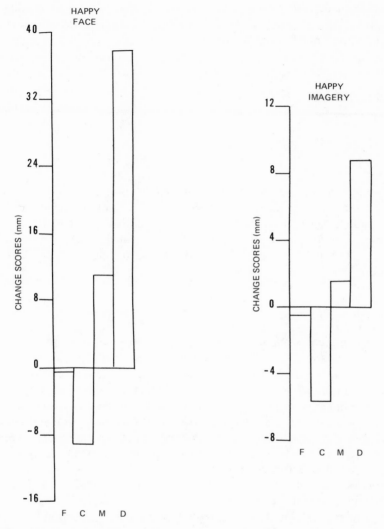

FIGURE 10-6. Average change from baseline in muscle activity for the frontalis (F), corrugator (C), masseter (M), and depressor (D) in a voluntary smile and imagery-induced joy (N = 12). (Data from Schwartz et al., 1974.)

guished mirth from the control condition. The measure that distinguished mirth from both sadness and the control condition was respiration irregularity, and this was seen largely as a function of the laughter that occurred in the mirth condition. In summary he considered changes in respiration as more characteristic of mirth while changes in the cardiovascular system were more characteristic of sadness. However, this study was not successful in providing a number of clearly distinguishing physiological reactions for sadness and mirth as induced by these particular stimuli.

Understanding and Experiencing Joy

Joy seems to be such a natural occurrence in the life of the healthy infant and child that it is puzzling why it is apparently so difficult for young people and adults to get a good understanding of this emotion and a perspective on its place in human life. Perhaps the best of all possible worlds is simply to experience joy from time to time and not bother with being so analytical about it. But students of the emotions need to take a closer look to see if a careful study of this emotion will make it more available to us and make us more appreciative of the experience and its functions. Let us take a further look at the meaning of joy and the conditions that impede or facilitate it.

More on the Phenomenology of Joy

1. Joy increases the individual's capacity to savor and appreciate the world. This means that the joyful person is more likely to see beauty and goodness in nature and in fellow human beings. While experiencing joy, people are more inclined to savor an object than to dissect it or analyze it. They appreciate the object as it is rather than wanting to change it. They feel closeness with the object rather than wanting to objectify it and put it at a distance. The object is seen as enhancing the self of the perceiver. Perhaps one reason why some mystical experiences bring great joy to us is because we stand before a mystery in awe, and realizing that we cannot fully understand it or exhaust its meaning by objective analysis, we savor it and appreciate it (Meadows, 1968).

2. Joy makes you feel that you have a distinctive bond between yourself and the world. Joy is more than a positive attitude toward self and the world. It is a special kind of link or bond. This has been described as a keen sense of belonging, or of oneness with the object of joy and with the world.

3. Although it may not be an integral part of the joy experience, joy is often accompanied by feelings of strength and vigor. Both personal experiences and empirical research have produced evidence of this feature of joy. Studies with the Differential Emotions Scale have shown a significant and positive correlation between scores on the joy experience scale and on the scale measuring vigor. The combination of joy and the feelings of strength

and vigor are also associated with the feelings of confidence and competence.

4. Perhaps as a corollary of the tendency for joy to be associated with feelings of strength and competence, joy also tends to be accompanied by a feeling of transcendence or freedom (Meadows, 1968), the feeling that you are more than or different from your usual self and that for a moment you exist in the realm of the extraordinary. In ecstatic joy you may feel that you are light and bouncy, or that you could soar, or that you really are soaring and that everything takes on a different perspective because of your unusual vantage point.

5. Joy is often accompanied by a sense of harmony and unity with the object of joy and, to some extent, with the world. Some people have reported that in ecstatic joy they tend to lose individual identity, as in the case of some mystical experiences associated with meditation.

Before leaving the phenomenology of joy it should be noted that some of the foregoing characteristics of the joy experience may involve the products of joy or the interaction of joy with perceptual and cognitive processes. There are great individual differences in the way that joy interacts with perception, memory, thought, and imagery, and consequently there may be great individual differences in the way people describe the joy experience and those phenomena that are typically associated with it.

There is an unsolved problem with respect to the role of activeness in the phenomenology of joy. Many people, including such theorists as Dumas (1948), make a distinction between active and passive (or receptive) joy. This may not really be a theoretically useful distinction. One might argue that the joy experience is a distinct subjective or phenomenological process. Although it varies in intensity, it is qualitatively a unitary phenomenon. The variation in intensity may in part explain the origin of the concepts of active and receptive joy. A low intensity of the joy experience would more nearly correspond with the notion of receptivity while a high intensity of joy would more likely correspond to the notion of activity. In the direction of passivity or receptiveness there is another quite distinct state of consciousness which may be conceptually confused with low-intensity joy. This is the feeling state which has been termed calmness-tranquility. This concept has emerged as a relatively independent empirical scale in various factor analytic investigations (Izard, Dougherty, Bloxom, & Kotsch, 1974). Joy plus tranquility may yield what some people call receptive joy.

We have already noted that joy tends to be associated with a sense of vigor and with feelings of strength, confidence, and competency. While these latter events are more correctly described as affective–cognitive orientations there is a strong tendency for them to be associated with intense joy. The concept of active joy, therefore, may derive from the tendency for intense joy to be associated with feelings of confidence and vigor. Other variations in the phenomenology of joy probably also result from variations in joy–cognition interactions.

Obstacles to the Experiencing of Joy

William Schutz has written a little book called, *Joy: Expanding Human Awareness* (1967). In this book he discussed what he views as some of the obstacles to joy. He defined joy almost completely in terms of self-fulfillment. "Joy is the feeling that comes from the fulfillment of one's potential" (Schutz, 1967, p. 15).

Although self-fulfillment often leads to the joy experience, it is very likely that self-fulfilling acts include other emotions besides joy, particularly excitement. In any case, to the extent that self-fulfillment is a prerequisite of joy, then it would follow that self-fulfillment cannot be pursued and captured any more than joy itself.

In Schutz's theory obstacles to the fulfillment of one's potential are obstacles to realizing joy. He pointed out that such obstacles come from everywhere. Several specific obstacles were discussed.

1. One pervasive obstacle to self-fulfillment and the realization of joy are some of the methods used to organize social institutions. Sometimes rules and regulations squelch creativity, lead to over-control, and impose mediocrity.
2. Society is often characterized by relationships that are superficial and hypercritical.
3. Dogma relating to child rearing, sex, and some religious organizations make it difficult for the individual to know himself and to like and trust himself.
4. Confusion about maleness and femaleness and uncertainty about one's sex role tend to block self-knowledge and self-fulfillment.
5. Another obstacle to self-fulfillment and joy is the high value placed by our society on material success and achievement.
6. In addition to the foregoing obstacles relating to personal and social functioning, poor physical condition of the body can also inhibit self-fulfillment and the realization of joy. A body that is not physically fit is less capable of realizing the sensations and experiences that lead to fulfillment and joy.

How Do You Find Joy?

As already suggested, it appears that one cannot achieve joy in the same way that one achieves a skill or "success" (Frankl, 1962). But this conclusion is based more on observations and reports of a personal nature than on rigorous experimentation. Many people undoubtedly have found that goal-directed activities and goal attainment often lead to joy, but in these cases the goal itself was not joy. When a person's efforts become pursuits for joy itself, they tend to change in nature and joy eludes the pursuer.

For the most part, people pursue goals because the goal-oriented activity and the possibility of goal attainment excites them. Often people do things because they are both exciting and enjoyable, but when joy comes into the picture the activity or pursuit may slow down and change in other ways as well.

Schutz, like Maslow (1971) and Rogers (1961), maintains that openness and honesty are essential ingredients in the process of realizing one's full potential and in experiencing joy. "A man must be willing to let himself be known to himself and to others, he must express and explore his feelings, and open up areas long dormant and possibly painful, with the faith that in the long run the pain will give way to a release of vast potential for creativity and joy. This is an exhilarating and frightening prospect, one which is often accompanied by agony, but which usually leads to ecstasy" (Schutz, 1967, pgs. 16–17).

To realize one's potential one has to attend to the biological, psychological, and social aspects of one's nature. It has already been noted that a body in poor physical condition can be an obstacle to self-fulfillment and joy. Self-fulfillment and joy come more readily when the body functions smoothly with a measure of grace and without undue strain. Good posture, good muscle tone, and a nervous system that is neither too sensitive nor too insensitive facilitate self-fulfilling activity and the experiencing of joy. This is an area in which anyone can make progress if he or she is willing to extend the effort. Strength, stamina, and physical skills that lead to a sense of fulfillment can be obtained through exercise and practice. Such achievements often lead to an increased sensory awareness and to a new appreciation and sensitivity to bodily feelings and inner experiences.

A second area that can be developed is what Schutz called personal functioning. In addition to the biological aspects already noted, Schutz maintained that logical thinking and creative potential could be nurtured. He also advocated the development of bodily functions that control the emotions. "Awareness of emotions, appropriate expression of feelings (and their relations to other functions such as thinking and action) can be trained" (p. 18). This observation is very similar to some of the notions about emotion control discussed in differential emotions theory.

The third area that can be developed in such a way as to facilitate self-fulfillment and joy is what Schutz called social functioning. Schutz's theory of interpersonal needs and interpersonal functioning is summarized in Shutz's own words:

This theory asserts that our needs from and toward other people are three: *inclusion, control,* and *affection*. We achieve interpersonal joy when we find a satisfying, flexible balance in each of these areas between ourselves and other people. *Inclusion* refers to the need to be with people and to be alone. The effort in inclusion is to have enough contact to avoid loneliness and enjoy people; enough aloneness to avoid enmeshment and enjoy solitude. The fully realized man can feel comfortable and joyful both with and without people, and knows with how much of each—and when—he functions best. In the area of *control* the effort is to achieve enough influence so that a man can determine his future to the degree that he finds most comfortable, and to relinquish enough control so that he is able to lean on others to teach, guide, support, and at times to take some responsibility from him. The fully realized man is capable of either leading or following as appropriate, and of knowing where he personally feels most comfortable. In *affection* the effort is to avoid being engulfed in emotional entanglement (not being free to relate without a deep involvement), but also to avoid having too little affection and a bleak, sterile life without love, warmth, tenderness, and someone to confide in. The fully realized man is aware of his needs, and functions effectively not only in close, emotionally involving situations, but also in those of lesser intensity. As in the other two areas, he is able to both give and take, comfortably and joyfully. (pp. 18–19)

According to Schutz, even if all the other requirements of body (physical) conditioning, personal functioning, and social functioning are met, self-fulfillment remains dependent in part upon the support of society. A repressive society with dehumanizing institutions and humiliating laws and practices or one that is characterized by bigotry and prejudice will place considerable restriction on self-fulfillment and the realization of joy. Thus a society characterized by optimal openness, honesty, and freedom is necessary for optimal self-fulfillment and joy experiencing.

Finally, it cannot be overlooked that one of the most important aspects of the effort toward self-fulfillment and joy consists of unlearning or undoing some of the events brought about by society and our present life style. Perhaps most people will have to overcome some degree of shame, shyness, guilt, or fear before undertaking the more positive activities that facilitate self-fulfillment and joy. We may be afraid to be open and honest and to express our emotions, even when expression is very much in order. We may be afraid that we will express the wrong feeling at the wrong time. Some may feel guilty over failure or over failing to try. Some may feel shame as they engage in the process of self-expression. Learning to control fear, shame, shyness, and guilt is one of the most difficult aspects in the effort toward self-fulfillment and the joy experience.

Summary

The individual's first social smile occurs in response to the presence of another person, and human beings remain probably the most significant source of joy in human life. In differential emotions theory the joy experience is distinguished from drive satisfaction or sensory pleasure, although the latter may reduce the threshold for joy.

Phenomenologically joy is characterized by a sense of confidence, contentment, and often by a feeling of being loved or of being lovable. Joy experiences vary along an active–receptive dimension. The expression of joy is readily recognized but the social smile may function more as a greeting than as an indicator of joy experience. According to Tomkins's theory joy is activated by a reduction in the gradient of neural stimulation. There is some evidence that selective sensitivity of receptors and neuro-mechanisms also play a role in joy activation.

The discussion of the causes of joy at the phenomenological level must be tempered by the fact that joy seems to be more a by-product than a direct result of deliberate thought or action. Joy may follow from the reduction of stimulation from undifferentiated stress or negative emotion states, from the recognition of the familiar, or from creative endeavor.

In evolutionary perspective joy complements the emotion of interest in guaranteeing that human beings will be social creatures. The effects of reciprocal smiling on facilitating mother–infant interactions and attachment probably increase the infant's chances of survival and help provide the social framework within which the infant can learn and grow. At the psychological level joy can increase frustration tolerance and promote confidence and courage. Joy's slowing-down effect makes it an antidote for the "rat-race" or "success-or-death" syndrome.

Although joy cannot be taught directly parents can share their joy and serve as models demonstrating the kinds of life styles that facilitate joy experiences. Biogenetic, socioeconomic, and cultural factors play a role in the development of the joy threshold. Given a reasonable degree of biological well-being and a relatively unrestrictive environment, children will show an amazing capacity to create their own fun and games.

A smile of sorts may appear on an infant's face in the first hours of life but the social smile does not appear until several weeks later. The smile seems to be preprogrammed, and the effectiveness of activating stimuli change with increasing age. The indiscriminate smiling of the 3- to 5-month-old infant in response to the human face probably testifies to the importance of smile-elicited affectionate behavior in the infant's welfare and healthy development. The effect of mutual smiling on the mother–infant relationship and infant development underscore the importance of emotion and emotion expression as motivational variables in human affairs.

Laughing develops a little later than smiling and progresses through certain developmental stages of its own. Theory and research have linked laughing to certain aspects of cognitive development, but the emotion dynamics in laughing have been little investigated. Laughter, like smiling, can foster interpersonal affective ties and social development. It can also foster opportunities for new experiences and learning.

Joy interacts with other emotions and with perception, cognition, and action. Joy can slow down performance but it can also create a kind of openness and receptivity associated with intuition and creativity.

Different thresholds for joy tend to create different styles of life. Some people experience a conflict between excitement and joy as they ponder the relative importance of tranquility and the vigorous pursuit of goals.

"Emotional needs" can be defined precisely in differential emotions theory as a kind of dependency on particular persons, objects, or situations for the realization of positive emotions or the prevention of negative emotions. Some degree of such emotional needs may be a normal part of effective social relationships but too great an emotional dependency can stifle growth and development.

Empirical studies of joy in adults have increased our understanding of the antecedents and consequences of joy and of joy phenomenology. Other studies have shown sex-linked changes in frequency of joy experiences or happiness during college years. One in-depth study of happiness has shown significant relationships between personality characteristics, joy thresholds, and types of joy experiences. Psychophysiological studies suggest the possibility of differentiating joy from other emotions on the basis of neurophysiological functions, especially in terms of facial electromyography.

While it is probably not possible successfully to pursue joy for its own sake it is feasible to reach a better understanding to certain obstacles to joy, such as over-control and restrictive dogma relating to child rearing, sex, and moral–ethical development. Learning to control negative emotions and unlearning unduly restrictive inhibitions can develop the kind of openness to experience that facilitates self-fulfillment and joy in living.

Bradburn's (1969) extensive empirical study of psychological well-being is generally consistent with the other studies reviewed in Chapter 10. He showed that people who participate more in their environment (become involved socially) and have more new or varied experiences report more positive affect. High socioeconomic status, which helps reduce the amount of drabness and monotony in life, was found to be positively correlated with positive affective experiences. Bradburn's data suggested, however, that money and status "may enable one to increase his joys, but it cannot decrease his sorrows" (p. 226).

SURPRISE–STARTLE

Surprise is not an emotion in the same sense as joy or sadness is. It does not have all the characteristics of the other emotions, but it has some very useful functions.

How Surprise Occurs

Surprise or startle is activated by a sharp increase in neural stimulation. The external condition for surprise is any sudden and unexpected event. The event may be a clap of thunder, the boom of fireworks, or the unexpected appearance of a friend.

What It Looks Like to Be Surprised

The look of surprise, as shown in Figure 11-1, is easy to recognize. The brow is lifted, creating wrinkles across the forehead. The eyebrows are raised, giving the eyes a large, rounded appearance. The mouth is opened in an oval shape. In more intense surprise and startle, characteristic postural changes accompany the facial expression. If the person is standing, the knees buckle a little and the body bends forward, prior to movements of withdrawal.

What It Feels Like to Be Surprised

Everyone is familiar with the feeling of surprise, but it is difficult to describe. One reason for this is the fact that the feeling does not last very long. However, the most important reason is because the mind seems to be

FIGURE 11-1. The surprise expression in an American girl (from Tomkins's Affect Pictures).

blank in the moment of surprise. It is as though ordinary thought processes are momentarily stopped. Thus there is very little thought content associated with surprise, and virtually none with startle. It is a little like receiving mild electric shock; your muscles contract rapidly and you can almost feel the tingle of the electrical activity that occurs in the nerves and makes you jump. In the moment of surprise, you do not know exactly how to react. There is a feeling of uncertainty created by the sudden unexpected event.

Figure 11-2 shows the profile of dimensions in the surprise situation. The graph, adapted from the Bartlett–Izard study, shows that a surprise situation is characterized by a high degree of pleasantness. This is consonant with the common sense observation that most people think of surprise in a positive way. If young people are asked to recall a time when they were surprised, they usually recall a situation that turned out to be happy and pleasant. Situations that evoke surprise are usually experienced as being about as pleasant as situations that elicit a high degree of interest. Situations that cause surprise are generally remembered as less pleasant than situations that cause joy but as much more pleasant than situations causing any negative emotion—distress, anger, disgust, contempt, fear, and shame.

In the surprise situation the mean for pleasantness was significantly higher than the means for self-assurance and impulsiveness, and the latter means were significantly higher than the mean for tension. Impulsiveness was significantly higher in surprise than all the emotions studied except for anger and joy. Self-assurance was significantly higher in surprise than for any of the negative emotions. The mean for tension in the surprise situation was significantly lower than for any of the negative emotions, approximately equal to the mean for the interest situation, and significantly higher than was the case for the joy situation. The data for the dimension of tension furnish some support for the differential emotion concept of surprise as occupying a place in between the positive and negative emotions. Even though middle-class American students typically image a surprise situation that is characterized by pleasantness and self-assurance, the amount of tension felt is as near to that felt in distress as that felt in joy. Since the means for tension are significantly higher in all of the negative emotions than in surprise and the two positive emotions of interest and joy, it is reasonable to conclude that the subjective experience of tension is experienced as negative once it reaches a certain level. However, a level of tension significantly higher than that experienced in joy can still be experienced in relation to the positive affect of interest–excitement.

Figure 11-3 shows the profile of emotions in the surprise situation. The differences between each successive pair of means shown on the graph are

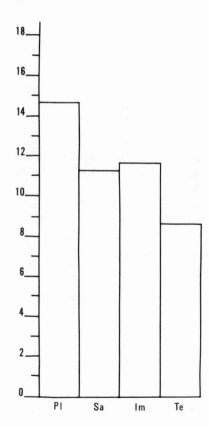

FIGURE 11-2. Profile of dimensions in the surprise situation. The DRS dimensions are abbreviated: (Pl) pleasantness, (Sa) self-assurance, (Im) impulsiveness, (Te) tension.

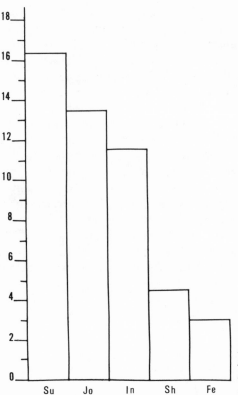

FIGURE 11-3. Profile of emotions in the surprise situation. The emotion (DES) scales are abbreviated (Jo) joy, (In) interest, (Su) surprise, (Sh) shyness, (Fe) fear.

significantly different. The surprise/joy/interest pattern is the most typical combination of emotions for the type of subjects sampled in the Bartlett–Izard study. The data show that the negative emotions most likely to be involved in a surprise situation in this class of subjects are shame and fear. Sometimes an individual is ashamed of the fact that he was "caught by surprise." Such a situation may be characterized by the feeling that the individual is overexposed. The appearance of fear in the larger pattern has a sufficiently low mean to suggest that in the population sampled, fear is not frequently associated with an imaged surprise situation. The fact that it occurs at all may lend some support to the notion that surprise and fear have similar or overlapping components at the neurophysiological level.

The Significance of Surprise

From the foregoing description of the experience of surprise, it is clear that it is a highly transient feeling. It comes quickly and goes away quickly.

Unlike other emotions, surprise does not motivate behavior for long periods of time. In some respects surprise is not a real emotion like the other fundamental emotions considered in this book.

If surprise is so fleeting and motivates very little thought or action, what is its function? Its primary function is to help prepare the individual to deal effectively with the new or sudden event and with the consequences of this event. It is important for the person to be able to deal with sudden changes. From an evolutionary standpoint, failure to change one's motivational set after the sudden appearance of some predatory animal or threatening situation could result in serious harm or death.

A person is always experiencing one emotion or another and often more than one. Some emotions, once they are activated, have great psychological inertia—they tend to continue. Distress is a good example of an emotion that is difficult to stop quickly. All mental health professionals know how difficult it is to break up a depression, a complex of emotions and feelings in which distress dominates. The sudden appearance of a poisonous snake or speeding automobile in the path of a depressed person could mean certain death if surprise did not facilitate a change in his or her emotion state.

Thus the function of surprise is to clear the nervous system of ongoing activity that would interfere with adjustment to a sudden change in our environment. Silvan Tomkins (1962) has aptly called it the "channel-clearing emotion." It clears the neural pathways for new and different activity.

TABLE 11-1

Antecedents and Consequences of Surprise
(N = Approximately 130 College Students)

Responses	Percentage of subjects giving responses
Antecedents of surprise	
Feelings	
1. Surprise synonyms: startled, shocked	31.4
2. Unexpectedly aware of something	22.3
3. Lost, bewildered, confused	12.4
4. Physically/mentally stimulated	8.3
5. Misled, hurt, used by others	7.4
6. Distress synonyms: depressed, sad	4.6
7. Shame synonyms: embarrassed, shy	.7
8. Other	12.4

Continued

TABLE 11-1 (continued)
Antecedents and Consequences of Surprise
(N = Approximately 130 College Students)

Responses	Percentage of subjects giving responses
Thoughts	
1. Something wrong, stupid	27.3
2. Of some specific person, activity	23.9
3. Unexpected awareness	19.8
4. Something original, creative	16.5
5. Other	12.4
Actions	
1. Something original, creative	33.9
2. Unexpected success or failure	33.1
3. Something stupid, makes mistake	15.7
4. React to stimulus	7.4
5. Other	9.9
Consequences of surprise	
Feelings	
1. Surprise synonyms	37.6
2. Bewildered, confused	14.3
3. Fear synonyms	10.5
4. Interest synonyms	10.0
5. Happy or sad, depending on the context	6.8
6. Enjoyment synonyms	4.5
7. Shame synonyms	2.3
8. Other	14.3
Thoughts	
1. About what caused surprise	39.9
2. Shouldn't have been surprised	33.9
3. Anticipate consequences, response	11.2
4. Of possible reward	.7
5. How to regain control of self and situation	.7
6. Other	13.5
Actions	
1. Try to understand cause	28.5
2. Regain control of self or situation	21.8
3. Express surprise, verbally or physically	18.8
4. Depends on situation, whatever is appropriate	9.2
5. Anticipate consequences, reaction	7.5
6. Something panicky, irrational	3.0
7. Express enjoyment	2.3
8. Other	9.2

If Rafe is given pleasant surprises relatively often he will come to view the overall effect of surprise as positive, though strictly speaking it is neither positive nor negative. If Rebecca has relatively frequent unpleasant surprises, she may come to view the effect of surprise as negative and become less capable of dealing with situations of surprise. If the socialization of surprise is very severe, the individual may become fearful or ineffective in the presence of anything novel or different whether or not it appears suddenly.

The study of antecedents and consequences of surprise in college students is presented in Table 11-1.

Charlesworth (1969) presents an extensive review of the literature on surprise, defining it specifically as a function of *mis*expected (as distinguished from *un*expected) events. Surprise so defined cannot occur until five–seven months of age, when cognitive development enables the infant to form expectations or assumptions. Working within this conceptual framework, Charlesworth makes a good case for assigning an important role to surprise in cognitive development. He sees it as instigating, "illuminating," and reinforcing a variety of responses that contribute to changes in cognitive structures. He attributes to surprise some of the characteristics that differential emotions theory assigns to interest.

In contrast to Charlesworth's position, Bower (1974) reports evidence of startle or surprise (terms he uses interchangeably) a few hours after birth. The two investigators agree, however, on the value of surprise as a measure of certain cognitive processes and possibly as an index of stages of cognitive development.

12

DISTRESS–ANGUISH, GRIEF, AND DEPRESSION

Distress is a highly important fundamental emotion that has many functions. It played a role in the evolution of human beings and it continues to serve important biological and psychological functions. Distress and sadness are generally considered synonymous. Ekman and Friesen (1975), while conceiving sadness as a form of distress, however, draw some distinctions between the two. They see distress as more active, as a stronger motivation to protest as well as to cope. While considering sadness a form of distress is not substantially inconsistent with differential emotions theory, the latter holds that the underlying emotion experience is the same. The total subjective experience in a distress situation may vary as different affects and cognitions interact. Ekman and Friesen's distinction between distress and sadness may be more a function of the cognition and imagery that interacts with distress than a result of differences in the experiential emotion (distress). For example, the protest and activity that Ekman and Friesen believe to be features that distinguish distress from sadness may result, in part, from a distress–anger interaction.

Grief is normally made up mostly of distress or sadness, though it is often a pattern of emotions and affective–cognitive structures that involve fear, guilt, or anger. Grief is typically a reaction to loss; one can grieve about any kind of loss, but here the focus will be on grief resulting from permanent separation or death of a loved one.

Depression also has distress as the key emotion, but it is always a complex pattern of emotions, changes in drive states, and affective–cognitive interactions. In addition depression may be instigated or influenced by a variety of neurophysiological and biochemical factors. The term depression is highly complex and unfortunately means many different things even to the scientists who study it.

The first section of this chapter will consider the fundamental emotion of distress and some of its interactions with other fundamental emotions. The second section will consider normal and psychopathological grief. In section three, several theories of depression will be briefly considered followed by a presentation of the differential emotions theory of depression and some empirical evidence to support it.

Distress–Anguish

While interest is normally the most frequently experienced positive emotion, distress is the most common negative emotion. Distress serves important biological and psychological functions.

Activation and Causes of Distress

According to Tomkins (1963), distress is a density-level affect. Distress occurs as a result of a continued excessive level of stimulation. The possible sources of stimulation (causes) are numerous—pain, cold, noise, heat, bright lights, loud speech, disappointment, failure, loss. Tomkins believes that pain, hunger, and any intense or enduring emotion, including distress itself, can serve as an innate activator of distress. He also believes that excessive repetition of imagery generated in the brain itself can serve as an innate activator. The learned activators of distress are numerous indeed. A memory of an innate activating condition as well as memories or anticipations of distressing conditions may activate this general, highly negative emotion.

The first occasion for distress is birth itself, the physical separation of the infant from the mother. Salk showed that infants placed in a nursery with the muffled heartbeat of a mother produced by a loudspeaker were able to gain more weight and cried less than those infants placed in the usual hospital or home nursery (cited in Tomkins, 1963). Tomkins speculated that the sound of the muffled heartbeat simulated a return to the prenatal condition.

Separation, whether physical or psychological, remains throughout life one of the basic and most common causes of distress. When we have to leave our family or dear friends we feel distressed, but we may be separated or alone psychologically, even when we are in a crowd of people. Psychological separation takes many forms—inability to communicate with others, express our true feelings, or obtain sympathy. Or, we may feel left out, that we do not belong.

Another important cause of distress is failure, either real or imagined. Rafe may become distressed because he did not do well at work or at school. In this realm, causes of distress are relative to the person's standards. Rafe may be very happy to make a B, while Rebecca would be very distressed because she strongly desires and expects an A. Another young woman may be distressed because she did not live up to her parents' expectations. Sometimes it is a combination of these things. Distress may also be caused by real or imagined failure in social relationships, romance, or sports.

It is very important for parents to recognize and understand objects of distress for both themselves and their children, and to treat distress in a serious manner instead of merely administering simple, thoughtless discipline. The child often has to contend with distress that is elicited by events beyond his or her control, and sometimes the sources of distress are beyond anyone's control. As Tomkins put it:

> Not only does the spectrum of sources of distress grow wider with development, but there are many sources of distress which so much depend on environmental vicissitudes as to be essentially independent of personality and personality development. Thus serious economic depressions, wars, illnesses and injuries of the self and of love objects, death of loved objects, and similar misfortunes may subject children, adolescents, and adults alike to severe distress over which they can exercise little control. Neither personality nor life ends in childhood and there is no way of guaranteeing that a child who has experienced only excitement and enjoyment may not, beginning in adolescence, be vulnerable to severe distress the rest of his life through circumstances over which he can exercise little control. (Tomkins, 1963, p. 53)

Since distress is an inevitable part of life, it is important that children learn to recognize its causes and to deal with it effectively. Some of the consequences of different styles of socialization of distress will be considered later.

The Expression of Distress

Everyone is familiar with the look of a sad face, but few people stop to analyze what happens to the face when it assumes the expression of distress. The expressions shown in Figure 12-1 are recognized by most people as portrayals of distress or sadness.

In the full expression of distress the eyebrows are arched upward and inward, sometimes forming a π-shaped arch in the lower middle forehead. The inner corners of the upper eyelids are drawn up, and the lower eyelid may appear to be pushed upward. The corners of the mouth are drawn downward, and the chin muscle pushes upward and raises the center of the lower lip. Of course, the prototype of the distress expression and its most usual form in infancy and childhood, as well as in the adult in moments of strong grief, is the act of crying. However, the keen observer of people

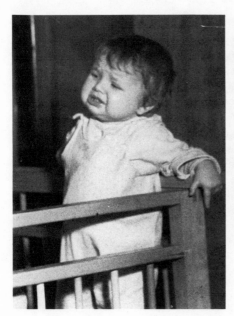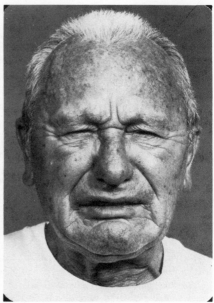

FIGURE 12-1. The facial pattern of distress in a toddler and an old man differs mainly in terms of the permanent wrinkles that come with age (photo of old man from Tomkins's Affect Pictures). The development of some emotions (e.g., fear) and their full facial expressions come later than distress, which appears in the neonate.

knows that it is necessary to look for the other signs of distress in the adult, because crying does not always signal simple distress. Crying may occur in a moment of great delight (tears of joy) or in anger and profound frustration. On these occasions some distress is often experienced but its cause may not be obvious—the joyous occasion may call to mind a previous separation and the frustration may elicit images of failure and discouragement.

As Tomkins (1963) observed, people learn to attenuate, modify, or completely transform the facial expression and vocal cry of distress. Beginning in late childhood, one begins to learn to abbreviate the cry, lower the volume, and to straighten up the face quickly. Crying becomes infrequent in adulthood, less frequent in men than in women, due to cultural forces and possibly to sex-linked characteristics as well. The distress expression may be completely transformed into a long, sagging face and whining voice. The sad appearance of the face and the plaintive tones embedded in the speech are transformations of the infant's cry for help.

How It Feels to Be Distressed

Even so common a feeling as that of distress is not altogether easy to describe. To feel distressed is to feel sad, downhearted, discouraged. In distress, we may feel lonely, isolated, miserable, out of touch with people, especially people who care about us. We may feel that we have failed and been rejected. The rejection may be real or imagined or it may even be self-rejection. Dissatisfaction with the self is often a part of the experience of distress. We may feel that we can not do what we really strongly desire to do. We may feel that our world is dark and gloomy—we have the "blues." Time seems to drag along slowly or stand still. We feel more helpless and dependent than usual. We feel a loss of something; we feel miserable.

The profile of experiential dimensions in the distress situation is presented in Figure 12-2. The highest dimensional mean in distress is tension, but it is quite in keeping with differential emotions theory that tension is lower in distress than in any other negative emotion. Thus, as already indicated, and as pointedly emphasized by Tomkins (1963), distress is much more tolerable than fear or the other negative emotions. Interestingly, impulsiveness, the second highest experiential dimension in distress, is lower for this emotion than any other emotion studied in the Izard–Bartlett experiment. The experiment showed that self-assurance in distress is not

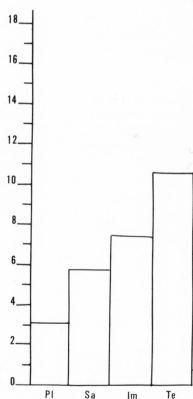

FIGURE 12-2. Profile of dimensions in the distress situation. DRS abbreviations: (Pl) pleasantness, (Sa) self-assurance, (Im) impulsiveness, (Te) tension.

significantly different from that in shyness and guilt but is significantly higher than in fear. As to be expected, the dimension of pleasantness is as low in distress as in any of the negative emotions. It is as low in distress as it is in fear, anger, and guilt, and significantly lower than it is in shyness.

The profile of emotions in the distress situation is presented in Figure 12-3. To indicate the reliability of emotion profiles obtained in imaged distress situations, the profile from another study is shown in Figure 12-4. The range of scores in the data for Figure 12-4 was 3–15, since this study used the standard DES with each emotion represented by three 5-point scales. The profiles in the two samples are essentially quite similar. Distress is extremely high. After the key emotion of distress, the next highest emotion, fear in one sample and interest in the other, is only about 50% the magnitude of the key emotion. The slight differences in the fear and interest

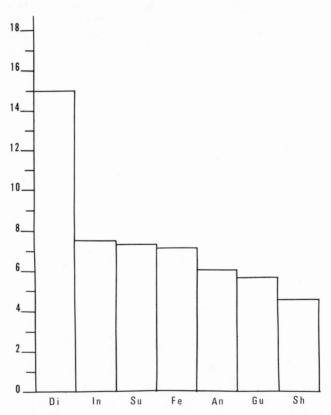

FIGURE 12-3. The profile of emotions in an imagined distress situation. The emotion (DES) scales are abbreviated: (In) interest, (Su) surprise, (Di) distress, (An) anger, (Gu) guilt, (Sh) shyness, and (Fe) fear.

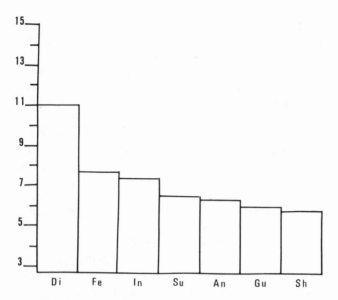

FIGURE 12-4. *Profile of emotions in imagined distress situation (N = 68). Emotions are abbreviated: (Di) distress, (Fe) fear, (In) interest, (Su) surprise, (An) anger, (Gu) guilt, and (Sh) shyness.*

means were not significant in either study. As can be seen in the two profiles, many emotions are elicited in a situation that people visualize as primarily distressing.

Of all the emotion situations examined in several different studies, the emotion profile in the distress situation is one of the most complicated. Only the guilt and shyness situations have an equal number of elevated emotions. It is worth noting that in the profile of emotions in the distress situation fear and interest are significantly higher than anger. Anger and other indexes of hostility are not as prominent in distress situations as in depression, as will be shown in the section on depression (p. 309ff.).

The Functions and Significance of Distress

Darwin suggested that tears prevent the unhealthy drying of the mucous membranes of the eyes and nose. Tears also contain the enzyme lysosome that protects the mucous membranes from dangerous bacteria. Three psychological functions of distress have been summarized by Tomkins (1963). First, distress communicates to the self and to others that all is not well. This is accomplished, in one primary instance, by the cry of the infant, but as has been noted, the infant, like the adult, may cry for reasons other than distress. In any event the expression of distress tells

Rafe that he is troubled and it tells others he needs some kind of help. Under some conditions the help can come only from Rafe himself, motivated by his own distress. Help may also come from others. Our everyday experiences tell us that a distressed face, particularly the distressed face of a child, tends to elicit empathy and sympathetic responses from the observer. This effect of the distress expression was demonstrated in a study by Savitsky and Sim (1974). They showed judges a series of standardized one-minute videotape segments of individuals playing the role of juvenile offenders and expressing either distress, anger, joy, or no emotion in an interview with a person in the role of a social worker. The supposed offenders had all committed offenses that were pre-judged to be equal in seriousness. The subjects' task was to decide what punishment they would recommend for the offenders. Savitsky and Sim found that significantly less punishment was recommended for the interviewees who expressed distress than for those who expressed either anger or joy.

Second, distress motivates Rebecca to do what is necessary to reduce her distress, to remove the source, or change her relationship to the object causing distress. Third, distress provides "negative motivation" that is not too toxic or too intolerable. The Bartlett–Izard study has shown that people report feeling less tension in distress than in any other negative emotion.

To some degree "negative motivation" is necessary to make us responsive to our own problems and to the problems of the world. But if a problem frightens us, we are more likely to flee from it than to try to cope with it. Fear is too toxic and intolerable to provide continuing motivation for sustained work toward the solution of a problem. For example, if Rafe has a problem in speaking before a group or an authority, he will have a handicap in expressing himself until his speech problem is solved. If speaking on such occasions distresses him, he will be motivated to improve his ability for this kind of performance; but if the thought of speaking on stage or to an authority frightens him, he will tend to avoid these situations and the problem goes unsolved.

> Distress is not a toxic crippling affect which necessarily generates avoidance strategies, but rather promotes remedial strategies which can attack the sources of distress. The presence of distress indicates a potential for remedial action either by the individual, or with his support. Therefore, one might assess the level of normal development by the width of the distress spectrum. To the extent to which there are many kinds of distress insensitivity on the part of any individual, there is developmental retardation . . . A profile of distress sensitivity might also be used as a measure of the development of society. Any society which is not distressed by its illnesses, its injustices, its discrepancies between abilities and achievements, its lacks of excitement and enjoyment, or its fears, humiliations and hostilities is an underdeveloped society. (Tomkins, 1963, p. 54–55)

Finally, distress serves another very fundamental purpose, a purpose that was served by distress in the evolution of human beings and is still served today. Distress (at least in the grief situation) facilitates cohesiveness of one's group, be it one's family, one's club, or one's society (Averill, 1968). Since separation causes distress, the avoidance or anticipation of distress is a strong force acting to keep one close to one's loved ones and friends. If we did not miss (feel distress over separation from) loved ones and friends, one of the great forces binding us to other people would be lacking.

When a large group of young people were asked to imagine and write down what it would be like to live in a world without distress, almost all of them thought it would also be a world without joy and love, without families and friends. Indeed, many of them wondered if it would really be a world of human beings.

The Socialization of Distress

In the opinion of Tomkins (1963), there are four main types of socialization of distress: (a) punitive or right wing, (b) rewarding or left wing, (c) incomplete rewarding, and (d) mixed. He wrote:

> We consider socialization of distress–anguish punitive whenever the distress cry itself is punished or rejected or whenever there is a failure of help in remedial action to reduce the source of distress, or both. This punitive socialization may or may not be consistent or general. (Tomkins, p. 88)

The Punitive Socialization of Distress. The punitive type of socialization of distress occurs when the parent or guardian habitually chooses to show a negative or punitive response to the distress cry of the child, regardless of the stimulus which has caused the distress in the child. A good example of this is demonstrated by the parent who scolds young Rafe for refusing to go to bed and on another occasion scolds him the same way for coming indoors crying after he has fallen and skinned his knees. Repeated indiscriminate punishment of distress produces even more distress in Rafe and his reactions to distress compounded will bring on more punitive measures from the parent. Tomkins calls this a multiple-suffering bind, in which there is "no way out" and no way to express distress or distress-induced anger without experiencing more punishment. In the end, this will cause compulsive behavior, isolationism, low frustration tolerance, poor individuation, excessive avoidance of distress, externalization of all types of distress, habitual apathy, and fatigue in a distress-laden individual. If the parent does follow up the punishment with a form of remedial help, then with time and patience the child may be able to gain a respectable degree of self-confidence and self-assurance.

> One of the further consequences of the punitive socialization of distress through the evocation of fear is the complication of the problem of physical courage. The human being responds innately to pain from his body with the cry

of distress. If this innate response is inhibited by fear, the individual's fear of pain will be greatly increased . . . Although pain is not easy for the human being to tolerate, it can produce panic the more distress itself has been linked with fear . . . It seems likely that the greater tolerance of pain, in our culture by women and in Oriental cultures by both men and women, is due to the less punitive early socialization of the distress cry. . . . (Tomkins, 1963, p. 93)

Rewarding the Distress Response during Socialization. In employing the rewarding type of socialization of distress, the parents attempt to comfort the child and make evident their attempts actively to reduce the severity of the stimulus for distress. It is more important that the parents act on the stimulus of distress, for if they only offer kind words and sympathy the child will be plagued with a severe case of chronic infantilism throughout adolescence and adulthood. If the parents do come to the rescue and offer not only comforting words but also the action upon the negative stimulus, then the child's freedom to express, cope with, and overcome distress will be much more broad and natural. With such treatment Rebecca will tend more to trust other people; she will be more likely to be honest, helpful, understanding and sympathetic with herself and others. She will have more physical courage and a much higher tolerance of frustration. She will successfully and rightfully experience distress in a context of love and joy (which inhibit or reduce distress), and she will have a much more optimistic attitude toward herself and life in general. This style of socialization of distress appears to have more desirable effects than the punitive approach. The style adopted depends largely on the past experiences and the deeply rooted affective–cognitive orientations of the parents, but the biologically based characteristics of the child (e.g., positive and negative emotion thresholds) also play a role. The infant with a low distress threshold will cry more often and perhaps more intensely than one with a high threshold, and frequent bouts of crying are more difficult to live with than frequent states of calmness or joy. The infant who smiles easily affects parents differently than the infant who cries easily.

The Incomplete Rewarding of Distress. According to Tomkins, when the parents employ the method of distress socialization known as incomplete rewarding, they are nurturing what may eventually develop into alcoholism and drug addiction. This type of socialization is displayed by the parents who simply kiss, hug, and pat their crying children without any effort to act upon the distressor or to make the object of distress obvious to their children so that they may be able to cope with it in the future. If the parents continue to act in this manner, the children will, as adults, be forced to find sedation, whether it be physical, mental, emotional, or social, when they are faced with a distress-eliciting situation.

Mixed Methods of Socializing Distress. All forms of distress socialization are not as patterned and concise as the foregoing categories; there is a special class which includes all those mixtures of socialization methods which are so often employed by so many parents. These mixtures can be in numerous combinations, such as parents who reward the crying infant, but punish the toddler. There may be a split in the punitive and rewarding socialization methods between the father and the mother. Tomkins maintains that results of a mixed socialization of distress are retardation in personality integration, social restlessness, and an interest in promoting interpersonal communication and resolving social conflict. Also, individuals who experience such socialization will show varying reactions to different aspects of their environment, based on the type of distress socialization they were given in these varying situations. An example of this is seen when there is rewarding socialization of that distress which is displayed in private and punitive socialization of that distress which is displayed publicly.

The Interactions of Distress with Other Emotions

Since distress is the most commonly experienced negative emotion, it frequently combines or interacts with other emotions. The more significant of these interactions involve other negative emotions, but it is possible for distress to interact with the positive emotions, as noted in chapters 9 and 10. The interaction of distress with enjoyment produces the experience described as tears of joy. Distress–interest interactions can take many forms; the child who exhibits a strong interest in injured pets or disabled people illustrates this interaction. Such interest may have generalized from concern over a chronically ill or crippled parent or sibling. Such an individual is more likely than not to develop a strong social orientation and choose an occupation or profession in human services or biological sciences.

Distress–Anger Interactions. Tomkins (1963) hypothesized that distress is an innate activator of anger. If both are density level affects, the steady-level stimulation of continuing distress would lower the anger threshold. Most people have had the experience of feeling discouraged and downhearted, followed by the experience of feeling angry with themselves or with someone else for their misery (see Figure 12-5). The distress–anger interaction can cause a father to react to his child's distress with a display of anger. The father may not be angry with the child, but with the source of distress. The anger may also be a counteraction to fear, suggesting the possible existence of a distress–anger–fear bind. Such a complex affective orientation could have its origin in an experience like this: a young boy is left alone in an automobile while his father goes shopping. It is a strange area of town and it is almost dark. The boy begins to feel lonesome and begins to cry in distress. As time passes the boy may feel some anger toward the father for abandoning him for so long. A feeling of abandonment

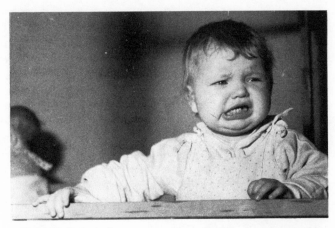

FIGURE 12-5. A distress–anger interaction in a ten-month-old.

in a strange place with darkness falling elicits fear in the child. The fear exacerbates the distressful crying and is very difficult to tolerate. If the boy manages to get angry with his father, the anger counteracts and attenuates the fear as well as the distress. Repetition of such situations may teach the boy to become angry at disappointments and setbacks, lest he suffer the distress–fear bind. The way in which a distress–anger interaction can contribute to normal and psychopathological depession will be discussed in the section on depression.

The Distress–Fear Bind. The toxic debilitating effects of fear make the linkage of distress and fear a factor important for adjustment. Such a linkage can occur under a variety of conditions. For example, if a young child cries when left alone and the parent punishes the child for crying, distress may become a learned activator of fear. If this fear–distress bind generalizes so that whenever this person faces a difficult, distressful problem or situation he or she becomes afraid, the relative frequency of the distress experience will make the toxic effects of fear so common that the problems of coping with life become overwhelming. Such a person will likely stop trying to solve difficult problems, live in dread of the new situations and uncertainties each day may bring, and become very cautious about trusting and liking one's self and other people. This individual will spend more energy in attempting to avoid the distress experience itself and the circumstances that provoked it than in attempting to control the sources of distress. "A generalized pessimism which contaminates achievement motivation and communion enjoyment, and which produces a pervasive hypochondriasis, is not infrequently the consequence of the linkage of distress to fear" (Tomkins, 1963, p. 91). When an early and strong linkage of distress and fear snowballs, the result is likely to be severe maladjustment.

The distress–fear bind may produce a lack of physical courage. As indicated in Chapter 7, pain often elicits distress. If there is a strong distress–fear linkage, then the sequence is likely to be pain→distress→fear, with subsequent panicky behavior rather than courageous action. The role of a fear–distress bind in impeding individuation and in the development of anxiety and anxiety neurosis will be discussed in Chapter 14.

The Distress–Shame Interaction. If the parents show rejection or indifference (contempt) toward Rebecca when she cries in distress, or if they let her "cry it out," she may learn to hang her head in shame whenever she feels like crying. If through such a process distress becomes an activator of shame, the toxicity of the combined distress–shame experience may make Rebecca a withdrawn and painfully shy person. The distress–shame experience would become as common as the numerous activators of distress—sickness, fatigue, loneliness, threats of loss of love, difficulties in problem solving. The frequent experience of distress combined with shame could make Rebecca feel incompetent, apologetic, and even contemptuous of herself.

"Ultimately, also, such socialization of distress is capable of producing a profound resignation to destiny because of an awareness that when one needs help most, one's cry for help will not be heard, or if it is heard it will make no difference" (Tomkins, 1963, p. 99).

If Rafe's father shames him when he cries in distress, and at the same time emphasizes that he should do something about his problem rather than crying about it, Rafe may come to feel shame in difficult situations for two reasons. First, he may feel shame because he feels like crying, and second, he may feel shame because he feels passive and unable to do anything constructive about the situation. According to Tomkins (1963) such a distress–shame bind can result in the externalization of distress. What this would mean for Rafe is that his chief concern in life would become the troubles and complaints of himself and others, but his focus would be on external objects and situations, not on his own distress experience. Not being tuned to his own distress experience, he would become unable to recognize distress in others and thus be incapable of showing sympathy.

Distress–Cognition Interactions

Interactions of distress with perceptual–cognitive processes begins very early in life. Ball and Tronick (1971) found that infants two to eleven weeks of age showed clear signs of distress (fussing, crying) upon perception of a looming shadow. Their findings suggest that the infant's responses to the distress were adaptive. They made protective and withdrawal movements that reliably signaled to observers that they were 'trying to avoid something.

Cognitive Transformations vs. Affect Induction in Delay of Gratification. Mischel (1974), although working within the framework of a cognitive theory of motivation, has conducted a series of studies that demonstrate the effects of cognitively induced affects, including distress or sadness, on subsequent thought and action. The series of experiments examined the effects of different types of imagery and ideation on willingness or ability of nursery school children to delay gratification. The procedural element common to these experiments consisted of showing the subject (age range 3–6) two food rewards (e.g., pretzel, marshmallow) and determining which the child most preferred. Prior to leaving the child alone in the experimental room with the reward the experimenter says to the child: "If you wait until I come back you can eat this one," pointing to the chosen object, "but if you don't want to wait until I come back, you can ring this bell and bring me back anytime you want, but if you do so you can only have this one" (pointing to the unchosen object).

Under these conditions Mischel and his students (e.g., Mischel & Ebbesen, 1970; Mischel, Ebbesen, & Zeiss, 1972; Mischel & Moore, 1973; Mischel & Baker, 1975) report that the length of time the child will wait in order to obtain the most preferred food reward (length of delay of gratification) is a function of the cognitive processes in which the child engages. The experimenters attempted to manipulate the child's ideation through verbal instructions and by leaving or not leaving the food rewards in the child's visual field. They found, for example, that the children would wait much longer when instructed to think "fun things" than when instructed to think about the food rewards.

The evidence from this ingenious series of experiments indicates that the various manipulations and the consequent effects are highly reliable, but some of the experimental findings, as well as some of Mischel's own reasoning, suggest that he tends to oversimplify his interpretation of the effects by attributing them solely to ideation or type of ideation. In summing up, Mischel states, "our overall findings on cognitive stimulus transformation clearly reveal that how children represent the rewards cognitively (not what is physically in front of them) determines how long they delay gratification" (Mischel, 1974, p. 48). He emphasizes that it is "*how* the subject ideates . . . rather than whether or not he does. . . ." Surely Mischel did not really intend to convey that the subject did or did not ideate, depending upon the experimenter's instructions. Perceptual and cognitive processes like affective ones are continually present in ordinary consciousness.

In elaborating the concept of ideation-as-cause, Mischel noted that any cognitive representation of the rewards that emphasized their motivational (consummatory, arousal) qualities, generates "excessive frustration" and reduces the ability of young children to delay gratification (in this case eating a preferred food reward). On the other hand, he argued that ideation about the nonconsummatory or less arousing qualities of the food rewards facilitates delay of gratification. With this argument Mischel, without explicitly acknowledging it, admits affect into his concept of the causal chain. He is saying, in effect, that if the cognition results in affective arousal the results are quite different than if it does not.

Another of Mischel's experimental findings that runs counter to his conception of cognition-as-primary-cause came from one of the experiments in which the children had the food rewards in the visual field. There were three conditions: in one condition the children were given an attractive toy to play with while they waited; in the second condition the children were instructed to think "fun things"; in the third condition the children were given neither toy nor cognitive instructions. In this experiment the toy served equally as well to delay gratification as did the instructions to think "fun things." This finding showed that experimental manipulation of cognitive processes was no more effective than a toy that engaged the child in play activity.

Another experimental finding that Mischel does not effectively relate to his final conclusion came from an experiment in which he used three kinds of affective imagery, including distress- or sadness-related imagery, as experimental conditions (Mischel, Ebbesen, & Zeiss, 1972). In this experiment the conditions were these: think about fun things, think about sad things, and think about the rewards themselves. The children in the think-fun condition delayed gratification significantly longer than those in either of the other two conditions. But the children in the think-sad condition did not differ in waiting time from those in the think-rewards condition. This experiment shows differential effects for cognitively induced positive and negative affect, if we assume that the think-fun and think-sad conditions altered the children's affect and elicited emotions.

Mischel's conclusion that the critical determinant of delay of gratification was how the child ideates (e.g., whether the child ideates about affect-inducing qualities of the reward) juxtaposes his position and differential emotions theory. According to Mischel the significant experimental effects were a function of cognitive processes—verbal instructions of the experimenter and consequent imagery and ideation of the child. But there is a second independent variable, more fundamental in a causal, motivational, or dynamic sense; namely, the affect induced by cognitive processes. The affects induced by the experimental manipulations probably include heightened hunger drive (in the think-rewards condition), a combination of interest and joy (in the think-fun and the toy-play conditions), and distress or sadness (think-sad condition). It is quite possible that other parts of the procedure induced anger (seeing a tasty morsel that whets one's appetite, but which one cannot eat) and fear (Jersild & Holmes, 1935), at least in the form of mild apprehension (being left alone in a room with constrictions on one's thoughts and actions).

It seems reasonable to assume that cognitively (think-fun) or behaviorally (toy-play) induced interest and enjoyment facilitated goal-directed behavior as measured in terms of delay of gratification, while cognitively induced distress or distress–hunger drive interactions (think-sad and think-reward conditions) reduced the children's ability to wait for a preferred food reward. The power of affects and affective–cognitive interactions to inhibit and otherwise alter behavior has already been discussed. We noted how excitement can cause one to entirely forget about consummatory activities and how distress, especially in children, calls for reassurance and comfort. Thus differential emotions theory and Mischel's position are close conceptually, the difference being that the former sees affect as the basic motivational condition and the cognitive manipulations as the causes of the affects.

Distress, Altruism, Self-gratification, and Conscience Development. The differential emotions theory interpretation of Mischel's findings is supported by three other experiments using quite different dependent variables—altruistic activity, self-gratification, and resistance to temptation. The Moore, Underwood, and Rosenhan (1973) experiment reviewed in Chapter 10 showed that cognitively induced joy makes children significantly more altruistic (left more pennies for nonparticipants) than did a neutral condition. Further, the children who experienced distress or sadness were significantly less altruistic than the control subjects.

In the second study (Underwood, Moore, & Rosenhan, 1972), the experimenters used the same manipulations but measured as the dependent variable only self-gratification (amount of money taken by each child during the experimenter's 60-second absence from the room). That is, the children were not restricted as in the earlier experiment by the instruction that they might want to leave some pennies for nonparticipants. For male children the cognitively induced positive affect resulted in significantly more self-gratification than did the negative affect or the control condition, the latter two not having differential effects. For female subjects, both the joy and the distress produced significantly more self-gratification than the control condition, but they did not differ significantly in the two affect conditions. The investigators concluded that it was the emotion or affective experiences that determined the observed spectrum of effects. The differential effects of the two emotion experiences in male and female children requires further study.

In the third experiment, which involved seven- and eight-year-old children, Fry (1975) found that a positive affect (think-happy) condition resulted in greater resistance to temptation than did either a negative affect (think-sad) condition or a neutral condition. The children in the think-sad condition showed significantly less resistance to temptation than did those in the neutral condition. Fry attributed the experimental effects to the imagery-induced affective (joyful, sad) states and pointed up the implications of this conclusion for child-rearing practices. He inferred that conditions that make for joyful or happy experiences increase ability to resist temptation while distressful experiences have the opposite effect.

The cross-cultural studies of emotion recognition and emotion labeling (e.g., Izard, 1971; Ekman, Friesen, & Ellsworth, 1972), the psychophysiological studies of affective imagery and emotion expression (Schwartz *et al.* 1973; Schwartz, Fair, Greenberg, Mandel, & Klerman, 1974), and the studies of affective imagery-induced changes in self-reported emotion experience (Izard, 1972) and behavior (Underwood *et al.,* 1972; Moore *et al.,* 1973; Fry, 1975) provide a strong inferential base for the assumption that experimentally manipulated cognitive processes actually induce real emotion experience that functions as motivation. Rosenhan and his colleagues (Rosenhan, Underwood, & Moore, 1974) clearly support this assumption, and although Mischel did not explicitly attribute a causal role to emotion, he assumes that his ideational instructions induced affective experience.

Expression-Motivated Behavior. In another ingenious study of altruistic actions, Neverovich (1974) used a variety of manipulations to induce distress or concern for others and measure the subsequent effects on altruistic activity. In each condition she had a group of four- to five-year-old children and a group of five- to six-year-old children. In condition one a child was brought into the experimental room and shown a disorderly array of toys. The child was asked to put the toys in order "so your friends can play with them later; if you do not put the toys in order your friends will not be able to play with them and they will be sad." At the end of 20 minutes the child was asked whether he or she wanted to continue working on ordering the toys or go for a walk, a diversion uniformly perceived as interesting and enjoyable by Russian children. In this condition only four out of twelve of the four- to five-year-old children elected to remain in the room and finish the task of placing the toys in proper order. Six out of twelve of the five- to six-year-olds elected to remain and complete the task for sake of their friends. In the second condition the children were given the same verbal instructions, but in addition they were shown pictures of children with sad faces looking at the toys in disarray, unable to play with them. In this condition seven out of twelve of the four- to five-year-olds elected to forego the walk and remain to complete the task of ordering the toys; eleven out of twelve of the five- to six-year-olds did the same. In the third condition, in which the children were shown photographs of a child who was both sad and sick and unable to play with the toys because they were in disarray, even more of the children elected to forego the walk and complete the task. Neverovich interpreted the improvement in task performance as a function of the distress experience induced in the subjects by a combination of verbal instructions and photographs of other children showing distress that would be relieved by the subject's task-oriented activities.

Antecedents and Consequences of Distress. For purposes of the study of its antecedents and consequences, distress was defined by the terms sadness, discouragement, downheartedness. The responses obtained in the study are presented in Table 12-1.

TABLE 12-1
Antecedents and Consequences of Distress
(N = Approximately 130 College Students)

Responses	Percentage of subjects giving responses
Antecedents of distress	
Feelings	
1. Distress, sadness, discouragement, etc.	33.9
2. Feeling lonely, isolated, rejected	30.9
3. Physically, mentally upset	14.0
4. Feelings of failure, disappointment in self, incompetence, inadequacy	13.2
5. Other	9.5
Thoughts	
1. About a specific personal problem	42.0
2. About failure, incompetence, etc.	19.8
3. Of sadness, death	16.7
4. About loneliness, rejection	8.7
5. Other	13.2
Actions	
1. Something stupid, a mistake	36.1
2. Something to hurt others	15.9
3. Others impose their will on subject	11.9
4. Something morally, legally wrong	7.1
5. Passive, does nothing	7.1
6. Retreat, withdraw	5.5
7. Other	16.7
Consequences of distress	
Feelings	
1. Distress, sadness, discouragement, etc.	43.5
2. Mentally, physically upset	22.1
3. Loneliness, rejection	13.7

TABLE 12-1 (continued)
Antecedents and Consequences of Distress
(N = Approximately 130 College Students)

Responses	Percentage of subjects giving responses
4. Feel need to be alone	5.3
5. Anger	3.0
6. Feel misled, used, hurt by others	2.3
7. Feel like a failure, incompetent, etc.	2.3
8. Other	7.6
Thoughts	
1. Life in general is bad	42.8
2. About the cause of sadness, distress	22.9
3. How to overcome sadness, more pleasant things	22.5
4. About failure, incompetence, etc.	3.8
5. About loneliness, rejection	1.5
6. Other	6.9
Actions	
1. Tries to get over it	29.8
2. Expresses sadness, verbally, physically	17.5
3. Does something specific	15.2
4. Retreats from others	13.7
5. Remains passive, does nothing	5.3
6. Thinks of all sadness in life	5.3
7. Talks to someone	3.8
8. Does something impulsive, irrational	.7
9. Other	8.4

Grief

Differential emotions theory holds that grief is a complex pattern of fundamental emotions and emotion–cognition interactions. The experiential phenomena of grief result from the interaction of distress with other affects and from affect–cognition interactions. In keeping with the central purpose of this volume, the focus here will be on the experiential and motivational significance of grief, with some attention to its determinants, its functions, and its interactions with cognitions and action.

Determinants of Grief

Theorists and investigators generally agree that the prime cause of grief is loss. The loss may be temporary (separation) or permanent (death), real or imagined, physical or psychological. The cause of the most profound and extended grief is the loss of the person one loves the most dearly. Peretz (1970) has pointed out three other forms of loss. One of these is the loss of some aspect of self-attractiveness, vigor, loss of some sensory or motor capacity, loss of intellectual power, or loss of positive self-attitudes such as self-esteem. A third form of loss is that of material objects such as money, treasures, homeland. A fourth form of loss is developmental loss or the type of loss that occurs in the process of growth and development (e.g., loss of the nurturing breast, baby teeth, status as center of parental attention). Peretz points out that loss is simultaneously a real event and a perceptual or psychological one by which the individual bestows personal or symbolic meaning upon the loss. Thus a real loss may constitute symbolically a loss of honor or "loss of face." He also noted that serious losses also carry with them the threat of additional, future losses.

The determinants of grief may be sorted into biological, cultural, and psychological classes, although each of these classes tend to be interrelated and interactive. Some of the determinants of grief also play a role in the grief–cognition–behavioral interactions that characterize the individual and the social matrix within which grief occurs.

Biological Determinants. Since grief is conceived as an interaction of distress and other fundamental emotions, it is reasonable to infer that grief has genetic determinants and biologically adaptive values. In an insightful and scholarly analysis of the nature and significance of grief, Averill (1968) made an excellent case for the assumption of a biological basis for grief. His argument rests on the well-supported assumption that human beings and higher primates in general are group-living forms whose survival and well-being are enhanced by social relationships (Jolly, 1966; Hamburg, 1963). In evolutionary perspective and to some extent in contemporary life, the social group affords protection from aggressors (or predators) and efficiency in locating and maintaining food. In turn, separation from the group diminishes chances for survival. In sum, Averill holds that "grief is a biological reaction, the evolutionary function of which is to insure group cohesiveness in species where a social form of existence is necessary for survival. This is accomplished by making separation from the group, or from specific members of the group, an extremely stressful event both psychologically and physiologically" (p. 729). Averill argues that grief is a more powerful force for social cohesion than positive incentives alone since the latter would offer little help during periods of satiation and satisfaction. In a later section we shall see how each of several fundamental emotions involved in grief may serve biological as well as social and psychological functions.

Cultural Determinants. In his analysis of the bereavement behavior complex, Averill (1968) delineated two components, grief and mourning.

He defined mourning as conventional bereavement behavior, determined and prescribed in large measure by sociocultural influences. Mourning practices vary extensively from culture to culture. The Japanese may smile at aquaintances and strangers during bereavement in order not to burden the other with their sorrow. The bereavement behavior of individuals in some societies appear to the Western eye as celebrations, but on more careful examination, such behavior follows well-defined cultural rules and customs.

The experiential–motivational phenomena associated with grief may also vary to some extent from culture to culture, depending upon the extent to which the different cultures inhibit or facilitate the interactions of distress with various fundamental emotions. For example, Block (1957) showed that grief and guilt were highly correlated in members of his American sample but orthogonal in his sample of Norwegians. Sociocultural practices also influence the intensity and duration of grief. An example is the child-rearing system of the Ifaluk, a Micronesian culture (Spiro, 1949, cited in Averill, 1968). Since the rearing of an Ifaluk child involves parents, siblings, and many persons outside the family, the grief displayed upon loss of a family member may be intense, but it is exceedingly brief in comparison with that shown in other cultures. A similar phenomenon has been observed among nonhuman primates, though in this case species characteristics play a role. Rhesus macaque monkeys, who form close one-to-one mother–infant attachments, show more profound separation grief than do bonnett macaque monkeys among whom mothering is widely shared among the adult females of a clan.

Perhaps the most significant cultural determinant of grief is that of role loss. Roles of father, mother, child, husband, etc., are prescribed by culture and loss of a loved one often means the loss of a role (e.g., loss of wife means loss of role as husband). As Averill and others have pointed out, role loss is essentially a disruption of a functional relationship through the loss of a significant other person. Role loss or changes in roles are significant determinants of grief when they entail loss of self-esteem (Bibring, 1953). Role changes or any other phenomena that deprive the individual of meaningful relationships or meaningful relations with the environment can produce grief (Becker, 1962; Das, 1971).

Psychological Determinants. Psychological causes of grief derive from an affectional attachment with the person, object, idea, or other symbol. Separation or loss from the object of attachment thus means loss of a source of joy and excitement, and depending upon the age of the person and the nature of the object, loss of affection, security, and sense of well-being. The factor common to all psychological causes of grief is a perceived loss of something valued and beloved and to which there was a strong affectional attachment.

Expressive and Experiential Characteristics of Grief

The predominant expression on the face of the grieving person is that of distress or sadness. The expression of grief may sometimes consist of blends, however, since other fundamental emotions are often involved.

The predominant experiential quality of grief is consonant with that of the predominant emotion of distress or sadness. As other emotions interact, the experiential phenomena of grief become more complex. As already noted Block's (1957) study of the phenomenology of grief, by means of semantic differential scales, showed a strong tendency for guilt feelings to be associated with grief. Block's study also showed that grief was highly correlated with the concepts of worry and envy and highly negatively correlated with the concept of contentment. The aspects of grief associated with emotion–emotion interactions and emotion–cognition interactions may vary from culture to culture. As already pointed out, Block found a substantial difference in the association of grief in American and Norwegian cultures. He also found substantial differences between samples of these two cultures in the association of grief with worry, envy, and contentment. The general trend of Block's findings are consistent with Izard's (1971) finding that cultures differ in their attitudes toward the fundamental emotions and hence in the frequency with which certain emotions interact with others.

The Functions of Grief

It has already been pointed out that grief serves a biological and social function in facilitating social affection and group cohesiveness. As are all emotions or patterns of emotions, grief is contagious—particularly so—and this contagion facilitates empathy and strengthens bonds among all those who are bereaved. These effects tend to generalize to the wider community since mourning rituals are typically highly visible to the public.

The foregoing function of grief is biological and social, but grief also has inherently adaptive functions for the individual. Normal grief is psychologically adaptive for the individual since it enables her or him to "work through" and adjust to the loss. In a sense, grief is a way of paying homage to the loved one that was lost. The stressful experience of grief motivates the individual to re-establish an adequate level of personal autonomy. According to Bowlby (1960, 1961, 1963), grief is adaptive for the individual because it functions as motivation to recover the lost object. Further, some expressions of grief can serve a communicative function, eliciting empathy and succor. Finally, grief and its expression communicate to significant others and to the wider community the fact that the bereaved individual is a loving and caring individual. Other functions of grief will be touched on in the following sections.

Grief in the Context of Attachment and Separation

In a monumental, two-volume work Bowlby (1969, 1973) presents a theory of attachment and separation and the psychological problems related to these phenomena. We have already considered Bowlby's theory of the prototypical interpersonal attachment, the mother–infant bond. It is in the context of the breaking of this bond, the separation response syndrome, that Bowlby discusses grief. Bowlby maintains that whenever a young child has normal opportunities for social development and forms attachment to a mother figure, its unwilling separation from the mother produces distress. Following separation, the infant or young child's behavior follows a typical sequence: protest, which consists of vigorous efforts to recover the mother or caregiver; despair, which is characterized by grief and mourning; and detachment, which consists of the development of various defenses to compensate for the loss. Responses to separation are, in part, a function of age. Since attachment does not become fixed and strong until about the age of six months, the separation response syndrome does not occur until sometime in the second half of the first year of life. From this period through early childhood even brief separations may elicit distress and the various phases of the separation response syndrome. Older children may be able to comprehend the relative insignificance of brief separations and are distressed only by longer ones. Adults are upset when separations are prolonged or permanent, as in the case of the death of a loved one.

According to Bowlby, the protest phase of the separation response syndrome is characterized, first and foremost, by the emotion of fear. Separation connotes being left alone, and Bowlby has marshaled considerable evidence supporting his notion that being alone is one of several natural clues to increased danger and hence a condition that often elicits fear. The fear serves as motivation to escape the danger, primarily through efforts to gain proximity to the absent mother. As fear abates, the infant may show anger, "a reproach for what has happened and a deterrent against its happening again" (Bowlby, 1973, p. 253). Bowlby's postulate that fear and anger interact in the wake of separation is consistent with the differential emotions theory of grief that will be explicated in more detail in a later section.

In the despair phase of the separation response syndrome, the infant shows signs of grief and mourning. In Bowlby's system grief is defined largely in terms of despair or distress since other participating emotions are treated separately in the other phases of the syndrome.

In the detachment phase of the separation response syndrome, the child develops various defenses. The infant and young child's chief means of recovery from the trauma of separation is the development of another healthy affectional attachment. Older children, adolescents, and adults may use any of a variety of defenses against distress or separation. Perhaps the chief defense is that of suppression or repression. The individual may attempt to repress all ideation associated with the distress experience. As Peretz (1970) has pointed out, the individual may also use the defenses of isolation of affect, displacement (especially of the anger component), substitution, and denial.

Emotion Dynamics in Grief

It is generally agreed that separation or loss is the principal determinant of grief. Bowlby may be quite right in pointing out that in infancy and early childhood the first emotion response to separation is fear. Bowlby's observation is not inconsistent with differential emotions theory since he does not consider grief to be present until the beginning of the second phase of the separation response syndrome, the phase of despair. In the adult, loss of a loved one probably elicits distress first, and in most cases it remains the predominant emotion. In terms of differential emotions theory, differences in individuals and in social relationships may give rise to a combination of the following fundamental emotions in grief: distress, fear, anger, guilt, and shame. Peretz (1970) has also recognized the presence of all of these emotions in grief.

Distress and Fear. While fear may be the first reaction of the infant to separation or loss, grief obtains only after distress becomes dominant. The first reaction to loss is probably distress in the older child and adult. Any individual, however, may experience fear or a distress–fear interaction when the individual surmises that his safety or security is jeopardized by the missing or lost loved one.

Distress–Anger. Since distress is the primary emotion in grief, the eventual occurrence of anger and aggression is not surprising. If Tomkins's assumption is correct, extended distress is an innate activator of anger, and the distress experience is usually prolonged in grief. Anger may also occur as a result of the individual blaming the absent or lost loved one for deserting him or her or as a result of blaming someone else for the separation. Further, as Averill has pointed out, the loss of a significant individual can be a highly frustrating experience. A relationship is lost, plans involving the other person cannot be carried out, and desires and fulfillment depending upon the other person cannot be gratified. Such disruption of behavior and such unfulfilled expectations can easily elicit anger.

Distress–Fear–Anger Interactions. Bowlby reports the results of a study by Heinicke and Westheimer (1966) which clearly demonstrated the appearance of anger and hostile behavior in children who were separated from their parents and housed in a residential nursery for two or more weeks. In comparison with children who remained in their own homes, the separated children exhibited hostile behavior in a doll-play test four times as frequently. The resilience of children is well-demonstrated by the fact that the administration of the doll-play test six and ten weeks subsequent to the return home of the separated children showed them to be no different in hostility from children who remained home throughout the period of the observations. According to Bowlby the anger in this distress–fear–anger interaction may be either functional or dysfunctional. Its positive value may be in assisting the individual in overcoming the obstacles to reunion and in discouraging the loved one from going away again. It may be dysfunctional when anger resulting from the highly distressful experience of repeated separation leads to destructive aggression or violence.

Distress–Guilt–Shame Interactions. Guilt, particularly in the American culture (Block, 1957), is a quite common component of grief. Grief may result from the fact that one regrets that one did not have a better relationship with the deceased or did not do as much for the lost beloved as one thinks might have been possible. Shame may occur when the individual feels that others are condemning him or her for not being closer to the deceased or more helpful during the period of illness.

Grief and Psychopathology

In a volume edited by Schoenberg, Carr, Peretz, and Kutscher (1970) a number of contributors present theory and evidence that support the notion that illness and death become more likely following the loss of a loved one. For example, Carr and Schoenberg, while noting that the evidence relating object loss to somatic symptom formation is mainly correlational, suggest that object loss and grief may contribute to such diverse somatic reactions as cancer and glossodynia. They presented evidence for significant increases in medical office consultation rate and in death rate of widowed people. Other contributors to the volume consider psychological and somatic reactions to other types of loss and possible therapeutic procedures for the management of these phenomena.

Depression

There are six major approaches to the study of depression: neurophysiological–biochemical, psychoanalytic, biogenetic, sociocultural, cognitive, behavioral, and differential emotions theory. All these approaches have been discussed in considerable detail by Izard (1972), and each is the subject of a growing body of literature. These approaches will be briefly summarized below.

Neurophysiological and Biochemical Approaches

Research on the biochemistry of depression has focused on the biogenic amines and on water and electrolyte balance. To date, the biogenic amine hypothesis has received the greatest attention (Davis, 1970). This hypothesis states that the synthesis and metabolism of the biogenic amines are importantly related to depression and mania. More specifically, depression is associated with a low level of amines in the brain, mania with a high level (Kety, 1970). The amines receiving most attention are norepinephrine, dopamine, and serotonin. Some studies have shown complex interrelationships among these amines, with levels differing with type or severity of depression (e.g., Asberg, Thoren, & Traskman, 1976). At present, most of the evidence indicates that norepinephrine deficiency in the brain and sympathetic nervous system is the single most critical factor in the biochemistry of depression. One study suggested that the mechanism for the influence of steroids on depression may be one that mediates an increase in norepinephrine in the nervous system (Maas & Mednieks, 1971).

Research has suggested that cyclic AMP is also involved in depression (Paul, Ditzion, Pauk, & Janowsky, 1970). This possibility is enhanced by the fact that cyclic AMP has been rather well-established as an intracellular mediator of the effects of some of the catecholamines and possibly some electrolytes and body fluids (Sutherland, 1970).

Research on the biochemistry and neurophysiology of depression has led to the clinical use of a number of antidepressant drugs. One class of such drugs is the monoamine oxidase inhibitors (MAOI) which block the catabolism of naturally occurring amines and thereby provide an increase in the level of norepinephrine in the brain and the sympathetic nervous system. Unfortunately, MAOI drugs have not only proved ineffective with many depressives but may also lead to a number of side effects, especially when taken in conjunction with certain foods and beverages (Goodman & Gilman, 1970). A second class of antidepressant drugs is the tricyclic type, of which the most frequently used are imipramine and amitriptyline. Though the biological mechanism for the action of tricyclic drugs is different from that of the MAOI drugs, the net effect is the same—increasing the amount of free functional norepinephrine in the nervous system. The tricyclic drugs also have been found limited in effectiveness and also may lead to serious complications and adverse side effects (Davis, 1970).

The problems with antidepressant drugs do not rule out their use with some patients. Authorities in biochemistry and psychopharmacology caution, however, that the use of antidepressant drugs requires an extensive knowledge of their effects, of the patient's history, and of the particular type of depression being treated.

Differential emotions theory has some implications for neurophysiological and biochemical investigations of depression. If we assume that distress is the key emotion in depression, then depression involves increased activity of the trophotropic system. In the case of dominance by the trophotropic system, there would also be parasympathetic dominance, cortical synchronization, and a tendency toward sleeplike EEG potentials.

If we assume that depression involves a combination or pattern of emotions, including anger, both inner- and outer-directed, then it is necessary to allow for the possibility that the ergotropic system is also involved. With ergotropic dominance, there would be increased sympathetic activity, cortical desynchronization, and indexes of behavioral and EEG arousal.

Differential emotions theory holds that depression represents a particular interactive balance between the trophotropic and ergotropic systems. Such a balance implies either a certain level of simultaneous functioning in these two systems or an alternation of dominance by the two systems. The balance may shift with type or severity of depression, as different emotions increase or decrease in intensity. In any case, the assumption that both systems are involved highly complicates the neurophysiology and biochemistry of depression.

Biogenetic, Sociocultural, and Cognitive Views

The picture of depression is not complete without a consideration of biogenetic, sociocultural, and cognitive factors. Theory or research in each of these areas has contributed something to our understanding of the subject.

Kraines (1957) presented a rather detailed biogenetic theory of depression. He considered the etiology of depression to be essentially physiological (hereditary and hormonal influences). Kraines defines the mechanism of depression as dysfunction in three areas of the brain: the diencephalon, rhinencephalon, and the reticular formation. He maintains that biogenetic theory explains the cyclic nature of depression and the efficacy of radical therapies, phenomena not so readily explained in terms of psychoanalytic or cognitive theory.

Kraines summarizes the evidence for the role of heredity in depression. He points out, for example, that among monozygotic twins, when one member of a pair has a psychotic depression, chances are between 70 and 96 in a hundred that the remaining twin will also suffer from manic depressive psychosis.

Kraines points out a relationship between biological factors and a number of depressive symptoms. He attributes visual paresthesias to disturbance in the optic thalamus and emotional isolation to inappropriate transmission or ineffective integration of the sensory processes involved in emotion. The research on the biochemistry of depression and on body types and depression are compatible with Kraines's biogenetic theory.

A number of studies have found apparent relationships between sociocultural factors and the occurence of depression. Depression has been reported less frequently in Africa and Ireland than in England (Silverman, 1968). Some studies have suggested that blacks suffer less frequently and less severely from depression (Prange & Vitols, 1962; Tonks, Paykel, & Klerman, 1970). However, some sociocultural factors such as family background and ethnic membership may be confounded with hereditary factors.

Fromm-Reichmann (1953) made an intensive study of the families of twelve manic-depressive patients and found that each family was set apart from the social milieu by some factor—minority-group membership, deteriorating social position, high status need. She found that depressive children tended to perceive their parents differently from their normal siblings and, as a result, different parent–child relationships obtained.

Beck (1967) has presented a comprehensive cognitive theory of depression. His central theses are very similar to those of the cognitive theorists reviewed in the study of anxiety. Essentially he maintains that cognition is the primary determinant of emotions, moods, and behavior. He describes as the primary triad of cognitive determinants one's way of viewing oneself, one's world, and one's future. A negative view of self causes depressives to see themselves as inadequate and unworthy and to attribute their misery to personal defects. Their negative view of the world leads them to interpret their interactions as failures, steps toward defeat and disparagement. Their negative view of the future causes them to anticipate an indefinite continuation of their suffering. Beck explains most of the typical depressive symptoms such as paralysis of will, suicidal wishes, and self-devaluation as the result of one or the other of these cognitive determinants.

Differential emotions theory raises a number of critical questions for Beck's theory. The most important of these is the question of how the individual comes to have persistently negative views of self, world, and future. To say that these are built up through experience and the reaction of others is not a very specific analysis of etiology.

Instead of seeing a pattern of emotions as defining and determining depression, Beck sees a cognitive organization or schema that determines how an object or idea will be perceived and conceptualized. The schemata of depression involve such themes as personal deficiency and negative expectations. Beck does not address himself to the problem of the determinants of the necessary selectivity of perception and cognition that go into the making of a schema. Differential emotions theory holds that such schemata develop from emotion–cognition interactions, with fundamental emotions or patterns of emotions serving as the primary determinants. Beck does, however, recognize the importance of emotions, once they have been cognitively induced.

Beck presents a comprehensive and very useful analysis of the symptomatology and phenomenology of depression. He summarizes the attributes of the depressive in four major groupings. He suggests that emotional manifestations are exemplified by the frequently observed sadness or dejected mood and that cognitive manifestations are exemplified by the depressive's tendency to see himself as deficient in attributes that are particularly important to him. Beck holds that motivational manifestations are exemplified by passivity, dependence, withdrawal wishes, and paralysis of the will and that vegetative and physical manifestations are exemplified by loss of appetite and sleep disturbance.

Some of Beck's groupings seem to overlap. Surely emotional manifestations and motivational manifestations have common roots in emotion processes. Also cognitive manifestations and physical and vegetative manifestations are probably influenced by one or more of the fundamental emotions.

Behavioral Learning Theories of Depression

As Wright and McDonald (1974) observed, behaviorists who have addressed the problem of depression have been more concerned with therapeutic procedures than with theoretical models. Learning-theory approaches to the analysis of depression received impetus, however, when Seligman and his associates (Seligman & Maier, 1967; Seligman, Maier, & Geer, 1968) began the experimental work that laid the foundation for the concept of depression as learned helplessness. Seligman and his associates showed that dogs that received a large number of inescapable electric shocks ultimately learned to become passive and accept the electric shock in apparent helplessness. According to Seligman, the dog learned that there was no adaptive response, and since there was nothing he could do to escape the shock, he learned passivity and helplessness. By using yoked controls who received the same amount of shock, but who were able to control or escape it, the experimenters were able to conclude that it was not the amount of shock or physical trauma that produced the passivity or learned helplessness in the experimental animals. Further, Maier (1970) showed that training dogs to stand still in order to escape shock did not result in a passivity that generalized to other situations where the animal could escape shock by jumping over a barrier. Rather, helplessness results when the animals learn that environmental outcomes are independent of instrumental responding. The motivation to act on the environment in order to control outcomes is thereby reduced. The resulting behavioral apathy becomes pathological when it interferes with the general process of learning that responses alter or control environmental events.

Seligman and his colleagues have maintained that the "learned helplessness" phenomenon resulting from an extended series of inescapable electric shocks is analogous to reactive depression in human beings. They suggest that what depressing situations have in common is that they are situations in which one thinks one has no control over events, particularly over those aspects which are perceived as most important. In generalizing his work to human beings, Seligman was influenced by the work of Beck (1967) and that of Kelly (1955). Kelly's theory of personality as a function of personal constructs emphasized the need of human beings to predict and control their environment.

Seligman (1975) has suggested that the opponent-process theory of emotion (Solomon & Corbit, 1974) is compatible with his own theory of the development of depression. A noxious event (electric shock in Seligman's animal paradigm) produces fear and panicky, dysadaptive responses. With repetition of the frenetic activity sequence, the organism learns that the fear-motivated responses are dysadaptive. As the experience is repeated, helplessness and the feelings accompanying depression increase. Ultimately depression serves as an inhibitor of fear and keeps the latter within tolerable limits (fear and depression operate as opponent processes). After termination of the noxious event, fear may be relieved while the opponent process of depression remains. As already noted, some psychoanalytic theory (e.g., Rado, 1968) and differential emotions theory recognize emotion–emotion interactions inherent in the profile of emotions in depression and one of these is that between distress and fear. In some respects fear is incidental rather than causal in Seligman's theory of depression; nevertheless, his experimental paradigm begins with shock-induced fear, and the question as to what other affective states might leave the organism susceptible to the development of learned helplessness and depression is left unclear.

The provocative experimental findings and the consequent model developed by Seligman and his associates have evoked considerable interest among those concerned with the understanding and treatment of depression. The most serious problem with the theory may be its limited scope. Seligman himself acknowledges that it applies only to reactive depressions and he implies that it does not account for all of these. If we assume antecedent situations that elicit fear plus only dysadaptive responses, then Seligman's model may be useful in conceptualizing one type of affect–cognition–action sequence that leads to what a number of theorists (e.g., Bibring, 1968; Beck, 1967) have recognized as symptoms of depression—feelings of hopelessness or helplessness.

Klinger (1975) has presented an "incentive theory of depression."

According to this theory, when the organism recognizes that a particular goal is beyond reach, a process of disengagement occurs prior to consummatory activity. The "incentive–disengagement cycle" consists of three phases. In the first phase, the individual responds to the loss of object with intense concentration and invigorated responses in an effort to retrieve what was lost. The second phase is characterized by anger and aggression toward the object. Finally, when activities of phase one and phase two prove unrewarding, the organism becomes completely disengaged from the incentives that ordinarily produce adaptive responses, and this complete disengagement leads to or constitutes depression.

Klerman's (1974) insightful review raises some questions for learning-theory approaches. He concluded that rather than being a set of learned dysadaptive responses, depression serves several adaptive functions in animals and infants: (a) social communication, (b) psychological arousal, (c) subjective responses, and (d) psychodynamic defenses. He maintains that depression in infants acts as a signal of distress and helplessness and elicits helping responses from parents or caregivers. Although Klerman was not confident about the adaptive function of depression in adults, he concluded that it was an inherently adaptive process at any age. In support of his point he noted that reactive depression is generally self-limiting in duration (a factor which he thought indicated its benign quality). Klinger (1975) even raised the possibility that interference with the normal course of depression (e.g., with antidepressant drugs) may prove harmful in the long run.

A number of other behavioral–learning-theory models of depression have been proposed (e.g., Forster, 1972; Lewinsohn, 1974; Liberman & Raskin, 1971; and Costello, 1972). While some of these theories apply to different types of depression, most of them are not incompatible with Seligman's position. All of them have a learning theory base.

In his behavioral analysis Forster (1972) suggests that depressed persons are characterized by the loss of certain adaptive behaviors and by an increase in escape and avoidance behaviors such as complaints, requests, crying, and irritability. Complaints and requests are the depressive's efforts to remove aversive conditions. More important than the ineffective avoidance efforts is the decrease in frequency of types of behavior that were originally positively reinforced. The reduction of adaptive behavior that was positively reinforced is a function of three different factors. First, there are things that limit the repertory of available responses in particular situations. The process of limiting the available responses can be exemplified by Forster's treatment of the role of anger in depression. Since anger is typically directed toward another person, it may reduce the possibility that the object of anger will provide positive reinforcement for the expressor. Further, the expression of anger is often punished, and in order to avoid punishment a person may repress the punished behavior. In the process, potentially adaptive responses may also be repressed, resulting in an unnecessary constriction of the individual's repertory of activities that could lead to positive reinforcement. A second factor that constricts adaptive behavior that was once positively reinforced develops as a result of inconsistent rewards and punishments. The individual becomes unable to understand and predict the contingencies of reinforcement. If parents or caregivers administer rewards and punishments arbitrarily to adaptive and maladaptive types of behavior, the child may develop inaccurate perceptions of actual contingencies, become confused, and develop the feelings of hopelessness and helplessness pictured in many theories of depression. The third factor discussed by Forster consists of changes in environment. If the environment, particularly the social environment, is altered in such a way that previously reinforced responses are no longer positively reinforced, these responses will tend to drop out of the individual's repertory. Following clinical tradition, Forster gives as a prime example of this problem the loss of a loved one or significant other who has been a source of positive reinforcement.

Lewinsohn's (1974) position is similar to that of Forster. He maintains that the dysphoria of depression is a result of a low rate of positive reinforcement. Lewinsohn's treatment of affects and affective–cognitive interactions in depression (feelings of guilt, pessimism, and loss of self-esteem) is rather cursory. He suggests that these more discrete phenomena derive from one's effort to label one's vague and general feelings of dysphoria. Liberman and Raskin (1971) propose a behavioral theory similar to the preceding ones, adding the proposition that the depressed person's problem is exacerbated by reinforcement of maladaptive behavior.

By virtue of their orientation, the behaviorists in general do not deal extensively with the discrete affects and affective–cognitive interactions in depression. An exception is Forster's insightful analysis of the role of anger in depression. The usefulness of these theories may be in providing ways of conceptualizing the origin of particular responses or activities of depressives. Costello (1972) has argued that a strict learning-theory approach and the concept of loss of reinforcement cannot adequately explain many of the clinical cases of depression. He gives as an example the man who loses his wife and refuses to eat. What has happened is that eating has, at least temporarily, lost its effectiveness as a reinforcer. Costello remains in a learning-theory tradition by maintaining that it is not loss of reinforcement of adaptive behavior but loss of reinforcer effectiveness that better explains the phenomenon of depression. Costello attempts to supplement his learning theory by incorporating the idea that biochemical and neurophysiological changes can contribute to loss of reinforcer effectiveness.

Psychoanalytic Theory of Depression

First, consider the origin and role of the various discrete emotions in depression, as presented by the psychoanalysts. All agree that distress (sadness, dejection, despair) is part of the picture of depression (see, for example, the fine collection of papers in Bibring, 1968). According to the psychoanalysts the distress results from real or imagined loss that threatens the individual's self-esteem, self-confidence, and emotional security. They hold that the predisposition to distress is laid in the oral (early) stages of infancy at the height of the individual's helplessness and dependency. As Rado (1968) put it, the patient's "mute cry for love is patterned on the hungry infant's loud cry for help."

Second, almost all the psychoanalytic theorists agree with Abraham's (1968) early observation that anger is part of the picture of depression. All the psychoanalysts agree that the anger and hostility of depression stem from the early frustrations and the tendency toward fixation at the oral and anal sadistic stages of psychosexual development. Fromm-Reichmann (1953) and Bibring (1968), however, relegated anger and hostility to a lesser role.

Guilt figures prominently as an emotion involved in depression, and for Rado the mood of gloomy repentance is the predominant one. The phrase "gloomy repentance" implies some combination of distress and guilt. Guilt arises, according to the psychoanalytic system, as a result of the depressed individual's relatively uncontrollable anger and rage and the behavior which the latter determines.

Fear or anxiety is mentioned by a number of psychoanalytic theorists, some viewing it as due primarily to the fear of losing sexual potency. By inference one could see fear resulting from the individual's feeling of inadequacy and incapacity in the face of threat or danger. Janet (1928) spoke of fear of action as a key determinant of depression, and Bowlby (1969, 1973) sees fear as part of the separation syndrome in young children.

The emotion of shame figures in the dynamics of depression in some psychoanalytic views and not in others. Freud (1968) felt that the depressed person lacked shame, whereas Fromm-Reichmann emphasized that shame was present and important. Most of the psychoanalysts agree that loss of self-esteem, self-confidence, and self-respect figures as a prominent dimension of depression. One could consider this loss of self-esteem and the accompanying feelings of inferiority as indexes of the emotion of shame.

Psychoanalysts use discrete emotions in the description of depression much more than they do in analyzing anxiety. One or another of the psychoanalytic investigators has touched on most of the components of depression that are hypothesized by differential emotions theory.

Differential Emotions Theory and an Empirical Analysis of Depression

Differential emotions theory holds that depression is a variable combination or pattern of affects and affective–cognitive interactions. Depression is an even more complex pattern than anxiety: More emotions are activated and there are more possibilities for conflicts in the emotion–emotion dynamics. The fundamental emotions involved in depression are distress, the key emotion, and anger, disgust, contempt, fear, guilt, and shyness. It is hypothesized that anger, disgust, and contempt (hostility) is expressed both toward the self and toward others.

Although the fundamental emotions are considered the primary and most important elements of depression, there are other factors which are frequently present—decreased sexuality, decreased physical well-being, and increased fatigue. These elements may be most properly considered as immediate effects or by-products of depression. Nevertheless, they have motivational properties and, consequently, influence the other components of the depression and its course.

Differential emotions theory suggests that the lack of sexual interest and concern over sexual adequacy is determined in part by the combined effects of inner-directed hostility on the one hand and the fear and guilt components of depression on the other. The concern over physical well-being results in part from the elevated nonemotion factor of fatigue as well as from the feeling of debilitation and motor retardation that results from emotion–emotion conflicts. The increased fatigue is determined in part by the expenditure of energy in the emotion conflicts inherent in the depression pattern.

Analysis of Depression with the DES. The application of differential emotions theory to the analysis of depression was accomplished by means of the DES. In modifying the DES for the study of depression (Izard, 1972), the items relating to anger, disgust, and contempt were included once for measurement of feelings toward self and again for measurement of feelings toward others (inner- and outer-directed hostility components). Subscales were added for sexuality, vigor or physical well-being, and fatigue. Finally, the items from the depression scale of Zuckerman's (1960) MAACL were added. The Zuckerman items scored positively for depression were designated Z and those scored negatively as Z−. The DES items, the new subscale items, and the Zuckerman items were placed in random order and the total scale was designated the DES + D.

In the study of normal depression, all subjects in the sample visualized the depression situation and completed the DES + D. Table 12-2 presents the profile of emotions for normal persons recalling and imaging a depression situation. The profile for the emotions represented by the *a priori*

TABLE 12-2

Rank Order of Scale Means of a Priori and Empirical Factors in a Recalled or Imagined Depression Situation[a]

A priori scales (from DES items)		Empirical factors (from DES + D items)		
Factor	Scale $\bar{x}$		Scale $\bar{x}$	Alpha
Distress	4.24	Distress + Z	3.8	.89
Disgust	3.14	A/D/C: hostility,	3.1	.86
Contempt	2.86	inner directed[b]		
Anger	2.85	Fear	2.8	.90
Fear	2.80	Fatigue	2.6	.77
Fatigue	2.64	Sociality/sexuality	2.5	.61
Guilt	2.41	Guilt	2.4	.83
Surprise	2.23	A/D/C: hostility,	2.3	.93
Interest	2.20	outer directed[b]		
Shyness	2.05	Surprise	2.2	.92
Enjoyment	1.14	Physical well-being (vigor)	2.0	.85
		Shyness	2.0	.80
		Joy + Z–[c]	1.2	.78

[a]From Izard, 1972 ($N = 332$ college students).
[b]A/D/C = anger/disgust/contempt.
[c]Z– items are those scored negatively on the Zuckerman MAACL depression scale.

scales of the DES are shown in column 1. The DES a priori scales describe the subjects' feelings toward or within themselves. The obtained profile is quite similar to that predicted by differential emotions theory. Distress is the key emotion and is elevated substantially above all other emotions in the pattern.

The second-, third-, and fourth-ranking emotions in the a priori depression profile are disgust, contempt, and anger, the three emotions designated as the hostility triad. These elevated means represent hostility directed toward the self. The rank of this component in the pattern is indicative of its relative importance in the depression situation. The fifth- and sixth-ranking emotions are fear and guilt, two emotions that are related in complex ways to each other as well as to the other emotion components of depression. The nonemotion factor of fatigue is actually the sixth highest mean in the profile. The reasons for its presence in the pattern have already been discussed.

A more complete picture of depression is presented in column 2 of Table 12-2, which shows the empirical factors derived from the factor analysis of the DES + D. In the factor analysis, most of the Z items merged with the DES distress scale and the Z– items with the DES joy scale.

Looking at the empirical factors that correspond to or represent fundamental emotions, it can be seen that the rank order of the emotions as represented in the empirical factors is virtually identical with the rank order of the emotions in the pattern based on *a priori* scales. The differences are due largely to the presence of the new affective factors (sexuality, vigor, fatigue) which hold positions among the emotion factors.

Between the emotions of fear and guilt in the empirical profile is the sixth-ranking factor, sociality/sexuality, which consists of items from the Zuckerman depression scale. The decreased sociability and loss of interest in sexual activity undoubtedly relate to the inhibiting emotions of fear and guilt and also to the feelings of incompetence and inadequacy brought about by inner-directed hostility. The decreased sexual involvement may also be related to the individual's lowered sense of vigor or physical well-being. The decrease in physical well-being is undoubtedly a function both of the factor of fatigue and the emotion–emotion conflicts, which make heavy demands on the energy of the depressed individual.

The eighth-ranking component in the empirical factor pattern for depression is outer-directed hostility. The outer-directed hostility may serve an adaptive function by keeping inner-directed hostility from mounting higher and higher. Outer-directed hostility may also serve to allay some of the guilt and fear in the pattern.

The presence of fear in the depression pattern may be adaptive in two ways. First it may continue to function as motivation for the depressed individual to remove himself from the situation or otherwise to change the scene. The fear may also serve as a check against excessive inner-directed hostility and thus decrease the chances of suicidal behavior.

The study of depression in normal college students was replicated in a sample of 330 high school students from the middle and upper middle socioeconomic groups. The DES + D affect profiles from the two studies were remarkably similar, attesting to the construct validity of the DES + D factors and the meaningfulness of the differential emotions theory analysis of depression. In both samples distress and hostility-in were first and second respectively, and guilt fifth. Fatigue was fourth in the college group, third in the high school sample. Among the first six factors the biggest difference between the college and high school profiles was a reversal of the ranks for fear and hostility-out, third and sixth in the college group and sixth and fourth in the high school sample. The higher hostility-out in the younger subjects suggests that on the average they are closer to the peak of the rebellious period that frequently characterizes adolescence. The higher hostility-out in this group may suppress the fear component and account for its relatively lower rank.

Patterns of Emotions of Depressive Clients in Psychotherapy. The Differential Emotions Scale has been used as a tool to facilitate psychotherapy with depressive persons. Table 12-3 presents a DES profile for two psychotherapy clients. Both of the profiles are basically similar to the profile of depression obtained from normal subjects recalling or imagining a depression situation. The fact that these profiles differ from each other and from the average profiles in imaged depression is quite as expected in terms of differential emotions theory. The depression pattern may vary from individual to individual or from time to time within the same individual. The particular pattern as it exists at the time can be used to guide the therapist in his treatment of the client.

In the case of the first profile in Table 12-3, the housewife and her husband were having extramarital affairs with the knowledge and consent of each other. Actually the housewife could not fully consent and could never adapt happily to the quadrangle affair. Distress was the most prominent emotion in her pattern, but surprise was also high. She was continually astonished to find herself in this situation. Anger, guilt, and fear were also elevated.

The client represented in column 2 was considerably more debilitated and retarded in his functioning than was the housewife. This could be inferred from the fact that fear, the most toxic and debilitating emotion, was second only to distress in the profile. For this client, the disgust and contempt were largely inner-directed. Guilt and shyness also played an important role in this young man's reactive depression.

Patterns of Emotions and Feelings in Hospitalized Depressive Patients. Marshall and Izard (1972b) administered a modified form of the DES + D to 30 female and 10 male hospitalized depressives. Table 12-4 compares the rank order of the DES + D factor scores for the depressed

TABLE 12-3
DES Profiles of Two Depressed Psychotherapy Clients [a]

Housewife suffering from marital upheaval (age 29)		College male suffering from loss of father and feelings of personal inadequacy (age 20)	
Distress	15	Distress	15
Surprise	7	Fear	14
Anger	7	Disgust	13
Guilt	7	Guilt	13
Fear	7	Shyness	11
Fatigue	5	Contempt	10
Interest	5	Fatigue	9
		Anger	8

[a]Adapted from Izard, 1972. DES scores range from a maximum possible of 15 to a minimum possible of 3.

TABLE 12-4

Rank Order of DES + D Factors for High School Students Recalling and Visualizing a Depression Situation and for Depressive Patients

Factor	High school ($N = 313$)	Depressive patients ($N = 40$)
Distress	1	1
Inner-directed hostility	2	3
Fear	3	2
Fatigue	4	7
Guilt	5	4.5
Outer-directed hostility	6	8
Physical well-being	7	6
Shyness	8	4.5

patients with that of the high school sample described earlier. Considerable similarity obtained between the profile of emotions and feelings for the depressed patients and that for the high school students describing a recalled and visualized period of depression. Differences of two or more were found between the ranks of three of the factors. One of these was not predicted, but the other two were quite as expected in a comparison of depression in hospitalized patients and normals. The patients reported relatively less fatigue than the high school students. This was somewhat surprising, until we considered the differences in environmental conditions and treatment. The patients may not experience as much fatigue because of their confinement, freedom from usual responsibilities, relative inactivity, and use of antidepressant drugs. As expected the depressed patients reported relatively less outer-directed hostility. This is consistent with both the developmental phenomenon already mentioned, with clinical observation, and with differential emotions theory, which suggests that outer-directed hostility could be adaptive in allaying inner-directed hostility and militating against the fear and guilt components of depression.

The largest difference between the depressed patients and the high school students was on shyness, where the depressed patients had a considerably higher rank. This tends to favor differential emotions theory and Fromm-Reichmann's position that shame is important in depression. It disconfirms the Freudian notion that the depressive is one who lacks shame and shyness and makes defensive use of exhibiting his miseries and woes. The differences on shyness and outer-directed hostility could result in part from differences in severity of depression and overall psychological adjustment. Despite these minor differences in relative rank order of affects, the profile of normals recalling and imaging a depression situation is essentially similar to that of hospitalized depressive patients.

Schultz (1976) showed that therapist-directed imagery and fantasy relating to anger, pleasure, and relaxation resulted in a lessening of depression in hospitalized depressives. His finding is compatible with the principle of emotion interaction (e.g., anger inhibiting or attenuating distress) and with the positions of Beck (1967) and Lazarus (1968).

An EMG Analysis of Discrete Emotions in Normal and Depressed Persons. Schwartz, Fair, Salt, Mandel, and Klerman (1976) asked normal and depressed individuals to self-generate happy, sad, or angry thoughts and feelings, and the thoughts and feelings associated with a typical day of their life. Using surface electrodes they recorded the EMG activity of the frontalis, corrugator, depressor anguli oris, and masseter muscles of the face. As in their earlier study, this experiment showed clearly different profiles of facial muscle activity in the happy, sad, and angry conditions (see Figure 12-6 adapted from Schwartz *et al.*, 1976).

In the experimental conditions the profiles of the normal and depressed patients were rather similar in form. For example, in the happy condition the depressed subjects showed considerably less change in the corrugator muscle and somewhat greater change in this muscle in the angry condition. The EMG profiles as a group distinguished between the normal and depressive individuals. The depressives showed an attenuated pattern in the image-happy condition. Further, the profiles for the two groups while imaging a typical day were strikingly different. The profile for the typical day in normals is rather similar to that of the profile for the happy condition, while the profile for the depressed patients visualizing a typical day looks like a mix of the sad (distress) and anger profiles. The finding of a distress–anger pattern in the life of depressed individuals is consistent with both psychoanalytic theory (Abraham, 1968; Freud, 1968) and differential emotions theory (Izard, 1972).

Normal Subjects' Descriptions of the Causes of Sadness, Distress, and Depression. In studies of imaged sadness, distress and depression situations, students were asked to write a brief description of the imaged situation. Although differential emotions theory holds that sadness and distress are essentially the same fundamental emotion, it recognizes that the total subjective experience may differ in situations thought of as sad or as distressful, depending on what other affects and what cognitions interact with the distress. Here, the concepts of distress, sadness, and depression were studied separately to check the extent to which they overlap in terms of attributed causes. The data, presented in Table 12-5, show that in the minds of college students there is considerable overlap among the connotations of the terms distress, sadness, and depression. Some of the empty cells in the table, as well as some of the differences among percentages across affect categories, may be accounted for by the fact that the study of depression was done earlier, using different raters and a slightly different

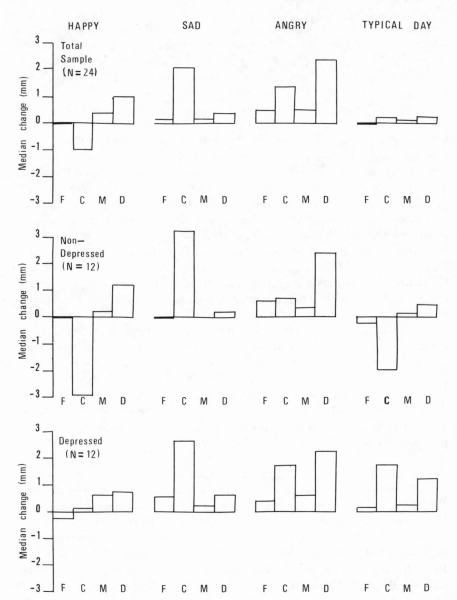

FIGURE 12-6. Changes in EMG profiles of depressed and nondepressed individuals imaging a happy, sad, and angry situation and a typical day. (Schwartz, et al., 1976).

TABLE 12-5

Classification of Free Response Descriptions of the Imaged Distress, Sadness, and Depression Situations
(College Students)

Response classification	Affect concept		
	Distress (N = 48)	Sadness (N = 106)	Depression (N = 332)
1. Academic failure, pressure of school work, and competition for grades and related problems	35.4	6.6	22.3
2. Heterosocial (boy–girl) problems	8.3	25.5	21.0
3. Loneliness, separation from loved ones, being left out	4.2	13.2	14.7
4. Loss or failure in nonacademic competition, sports, campus elections, honors		6.6	5.7
5. Death or illness of loved one or friend	6.2	31.1	4.7
6. Difficulties with parents or relatives		6.6	3.3
7. Responses combining two or more categories			10.0
8. Problems of other people		7.5	
9. Physical injury, harm to self or others	20.8		
10. Feeling of hopelessness inability to cope	10.4		
11. Categories with less than 3% of the total responses	14.5	2.8	18.3

classificatory scheme. For example, response category 8 was not used in the study of distress and sadness.

Nevertheless, there are some differences that are substantial enough to be noteworthy, particularly since they tend to confirm Ekman and Friesen's (1975) notions about distinctions between distress and sadness. A much larger percentage of students considered academic failure, the pressure of school work, and the competition for grades as causes for distress than was the case for sadness. The percentage of responses for depression fell in between those for distress and sadness. Considerably more individuals perceived loneliness and separation from loved ones as cause for sadness or depression than was true for distress. About 31% of the sample perceived physical injury, harm to self or others, feelings of helplessness, and inability to cope as causes of distress, whereas no members of the other two samples saw these phenomena as causes of sadness or depression.

Summary

Distress is the most ubiquitous of the negative emotions, and it is typically the dominant emotion in grief and depression. However, since it is less toxic than fear, it can serve constructive purposes by motivating problem-solving activity.

At the neural level, distress is activated by a continued moderate level of stimulation. Psychological causes of distress include many problem situations of everyday life, high drive states, other emotions, imagery, and other cognitive processes. The prototypical distress situation is the physical separation of the infant from the mother. The innate expressions of distress include arched eyebrows, transverse forehead wrinkles, and downturned mouth. Transformed distress expressions include the long, sagging face, and whining voice. The experience of distress is typically described as sadness, downheartedness, discouragement, loneliness, isolation. While distress can become quite noxious, it is characterized by less tension than any other negative emotion. Consistent with the differential emotions theory of the dynamics of distress in grief and depression, normal subjects imaging a distress situation report fear as the second strongest emotion in distress-eliciting situations.

Distress is biologically useful when it results in tears that prevent unhealthy drying of mucous membranes and that produce lysosome which wards off dangerous bacteria. At the social and psychological level, distress communicates to self and to others that all is not well. Distress expression tends to elicit sympathy and help from others. Distress also serves as a cohesive force in social relationships.

The punitive socialization of distress can cause compulsive behavior, low frustration tolerance, poor individuation, and loss of physical courage. The incomplete rewarding of distress and mixed methods of socializing distress can produce problems in personality development.

The ubiquity of distress means that it frequently interacts with other emotions in day-to-day life. A distress–anger interaction can cause a father to respond to his child's distress with a display of anger. A distress–fear bind can impede individuation and lead to "anxiety neurosis." When a child is repeatedly blamed for crying, a distress–shame bind can develop and produce a painfully shy person. Distress–cognition interactions are common operations in consciousness. The work of a number of investigators has shown that experimentally manipulated cognitive processes can induce distress experience and alter subsequent thought and activity.

Grief over loss of a beloved person or a highly valued object is a virtually universal human experience. The most profound grief comes from the loss of a loved one. While distress or sadness is the dominant emotion in grief, the conditions eliciting grief frequently evoke other interacting emotions. The extent to which fear, anger, guilt, and shame interact with distress during the period of grieving depends upon the particular individual's life experience and the prevailing conditions at the time of loss. It has been argued that grief is biologically based and biologically adaptive, serving as a cohesive force in maintaining social organization in species that are essentially group-living forms. Grief can also be interpreted as useful to the individual and the observing community. Intense grief, such as that over loss of a lifelong mate, can render the grieving person more susceptible to disease and death. A number of clinical investigators have concluded that grief can take on pathological characteristics.

Consistent with the notion that distress is the most ubiquitous negative emotion, depression is considered the most common psychological or psychopathological problem. There are a number of viable theories of depression. Most of them agree that it is a complex phenomenon involving neurophysiological and biochemical factors, a number of affects, and various affective–cognitive interactions. The major exception is strict behavioristic theory.

Studies of monozygotic twins have implicated genetic determinants of depression. Biochemical studies have shown relationships between depression and the synthesis and metabolism of biogenic amines. Cyclic AMP is also considered to play a mediational role. Biochemical research has led to the development of antidepressant drugs, but their therapeutic value has not been completely determined. Beck's cognitive theory of depression holds that the individual's view of oneself, one's world, and one's future constitutes the principal determinant in depression. He has presented a highly useful analysis of the symptomatology and phenomenology of depression.

There are a number of behavioral or learning-theory approaches to the study of depression. Though some of them recognize biological factors, most of them emphasize only the role of learning. One holds that repeated exposure to inescapable pain or threats leads to fear, distress, and learned helplessness and hopelessness (depression). Another behavioral theory holds that depressives have lost certain adaptive behaviors and have increased escape and avoidance behaviors as a result of inappropriate or absent reinforcing conditions. Another holds that depression results from the loss of reinforcer effectiveness, as it applies to certain types of adaptive behavior.

Psychoanalytic theory has recognized the role of a number of discrete emotions in depression. Neoanalytic theories have extended the causal concept of loss to include loss of self-esteem, loss of confidence, and loss of self-respect.

Differential emotions theory holds that depression is a pattern of fundamental emotions including the key emotion of distress and variable combinations of anger, disgust, and contempt (inner- and outer-directed hostility), fear, guilt, and shyness. It also recognizes the role of other affective factors such as decreased sexuality, increased fatigue, and loss of sense of physical well-being. Empirical studies of normal subjects and hospitalized depressives with the DES support the differential emotions theory conception of depression. Further, the DES profile of emotions and affective–cognitive structures in normal and pathological depression are quite similar. The differences are readily explained in terms of varieties of depression or overall psychological status of the normal subjects and depressives.

DES profiles of depressed individuals in psychotherapy show the main features of the depressive profile, but they also illustrate variations in the importance of different emotions depending upon the individual client and the life situation.

EMG studies of facial muscle activity in normal and depressed persons yielded results quite consistent with differential emotions theory. Facial muscles involved in the expression of joy and distress (sadness) distinguished between the two groups.

Since distress is the key emotion in depression it is reasonable to expect overlap in the meanings attributed to the two terms. A study of connotations of distress, sadness, and depression showed considerable overlap in the kinds of things perceived as their causes. Differences that were observed are consistent with Ekman and Friesen's distinctions between distress and sadness, which they consider as two forms of the same emotion.

13

ANGER, DISGUST, AND CONTEMPT AND THEIR RELATIONSHIP TO HOSTILITY AND AGGRESSION*

Anger, disgust, and contempt are distinct fundamental emotions. They can be differentiated at the expressive level, as evidenced by Table 1-1. As shown in the table, many different cultures show relatively high agreement in differentiating the facial expressions of these three emotions. There are also differences at the experiential level: One may feel irritable in anger, strong distaste in disgust, and cool and distant in contempt. In day-to-day experiences, however, anger, disgust, and contempt often seem to go together. Situations that elicit one of these emotions often elicit one or both of the others. In the first section of this chapter, anger, disgust, and contempt will be considered separately as discrete fundamental emotions. In later sections these emotions will be considered in relation to hostility and aggression.

The Distinguishing Characteristics of Anger, Disgust, and Contempt

Anger

How Anger Occurs: Its Causes and Activation. Though not known to be a universal cause, a very common stimulus to anger is the feeling of being either physically or psychologically restrained from doing what one

*An earlier version of some parts of this chapter appeared in Pliner, Krames, and Alloway (Eds.), *Nonverbal Communication of Aggression.* New York: Plenum, 1975.

intensely desires to do. The restraint may be in terms of physical barriers, rules, and regulations, or one's own incapability. If the restraints are subtle or disguised the immediate response may not be anger. However, if the barrier really prevents the attainment of a highly desirable goal or some aspect of self-expression, anger is almost certain to occur eventually. Low levels of anger may be suppressed for a long time, at some cost to health and with the risk of an ultimate explosion of rage.

Other causes of anger include personal insult, everyday frustrations (blocking or interfering with goal-oriented behavior), interruption of interest or joy, being taken advantage of, and being compelled to do something against one's wishes. While these things elicit anger in many people, there are, of course, individual and cultural differences in causes of anger. Further, some of these things may cause emotions other than, or in addition to, anger. Since most causes of anger are a function of personal experiences, cultural conditioning, and learning, there are not many stimuli (or situations) that cause anger and only anger. Tomkins has proposed that prolonged, unrelieved distress is one inborn activator of anger.

According to Tomkins's theory, anger is a density-level emotion. That is, its neural activation occurs as a result of a moderately high and steady level of neural activation. Since distress is also activated by a steady (but lower) level of neural stimulation, it can be seen how prolonged distress would increase the likelihood of anger activation. Any increase in the level of stimulation experienced in distress may send the density of neural firing above the threshold for anger. Apparently consistent with Tomkins's theory is Zillman and Bryant's (1974) finding that prior stimulation ("excitatory residues") facilitates both anger and aggressive action.

What It Looks Like to Be Angry. Figure 4-9 (p. 88) shows most of the components of the expression of strong anger. In the innate expression of anger, the muscles of the brow move inward and downward, creating a frown and a foreboding appearance about the eyes, which seem to be fixed in a hard stare toward the object of anger. The nostrils dilate and the wings of the nose flare out. The lips are opened and drawn back in a rectangle-like shape, revealing clinched teeth. Often the face flushes red. Children are usually taught to control their anger and this includes controlling or partially controlling the expression. Because of this children gradually learn to partially conceal or disguise the expression of anger. In Figure 13-1, sister's playful attempt to stop thumb sucking elicits an uninhibited anger expression from the toddler, and a 10-year-old boy shows an anger expression with tightly compressed lips that disguise the bare-teeth look. Individuals' expressions of anger may vary considerably, but on the face of an angry person there is almost always one or more of the innate components of the natural expression which signals his or her internal state.

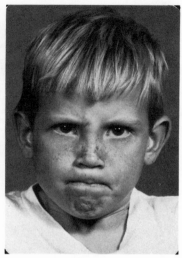

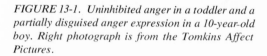

FIGURE 13-1. Uninhibited anger in a toddler and a partially disguised anger expression in a 10-year-old boy. Right photograph is from the Tomkins Affect Pictures.

What It Feels Like to Be Angry. In anger the blood "boils," the face becomes hot, the muscles tense. There is a feeling of power and an impulse to strike out, to attack the source of anger. The stronger the anger the stronger and more energetic the person feels and the greater the need for physical action. In rage the mobilization of energy is so great that one feels one will explode if one does not bite, hit, or kick something, or "act out the anger" in some way.

The Bartlett–Izard study (see Figure 13-2) showed that anger causes the person to feel great tension, second only to that in fear, and far more self-assurance than in any other negative emotion. The sense of physical strength and self-assurance tends to make the person feel brave and courageous. We do not always associate anger with courage because in many cases the anger is quickly reduced by feelings of fear or guilt over the possible consequences of the anger.

Figure 13-2 also shows that the experience of anger is accompanied by a strong feeling of impulsiveness. The mean for the dimension of control, not shown on the graph, was lower in anger than in any other emotion. Although the control mean in anger did not differ significantly from that of several other emotions, the combination of high impulsiveness and low control helps explain why the rules for anger expression and "acting out anger" are carefully laid down during socialization. The combination of muscle tension (strength), self-assurance, and impulsiveness help explain the individual's readiness to strike out or engage in some kind of motor activity. Anger is a relatively unpleasant feeling, though the mean on the

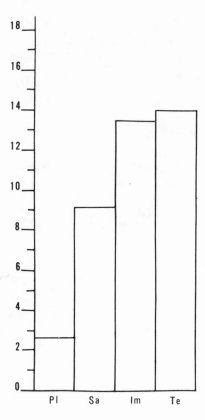

FIGURE 13-2. Profile of dimensions in the anger situation. The DRS dimension are abbreviated: (Pl) pleasantness, (Sa) self-assurance, (Im) impulsiveness, (Te) tension.

pleasantness dimension was not significantly lower in anger than in fear, distress, or guilt. The DRS study also showed that, on the average, individuals feel significantly more extraverted in anger than in any other negative emotion.

Figure 13-3 shows the pattern of emotions in the imaged anger situation. As can been seen from the graph the pattern is dominated by what has been termed the hostility triad, anger–disgust–contempt (Izard, 1972).

The mean for the key emotion of anger is higher than that of any other key emotion in the situations for negative emotions. Further, the dynamically related emotions of disgust and contempt, which occupy the second and third places in the anger situation, are considerably elevated.

For the most part, the emotions with the highest means in the anger pattern interact harmoniously and sustain a high level of activity that is clearly focused and directed. Distress, which is moderately elevated, is the most difficult emotion to analyze as a part of the dynamics of the anger pattern. As already noted, anger and distress, according to Tomkins (1963), are activated by similar gradients of neural firing. This may help explain the presence of distress in the pattern, but not its role. The role of distress might be to moderate the intensity of anger and the related emotions of disgust and contempt. Should anger lead to aggression, distress could serve as a basis for empathy with the victim and thus serve as a sort of safety valve. It is also quite possible that as a result of social experience and learning, individuals may feel some distress (sadness, discouragement) in anger situations because anger is so seldom expressed in openly satisfying and rewarding ways in our society and because it often arises in the face of disappointment resulting from thwarting or postponement of goals. It should be noted that in the anger situation, fear is lower both in absolute value and in relative rank than in any other negative emotion situation. This follows from the fact that anger inhibits fear. The probable role of fear in the anger situation, like that of distress, is to exercise a moderating effect on the potentially dangerous hostility triad.

The Significance of Anger. In the evolution of human beings anger was important for survival. Its value lay in its ability to mobilize one's energy and make one capable of defending oneself with great vigor and strength. With the rise of civilization this function of anger became so rarely needed that it is now considered by many scientists as more of a liability than an asset. Ethologists say it is an example of cultural evolution outrunning biological evolution. Now, except in rare cases of self-defense

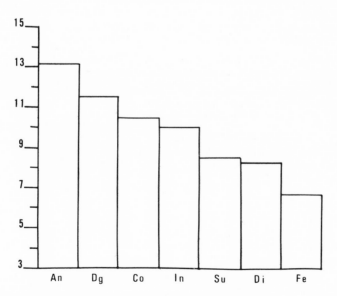

FIGURE 13-3. *Pattern of emotions in the imaged anger situation* (N = 36): *Minimum score, 3; maximum score, 15. Abbreviations of emotions as follows: (An) anger, (Dg) disgust, (Co) contempt, (In) interest, (Su) surprise, (Di) distress, and (Fe) fear.*

or defense of loved ones, the angry attack is almost always a violation of legal and ethical codes and not only causes harm to the victim but gets the aggressor in serious trouble.

One form of adaptation has been learning to respond to anger with words and with enough tact to keep from angering the other person and cutting off communication. This form of response to anger may be adaptive and healthy in case of attack on an individual's personal integrity, or when the anger is a result of needless constraints and oppression. In such cases a little controlled anger can provide the psychological strength (self-confidence) one needs to speak up for one's self. There are clinical and experimental data which show that failure to respond appropriately and constructively to justifiable anger can interfere with clear thinking, "poison" relationships, and cause psychosomatic disorders (e.g., see Holt, 1970).

The responses from the study of the antecedents and consequences of anger are presented in Table 13-1.

TABLE 13-1
Antecedents and Consequences of Anger
(N = Approximately 130 College Students)

Responses	Percentage of subjects giving responses
Antecedents	
Feelings	
1. Of being misled, betrayed, used, disappointed, hurt by others	40.8
2. Anger–rage synonyms	17.6
3. Hatred, dislike, disapproval of others, detrimental thoughts	12.0
4. Aggressive, revengeful, like attacking others	8.0
5. Of failure, disappointed in self, self-blame, inadequacy	5.6
6. Sense of injustice in world	3.2
7. Distress–anguish synonyms	.8
8. Other	12.0
Thoughts	
1. Of hatred, dislike, disapproval of others: detrimental thoughts	31.2
2. Of being misled, betrayed, used, disapproved, hurt by others	19.2
3. Of having failed, disappointing self, blaming self, inadequacy	10.4
4. Injustice, world problems	10.4
5. Of destruction, revenge	14.4

TABLE 13-1 (continued)
Antecedents and Consequences of Anger
(N = Approximately 130 College Students)

Responses	Percentage of subjects giving responses
6. Irritating, things go wrong	8.0
7. Other	6.4
Actions	
1. Something wrong, stupid	34.4
2. Something violent, rash, let off steam	16.8
3. Something unappreciated by others	12.0
4. Something that you don't want to do, others impose their will	8.8
5. Aggression, revenge	8.0
6. Something legally or morally wrong or harmful	7.2
7. Other	12.8
Consequences	
Feelings	
1. Anger synonyms	28.8
2. Hot, tense, etc.	24.2
3. Revengeful, like attacking others, destructive	24.2
4. Hatred, dislike, disapproval of others	6.8
5. Distress synonyms	2.3
6. Angry	1.5
7. Justified	1.5
8. Other	10.6
Thoughts	
1. Of revenge, attacking others, destruction	43.9
2. Of ways to regain, maintain control of self, situation, or change situation	13.6
3. Hatred, dislike, disapproval of others	12.1
4. Of expressing anger, verbally or physically	7.6
5. Negative, hostile thoughts (unspecific)	7.6
6. About event which caused anger	4.5
7. Angry, detrimental thoughts toward self	4.5
8. Other	6.1
Actions	
1. Tries to regain or maintain control of self or situation	35.6
2. Verbal attack or physical action against object of anger	24.2
3. Takes action, aggresses against object or situation causing anger	18.9
4. Does something impulsive or irrational	11.4
5. Other	9.8

Disgust–Revulsion

In some ways disgust is closely related to anger, yet it has some distinct features. By itself it is not as potentially dangerous as anger.

How Disgust Occurs. Things that are deteriorated or spoiled, either organically or psychologically, cause disgust. Some theorists maintain that disgust evolved from the hunger drive and the behavior associated with it. Thus the prototype of a disgusting situation is something that "tastes bad." When a person experiences some condition (a dirty, smelly room or person) or even some unseemly behavior (that of another or of oneself) he may say, "That puts a bad taste in my mouth."

What It Looks Like to Be Disgusted. Figure 4-10 (p. 89) is a rather good picture of disgust. In the full expression of disgust, one appears as though one is gagging or spitting out. The expression of disgust also shows a pulling upward of the upper lip and a wrinkling of the nose. This tends to make the eyes appear to be squinting. More details and illustrations of the disgust expression can be found in Ekman and Friesen (1975).

What It Feels Like to Be Disgusted. The feeling of disgust is like feeling "sick at the stomach," with a bad taste in the mouth. One wants to remove or get away from the object of disgust. If disgust is very intense it may actually make one "sick at the stomach" by creating nausea.

As can be seen by comparisons of Figures 13-3 and 13-4, the profiles

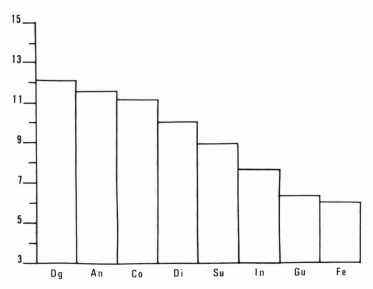

FIGURE 13-4. Pattern of emotions in the imaged disgust situation: minimum score, 3; maximum score, 15. Abbreviations of emotions as follows: (Dg) disgust, (An) anger, (Co) contempt, (Di) distress, (Su) surprise, (In) interest, and (Fe) fear.

for anger and disgust are quite similar, but there are some noteworthy differences. In the anger situation, interest is considerably higher and distress somewhat lower than in the disgust situation. This suggests that the object of anger captures the alert attention of the person more than does the object of disgust, which is more likely to motivate the turning of attention elsewhere.

The Significance of Disgust. When something disgusts us we want to remove it or change it in such a way that it is no longer disgusting. In evolution, disgust probably helped motivate organisms to maintain an environment sufficiently sanitary for their health and to prevent them from eating spoiled food and drinking polluted water. Disgust is not a perfect detector of dangerous contamination, but it helps. Also, disgust probably plays a role in the maintenance of body hygiene. Foul body odors or a grossly dirty appearance may be disgusting to the self and others. Failure to clean up the environment may prove disastrous for the group and failure to maintain body cleanliness that meets the group's standards may lead to rejection and isolation of the individual.

Disgust can be directed toward an idea or a personality, including one's own. Disgust combined with anger can be very dangerous, since anger can motivate "attack," and disgust the desire to "get rid of." Disgust, like anger, can be directed toward the self, and self-disgust can lower self-esteem and cause self-rejection. As seen in Chapter 12, research with normal people and hospitalized patients has shown that inner-directed anger and disgust are usually characteristic of depression.

The responses from the study of the antecedents and consequences of disgust are presented in Table 13-2.

Contempt–Scorn

It is rather difficult to analyze the role of contempt in evolution and to find its adaptive or constructive functions in contemporary life. Nevertheless, it seems worthwhile to speculate on the nature and possible adaptive functions of contempt in evolutionary-biological perspective and in day-to-day interactions.

How Contempt Occurs. In evolutionary perspective, contempt may have emerged as a vehicle for preparing the individual or group to face a dangerous adversary. For example, a young man might prepare for defense of himself or of his group with such thoughts as: "I am stronger than he, I am better." Eventually this message might become a rallying signal for all the men in preparation for defense or attack. Perhaps those who were quite persuaded marshaled more courage (and felt less empathy for the enemy) and were more successful in surviving the hazards of hunting and fighting. Still today the occasions that elicit contempt are situations in which one needs to feel stronger, more intelligent, more civilized, or in some way

TABLE 13-2
Antecedents and Consequences of Disgust
(N = Approximately 130 College Students)

Responses	Percentage of subjects giving responses
Antecedents	
Feelings	
1. "Sick of something," repelled, tired	27.7
2. Of failure, disappointment in self, anger toward self, incompetency	26.8
3. Of dislike, disapproval of actions of others	17.7
4. Disgust synonyms	11.5
5. Distress synonyms	6.9
6. Anger synonyms	3.8
7. Contempt synonyms	3.1
8. Other	4.6
Thoughts	
1. Hatred, dislike, disapproval of actions of others	24.6
2. Of failure, disappointment in self, anger toward self, incompetency	22.3
3. War, politics, racism	20.8
4. Smelly, unpleasant things	14.6
5. Unclear thoughts	4.6
6. Lonely, isolated, rejected	3.8
7. Other	5.4
Actions	
1. Blames self	30.8
2. Something wrong, stupid, a mistake	25.4
3. Has to do something unpleasant, others impose their will	15.4
4. Does something unappreciated by others	12.3
5. Does something legally or morally wrong or harmful	10.8
6. Other	5.4
Consequences	
Feelings	
1. Physical disgust: nausea, fatigue, sick, etc.	25.5
2. Disgust synonyms	18.8
3. Anger synonyms	15.0
4. Contempt synonyms	14.3
5. Like giving up, apathetic	7.5
6. Feels misled, betrayed, used, or hurt by others	3.8
7. Has failed, blames self, etc.	3.8

TABLE 13-2 (continued)
Antecedents and Consequences of Disgust
(N = Approximately 130 College Students)

Responses	Percentage of subjects giving responses
8. Feels bad, lousy, terrible	3.0
9. Other	8.3
Thoughts	
1. How bad the situation is	30.8
2. Thinks about event which caused the disgust	15.0
3. Of others, trying to forget, escape situation	15.0
4. Has failed, blames self, etc.	11.5
5. Hatred, dislike, disapproval of others	10.5
6. About a solution to the problem	9.8
7. Contempt synonym	3.0
8. Other	11.3
Actions	
1. Gets away from situation	39.8
2. Finds a solution to problem	21.1
3. Verbally or physically hostile	12.8
4. Evaluates attitude, tries to do better	4.5
5. Covers up feelings, puts up a front	3.0
6. Gets mad	3.0
7. Acts superior	2.3
8. Talks to someone, gets with friend	2.3
9. Other	11.3

better than, the person one is contending with. Situations that elicit jealousy, greed, and rivalry are breeding grounds for contempt.

What It Looks Like to Be Contemptuous. Figure 4-11 (p. 90) is a good portrayal of contempt. The eyebrow is cocked, the face stretched longer and the head lifted up, giving the appearance that the person is looking down on someone. At the same time the expression of contempt gives the impression that the contemptuous person is pulling away, creating distance between self and the other.

How It Feels to Be Contemptuous. As suggested by the foregoing paragraph, the feeling of contempt is the feeling of being superior, of being better than someone, some group or some thing. It may also be the feeling that one's family, one's culture, or one's society is superior to and better than someone else's. Contempt, like anger and disgust, is to some degree a feeling of hostility. In contempt one feels prejudiced against some object, idea, person, or group.

The profile of emotions in the contempt situation is presented in Figure 13-5.

The Significance of Contempt. In evolutionary perspective contempt may have played a constructive role in developing self and group defense against the elements or predators. Once the contempt is turned against other human beings (or the self) it seems difficult to find anything positive or adaptive in this emotion. Perhaps it serves a socially constructive purpose when it is directed in moderate degree against those objectively deserving it: those who foster waste, pollution, immorality, oppression, crime, or war.

It is easy to analyze the negative functions of this emotion. Contempt is the principal emotion in all kinds of prejudice, including racial prejudice. Of the three emotions in the hostility triad—anger, disgust, contempt—contempt is the most subtle, the coldest. Anger is a "hot" emotion, usually impelling forthright action. Contempt is cold and distant, more likely to foster aggression characterized by trickery and deceit. The feeling of contempt toward a human being tends to depersonalize the target individual, to cause the person to be perceived as something less than human. It is because of these characteristics that contempt can motivate murder and mass destruction of people—"cold-blooded killing." Some antecedents and consequences of contempt are presented in Table 13-3.

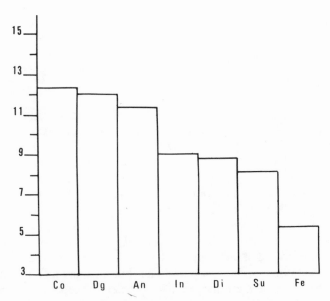

FIGURE 13-5. *Pattern of emotions in the imaged contempt situation: minimum score, 3; maximum score, 15. Abbreviations of emotions as follows: (Co) contempt, (Dg) disgust, (An) anger, (In) interest, (Di) distress, (Su) surprise, and (Fe) fear.*

TABLE 13-3

Antecedents and Consequences of Contempt

Responses	Percentage of subjects giving responses
Antecedents	
Feelings	
1. Of superiority	59.3
2. Feels misled, betrayed, used, disappointed, hurt by others	10.6
3. Disapproval, disturbed by actions of others	8.9
4. Disgust synonyms (revulsion, aversion)	3.2
5. Shame synonyms (embarrassed, shy)	2.4
6. Anger synonyms (irritated, annoyed, mad)	1.6
7. Other	13.8
Thoughts	
1. Disapproving of actions of others	40.6
2. Contempt synonyms	33.3
3. Of being misled, betrayed, used, hurt by others	7.3
4. Shame synonyms	4.9
5. Of being embarrassed	3.2
6. Other	10.6
Actions	
1. Acts superior, condescending	19.5
2. Succeed when others thought you could not, do superior work	15.4
3. Act sarcastic, hateful, hurt others	13.0
4. Something wrong, stupid, mistake	11.5
5. Disapprove, dislike actions of others	10.6
6. Act selfishly	5.7
7. Other	5.7
Consequences	
Feelings	
1. Of superiority	60.6
2. Confident, good, elevated	7.6
3. Anger synonyms	5.3
4. Shame synonyms	5.3
5. Hatred, dislike, disapproval of others	3.8
6. Disgust	3.0
7. Envy, jealousy, of others	3.0
8. Other	11.4

Continued

TABLE 13-3 (continued)
Antecedents and Consequences of Contempt

Responses	Percentage of subjects giving responses
Thoughts	
1. Of being and feeling superior	37.9
2. Of hatred, dislike, disapproval of others	19.7
3. How to ignore, avoid object or situation	15.1
4. Questions reasons for behavior, thinks of what was done and why	6.8
5. Try not to feel contempt	5.3
6. Anger synonyms	1.5
7. Other	12.9
Actions	
1. Expresses contempt, either verbally or physically	38.6
2. Ignores, avoids object of contempt or situation	20.5
3. Tries not to show emotion, or feeling	9.1
4. Tries to regain control of self or situation	7.6
5. Tries to understand the other point of view	4.5
6. Other	19.7

Anger, Disgust, Contempt in Relation to Hostility and Aggression

The first task of this section is to distinguish between hostility and aggression and to give aggression a relatively more specific definition than it is sometimes accorded. The major distinction proposed here is that hostility consists of affective experience (emotions, feelings) and affective–cognitive orientations while aggression consists of actions intended to harm.

Distinctions between Hostility and Aggression

Hostility is a complex affective–cognitive orientation. It consists of a variable set of interacting emotions, drives, and affective–cognitive structures. The emotions most prominent in the pattern of hostility are anger, disgust, and contempt. Hostility also involves drive states, affect–affect interactions, and, usually, imagery or wishful thinking about harm, embarrassment, or defeat of the object of hostility. Such imaging and wishing does not necessarily include an intent actually to harm the object. Hostility has both experiential and expressive components, but it does not include verbal or physical activity. Anger, disgust, and contempt influence perceptual processes and tend to foster cognitive processes consonant with the underlying affect, and the result is hostility. Since hostility communicates negative emotion (e.g., by way of anger expression), it can harm or embarrass the target, but the harm is primarily psychological.

Within the theoretical framework of differential emotions theory aggression is defined as hostile action or hostile behavior. Aggression is a physical act which may or may not be instigated and maintained in part by one or more of the emotions in the hostility pattern. It is intended to harm, embarrass, or defeat the object. The term "physical act" includes speech as well as all other physical actions. The harm may be psychological or physical, a blow to the body or to the self-concept. Thus, the hurt caused by aggression may be from genuine pain, negative emotions, or both. In general, aggression follows from hostility and the imagery and ideas it produces. However, aggressive action can influence the ongoing hostility. Thus, hostility is considered as the complex motivational condition, and aggression the subsequent behavior. Although this chapter will have more to say about aggression, its central concern is with hostility and with the affects and patterns of affects that constitute it.

The conceptual framework outlined by these definitions indicates that emotion expression (e.g., facial, vocal, postural expression) may be agonistic, but it is not aggression itself, since the latter is defined as physical action apart from the emotion process. Affect expression does communicate anger, disgust, contempt, or hostility and in doing so can cause emotional hurt and do psychological damage. Thus, there is a need for regulation and control of hostility (affect expression), as well as aggression. The distinction between hostility (affects, hostile cognition, affect expression) and aggression (actions intended to harm) may help establish more refined principles of control for all types of agonistic phenomena.

Verbalizations (e.g., "angry words") directed toward another person occupy a middle ground between expression and physical action. They are a kind of motor act, but their harm is typically only psychological (like that of hostility). Linguistic attack is something more than emotion expression (considering expression as a component of emotion); it is a consequence of emotion rather than a part of it. Thus it is more properly considered a form of aggression.

The present definition of aggression is similar to that proposed by the ethologist Hinde (1971), except that in restricting aggressive behavior to physical acts directed toward the causing of physical harm he makes no allowance for verbal aggression.

Patterns of Affects in Situations that Elicit Anger, Disgust, Contempt, and Hostility

Studies paralleling those for the fundamental emotion of distress and the affect pattern of depression have also been completed for the fundamental emotions of anger, disgust, contempt, and the affect pattern of hostility. The profiles of emotions in visualized hostility, anger, disgust, and contempt situations are presented in Table 13-4. These results differ in some ways from those obtained in the studies of the distress and depression situations. While the distress and depression situations had emotion profiles that were quite distinct from each other and those of any of the other fundamental emotions, this was not the case for hostility. The profiles of emotions for the imaged "hostility" and anger situations were virtually identical. Further, except for the expected difference for the key emotion (the one named in a given imaging instruction) the profiles for disgust and contempt were very similar in shape to those for hostility and anger.

Of the four profiles, that for contempt is the most deviant from the others. If we take the sum of the mean scores for anger, disgust, and contempt as a general index of the intensity of hostility, then the contempt situation elicited the lowest amount of hostility. The largest part of the difference is accounted for by the fact that the contempt situation elicited substantially less anger than the hostility or anger situations and slightly less than the disgust situation. The contempt profile differs in some other ways. First, the amount of distress elicited in the contempt situation is substantially lower than the other three. The amount of fear in the contempt situation is substantially less than that in the hostility and anger situations and somewhat less than that of disgust. There is also slightly less guilt and shyness in the contempt situation than in the others. The direction of the

TABLE 13-4

Profiles of Emotions in Visualized Hostility, Anger, Disgust and Contempt Situations[a]

	Situation			
Emotion	Hostility, N = 213	Anger, N = 30	Disgust, N = 33	Contempt, N = 37
Anger	12.46	12.53	10.39	9.86
Contempt	10.28	10.60	9.88	10.49
Disgust	10.05	10.97	10.70	9.19
Distress	8.99	9.33	8.97	7.78
Interest	8.58	8.93	7.79	8.68
Surprise	7.66	7.87	7.09	6.62
Fear	5.62	5.97	5.27	4.89
Guilt	5.42	6.33	5.33	5.00
Shyness	4.64	4.57	4.61	4.08
Joy	3.43	3.80	3.70	5.16

[a]Scores derived from the Differential Emotions Scale; maximum score, 15; minimum score, 3.

difference is reversed in the case of joy, which is highest in the contempt situation. Virtually no joy is reported in the hostility, anger, or disgust situations, but the mean in contempt is well above the absolute minimum of 3.00.

One might conclude from this that the situations that elicit contempt are less likely to result in aggression than those that elicit anger and disgust. If this conclusion is correct, contempt is the most benign of the three emotions in the hostility triad. However, if we look again at the profile of emotions in contempt, there are some factors that militate against this conclusion. The contempt situation elicited the least amount of distress, guilt, and fear, three emotions that might serve to inhibit aggression. Further, the contempt situation is somehow more enjoyable, and presumably the concomitant experience and subsequent behavior are more tolerable.

It is no accident that we speak of the "heat of anger," for the flushed face of the angry individual feels and looks hot. Aggression that occurs in anger is more likely to be a direct result of relatively intense emotion in an individual whose energy has been highly mobilized. On the contrary, contempt can be considered the "cool" emotion in the hostility triad. It seems reasonable that it is the contempt situation in which the "cold-blooded" aggressor operates, since contempt is a distancing and devaluing emotion. This description also has validity in the language of common usage, as indicated by such phrases as "murder in cold blood," or "cold-blooded killer."

One possible factor contributing to the similarity of the hostility and anger profiles was the instruction to visualize a situation of intense hostility. In a follow-up study the term "intense" was omitted and several drive and affective–cognitive scales replaced six of the emotion scales that were not considered especially important in the hostility profile. The results are presented in Table 13-5. The rank order of emotion means, disregarding the other scales, is very similar to that for hostility and anger in Table 13-1. Apparently the term "intense" had no special effect in the instructions of the previous study. In fact, the second study showed a somewhat higher hostility (anger–disgust–contempt) index. As in the first study, females had substantially higher scores on distress than did males.

Table 13-5 shows that drives and affective–cognitive orientations are part of the hostility pattern. As expected, vigor, egotism, and skepticism were substantially elevated and tranquility and sex were depressed. (In a few individual profiles sex was elevated. These subjects described hostility situations involving a person of the opposite sex.) The data of Table 13-5 show that hostility is a complex pattern of emotions, drives, and affective–cognitive orientations.

The foregoing analysis supports the notion that there are a variety of

TABLE 13-5
Profile of Affects in an Imaged
Hostility Situation [a]

Scale	Mean
Anger	13.34
Contempt	12.73
Disgust	11.48
Distress	8.57
Vigor	9.48
Skepticism	8.27
Egotism	7.16
Fear	6.05
Sociality	5.14
Guilt	5.09
Sex	3.64
Tranquility	3.66

[a]Scores derived from the Differential
Affects Scale: maximum score, 15; minimum score, 3.

emotion profiles that involve enough hostility to increase the likelihood of
aggression. Awareness of the similarities and differences among these
situations and their emotion profiles may increase our understanding of the
motivations underlying or accompanying aggressive acts.

The rank ordering of emotion means in the hostility situation was
identical for males and females. Females reported slightly higher scores in
anger, disgust, and contempt, but they exceeded the males even more in
distress and surprise. The greater mean in distress suggests that the hostility situation elicits in the female an emotion which could tend to inhibit
aggressive acts. The relatively greater surprise may simply mean that it is
more unusual and hence a bit astonishing for the female to find herself
experiencing (or admitting) intense hostility feelings.

The Interactions of Anger, Disgust, and Contempt with Other Affects and Cognitions

The interactions of anger, disgust, and contempt with the pain and sex
drives were discussed in Chapter 7. Acute pain can activate or amplify
anger, and chronic pain can lower the anger threshold. The combination of
anger, disgust, or contempt with the sex drive can result in deviant, abusive
sexual activity.

The interactions of anger, disgust, and contempt with distress were
discussed in Chapter 12. Anger can alleviate or substitute for distress in
certain more or less transient conditions. Some combination of anger,

disgust, and contempt constitute the inner- and outer-directed hostility that often forms an important component of depression.

As will be seen in Chapter 14, anger can interact with fear in a number of ways. Anger attenuates or inhibits fear and controlled anger can be used adaptively or therapeutically for this purpose. On the other hand, fear–anger interactions together with certain affective–cognitive structures can constitute a maladaptive syndrome that some would designate as anxiety.

Anger, disgust, and contempt have constricting effects on perception and cognition. The admonitions of common sense that advise one to "bury anger" and not to "carry a grudge" are not without wisdom. Apart from the possibility of psychosomatic symptoms, hostility limits mental productivity. Hostility, which includes affective–cognitive orientations, can, and often does, result in aggression. Human aggression, which will be discussed in the next section, typically involves an affective–cognitive interaction.

Emotion Expression, Interindividual Emotion Communication, and Aggression

How does the expression of anger or hostility affect the perceiver? What is the relationship between anger expression and aggressive acts? More generally, how does emotion communication influence both prosocial and agonistic behavior? These questions have been approached through several lines of investigation.

In many laboratory studies of aggression with human subjects, the subject has been isolated from the recipient, a person who may or may not be present in another room. This procedure—in addition to limiting considerably the generalizability of the results—does not represent the approach most relevant to the present discussion. The approach that is the most relevant focuses on aggression in face-to-face encounters. A study by Zimbardo (1969) showed that the physical presence of the victim influenced the behavior of the aggressor. It has been disappointing that so few investigators have followed the implication of Zimbardo's finding and that there are so few studies that have examined the effects on the aggressor of the victim's communication. Some of the studies that have developed this area have focused on the effects of eye contact or interocular responses, and these have been well-summarized by Ellsworth (1975) and Exline *et al.* (1975).

Aside from the work on eye contact the bulk of the work on the effect of the victim's communication on subsequent aggression has come from ethology. Ethological studies have shown that expressive behavior often eliminates or reduces overt aggression in coral-reef fish (Rasa, 1969), elephant seals (Le Boeuf & Peterson, 1969), and baboons (Kummer, 1968).

Both expressions of threat and expressions of submission or appease-
ment have been judged as effective in influencing agonistic behavior among
nonhuman primates. In rhesus macaque monkeys submissive expressions
range from the fear grimace to presenting the rump as in sexual invitations.
These expressive communications have been judged as effective in inhibiting aggressive behavior (Hinde & Rowell, 1962). The effect of a threat
expression may vary considerably with the status of the animal and the
situation. A high-status animal in its own territory will frequently succeed
in avoiding fights by means of threat displays. But a territorial intruder or
low-status animal may provoke fighting with a threat expression. Morris
(1968) suggested that people can avoid an attack by a potential aggressor by
displaying fear and humility and by avoiding threatening expressions.

Morris's inference is based primarily on observations of nonhuman
animals. Most theories of human aggression have not addressed the question of the effect of the victim's threat expression on the occurrence of
subsequent aggression, and predicting the effect of the victim's expression
is not at all easy. Undoubtedly there are some variables in human subjects
(see Figure 13-6) that correspond in some way to status and territory among
nonhuman primates, but it is much easier to determine status relations
among a group of socially living rhesus macaque monkeys than it is to
assess the status of a human subject who walks into the laboratory. The
equations for predicting the effect of expression on subsequent aggression
are always multivariate and both organismic and environmental variables
are involved. A couple of examples will illustrate the complexity of the

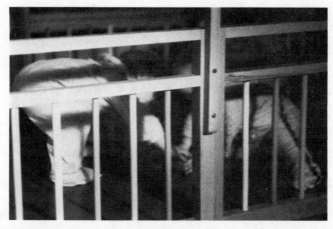

FIGURE 13-6. This "possession contest" in 10–12-month-old infants ended without any sign
of anger or aggression, but a similar encounter would produce both after attachment to the
object is formed in the second year of life.

problem of prediction. If an aggressor is not particularly angry or ego-involved in the encounter, the anger expression of the potential victim may signal a counterattack that the aggressor would choose to avoid. In this case the threat expression would decrease or avoid further aggression. On the other hand if the potential aggressor sees himself as a winner, the anger expression of the potential victim may provoke greater aggressive behavior. In summary, hostile communication (via affect expression) tends to change the threshold of aggression, but the direction of the change may vary with social status, territorial prerogatives, and other ecological factors.

The ethically controversial studies of Milgram (1963, 1964, 1965) showed that the aggressive responses made by subjects in response to the request of an "authority" was significantly influenced by the victim's presence and proximity. Immediacy was varied from a condition in which there was no visual or vocal contact (remote condition) to a condition in which the subject forced the victim's hand onto the shock plate (touch-proximity condition). Immediacy, which undoubtedly altered affective–cognitive interactions in the subject, proved to be a potent deterrent of aggression. The percentage of subjects who obeyed the experimenter and continued to give shocks to the maximum (labeled "danger: severe shock"), in spite of screams of pain and urgent protests from the victim, varied from 66% in the remote condition to 30% in the touch-proximity condition. Thus, while immediacy made a large difference in the subject's willingness to agress on command, 30% of subjects recruited from the community represent a rather sizable segment who were apparently willing to risk executing a subject because an authority (experimenter) told them to do so. The reduction in aggressive responses as a result of the immediacy of the victim is consonant with Zimbardo's (1969) concept of individuation as a deterrent of aggression and with the contention of ethologists (e.g., Ardrey, 1966; Lorenz, 1966) that wars are more likely because our vast weapon technology makes it possible to kill at great distances.

Other studies have attempted to assess the effect of the victim's nonverbal communication but the results of these studies are not consistent. Wheeler and Caggiula (1966), Feshbach, Stiles, and Bitner (1967), and Hartman (1969) found that a victim's indication of pain was followed by an increase in shock aggression. In the latter two studies the subject had previously been insulted. On the other hand, Buss (1966a,b) and Baron (1971a,b) have found that pain cues from the victim reduced the subject's aggressive responses. One of the reasons for the inconsistency in the results of these studies may have been the failure to specify the emotion state of the subject, the relative status of experimenters and subjects, and the precise nature of the nonverbal cues emitted by the victim. In many cases, the nonverbal cues were simply described as grunts and groans, without any indication as to the specificity of such communications. Baron's study, which showed a sharp reduction in aggressive responses as a result of pain cues, represents an exception. Subjects observed a "pain meter" to see the effect their shock was having on the victim. While Baron's feedback was specific it had the disadvantage of removing the victim from the possibility of face-to-face encounter with the aggressor.

Effects of Perceiving an Anger Expression

The Savitsky *et al.* study communicated well-defined expressions of specific emotions to an aggressor via a confederate victim's face. Half the subjects (aggressors) were insulted by a confederate victim and the other half were treated neutrally and not insulted. Then subjects were assigned to a victim who expressed facially either fear, anger, joy, or a neutral countenance following the delivery of shock by the subjects. The experimenters hypothesized that the victim's expression of discrete emotions would significantly influence the subject's aggression. They had a number of specific expectations based on the assumption that their insult manipulation would arouse anger in the subjects, but as it did not, only their results relating to the facial expression manipulation are of interest. The DES was used to assess the emotional state of the subjects during the experiment, and the subjects also completed a DES to describe the emotions of the victim. In addition the subjects completed a first-impression rating scale as an additional description of the victim.

The subject's task was to teach the victim a paired-word list and to administer shock for incorrect responses for the purpose of facilitating learning. He was told that the best level of shock varied from person to person and that he was free to use his judgment in the matter. Each subject was exposed to a victim with a fearful expression, an angry expression, a joyful expression, or with an emotionally nonspecific or neutral expression. The subject's DES ratings of the victims showed that facial expressions were clearly perceived and differentiated.

Two of the emotion-specific facial expressions did significantly influence the aggression of the subjects. Subjects who were exposed to a smiling victim gave a consistently higher level of shocks. Apparently subjects in this group perceived their victim as not being harmed and as enjoying the task. It is reasonable to assume that the victim's apparent enjoyment elicited some enjoyment in the subjects (Tomkins, 1962). For these subjects, the learning task and the administration of shock may have taken on the character of a game. Since the victim appeared to enjoy the penalties (shock), the subject enjoyed delivering them. It is possible that some subjects were also motivated to increase shock in order to get the subject to be more serious about the task. Interestingly, the smile in our study had an effect similar to the aversive glance in a study by Ellsworth (1975).

Subjects exposed to the anger expression decreased their aggressive responses. The decrease in shock aggression on the part of the subjects may have been motivated by anticipation of subsequent retaliation or an embarrassing confrontation with the victim. The victim's anger expression may also have threatened the subject and acted directly as an inhibitor of aggression.

Since the analysis of the subjects' self-reported emotion scores suggested that they were not anger-aroused, the experimenters assumed that their results were descriptive of the category of aggression that has been termed instrumental aggression. The subjects were using the shock as a means of facilitating learning and apparently did not perceive themselves as hurting or harming the victims.

The Effects of Not Expressing Anger

Holt (1970) reasons that failure to express anger can be maladaptive. He uses the term expression here to include both emotion expression (facial, vocal changes) and aggressive actions, primarily verbal aggression. Anger expression and appropriate anger-related behavior can be constructive when the angry person wishes to "establish, restore, or maintain a positive relationship with the other. He acts and speaks in such a way as to give direct and genuine expression to his own feelings, while maintaining enough control so that the intensity is no greater than what is necessary to convey their true quality" (Holt, 1970, pp. 8–9). For Rafe to use anger constructively, his anger expression and verbal aggression must communicate fully and clearly how he perceives the anger-instigating situation and how it affects him, and he must make it clear why he feels the way he does. Holt implies that this kind of behavior leaves communication lines open to both parties and no one has to be seen as "losing." On the contrary, destructive anger expression and verbal aggression come from the person who wants to win at any cost to the other person or to the relationship. A well-designed and research-supported therapeutic procedure for controlling anger has been presented by Novaco (1975).

Holt goes on to present arguments and clinical evidence suggesting that anyone who repeatedly fails to express anger and appropriate anger-related behavior tends to develop one or more of a variety of psychosomatic symptoms. Though not necessarily the sole cause, unexpressed anger has been "implicated by psychoanalysts in the etiology of rheumatoid arthritis, hives, acne vulgaris, psoriasis, peptic ulcer, epilepsy, migraine, Raynaud's disease, and essential hypertension" (p. 9).

In considering the problem of expressing or not expressing anger and aggressive tendencies it is appropriate to consider briefly the relationship between aggression and sex. As discussed in Chapter 7, a number of experimental studies with animals showed that the male hormone (testosterone) apparently has some association with aggressive behavior. Experiments have shown that injections of testosterone will make young female rats and monkeys more aggressive. Perhaps from both biological and cultural factors, aggressiveness and sexual potency are often associated with one another. Fathers who fear that their sons will grow up to be cowards or homosexuals may be particularly concerned that their sons be appropriately aggressive. Many people have a tendency to associate manliness, masculinity status, and aggression; it is an easy step to make the association between aggressiveness and sexuality. In an impressive paper, Feshbach (1971) presented evidence and arguments to support the conclusion that it is the inhibition of "aggressive affect" (what has been discussed in this chapter as anger/disgust/contempt/hostility) that decreases or inhibits the sexual drive and sexual potency. The inhibition of aggressive acts do not necessarily have this deleterious effect.

Aggression and the Need to Understand Ourselves

In his book, *Statistics of Deadly Quarrels,* Richardson (1960) pointed out that in the 126 years between 1820 and 1945 man killed his fellow man at the rate of one every 68 seconds in wars, skirmishes, quarrels, or murders. The killings during this period totalled 59,000,000 people.

Tinbergen (1968), a 1973 Nobel Laureate, concluded that human beings' propensity to kill their fellow beings characterizes them as unhinged killers. He said,

> There is a frightening, and ironical paradox in this conclusion: that the human brain, the finest life preserving device created by evolution, has made one species so successful in mastering the outside world that it suddenly finds itself taken off guard. One could say that our cortex and our brainstem (our "reason" and our "instincts") are at loggerheads. Together they have created a new social environment in which, rather than ensuring our survival, they are about to do the opposite. The brain finds itself seriously threatened by an enemy of its own making. It is its own enemy. We simply have to understand this enemy. (Tinbergen, 1968, p. 1416)

Some literary and scientific thinkers have considered man a creature that thrives on conflict and crisis. In *The Skin of Our Teeth,* Thornton Wilder, the brilliant American playwright, sketches man's progress from the dawn of history to modern day by depicting man in a series of crises that range from the avalanche of ice that covered much of the earth in the ice age to the atom bomb that destroyed most of mankind in the "last great war." The great historian Toynbee maintains that human beings raise themselves to new levels of creativeness by meeting the challenges that they face. Gardner Murphy, one of our most learned psychologists, put it this way: "Man, if he is to be man at all, must somehow create and somehow escape his engines of destruction. He is the kind of animal who lives from one crisis to another, and it is his nature to surmount them. He will surmount those of the present century because he continues to be man" (Murphy, 1958, p. 3).

Human beings may indeed reach some new understanding of themselves through facing and overcoming crises, but today people are capable of confronting themselves with crises that cannot be overcome—e.g., total nuclear war. Thus, human beings are faced with the crisis of surmounting their dependency on crisis. In a less paradoxical way we must accept as a crisis of our times the need to understand basic human nature, to understand ourselves as living beings with capacities for a virtually limitless range of aggressive acts, including the destruction of the human species.

Human beings are not only capable of hostility and aggression that lead to crime, murder, massacre, and even global conflicts and crises, they are capable of hiding their crimes and escaping punishment. Take an example from a black college campus on May 14, 1970, when uniformed policemen (highway patrolmen) accompanied by city police and hundreds of national guardsmen fired into a crowd of black students and into a women's dormitory, killing two students and injuring more than a dozen others. A psychologist, a team of lawyers, and a Presidential Commission independently studied the incident and concluded that the killing of the students was totally unjustified. Yet, a local grand jury impaneled to investigate the case cleared all lawmen involved, indicting no one. The Presidential Commission said that the policemen not only killed the black students needlessly but later lied to their superiors and to the FBI to help cover up the crime. Judging from the history of such incidents it is not likely that anyone will suffer much for the killing and wounding of these black students. Indeed, past experience suggests that little will be done to find and punish the guilty.

Summary

Anger, disgust, and contempt are discrete emotions, but they frequently interact in human experience. Any combination of these three emotions together constitute the main affective component of hostility. Many of the causes of anger can be subsumed under the rubric of frustration or restraint. Pain and prolonged, unrelieved distress may be natural (unlearned) activators of anger. The anger expression includes the frown and either bared teeth or compressed lips. The experience of anger is characterized by a high degree of tension and impulsiveness. The feeling of self-assurance is far greater in anger than in any other negative emotion. Situations that elicit anger often elicit some degree of disgust or contempt.

The adaptive functions of anger are more readily understood in evolution-ary perspective than in day-to-day life. Anger mobilizes energy for defense of self and imbues the individual with a feeling of vigor and strength. Anger in contemporary human affairs may be occasionally justified and con-trolled anger may be used adaptively or therapeutically to inhibit fear.

Disgust is a response to the distasteful. In evolution it may have served adaptive functions in relation to the hunger drive and in relation to the maintenance of physical and psychological health.

Contempt is associated with feelings of superiority. It is difficult to find the biosocial adaptiveness of contempt unless it is directed toward personal wrongdoing or the evils of society. Contempt is the principal affective component of prejudice and, since it is the coldest of the three emotions associated with hostility, it is probably the affective component in "cold-blooded" destructiveness.

Hostility is defined as some combination of the fundamental emotions of anger, disgust, or contempt with certain drive states and affective–cognitive structures. Hostility usually, though perhaps not always, includes imagery or wishful thinking about harm, embarrassment, or defeat of the target of hostility.

For heuristic purposes differential emotions theory differentiates between hostility (affective–cognitive processes), affect expression (includ-ing anger expression, hostility expression), and aggressive acts. Aggression is limited by definition to verbal or physical actions definitely intended to harm.

The profiles of emotions in imaged hostility and anger situations are very similar. The pattern is fairly similar between hostility, disgust, and contempt, though in the imaged situations for the latter two emotions there are some potentially important changes in the magnitude and relative rank of emotion means.

Anger, disgust, and contempt have important interactions with other affects and with cognition. Stable interactions between any of these emo-tions and cognitive structures can be considered as a personality trait of hostility. The management of anger, disgust, and contempt presents some problems. The unregulated influence of these emotions on thought and action would create a serious adjustment problem, while the suppression of thought and action related to these emotions can produce psychosomatic symptoms.

There is some evidence that emotion communication plays a signifi-cant role in interpersonal aggression. There are a number of other impor-tant variables including proximity of the parties and eye contact, and much more research is needed before we achieve full understanding and control of destructive aggression.

14

FEAR AND THE
FORMS OF ANXIETY

Fear affects every human being, and at one time or another it leaves its mark on each of us. It locks into our minds experiences that we can often easily recall and that sometimes erupt into consciousness through our dreams. Fear is the most toxic of all the emotions. Intense fear can even kill: Animals, including human beings, are sometimes literally frightened to death.

Yet fear is not all bad. It can serve as a warning signal and redirect thought and action. From an evolutionary-biological perspective, Eibl-Eibesfeldt (1971) points out that fear can be adaptive and facilitate social bonds by releasing "flight to one another" and collective defense.

The concept of anxiety has occupied an important place in psychological theory and research since Freud (1959) emphasized its role in neurosis. The concept has suffered for lack of a clear and widely accepted definition. Most definitions have tended to treat it as a unitary state (or trait) and failed to recognize its complexity. The second section of this chapter defines anxiety as a complex combination of affects and affective–cognitive structures and then reports some studies relating to this conception.

Fear

In contemporary civilizations there is an ever-increasing number of objects, events, conditions, and situations that frighten or are potentially frightening. Perhaps this helps account for the fact that fear has probably been the subject of scientific investigation more frequently than any other fundamental emotion. Fear and anxiety taken together are far more prevalent concerns of both experimentalists and clinicians than any other set of affective phenomena. Extensive reviews of the theory and evidence on the origins, development, and management of fear have provided excellent background for further research and better understanding of this important emotion (Bowlby, 1973; Gray, 1971; Lewis & Rosenblum, 1974; Rachman, 1974). An understanding of fear does not remove dangerous or frightening situations, but it may provide an added measure of control over this toxic emotion.

The Activation of Fear

At the neurophysiological level, fear is a density-increase emotion; it is activated by a rather rapid increase in the density of neural firing. According to Tomkins (1962), there are three density-increase emotions—surprise-startle, fear-terror, and interest-excitement. The innate and learned differentiation of these three emotions equips the human being for every major contingency of stimulation increase. The most sudden and sharpest increases in density of neural firing activate startle. The next sharpest increases activate fear. Less sudden, less sharp increases in stimulation activate interest. Tomkins (1962) has presented the case for the differentiation of these three affects based on differences in the gradient of stimulation. However, the hypothesis that the selective activity of receptor organs plays a part in fear activation (Izard, 1971) is supported by Bowlby's (1973) and Gray's (1971) discussions of innate determinants or "natural clues" for fear.

There are undoubtedly overlapping components in the emotions of startle, fear, and excitement. This, plus the fact that there exists an unstable equilibrium between them, has important implications for anxiety theory and research. We shall return to this in a later section.

The Causes of Fear

Causes of fear may derive from internal and external events, conditions, or situations that signal danger. The threat, as well as the potential harm, may be physical or psychological. As Bowlby (1973) pointed out, the cause of fear may be either the presence of something threatening or the absence of something that provides safety and security (e.g., an infant's mother). And as Gray (1971) observed, fear may be elicited by the nonoccurrence of an event at the expected time or place. The causes of fear are influenced by their contexts (Sroufe, 1974), by individual differences in temperament or predisposition (Kagan, 1974; Charlesworth, 1974), and by experience or person–environment interactions. Finally, the causes of fear are in part a function of age or maturation (Jersild & Holmes, 1935; Gray, 1971; Izard, 1971; Bowlby, 1973).

It is also possible to experience fear that has no relationship to another person or object. When fear is activated without discernible object, it is experienced phenomenologically as objectless fear. Rafe may wake up feeling afraid and describe his mood as one of apprehension. He may be able to verbalize the fact that he is tense and jittery, and this mood may have one of a great variety of causes. It may have resulted from a distress–fear linkage, formed in childhood, such that his feeling of sadness and loneliness activate fear. It is obvious that this distress-activated fear would have no object. Because of the ubiquity and frequency of distress, an early and strong linkage of distress and fear may produce an "anxiety" neurosis.

Second, an object of fear may or may not be the primary cause of the fear. For example, Rebecca, who suffers a distress–fear bind, becomes distressed as she begins to contemplate a forthcoming examination on which she wants badly to make a good showing. Her distress activates fear, but she perceives the exam, not the distress, as the source or object of fear. The exam makes her afraid only indirectly, because it distresses her. Thus the identification of objects as causes of fear may not always be correct. In the foregoing example where the fear activator was distress, the individual mistook the exam or proximal cause of her heightening fear as the sole and original cause of the fear.

Rebecca may also feel guilt because she has goofed-off instead of studying for the exam. At the same time she may have some genuine interest in the subject and her relationship with her professor. The combination of fear, distress, guilt, and interest are often components of what is commonly called "anxiety."

Specific activators or causes of fear may be divided into four classes: (a) environmental events or processes, (b) drives, (c) emotions, and (d) cognitive processes—thinking, remembering, imaging. Causes within each of these classes may be primarily innate or primarily learned. The term innate here, as elsewhere in this volume, refers to an evolutionary genetic tendency or predisposition to respond in a certain fashion to an identifiable class of events or stimulus situations. In the language of ethology the relationship between the situation and the behavior is environmentally stable. As implied by this definition, most such genetic predispositions are subject to some degree of modification through experience.

Environmental Events. The term event here means something more than is usually conveyed by the term stimulus. It refers to a happening or a process and its definition is dependent, in part, on the context of occurrence. This section will examine some of the major classes of innate and learned events that instigate fear or that trigger the neural processes that have been described as fear activation.

1. Innate determinants. Classifications of innate determinants of fear have been offered by a number of writers. Gray (1971) has proposed that all fear causes can be put in four categories: intensity, novelty, special evolutionary dangers, and causes arising from social interaction. Pain and loud noise are examples of intense stimuli, while strange persons or objects exemplify novelty. Gray considers lack of stimulation or the failure of a stimulus to occur at an expected point in time and space as a kind of novel stimulus. Any situation or condition that is responsible for the death of a significantly large proportion of the members of a species over a large span of time may give rise to what Gray has called special evolutionary danger signals. Darkness and heights are considered to be examples of this class. An anger or threat expression is an example of a fear stimulus arising out of social interaction with conspecifics.

While some of Gray's categories apply to both innate and learned stimuli, Bowlby (1973) has developed a list of innate determinants which he calls "natural clues and their derivatives." The derivatives are presumably more subject to modification through experience than are the natural clues themselves. The natural clues to fear are being alone, strangeness, sudden approach, sudden change of stimuli, height, and pain. In arguing against the traditional psychoanalytic view that normals experience fear only in the presence of something likely to hurt or damage, Bowlby stated: "So, far from being either phobic or infantile, it is argued that the tendency to fear all these common situations is to be regarded as a natural disposition of man, a natural disposition moreover, that stays with him in some degree from infancy to old age, and is shared with animals of many other species" (Bowlby, 1973, p. 84). According to Bowlby the natural clues to danger derive from situations that actually have a high probability of involving increased risk of danger. This is not necessarily true of learned or cultural clues.

Derivatives of the natural clues to fear include darkness, animals, and strange objects and persons. The latter derive from the natural clue of strangeness, but their potency as fear instigators is a function of the context in which they occur (Sroufe, 1974). Fear of darkness, according to Bowlby, may be a function of a combination of the natural clues of being alone and strangeness. Fear of animals may be a combination of the natural clues of strangeness and sudden approach (as in the case of a would-be friendly dog). All of these derived causes, though extremely common, are relatively more subject to cultural influences and the context of occurrence.

Bowlby and others (Lewis & Rosenblum, 1974) have pointed out that the natural clues to fear are age-related, or dependent on developmental or maturational processes. For example, a number of researchers (e.g., Bronson, 1974; Sroufe, 1974) have hypothesized that the occasionally observed "fear of strangers" cannot occur in the first few months of life simply because the child has not developed a perceptual–cognitive capacity to discriminate familiar from unfamiliar faces. This ability emerges between roughly six and nine months of age, and it is during this age span that most observers report occasional fear of strangers in infants. Fear of animals and of the dark usually do not occur in the first year and a half or so of life, but they are observed with great regularity in children from age three upwards. The classic study of causes of fear in relation to age was conducted by Jersild and Holmes (1935). The stimuli for fear were experimentally contrived, but they would probably be considered by Bowlby as simulating natural clues and their derivatives. In the age period of one to six years, fears of noises and strange associations declined, fear of animals increased to about age four then leveled off, and fear of imaginary situations increased markedly with increase in age and cognitive abilities.

Given Bowlby's immersion in the phenomenon of attachment and separation, it is easy to understand that he considered being alone as the most fundamental and important of the natural clues for fear. He argued that being alone during childhood, sickness, or old age is less safe, considered strictly in terms of probability of danger, than being with a companion. He pointed out that being alone was a particularly potent instigator of fear when it was combined with any combination of strangeness and sudden changes in stimulation from visually or auditorally perceived objects. In summing up he paraphrased Shakespeare: "Being alone, like conscience, 'doth make cowards of us all'" (Bowlby, 1973, p. 119).

2. *Cultural clues for fear—clues derived from observation and learning.* Although a number of specific instigators of fear discussed in the preceding section are considerably influenced by cultural conditions and life experience, there are a wide variety of clues for fear that are mainly, if not altogether, the result of observation or learning. While living under the threat of military attack, even a barely audible air raid siren might elicit fear.

Bowlby pointed out, however, that many of the cultural clues for fear bear some relationship to the natural clues. Cultural clues for fear, upon closer examination, may prove to be natural clues disguised by some form of misattribution, rationalization, or projection. Fear of imaginary monsters, burglars, or ghosts, for example, may be a rationalization of the fear of darkness. Similarly, an adult may rationalize fear of thunder on the grounds that it is really the likelihood of being struck by lightning that is frightening.

Bowlby also discusses clues that are learned and that form the bases for sophisticated processes of assessing and avoiding dangerous situations. He pointed out, for example, that learning to determine whether a dog is dangerous or not is by no means a simple matter. Clues for such appraisals come not only from the animal, but from the presence or absence of collar and appropriate identification, proximity to an apparent owner, and various other aspects of the context.

Rachman (1974) has presented an excellent summary of the processes by which cultural clues for fear are learned or how natural clues may be exaggerated by learning. The traditional explanation of learned clues is that of traumatic conditioning, as discussed earlier. In brief this hypothesis states that events or situations that elicit pain (or threat of pain) become capable of eliciting fear independent of any actual sensations of pain. The proponents of this hypothesis hold that the fear-provoking qualities of such conditional stimuli motivate avoidance actions. Rachman holds that traumatic conditioning does account for a number of fears based on learning, but that it by no means can account for all fears. That is, he acknowledges the existence of natural clues for fear and notes that certain fears are far too common to be accounted for by traumatic conditioning. Thus, snakes are feared by many people who have never had any contact, much less a painful one, with a snake. Rachman also pointed out that a number of psychiatric patients who were administered painful electric shocks as part of aversion therapy (for sexual deviancy, alcoholism) received therapeutic benefits from the treatment without learning to be afraid of electric shock. Rachman also recognized that many fears are based on vicarious learning experiences in which no pain or trauma is involved.

3. Fear, distress, surprise, or other emotion. The work of the investigators cited in the foregoing sections constitute a significant contribution to the understanding of the sources and significance of fear. One important issue, however, must be confronted before further research can advance our knowledge of the development of this critical emotion. Much of the research reviewed in the foregoing sections does not necessarily relate to the specific emotion of fear. In all studies with prelingual infants, the investigator must infer the presence of fear from externally observable expressions and activities on the part of the subject. The literature is notably deficient of validated lists of responses that characterize fear as distinguished from distress or even from anger or some other emotion.

One of the more careful analyses of the problem is that of Bowlby's. He listed a number of observable expressive and motor activities that he considers as indexes of fear. "They include wary watching combined with inhibition of action, a frightened facial expression accompanied perhaps by trembling or crying, cowering, hiding, running away, and also seeking contact with someone and perhaps clinging to him or her" (Bowlby, 1973, p. 88). Bowlby made no claim to having developed an exhaustive list, and his language was tentative when he described four reasons why these diverse forms of behavior could be grouped together. (a) Many, though not all of them, tend to occur simultaneously or sequentially; (b) events that elicit one of them tend to elicit others (though not necessarily all others); (c) most though not all of them serve a single biological function, that of protection; (d) after the acquisition of language the persons exhibiting these responses say, when asked, that they are "feeling afraid or anxious or alarmed" (p. 88). But crying is the prototypical response in distress and it may accompany anger or joy. Furthermore, a self report of "feeling anxious" is by no means a clear and unequivocal indication of fear and fear alone (Izard, 1972).

The list of fear indicators proposed by Charlesworth (1974) include: "Momentary arresting or slowing of ongoing behaviors or prolonged freezing, heightened vigilance or awareness, stimulus–distance maintaining or expanding behavior, serious or fearful facial expressions . . ." (p. 263). Charlesworth complicated the picture, however, with the observation that fear can be accompanied or followed by withdrawal, flight, wary exploration, and even smiling or laughing. Obviously these lists of fear indicators as well as the lists of fear causes like those of Bowlby and Gray, are in need of refinement and revision.

The careful experimental analysis of infants' responses to the presence or approach of a stranger supports the notion that some of the relatively well-accepted indicators of fear may have been prematurely adopted. Bronson (1972, 1974) noted that infants three or four months of age stared long and intently at a stranger. Bronson inferred that infants at this age were attempting to fit "the strangers face into an existing facial schema" (1974, p. 256). He assumed that babies who eventually smiled after staring at the stranger somehow resolved their uncertainty. Others continued to stare until they began crying. Bronson thought that such infants had failed in their efforts at assimilation. Though not made explicit by Bronson, his data and his reasoning suggest that prolonged unsuccessful attempts at assimilation underlie the earliest instances of crying at a stranger and that such crying reflects distress rather than fear.

Bronson concluded that babies of six and a half months or older had no difficulty in differentiating a stranger from familiar people, and the frequent instances of crying at this age were attributed to other causes. Bronson proposed that the underlying cause of crying in this age group was the infants' inability to accommodate the strangers sequential activities into established expectations regarding interpersonal exchange. Bronson suggested that at nine months of age the infant immediately assimilated the stranger's appearance "but into a schema derived from previous unhappy encounters with similar persons" (1974, p. 256). Even in describing the events at this age, Bronson's language (e.g., "unhappy encounters") suggests that the infant's vocal response may be a cry of distress. While Bronson's reasoning is admittedly speculative, the picture he presents, together with his observational data provides other grounds for questioning Bowlby's assumption that all of the traditionally accepted indicators of infant fear relate to a single adaptive system.

In some ways Kagan's work on the development of negative affect in infants supports a more differentiated analysis of affects; he suggests that there are at least four "distress states" that have been called fear. The problem with Kagan's analysis is that he has used the term distress in a rather general fashion, considering it as virtually equivalent to a state manifested by crying. According to Kagan, the causes of distress states are (a) unassimilated discrepancy, (b) anticipation of an undesirable event, (c) unpredictability, (d) recognition of inconsistency between belief and behavior, and (e) recognition of dissonance among beliefs. Only the fifth of these is identified by Kagan as a source of the distress state "typically called anxiety." This suggests that Kagan recognizes the other distress states as something other than fear.

Two other investigators have raised problems with the taxonomy of fear causes and fear indicators. The work of Sroufe and his collaborators (e.g., Sroufe, Waters, & Matas, 1974; Sroufe & Wunsch, 1972) has shown that a number of the frequently used stimuli for fear actually produce laughter, interest, and approach behavior. Rheingold (1974) noted that many investigators have reported expressions of surprise in response to experimental manipulations designed to elicit fear. She also pointed out that infants often respond positively and in an affiliative fashion to strangers. It seems reasonable to assume that under certain conditions, a positive response to a stranger would be more adaptive than a fearful response.

Drives and Homeostatic Processes as Causes of Fear. In comparison with emotions and cognition, drive and homeostatic processes constitute the least significant class of fear causes. A drive becomes psychologically important when it increases to a point where it signals a critical deficit and activates emotion. In some of these cases the emotion activated is fear. Tomkins gave the following example: ["When the need for air becomes critical enough to require drive activation it also activates affect, ordinarily a massive fear reaction, which quickly reaches panic proportions if the obstruction to drive satisfaction is not immediately removed. The need is so vital that the massive affect in addition to the awareness of suffocation represents an important safety factor in guaranteeing immediate attention to drive satisfaction"] (Tomkins, 1962, p. 46).

As indicated in the foregoing section, pain, whether deficit-determined or exogenous, may instigate fear. Fear can amplify the pain, but it can also hasten escape responses and avoidance of further pain. The discussion of pain–emotion interactions in Chapter 7, however, showed that pain may also elicit distress, distress combined with fear, or other combinations of emotions.

Other Emotions as Causes of Fear. Potentially, any emotion may activate fear (or any other emotion) by the principle of contagion discussed in Chapter 5. Similarities at the neurophysiological level make startle and excitement likely candidates for roles in fear activation. As indicated earlier, a basic interest–surprise–fear relationship derives from similarities in the neurophysiological mechanisms underlying these emotions. Tomkins (1962) holds that "The sudden reduction of intense, enduring fear, if complete, releases joy, but if incomplete releases excitement" (p. 290). Indirect support for the close relationship of fear and excitement can be found in Bull's (1951) study of hypnotically induced fear. She reported that her frightened subjects were caught in a conflict between the wish to investigate and the wish to escape. She considered this as evidence of the dual nature of fear. Differential emotions theory interprets the conflictful behavior as a result of the oscillation between fear (motivating escape behavior) and interest (motivating investigatory activities).

Specific excitement– or surprise–fear connections may be learned. Any of the other emotions may also become learned activators of fear. Of course, fear itself is an innate activator or amplifier of fear. Thus, the experience of fear is frightening.

Cognitive Processes. Fear (or any emotion) may be activated by a cognitively constructed cause. Indeed, cognitive processes constitute the most general and pervasive fear-instigators. For example, fear of a specific object may be activated by a cognitive construction in memory or anticipation. Unfortunately, such a cognition may not be accurate or precise. So one may learn to fear the wrong situation or too many situations or all situations and life in general. The memory or anticipation of fear itself is sufficient to activate fear. If an individual mistakenly identifies a person as a source of fear, he may nonetheless experience fear in thinking about this person, then in anticipating meeting him, and for the third time in actually seeing him again. In this way a person, object, or situation may become a source of fear first (a) through hypothesis formation, then (b) through anticipation, and finally (c) through confrontation of the constructed dread object (Tomkins, 1963, p. 66).

A cognitive construction having great power to evoke fear (and shame) can develop in early childhood, if the individual, say a first-born, construes the mother's response to a later-born as betrayal and desertion. Tomkins has presented a cogent example of this situation in his analysis of castration fear. The stage is set by inner conflict—the conflict between affect expression and the internalized demand for affect inhibition. Tomkins theorizes that Freud mistook this fear-producing conflict as one between the drives and the threat of castration. "Castration anxiety and penis envy are not, to our way of thinking, genital masks for oral dangers; both are symbols of the threat to positive affect from negative affect—in short, the danger to love from hate" (Tomkins, 1963, pp. 526–529).

The Facial Expression of Fear

While the research on the development of fear in infants suggests that some of the most frequently used indicators of fear may signal distress, the facial expression of fear (at least in older children and adults) can be reliably distinguished from the facial expression of distress. Emotion expression and recognition has not been studied as extensively in infants as in older children and adults. The evidence from the latter groups suggests that careful analysis of facial expressions in infants should ultimately provide the most reliable and objective indexes of fear (and of other discrete emotions as well). In the extensive cross-cultural research on facial expressions, fear was confused with only one other emotion, surprise, and that occurred only in the preliterate samples studied by Ekman, Sorenson, and Friesen (1969). Examples of the fear expression are shown in Figure 14-1.

In fear, the eyebrows are approximately straight and appear somewhat raised. The inner corners of the brow are drawn together and there are horizontal wrinkles that usually extend across about two-thirds or three-quarters of the forehead. These horizontal wrinkles usually do not run completely across the forehead as they do in the case of surprise. Ekman and Friesen (1975) maintained that when fear is expressed only in the brow region, the meaning of the expression is slight apprehension, worry, or controlled fear.

Fearful eyes are more widely opened than eyes in a normal or interested pose. The lower eyelid is tensed and the upper eyelid slightly raised.

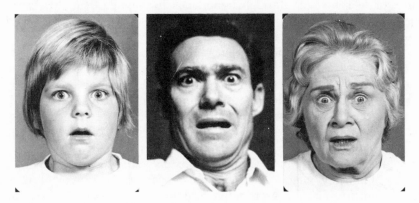

FIGURE 14-1. Expressions of fear varying in intensity and completeness. Photographs on the extreme left and right are from the Tomkins Affect Pictures.

According to Ekman and Friesen, the eyes in surprise are distinguished from those in fear by the fact that in the former emotion the lower lids are relaxed. For this reason surprise eyes may appear somewhat larger than fear eyes. In the innate expression of fear, the mouth is opened and the lips are tense and drawn back tightly. Learned variations on the innate expression may give the mouth the appearance of being less tightly drawn back, but there is usually tension in one or both of the lips. In surprise the lips are more relaxed and the shape of the mouth is more oval in contrast to the narrower elliptical shape of fear.

Normally the intensity of fear, which varies from apprehension to terror, is correlated with the amount of tension in the various muscles in the brow, eye, and mouth region that participate in the fear expression. One of the more evident clues to intense fear is the extent to which the corners of the mouth are drawn back, tensing and stretching the lips over the teeth.

It is not presently known whether the expressive movements of the brow, eye, and mouth region develop at differential rates. Nor is it known whether the infant's first expressions of fear are blended with surprise or distress. Research is this area is sorely needed.

The Subjective Experience of Fear

Fear is an emotion of great potency, one that has a very marked effect on the individual's perception, thought, and action. It is the most constricting of all the emotions. In extreme fear the effects on perception have been characterized as "tunnel vision," a condition in which the victim becomes functionally blind to a large proportion of the potential perceptual field. Fear can cause thinking to be slow, narrow in scope, and rigid in form. It brings about a tensing and tightening of muscles and other motor mechanisms, and in terror the individual may "freeze" and become immobile. Fear greatly reduces behavioral alternatives.

[Fear, depending on its intensity, is experienced as apprehension, uneasiness, uncertainty, complete insecurity. One has the feeling that one lacks safety, a feeling of danger and impending disaster. One feels a threat to one's very existence; this may be sensed as a threat to the body, the psychological self, or both.]

A Study of Hypnotically Induced Fear. Despite the importance of the emotion of fear, very little is available on its phenomenology. Major works on emotion (May, 1950; Reymert, 1950; Arnold, 1960; Knapp, 1963) contain scarcely anything in the way of subjects' own descriptions of the experience of fear. A notable exception is the work of Nina Bull (1951), who studied individuals in whom she had induced a "pure" experience of fear via hypnotic trance. After the emotion subsided but while still in the hypnotic state, subjects described the experience. Bull maintained that her seven subjects reported a consistent pattern of events. Perhaps the most prominent feature of the experience was a tensing-up or freezing of the body. Equally salient was a strong feeling of wanting or needing to escape, to run, to hide, to get away. Here are some examples from the subjects' reports. Subject B: "I wanted to turn away . . . I couldn't . . . I was too afraid to move . . . I couldn't move my hand . . ." Subject D: "I wanted to turn away . . . I became very tense . . ." Subject F: "My whole body stiffened . . . wanted to run away . . . I was petrified and couldn't move . . ." Subject E (II): "First my jaws tightened, and then my legs and feet . . . my toes bunched up until it hurt . . . I wanted to shrink away, make myself as inconspicuous as possible" (Bull, 1951, pp. 58–59). Bull interpreted her data as indicative of a conflict, experienced as a freezing-up in fear on the one hand and wanting to escape on the other.

Bull believes there is another duality in the nature of fear. "Thus the feeling of fear in its simplest form is definitely dual in character, and owes its existence to an uncomfortable struggle between the reflex of investigation (the 'what is it?' reflex of Pavlov) and the reflex of escape. These competing tendencies give fear a unique position in a sequence between the primary start or shock of surprise and eventual specific adaptive behavior, for which it is a kind of fumbling in the dark before a wholly satisfactory appraisal of the danger has been made. It means that fear is primarily bound up with the feeling of *uncertainty* as to (a) the exact nature of the danger stimulus and, therefore, (b) how to act with reference to it" (Bull, 1951, p. 100). This suggests that adaptive, effective behavior in the face of a fear-evoking object or situation may require cognitive processes to appraise and differentiate the object or situation. Cognition may also be required to generate or select a plan of escape or other appropriate action. Motor responses are required to execute the plan. The sequences of fear–cognition–action are basically the same even in those situations where we are able to talk our way out of danger. According to differential emotions theory the "reflex of investigation" is not adequate to support these cognitive and motor activities in a complex and prolonged fear experience. Rather, under such conditions, extended adaptive effort in perceiving, attending, planning, and acting would require the motivational experience of the emotion of interest–excitement. In terms of differential emotions theory, the "duality of fear" observed by Bull is a function of a fear–interest interaction.

Experiential Dimensions and Patterns of Emotions in the Fear Situation. The experiential dimensions in the fear situation (Bartlett–Izard study) are presented in Figure 14-2. As expected, the dimension of tension showed a higher mean in the fear situation than in any other emotion situation. The mean for tension was significantly higher than any other dimension measured in the study and almost 50% higher than the next

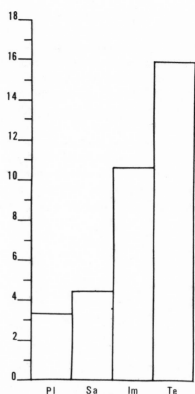

FIGURE 14-2. The profile of dimensions in the fear situation. The DRS dimensions are abbreviated. (Pl) pleasantness, (Sa) self-assurance, (Im) impulsiveness, (Te) tension.

highest mean shown in Figure 14-2, that for impulsiveness. The mean for impulsiveness was substantially lower than in the anger situation, about equal to that in the distress situation, and somewhat higher than in any of the other negative emotion situations.

The moderately high impulsiveness felt in the fear situation could be considered as adaptive in view of the fact that the individual needs to experience a readiness to respond. On the other hand, the impulsiveness could lead to maladaptive behavior in the form of panicky responses that are not effective in dealing with the situation. On the dimension of active-ness (not shown in Figure 14-2), the subjects had a higher mean than was the case for any other negative emotion situation except anger. The combi-nation of feelings suggested by this pattern—highly tense, active, impul-sive—supports the idea that strong fear effectively supports only one type of behavior, that of avoidance or escape, which may take the form of "flight to one another" for protection. Other types of fear-related behavior are a function of the interaction of fear with other emotions.

The mean for self-assurance was lower in the fear situation than in any other negative emotion situation. The differences in self-assurance between the fear situation and distress situation, and between the fear situation and the anger situation were significant ($p < .01$).

The patterns of emotions in the fear situation are presented in Figure 14-3. The differences among the first four emotions shown in the profile (fear, interest, surprise, and distress) are all statistically significant ($p < .01$). The next three emotions in the profile (anger, guilt, and shyness) are significantly lower than any of the preceding four emotions but not significantly different from each other. The relatively low means of these three emotions suggests that ordinarily none of these fundamental emotions plays a highly significant role in a fear situation, but for some individuals any of these emotions may be a part of the emotion dynamics.

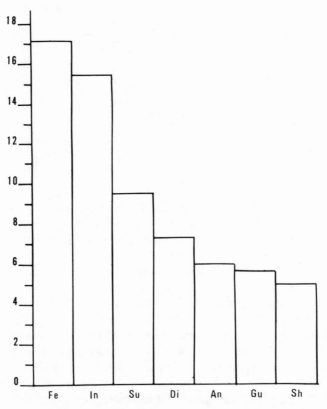

FIGURE 14-3. The profile of emotions in the fear situation. The emotion (DES) scales are abbreviated: (Fe) fear, (In) interest, (Su) surprise, (Di) distress, (An) anger, (Gu) guilt, (Sh) shyness, and (Jo) joy.

Perhaps the most important aspect of the emotion profile in the fear situation, is the fact that the three highest emotion means (fear, interest, and surprise) are the three that according to Tomkins are stimulation-increase emotions. The profile furnishes indirect support for the interrelatedness of these emotions at the neurophysiological level.

The high fear and moderately high interest in the fear-situation profile supports the differential emotions theory hypothesis that the duality of fear discussed by Bull and Kierkegaard actually consists of fear-motivated avoidance and interest-motivated approach and exploration. How the individual eventually responds to the fear situation will depend on the relative intensity of fear and interest and the interactions of other emotions in the profile.

Development and Socialization of Fear

One of the most common of parental techniques for the socialization of emotion involves the use of one emotion to influence another. Many emotions are socialized by shaming techniques. A child's fear may be attenuated by the evocation of shame: "You ought to be ashamed for acting like a scaredy-cat." In later years and throughout life the anticipation of shame that would follow a show of cowardice may serve as a regulator of fear or fear expression. If Rafe's fear is habitually controlled by shame, he becomes vulnerable to shame whenever he senses danger or any threat which frightens him.

Tomkins (1963, 1965) has discussed the role of socialization in the acquisition of knowledge and the development of ideologies. He posits a basic ideological polarity in Western thought. The issues in the polarity are these: "Is man the measure, an end in himself, an active, creative, thinking, desiring, loving force in nature? Or must man realize himself, attain his full stature only through struggle toward, participation in, conformity to, a norm, a measure, an ideal essence basically prior to and independent of man?" (Tomkins, 1965, p. 79). Patterns of socialization, particularly the socialization of fear, play a vital role in determining whether an individual will develop affective–cognitive organizations that resonate to left-wing, humanistic ideology or right-wing, normative ideology. A brief description of right-wing and left-wing socialization of fear is presented below. A more detailed analysis can be found in Tomkins (1965) and Izard and Tomkins (1966).

Left-Wing Socialization of Fear. Fear socialization techniques which will produce affective–cognitive orientations that resonate with left-wing ideology will include one or more of the following components.

(a) The experience of fear is minimized. The child is exposed to a parent who refrains from terrorizing the child. Even when the parents themselves may be frightened for the safety of the child, they try to protect the child without communicating their own fear. The parents believe and communicate to the child that fear is noxious and not to be invoked except under emergency conditions.

(b) There is a verbalized ideology exaggerating the noxiousness of fear. This is in some measure self-defeating, since the child is made more timid about fear than he or she need be. However, the general benevolence of the intention limits somewhat this secondary effect.

(c) The parents make restitution for fear. If they have willingly or unknowingly frightened the child, they atone for this by apology or explain that this was not their intention. They also reassure and re-establish intimacy with the child.

(d) Tolerance for fear per se is taught. If Rebecca becomes afraid, her parents attempt to teach her not to be overwhelmed by the experience, to accept it as part of human nature, and to master it. This presupposes parents who are somewhat at home with their own fear, who can tolerate it in themselves and others sufficiently to teach tolerance of it to their children. In particular, the masculinity of the father must not hinge excessively on shame about being afraid.

(e) Counteraction against the source of fear is taught. For example, Rafe is not only taught to tolerate the experience of fear, but he is also taught to counteract the source of fear while he is experiencing fear. Such a technique was used in World War II to prepare combat troops to face fire; they were required to crawl forward while shots were being fired just above their heads. Rafe may be similarly taught to confront various sources of fear, first with the aid of the parent as an ally, and then gradually more and more on his own. Visits to the doctor and dentist, confrontations with bullies, and confrontations with persons of authority, are all occasions for learning to counteract fear by going forward rather than retreating; and in the type of socialization being described here these steps would ideally be graded to Rafe's ability to master them.

(f) There is concern that the child not become chronically fearful. The parents, upon detecting any signs of fear in the child, attempt some type of remedial action or refer the child to a therapist. Fearfulness is regarded as an alien symptom and is treated as any other problem might be treated, with speed and concern. They are generally concerned lest the child's spirit be broken.

Right-Wing Socialization of Fear. Socialization of fear which will produce affective–cognitive orientations resonant with right-wing ideology will include one or more of the following components.

(a) The experience of fear is not minimized. The child is exposed to parents who rely upon terror as a technique of socialization. When the parents themselves are frightened they communicate this to the child. The parents may be chronically afraid so that the child becomes fearful through identification. When the socialization is normative, terror may be used to guarantee norm compliance. The child may be terrorized into "goodness."

(b) There is a verbalized ideology minimizing the noxiousness of fear. This has a double consequence: On the one hand, the child is made less afraid of fear through identification with such a parent, but the child is also made more fearful because this parent has no hesitancy in using fear frequently as a socialization technique.

(c) There is no restitution for the use of fear. If the parents have willingly or unknowingly frightened the child they make no restitution. There is no apology nor explanation that the frightening experience was not intentional. Nor do they attempt to reassure or re-establish intimacy with the child. If the fear has taught the child norm compliance the parents regard it as entirely justified.

(d) Tolerance for fear is not taught. If Rafe becomes afraid, he is permitted to "sweat it out" alone, or his burden is increased by shaming him for his fear. Some normative socializations, especially those aiming to produce toughness or independence, do attempt to teach the child to overcome his fear, but this is frequently done by invoking shame and other negative sanctions for cowardice. Other types of normative socialization emphasize the value of fear as a deterrent so there is no motive to attenuate the experience of terror.

(e) Counteraction against the source of fear is not taught. It is either disregarded or derogated. If it is derogated the parents may also force Rafe to counteract his fear at such a price that he would rather risk still more fear than suffer further humiliation. Under those circumstances in which counteraction proves impossible, the individual socialized through contempt will suffer deep humiliation, whereas one socialized by the parent-as-ally will not.

(f) There is no concern about fearfulness in the child. The parents characteristically are insensitive to signs of fear in the child and disregard or minimize them. The parents deprecate as an alarmist anyone who suggests the child might need help. So long as the child is meeting the norm the parents are not concerned with the hidden costs (Tomkins, 1963).

In the foregoing schema, the socialization process was depicted at the right and left extremes, neither of which is intended to represent the ideal or correct form. Actual parental techniques of socialization vary widely and often include right- and left-wing elements. Determining optimal socialization attitudes and procedures remains one of the greatest challenges to psychological science.

Some Antecedents and Consequences of Fear

College subjects' free-response descriptions of the antecedents and consequences of fear are quite consistent with the psychology of fear presented in the foregoing sections. The data are presented in Table 14-1.

Some Interactions of Fear with Other Emotions

Some of the interactions of fear with other emotions were presented in earlier chapters. There will be further discussion of fear interactions in the section beginning on p. 376, since an emotion–emotion interaction in which fear is dominant may be considered a form of anxiety.

Fear–Distress Interactions. According to Tomkins (1963), a fear–distress bind can increase the difficulty of solving the essential problem of individuation and of tolerating loss of love. The threat of loss of love and communion that often accompanies the process of becoming individuated from one's parents, friends, and spouse is distressing, first of all. The addition of fear to distress may jeopardize individuation and foster "anxious" attachment as a haven from the terror of loneliness and the unknown. Loneliness may be distressing without being terrifying if there is no fear–distress bond. However, if Rafe is made to experience fear whenever he feels like crying, he will be especially vulnerable to the threat of separation.

TABLE 14-1
Antecedents and Consequences of Fear
(N = Approximately 130)

Responses	Percentage of subjects giving responses
Antecedents	
Feelings	
1. Threatened, in danger, in trouble, overpowered	31.2
2. Fear synonyms	26.4
3. Alone, lost, isolated, rejected	16.0
4. Threat to self-esteem, impending failure, feels inadequate	15.2
5. Other	11.2
Thoughts	
1. Of threatening, danger, or trouble	36.8
2. Of death, loneliness, sadness	28.0
3. Of loss of self-esteem, failure, of being inadequate	19.2

TABLE 14-1 (continued)
Antecedents and Consequences of Fear
(N = Approximately 130)

Responses	Percentage of subjects giving responses
4. Of things not understood (supernatural, etc.)	4.0
5. Other	12.0
Actions	
1. Something legally or morally wrong, harmful	32.0
2. Something dangerous	22.4
3. Something that threatens self-esteem	20.0
4. Panicky, irrational things	8.0
5. Trying to escape, run away, withdraw, protect self	7.2
6. External force (caught using drugs, drafted, etc.)	5.6
7. Other	4.8
Consequences	
Feelings	
1. Fear synonyms	31.5
2. Nervous tension	17,7
3. Inadequate, insecure	14.6
4. Need to escape, run away, withdraw, protect self	10.0
5. Lost, lonely, isolated, rejected	6.2
6. Surprise synonyms	3.8
7. In danger, physically threatened	3.1
8. Shame synonyms	3.1
9. Other	10.0
Thoughts	
1. How to escape, withdraw, protect self	43.1
2. Anticipating possible consequences or reaction to event	29.2
3. How to regain control of self or situation	8.5
4. Trying to understand causes or reasons for emotion	5.4
5. Other	13.8
Actions	
1. Run away, withdraw, protect self	45.4
2. Face situation, cope, try to act courageously	33.1
3. Something panicky, impractical	9.2
4. Talk to someone, get with trusted friend	2.8
5. Takes action or aggresses against object or situation	2.3
6. Other	9.2

When there is a strong distress–fear bond, signs of distress in others may arouse fear in the self. For example, Rafe may become fearful if someone else expresses his or her discouragement and apparent failure or a feeling of loneliness. "All such attempts at communion through the expression of distress may evoke from the distress-frightened listener not sympathy but fear" (Tomkins, 1963, p. 95).

Fear–Contempt–Disgust Interactions. Tomkins points out that if parents frequently respond to their child with disgust or contempt, the child will learn to expect such disgust or contempt. If the expected parental contempt is internalized the self may be bifurcated, with one part of the self acting as judge and the other part as offender. The judging self finds the offending self disgusting. In this case the accused self may become afraid of the judging self, fearing that the accuser is right. One now fears oneself as one once feared the tongue-lashing from the parents.

Fear of Fear and the Neurotic Paradox. As Tomkins (1963) noted, cognitively constructed causes of fear may be both inaccurate and imprecise. This tends to make the individual develop a more comprehensive system of defenses than is demanded by reality. Thus Rafe has to defend himself against dangers that exist only in his perceived world. Effective defense or avoidance of these dreaded objects is rewarding in that it results in fear reduction. The continuing reward for avoidance makes it difficult for him to re-evaluate the source of his fear and thereby discover its impotency and learn not to be afraid. He *fears the fear* that confrontation of the object would evoke. These imprecise, inaccurate, cognitively constructed sources of fear and the avoidance behavior that precludes confrontation and mastery of them create the neurotic paradox, the resistance to extinction of such unrealistically exaggerated fears.

For the anxiety neurotic who has had the continuing experience of being afraid of fear, it is insufficient to demonstrate that it is no longer necessary to fear the *object* which was the original source of fear. Rather, such people must now be taught to tolerate their own fear, since it is the anticipation of their own fear that has become the major activator of further fear (see Tomkins, 1963, for further discussion).

The Fear–Shame Bind. If the socialization of fear has been accomplished by means of shaming techniques, the individual may be vulnerable to shame whenever he senses any threat which frightens. A strong fear–shame bind can result in a high degree of psychological entropy. If the fear expands to terror and the shame to humiliation, the combined effects of the two debilitating affects can produce paranoid schizophrenia (Tomkins, 1963). In Tomkins's view, the paranoid experiences fear of being caught and found guilty of sexual or hostile intent or deed or of being made to feel more and more inferior until perceived impotence brings on humiliation.

Some Techniques for Reducing or Controlling Fear

Rachman presented a good review of the literature on the therapeutic management or control of fear through the processes of habituation and modeling. He defined the habituation that results from repetitive stimulation as a decrease in sensitivity to stimulation and a decrease in readiness to respond. A concept like habituation was implemented by Wolpe in his desensitization treatment technique (Wolpe, 1958). This technique consists of relaxation procedures coupled with the repetitive presentation of a graded (increasingly fearful) series of stimuli.

Rachman also summarized the reduction technique of flooding or implosive therapy developed by Stamfl (1970). This method requires patients to imagine highly traumatic events selected on the basis of psychodynamic explorations conducted by the therapist. Rachman questioned Stamfl's theoretical explanations of the effects of the technique but agreed that the clinical effects are encouraging.

A third method of reducing and managing fear is the well-known modeling technique developed by Bandura and his associates (e.g., Bandura, Blanchard, & Ritter, 1969). This technique is essentially one of vicarious learning or social imitation. For example, the experimenter or therapist models courageous behavior in approaching and handling objects that frighten the phobic individual.

None of the foregoing fear-control techniques makes explicit use of differentiated emotion concepts, emotion dynamics, or affective–cognitive interactions. Descriptions of clinical applications of these techniques suggest that they do involve underlying emotion dynamics and emotion–cognition–behavior interactions. Izard (1971, Chapter 15) has presented some therapeutic techniques that are derived from differential emotions theory. Some of these are similar in form to certain techniques of behavior therapy, modeling, and role-playing, but they emphasize interpersonal exchange in terms of the specific discrete emotions that require attention. They take into account the principles of emotion processes discussed in Chapter 5, and they are similar to some of the techniques applied successfully in the framework of psychodynamic therapy by Singer (1974). For example, they make explicit use of the principle of emotion contagion (a principle that operates in modeling and role-playing techniques) and the principle of emotion–emotion activation and regulation. The latter principle can be implemented by using imagery-induced interest (or, if necessary, anger) to control debilitating fear or imagery-induced joy to attenuate distress. The principle of interactive subsystems is implemented by using the action system (acting or role-play techniques) to induce desired emotions or inhibit undesired ones.

Fear Interactions with Other Emotions as Forms of Anxiety

Any discussion of anxiety would be incomplete without reference to Freud, but Freud (1959) described anxiety largely in terms of the fundamental emotion of fear, and his concept of signal anxiety is roughly equivalent to fear anticipation, an affective–cognitive orientation. Anxiety (fear) results from exposure to danger, signal anxiety (fear anticipation) from perceived threat of danger.

According to Freud, all danger situations involve separation or loss of a loved object, or loss of its love. He thought that birth was the prototypic danger experience, and that the other most important danger situations were loss of mother as an object, threat of loss of penis, loss of cathected objects (objects of emotional attachment), loss of love, or loss of the superego's love.

Freud observed that the nature of danger situations changes with age. In early childhood, the danger is the loss of objects. During the phallic phase of development (early childhood), it is the perceived or imagined threat of castration. After the superego develops, social anxiety (fear–shame or fear–shyness interactions) may become an internal substitute for an external danger, and moral anxiety (fear–guilt structures) may develop as a completely intraindividual phenomenon.

Although Freud did not explicitly say so, he apparently thought that the *threat* of danger was the result of a cognitive process, and that signal anxiety (fear anticipation) follows from an appraisal process. The general sense of his statements about perceived threat suggests that he viewed this source of anxiety or fear-anticipation as the one which allowed for individually learned fear responses and individual differences in response to different situations. Freud can therefore be credited with two important ideas: (a) individuals differ in their perception and appraisal of potential danger in the world about them; (b) what triggers anxiety or fear anticipation in nondangerous situations is a result of individual learning and appraisal processes. Thus Freud laid the foundation for the cognitive theories of emotion, but his theory differs from most cognitive theories in one important fashion. He allowed for the possibility that appraisal may be determined, or at least influenced, by innate processes (mnemic images).

Freud viewed signal anxiety (fear anticipation) as having an adaptive function. In foreseeing the possibility of danger, it prepares the individual to avoid the danger or prevent the danger situation from occurring. More specifically, he saw signal anxiety (fear anticipation) as restricting and regulating emotion (discharge) and as facilitating adaptive behavior (operation of normal defenses). However, when defenses are inadequate, anxiety (fear) increases and becomes disrupting, disorganizing, and maladaptive.

Unrealistic appraisal (perceiving danger where none exists) and inadequate defenses lead to anxiety (fear) neurosis.

While Freud's idea of ordinary or reality anxiety seems equivalent to fear, his notions of signal anxiety, and social and moral anxiety, clearly involve other affects and cognition. An analysis of numerous other conceptions of anxiety shows that they represent complex multifaceted phenomena involving fear and one or more additional affects as well as various affective–cognitive structures (Izard, 1972). Sarason and his colleagues (e.g., Sarason, 1966; Sarason, Davidson, Lighthall, Waite, & Ruebush, 1960) describe anxiety in terms of fear, hostility, distress, and guilt. Grinker and Speigel's (1945) definition includes concepts related to fear, distress, and guilt. Sullivan (1953) recognized fear, shame, and psychophysiological arousal. There are numerous other definitions of anxiety that contain language related to some combination of the several descrete emotions mentioned above (e.g., Cattell & Scheier, 1961; Basowitz, Persky, Korchin, & Grinker, 1955; Maher, 1966; Gottschalk & Gleser, 1969). A few contemporary theorists have tended to equate anxiety (or at least its affective component) with fear (May, 1950; Epstein, 1972; Spielberger, 1966; Levitt, 1967), but a close examination of their work suggests the presence of other affects.

Bowlby (1973) considers anxiety as closely allied to fear, as is the case in the psychoanalytic tradition and most of psychiatry, but he does not equate the two concepts. He thinks the two terms refer to closely related states and share common causes and manifestations.

Bowlby's distinctions between fear and anxiety have to be considered in the context of attachment and separation. When an infant develops a relationship with the mother or caregiver such that the infant's behavior is described as clinging, jealous, possessive, greedy, immature, and overdependent, Bowlby prefers to eschew the foregoing descriptors and label the phenomena as "anxious attachment." The frequent clinical use of the traditional descriptors suggest that anxiety in this context is a complex of emotions and affective–cognitive structures. But Bowlby sees a form of fear as the central affect. In referring to his preference for the term "anxious attachment" (as opposed to the term overdependency) he remarked: "This makes it clear that the heart of the condition is apprehension, lest attachment figures be inaccessible and/or unresponsive" (1973, p. 213). In further discussion of the infant's responses to separation, Bowlby links the emotion of anger to the anxious attachment complex. In some respects, however, Bowlby's idea of anxious attachment seems to be better described as a fear–anger interaction than by the elusive concept of anxiety.

Differential emotions theory hypothesizes that anxiety as typically conceptualized consists of the dominant emotion fear and fear-interactions with one or more of the other fundamental emotions, particularly with distress, anger, shame, guilt, and interest. Anxiety, like depression, may also involve drive states (e.g., pain, sex, fatigue) and biochemical factors. The remainder of this chapter will consist of a brief review of some of the studies of the neurophysiological and biochemical factors in fear and anxiety and a summary of studies with the DES that lend support to the differential emotions theory of anxiety. The evidence suggests that the term anxiety, unless modified by more specific qualifiers, can never obtain the requisite precision to guide definitive scientific investigation.

Conceivably one could speak precisely of *forms of anxiety,* if for each form the combination of affects (e.g., fear–distress–anger, fear–shame–guilt) were carefully specified. Thus, in the context of differential emotions theory, anxiety is used only as a general, imprecise term that refers to any interactive combination of fear, other affects, and certain affective–cognitive orientations. It is, at best, a term of convenience, appropriate only when it is not possible to specify more precisely the actual pattern or combination of affects.

Differential emotions theory recognizes affect combinations that may be called anxiety. For example, guilt-prone individuals may experience fear–guilt or fear–shame–guilt patterns. For others there may be fear–distress, fear–anger, or fear–distress–anger combinations. However, fear must always be the dominant emotion in the pattern, if the pattern is to be considered a form of anxiety.

The way the affect components interact may also vary from individual to individual. A prominent distress component may amplify the fear component in some individuals and the shame component in others. An interest–excitement component may oscillate with fear or inhibit distress. A great variety of emotion dynamics can exist, making careful analysis a complex task. Assessment must also consider the fact that each form of anxiety may reflect different blends of facial expressions as different emotions are activated simultaneously or in rapid sequence.

Neurophysiology of Fear and Anxiety

There are several reasons for considering the neurophysiology of both fear and anxiety. First, investigators have often equated the two concepts or inadequately differentiated them in the literature. Second, studies of fear alone must be considered since fear is the dominant component of anxiety. Third, there is the possibility that the alternation in the experience of intense fear and mild to moderate fear may produce neurophysiological and biochemical activities very like those in forms of anxiety. This follows from the assumption that intense fear is trophotropic in nature and moderate to mild fear ergotropic. Gellhorn (1965, 1967) has marshaled considerable supporting evidence for his conception of anxiety as characterized by the simultaneous and antagonistic functioning of both the ergotropic and trophotropic systems. This would mean the simultaneous functioning of the sympathetic and parasympathetic nervous systems. Such simultaneous functioning of the two systems is consistent with differential emotions theory, since some anxiety components (moderate fear, anger, interest) are ergotrophic–sympathetic and some (distress) are mainly trophotropic– parasympathetic.

The Neurophysiology of Acute (Sudden, Intense) Fear. Gellhorn's (1965, 1967) analysis of the neurophysiological basis of fear and anxiety began with a distinction between acute (sudden, intense) fear and chronic fear. He maintained that the trophotropic syndrome prevails in acute fear. Electroencephalogram (EEG) potentials are slowed, the parasympathetic activity increases, and striate muscle tone, heart rate, and blood pressure decrease. Despite the dominance of the trophotropic system in acute fear, ergotropic discharges may produce pupillary dilation, sweating, and increased blood flow through the muscles. In light of his theory, Gellhorn reversed Cannon's interpretation of the cause of voodoo death and hypothesized that voodoo death results from circulatory collapse brought about by acute fear and the consequent massive increases in trophotropic discharges. His view is consistent with the fact that the voodoo victim thinks that survival is hopeless and doom inevitable.

The Neurophysiology of Chronic Fear (Anxiety). Gellhorn defined anxiety as chronic fear, but the idea of fear persisting over time and across different life situations allows for the possibility of interactions with other fundamental emotions. Anger is specifically implicated in his analysis of what he called subacute fear.

Gellhorn's neurophysiological analysis of anxiety is based on his idea that the antagonistic ergotropic and trophotropic systems normally function in a balanced and reciprocal fashion—an increase in ergotropic activity is accompanied by a decrease in trophotropic activity and vice versa. Anxiety obtains as a result of simultaneous upward discharges of the ergotropic *and* trophotropic systems. Breakdown in reciprocity of the two systems fails and their subsequent concurrent functioning creates conflicting demands on the organism. Gellhorn (1965) recognized different "patterns of anxiety" (p. 499). First, there is the excitatory form characterized by restlessness, hyperactivity, sympathetic responses, and ergotropic dominance—possibly a fear–anger pattern. Second, the inhibitory form is characterized by hypoactivity, parasympathetic responses, and trophotropic dominance— possibly a fear–distress pattern.

Gellhorn presented considerable evidence for the notion that anxiety is characterized by both ergotropic and trophotropic activity, with typically ergotropic dominance. For example, he noted that most of the procedures used to induce experimental neuroses—difficult discrimination, massive pain, nociceptive stimulation applied during an alimentary conditioned reflex—involve both the ergotropic and trophotropic systems. The application of an unconditioned stimulus such as electric shock or an air blast acts mainly on the ergotropic system, and when it is applied during eating there is concomitant heightened trophotropic activity (Gellhorn, 1967).

Gellhorn mentions two other biological factors in anxiety. First, hereditary predispositions affect hypothalamic tuning and ergotropic–trophotropic balance. Second, other individual differences influence the patterns of somatic symptoms in anxiety.

Epinephrine Level, Norepinephrine–Epinephrine Ratio, and Anxiety. An increase in epinephrine and a concomitant decrease in the norepinephrine–epinephrine ratio are associated with a shift in the ergotropic–trophotropic balance to the trophotropic side (Gellhorn, 1965). At the phenomenological level, this condition might be experienced as an increase in acute fear or in distress and a decrease in anger or aggressiveness.

Funkenstein (1955) investigated normal subjects (medical students) during a stressful period (waiting to hear about internship applications) and found that those who were angry at others for the stressful situation had a mild response to a parasympathomimetic agent and that those who were angry at themselves (depressed) or afraid (anxious) had a strong reaction. Subsequent studies showed that when subjects responded to stress with anger toward others (outer-directed anger), their physiological reactions were like those induced by injection of noradrenalin (norepinephrine), but when the same subjects reacted with fear, their responses were like those induced by injection of adrenalin (epinephrine). Similar findings have been reported by Ax (1953), Schachter (1957), Martin (1961), and Breggin (1964). Furthermore, a review by Fehr and Stern (1970) generally supports the notion that fundamental emotions such as anger and fear have specific and distinct hormonal and autonomic patterns.

The Corticosteroids and Anxiety. Gellhorn (1965) argued that the increased steroid level during anxiety was further evidence of strong ergotropic discharges. Consistent with this conclusion, Wehmer (1966) showed that film-induced anxiety produced an increase in plasma 17-hydroxycorticosteroids (17-OH-CS), heart rate, and self-reported negative emotions.

Brady's (1970) experiments on induced "anxiety" in rhesus monkeys also markedly increased the 17-OH-CS level in the blood. In other experiments, Brady showed that "conditioned anxiety" produces highly significant increases in both epinephrine and norepinephrine, supporting Gellhorn's (1965) position that anxiety involves both the trophotropic and ergotropic systems and the differential emotions hypothesis that fear and anger can constitute one form of anxiety.

Empirical Studies of Anxiety as a Combination of Emotions

A series of studies with the Differential Emotions Scale showed that anxiety, as conceived by psychologists and as defined or imaged by college students, could be broken down into a number of relatively independent affective factors (Izard, 1972). These studies will be summarized briefly.

The first study was a factor analytic investigation of the DES combined with the items of the Spielberger–Gorsuch–Lushene (1970) State Trait Anxiety Inventory (STAI). The combined instrument (DES+A) was administered to 339 college students, who were instructed to complete the scale while recalling or visualizing situations in which they felt anxious. The factor analysis of the data from this study showed that anxiety, as defined by STAI, was indeed a complex of affective factors. Most of the anxiety-related terms of the STAI loaded on a fear factor that included all of the fear items of the DES. A few of the STAI items loaded on a factor that combined the distress and guilt items of the DES and most of the nonanxiety items of the STAI (e.g., content, secure, confident) loaded on a joy factor that included all of the joy items of the DES. Thus the factor analysis of the STAI in a context with items representing a variety of discrete emotions showed that this widely used anxiety scale is actually a multifactor instrument representing several of the discrete emotions hypothesized by differential emotions theory as components of anxiety.

The DES was administered to a large group of black college students immediately after their campus had been invaded by armed national guardsmen and local police. During the occasion police fired into a crowd of students and into a dormitory, injuring several students and killing two. The students were asked to recall the scene and its aftermath and to describe their feelings about it by completing the DES. As predicted, they showed significantly elevated means on fear, distress, shame, anger, and interest, most of the hypothesized affective components of anxiety.

In another study (Bartlett & Izard, 1972), 160 college students were divided into high- and low-anxiety groups on the basis of their STAI scores. These students then took the DES under two conditions. First, in the quiet of their own dormitory rooms they were requested to imagine a situation that made them anxious and then to keep the situation vividly in mind while completing the DES. On a second occasion, just prior to a midterm examination (real anxiety condition) the subjects were requested to complete the DES. Figure 14-4 shows the profiles of DES means for the high- and low-anxiety subjects in the real and imagined anxiety conditions.

The profiles for the high-anxiety subjects are quite consistent with predictions on the basis of differential emotions theory. The highest means are fear, interest, guilt, anger, and shame (shyness). The marked similarity in the profiles for the real and imagined anxiety conditions lend support to the imaging technique in the study of emotions.

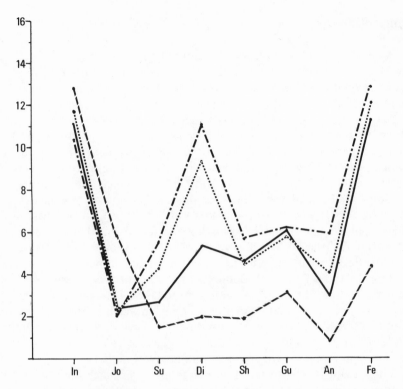

FIGURE 14-4. *Profiles of DES means for high-anxiety subjects under real (——) and imagined (—·—·—·—·) conditions and low-anxiety subjects under real (— — —) and imagined (- - - - - -) conditions.*

Summary

Intense fear is the most dangerous of all emotion conditions. In mild to moderate intensities, it often interacts with both positive and negative emotions. Fear is activated by a sharp increase in density of neural firing. At the neurophysiological level, fear seems to have some overlapping components with startle and excitement, at least in the initial stages of the emotion activation process.

There are both innate (natural) and learned (cultural) causes or clues for fear. The threshold for fear, like that of any other fundamental emotion, is influenced by biologically based individual differences, idiosyncratic experience, and the total sociocultural context of the occasion. The innate releasors or natural clues for fear include being alone, strangeness, height, sudden approach, sudden change of stimuli, and pain. While any of these conditions tend to increase the probability of fear, their effect on any given individual at any given time depends upon the previously listed factors that influence the fear threshold. The widely reported fear of darkness, animals, strange objects, and strange persons has led some theorists to consider these conditions as derivatives of natural causes.

Many of the learned or sociocultural factors that instigate or influence fear bear some relationship to the innate or natural causes and their immediate derivatives. For example, an adult may rationalize fear of thunder on the grounds that it signals an increased likelihood of being struck by lightning. Socioculturally based fears can be learned through the processes of traumatic conditioning or vicariously through a parent, adult, or sibling who serves as a fearful model.

The causes of fear also include certain drive states (e.g., pain) and other emotions. By the principle of contagion, fear can serve as an activator of itself, and through learning any emotion may activate fear. Fear may also be instigated by cognitive processes; cognitive constructions constitute one source of objectless fear.

Studies of the development of fear in infants suggest that this emotion does not appear until the second half of the first year of life. The data are not conclusive, however, since the frequently used indicators of infant fear may also signal other emotions such as distress. Definitive analyses of infant facial expressions hold promise for the study of the development of emotions, but the technique has been little used.

The facial expression of fear is readily distinguished from other emotion expressions. In fear the eyebrows are raised somewhat but kept approximately straight; the inner corners of the brow are drawn together, and there are horizontal wrinkles extending partway across the forehead. Fear eyes are more widely opened than interested eyes. The lower lid is tensed, the upper lid is slightly raised, and the corners of the mouth are drawn back, creating tension in the lips.

The experience of fear can range from apprehension to terror. In fear the person senses uncertainty, insecurity, and imminent danger. The person feels a high degree of tension and a moderate degree of impulsiveness.

The adult personality is significantly influenced by the manner in which fear is socialized during childhood. In left-wing socialization of fear, fear experiences are minimized, parents refrain from frightening the child, and tolerance for fear and fear counteraction techniques are taught. In right-wing socialization of fear, parents communicate their own fear to the child, the noxiousness of fear is minimized, and parents may willingly frighten their children without making restitution. Tolerance for fear and counteraction techniques are not taught, and parents show little concern about the fearfulness of their children.

Fear interactions with other emotions can also greatly influence personality and behavior. Fear–distress interactions can increase the problems of individuation and decrease the capacity to tolerate loss of love. If Rafe is punished and frightened whenever he cries, he may become especially vulnerable to a threat of separation. A strong distress–fear bond may greatly decrease a person's ability to be sympathetic with other people in distress.

The interaction of fear and self-contempt may lead to heightened self-distrust or even fear of self. A severe fear–shame bind can produce paranoid schizophrenia.

A number of techniques for reducing or controlling fear have been reported to be effective. These include habituation or desensitization treatment, flooding or implosive therapy, and modeling, which is based on vicarious learning or social imitation. Differential emotions theory provides the basis for a number of therapeutic techniques. These include techniques based on principles of emotion processes such as emotion contagion, which operates in modeling and role-playing techniques, and emotion–emotion activation and regulation, by which imagery-induced joy might be used to attenuate distress and depression.

On the whole clinicians and clinical investigators have considered fear and anxiety as closely allied states and processes, but most descriptions of anxiety include fear along with other affects. Differential emotions theory hypothesizes that anxiety, as typically conceptualized, consists of fear as the dominant emotion, fear interactions with one or more of the other fundamental emotions, particularly with distress, anger, shame, guilt, and interest, and of affective–cognitive interactions. The theory also recognizes that anxiety, like depression, may involve drive states and biochemical factors.

Some of the work on neurophysiological and biochemical factors in fear and anxiety supports the differential emotions theory. For example, Gellhorn's analysis of anxiety as simultaneous and antagonistic functioning of the ergotropic and trophotropic systems clearly allow for such combinations of emotions as fear–anger and fear–distress, both of which may be considered as forms of anxiety.

Empirical studies with the Differential Emotions Scale also support the differential emotions analysis of anxiety. These studies showed that both real and imaged anxiety situations involve fear as the dominant emotion and increases in one or more of the emotions of distress, shame, guilt, anger, and interest.

SHAME AND SHYNESS

Shame and shyness play a highly important role in human affairs, but they have been much less studied than emotions such as anger and fear. The apparent relationship between anger and at least some forms of aggression and the relationship between fear and the complex concept of anxiety have resulted in extensive studies of at least certain aspects of these emotions. The social and clinical significance of both normal and deviant anger- and fear-related behavior and the effects of these emotions upon individuals and groups have caught the attention of scientists for many decades. The effects of shame on the individual and on social relations, however, has not been so evident or compelling for most behavioral scientists.

Perhaps shame deserves a more important place in emotion research and in the behavioral sciences in general. In a survey of 800 high school and college students Zimbardo, Pilkonis, and Norwood (1974) found that 82% considered themselves "dispositionally shy" (shy at some time during their lives) and 42% described themselves as presently shy. There can be little question about the importance of shame in the socialization process and in the development of the individual personality. Shame and shyness also have important relationships to the positive emotions of interest and joy and to the sex drive.

Definition of Shame: Biological and Psychological Characteristics

Before defining the concept of shame it is necessary to consider the two closely related concepts of shyness and guilt. Shame, shyness, and guilt are sometimes considered as aspects of the same emotion, sometimes as quite distinct emotions, and sometimes as quite different emotions with some common characteristics.

Darwin (1872) used all three terms—shame, shyness, and guilt—but he apparently used shame and shyness as virtually synonymous terms. Occasionally he implied that there were some differences between shame and shyness, but he did not specify these differences. He did point out the difference between shame and guilt and this will be considered in the next chapter. Darwin thought that shame belonged to a large group of related emotions—shame, shyness, guilt, jealously, envy, avarice, revenge, suspicion, deceit, vanity, conceit, ambition, pride, and humility. Most contemporary emotion theorists would agree that all of these concepts definitely have an emotion conponent and an emotion connotation, but few would argue that each is a basic and distinct emotion with different neurochemical substrates.

The astuteness of Darwin's observational powers is again evident in the fact that almost all the concepts in the "shame group" are related in some important way to shame, shyness, or guilt. The shy woman who feels restricted in interacting socially may be more likely to feel jealous when her husband enjoys social encounters. The person who is shamed (disgraced) may seek revenge. Deceit may be used to hide guilt. Vanity and conceit may be defenses against shame or shyness. A person may become quite ambitious and develop great pride in order to avoid shame. Humility can be seen as a direct correlate of shame.

It has been generally assumed that Darwin considered each of the concepts in the "shame group" as representing a distinct emotion. Actually, though, he referred to these concepts consistently as representing "mental states" or "states of mind." Although not a very precise term, "state of mind," considered as an equivalent of affective–cognitive structure, describes such concepts as revenge, conceit, pride, and humility better than does the term emotion.

Darwin considered guilt as a state of mind resulting primarily from moral transgression. When we consider the activation of shame, we shall see one way in which Darwin related the emotions of shame and guilt. In this chapter shame and shyness are considered together, as aspects of the same emotion, but guilt will be treated separately in Chapter 16.

The Expression of Shame and Its Physiological Aspects

The physical expression of shame is relatively easy to describe. If Rafe feels shame he typically averts his gaze, and turns his face away, usually by turning his head to the side and downward. His head and body movements tend to have the effect of making him appear smaller (see Figure 15-1). Darwin thought that the eyes were the primary expressive device of shame. The "eyes are turned ascant" and "waver from side to side." The eyelids are lowered and held partly closed from time to time.

FIGURE 15-1. Shame interacting with enjoyment in a 10-year-old boy of northern India.

The tendency to curl up and make the body appear smaller was dramatically exemplified by a young woman who was participating in the making of a film on hypnotically induced emotions. When shame was induced she averted her eyes, lowered her head, and then immediately curled up in the chair with her knees against her breasts and her arms around her legs. In the posthypnotic inquiry she reported that she felt like a little rabbit all curled up in a furry ball, trying very hard not to be seen.

One of the physical attributes of shame is that rather mysterious phenomenon of blushing, which Darwin considered the most peculiar and most human of all the emotion expressions. Darwin was apparently correct in maintaining that blushing does not occur in nonhumans. (Darwin thought that animals did exhibit shame or shyness, and he gave examples of this behavior in dogs.)

It is generally believed that blushing cannot be controlled voluntarily. It is a result of certain activities of the autonomic nervous system. Darwin, as well as many contemporary emotion theorists, considers blushing a result of the emotion of shame. The fact that blushing is a function of the autonomic nervous system and an effect of shame experience places it in a different category from the facial expressions of emotions previously considered.

It is not certain that blushing is an inevitable accompaniment of shame. Some people reportedly feel shame without blushing. In any case, there are wide individual differences in the frequency of blushing, and the threshold for blushing apparently changes with age. In general, children and adolescents seem to have a lower threshold for blushing than do adults. It is not known whether this is a result of biological changes that occur as the person grows older or whether it is a result of psychological changes in the blushing threshold.

As already indicated, it is customary to consider blushing as a completely involuntary reaction that cannot be controlled at will. However, recent research on control of autonomic functions by means of biofeedback or by means of certain meditational practices makes it appear quite reasonable that blushing could be brought under voluntary control, from the standpoint of both production and inhibition, as one grows from childhood through adolescence and adulthood. Of course it is also quite possible that at the same time the individual has learned other methods (or defenses) for the control of blushing by means of avoiding shame-eliciting situations.

Tomkins (1963) has suggested that blushing is an immediate effect of shame but is also a cause of further shame. By calling the attention of others to our embarrassment, blushing tends to make worse the shame we already feel. Thus the inhibition of blushing may well attenuate the shame experience. The person who "never blushes" may indeed be one who feels little shame.

Blushing is apparently caused by an autonomic nervous system reaction that results in inhibition of the normal tonic and contracting activities of the capillaries of the face, allowing these vessels to fill with blood. The increased blood flow results in the flushed red appearance of the face. Darwin noted the possibility that the same kind of capillary action that causes blushing in the facial skin may occur in the part of the brain that controls blushing, thus resulting in the "confusion of mind" that occurs in shame.

Darwin thought that blushing was confined mainly to the face for two reasons. The first reason is the exposure of the face to the air, light, and temperature variations. He reported that people who go naked to the waist blush on their torsos as well as on their faces. Secondly, the attention of the self (and of others) is "directed much more frequently and earnestly to the face." The face, more than any other part of the body, is subjected to self-attention, by virtue of its being the "seat of beauty and ugliness" and the most "ornamented part of the body."

Although it is commonly accepted that visual stimulation is the most important type of input in the generation of shame and blushing, there is some evidence that it is not essential in shame activation. Darwin reported instances of blushing in a blind and deaf girl and cited instances of other blind children who were "great blushers." Darwin also reported instances of people who maintained that they blushed in complete solitude. I also have obtained considerable anecdotal evidence that individuals blush when they are alone. Apparently the memory of an embarrassing incident which occurred in the presence of another person or thoughts about the attitudes, remarks, or actions of other people can serve as sufficient stimulus to elicit the emotion of shame and the phenomenon of blushing.

In the survey of Zimbardo *et al.*, 53% of the shy respondents reported blushing. Other physiological reactions reported as accompaniments of shyness were increased pulse (54%), perspiration (49%), butterflies in the stomach (48%), and a pounding heart (48%). Shy people also reported that they talked less (80%), had a low speaking voice (40%), made less eye contact (51%), more frequently avoided others (44%), and more frequently avoided taking action (42%). Cattell (1965, 1973) holds that shy people have a biologically determined temperament characterized by a sympathetic nervous system that is unduly susceptible to conflict and threat.

As Tomkins has pointed out, the adult modifies the shame expression because it is not socially desirable for him to express shame too openly, too intensely, or too often. One modification of the shame response is for the individual to simply take a quick look downward. Sometimes an individual may hold the head high, in effect, substituting the look of contempt for the look of shame. A person may look chronically humble so that a shame expression will not be so noticeable. Finally, a person may hold the head back, the chin out, but still have a downward cast of the eyes.

The Phenomenology of Shame

In some respects the psychological characteristics of shame are difficult to describe, but virtually everyone has experienced shame or shyness at some time. The survey of Zimbardo *et al.* found only one percent of their sample of 800 who reported never having experienced shyness. Thus, most people know intuitively what this experience is like. Darwin and all serious students of shame have pointed out that in shame a person feels a heightened degree of self-consciousness, self-awareness, or self-attention. In shame, our whole consciousness is suddenly and for a moment filled with the self. We are aware only of the self or some aspect of the self that we consider indecorous or inadequate. It is as though something we were hiding from everyone is suddenly under a burning light in public view. At the same time we feel totally ineffective and incompetent. We feel at a loss for words and actions. As Darwin put it, when one blushes in shame, one loses one's "presence of mind" and often utters "inappropriate remarks." The shamed person may also stammer and make awkward movements and strange grimaces.

Tomkins (1963) gave a very vivid description of shame. He considers shame, shyness, and guilt as one emotion served by the same neurophysiological mechanisms. He maintains, however, that at least at the conscious, phenomenological level shame and guilt are quite different phenomena. He describes shame as the emotion of indignity, defeat, transgression, and alienation:

> Though terror speaks to life and death and distress makes of the world a veil of tears, yet shame strikes deepest into the heart of man. While terror and distress hurt, they are wounds inflicted from outside which penetrate the smooth surface of the ego; but shame is felt as an inner torment, a sickness of the soul. It does not matter whether the humiliated one has been shamed by derisive laughter, or whether he mocks himself. In either event he feels himself naked, defeated, alienated, lacking in dignity and worth (Tomkins, 1963, p. 185).

Tomkins described shame as the most reflexive of the emotions, an experience of the self by the self, in which the phenomenological distinction between the subject and the object of shame is lost and in which the increased consciousness, awareness, and visibility of the face generates the torment of self-consciousness.

Helen Lewis (1971) has also written a detailed description of the phenomenology of shame. (She treats shame and guilt as separate emotions and some of her work on guilt will be considered in the following chapter.) In shame, the self is experienced as the object of contempt and scorn. The shamed person feels ridiculed, reduced, little. Feelings of helplessness, inadequacy, and even paralysis flood consciousness. There are noxious body stimuli from blushing and sometimes from tears and rage when the shame elicits distress and anger. The shamed adult feels childish with all weaknesses exposed in full view of the self and others. The self feels as though it can function poorly or not at all as a perceiver, thinker, and doer. The "ego boundaries" become permeable.

In shame the individual sees the "other" as the source of contempt, scorn, and ridicule. The other appears as a powerful ridiculing being sometimes expressing derisive laughter. The other appears intact and capable. The other may also appear as "going away" or abandoning. In defining shame, Lewis uses the synonyms shyness, bashfulness, modesty, embarrassment, chagrin, and mortification.

The Zimbardo *et al.* survey found that shyness and shyness–cognition interactions were characterized by "self-consciousness (in 18% of the group), concern for impression management (67%), concern for social evaluation (59%), thoughts about the unpleasantness of the situation (56%), thoughts about shyness in general (46%), and forms of cognitive distraction aimed at averting all the above" (p. 12). They hypothesized that the self-preoccupation of the shy person stemmed "from overindulging the normal feedback processes of self-monitoring and social evaluation" (p. 11).

Lynd (1961) suggests that the feeling of shame includes an unexpectedness or "astonishment at seeing different parts of ourselves, conscious and unconscious, acknowledged and unacknowledged, suddenly coming together, and coming together with aspects of the world we have not recognized . . . the sudden sense of exposure, of being unable to deal with what is happening, characterize shame" (p. 34). Erikson (1950, 1956) expresses a similar view of shame phenomenology and adds the notion that shame also includes the feeling of a sudden loss of self-control.

Modigliani (1971) defined shame or embarrassment as a loss of situational self-esteem and conducted a laboratory study of responses to "private" and "public" success and failure on an intellectual task. Experimental conditions (task failure) for inducing embarrassment occurred both in private and public (group) and was either mitigated or not by cognitive input regarding the difficulty level of the task. The mean for self-reported embarrassment was highest for subjects who experienced public failure and lowest for those who experienced public success. The data showed that slight embarrassment occurred even in the private failure condition and the author interpreted the cause as "anticipated presence of others." The results also showed a significant negative relationship between amount of embarrassment and eye contact.

The foregoing descriptions of the phenomenology of shame have a number of common themes. Shame involves the self in a very unusual and particular way. There is an extremely heightened consciousness of self and often of some particular aspect of self. The heightened self-awareness results in unusual and distinct self-perceptions. The self is seen as small, helpless, frozen, emotionally hurt. The self is seen as foolish, inept, out-of-place. The domination of consciousness by the self and by self-imaging results in a temporary inability to think logically and efficiently. In shame one feels a loss of words, especially of the right words, the appropriate ones for the occasion. Later one thinks of just the thing that one wishes one could have said in the speechless moment of embarrassment. Shame is usually accompanied by some measure of failure or defeat. At the very least we "lose our cool," and our customary style of expression is at least momentarily destroyed. In one respect we are anything but alienated. We are standing in flaming light before piercing eyes. However, we are quite alienated in the sense that we cannot easily reach out, touch, or communicate with the other person.

The profile of emotions in a "shyness situation" (Izard, 1972) provides rather firm support for the theoretical notions about shame and shame dynamics developed in this chapter. The DES profile for students' recalling or imaging a situation in which they experienced intense shyness is presented in Figure 15-2. It is noteworthy that the interest–excitement mean is the third highest in the profile, and the interest mean is not significantly lower than the second highest mean, that for fear. This is a higher mean on interest than that obtained in any other negative emotion situation except for anger, where the interest score was 9.72. Even more remarkable is the

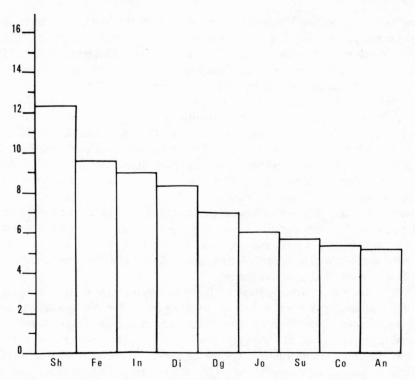

FIGURE 15-2. The profile of emotions in the shyness situation (N = 58). The emotion (DES) scales are abbreviated: (Sh) shyness, (In) interest, (Fe) fear, (Di) distress, (Dg) joy, (Co) contempt, and (An) anger.

fact that the mean score for enjoyment (6.36) is elevated in the shyness situation. Shyness was the only one of the six negative emotions in which the mean for enjoyment was substantially elevated. The position of interest and enjoyment in the shyness situation profile strongly supports the notion that shyness is most likely to occur in situations where interest and enjoyment are also experienced. This is also consistent with Tomkins's notion that shyness is activated by the partial but not complete reduction of the neural activity in interest or enjoyment.

The prominent position of fear in the DES profile for the shyness situation is also consistent with our explanation of the dynamics of shame and shyness. Shame and shyness are responses relating to the person's well-being, the self-concept, and self-integrity. It is quite reasonable that an emotion so closely related to the core of the personality should be dynamically related to the emotion of fear. In some situations shame and shyness may serve as frontrunners, motivating the individual to cover or withdraw the extended or exposed self before more serious threat elicits the very toxic emotion of fear.

The profile of dimensions in the shyness situation is presented in Figure 15-3. Of particular interest is the combination of high tension and high pleasantness relative to the other negative emotions. The tension in shyness, while lower than that in fear, is roughly equal to that in anger and guilt and significantly higher than that in distress. The pleasantness reported in the shyness situation is lower than that in the positive emotions but significantly higher than in any of the other negative emotions.

The Activation and Causes of Shame

As in the case of the other fundamental emotions, the activation of shame at the neural level is considered separately from the conscious causes of shame. Although the precise mechanisms involved in the neural activation of shame have not been determined there is fairly general agreement regarding a variety of causes of shame at the conscious level.

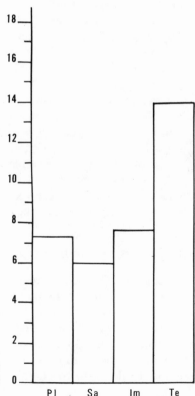

FIGURE 15-3. The profile of dimensions in the shyness situation. DRS dimensions are abbreviated: (Pl) pleasantness, (Sa) self-assurance, (Im) impulsiveness, and (Te) tension.

Activation of Shame at the Neurological Level

Tomkins (1963) considers shame as an emotion that is activated by a decrease in the density of neural firing. Specifically, shame is activated by the partial reduction of the neural activity of the ongoing emotion of either interest–excitement or enjoyment–joy.

Tomkins's interesting hypothesis regarding the neural mechanism for the activation of shame has several implications for the psychology of this important emotion. First, if we assume that the hypothesis is valid, then shame occurs only when the individual is experiencing one of the positive emotions, either interest or enjoyment. Thus, both neurologically and psychologically shame is more closely associated with the positive emotions than any of the other negative emotions. Since the hypothesis states that shame is activated by only the partial reduction of the neural activity of a positive emotion, there is greater likelihood that the interrupted positive emotion will continue at some level or will alternate in consciousness with shame, particularly if the shame is not too intense.

The study of Bartlett and Izard (1972) on feeling states accompanying different fundamental emotions lends some indirect support to the notion that shame is associated with the positive emotions. Although shame was rated high on tension and low on self-assurance, it received a far higher rating on the dimension of pleasantness than any of the other negative emotions.

There is a strong possibility that changes in the cardiovascular system—particularly the blushing phenomenon—play a role in the neurochemical processes of shame. Since the cardiovascular changes are probably subsequent to the initial subjective experience of shame, the cardiovascular changes such as that involved in blushing probably serve more of a regulatory function in the shame process. As Tomkins has pointed out, the effect of blushing on the experience of shame is at least partly psychological: it increases the already heightened consciousness of the face and also calls greater attention to the face by the observer, and thus amplifies the shame experience.

The Causes of Shame

One possible source of shame can be traced to early shame experiences with strangers. In the young infant the human face is typically a stimulus for excitement and joy. On seeing the human face, the infant usually desires social contact and attempts to increase communication with the other person. As a child is learning to differentiate the face of the mother from the face of a stranger the first glimpse of the stranger will elicit the infant's desire to communicate. Recognition of the face as different and strange inhibits the infant's interest and enjoyment and reduces the desire to communicate. Shame or shyness results from the infant's mistake in recognition that led to the "familiar responses" to an unfamiliar person. If in childhood there is a series of negative experiences with strangers, one eventually learns that one is always subject to shame when one meets a stranger. As Tomkins puts it:

> The expectation of an impediment to communication somewhat attenuates the excitement he experiences the next time he sees a stranger. Shame is then evoked again, and the child has taken the crucial steps in constructing in his imagination the class of people in whose presence one feels shy. Future experiences in which this expectation is confirmed will then produce a learned shyness which is much more severe and generalized than the innate response to innate activators. (Tomkins, 1963, p. 2, 142).

Many people have had the experience of seeing someone in a crowd and eagerly trying to greet and communicate with the individual only to find suddenly that the person whose attention has been claimed is a total stranger. The shame experienced in such a situation may be mild or intense, depending upon the circumstances. Since an unanticipated friend–stranger differential can elicit shame, Tomkins hypothesizes that as soon as the infant learns to differentiate the face of the mother from the face of the stranger (sometime around the fourth month of life) the infant is vulnerable to shame. Henceforth, according to Tomkins, "shame is inevitable for any human being insofar as desire outruns fulfillment sufficiently to attentuate interest without destroying it" (Tomkins, 1963, p. 185).

Much of a healthy childhood and a great deal of the creative life of an adult is spent in some form of exploration that is accompanied by interest and enjoyment. Tomkins believes that in this condition any barrier to further exploration that reduces positive emotion will produce shame. However, it seems that certain barriers may not heighten self-consciousness or call undue attention to the self, and hence may not evoke shame. If Rafe is happily and excitedly exploring a mountain forest and he comes to a gorge in his path, his positive emotion may be partly reduced but the cause (barrier) is completely impersonal and reflects in no way upon the self. In such a situation the individual may momentarily feel less excitement and enjoyment and perhaps even mild distress but it would be no occasion for shame. On the other hand, if Rafe the explorer had promised to take his girl friend Rebecca to some point of interest beyond the gorge he might, depending on his sensitivity to Rebecca's expectations of him, experience some embarrassment over his temporary inability to fulfill his promise on schedule.

Lewis's (1971) position, influenced by both the psychoanalytic tradition and experimental psychology, is that failure to live up to one's ego ideal constitutes a pervasive source of shame. The gap between a self-concept and an ideal self-concept is a good example of Tomkins' principle of desire outrunning achievement. Rafe never quite becomes his ideal self. The more nearly he approaches the ideal self the more likely he is to revise his concept of the ideal, thus keeping it ever beyond attainment. Failure to live up to the ego ideal can certainly be seen as a condition which would weaken interest at least from time to time, but not destroy it.

According to Lewis, shame can occur only in the context of an emotional relationship with another person, and only in relation to a person whose opinions and feelings are valued (Lewis, 1971, p. 42). The threshold for shame is correlated with sensitivity to the feelings and opinions of others about the self.

Contempt from self or others can activate shame. The feeling that the self or any aspect of self is inadequate, inept, or unbecoming is another precondition for the experience of shame. Fantasies about the inadequacy or unseemliness of the self may generalize to all aspects of the individual. If Rafe is dissatisfied with his physique, and attention is suddenly focused upon it, shame results. Similarly, Rafe as a teenager may be tortured with shame when attention is suddenly focused upon his "big ears" or "wide nose," or on his plumpness, frailty, clumsiness, complexion, *ad infinitum*.

Rafe may think that his thought and speech is inadequate or inappropriate. What young man cannot remember vividly the frequent embarrassment created by his voice changing its pitch during adolescence? Later in life he may be embarrassed by his grammar, or by the quality of his thought as reflected in the substance of his speech.

Darwin alluded to the fact that although shame is most frequently elicited by blame, criticism, or derision, it can also occur in response to praise. Most young people can recall some embarrassment on an occasion when doting parents pointed out some virtue of their darling child. Darwin's observation appears sound but the activation of shame by praise is a topic that has received very little attention. Why should such praise elicit shame? In such a situation at least one of the conditions for the activation of shame is evident—attention to the self is greatly increased. Tomkins's criteria of partial reduction of interest or enjoyment might be met also. It might well be that the child's interest or enjoyment in participation in an adult affair is partly reduced by the focusing of attention on the self and the feeling of inability to respond appropriately. The feeling in children on such occasions could occur because they feel that they have suddenly been overexposed or described in terms they feel they cannot live up to.

Lynd (1961) noted that under some conditions the perception of inappropriateness or incongruity elicits shame. She recognized that in other circumstances incongruity elicits interest or joy. Thus we have another basis for hypothesizing a dynamic relationship between the positive emotions and shame.

As is the case for all emotions, situations vary greatly in their potency for producing shame in different individuals. The situation that evokes shame in one person may evoke excitement and challenge in a second and anger and aggression in a third. Still others may respond to the same situation with distress or fear. Even within the same individual, what produces shame in one situation or under some conditions may produce an entirely different reaction on other occasions and under other conditions. A common theme across a great variety of situations that can prove to be sources of shame is the excitement or enjoyment that these situations typically elicit. Thus, in whatever situations we have invested interest and enjoyment we may find occasions for shame. The most common and ubiquitous objects involved in the activation of shame are the self (or self-concept), the body, love, work, friendship, close interpersonal relationships, or even brief encounters that have special meaning for the individual.

A summary of the free responses for shyness on the antecedents and consequences test are presented in Table 15-1. These responses are generally consistent with the theoretical description of shame and shame–shyness dynamics, although some subjects apparently did not clearly distinguish shame and guilt.

Zimbardo *et al.* asked the shy people in their study to indicate the kinds of situations and people that elicited their feelings of shyness. The data are presented in Table 15-2. These responses are generally consistent with the data from the antecedents and consequences survey with the theories of Lewis, Lynd, Erikson, and others who distinguish between shame and shyness on the one hand and guilt on the other.

TABLE 15-1
Antecedents and Consequences of Shame

Responses	Percentage of subjects giving responses
Antecedents	
Feelings	
1. Of disappointment in self, inept	31.0
2. Self-conscious (shame synonyms, e.g., embarrassed, shy)	25.0
3. Has done something to hurt others	16.4
4. Of being legally or morally wrong	12.5
5. Isolation, rejection, loneliness, lost	4.7
6. Distress synonyms	2.3
7. Other	7.8
Thoughts	
1. Of failure, disappointment, blameworthiness	32.0
2. Has done something to hurt others	21.8

Continued

TABLE 15-1 (continued)
Antecedents and Consequences of Shame

Responses	Percentage of subjects giving responses
3. Unclean, immoral thoughts	21.1
4. Something wrong, stupid	10.9
5. People are laughing at (rejecting) you	3.1
6. Other	10.9
Actions	
1. Has done something legally or morally wrong, harmful	35.9
2. Has done something wrong, stupid, made a mistake	28.9
3. Has done something to hurt others	21.9
4. Did nothing	2.3
5. Other	10.9
Consequences	
Feelings	
1. Shyness, embarrassment (other shame synonyms)	28.0
2. Feels inadequate, disappointed, like a failure	25.8
3. Feels bad, terrible, lousy, discouraged, sad	24.3
4. Lonely, isolated, rejected, lost	6.1
5. Unclean, morally unfit	2.3
6. Other	13.6
Thoughts	
1. Has failed, is disappointed, blames self	30.3
2. Questions reasons for behavior, thinks about what was done and why	23.5
3. Rationalize, escape from feeling	18.2
4. How to atone, make amends, is sorry	10.6
5. Of being set apart (people are looking), lonely, rejected	3.8
6. Other	13.6
Actions	
1. Repents, atones, makes amends, changes, improves, does not repeat offense	48.5
2. Is deliberately alone, retreats from others	22.0
3. Rationalize, forget it, escape from feeling	12.9
4. Questions, reasons for behavior, questions what was done and why	4.5
5. Punishes self	3.8
6. Other	8.3

TABLE 15-2

Inventory of Shyness Elicitors and Reactions
(N = 320 College and High School Students)[a]

Sources and symptoms of shyness	Percentage of students who label themselves shy
Situations	
Where I am focus of attention—large group (as when giving a speech)	72.6
Large groups	67.6
Of lower status	56.2
Social situations in general	55.3
New situations in general	55.0
Requiring assertiveness	54.1
Where I am being evaluated	53.2
Where I am focus of attention—small group	52.1
Small social groups	48.5
One-to-one different sex interactions	48.5
Of vulnerability (need help)	48.2
Small task-oriented groups	28.2
One-to-one same-sex interactions	13.8
Other people	
Strangers	69.7
Opposite sex group	62.9
Authorities by virtue of their knowledge	55.3
Authorities by virtue of their role	39.7
Same-sex groups	33.5
Relatives	19.7
Elderly people	12.4
Friends	10.9
Children	10.0
Parents	8.5

[a]Adapted from Zimbardo *et al.*, 1974.

The Evolutionary-Biological and Psychological Functions of Shame

It seems safe to assume that the various human emotions evolved over thousands and thousands of years as our progenitors and their processes of adaptation became more and more complex. Since our emotions are a product of our evolutionary-biological heritage, we can infer that each emotion served an inherently adaptive function in the phylogenesis of human beings. It is fairly easy to deduce the role of certain emotions in adaptation, but the role of shame is not so obvious. On the surface, shame seems to have only negative consequences for the individual. A closer look may show that this superficial assessment of the value of shame is not altogether accurate.

Evolutionary-Biological Perspectives

Shame has some functions which may have survival value for the individual. First, shame sensitizes the individual to the opinions and feelings of others and thus acts as a force for social cohesion. It assures the group or society that the individual will be responsive to criticism, particularly criticism directed toward central aspects of the self. Thus a man who did not fulfill his responsibility with regard to such things as group defense, risk-taking involved in the essentials of life (exploring, food gathering, hunting), could be subjected to humiliation and isolation. Avoidance of shame can thus be seen as powerful motive, as powerful as the value the person places on his dignity and honor. As Tomkins stated it:

> Men have exposed themselves repeatedly to death and terror and have even surrendered their lives in the defense of their dignity less they be forced to bow their heads and bend their knees. The heavy hand of terror itself has been flaunted and rejected in the name of pride (the shield against shame) . . . better to risk the uncertainties of death and terror than to suffer the deep and certain humiliation of cowardice. (Tomkins, 1963, p. 132–133)

Even in modern times the threat of shame has motivated many young men to risk pain and death in wars, even in a war which they did not understand and for which they had no sympathy.

It is also possible that the threat of shame served some kind of regulatory function in the sexual life of prehistoric human beings. Many men find shyness and modesty sexually appealing. It is quite possible that a sense of shame (shyness, modesty) played an important role in pair bonding and in the reduction of conflicts and physical aggression over women. The emotion of shame is probably the fundamental motive that leads people to seek privacy for sexual relations. The observation of rules regarding privacy in sexual relations will also serve the interest of social order and harmony. In many respects shame continues to serve these functions in contemporary society.

A final reason for the evolution of shame was the role that it played in the development of skills and conpetencies necessary for the survival of the individual and the group. The self most subject to shame is the self without skills or competencies. To avoid the shame of ineptness the individual is motivated to find his strength and develop it. Individuals with highly developed and varied skills and competencies make for a stronger and more defensible group.

The Psychosocial Functions of Shame

There is considerable overlap between the biological and psychosocial functions of shame. What is of significance for people biologically will certainly have significance for them psychologically, and what has significance for the psychological well-being of people may certainly affect their overall biological adaptation. Nevertheless, there are several functions of shame which are rather distinctly psychological in nature. These are summarized below. A more detailed discussion of various aspects of shame in personality development and adjustment can be found in Erikson (1956), Lewis (1971), Lynd (1961), and Tomkins (1963).

1. Shame focuses on the self or some aspect of the self, and makes it the focus of evaluation.

2. The heightened awareness of self and the exaggerated self-consciousness produced by shame tends to bring about more self-imaging than is characteristic of guilt or other emotions. In shame, people picture themselves in all kinds of predicaments and in shame dreams often stand naked in the presence of others. Cognition in the wake of shame works toward strengthening the self or decreasing vulnerability.

3. As Lewis (1971) has indicated, shame increases the permeability of the boundaries of the self. A person is more vulnerable in a state of shame. Sensitivity to shame makes it quite possible to experience shame for another person. A schoolboy may blush crimson for his pretty but inept young schoolteacher when the principal walks into her class and finds it in disorder.

4. The fact that shame generally is elicited by the words and actions of others guarantees a degree of sensitivity to the opinions and feelings of other people, particularly other people with whom we have emotional relationships and whose opinions we value.

5. Due to the fact that shame involves heightened self-awareness and blushing, it involves a greater awareness of the body than other emotions. This sensitivity to the self and body that obtains in shame may serve certain useful functions of both biological and psychological nature; it may inspire the individual to practice good hygiene, and hence to guard his health. It may also motivate one to attend to one's grooming and clothing and thus enhance one's sociability.

6. Darwin, Lewis, and others maintain that shame has a highly adverse impact upon a person's rational intellectual processes. In comparing it with guilt, Lewis observed that shame is "a less differentiated, more irrational, more primitive, more wordless reaction. There is little cognitive content in shame." However, reflection (looking back) on the shame experience may inspire a great deal of thinking and imaging. Few people have suffered intense shame and not had fantasies of triumph over the one who evoked the shame.

7. Shame increases self-criticism and momentary feelings of impotence. In the Dural–Wickland studies discussed earlier, the experimenters induced objective self-awareness by causing the subject to see himself or herself as in error, inept, or in some way discrepant from his or her standard of correctness. Their results suggest that such objective self-awareness is an aspect of the shame experience. Duval and Wicklund indicated that objective self-awareness typically results in an attempt either to reduce the discrepancy or to avoid the conditions that created the state. Further, the objectively self-aware person becomes more self-critical. They argued that the focus of attention upon the self forces the individual to be aware of intraself discrepancies and to suffer a reduction of self-esteem, a reduction that results from falling short of one's personal standards of correctness. Another way in which Duval and Wicklund's concept of objective self-awareness coincides with a concept of shame is their belief that objective self-awareness tends to engender feelings of passivity and impotence. Further, Duval and Wickland pointed out that one of the important determinants in the emergence of objective self-awareness is the individual's awareness of being observed by others. This is very much in keeping with the idea that shame focuses or gives direction to the operations of consciousness that bring about objective self-awareness.

8. Although efforts to avoid shame may subserve conformity, confronting and coping successfully with shame experiences can facilitate the development of autonomy, personal identity, and mutual love. In his discussion of the growth and crises of the healthy personality, Erikson (1956) sees shame and doubt pitted against the development of personal autonomy. He holds that in most Western societies toilet training (the anal stage of psychosocial development) provides the original setting for the shame–autonomy conflict. In this period the child struggles to learn self-control, when a loss of control means that one has exposed oneself "prematurely and foolishly," or shamefully.

> This stage, therefore, becomes decisive for the ratio between love and hate, for that between co-operation and willfulness, and for that between the freedom of self-expression and its suppression. From a sense of self-control without loss of self-esteem comes a lasting sense of autonomy and pride; from a sense of muscular and anal impotence, of loss of self-control, and of parental over-control comes a lasting sense of doubt and shame. (Erikson, 1956, p. 199)

Lynd (1961) pursued Erikson's theme and developed the idea that confronting and transcending shame is essential to the sense of personal identity and freedom. She sees willingness to risk exposure and shame as a corrective for people's tendency to manipulate each other and for the tendency of long-term intimacy to diminish mutual love.

> Enlarging the possibilities of mutual love depends upon risking exposure. This risk of exposure can come about only with respect for oneself, respect for the other person, and recognition of nonpersonal values and loyalties that both

persons respect. Through such love one comes to know the meaning of exposure without shame, and of shame transformed by being understood and shared. Aristotle distinguishes between feeling ashamed of things shameful "according to common opinion" and things shameful "in very truth." In love there can be the exploring together of the meaning of things shameful "in very truth." (Lynd, 1961, p. 239)

Shame and the Defense of Self and Personal Integrity

Shame is responsive to criticism of the individual's most intimate possession, the integrity of the self. Shame protects self-integrity by increasing the individual's responsiveness to any indication that the self is overextended or overexposed. Shame and successful coping with shame experiences play an important role in the development and maintenance of the self-concept and personal identity. The normal individual's desire to avoid shame or to develop a high threshold for shame serves as an important motive in the development of a set of intellectual, physical, and social skills that give the individual a sense of adequacy and competency. However, if the individuals' early experiences, particularly their shame-socialization experiences, have given them concepts of themselves as dependent, inadequate, and inept people, they are likely to capitalize on certain types of ego defenses (Lewis, 1971).

Denial is one of the characteristic defenses against shame. Denial comes into play as a defense because shame is such a painful emotion, because it is difficult to tolerate, and because it is difficult to disguise or conceal. When Rafe feels shame, he wants to remove himself physically or psychologically from the source of shame. One way of accomplishing this, in the psychological realm at least, is to deny the existence or the importance of the source. Rafe also can try to deny that he feels shame. This is very difficult since he needs first of all to convince himself, and the self is typically acutely aware of the experience of shame. Nevertheless, if he is dependent on denial as a defense, he will stand with crimson face, lowered head or averted gaze, and staunchly affirm that he is not embarrassed.

A second way in which an individual defends himself against shame is by the ego defense mechanism of repression. People try to repress (forget, remove from consciousness) their thoughts about embarrassing situations or situations in which they have experienced or may experience shame. Repression has more serious consequences for the psychological adjustment and well-being of the individual than does the defense mechanism of denial. In using denial people merely disclaim their embarrassment at the moment they experience shame, but this does not preclude their thinking about or working through the situation at a later time. In using the mechanism of repression people deny themselves the possibility of thinking through the situation and making self-repair, "restitutions within the domain of the self, i.e., some narcissistic affirmation" (Lewis, 1971, p. 89).

The effort to repair and strengthen the self after experiencing intense shame often continues for several days or weeks. Even months, and in some cases years, after an intensely embarrassing situation an individual may recall the situation and rehearse techniques for coping with it. Through such rehearsal in fantasy and imagination the individual may develop many interpersonal techniques for coping with situations or conditions likely to elicit shame. When Rafe meets such a situation in the future he can practice the technique he has rehearsed in fantasy and then rehearse again and adjust the technique if necessary. These processes can lead to a sense of adequacy and enhance self-identity.

A third ego defense mechanism that the individual may use as a shame defense is affirmation of the self. If Rebecca uses this defense she will respond to shame by affirming some aspect of her self that may be totally unrelated to the shame situation. In other instances she may affirm the aspect of herself that has been criticized. Thus if she is frequently embarrassed because of her short stature she may respond to shame either by developing mental abilities that distract attention from her physique or by developing special motor skills that enhance her physical attractiveness and compensate for her short height.

There are many and diverse ways that the individual can use the defense of self-affirmation. A young man may cover his shame over his ineptness or inexperience in heterosexual situations by talking of his adventures with the opposite sex, embellishing or fabricating the events to suit his needs. A young woman continually frustrated in heterosexual situations may capitalize on her scholastic abilities and largely displace her heterosexual life with intellectual pursuits that gain the favor of her parents and professors and the admiration of other academically oriented students (one of whom may fall in love with her).

According to Lewis, the most radical ego defense against shame is the affective disorder of depression. In Lewis's theory the depression results from "undischarged shame." Thus if a person frequently experiences shame, especially intense shame or humiliation, and is incapable of responding effectively or of using one of the more adaptive ego defense mechanisms (denial, self-affirmation), then the individual is likely to experience distress, inner-directed hostility, fear, and guilt—the emotion components of depression (Izard, 1972). Although there are frequently external causes, particularly external precipitating events, depression, like shame, is typically about the self, self-centered. The individual feels personally dejected, unworthy, incapable, and generally miserable. In depression, as in shame, the fault is generally considered to be personal and self-related and as a result there is typically self-blame. In depression, as in shame, the fault or the defect is not easily rationalized or justified. Lewis (1971) has suggested that women are more prone to shame than are men. She interpreted this as consistent with the fact that women are more field dependent and more prone to depression.

The Development of Shame and Shyness in the Child

Shame often occurs in the context of emotional relationships, in situations where at least some emotion is invested. Social situations that elicit shame are ones in which the individual is responsive to the emotions, attitudes, opinions, and actions of others. Thus, it is highly important to examine the origin and development of shame in the infant and child for whom emotional relationships are pervasive and dominant. Every adult has at some time seen shame on the face of a young child, or shyness in the behavior of the toddler. Often a friendly effort to get acquainted with Rebecca the toddler, even a simple inquiry as to her name, will cause her to avert her gaze, lower her head, and curl up in her mother's lap, or cling tightly to her.

A few years later she may blush in shame and respond shyly to the praise or compliment of an adult. This kind of situation is beautifully illustrated in the story *Jonathan Livingston Seagull* (Bach, 1970). Jonathan was no ordinary seagull. His adventuresome experience and love of learning had enabled him to develop flying skills that had brought him to a new planet where he lived among a species of telepathic gulls with extraordinary flying abilities. After the elder gull, Chiang, had just taught Jonathan to fly anywhere and anytime at perfect speed, he received the congratulations of other members of this special species of gull. They were telling him how he flew with such grace and speed:

> He stood their congratulations for less than a minute. "I'm the newcomer here! I'm just beginning! It is I who must learn from you!"
> "I wonder about that, Jon," said Sullivan, standing near. "You have less fear of learning than any gull I've seen in ten thousand years." The flock fell silent, and Jonathan fidgeted in embarrassment. (p. 60)

Biogenetic Factors

Shame, like each of the other fundamental emotions, depends upon a particular neurochemical process. The mechanisms involved in this process are subject to the same genetic laws that control other structural and behavioral characteristics. As with other emotions, little is known about the specifics of the genetic transmission of the shame mechanism. A cross-cultural study by Blurton Jones and Konner (1973) suggests that there are genetically determined sex differences in the shame threshold or the tendency to experience shame. This inference is based on their finding that boys received significantly higher scores than girls on several indexes of sociability.

Sociocultural Factors

Although sex-linked genes may influence the tendency to experience shame, the individual's social milieu and culture constitute other important determinants of the shame threshold. Each culture and subculture transmits certain norms or rules, the violation of which may lead to shame. Some aspects of the socialization of shame will be considered in the next section. This section will focus primarily on some findings from cross-cultural research on attitudes toward shame. These findings illustrate some differences between cultures that probably originate from cultural differences in child-rearing practices, and the child–adult and child–child interactions that constitute the socialization process. The data to be discussed were obtained by administration of the *Emotion Attitude Questionnaire* (EAQ) (Izard, 1971) to groups of American, English, German, Swedish, French, Swiss, Greek, and Japanese college students. The seven cultural samples varied in size from 41 to 153. Prior to the administration of the EAQ, the students had taken the *Emotion Recognition Test* and thus were familiar with photographs representing each of the fundamental emotions and with the names and definitions of the emotions.

EAQ question 1 asked: "Which emotion do you understand best?" Considering the average percentages of subjects from all cultures selecting each emotion, joy, as expected, was chosen more frequently than any other emotion, and not surprisingly shame was chosen less frequently than any other emotion. There are several reasons for the generally low frequency with which individuals indicated that shame was the best-understood emotion. The shame face tends to hide itself and the experience of shame elicits a tendency toward concealment and isolation. It is a threat to the self-concept (or ego) to be seen with a look of shame on the face, particularly during adolescent years when the self- and body-image are relatively more vulnerable (at least in most cultures). In the socialization process children are taught to hide their shame. These factors lead to a great reluctance to admit to the experience of shame, much less to reflect upon it and try to understand it. In addition to these forces, the experience of shame tends to hamper logical thought and frequently there is little meaningful cognitive content accompanying the shame experience. This too makes it difficult for us to reflect upon and analyze and understand the shame experience.

In comparing the responses across cultures it was found that a larger percentage of the Greeks than of any other cultural group indicated that they understood shame better than any other emotion. For Greek men, there were 29% who indicated that shame was the best-understood emotion, and this figure is two standard deviations larger than the mean frequency for all cultures. There is no specific evidence as to why the Greeks deviated in this way. It is generally agreed by psychological and anthropological observers that the Greeks are relatively high on sociability and emotion expressiveness, especially Greek males. Enjoyment and self-confidence in social situations reduce the sources of shame.

The second EAQ question was: "Which emotion do you understand the least?" In answering this question far more Japanese than any other cultural group selected the emotion of shame. The percentage for Japanese males was 68, two standard deviations higher than the average frequency for the eight cultures considered together. The next highest frequency, that of Swedish males, was 40%. There is strong evidence that shame is a highly important emotion in the Japanese culture (Benedict, 1946), especially in the Japanese culture prior to the influx of Western influence. An act bringing shame upon the self, or more importantly, upon one's family and the Japanese society was perhaps the greatest of indignities. In these earlier times shame must have been considered a highly intolerable emotion. Zimbardo *et al.* reported that nearly two-thirds of their Japanese sample considered themselves as shy and that unlike Americans they spontaneously mentioned positive consequences of shyness. Since the EAQ data suggest that a strong negative attitude toward shame continues to prevail in Japan, it seems likely that the Japanese distinguish between shame, which may be a mortifying experience, and shyness as a trait, which may be associated with an appealing modesty.

The third question of the EAQ asked: "Which emotion do you dread the most?" Here again the responses of the Japanese are quite distinct from the Western cultures, including the Greeks. Seventy-two percent of the Japanese males and 69% of the females indicated that contempt was the most dreaded of all the emotions. Both these figures are more than two standard deviations greater than the average frequency for the eight cultural samples combined. The data from the previous EAQ questions, as well as the interpretation of the Japanese psychologist who collaborated in this research, indicated that the Japanese students interpreted this question to mean "what emotion expression from other people do you dread the most?" The use of the look of contempt to elicit shame is well-known in Eastern and Western cultures, but apparently the look of contempt is generally considered an adequate cause for shame by virtually all of the Japanese. Thus for the Japanese, being looked upon with contempt is equivalent to being found in a shameful condition or situation. In the days of the samurai the look of contempt was an unbearable stimulus. When a samurai was looked upon with contempt he had but two alternatives: to kill the person who held him in contempt, or to kill himself.

Marsella, Murray, and Golden (1977) used the semantic differential technique (Osgood, Suci, & Tannenbaum, 1957) to study ethnic variations among Hawaiian students in their attitudes toward shame and other emotions. The subjects rated the emotions on semantic scales such as low–high and good–bad. They found that Caucasian-Americans rated shame "more low, weak, and dull" than Chinese Americans and Japanese-Americans. One of the authors' tentative conclusions was that shame was less clearly identifiable and understood by the Caucasian-Americans.

There are many more cultural differences in the experiencing and expression of shame than we have touched upon here. It is reasonable to assume that the differences discussed in the foregoing paragraphs reflect real differences in shame thresholds and in the antecedents and consequences of the shame experience and shame expression. Although the data did not always justify clear explanations of the observed cross-cultural and sex–cultural differences they did clearly demonstrate that these differences exist.

The Socialization of Shame and Shyness

The healthy child is curious and active. A wide variety of things interest the child and prove possible sources of enjoyment. The young child's low threshold for excitement and for excitement-generated activity leads to a kind of natural self-expression or self-extension, often channeled into exploratory behavior. However, the child's excited response to a wide variety of stimuli will inevitably generate behavior that will be seen by parents, other adults, or other children as inappropriate or wrong. From children's vantage point they are not really indecorous; they are merely indulging in natural self-expression, yet they are shamed. Children's great capacity for excitement and joy and the activity that these emotions generate greatly increases the range of possibilities for censurable behavior. The importance of a positive and nonpunitive socialization of shame is evident.

The socialization of shame is made difficult by the fact that shame is paradoxical. The experience of shame confronts the individual with puzzling contradictions; for example, it can facilitate both conformity and autonomy. The socialization of shame proceeds as the result of a series of confrontations of differences that range from trivial matters to serious conflict.

If Tomkins is correct in assuming that the infant can experience shame as soon as he or she can differentiate the face of the mother from the face of a stranger, then the infant is vulnerable to shame by the age of four or five months. During the first half-year of life, it is the human face that has provided the infant the greatest source of excitement and joy. For about half of this time (about two to five months) the human face, any human face, is an innate releaser of the smile of joy on the face of the infant. Yet, paradoxically, face-to-face encounters that once elicited only joy become the principal context for shame experiences, and one of the immediate effects of the shame response is to reduce face-to-face communication.

Another shame paradox is the nature of the association of excitement and joy with the activation and experience of shame. People experience shame in a way that focuses attention on the self. According to Tomkins, experiencing some level of interest or enjoyment is a necessary precondition for the activation of shame. Yet when the experience of shame is felt, it sharply inhibits the continuation of interest or enjoyment.

The potential for experiencing shame begins very early in life and continues until death. In childhood a continual source of excitement and joy comes from efforts to please parents and win their praise and approval. Often the effort to please is itself exciting and enjoyable for the child. But if the child's effort to please meets with disapproval and reprimand, interest in the activity decreases and shame is likely to result.

Over the years the child Rebecca develops, through observation of her parents and other loved or admired people, an ideal self-image or the image of an ideal self (self-ideal). Unlike her parents her self-ideal is always present, and the self-ideal typically "incorporates," or is greatly influenced by one's concepts of one's parents. The greater the distance between Rebecca's real self-concept and her self-ideal the more likely she will experience shame as she fails to live up to her self-ideal. Similarly, the more intensely she desires to live up to her self-ideal, the more vulnerable she is to failure and resulting shame and the more likely the shame will be intense.

Another of the shame paradoxes is the link between the shame experience (the phenomenon of experiencing shame) and the development of emotional ties. As already noted, shame is most likely to occur and is most likely to be intense when it happens in the context of an emotional or meaningful relationship. Yet when shame occurs, it temporarily destroys or greatly hampers social communication and interpersonal contact. We like to look at the person whom we love or admire, and in turn we like to have them look at us. But when shame occurs it is certain to reduce facial and social communication. One of the defenses against shame is to hold the head stiffly high and to look upon others with contempt, an emotion that depersonalizes, creates social distances, and degrades interpersonal relations. The false contempt only increases the feeling that we are wrong, defeated, and in a sense isolated while we are actually in the presence of the very people we care about. It is unfortunate that one of the most frequently used techniques for avoiding shame and for developing a higher shame threshold is to fantasize triumph over the source of shame. One can readily see the double jeopardy in the overused "shame-on-you" technique by parents and teachers of the young. The fantasy of triumph is sometimes realized by bringing defeat and shame to the one who did the shaming.

Shame, Self-Development, and Self-Improvement. The conditions and situations that elicit shame are as variable as individuals and self-concepts. This makes the understanding of the socializations of shame extremely difficult. Another complication in the understanding of shame socialization is the fact that there are often delayed and indirect consequences of having been shamed. Probably by the time one reaches late childhood one can sometimes postpone an emotion experience until some time after the emotion-eliciting stimulus has passed. This cannot be so for shame. It is extremely difficult, if not impossible, to postpone the experience of shame. The fact that shame is difficult to hide and virtually impossible to postpone means that it is very likely that others will see it. But as we recall our shame we may be motivated to behave in various ways as a result of having been shamed. We may also be motivated to do certain things in order to avoid future shame. Another reason why it is difficult to understand shame socialization is the fact that a person may feel shame for many things and on many occasions when no one was really being critical or attempting to cause shame. The dynamics of shame socialization involve the complex interactions of the attitudes, values, and opinions of others with a particular personality or self-concept.

We have already noted that one of the functions of shame and shame-avoidance is to foster the development of a strong, autonomous, independent self. However, shame cannot function in this way for a child who has suffered a punitive socialization of the shame experience itself. If the child Rafe is punished for being embarrassed and showing shame, or if he is often made to feel ashamed, he may develop a general distrust and fear of other people. His exaggerated efforts to avoid shame may cause him to insulate himself against all emotion, at least insofar as possible, and thereby become highly rigid and restricted. If this happens his subsequent shame experiences are likely to be intense and to render him completely inept and incapable of dealing with the situation. On the other hand, if when Rafe experiences shame his parents are encouraging and attempt to teach him techniques for coping with the situation or condition that elicits shame, he will not only develop effective shame-avoidant techniques but also a stronger, less vulnerable self. Trust in his parents will grow and this trust will very likely generalize to other people. The repeated experience of parental help in coping with shame and shame-eliciting situations tends to increase his willingness and ability to offer sympathy and help to others. According to Tomkins, the positive socialization of shame leads not only to increased cooperativeness and sympathy but to an "increased willingness and ability to offer help to the self, the generation of resonance to the idea of progress, the development of physical courage, the development of shame tolerance in problem solving, to individuation and the achievement of identity" (see Tomkins, 1963, pp. 313–317).

The intensive manner in which shame brings the self into focal awareness has several important psychological consequences. One knows immediately the effect of experiencing some aspect of one's self in a highly intense fashion. Shame creates a psychological instability in which the self-as-self and the self-as-object are intermixed. The "ego-boundary" or self-boundary is more permeable. The instability and permeability of the self in shame provides strong motivation for the individual to want to know the self and the boundaries of the self. And every child needs to learn the nature and limits of the self for which he or she will be responsible. Thus one of the positive functions of shame is to increase self-knowledge—to facilitate the realization of the ancient adage, "know thyself."

Shame and Sexual Development. Everyone is familiar with the association between the emotions of shame, shyness, and guilt on the one hand, and sex characteristics and sexual behavior on the other. This strong association holds to a greater or lesser degree in most cultures of both Western and Eastern civilizations. There are, of course, many cultural variations with regard to what sex-linked features or what sexual behavior elicits shame or pride. Despite these variations the evidence from folklore, literature, and anthropology strongly support the notion that those features which identify the individual as male or female are, under certain conditions, sources of shame or pride. Likewise, in virtually every society that has been studied by social scientists, there are some aspects of sexual behavior that elicit shame, shyness, or guilt, and, similarly, certain types of sexual behavior which are sources of pride and self-confidence.

There are several reasons for the strong and prevalent relationship between shame and sex. The highly intimate and emotional character of the sexual relationship makes it a fertile ground for shame and shyness. Any interruption of the excitement and joy that are so much a part of healthy sexual relationships can activate shame and shyness. This is undoubtedly one of the basic reasons why in virtually all societies, except under unusual conditions where sex is exploited, sexual intercourse occurs in privacy.

The widespread use of privacy for sexual intercourse testifies to its intimate and self-revealing character. The persons engaging in sexual intercourse typically feel that they are exposing themselves fully. The persons not only reveal their bodies physically, they reveal themselves. Many more self-revealing and personally relevant statements are made in sexually intimate encounters than in ordinary conversation. Because of the emotional, highly intimate, and self-revealing nature of the sexual relationship some degree of shyness and modesty usually obtains even when both participants are completely free of guilt.

The character of the sexual relationship is one of the reasons why the external genital organs are covered and kept from public view in virtually all human societies. Even in preliterate cultures where people are scantily clothed the sex organs are more often covered than any other part of the body. In some preliterate groups the only clothing used is that which covers the sex organs.

As already noted, the emotion of shame is used as a means of controlling open sexual competition and sexual aggression. One way in which shame accomplishes this purpose is through its effect on the individual's habits of dress (concealment of the sex organs). Open sex competition and aggression among like-sex individuals over opposite-sex individuals could not only lead to defeat and disgrace on an individual basis, but could render an entire group or society more vulnerable to defeat and disgrace as a function of the lack of harmony and cooperation.

An even more fundamental problem than the shame–sex bond is the question of the origin of the relationship between shame and intimacy. The origin of the shame–intimacy bond may have its foundation in the mother–infant relationship. The relationship between mother and infant is close, intense, and intimate. It is replete with face-to-face contact and face-to-face communication. In these face-to-face communications infants extend themselves, expose themselves, and give of themselves openly and freely. It may well be that infants' first experiences of shame are activated on an occasion when they think they are beginning another intense and intimate encounter with the beloved face of the mother and the face turns out to be that of a stranger. The interruption, interference, and partial attenuation of the infant's excitement and joy leads to shame.

Childrens' low threshold for interest–excitement and consequent exploratory activity almost inevitably lead them to visual and tactual exploration of their sex organs. It is also quite common for the young child to attempt to explore the sex organs of a member of the opposite sex. To the extent that such exploratory behavior is punished, the bond between shame and sexual activity is strengthened. In extreme cases, sexual activity or even the anticipation of sexual activity can evoke such intense shame as to inhibit and virtually destroy the individual's sexual life.

The older child and adolescent is faced with another shame–sex paradox. For a girl or boy to develop an appropriate sex identity he or she needs to be proud of his or her sexual development and of those characteristics which are biologically or culturally associated with membership in his or her sex. Yet display of sex organs is forbidden and the display rules governing secondary sexual characteristics are more or less strict in various cultures and subcultures. Most children at one time or another feel some shame about one or another of their sexual characteristics. Child-rearing practices and peer relationships can have very important influences on personality or self-development during those stages of life when the child and adolescent are highly sensitive about the status of their sexual characteristics.

The complex and long-lasting processes of personality development make it clear that primary and secondary sex characteristics are only one set of the determinants that influence femininity and masculinity. For example, a girl may develop highly adequate sex-pride and sex-identity on the basis of pride in her hair, her eyes, her voice, her face, her legs, her breasts, or her general good looks. A buxom woman may be very unfeminine, and a young man with a high-pitched voice and small penis may be a tiger on the football field and completely adequate in his sexual relationships.

Intimacy, Eye-Contact, and Shame. If the mother–infant relationship is the origin of intimacy and the shame–intimacy bond, so too it is probably the origin of the intimacy and personal involvement associated with extended gazing at another person's eyes. Mother and infant spend many hours gazing into each other's eyes. Indeed, facial expression and visual contact constitute the very basis for this primal social relationship. It is highly reasonable to assume that the mother–infant relationship, perhaps combined with certain genetic tendencies, create the bond between eye-contact and feelings of involvement and intimacy. The self-involving and intimacy-facilitating functions of eye-contact make this interpersonal phe-nomenon a likely determinant of shame or shyness.

The relationship between eye contact and intimacy has a component of sensory pleasure. Mother–infant face-to-face communication and eye con-tact occur in the context of nursing, cuddling, fondling, as well as in the context of the emotions of excitement and joy. The association between eye contact and sensual pleasure may take on a more or less specific sexual connotation. It is probably the connotation of personal involvement and sexual intimacy that led to the widespread taboo on extended eye-contact between nonintimates.

The observations and research of psychologists support the idea of a close relationship between eye contact and intimacy. Simmel (1921) spoke of eye contact as the most perfect reciprocity in human relationships. Heider (1958) and Tomkins (1963) have maintained that eye contact pro-vides a vehicle for a very special kind of communion between persons. Rubin (1970) showed that couples who are deeply in love spend more time gazing into each others' eyes than couples who are not so much in love. Ellsworth and Ludwig (1972) reviewed the evidence relating to eye contact and social interaction and concluded that while eye contact is not necessar-ily positively associated with interpersonal attraction, it always indicates interpersonal involvement.

As already noted, it is quite possible that individuals may have ambiva-lence about eye contact or that eye contact may generate either positive or negative feelings depending upon the persons and the situation. Experi-ments by Ellsworth and Carlsmith (1968) and Ludwig and Ellsworth (1974) showed that interviewers seeking personal information or providing poten-tially negative evaluations are liked better by the interviewees when they do not look directly into the eyes of the respondent. In the first of these experiments Ellsworth and Carlsmith reported that the interviewer elicited relatively more personal references when she averted her gaze. The investi-gators concluded that eye contact may inhibit rather than facilitate intimacy and self-disclosure when the individual is made to feel uncomfortable or vulnerable—the conditions that we have already described as those in which shame is most likely to occur. Another study showing a connection between eye contact and shame was reported by Exline, Gray, and Schuette (1965). They found that subjects avoid eye contact when answer-ing personal or potentially embarrassing questions.

Verbal self-disclosure in the adolescent or adult may be viewed as an extension of the infant's and child's self-expression, self-extension, and self-exposure discussed earlier. Thus the extent to which Rafe engages in self-disclosure may be a function of his feelings of shame or of his anticipation of being shamed as he is in the process of extending or exposing himself to another person.

Ellsworth and Ross (1974) conducted an experiment designed to evaluate the influence of a listener's eye contact or visual behavior on a speaker's self-disclosure. The study is reviewed here, on the assumption that self-disclosure is behavior controlled in large part by the emotion of shame or the anticipation of this emotion. Ellsworth and Ross wanted to uncover some of the psychological processes that mediate the relationship between visual behavior and verbal intimacy. The subjects participated in the study with the belief that they were engaging in an experiment that was evaluating certain aspects of encounter groups. Male and female subjects were given instructions that encouraged them to make personally revealing statements in a five-minute monologue addressed to a same-sex listener. The listener had been previously instructed to follow one of four styles of eye contact: (a) continuous direct gaze, (b) direct gaze contingent upon intimate statements, (c) continuous gaze aversion, or (d) gaze aversion contingent upon intimate statements. The subject who participated as the speaker, the listener, and a "blind" observer rated the intimacy of the speaker's monologue. The results were different for females and males. For the females, the direct gaze into the eyes, whether constant or contingent upon a personally revealing statement, promoted intimacy between the female speaker and the female listener. Gaze avoidance had the opposite effect. The female speakers' ratings of the amount of direct eye contact received correlated positively and significantly with their ratings of feelings of satisfaction with the experimental task ($r = .43$), their liking for the listener ($r = .77$), and with their perception of being liked by the listener ($r = .53$). For the male speakers who were talking to male listeners, direct gaze appeared to foster reticence and gaze avoidance tended to promote intimacy.

The Interactions of Shame with Social Behavior and Other Affects

Shame has an important role in social interactions and the development of social life. It has significant interactions with the sex drive and certain of the discrete emotions.

Shame, Sociability, and Conformity. Shame is used to develop and maintain conformity to the group's norms; shaming techniques are most readily observed when there is the need to inhibit or regulate deviations from the norm. Shame also promotes sociality by acting as a restraint on self-centeredness or egotism and thus fostering the investment of positive emotions in others and in relationships with others. At the same time, conformity and the sense of belongingness increase people's self-confidence and security and render them less vulnerable to shame. Paradoxically, the greater their identification with the group and the stronger their sense of belongingness the more vulnerable they are to the censure of the group and the more likely will their behavior be influenced by the anticipation of possible shame and by shame-avoidance strategies and techniques.

Shame and the Sex Drive. In the foregoing discussion of the socialization of shame it was pointed out that there is usually a relationship between shame and intimacy and that often intimacy has a sensual or directly sexual connotation. It is not at all surprising, then, that there would be important interactions between the emotions of shame and shyness and the sex drive. Mild degrees of shyness are often perceived as attractive and even as sexually exciting. The maintenance of some degree of shyness or modesty may be quite important in maintaining and enhancing long-lasting sexual relationships.

Of course, sexual intercourse within the context of a love relationship should be relatively free of shame, shyness, guilt, or any of the negative emotions. But of all the negative emotions, shyness is the most pleasant and probably the most tolerable during sexual intimacy. A mild shame or shyness during the moments of sexual intimacy, especially in the developing stages of the sexual relationship of two people who are in love with each other, may serve by virtue of a contrast effect, to heighten the excitement, joy, and sensual pleasure of the sex experience. Of course if shame or shyness is sufficiently intense the sex drive will be inhibited and sexual relations will be devoid of excitement, if not impossible. The child who is excessively shamed for sexual exploration may never be able to enjoy sexual relations without shame. In severe cases, sexual life will be destroyed.

It is quite common for children at some stages of their development to feel both affection and tenderness on the one hand and sexual stimulation on the other in relation to the parent of the opposite sex. This is the context for the problems which Freud described as the Oedipus complex. According to Freud the key emotion in the development and maintenance of the Oedipus complex is fear. Tomkins maintains that the common difficulty in feeling tenderness and lust toward the same person (the condition characterizing the Oedipus complex) is a consequence of shaming children rather than the consequence of frightening them.

In a study of sexual standards, sexual experience, and emotion responses to imaging (visualizing) sexual intercourse (Izard, Spiegel, Alessio, & Kotsch, 1974), an analysis of DES trait scores showed that males experienced more shyness in their day-to-day lives than did females. This tends to disconfirm the hypothesis of Lewis (1971) that women are more prone to shame and shyness than are men. However, on the DES that measured state-shyness immediately after visualizing sexual intercourse, women reported more shyness than men. The virgin women reported significantly more shyness than the nonvirgins, and the difference here was quite substantial. With regard to sex standards, women who believed in coitus without affection reported substantially more shyness subsequent to imaging the sexual scene than did men who believed in coitus without affection.

Fear, shame, and shyness may play important roles in sexual adjustment. Homosexuality may be, at least in part, a result of one's susceptibility to fear and intense shame as one anticipates and approaches sexual relations with members of the opposite sex. The emotion dynamics of a homosexual in psychotherapy were discussed by Izard (1972). The DES emotion profile for this patient showed extremely high scores on both fear and shyness. He was described clinically as a "highly anxious" individual.

The clinical concept of "anxiety" often includes a component of shyness, in addition to fear, distress, and guilt. Shyness is also an emotion component of some forms of depression. A study of depressive patients by Marshall and Izard (1972b) showed that shyness was one of the more important emotions in the emotion profile of depressive patients. Distress, inner-directed anger (hostility), and fear were the three emotions receiving the highest scores, while shyness and guilt were next in order of magnitude.

Shame Interactions with Other Emotions. Everyday experience, theoretical considerations, and the analysis of the DES profile in the shame–shyness situation indicate that shame is often experienced at the same time as other affects. As with other emotions, the experiencing of shame concomitantly with drives and other emotions results in the development of associations or bonds between shame and other affects. In this way shame may become an activator of other emotions and other emotions may come to activate shame. Similarly, shame may serve in some way to defend the individual against other emotions and other emotions may be used as anticipatory defenses or methods of coping with shame. The interactions of shame with interest, joy, distress, anger, and fear were discussed in previous chapters.

Tomkins thinks that shame and contempt rarely exist separately. Contempt from another or from the self is an activator of the shame experience. Under certain conditions shame can be reduced by self-contempt, by a rejection of that aspect of the self of which one is ashamed. However, at the same time the more the individual is invested in that part of the self that caused shame and the stronger the wish not to lose that part of one's self, the more likely will the self-contempt that rejects that aspect of the self lead to shame (Tomkins, 1963).

Summary

Shame, shyness, and guilt may have common neurophysiological substrates but they are not the same in consciousness. Factor-analytic studies with the DES have yielded two independent factors, one corresponding to shame and shyness and the other to guilt. Shame and shyness have often been used interchangeably in the literature and they have not been differentiated empirically. Shame and shyness are used more or less interchangeably in this chapter, and guilt will be treated separately in the next.

A large majority of young Americans report that they were shy at some time during their lives. Even a greater percentage of Japanese students report shyness as a personal characteristic.

Shame is expressed by lowering or turning the head, averting the gaze, lowering of the eyelids, and blushing. Blushing often emphasizes the shame experience by calling further attention to the face. People also report physiological reactions that suggest sympathetic arousal in the shame–shyness experience, but these do not distinguish shame from other emotions that are accompanied by sympathetic arousal.

The shame experience begins with a sudden and intense heightening of awareness of the self. Awareness of the self so dominates consciousness that cognitive processes are sharply inhibited, causing a loss of presence of mind and increasing the likelihood of stammering inappropriately and coping clumsily. Shame typically occurs in the presence of other people who play some role in activating the shame, but shame can occur in privacy. Self-consciousness, concern over the impression one makes, and concern over social evaluation are frequent in shy people. There is a tendency for shame to make the self seem small, helpless, and inept, and to generate a feeling of defeat or failure. Paradoxically, shame sometimes occurs after a positive and complimentary evaluation by others.

Situations that elicit shyness are likely to activate interest or fear. Shyness is characterized by a relatively high degree of tension and impulsiveness, but it is characterized by a significantly greater degree of pleasantness than any of the other negative emotions.

At the neurological level, shame often is activated by the partial reduction of the neural activity of the ongoing emotion of either interest–excitement or enjoyment–joy. At the psychological level, shame may be activated by any situation which focuses attention on the self or some aspect of the self that is found wanting. Any experience that gives one the feeling of inappropriate self-disclosure can elicit shame. The prototypical shame experience probably occurs when the infant mistakenly makes "familiar" overtures to an unfamiliar face. In later life, failure to live up to one's self-ideal may constitute a pervasive source of shame.

Shame has two functions that suggest its role in evolution. It sensitizes the individual to the opinions and feelings of others and thus facilitates a degree of social conformity and social responsibility. Shame may also play a role in regulating sexual life and in facilitating the development of skills and competencies.

Shame increases the permeability of the boundaries of the self. At the same time it may play a significant role in the development of self-control and autonomy. Confronting and transcending shame can increase the sense of personal identity and freedom.

People use the defense mechanisms of denial, repression, and affirmation of self in dealing with shame. Frequently experienced shame that is not dealt with effectively can lead to distress and depression.

Attitudes toward shame very widely across cultures and these differences in attitude lead to different methods of socializing this emotion. Children's interest-instigated activities lead them into shame eliciting situations. Parental handling of shame experiences in young children require sensitive attention since shame tends to hamper social communication and interpersonal contact. It is difficult to deal effectively with an emotion that tends to reduce facial and social communication.

Properly dealt with, shame can play a positive role in self-development and self-improvement. Since it calls attention to the self or some aspect of the self, reflection on the shame experience can increase self-knowledge.

The highly intimate and emotional character of the sexual relationship makes it a fertile ground for shame and shyness. Sexual intercourse leads to self-exposure and self-exposure may be a precursor of shame.

An early source of the shame–sex interaction comes from children being caught unawares while exploring their sexual organs. Shame is readily elicited during periods when sexual organs and secondary sexual characteristics are developing.

The mother–infant relationship is probably the origin of the shame–intimacy relationship and of the relationship between eye contact and personal involvement or intimacy. The association between eye contact, intimacy, and sensual pleasure is probably the source of the widespread taboo on extended eye contact between nonintimates.

Shame has important interactions with social behavior and other affects. It plays a role in the development of sociality. Under favorable circumstances, some degree of shyness or modesty may enhance sexual relationships but under less favorable conditions, it can inhibit or destroy them. Shame interactions with interest, joy, distress, anger, and fear were discussed in previous chapters. Here it was noted that contempt was often an activator of shame, and that the contempt may be from self as well as from others.

Shame–shyness has unique motivational–experiential characteristics and the shame experience or the trait of shyness can be of great significance to the individual and to society.

16

GUILT, CONSCIENCE, AND MORALITY

> One important point with regard to morality should not be forgotten: unless it has a fervor of emotion, unless it is touched with spiritual warmth, it is nothing but formal rectitude. True morality, like beauty, needs more than intellect. It includes a feeling of good will for others that is warmed by an inner fire. (Sinnott, 1966, pp. 181–182)

Perhaps all of the emotions play some part, directly or indirectly, in the development of conscience and morality. Fear, anger, and shame are likely to emerge if harsh physical punishment is used in teaching right–wrong discriminations. Excitement and joy in caring for and helping others, especially when no reciprocation can be expected, may characterize the mature conscience and the highest form of moral behavior. Nevertheless, guilt is the emotion most essential to the development of the affective–cognitive structures of conscience and the affective–cognitive–action patterns of moral behavior.

In differential emotions theory guilt is considered a fundamental emotion, which emerged, like other fundamental emotions, through evolutionary-biological processes. The experience of guilt, like the experience of fear, is unlearned. As with fear, there are some innate activators or natural clues for guilt that operate under minimally favorable sociocultural conditions. In addition to the natural clues to guilt, each culture and each institution (e.g., family, religious organization) concerned with human ethics and morals prescribes certain standards of conduct and attempts to teach them to growing children. These prescriptions (moral and ethical principles) constitute the cognitive component of conscience. In the mature conscience they are linked with emotion to form affective–cognitive structures that guide the actions we call moral and ethical behavior. The compelling fact that makes guilt rather than fear the chief affect in conscience is this: The experience of guilt binds the person to the source of guilt and does not subside without reconciliation that tends to restore social harmony. Fear motivates escape from the source and subsides at a safe distance from threat of harm. The balance between fear–escape-behavior and guilt–responsible-actions provides an index of the maturity of conscience and conduct. The feeling of responsibility, the central guilt–cognition orientation in conscience, facilitates behavior that minimizes intense experiential guilt.

Since shame and guilt are in some respects closely related, one of our concerns in this chapter will be to compare the two emotions and thus point up the distinct features of each. People usually find it easy to tell the difference between these two emotions in their personal experiences, but they may not find it easy to describe the differences in or be aware of all the different effects of them.

Characteristics and Functions of Guilt

There are good reasons for people confusing shame and guilt or failing to distinguish clearly between them. The two emotions are often experienced in the same or similar situations. Both emotions tend to make people want to conceal something or to set something right, but as we shall see, what one wants to conceal or set right is quite different in shame and guilt.

The Determinants of Guilt

Eibl-Eibesfeldt (1971) argues that there is a biological basis for the development of ethical norms, and in agreement with differential emotions theory, he implies that there is a genetic basis for the subsequent development of a sense of personal responsibility and guilt. Ausubel (1955) does not directly endorse a biogenetic mechanism for guilt but he believes that it is so basically human and so fundamental to the development and maintenance of social norms that it will develop in all cultures if conditions are even minimally favorable. He hypothesizes three psychological conditions that are essential for the development of guilt: (a) acceptance of moral values (b) internalization of a sense of moral obligation to abide by these values, (c) a sufficiently self-critical ability to perceive discrepancies between actual behavior and internalized values.

Ausubel (1955) holds that there are some uniformities across cultures in the acquisition of guilt and guilt-related behavior. These uniformities stem from (a) basic aspects of parent–child relationships, (b) minimum cultural need for the socialization of children, and (c) certain trends or stages in cognitive and social growth. The single most important basis for the development of conscience and guilt, according to Ausubel, is the powerful need for parents and society to develop a sense of responsibility in growing children.

The phenomenological determinants of guilt are perhaps easier to explain than the determinants of any of the other negative emotions. Guilt results from wrongdoing. The behavior that evokes guilt violates a moral, ethical, or religious code. Usually people feel guilty when they become aware that they have broken a rule and violated their own standards or beliefs. They may also feel guilty for failing to accept or carry out their responsibility. Guilt, like all the other emotions, has a great deal of generality. Since it is associated with behavior in the broad sphere of morality, ethics, and religion, the causes of guilt vary widely from individual to individual, from one ethnic group to another, and from culture to culture. Some people may feel guilty over eating meat on Friday, others over eating meat any time, and yet others may not have any concern over eating meat or any other edible substance at any time. Some people may feel guilt when they do not work hard enough to meet standards set by themselves, their parents, or their reference group (primary social group), while others may feel guilty for being so preoccupied with their work that they do not take sufficient time to enjoy their family and friends.

Misconduct can also cause shame, but in this case the deed need not be wrong except in the sense of being misfitting, inept, or inappropriate. If we should feel shame because of moral, ethical, or religious misconduct, it would probably be because others observed our deed and have knowledge of it. The shame would then be a result of the heightened self-consciousness brought about this time by others' observations of the misconduct.

In contrast to guilt, shame can result from actions that have no implications for moral, ethical, or religious codes. This is what Ausubel (1955) calls "nonmoral shame." In his view "moral shame" follows from the negative moral judgment of others about actions not necessarily immoral in the eyes of the offender. Moral shame also occurs in association with guilt when one violates a moral standard and then images the censure of others. He holds that shame always involves external sanctions, either overtly expressed by others or imaged by the individual. Guilt, on the other hand, includes self-reactions that are independent of the judgment of other people. These self-reactions include self-reproach, lowered self-esteem, remorse, and in Ausubel's view a special type of moral shame.

It should be noted that the feeling of guilt is not dependent upon one's belief and adherence to written or explicit moral, ethical, or religious codes. The codes may be implicit and accepted intuitively. Almost everyone has an ethical framework which guides his interpersonal and social behavior, but very few people carry the structure and details of this framework in consciousness all the time.

Guilt occurs in situations in which one feels personally responsible. There is a strong relationship between one's sense of personal responsibility and one's threshold for guilt. Shame is most frequently evoked by the actions of other people. Guilt comes from one's own acts or one's failure to act. It should be emphasized that guilt may occur as readily and as frequently from omission as from commission, from failure to feel or think or act in a certain way at a certain time, as well as from actual feelings, thoughts, or acts that violate moral codes or beliefs.

While the feeling of guilt, like that of the other emotions, is the same the world over, the causes and consequences vary widely from individual to individual and from culture to culture. However, there are some spheres in which the misconduct–guilt relationship is virtually pancultural. There are few if any cultures in which violation of strictly held sexual taboos (e.g., incest) would fail to elicit guilt. The same is true for the act of murder especially of a member of one's own family or group. In addition to these extreme types of misconduct, all cultures have some moral and ethical standards relating to other sexual and aggressive acts. For this reason guilt is probably more widely associated with these spheres of feeling, thought, and action than with any other.

The Expression of Guilt

All of the other negative emotions have more distinct facial characteristics in their expression than does the emotion of guilt. This helps account for the well-known difficulty in detecting the culprit, even when the guilty one is too young to inhibit or disguise facial expression effectively.

There are some similarities in the expression of shame and guilt. As in the case of shame, guilt tends to cause the person to hang his head lower, to avert his gaze, and to take only quick glances at other people, especially the accusers. The guilty person generally tries to avoid eye-to-eye contact with other people.

Two features may distinguish guilt from shame. In intense guilt, the person's face takes on a heavy look, while the hot, flushed face (blushing) is more characteristic of shame. Guilt typically affects a person's expression and demeanor for a considerably longer period of time than does shame. As with all the other emotions, a person can learn to inhibit or disguise the expression of guilt and thus "cover up" his misconduct.

The Phenomenology of Guilt

In describing the phenomenology or subjective experience of guilt, and throughout this chapter, the concern is with moral, ethical, or religious guilt, not with guilt in the legal sense. Legally, a person may be incorrectly convicted and thus guilty in the eyes of the law, but such a person may never experience any feelings of guilt. There may even be cases in which the individual is justly convicted of some misdemeanor (e.g., Rafe's running a stop sign that he did not see), but he feels no guilt despite the fact that his misdeed may cost him a day in court and a fine.

If Rafe feels guilt, he has an intense, gnawing feeling that he is "not right" with the person or persons he has wronged. If he is religious he will have the additional burden of feeling that he is "not right" with God.

It is quite common for a person to feel guilty for wrongdoing against the self. One may feel that one's misconduct has affected only one's own character.

Guilt hangs heavy on one's mind. While shame befuddles one's thinking temporarily, guilt stimulates a great deal of thought, usually cognitive preoccupation with the wrongdoing and the development of schemes for setting things right again. Because people dread facing up to their misconduct, coming face to face with the one wronged in order to make amends, the scene is often rehearsed in memory and imagination, over and over again. People who can muster the courage to face up to their guilt and begin immediately working toward amelioration will not suffer as long from the agony of the cognitive rehearsal of the guilt situation as people who postpone facing up to their guilt.

The profile of emotions in the guilt situation is presented in Figure 16-1. The profile helps make certain important points about the dynamics of guilt and related emotions. The separateness of guilt and shyness is substantiated by the fact that shyness is only the fifth highest emotion mean in the profile of the guilt situation. As a number of theorists have suggested, fear is relatively prominent in the guilt situation. This suggests that for many people a guilt situation is often accompanied by a substantial amount of fear. However, the mean for fear is not quite as high as that for distress. Judging from this profile one would have to conclude that both distress and fear are likely to be significant motivations in the guilt situation.

The profile of dimensions in the guilt situation is presented in Figure 16-2. While the emotion profile for the guilt situation is quite distinct by comparison with the profile for other emotion situations, the profile of dimensions for guilt is not clearly distinguished from the profile of other negative emotions such as anger and fear. The dimension of pleasantness, however, is significantly lower in guilt than in shyness.

Origins, Functions, and Malfunctions of Guilt

Guilt, like all the other emotions, undoubtedly played a significant role in the evolution of human beings and human societies. Guilt served as a check on wanton waste and on sexual and aggressive exploitation. The

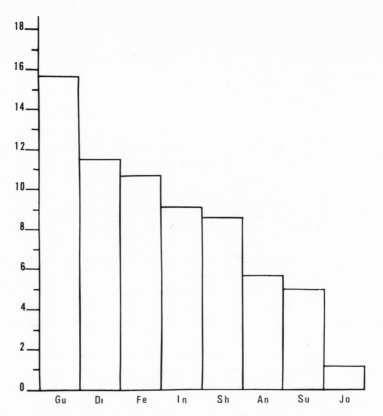

FIGURE 16-1. The profile of emotions in the guilt situation. The emotion (DES) scales are abbreviated: (Gu) guilt, (Di) distress, (Fe) fear, (In) interest, (Sh) shyness, (An) anger, (Su) surprise, and (Jo) joy.

anticipation of guilt or guilt avoidance heightens one's sense of personal responsibility. Guilt complements shame in fostering social responsibility.

In contemporary life, guilt and the anticipation and avoidance of guilt continue to serve these functions. Without guilt and shame people would lose their grip on morality and ethics. It seems quite likely that the absence or drastic reduction of guilt and shame was highly significant in the psychodynamics of Watergate and its aftermath.

Without guilt the rules of fair play would have to be monitored by a special police force, but who would train and monitor the police? A society in which no one had a sense of guilt would indeed be a poor and dangerous place in which to live. Fostering compliance with the rules of fair play is one of the constructive functions of guilt (or guilt anticipation and guilt avoidance), and several empirical studies which will be reviewed in the next section have shown that guilt does increase compliance.

The foregoing conclusion is not intended to suggest that blind compliance to any set of rules or to any system is necessarily good or adaptive. What is indicated is that the emotion of guilt plays a role in the development of personal and social responsibility and that without guilt or guilt anticipation there would be a significant loss in the need and desire to abide by the rules of fair play. The emotion of guilt helps us perceive the wronged individual as injured, suffering, hurt and in need of the appropriate words and actions that will heal the wound. The effect of guilt in making us feel responsible fosters growth toward adulthood and a greater psychological maturity.

After showing how different cultures and child-rearing practices result in different guilt antecedents and consequences, Meade (1950) suggested that guilt served a basic function for the human species. She wrote:

> But we may also consider whether, in addition to the specific nurturing situation, there may not be a biological basis for guilts of another order covered by the conception of the "metaphysical guilt of creatureliness" . . . guilt which arises inevitably from the nature of life and death itself, guilt over the domestica-

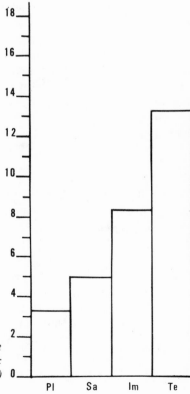

FIGURE 16-2. The profile of dimensions in the guilt situation. The DRS dimensions are abbreviated: (Pl) pleasantness, (Sa) self-assurance, (Im) impulsiveness, and (Te) tension.

tion which men endure who become responsible fathers and the pain which women take on who become mothers, guilt over all who have suffered and died as the human race struggled to its present position in the world—a deep guilt which is reactivated by any failure in the individual organism to grow, to attain full sex membership, to use its particular gifts and capacities. Such guilt, such consciousness of a debt to life which can be paid by living, may be so inherent in the nature of human beings, who live in a culture, that it is ineradicable and will always be both the mainspring of man's spiritual strivings and the guarantee of his humanity. (Meade, 1950, p. 372)

Guilt and Psychopathology

The role of guilt in psychopathology has not been the subject of very many empirical studies. A major reason for this is that theories of psychopathology frequently do not treat guilt as a separate and distinct motivational variable. Since Freud (1936) interpreted guilt as a type of anxiety, moral or "conscience" anxiety, many theorists of different orientations have failed to recognize guilt as having distinct and important characteristics of its own. For example, Mandler (1975) suggests that the only difference between anxiety and guilt may be the situational variables that give rise to the labels that the person uses to describe inner feelings. Thus, in his view, a person experiencing guilt is simply one who feels anxious about some real or imagined misdeed. Mandler pointed out that this type of anxiety (labeled by the individual as guilt) often leads to the use of the defense mechanism of undoing. This defense mechanism, typically characterized as guilt-motivated, consists of attempts by the individual to atone or to neutralize damage done by misdeeds.

Rosenhan and London (1970) recognized guilt as a separate and distinct motivational phenomenon. They suggested that one of the functions of guilt was to reduce anxiety and militate against serious psychological disorder. London (1970) pointed out that the delusions of psychotic depressives are often concerned with feelings of guilt and worthlessness.

Lewis (1971), who draws important distinctions between guilt and shame, has argued that while shame often plays an important part in depression, guilt can lead to obsessive–compulsive neurosis and paranoia. She recognized the lack of empirical research on the role of guilt in psychopathology but indicated that careful effort to differentiate the effects of shame and guilt should help in clarifying the formation of neurotic symptoms. It should be noted that not all writers in the field agree with Lewis regarding guilt as a factor in obsessions and compulsions. The more traditional view (e.g., Henderson & Gillespie, 1956) maintains that fear, not guilt, supplies the motive for obsessive thinking.

Previous chapters have presented Mowrer's view that conscience and real guilt (from acts one has committed but wishes one had not) are central in the development of neurosis. Mowrer believes that the neurotic gratifies wishes while hurting others and thus develops genuine grounds for realistic guilt. Peterson (1967) conducted a study of socialization which he interpreted as consistent with Mowrer's hypothesis. He found that children with neurotic characteristics (shy, anxious, withdrawn, and insecure) were poorly socialized, had failed to integrate socialization and behavior. Also supportive of Mowrer's view is a finding by Johnson, Ackerman, Frank, and Fionda (1968) showing that conscience as measured by resistance to temptation correlates positively with good adjustment. Ogren and Dokecki's (1972) insightful analysis of moral development and behavior disorders in young children also present some arguments consistent with Mowrer's position. They point to decentering (decrease in egocentrism) and social integration as common themes in Erikson's and Mowrer's theories of conscience development and note that moral immaturity may lead to a breakdown in peer-group interactions, neurosis, and even paranoid schizophrenia.

Theoretical Conceptions of Guilt

Guilt has been a major topic in theology and philosophy since their beginnings. In the more orthodox Jewish and Christian theologies a person is born in sin and finds salvation only through God's forgiveness. More or less liberal variations on this theme include sin against God and humanity as sources of guilt, and interaction with God (prayer and contrition) and with people (rectification) as means of absolving guilt. Many contemporary theologies and philosophies have psychological overtones in that they recognize a relationship between self-development and capacity for guilt. The "age of accountability" for one's conduct is considered a function of ability to discriminate between "right" and "wrong" and the "age of accountability" for a given act may differ with the difficulty of the discrimination.

In this section, the focus is on psychological conceptions of guilt. As is so often the case, one of the earliest contributions came from psychoanalysis.

A Psychoanalytic Conception of Guilt

In classical psychoanalytic theory, the stage is set for the development of guilt only after the basic structure of the personality has emerged (the id, the ego, and the superego). First to develop is the id, conceived largely as an innate set of impulses, instincts, or drives. It is largely sexual and aggressive in nature. The ego emerges as the child develops the capacities to conceptually separate the self from others, to think and choose, and to cope with and act upon the environment (reality). The superego, popularly thought of as the conscience, develops as children internalize or accept as their own a sense of proper conduct (rules of right and wrong behavior), either identical with or sufficiently similar to their parents or that of their reference group to be acceptable by those concerned. Psychoanalytic theory maintains that superego develops primarily as a function of mechanisms of incorporation or introjection (taking the thought or feeling of someone else as one's own) and identification (the process whereby the child assumes the identity of the parent or says in effect, "I am like him" or "I am like her"). Using these two mechanisms the superego incorporates the standards and values of the parents, with individual differences depending on the resolution of the Oedipus conflict.

Piers and Singer (1953) presented an interesting elaboration of basic psychoanalytic theory and discussed some distinctions between the dynamics of guilt and shame. They followed standard psychoanalytic theory in arguing that guilt arises from tension between the id and superego. Like Lewis (1971), they held that shame develops from tension between the ego and the ego-ideal. Shame occurs when people fail significantly in their efforts to obtain their goals and live up to the image of their ego-ideals. The "unconscious, irrational threat" that operates in shame is the threat of abandonment.

On the other hand, guilt is elicited by violation of a value or standard of conduct that characterizes the superego. Piers and Singer see a close relationship between guilt and fear, fear of the wrath of the parent figure. They hold that the "unconscious, irrational threat" that operates in guilt is the threat of mutilation or castration.

The Concept of Existential Guilt

Rollo May (1958) defined three forms of existential guilt. The first form of guilt is a result of "forfeiting of potentialities." Potentialities for development exist in the intellectual, social, emotional, and physical spheres. The individual's capacities for "being" are seemingly unlimited. However, people do not always choose to develop their potentialities. A person may neglect or completely abandon his potentiality in a given sphere of life. According to May such a forfeiture of human potentiality results in the first form of guilt. A similar view has been presented by Boss (1963) and by Bugental (1965).

> As the subject, we give actuality (life) to some possibilities by denying it to others. Therein resides our guilt. Guilt is always an aspect of our being: condemnation is the ultimate threat we must face. The guilt and condemnation here specified are outward and not neurotic. They are inherent in our situation, not judgements against our worth. (Bugental, 1965)

Khanna (1969) made some provocative criticisms of this concept of existential guilt. He noted that newborn children have a vast and virtually limitless number of potentialities and that they will inevitably give up some and develop others as a result of their upbringings, their social interactions, and their life situations. The existential implication that one must develop all of one's potentialities sets such an impossibly high standard that it becomes meaningless. As it is with any individual, Rafe must be free to develop those potentialities that he consciously chooses and to give up those that do not interest him, without feeling guilt in the usual sense. That is, such an exercise of choice should not cause him to feel guilt as he would experience it if he violated a code of conduct. Khanna pointed out that potentialities exist in anyone in a continually changing hierarchy so that at any given time he or she is preferring and responding to some to a greater extent than others. Rafe may rightly feel guilty for denying a potentiality that is important for his development and existence as a human being or for cultivating a potentiality that makes him an immoral person. However, to say that Rafe is guilty for actualizing his potential as an artist while denying his potential to become a scientist makes no more sense than to say that he is guilty because he is alive and makes choices.

The second type of existential guilt, according to May, develops as a result of one's separation from one's fellow man. It is not possible for us to see our fellow men exactly as they see themselves. It is not possible for us to have perfect empathy. It is not possible for us to be completely one with another individual. Thus there is a basic separateness or aloneness that characterizes every human life. And, according to the existential view, the insulation set up by this separateness creates barriers and conflicts in interpersonal relations. Khanna maintains that this separateness of human beings needs to be recognized and accepted but not considered as a reason for guilt. Other human beings are essential for the realization of a major aspect of our potentiality. Other people are essential but not for the purpose of complete identification with them. Inability to speak and feel in perfect harmony with another human being is a fact of human existence and human individuality which cannot be reasonably regarded as guilt.

The third form of existential guilt results from separation from nature. Khanna points out that this type of guilt is dependent upon the assumption of a value system which indicates that oneness with nature is right, good, and important, and that human beings somehow become separated from nature. Since by birth we are a real and genuine part of nature, a tricky problem arises in the definition as to what exactly constitutes "union" and what exactly constitutes "separation."

Khanna's comparisons and criticisms of existential guilt were made with reference to the standard or conventional meaning of the term—an emotion elicited by deviation from a code of conduct and an emotion that motivates the individual to get back in line or suffer punishment. Khanna concludes his critique by pointing out that the concept of existential guilt describes some very important aspects of human life but falters when it makes the concept of guilt so general that it is equivalent to being human. Khanna observes that existential guilt can meaningfully refer to instances where people's actions deviate from the hierarchy of values and standards that they have accepted and developed.

Some Learning Theory Conceptions of the Developmental Origins and Consequences of Guilt

O. H. Mowrer (1960b, 1961) has presented some interesting and provocative ideas on the origin of guilt, its effects upon the individual, and ways to deal with it in psychotherapy. In his view, guilt develops essentially as a function of the learning process. As young children are repeatedly rewarded for doing things that are considered good and right and repeatedly punished for doing things that are considered bad and wrong, they gradually develop their own sense (or concepts) of proper and improper behavior. Mowrer agrees with one of the traditional distinctions between shame and guilt, noting that shame occurs in the presence of another person while the mechanism of guilt can operate when the individual is entirely alone and in the absence of the source of punishment.

According to Mowrer, the sense of right and wrong are learned largely through the mechanism of identification and imitation. He criticized a strict behavioristic analysis and interpretation of guilt on the grounds that it is inadequate to deal with the highly generative and verbally abstract aspects of the phenomena of human guilt. Mowrer thinks that the methods used in the study and analysis of the development of guilt would have to parallel those used in the study of the development of language.

A number of theories take the position that a close relationship exists between guilt and fear (e.g., Mandler, 1975). Mowrer goes a step further and defines guilt as a type of fear, the fear that arises after performing a previously punished act. Mowrer defines temptation as the fear and conflict that occur before such an act. He defines conscience as representing both the capacity to resist temptation and the capacity for remorse.

Following his fundamentally learning-theory orientation, Mowrer maintains that discipline and punishment are essential in the development of guilt, although he does recognize the possibility of constitutional or hereditary differences in susceptibility to guilt or guilt training. (Punishment can also elicit fear, distress, and anger. For a detailed discussion of punishment, see Cheyne and Walters, 1970). Mowrer suggests that the development of guilt is facilitated when the learner feels dependent upon another person who is also the source of punishment or discipline. This is consonant with the theoretical material discussed in Chapter 15 wherein shame was considered as an emotion that occurs primarily, if not only, in the context of an emotional relationship.

Sarason (1966) presented a conception of guilt very similar to that of Mowrer. He, too, believed that the development of guilt was contingent on the use of punishment. He did not really carefully delineate his notion of guilt from his concept of fear and anxiety, except to note that guilt is related more closely to the individual's self-concept and attitudes.

In addition to the theories already reviewed, a number of other writers (e.g., Switzer, 1968) have drawn a close relationship between guilt and fear. Unger (1962) presented a rather detailed analysis of guilt in which fear or anxiety constitute an integral part, but unfortunately his definition of anxiety was highly ambiguous. He defined anxiety as "the conditionable 'residue' of noxious experience . . . a particular pattern of autonomic–visceral events and attendant feedback." For present purposes we shall consider his concept of anxiety as meaning fear (a term which he uses interchangeably with anxiety). He sees his position as an expansion of that of Mowrer.

Unger defines guilt as a two-stage mediating process. The first stage is a verbal evaluative response (e.g., "I shouldn't have done that!"). The verbal evaluation process of the first stage triggers the second stage, the autonomic–visceral reaction of fear. Unger's analysis attempts to specify the contingencies and conditions of parent behavior and parent–child relations which result in the development of guilt. He found a number of studies in support of his assumption that emotion can be verbally mediated and that semantic conditioning (e.g., Luria & Vinogradova, 1959) can put autonomic responsiveness under the control of verbal mediating processes.

Unger notes that postulating a prototypic verbal component in guilt implies that it is a uniquely human phenomenon. On this point he is in disagreement with a number of scientists from Darwin to Mowrer. The latter pointed to differences in guilt reactions among various species of dogs as evidence of an hereditary component in guilt susceptibility. However, Unger agrees with Mowrer and others that guilt develops in the context of an emotional relationship.

According to Unger, it is the individual's dependency and emotional tie to the other person (typically the parent or parent figure) that sets the stage for the development of dependency and separation anxiety which are fundamental in the development of guilt. Like Sarason and Mowrer and others who work within the framework of learning theory or general behavior theory, Unger defines guilt, or at least the affective component of guilt, as a type of fear.

In Unger's view, the nurturance of the infant and young child by a loving and caring parent develops a powerful dependency in the infant. The parent is closely associated with the infant day after day and week after week, and throughout the early months and years of life the parent is responsible for the termination and amelioration of hurtful and frustrating situations. Thus the presence and availability of the parent become matters of high importance for the young child and conversely the absence or nonavailability of the parent evokes "dependency anxiety"—the prelude to the development of guilt.

The nurturance of the child and the concomitant development of the capacity for dependency anxiety under conditions of parental absence or nonavailability set the stage for guilt training. According to Unger and other learning theorists this training begins, or at least begins to take effect, at around age four or five. When the parent observes the child's transgression the child is confronted by a stern-faced parent who says in a harsh voice, "How could you do that, that was a bad thing." The incident contains a verbal evaluation "Never do that again, bad, bad, shame on you," and the parent's words and actions, according to Unger, are interpreted by the child as signs of withdrawal and separation, and hence they elicit dependency anxiety. After a number of such training episodes, the child learns to evaluate his or her behavior in the absence of the parent. "I did a bad thing; Mommy or Daddy says that's wrong, I must not do that again." Unger maintains that these evaluation-mediating responses interweave with reverberating anxiety over a more or less extended period of time. Eventually the child learns to evaluate the situation in advance and avoid the transgression and hence the dependency anxiety that Unger sees as the affective component of guilt.

Unger cited the classical studies of Solomon and his associates (e.g., Solomon & Wynne, 1953; Wynne & Solomon, 1955) as evidence that extinction of guilt-mediated responses is difficult if not impossible. However, the stimulus in the series of studies by Solomon and his associates was painful, and the affect very probably was fear, and the strength of Unger's argument depends upon one's acceptance of his proposition that a form of fear constitutes the affective component of guilt.

Unger make some cogent arguments for the proposition that psychological ("love-oriented") disciplinary techniques are more potent in guilt training than physical or "materialistic" techniques. He cited studies by McKennan (1938), Whiting and Child (1953), Faigan (1953), Miller and Swanson (1956), Funkenstein et al. (1957), and Unger (1962) in support of this argument. He emphasizes that psychological techniques of guilt training would work only if there was a background of parental nurturance and a continuing affectionate relationship between parent and child. Love cannot be withdrawn where none exists.

Unger also makes a case for the soundness of clear and immediate punishment or discipline in guilt-training episodes. Sometimes parents make unpredictable threats of unknown punishments (for example, "God will punish you," "you can never make up for hurting your mother"). Under such threat, the child's evaluative response, "I did wrong," can reverberate over a highly protracted period of time and possibly mediate serious intrapunitive behavior aimed at relieving the guilt (dependency anxiety).

Sears, Maccoby, and Levin (1957) strongly support the thesis that identification with warm and accepting parents who use "love-oriented techniques of discipline" facilitates the development of a healthy conscience. They argue that withdrawal of love is particularly effective in morality training. They point out that the development of too strong a conscience may result in an inflexible, guilt-ridden individual while too weak a conscience can produce an immoral bully. The antisocial impulses of the latter type individual are controlled only by his fear of being caught and punished.

A study by Glueck and Glueck (1950) showed that psychological techniques of control were used more frequently by parents of nondelinquents and physical punishment more frequently by parents of delinquents. Affection, warmth, and feelings of attachment were much more characteristic of the nondelinquent population than of the delinquent one.

McKennan (1938) studied the relative effects of psychological and physical punishment by way of retrospective reports of Harvard students. The students were asked to report their reactions to each type of punishment. The memories they had of their reactions of physical punishment were "anger, stubborness, resentment, antagonism, annoyance, obstinacy, hatred, cold dislike, and so forth" (p. 500). The reactions they recalled in relation to discipline that made them feel inferior, unworthy, and temporarily unloved, were "felt ashamed, sorrowful, conscience-striken, repentent, desirous to apologize, anxious not to offend again, and so forth" (p. 498).

Maher (1966) defines guilt in a fashion very similar to Unger. He describes guilt as a particular instance of anxiety, the anxiety resulting from expectation of loss of love and similar punishments for one's own behavior. He also sees guilt and other criteria of conscience as dependent upon the use of punishment in moral training. Like Unger, he defines guilt as consisting of verbal evaluations plus emotional–visceral responses (essentially fear). Maher added the notion that the subjective experience of guilt tends to cause the individual to seek punishment. He supports Mosher's (1968) conclusion that sensitivity to situational cues regarding propriety of behavior is a function of strength of trait-guilt—the higher the guilt the less sensitive to situational cues and the more sensitive to internal processes.

Maher applied the concept of guilt as developed by Unger, Mosher, and others to an analysis of the psychopath. He described the psychopath as an individual who is essentially deficient in guilt or conscience. The background for this is laid by the fact that the psychopath is unable to form close personal relationships. There is the implication that the psychopath never experiences parental nurturance or at least does not have moral training in the context of a warm, affectionate relationship. Maher cited psychopaths' tendencies to antisocial acts and sexual promiscuity as evidence of their guilt deficiencies.

Maher suggested that as children psychopaths learn to use suitable expressions of repentance and promises in order to avoid punishment. They thus have repentance behavior reinforced while extinguishing the fear of punishment. They learn to use charm and social skill to get what they want. They get no training in learning to work and wait for long-term rewards. They do not learn to tolerate frustration. They learn to get affection or approval by being "good looking," "charming," and "clever." Psychopaths are remarkably capable of getting people to help them and to avoid punishment. As the result of not being punished for wrongdoing, they do not learn that their actions distress and harm other people.

Maher maintains that conscience consists of resistance to temptation, self-instruction to obey, and capacity for feeling guilt. He sees resistance to temptation as a function of avoidance learning and self-instruction to obey moral principles as a function primarily of imitation of the loved parent. Maher cited a number of studies in support of his analysis of the psychopath as a guilt-deficient individual. One of these studies showed that psychopaths perform more slowly on tasks where remote previous responses had been reinforced but performed in superior fashion on tasks when deficient performance was determined by immediate previous reinforcement.

In an incisive paper on the role of parental discipline in the development of conscience and guilt, Hoffman and Saltzstein (1967) differentiate between power-assertive disciplinary techniques and two types of non-power-assertive techniques: love withdrawal, in which parents give direct but nonphysical expression to their anger or disapproval, and induction of empathy, which involves the child being made aware of his or her own role in distressing or hurting others. Their experiment showed that simple love withdrawal was not as effective as the induction of empathic responses accompanied by communication to the child of his or her role in others' distress or pain.

Differential emotions theory allows for the possibility that withdrawal of love as a punishment technique for teaching morality can produce distress, anger, fear, guilt, or some combination of these depending upon the individual, the relationship, and the situation. When love withdrawal is perceived as threat of separation, distress might be the most likely result if such separation is seen as resulting in being left alone for a while without the joy, excitement, and comfort that are contingent on the presence and availability of the parent or loved one. Fear may be the result when the love withdrawal appears to leave the individual more vulnerable to hurt or harm. The individual sees loss of love as a loss of protection from danger. Guilt is more likely to obtain when the individual sees the withholding of love as a sign of disapproval of wrongdoing. Withdrawal of love may thus be seen as one of not being "right" with the loved one. In this case it is a kind of estrangement, a kind of inability to relate in the normal and affectionate way, an estrangement in which real or imagined wrongdoing stands as a barrier between the child and the parent or caregiver.

Hoffman and Saltzstein's (1967) empathy induction technique is seen in differential emotions theory as an application of the principles of emotion contagion and emotion communication. Techniques of conscience development based on these principles of interpersonal emotion processes may prove the most effective route to the development of a healthy conscience and a more uniformly ethical society.

Experimental Studies of Guilt

In the last few years a number of empirical investigations have been undertaken in order to experimentally induce, manipulate, and evaluate guilt. Most of these studies were based on drive-reduction learning theory, social-learning theory, and psychoanalytic theory—positions that have not traditionally fostered careful delineation of discrete emotions. Although this body of research sometimes confounds or fails to differentiate emotion states, it is helpful in furthering our understanding of guilt and the interaction of guilt with other emotions, cognition, and action. An excellent selection of research and theoretical articles from the growing literature on guilt are presented in Johnson, Dokecki, and Mowrer (1972).

The Interaction of Guilt and Anger

Gambaro (1967) conducted a study of the interaction of guilt and anger in a frustrating situation. Gambaro's experiment was rather sophisticated in that he did not simply assume that his frustrating condition would elicit anger. He used a self-report measure to check on the success of his manipulation in altering the subjective experience of anger.

Gambaro (1967) conducted a study of the interaction of guilt and anger tion-instigated anger would raise diastolic blood pressure and that expression of aggression under this condition would lower diastolic blood pressure. Further, he hypothesized that subjects scoring high on the Mosher Aggression–Guilt Scale (Mosher, 1967) would respond differently in the experimental conditions from subjects scoring low on this scale. There were four experimental conditions. In the first condition subjects were frustrated and then allowed to respond to their anger directly by administering electric shock to the frustrator (the experimental assistant). In the second condition the subjects were frustrated but were allowed only an indirect response to their anger—they could allow the experimenter to shock the frustrator. In the third condition the subjects went through the frustration sequence but were not allowed to respond overtly to their anger. In the fourth condition the subjects went through the experimental procedure but there was no frustration condition and no cause or opportunity for aggression. They completed "fill in" activities instead.

A self-report measure of anger, the check on the success of the frustration manipulation, showed that subjects under frustration rated themselves significantly angrier than did the control group. Further, the diastolic blood pressure of all subjects in the frustration conditions was significantly elevated above that of the control group. All subjects in the direct-response condition (those who were frustrated and allowed to shock the frustrators) showed a significantly greater decrease in diastolic blood pressure than did the subjects in the no-response group (those who were frustrated and allowed no overt response to their anger). The indirect response to anger (allowing the subject to shock the frustrator) showed no more change in diastolic blood pressure than did the no-response group. Although the high- and low-guilt subjects did not differ on the blood-pressure measure in the frustration conditions (both groups showed significant increases), the high-guilt subjects showed significantly less decrease in diastolic blood pressure than did the low-guilt group during the postfrustration activities. The high-guilt group in the indirect-response condition actually showed a slight mean increase in diastolic blood pressure.

This interesting study has important implications for understanding the dynamics of guilt, particularly as it is associated with the experience of anger and subsequent aggression. The study shows very clearly that the extent to which people feel guilt after they aggress (even when the aggression may be objectively justifiable), is significantly related to the effects their feelings and actions will have on their physiological functioning. Subjects who experience strong guilt over their aggressive actions (whether or not they may be considered objectively justifiable) may increase their physiological disturbance (increased diastolic blood pressure) if they respond to their anger through physical aggression. On the other hand, subjects who can operate on the "eye-for-an-eye, tooth-for-a-tooth" principle of aggression tend to get their system back in equilibrium (decrease in diastolic blood pressure) by responding to their anger through physical aggression. Of course, these generalizations must be tempered by careful consideration of the experimental conditions and their generalizability to real life situations.

Solomon, Turner, and Lessac (1968) conducted a study with dogs and concluded that their study had implications for guilt and guilt-related behavior in human beings. They taught dogs to "resist the temptation" of eating a more desirable canned dog food and to eat instead a less desirable dry meat. They taught them to discriminate between the "taboo food" and the acceptable food by means of punishment (a blow on the nose). They varied the length of delay between the dogs' yielding to temptation and eating the desirable canned dog food and the time of the punishment. The variations in delays of punishment did not affect the ease with which the dogs learned to resist the temptation and avoid punishment. However, patterns of "emotionality," reactions to absence of experimenter, and reactions to violation of the taboo varied greatly for different delays in the schedule of punishment. The authors concluded that their findings were relevant in child-rearing practices in that delays of punishment following a child's wrongdoing would be correlated with "the intensity of shame and guilt in children."

The authors' generalization from conditioning in dogs to the socialization of children should be weighed carefully but probably should not be ignored. If Rebecca is made to feel guilty, the timing and manner of her punishment will undoubtedly make some difference in what happens to her guilt feelings and to guilt-motivated thought and behavior. For example, if she is made to feel guilty and then has to wait a long time before she gets the expected punishment, she will have much longer to "live with the guilt," rehearse the guilt situation, and ruminate over its seriousness and its consequences. A mother should weigh carefully the possible effects of creating guilt in a child (caught in the midst of wrongdoing) and then telling her or him to "wait until your father gets home and you'll get the spanking of your life."

Guilt and Compliance

Freedman, Wallington, and Bless (1967) reviewed studies by Freedman and Fraser (1966), Wallace and Sadalla (1966), Brock and Becker (1966), and Carlsmith and Gross (1969) and concluded that their experimental results supported the conclusion that guilt increased compliance.

Freedman, Wallington, and Bless thought there were some weaknesses in some of the foregoing studies and they extended this line of research with a series of three additional experiments. In the first experiment, subjects were put into a situation in which they either denied or admitted to the experimenter the fact that they had been given previous knowledge of the experiment in which they were about to participate. All subjects were then asked to volunteer for a future experiment of either an unpleasant or neutral type. A significantly greater number of the subjects who withheld information from the experiment ("lie condition") volunteered for a future experiment than did subjects in the control condition. The pleasantness or neutrality of the future experiment had no effect on the number of individuals complying with the request to participate in a future experiment.

In a second experiment, subjects either sat at a wobbly table where they inevitably upset some supposedly carefully arranged index cards, or at a steady table where the cards remained in order. Following this treatment condition, the experimenter asked the subjects to volunteer for an experiment being run by a graduate student whose office and cards had been involved or for an experiment being conducted by a graduate student unrelated to the events of the day. Seventy-five percent of the subjects in the group who upset the index cards complied with the request to participate in a future experiment while only 39% of the control group volunteered. There was no difference in the frequency with which members of the guilt and no-guilt groups volunteered for the experiment with the graduate student who had nothing to do with the experimental situation, but there was a great difference in the number volunteering to help the graduate student whose index cards had been disarranged. In the guilt condition, nine out of ten of the subjects (who did not expect to be identified as the "culprit") volunteered to help by participating in the future experiment of the "victimized" graduate student, while only five out of fifteen volunteered in the nonguilt condition. The question as to the effect of having to face the "wronged" individual when volunteering to help ("do recompense") was examined in a third experiment.

The setup for the third experiment was similar to that for the second, except that all subjects were requested to help the victimized graduate student. Half were asked to help in such a way that it was necessary to meet him and work side by side with him; the other half were asked to help in a way that did not require meeting him. Again, there was significantly greater compliance with the request by the group in the guilt condition. There was no difference between the guilt and nonguilt groups in response to the request to help by working with the victim, but in responding to the request that did not require meeting the victim, eleven out of fifteen subjects in the guilt condition complied and only three out of seventeen in the nonguilt condition.

Unfortunately these studies did not measure the subjective experience of guilt, and hence made no direct check on the guilt manipulation. Guilt was operationally defined as a condition arising from actions contrary to normal standards of behavior ("telling a lie," "afflicting a hardship" on another person). The results indicated that such a "guilt condition" had a fairly potent influence on the subjects' willingness to comply to a request that involved some of their time and effort at some point in the future.

Interestingly, but not surprisingly, subjects in the guilt condition were much more reluctant to comply if compliance involved meeting and dealing directly with the person who had been "wronged." This might mean that the subject did not want to add to his burden of guilt the possibility of an unpleasant confrontation with the wronged person, but generalization to real life situations must be tempered by the fact that these were rather contrived situations in which the parties involved were strangers. However, the validity of the finding that experimental subjects suffering from experimentally induced guilt are reluctant to comply with a request requiring them to meet and deal with the victim was further supported by a study of Silverman (1967). This study involved 199 sixth-grade students. The students were presented with the temptation to falsify their answers on a test in order to win prize money. The experimenter (who was victimized by losing money to the cheaters) requested the students to volunteer to work with him in a future experiment. There was no significant difference in the number of volunteers among noncheaters, low cheaters, and high cheaters. This finding is consistent with Freedman, Wallington, and Bless and that of Wallace and Sadalla that transgression, *per se,* (guilt as operationally defined by these manipulations) is not sufficient to obtain compliance when compliance means having to meet and deal with the victim.

Development of Guilt as a Personality Trait

As in the case for other fundamental emotions, guilt and the interactions of guilt with other emotions, cognition, and action is considered as a trait or cluster of traits in the human personality. A number of other theoretical positions and numerous empirical investigations support the notion that guilt can be considered as a personality trait.

One of the earliest studies of the development of trait guilt was that of Whiting and Child (1953, pp. 218–262). They used the Yale Human Relations Research Files to do a cross-cultural study, focusing especially on data from preliterate cultures. They analyzed the individual's attitude toward illness and used willingness to accept blame for the problem as a measure of guilt. Influenced by psychoanalytic theory and behavioristic learning theory they looked through data on child-rearing practices in the various cultures to find correlates of guilt. They found that early weaning, early independence training, training in modesty, and inhibition of heterosexual play tended to produce a higher level of guilt. They concluded that the mechanism of identification mediated the development of guilt in these cultures. Parents who adopted child-rearing practices that resulted in early weaning, early development of independence, modesty, and control of heterosexual play were relatively more powerful models with whom the children could identify. In monogamous societies age of weaning correlated with the individual's willingness to take blame or responsibility for his illness (the index of guilt). The same was not true in polygamous societies. One of their interesting though speculative conclusions was that guilt was derived from identification with the male role. Their more generally accepted conclusion was that guilt plays an important role in social control (cf. Levine, 1973, p. 64).

The studies of Whiting and Child, as well as the work of Benedict (1934), Mead (1956), and Izard (1971) all support the notion that shame and guilt are transcultural phenomena. Some cultures seem to be more shame oriented and others more guilt oriented. Benedict (1946) characterized certain cultures as "shame cultures" and others as "guilt cultures." Johnson and Medinnus (1965), in their child psychology textbook, suggested that in American culture urbanites are moving from a guilt to a shame orientation. They pointed to several factors as determinants of this change—the influence of psychoanalysis and psychotherapy which point to the dangers of severe guilt socialization, alterations in American culture that cause parents to be unsure of their own value judgments, and the apparent increased power of the influence of peers on the development of moral and ethical standards.

Although there is a possible tendency to reduce the guilt orientation in American culture, Johnson and Medinnus noted that shame is more likely to be effective in small societies than in a large heterogeneous one like that in the United States. Their notion makes some sense in relation to the psychology of shame and guilt. Since shame is most often elicited in the individual by other people, then shame might be a more effective control in relatively closed groups where "everybody knows everybody." However, in urban societies, where individuals enjoy a great deal of anonymity and multiple group membership, it would be more necessary for the individual to exercise the internal control that derives from the incorporation of parental and adult standards that form the basis for conscience and guilt.

Traditionally people have thought of religion and religious training as one of the principle sources of conscience and guilt reactions. Most people with a strong religious upbringing recognize that religion played a role in the development of their consciences and in determining some of the causes and consequences of guilt. People who maintain strong religious affiliations continue to consider religious values and codes as guides to certain aspects of their conduct. However, even in the most devoutly religious, other factors such as morality, human ethics, and local customs relating to right and wrong play a role in the development of conscience and guilt thresholds.

London, Schulman, and Black (undated) examined the relationship between subjective experience of guilt and religious affiliation. There were some problems with the sampling, since it developed that there was a sex difference in responses to their questionnaire and the different religious groups were not balanced by sex. Regardless of religious affiliation, the male subjects reported significantly fewer guilt feelings than females. There was a statistically significant ($p < .05$) though not very substantial difference indicating that Jewish subjects had somewhat higher levels of personal guilt than Protestant subjects. The authors concluded that guilt feelings did not differ strikingly among denominations, but they thought that sex differences were more substantial. The authors' analysis of other aspects of the data led them to conclude that guilt as a contributor to psychopathology was probably equally important in all religious groups.

Katz and Ziegler (1967) reasoned that the development of guilt in the individual was positively correlated with the development of ability to make finer cognitive judgments and with growth toward maturity. This is consistent with the previously presented theoretical concepts on the relationship between, and the development of, personal and social responsibility. The authors did a survey of 120 fifth grade, eighth grade, and eleventh grade students. Their questionnaires were designed to measure differences between the individuals' concept of their "real selves," their "social selves," and their "ideal selves." Their results showed that discrepancy between the individual's real and ideal self-concepts was related to age and IQ. On the basis of their analysis of the data they argued that neither guilt nor anxiety functioned as a strictly negative agent in the "individual's total psychic economy." They saw the increasing disparity between individuals' concepts of their real selves and their concepts of their ideal selves as accompanying higher levels of development. They thought that the increasing age of the individual resulted in greater capacity for cognitive differentiation and for self-derogation and hence for the experience of guilt. They suggested that the data supported their contention that the increasing disparity between real and ideal self-concept and increasing development of guilt or capacity for guilt was related to maturity. The more mature the children the greater their self-demands, thus the more likelihood of experiencing guilt.

A similar study by Nicholas (1966) supported the conclusion that there is a significant relationship between guilt and a person's self-concept. His study pointed up another interesting aspect of these complex emotion–personality dynamics. He found a significant negative relationship between guilt scores and self-acceptance scores. Nicholas concluded that within certain "normal" limits there is no significant relationship between guilt and personality adjustment. Earlier research by Rogers (1959) and his colleagues had shown that high discrepancies between real and ideal self-concepts and low scores on self-acceptance are indexes of maladjustment.

The work of Rogers and his colleagues, as well as the studies reviewed above, are not really inconsistent with the notion that a certain threshold for guilt is essential for personal responsibility and social–emotional maturity. It is severe and chronic guilt or an extremely low guilt threshold that leads to serious psychological problems and maladjustment. This conclusion is further supported by a study of Fenyes (1967) in which she illustrated a relationship between a high level of moral judgment and the relative absence of inappropriate self-blame. Using a projective measure she also found that tendency to take other people's point of view into account was associated with a tendency to react with self-blame for another person's distress.

Guilt and Hostility

Mosher, his students, and colleagues have made significant contributions to the psychology of guilt. Beginning his work in the framework of Rotter's social-learning theory, Mosher reasoned that individuals who violated a religious, moral, or ethical code would be significantly influenced by actual or anticipated external punishment (fear-arousing condition) and by internal punishment (guilt). Mosher defined guilt as an expectancy of self-mediated punishment for violating or failing to attain internalized standards of proper behavior. (Internalized standards, which differential emotions theory interprets as the result of guilt–cognition interactions, have both an inhibiting [should not] component and a positively valued ideal–goal [ought to] component.) The "expectancy for guilt" was defined by Mosher as a function of the individual's social-learning history (socialization), during which time the internalization of standards were reinforced by producing approval and avoiding punishment. Mosher maintained that the behavior that would materialize in a situation that was potentially fear arousing and guilt arousing would be the function of three variables: (1) the value of the goal (or reinforcement) to be obtained by the behavior, (2) the strength of the expectancy that the behavior will lead to externally mediated punishment (the fear-arousing condition), and (3) the strength of the expectancy that the behavior will lead to self-mediated punishment (guilt).

Mosher's first instrument for the measurement of guilt was a sentence-completion test. He conducted several studies with this instrument and confirmed and elaborated some of the previously discussed findings relating to guilt as a personality trait. These studies tended to confirm his notion of a fear–guilt interaction as a basic factor in determining people's behavior in situations where they are confronted with a possibility of violating religious, moral, or ethical codes. For example, he showed that low-guilt subjects were more influenced by expectancy of external punishment than high-guilt subjects. He also found that the level of guilt was positively related to verbal conditioning of guilt-related content.

Partly as a result of these initial studies, Mosher decided that guilt experience could be subdivided into three aspects: (1) hostility guilt (guilt elicited as a result of feelings of hostility and by acts of aggression), (2) sex guilt (guilt associated with thoughts, feelings, and actions in the sexual sphere), and (3) morality–conscience guilt. Several studies were conducted by Mosher and his colleagues relating to the first two types of guilt. He showed that sex guilt was significantly related to perceptual defense against sexual stimuli (the higher the guilt, the higher the threshold for the perception of sex-related words). Mosher suggested that subjects low on sex guilt were more sensitive to cues suggesting the possibility of external punishment while subjects high on sex guilt tended to respond more in terms of internal standards. Although high sex guilt tended to facilitate verbal conditioning of self-related content, high hostility guilt seemed to inhibit the conditioning of material with hostile content. These and other experiments led Mosher to the interesting and quite reasonable conclusion that high guilt tends to override the force of situational cues in determining behavior. He obtained some empirical support for the notion that high-guilt subjects were actually less responsive to the probability of external punishment or disapproval. Conversely, subjects low on guilt were less responsive to the possibility of internal punishment (guilt feelings) and more sensitive to the possibility of external punishment or disapproval.

Guilt and Sexual Behavior

Mosher and his colleagues conducted a series of studies relating to sex guilt (for example, see Mosher and Galbraith, 1970). These studies led to the following conclusions: (1) there is a negative correlation between sex guilt and the ease with which a person free-associates to words with a sexual connotation; (2) subjects high on sex guilt show less awareness of the sexual and nonsexual connotations; (3) only low sex-guilt subjects show an increase in sexual associations on a word association task following sexual stimulation (e.g., looking at nude or scantily clad pin-up girls by male subjects).

The Mosher and Galbraith (1970) study is a good example of the kind of experiment that contributed to the foregoing conclusions. The authors examined the recall ability of high- and low-guilt subjects for associations given under sexually stimulating and sexually nonstimulating conditions. The subjects were divided into low and high sex-guilt groups on the basis of the scores on the Mosher Forced-Choice Guilt Inventory. Half of the high sex-guilt subjects and half of the low sex-guilt subjects were in each of the two sex-stimulation conditions. The sexual stimulation procedure required the subjects to rate 27 photos of nude or seminude girls on sexual attractiveness. Following this task the subjects were given a double entendre word association test. The test included 30 double entendres and 20 neutral words. The subjects were required to respond as rapidly as possible with the word that the stimulus word suggested to them. Word association latencies were measured with an openly displayed stop watch. Immediately after the word association test the original words were repeated and on this occasion the subjects were required to recall their original association. Again, the response latencies were recorded. Accuracy of recall was also scored.

The results showed that high sex-guilt subjects made the largest number of recall errors when in the sexual stimulation condition and fewest under the control condition. The high sex-guilt subjects even showed a slight impairment in recall ability for neutral words under the sex stimulation condition. Low sex-guilt subjects showed no impairment for recall of either sexual or neutral words: they even showed a slight improvement under the sexual stimulation condition. Mosher and Galbraith explained the poor recall of high sex-guilt subjects on the basis of negative emotions. Probably a combination of fear and guilt caused the subjects to give associations that were only weakly related or associated to the stimulus word. Thus recall was more difficult.

Mosher (1968) conducted a study of the effects of sex guilt (measured as a personality trait) on females' emotion responses to the reading of an erotic passage of literature. High and low sex-guilt subjects read either a neutral or erotic passage with a like-sex (female) experimenter either present or absent. Only the high-guilt subjects who read the erotic passage showed a significant increase in state guilt as measured by Nowlis' Mood Adjective Checklist.

Izard and Caplan (1974) did a follow-up of Mosher's study using both male and female subjects. Males who read the erotic passage reported significantly higher sexual arousal, interest, and enjoyment, and less disgust than did the females, but there were no differences between the males and females on fear. The liberalization of views on sex together with the greatly increased openness and vividness with which sex is treated in literature and in the media (particularly the movies) was seen as a significant factor in the difference between Mosher's study and the Izard–Caplan study, conducted five years later.

The Izard–Caplan study was replicated (Izard, Caplan, Walker, & Kotsch, 1977) with the modification that the experimenter and subject were of opposite sex. As in Mosher's study and the 1974 Izard–Caplan study the erotic passage was Chapter 72 of Calder Willingham's *Eternal Fire* (1963). The affects measured were sexual arousal, interest, joy, surprise, distress, anger, disgust, fear, shyness, and guilt. Our concern here will be primarily with the state measure of guilt and the relationships between Mosher's sex-guilt scale (a trait measure of guilt) and the foregoing emotions measured as states by the DES.

There were 112 male subjects and 112 female subjects. One-half of the subjects of each sex read either the academic or erotic passage with the observer present, and the other subgroups read one of the two passages with the observer absent. As in the 1974 Izard–Caplan study, the subjects were contacted by telephone and later visited in their own rooms for the administration of the experiment. The DES was administered before and after the reading of the passages. An analysis of the pretreatment DES scores showed that simply as a result of the presence of an opposite-sex experimenter in their rooms, males reported significantly greater sexual arousal, surprise, anger, disgust, fear, shyness, and guilt than did the females.

Since the design of this study and the Izard–Caplan study was the same except for the opposite-sex condition, the pretest data of the two experiments were compared to examine further the effects of an opposite-sex experimenter. This analysis showed that the presence of an opposite-sex experimenter brought about a highly significant increase in sexual arousal in males and a slight, though not significant decrease, in females. On the guilt scale the males showed a significant increase, and the females showed a decrease of equal magnitude, though it was not statistically significant. The data do not tell exactly why males were generally more emotionally responsive to the presence of opposite-sex experimenters in their rooms. It is quite reasonable that the increase in sexual arousal in males was a significant determinant of other observed changes. A big increase in sexual arousal may have activated guilt as well as other emotion responses.

Analysis of the joint effects of opposite-sex experimenter and the "literary treatment" (academic or erotic passage) showed that those who read a passage (whether neutral or erotic) with the opposite-sex observer present expressed more guilt than those who read their passage with the observer absent.

At the conclusion of the second DES, Mosher's sex-guilt scale was administered. Scores on the sex-guilt scale were correlated with scores from the DES. The trait sex-guilt scores showed modest, though statistically significant, negative correlations with sexual arousal ($r = -.19$, $p < .01$) and joy ($r = -.21$, $p < .05$). Trait sex-guilt was significantly positively correlated with disgust ($r = .31$, $p < .01$), and with the DES state measure of guilt ($r = .24$, $p < .01$). These are logical findings that could be predicted from an understanding of the psychology of guilt and of guilt–sex interactions. The findings are consistent with those presented by Mosher (1965).

We have already suggested that one of the determinants of the higher emotion scores for men in the opposite-sex experimenter study was the substantially greater sexual arousal on the part of the males. In the American culture it is generally thought that males are more readily sexually aroused by the presence of a member of the opposite sex than are females.

Because of the linkage of sex and guilt in socialization, the higher sexual arousal could help account for the males' higher guilt scores. But what of the males higher scores on anger, disgust, and fear? Perhaps part of the reason for the increase in these emotions was the male's frustration and uncertainty as to what to do about their increased sexual arousal. For the males the experiment reversed the traditional (stereotyped) male and female roles. A young woman (fellow college student) had, in effect, invited herself into a young man's room; further, she was the experimenter ("authority figure") and in charge of the situation. This relatively unusual social situation may have interacted with the relatively high sexual arousal to recruit the emotions of anger, disgust, and fear.

Izard, Spiegel, Alessio, and Kotsch (1974) conducted a study of the effects of moral–ethical standards relative to sexual behavior and sexual experience on emotion responses to imaging (visualizing) sexual intercourse. The study was conducted in the form of an anonymous survey handled entirely by student experimenters. From a booth that was placed at several points on the campus, 495 students accepted questionnairs as they passed by. To insure anonymity the participants were supplied with self-addressed envelopes and requested not to sign the experimental material. Of the 275 students who responded, 255 returned complete and usable research forms.

The major hypotheses were that sexual standards and sexual experience would be significantly related to emotion responses subsequent to imaging the sexual scene. It was also hypothesized that subjects with conservative sexual standards would respond with more negative emotions (particularly fear and guilt) than those with liberal standards.

The test materials that were passed out to the students contained four research forms: the DES II (the trait version of the DES), the Reiss Scale of Sexual Standards (Reiss, 1967) a modified Podell–Perkins Sexual Experience Scale (Podell and Perkins, 1957) and the DES (state measure of emotion). The items on the Sexual Standards Scale measured the participants belief in (or agreement with) behavior ranging from "kissing with affection" to "sexual intercourse without affection." The Sexual Experience Scale asked the participants to indicate the frequency with which they performed the various sex-related activities ranging from kissing to sexual intercourse. The data for each emotion trait and for each posttreatment emotion state (subsequent to visualization of the sexual scene) was analyzed in a 2 × 3 × 3 factorial design: 2 (male–female) × 3 (sexual virgin, relatively inexperienced, sexually more experienced) × 3 (standards that do not permit premarital coitus, standards that permit coitus with affection, and standards that permit coitus without affection). In this summary we shall be concerned primarily with responses related to shyness and guilt. Remember, the participants completed the DES II (trait measure of emotions) before seeing any of the rest of the test materials. They completed the DES (state measure of emotions) immediately after imaging and visualizing sexual intercourse.

The DES II revealed an interesting curvilinear relationship between amount of sexual experience and amount of trait guilt. The participants who had had sexual intercourse only one or a few times reported the highest amount of guilt, the more sexually experienced participants reported the least amount of guilt, and virgins occupied the middle position. Perhaps subjects who had had sexual experience only a few times were still working through their guilt feelings and such affective–cognitive preoccupation resulted in higher scores on trait guilt. This finding is consistent with results cited by McCary (1973).

The individual's level of sexual experience also had a significant effect upon the amount of state guilt aroused by visualizing sexual intercourse. In the case of the female participants, the more sexually experienced the individual the less guilt was aroused. In the case of the male group, men who had a single or only a few sexual experiences reported more guilt subsequent to visualization of sexual intercourse than did the men who were virgins or the men who were sexually more experienced. Thus the males' scores on the state measure of emotion following visualization of intercourse follow the same pattern as that of all subjects on the trait measure of guilt. Again the data suggested that, at least for males, the period when a person is first obtaining sexual experience is likely to be relatively more guilt laden than periods of virginity or sexual sophistication.

The sexual standards of the individuals also affected the amount of guilt aroused by visualizing the sexual scene. Participants who indicated that they did not believe in premarital intercourse reported greater guilt as a result of visualizing sexual intercourse than did participants who accepted premarital coitus. In general, the more liberal the participants' sexual attitude as measured by the sexual standards scale the less guilt they felt when they visualized sexual intercourse. The data are not entirely consistent with Lewis's hypothesis that men tend to be more guilt prone while women tend to be more prone to shame and shyness. As noted in Chapter 15, males report greater trait shyness than females. The same is true for trait guilt. Thus while men reported slightly more shyness and guilt in their day-to-day lives (irrespective of cause), women reported more shyness and guilt subsequent to visualization of sexual intercourse. Further, female virgins reported significantly more guilt in their day-to-day lives than did male virgins. This may help explain the fact that, at least until quite recently and perhaps still today, within a given age group more women are virgins than are men. It should be noted that Lewis's hypothesis applies to behavior in general, while these data relate only to sexual behavior.

Considerable research data support the conclusion that guilt as a personality trait (trait guilt) and guilt as a psychological state (state guilt) are reliable and valid psychological phenomena that have important consequences for personality and social behavior. Trait guilt may be defined in terms of an individual's guilt threshold or his or her generalized expectancy of self-mediated punishment for violating or anticipating the violation of interalized standards of proper behavior or codes of conduct. Thus guilt as a personality trait or tendency serves as a regulator of behavioral propriety and as an inhibitor of improper thoughts, feelings, and actions.

Research support for the construct of trait guilt was provided by Mosher's (1965) finding that guilt over hostility (hostility guilt) prevented the expression of verbal hostility in a verbal conditioning study. Also, Ogle and Mosher (1968) found that subjects high on trait guilt showed significant increases in state guilt after engaging in hostile–aggressive behavior in a laboratory situation. The Mosher and Galbraith (1970) finding that subjects high on sex guilt were inhibited in making sexual responses to the double entendre word association test was also evidence of the validity of the concept of trait guilt.

In addition to the laboratory studies already discussed, several studies of prison inmates have also supported the notion that trait guilt has as a real and important influence on important aspects of human behavior. Oliver and Mosher (1968) and Persons and Marks (1969) showed that prisoners' scores on the Mosher guilt scale were positively correlated with MMPI subscales associated with inhibition (Pt and Si scales) and negatively correlated with MMPI subscales indicative of acting-out behavior (F, Pd, Sc, and MA scales). Mosher and Mosher (1967) found that prisoners who commit offenses against property have higher guilt than prisoners who commit offenses against people. Persons (1970a) showed that there was a negative relationship between trait guilt and total number of crimes committed by an inmate. Further, he showed that there was a significant negative relationship between hostility guilt and crimes of violence (the lower the guilt the greater the number of violent crimes), and similarly the lower the prisoners' scores on sex guilt the higher the number of sexual crimes. A more detailed study of the relationship of the various Mosher guilt subscales in the prison population showed that the guilt–crime relationship was highly complex (Persons, 1970b). For example, both trait and state guilt showed a significant interaction with race and type of crime. Further studies of trait and state guilt in real life situations are needed.

Summary

In differential emotions theory guilt is the key affect in the development of personal and social responsibility and the phenomena of conscience. While there probably are some basic human conditions that universally elicit guilt, conscience consists mainly of affective–cognitive structures that include precepts inculcated by parents and societal institutions. These affective–cognitive structures motivate and guide moral and ethical behavior. Though guilt is predominant in the development of the feeling of responsibility, positive emotions may characterize altruism that is extended without expectation of reciprocation—the highest form of moral–ethical action.

Shame and guilt often occur together. Tomkins argues that they are essentially one emotion with two representations in consciousness. Ausubel holds that guilt involves a component of moral shame, but he recognizes that guilt includes other important self-reactions and that nonmoral shame is independent of guilt.

Most theorists agree that shame typically involves the real or imaged sanctions of other people and that guilt is mainly a function of internal sanctions, though external ones may also be involved. Guilt results from the violation of ethical, moral, or religious standards. While certain ethical standards may have a basis in evolutionary-biological history, the specifics of various codes are internalized through identification with parents and significant adults, imitation or modeling, induction of empathy, and other forms of social and experiential learning.

The expression of guilt is not as sharply defined as the expression of other negative emotions. Guilt may cause the person to hold the head lower and to avert his or her gaze.

The experience of guilt consists of a gnawing feeling that one is in the wrong, "not right" with others or with the self. The profile of emotions in guilt situations shows a relatively high mean for distress and fear. The frequency with which fear is elicited in guilt situations probably accounts for the lack of a clear differentiation between these two emotions in a number of theories. The guilt experience is characterized by a high degree of tension, a moderate degree of impulsiveness, and relatively little self-assurance.

Guilt complements shame in fostering social responsibility and it serves as a check on wanton waste and sexual and aggressive exploitation. The development of guilt and conscience fosters growth toward greater psychological maturity.

An overdeveloped conscience or too low a threshold for guilt may lead to serious adjustment problems or psychopathology. Several theorists hold that high guilt proneness can lead to obsessive–compulsive disorders and even to paranoid schizophrenia.

In Freudian theory the development of conscience and guilt is dependent upon the way the Oedipus conflict is resolved in the child's developing superego. Existential theorists hold that one inevitably experiences guilt because of one's failure to live up to one's full human potentialities. In Khanna's critique of existential theorists he points out their failure to differentiate between being guilty and being human.

Various learning theory conceptions of the developmental origins of guilt have contributed significantly to our understanding of conscience and morality. These theories have emphasized the role of various forms of social learning in the internalization of guilt. Most of them agree that a warm accepting relationship with a parent figure forms the best background for the development of a healthy conscience and an appropriate guilt threshold. Both theoretical arguments and a number of empirical studies suggest that some combination of temporary withdrawal of approval and the induction of empathic responses with understanding of one's role in bringing harm to others provide the best framework for discipline that leads to an appropriate guilt threshold and a mature conscience.

REFERENCES

Abelson, R. P., & Sermat, V. Multidimensional scaling of facial expressions. *Journal of Experimental Psychology,* 1962, *63*(6), 546–554.

Abraham, K. Notes on the psycho-analytical investigation and treatment of manic-depressive insanity and allied conditions (Originally published 1911). In W. Gaylin (Ed.), *The meaning of despair.* New York: Science House, 1968.

Adler, A. *Social interest: A challenge to mankind.* New York: Capricorn Books, 1964.

Ainsworth, M. D. *Infancy in Uganda: Infant care and the growth of love.* Baltimore: Johns Hopkins Press, 1967.

Allen, J. G., & Hamsher, J. H. The development and validation of a test of emotional styles. *Journal of Consulting and Clinical Psychology,* 1974, *42*(5), 663–668.

Allport, F. H. *Social psychology.* Cambridge, Mass.: Houghton Mifflin, 1924.

Allport, G. W. *Personality: A psychological interpretation.* New York: Holt, 1937.

Allport, G. W. *Becoming: Basic Considerations for a psychology of personality.* New Haven: Yale University Press, 1955.

Altmann, S. A. *Social communication among primates.* Chicago: University of Chicago Press, 1967.

Ambrose, A. The age of onset of ambivalence in early infancy: Indications from the study of laughing. *Journal of Child Psychology and Psychiatry,* 1963, *4,* 167–181.

Andrew, R. J. Evolution of facial expression. *Science,* 1963, *142,* 1034–1041.

Andrew, R. J. The origins of facial expressions. *Scientific American,* 1965, *213,* 88–94.

Anokhin, P. K. New data on the functional heterogeneity of the reticular formation of the brain stem. *Zh. Vyssh. Nervn. Deyat. im. I. P. Pavlova,* 1958, *9,* 484–499.

Anshen, R. N. (Ed.) Credo Perspectives: Their meaning and function. In E. W. Sinnott's *The bridge of life.* New York: Simon and Schuster, 1966.

Antrobus, J. S., Singer, J. L., & Greenberg, S. Studies in the stream of consciousness: Experimental enhancement and suppression of spontaneous cognitive processes. *Perceptual and Motor Skills,* 1966, *23*(2), 399–417.

Appley, M. H., & Trumbull, R. (Eds.) *Psychological stress issues in research.* New York: Appleton-Century-Crofts, 1967.

Ardrey, R. *The territorial imperative.* New York: Dell, 1966.

Argyle, M. *Bodily communication.* New York: International Universities Press, 1975.

Argyle, M., & Dean, J. Eye contact, distance, and affiliation. *Sociometry,* 1965, *28*(3), 289–304.

Arnold, M. B. *Emotion and personality,* Vol. I, *Psychological aspects.* New York: Columbia University Press, 1960(a).

Arnold, M. B. *Emotion and personality*, Vol. II, *Neurological and physiological aspects*. New York: Columbia University Press, 1960(b).

Arnold, M. B. In defense of Arnold's theory of emotion. *Psychological Bulletin*, 1968, *70*, 283–284.

Asberg, M., Thoren, P., & Traskman, L. Serotonin depression—a biochemical subgroup within the affective disorders? *Science*, 1976, *191*, 478–480.

Asratyan, E. L. Concurrent elaboration of different types of conditioned reflexes to the same stimulus (in Russian). In A. Tonkikh (Ed.), *Tret'e soveshchanic po fiziologicheskim problemam*. Moscow: 1938, p. 31.

Atkinson, J. W. *An introduction to motivation*. Princeton, New Jersey: Van Nostrand, 1964.

Ausubel, D. P. Relationships between shame and guilt in the socializing process. *Psychological Review*, 1955, *62*, 378–390.

Averill, J. R. Grief: Its nature and significance. *Psychological Bulletin*, 1968, *70*, 721–748.

Averill, J. R. Autonomic response patterns during sadness and mirth. *Psychophysiology*, 1969, *5*, 399–444.

Averill, J. R., Opton, E. M., Jr., & Lazarus, R. S. Cross-cultural studies of psychophysiological responses during stress and emotion. *International Journal of Psychology*, 1969, *4*, 83–102.

Ax, A. F. The physiological differentiation between fear and anger in humans. *Psychosomatic Medicine*, 1953, *15*, 433–442.

Bach, R. *Jonathan Livingston Seagull*. New York: Macmillan, 1970.

Bakan, D. *Disease, pain, and sacrifice: Toward a psychology of suffering*. Chicago: University of Chicago Press, 1968.

Ball, W., & Tronick, E. Infant responses to impending collision: Optical and real. *Science*, 1971, *171*, 818–820.

Bandura, A. Blanchard, E., & Ritter, B. The relative efficacy of desensitization and modeling approaches for inducing behavioral, affective, and attitudinal changes. *Journal of Personality and Social Psychology*, 1969, *13*, 73–199.

Bardwick, J. M. *The psychology of women*. New York: Harper and Row, 1971.

Baron, R. A. Magnitude of victim's cues and level of prior anger arousal as determinants of adult aggressive behavior. *Journal of Personality and Social Psychology*, 1971, *17*, 236–243. (a)

Baron, R. A. Exposure to an aggressive model and apparent probability of retaliation from the victim as determinants of aggressive behavior. *Journal of Experimental and Social Psychology*, 1971, *7*, 343–355. (b)

Bartlett, E. S., & Izard, C. E. A dimensional and discrete emotions investigation of the subjective experience of emotion. In C. E. Izard (Ed.), *Patterns of emotions: A new analysis of anxiety and depression*. New York: Academic Press, 1972.

Bartlett, F. *Thinking: An experimental and social study*. London: Allen & Unwin, 1958.

Basowitz, H., Persky, H., Korchin, S. J., & Grinker, R. R. *Anxiety and stress*. New York: McGraw-Hill, 1955.

Bauman, M. J., & Straughon, J. H. BRS as a function of anxiety, stress, and sex. *Psychological Record*, 1969, *19*, 339–344.

Beach, F. A. *Sex and behavior*. New York: Krieger, 1935.

Bechtereva, N. P. Personal communication. Institute of Medical Sciences, Leningrad, USSR, 1974.

Beck, A. T. *Depression*. New York: Harper and Row, 1967.

Becker, E. Toward a comprehensive theory of depression: A cross disciplinary appraisal of objects, games, and meaning. *Journal of Nervous and Mental Disease*, 1962, *57*, 281–304.

Beecher, H. K. *Pain: One mystery solved*. Science, 1966, *151*, 840–841.

Benedict, R. *Patterns of culture*. Boston: Houghton-Mifflin, 1934.

Benedict, R. *The chrysanthemum and the sword.* Boston: Houghton-Mifflin, 1946.

Bergson, H. L. *Laughter: An essay on the meaning of the comic* (translated by Cloudesley Brereton). New York: MacMillan, 1911.

Berkowitz, L. *Roots of aggression.* New York: Atherton 1969.

Berkun, M. M., Kessen, M. L., & Miller, N. E. Hunger reducing effects of food by stomach fistula versus food by mouth measured by a consummatory response. *Journal of Comparative and Physiological Psychology,* 1952, *45* 550–554.

Berlyne, D. E. Novelty and curiosity as determinants of exploratory behavior. *British Journal of Psychology,* 1950, *41,* 68–80.

Berlyne, D. E. The arousal and satiation of perceptual curiosity in the rat. *Journal of Comparative and Physiological Psychology,* 1955, *48,* 238–246.

Berlyne, D. E. *Conflict, arousal, and curiosity.* New York: McGraw-Hill, 1960.

Berlyne, D. E. Arousal and reinforcement. *Nebraska Symposium on Motivation, 1967.* Lincoln, Nebraska: University of Nebraska Press, 1967, *15,* 1–110.

Berlyne, D. E. What next? Concluding summary. In H. I. Day, D. E. Berlyne, & D. E. Hunt (Eds.), *Intrinsic motivation: A new direction in education.* Toronto: Holt, Rinehart, & Winston of Canada, 1971.

Bernstein, I. S. Activity patterns in pigtail monkey groups. *Folia Primatologica,* 1970, *12,* 187–198.

Beyers, C. K. Don't worry if you're shy. *The Nashville Tennessean, Parade,* January 18, 1976.

Bibring, E. The mechanism of depression. In P. Greenacre (Ed.), *Affective disorders.* New York: International Universities Press, 1953.

Bibring, E. The mechanism of depression. In W. Gaylin (Ed.), *The meaning of despair.* New York: Science House, 1968.

Bindra, D. The interrelated mechanisms of reinforcement and motivation, and the nature of their influence on response. In W. J. Arnold & D. Levine (Eds.), *Nebraska Symposium on Motivation, 1969,* Lincoln Nebraska: University of Nebraska Press, 1969, pp. 1–33.

Blackburn, T. Sensuous–intellectual complementarity in science. *Science,* 1971, *174,* 10003–10007.

Block, J. Studies in the phenomenology of emotions. *Journal of Abnormal and Social Psychology,* 1957, *54,* 358–363.

Blurton Jones, N. G. *Ethological studies of child behavior.* New York: Cambridge University Press, 1972.

Blurton Jones, N. G., & Konner, M. J. Sex differences in behavior of London and Bushmen children. In R. P. Michael & J. H. Crook (Eds.), *Comparative ecology and behavior of primates.* London: Academic Press, 1973.

Bogen, J. E. The other side of the brain, II: An appositional mind. *Bulletin of the Los Angeles Neurological Society,* 1969, *34,* 191–220. (Also in R. E. Ornstein (Ed.), *The nature of human consciousness,* San Francisco: W. H. Freedman and Co., 1973.)

Bolwig, N. Facial expression in primates with remarks on a parallel development in certain carnivores (a preliminary report on work in progress). *Behavior,* 1964, 22, 167–192.

Boring, E. G. *A history of experimental psychology.* New York: Appleton-Century-Crofts, 1950.

Boss, M. *Psychoanalysis and daseinsanalysis.* (Trans. by Ludwig R. Lefebre). New York: Basic Books, 1963.

Bostrom, R. N. Affective, cognitive, and behavioral dimensions of communicative attitudes. *The Journal of Communication,* 1970, *20*(4), 359–369.

Bower, T. G. R. *Development in infancy.* San Francisco: Freeman. 1974.

Bowlby, J. Some pathological processes set in train by early mother–child separation. *Journal of Mental Science,* 1953, *99,* 265–272.

Bowlby, J. Grief and mourning in infancy and early childhood. *Psychoanalytical Study of Children,* 1960, *15,* 9–52.

Bowlby, J. Processes of mourning. *International Journal of Psychoanalysis.* 1961, *42,* 317–340.

Bowlby, J. Pathological mourning and childhood mourning. *Journal of the American Psychoanalytic Association,* 1963, *11,* 500–541.

Bowlby, J. *Attachment and Loss,* Vol I. *Attachment.* New York: Basic Books, 1969.

Bowlby, J. *Attachment and Loss:* Vol. II. *Separation, anxiety, and anger.* New York: Basic Books, 1973.

Bradburn, N. M. *The structure of psychological well-being.* Chicago: Aldine, 1969.

Brady, J. V. Emotion: Some conceptual problems and psychophysiological experiments. In M. B. Arnold (Ed.), *Feelings and emotions: The Loyola Symposium.* New York: Academic Press, 1970.

Brandt, K., & Fenz, W. D. Specificity in verbal and physiological indicants of anxiety. *Perceptual and Motor Skills,* 1969, *29,* 663–675.

Breggin, P. R. The psychophysiology of anxiety. *Journal of Nervous and Mental Disease,* 1964, *139,* 558–568.

Brierly, M. Affects in theory and practice. *International Journal of Psychoanalysis,* 1937, *18,* 256–268.

Brill, A. A. Editorial note in S. Freud, *The basic writings of Sigmund Freud.* New York: Random House, 1938.

Brock, T. C., & Becker, L. A. "Debriefing" and susceptibility to subsequent experimental manipulations. *Journal of Experimental Social Psychology,* 1966, *2,* 314–323.

Bronson, G. W. Infants' reactions to unfamiliar persons and novel objects. *Monographs of the Society for Research in Child Development,* 1972, *37*(3), Serial No. 148.

Bronson, G. W. General issues in the study of fear: Section II. In M. Lewis & L. A. Rosenblum (Eds.), *The origins of fear.* New York: John Wiley, 1974, 254–258.

Brown, J. S., & Farber, I. E. Emotions conceptualized as intervening variables with suggestions toward a theory of frustration. *Psychological Bulletin,* 1951, *48,* 465–495.

Brownfield, C. A. Optimal stimulation levels of normal and disturbed subjects in sensory deprivation. *Psychologia,* 1966, *9,* 27–38.

Bruner, J. S., & Goodman, C. C. Value and needs as organizing factors in perception. *Journal of Abnormal and Social Psychology,* 1947, *42,* 33–44.

Buck, R., Miller, R. E., & Caul, W. F. Sex personality and physiological variables in the communication of affect via facial expression. *Journal of Personality and Social Psychology,* 1974, *30*(4), 587–596.

Buck, R., Savin, V. J., Miller, R. E., & Caul, W. F. Nonverbal communication of affect in humans. *Proceedings of the 77th Annual Convention of the American Psychological Association,* 1969, 367–368.

Bugelski, B. R. Words and things and images. *American Psychologist,* 1970, *25*(11), 1002–1012.

Bugental, J. F. I. *The search for authenticity.* New York: Holt, Rinehart & Winston, 1965.

Bull, N. The attitude theory of emotion. *Nervous and Mental Disease Monographs,* 1951, *81.*

Buss, A. H. *The psychology of aggression.* New York: Wiley, 1961.

Buss, A. H. The effect of harm on subsequent aggression. *Journal of Experimental Research in Personality,* 1966, *1,* 249–255. (a)

Buss, A. H. Instrumentality of aggression, feedback and frustration as determinants of physical aggression. *Journal of Personality and Social Psychology,* 1966, *3,* 153–162. (b)

Buss, A. H. Aggression pays. In J. L. Singer (Ed.), *The control of aggression and violence.* New York: Academic Press, 1971.

Butler, R. A. Discrimination learning by rhesus monkeys to visual exploration motivation. *Journal of Comparative and Physiological Psychology,* 1953, *46,* 95–98.

Butler, R. A. Incentive conditions which influence visual exploration. *Journal of Experimental Psychology*, 1954, *48*, 19–23.

Butler, R. A. The effect of deprivation of visual incentives on visual-exploration motivation in monkeys. *Journal of Comparative and Physiological Psychology*, 1957, *50*, 177–179.

Butler, R. A. The differential effect of visual and auditory incentives on the performance of monkeys. *American Journal of Psychology*, 1958, *71*, 591–593.

Buytendijk, F. J. J. The phenomenological approach to the problem of feelings and emotions. In M. L. Reymert (Ed.), *Feelings and emotions*. New York: McGraw-Hill, 1950, pp. 127–141.

Byrne, D. Interpersonal attraction and attitude similarity. *Journal of Abnormal and Social Psychology*, 1961, *62*, 713–715.

Candland, D. K. Discriminability of facial regions used by the domestic chicken in maintaining the social dominance order. *Journal of Comparative and Physiological Psychology*, 1969, *69*(2), 281–285.

Cannon, W. B. The James–Lange theory of emotions: A critical examination and an alternative theory. *American Journal of Psychology*, 1927, *39*, 106–124.

Cantor, J. R., Bryant, J., & Zillman, D. Enhancement of humor appreciation by transferred excitation. *Journal of Personality and Social Psychology*, 1974, *30*, 812–821.

Cantor, J. R., Zillman, D., & Bryant, J. Enhancement of experienced sexual arousal in response to erotic stimuli through misattribution of unrelated residual excitation. *Journal of Personality and Social Psychology*, 1975, *32*, 69–75.

Cantril, H. A transactional inquiry concerning mind. In Jordon M. Scher (Ed.), *Theories of the mind*. New York: The Free Press of Glencoe, 1962.

Carlsmith, J. M., & Gross, A. E. Some effects of guilt on compliance. *Journal of Personality and Social Psychology*, 1969, *4*, 321–322.

Carlson, R., & Levy, N. Self, values, and affects: Derivations from Tomkins's polarity theory. *Journal of Personality and Social Psychology*, 1970, *16*(2), 338–345.

Cattell, R. B. *The scientific analysis of personality*. Harmondsworth, England: Penguin, 1965.

Cattell, R. B. *Personality and mood by questionnaire*. San Francisco: Jossey Bass Co., 1973.

Cattell, R. B., & Scheier, I. H. *The meaning and measurement of neuroticism and anxiety*. New York: Ronald Press, 1961.

Charlesworth, W. R. Cognition in infancy: Where do we stand in the mid-sixties? *Merrill-Palmer Quarterly*, 1968, *14*, 25–46.

Charlesworth, W. R. The role of surprise in cognitive development. In D. Elkind & J. Flavell (Eds.), *Studies in cognitive development*. London: Oxford University Press, 1969.

Charlesworth, W. R. General issues in the study of fear: Section IV. In M. Lewis & L. A. Rosenblum (Eds.), *The origins of fear*. New York: John Wiley, 1974, 254–258.

Charlesworth, W. R., & Kreutzer, M. A. Facial expressions of infants and children. In Paul Ekman (Ed.), *Darwin and facial expression: A century of research in review*. New York: Academic Press, 1973.

Chevalier-Skolnikoff, S. Facial expressions of emotion in nonhuman primates. In P. Ekman (Ed.), *Darwin and facial expression: A century of research in review*. New York: Academic Press, 1973.

Cheyne, J. A., & Walters, R. H. Punishment and prohibition: Some origins of self-control. In T. M. Newcomb (Ed.), *New directions in psychology*, IV. New York: Holt, Rinehart & Winston, 1970, 281–266.

Church, J. *Three babies*. New York: Random House, 1966.

Cofer, C. N. *Motivation and emotion*. Glenview, Ill.: Scott, Foresman and Co., 1972.

Cofer, C. N., & Appley, M. H. *Motivation: Theory and research*. New York: Wiley, 1964.

Cohn, C. K., Dunner, D. L., & Axelrod, J. Reduced catechol-o-methyltransferase activity in the red blood cells of women with primary affective disorders. *Science*, 1970, *170*, 1323–1324.

Coles, R. *Children of crisis: A study of courage and fear*. Boston: Little-Brown, 1971.

Combs, A. W., & Snygg, D. *Individual behavior*. New York: Harper, 1959.

Constantinople, A. Some correlates of average level of happiness among college students. *Developmental Psychology*, 1970, *2*(3), 447.

Costello, C. G. Depression: Loss of reinforcers of loss of reinforcer effectivenss. *Behavior Therapy*, 1972, *3*, 240–250.

Cupchik, G. C., & Leventhal, H. Consistency between expressive behavior and the evaluation of humorous stimuli: The role of sex and self-observation. *Journal of Personality and Social Psychology*, 1974, *30*, 429–442.

Dahl, H. The appetite hypothesis of emotions: A new psychoanalytic model of motivation. In C. E. Izard (Ed.), *Emotions and psychopathology*. New York: Plenum Press, in preparation.

Daniels, D. N., Gilula, M. F., & Ochberg, F. M. (Eds.). *Violence and the struggle for existence*. Boston: Little-Brown, 1970.

Danish, S. J., & Kagan, N. Measurement of affective sensitivity: Toward a valid measure of interpersonal perception. *Journal of Consulting Psychology*, 1971, *18*(1), 51–54.

Darwin, C. R. *The expression of emotions in man and animals*. London: John Murray, 1872.

Darwin, C. R. A biographical sketch of an infant. *Mind*, 1877, *2*, 286–294.

Das, S. S. Grief and suffering. *Psychotherapy: Theory, Research, and Practice*, 1971, *8*(1), 8–9.

Davis, A., & Dollard, J. *Children of bondage*. Washington, D.C.: American Council on Education, 1940.

Davis, J. Theories of biological etiology of affective disorders. *International Review of Neurobiology*, 1970, *12*, 145–175.

Davis, K. E. Sex on campus: Is there a revolution? *Medical Aspects of Human Sexuality*. January, 1971, 128–142.

Davis, R. T., Setledge, P. H., & Harlow, H. F. Performance of normal and brain-operated monkeys on mechanical puzzles with and without food incentive. *Journal of Genetic Psychology*, 1950, *77*, 305–311.

Davitz, J. R. A dictionary of grammar of emotion. In M. B. Arnold (Ed.), *Feelings and emotions*. New York: Academic Press, 1970.

Deci, E. *Intrinsic motivation*. New York: Plenum Press, 1975.

Deglin, V. L. Clinical-experimental studies of unilateral electroconvulsive block. *Journal of Neuropathology and Psychiatry*, 1973, *11*, 1609–1621.

Deikman, A. Bimodal consciousness. *Archives of General Psychiatry*, 1971, *45*, 481–489.

Deikman, A. The meaning of everything. In Robert E. Ornstein (Ed.), *The nature of human consciousness*. San Francisco: W. H. Freeman, 1973.

Delgado, J. M. R. *Physical control of the mind: Toward a psychocivilized society*. New York: Harper and Row, 1971.

Dember, W. N., & Earl, R. W. Analysis of exploratory, manipulatory, and curiosity behaviors. *Psychological Review*, 1957, *64*, 91–96.

Dennis, W. An experimental test of two theories of social smiling in infants. *Journal of Social Psychology*, 1935, *6*, 214–223.

Dennis, W. Causes of retardation among institutional children: Iran. *Journal of Genetic Psychology*, 1960, *96*, 47–59.

de Rivera, J. A decision theory of emotions (Doctoral dissertation, Stanford University, 1961). *Dissertation Abstracts International*, 1962. (University Microfilms No. 62-2356.)

Dewey, J. *The theory of emotions: II*. The significance of emotions. *Psychological Review*, 1895, *2*, 13–32.

Dickey, E. C., & Knower, F. H. A note on some ethnological differences in recognition of simulated expressions of the emotions. *American Journal of Sociology*, 1941, *47*, 190–193.

Douglas, R. J. The hippocampus and behavior. *Psychological Bulletin,* 1967, *67,* 416–442.

Douglas, R. J., & Pribram, K. H. Learning and limbic lesions. *Neuropsychologia,* 1966, *4,* 197–220.

Driscoll, J. M., & Lanzetta, J. T. Effects of problem uncertainty and prior arousal on predecisional information search. *Psychological Reports,* 1964, *14,* 975–988.

Duchenne, G. B. *Mécanisme de la physionomie humaine.* Paris: Baillière, 1876.

Duffy, E. Emotion: An example of the need for reorientation in psychology. *Psychological Review,* 1934, *41,* 184–198.

Duffy, E. An explanation of "emotional" phenomena without the use of the concept "emotion." *Journal of General Psychology,* 1941, *25,* 283–293.

Duffy, E. The concept of energy mobilization. *Psychological Review,* 1951, *58,* 30–40.

Duffy, E. The psychological significance of the concept "arousal" or "activation." *Psychological Review,* 1957, *64,* 265–275.

Duffy, E. *Activation and behavior.* New York: John Wiley, 1962.

Dumas, G. La mimque des aveugles. *Bulletin de L'Académie de Médecin.* Paris, 1932, *107,* 607–610.

Dumas, G. *La vie affective.* Paris: Presses Universitaires de France, 1948.

Dunbar, F. *Emotions and bodily changes*(4th ed.). New York: Columbia University Press, 1954.

Duval, S., & Wicklund, R. A. *A theory of objective self-awareness.* New York: Academic Press, 1972.

Eibl-Eibesfeldt, I. *Love and Hate: The natural history of behavior patterns.* New York: Holt, Rinehart & Winston, 1971.

Eibl-Eibesfeldt, I. Similarities and differences between cultures in expressive movements. In R. A. Hinde (Ed.), *Nonverbal communication.* Cambridge, Mass.: Cambridge University Press, 1972, pp. 20–33.

Ekman, P. Body position, facial expression, and verbal behavior during interviews. *Journal of Abnormal and Social Psychology,* 1964, *68*(3), 295–301.

Ekman, P. Universal and cultural differences in facial expression of emotion. In J. R. Cole (Ed.), *Nebraska Symposium on Motivation, 1971.* Lincoln, Nebraska: University of Nebraska Press, 1972.

Ekman, P. (Ed.). *Darwin and facial expression: A century of research in review.* New York: Academic Press, 1972.

Ekman, P., & Friesen, W. V. Nonverbal leakage and clues to deception. *Psychiatry,* 1969, *32*(1), 88–106.

Ekman, P., & Friesen, W. V. *Unmasking the face.* Englewood Cliffs, New Jersey: Prentice-Hall, 1975.

Ekman, P., Friesen, W. V., & Ellsworth, P. C. *Emotion in the human face: Guidelines for research and an integration of findings.* New York: Pergamon Press, 1972.

Ekman, P., Friesen, W. V., & Tomkins, S. S. Facial affect scoring technique: A first validity study. *Semiotica,* 1971, *1,* 37–53.

Ekman, P., Leibert, R. M., Friesen, W., Harrison, R., Zlatchin, C., Malmstrom, E. J., & Baron, R. A. Facial expressions of emotion while watching televised violence as predictors of subsequent aggression. In *Television and social behavior:* a report to the Surgeon General's Scientific Advisory Committee, Vol. 5. Washington, D.C.: U.S. Government Printing Office, 1971.

Ekman, P., Sorenson, E. R., & Friesen, W. V. Pan-cultural elements in facial displays of emotion. *Science,* 1969, *164,* 86–88.

Ellis, A. The justification of sex without love. In Elenor S. Morrison & Vera Borosage (Eds.), *Human sexuality: Contemporary perspectives.* California: National Press Books, 1973.

Ellsworth, P. C. Direct gaze as a social stimulus: The example of aggression. In P. L. Pliner, L. Krames, & T. Alloway (Eds.), *Nonverbal communication of aggression.* New York: Plenum Press, 1975.

Ellsworth, P. C., & Carlsmith, J. M. Effects of eye contact and verbal content on affective response to a dyadic interaction. *Journal of Personality and Social Psychology,* 1968, *10*(1), 15–20.

Ellsworth, P. C., & Ludwig, L. M. Visual behavior in social interaction. *Journal of Communication,* 1972, *22,* 375–403.

Ellsworth, P. C., & Ross, L. Eye contact and intimacy. Unpublished manuscript, Stanford University, 1974.

Emde, R. N., & Koenig, K. L. Neonatal smiling and rapid eye-movement states. *Journal of the American Academy of Child Psychiatry,* 1969, *8,* 57–67.

Emde, R. N., Gaensbauer, T. J., & Harmon, R. J. *Emotional expression in infancy.* New York: International Universities Press, 1976.

Engen, R., Levy, N., & Schlosberg, H. The dimensional analysis of a new series of facial expressions. *Journal of Experimental Psychology,* 1958, *55*(5), 454–458.

Epstein, S. The nature of anxiety with emphasis upon its relationship to expectancy. In C. D. Speilberger (Ed.), *Anxiety: Contemporary theory and research.* New York: Academic Press, 1972.

Erickson, E. H. *Childhood and society.* New York: Norton, 1950.

Erickson, E. H. Growth and crises of the healthy personality. In C. Kluckhohn, H. A. Murray, & D. M. Schneider (Eds.), *Personality in nature, society, and culture* (2nd ed./rev.). New York: Knopf, 1956, pp. 185–225.

Exline, R. Visual interaction—the glances of power and preference. In J. K. Cole (Ed.), *Nebraska Symposium on Motivation,* 1971, Lincoln, Nebraska: University of Nebraska Press, 1972.

Exline, R. V., Ellyson, S. L., & Long, B. Visual behavior as an aspect of power role relationships. In P. Plines, L. Krames, & T. Alloway (Eds.), *Nonverbal communication of aggression,* New York: Plenum Press, 1975.

Exline, R., Gray, D., & Schuette, D. Visual behavior in a dyad as affected by interview content and sex of respondent. *Journal of Personality and Social Psychology,* 1965, *1,* 201–209.

Faigan, H. Childrearing in the Rimrock community with special reference to the development of guilt. Unpublished doctoral dissertation, Radcliffe College, 1953.

Fair, C. M. *The dying self.* Middletown, Conn.: Wesleyan University Press, 1969.

Fantz, R. L. Pattern vision in unborn infants. *Science,* 1963, *140,* 296–297.

Fantz, R. L. Visual perception from birth as shown by pattern selectivity. *Annals of the New York Academy of Sciences,* 1965, *118,* 793–814. Also in L. J. Stone, H. T. Smith, & L. B. Murphy (Eds.), *The Competent Infant.* New York: Basic Books, 1973, 622–630.

Fantz, R. L. Pattern discrimination and selective attention as determinants of perceptual development from birth. In Aline H. Kidd & J. L. Rivoire (Eds.), *Perceptual development in children.* New York: International Universities Press, 1966, 143–173.

Fantz, R. L. Pattern vision in newborn infants. In L. J. Stone, H. T. Smith, & L. B. Murphy (Eds.), *The competent infant.* New York: Basic Books, 1973. (Also in *Science,* 1963, *140,* 296–297).

Fantz, R. L., & Nevis, S. Pattern preferences and perceptual–cognitive development in early infancy. *Merrill-Palmer Quarterly,* 1967, *13,* 77–108. (a)

Fantz, R. L., & Nevis, S. The predictive value of changes in visual preferences in early infancy. In J. Hellmuth (Ed.), *The exceptional infant* (Vol. 1). Seattle: Special Child Publications, 1967 (b).

Fehr, F. S., & Stern, J. A. Peripheral physiological variables and emotion: The James–Lange theory revisited. *Psychological Bulletin,* 1970, *74,* 411–424.

Feigl, H. Mind–body, not a pseudo problem. In Jordon M. Scher (Ed.), *Theories of the mind*. New York: The Free Press of Glencoe, 1962.

Fenichel, O. *The psychoanalytic theory of neurosis*. New York: Norton, 1945.

Fenyes, G. Moral judgment and situations: Appropriateness for self-blame and resistance to temptation. University of California: *Dissertation Abstracts*, 1967, *78*(13), 1687–1683.

Fenz, W. D., & Epstein, S. Manifest anxiety: Unifactorial or multifactorial composition. *Perceptual and Motor Skills*, 1965, *20*, 773–780.

Feshbach, S. Dynamics of morality of violence and aggression: Some psychological considerations. *American Psychologist*, 1971, *26*, 281–291.

Feshbach, S., Stiles, W. G., & Bitner, E. The reinforcing effect of witnessing aggression. *Journal of Experimental Research in Personality*, 1967, *2*, 133–139.

Festinger, L. *A theory of cognitive dissonance*. Evanston, Ill.: Row-Peterson, 1957.

Fitts, W. H. *The self-concept and self-actualization: Studies on the self-concept and rehabilitation*. Dede Wallace Center, Nashville, 1971.

Forster, C. B. A functional analysis of depression. *American Psychologist*, 1972, *28*, 857–871.

Fox, S. S., & Rudell, A. D. Operant-controlled neural event: Formal and systematic approach to electrical coding of behavior in brain. *Science*, 1968, *162*, 1299–1302.

Frankl, V. E. *Man's search for meaning; an introduction to logotherapy*. A newly revised and enlarged edition of *From death-camp to existentalism*. Trans. by Ilse Lasch. Boston: Beacon Press, 1962.

Freedman, J. L., & Fraser, S. C. Compliance without pressure: the foot-in-the-door technique. *Journal of Personality and Social Psychology*, 1966, *4*, 195–202.

Freedman, J. L., Wallington, S. A., & Bless, E. Compliance without pressure: The effect of guilt. *Journal of Personality and Social Psychology*, 1967, *7*(2), 117–124.

Freedman, S. J., Gruebaum, H. U., & Greenblath, M. Perceptual and cognitive changes in sensory deprivation. In P. Solomon, P. E. Kubsansky, P. H. Leiderman, J. H. Mendelson, R. Trumbull, & D. Wexler (Eds.), *Sensory deprivation*. Cambridge, Mass.: Harvard University Press, 1961.

Freud, S. *Civilization and its discontents* (Trans. by Joan Riviere). New York: Jonathan Cape and Hanson Smith, 1930.

Freud, S. *The basic writings of Sigmund Freud* (Trans. by A. A. Brill). New York: Random House, 1938.

Freud, S. Inhibitions, symptoms, and anxiety. In J. Strackey (Ed.), *The standard edition of the complete psychological works of Sigmund Freud*. Vol. 20. London: Hogarth Press, 1959. (Originally published, 1936.)

Freud, S. Mourning and melancholia. In W. Gaylin (Ed.), *The meaning of despair*. New York: Science House, 1968.

Frijda, N. H. Emotion and recognition of emotion. In M. B. Arnold (Ed.), *Feelings and Emotions*. New York: Academic Press, 1970.

Frijda, N. H., & Phillipszoon, E. Dimensions of recognition of expression. *Journal of Abnormal and Social Psychology*, 1963, *66*, 45–51.

Fromm-Reichmann, F. An intensive study of twelve cases of manic-depressive psychosis. Final Report, Office of Naval Research Contract Nonr-751(00), Baltimore: Washington School of Psychiatry, 1953.

Fry, P. S. Affect and resistance to temptation. *Developmental Psychology*, 1975, *11*, 466–472.

Fulcher, J. S. "Voluntary" facial expression in blind and seeing children. *Archives of Psychology*, 1942, *272*, 5–49.

Funkenstein, D. H. The physiology of fear and anger. *Scientific American*, 1955, *192*, 74–80.

Funkenstein, D. H., King, S. H., & Drolette, M. E. Mastery of stress. Cambridge: Harvard University Press, 1957.

Galin, D. Two modes of consciousness and two halves of the brain. In P. R. Lee, R. E.

Ornstein, D. Galin, A. Deikman, & C. T. Tart (Eds.), *Symposium on consciousness* (AAAS, 1974). New York: Viking, 1976.

Gaylin, W. (Ed.), *The meaning of despair.* New York: Science House, 1968.

Gambaro, S. Blood pressure relations to expressed and unexpressed anger in low guilt and high guilt subjects. *Dissertation Abstracts, 1967, 27*(9-B), 3284–3285.

Gasanov, G. G. Emotions, visceral functions, and limbic system. In G. G. Gasanov (Ed.), *Emotions and visceral functions.* Moscow: Elm Press, 1974.

Gazzaniga, M. S. The split brain in man. *Scientific American, 1967, 217,* 24–29.

Geldard, F. A. *The human senses.* New York: John Wiley, 1972.

Gellhorn, E. Prolegomena to a theory of the emotions. *Perspectives in Biology and Medicine, 1961, 4,* 403–436.

Gellhorn, E. Motion and emotion: The role of proprioception in the physiology and pathology of the emotions. *Psychological Review, 1964, 71*(6), 457–472.

Gellhorn, E. The neurophysiological basis of anxiety: A hypothesis. *Perspectives in Biology and Medicine, 1965, 8,* 488–515.

Gellhorn, E. The tuning of the nervous system: Physiological foundations and implications for behavior. *Perspectives in Biology and Medicine, 1967, 10,* 559–591.

Gellhorn, E. The emotions and the ergotropic and trophotropic systems. *Psychologische Froschung, 1970, 34,* 48–94.

Gesell, A. Emotion from the standpoint of a developmental morphology. In M. L. Reymert (Ed.), *Feelings and emotions,* New York: McGraw-Hill, 1950, pp. 393–397.

Gewirtz, J. Attachment, dependency, and a distinction in terms of stimulus control. In J. Gewirtz (Ed.), *Attachment and dependency.* Washington, D.C.: Winston, 1972, pp. 139–178.

Gibson, D. C. The young child's awareness of affect. *Child Development, 1969, 40,* 629–640.

Gibson, E. J. *Principles of perceptual learning and development.* New York: Appleton-Century-Crofts, 1969.

Gibson, E. J. Visual perception: Depth, constancies, and cognition. *American Scientist, 1970, 58,* 98–107.

Gibson, J. J. *The senses considered as perceptual systems.* Boston: Houghton-Mifflin, 1966.

Glueck, S., & Glueck, E. *Unraveling juvenile delinquency.* Cambridge, Mass.: Howard University Press, 1950.

Goldfarb, V. Emotional and intellectual consequences of psychologic deprivation in infancy: A re-evaluation. In P. H. Hock and J. Zubin (Eds.), *Psychopathology of childhood.* New York: Grune and Stratton, 1955, pp. 105–119.

Goldstein, K. *The organism.* New York: American Book, 1939.

Goodenough, F. L. Expressions of emotions in a blind–deaf child. *Journal of Abnormal and Social Psychology, 1932, 27,* 328–333.

Goodman, L. S., & Gilman, A. (Eds.), *Pharmacological basis of therapeutics* (4th edition). New York: Macmillan, 1970.

Gottschalk, L. A., & Gleser, G. C. *The measurement of psychological states through the content analysis of verbal behavior.* Los Angeles: University of California Press, 1969.

Grant, E. C. Human facial expression. *Man, 1969, 4,* 525–536.

Gray, J. A. *The psychology of fear and stress.* New York: McGraw-Hill, 1971.

Gray, W. Emotional–cognitive structuring: A new theory of mind. *FORUM for Correspondence and Contact, 1973, 5,* 1–6.

Grinker, R. R., & Speigel, J. *Men under stress.* Philadelphia: Blakiston, 1945.

Guhl, A. M. Peck-orders established in spite of debeaking. *American Poultry Journal, 1956, 20,* 4.

Haggard, E. A., & Isaacs, F. S. Micromomentary facial expressions as indicators of ego mechanisms in psychotherapy. In L. A. Gottschalk & A. H. Averback (Eds.), *Methods of research in psychotherapy.* New York: Appleton-Century-Crofts, 1966, pp. 154–165.

Hale, E. B. Observation on the social behavior of hens following debeaking. *Poultry Science,* 1948, *27,* 591–592.

Hall, C. S., & Lindzey, G. *Theories of Personality.* New York: John Wiley and Sons, 1970.

Hamburg, D. A. Emotions in the perspective of human evolution. In P. H. Knapp (Ed.), *Expression of the emotions in man.* New York: International Universities Press, 1963.

Hardy, J. D., Wolff, H. G., & Goodell, H. *Pain sensations and reactions.* Baltimore: Williams and Wilkins, 1952.

Harlow, H. F. Learning and satiation of response in intrinsically motivated complex puzzle performance by monkeys. *Journal of Comparative and Physiological Psychology,* 1950, *43,* 289–294.

Harlow, H. F. Motivation as a factor in the acquisition of new responses. *Nebraska Symposium on Motivation,* 1953, *1,* 24–49.

Harlow, H. F. The heterosexual affectional system in monkeys. *American Psychologist,* 1962, *17,* 1–9.

Harlow, H. F. *Learning to love.* San Francisco: Albion, 1971.

Harlow, H. F., & Zimmerman, R. R. Affectionate responses in the infant monkey. *Science,* 1959, *130,* 421–432.

Harrison, A. A., & Zajonc, R. B. The effects of frequency and duration of exposure on response competition and affective ratings. *The Journal of Psychology,* 1970, *75,* 163–169.

Hartman, H. Comments on the psychoanalytic theory of the ego. *Psychoanalytical Studies of Children,* 1950, *5,* 74–95.

Hartman, O. P. Influence of symbolically modeled instrumental aggression and pain cues on aggressive behavior. *Journal of Personality and Social Psychology,* 1969, *11,* 280–288.

Hass, H. *The human animal.* New York: Putnam's Sons, 1970.

Hawkins, C. K., & Lanzetta, J. T. Uncertainty, importance, and arousal as determinants of predecisional information search, *Psychological Reports,* 1965, *17,* 791–800.

Hebb, D. O. *The organization of behavior.* New York: John Wiley, 1949.

Hebb, D. O. Drives and CNS (conceptual nervous system). *Psychological Review,* 1955, *62,* 243–254.

Hebb, D. O. *The organization of behavior.* New York: Science Editions, 1961.

Hebb, D. O., & Thompson, W. R. The social significance of animal studies. In G. Lindzey (Ed.), *Handbook of social psychology,* Vol I. *Theory and method.* Cambridge, Mass.: Addison-Wesley, 1954, pp 532–561.

Heider, F. *The psychology of interpersonal relations.* New York: John Wiley, 1958.

Heinicke, C., & Westheimer, I. *Brief separations.* New York: International Universities Press; London: Longmans, 1966.

Henderson, D., & Gillespie, R. D. *A textbook of psychiatry.* London: Oxford University Press, 1956.

Hendrichsen, C., Kimball, R., & Kimball, D. Hippocampal lesions and the orienting response. *Journal of Comparative and Physiological Psychology,* 1969, *67,* 220–227.

Hendrick, I. Instinct and the ego during infancy. *Psychoanalytic Quarterly,* 1942, *11,* 33–58.

Hernandez-Peon, R. A neurophysiologic model of dreams and hallucinations. *Journal of Nervous and Mental Disease,* 1966, *141,* 623–650.

Hess, W. R. Stammganglien-Reizversuche. (*Verh, Dtsch. Phys. Ges.,* Sept., 1927.) *Ber. Gesamte Physiol. Exp. Pharmakol.,* 1928, *42,* 554–555.

Himwich, H. E. Emotional aspects of mind: Clinical and neurophysiological analysis. In Jordon M. Scher (Ed.), *Theories of the mind.* New York: The Free Press, 1962.

Hinde, R. A. Ethological models and the concept of drive. *British Journal of the Philosophy of Science,* 1956, *6,* 321–331.

Hinde, R. A. Unitary drives. *Animal Behavior,* 1959, *7,* 130–141.

Hinde, R. A. *Animal behavior: A synthesis of ethology and comparative psychology.* New York: McGraw-Hill, 1966.

Hinde, R. A., & Rowell, T. E. Communication by postures and facial expressions in the rhesus monkey *(Macaca mulatta). Proceedings of the Zoological Society of London,* 1962, *138,* 1–21.

Hoffman, M. L., & Saltzstein, H. D. Parent discipline and the child's moral development. *Journal of Personality and Social Psychology,* 1967, *5,* 45–57.

Hofstatter, P. R. Dimensionen des mimischen ausdrucks. *Zeitschrift fuer Angewandte und Experimentelle Psychologie,* 1955–56, *3,* 503–509.

Holmes, D. S. Differential change in affective intensity and the forgetting of unpleasant personal experiences. *Journal of Personality and Social Psychology,* 1970, *15*(3), 234–239.

Holt, R. R. On the interpersonal and intrapersonal consequences of expressing or not expressing anger. *Journal of Consulting and Clinical Psychology,* 1970, *35*(1), 8–12.

Holt, R. R. Beyond vitalism and mechanism: Freud's concept of psychic energy. In *Science and Psychoanalysis,* New York: Grune & Stratton, 1967, *1,* 1–41.

Holt, R. R. Drive or wish? A reconsideration of the psychoanalytic theory of motivation. In M. M. Gill & P. S. Holzman (Eds.), Psychology versus metapsychology: Psychoanalytic essays in memory of George S. Klein. *Psychological Issues* 1976, *9*(4), 158–197.

Huber, E. *Evolution of facial musculature and facial expression.* Baltimore: The Johns Hopkins Press, 1931.

Hull, C. L. *Principles of behavior.* New York: Appleton-Century-Crofts, 1943.

Hunt, J. McV. Intrinsic motivation and its role in development. In D. Levine (Ed.), *Nebraska Symposium on Motivation.* Lincoln: University of Nebraska Press, 1965, 189–282.

Huxley, A. *The doors of perception.* New York: Harper & Row, 1954.

Issac, W. Evidence for a sensory drive in monkeys. *Psychological Reports,* 1962, *11,* 175–181.

Ittelson, W. H., & Kilpatrick, F. P. Experiments in perception. *Scientific American,* 1951, - 185, 50–55.

Izard, C. E. Positive affect and behavioral effectiveness. Unpublished manuscript, Vanderbilt University, 1959.

Izard, C. E. *The face of emotion.* New York: Appleton-Century-Crofts, 1971.

Izard, C. E. *Patterns of emotions: A new analysis of anxiety and depression.* New York: Academic Press, 1972.

Izard, C. E. Patterns of emotions and emotion communication in hostility and aggression. In P. Pliner, L. Kramer, & T. Alloway (Eds.), *Nonverbal communication of aggression.* New York: Plenum Press, 1975.

Izard, C. E., & Caplan, S. Sex differences in emotion responses to erotic literature. *Journal of Clinical and Consulting Psychology,* 1974, *42,* 468.

Izard, C. E., Dougherty, F. E., Bloxom, B. M., & Kotsch, W. E. The differential emotions scale: A method of measuring the subjective experience of discrete emotions. Unpublished manuscript, Department of Psychology, Vanderbilt University, 1974.

Izard, C. E., Caplan, S., Walker, S., & Kotsch, W. E. Changes in emotions in response to erotic literature and opposite-sex experimenter. In preparation, 1977.

Izard, C. E., Izard, C. E., Jr., & Makarenko, Y. A. Observations on a communal group of infants. In preparation, 1977.

Izard, C. E., & Nunnally, J. C. Evaluative responses to affectively positive and negative facial photographs: Factor structure and construct validity. *Educational and Psychological Measurement,* 1965, *25,* 1061–1071.

Izard, C. E., Spiegel, M., Alessio, G., & Kotsch, W. E. Sex standards, sex experience, and emotion responses to imaging sexual intercourse, unpublished paper 1974.

Izard, C. E., & Tomkins, S. S. Affect and behavior: Anxiety as a negative affect. In C. D. Spielberger (Ed.), *Anxiety and behavior.* New York: Academic Press, 1966, pp. 81–125.

Jacobson, E. *Progressive relaxation*. Chicago: University of Chicago, 1929.

Jacobson, E. *Biology of emotions*. Springfield, Ill.: Charles Thomas, 1967.

James, W. What is emotion: *Mind*, 1884, *4*, 188–204.

James, W. *The principles of psychology*. New York: Holt, 1890. (Reprinted, New York: Dover, 1950.)

Janet, P. Fear of action as an essential element in the sentiment of melancholia. In M. L. Reymert (Ed.), *Feelings and emotions: The Wittenberg symposium*. Worcester, Mass.: Clark University Press, 1928.

Janis, I. L., Kagan, J., Mahl, G. F., & Holt, R. R. *Personality: Dynamics, development, and assessment*. New York: Harcourt, Brace, and World, 1969.

Jersild, A. T., & Holmes, F. B. Children's fears. *Child Development Monograph*, No. 20. New York: Teachers College, Columbia University, 1935.

John, E. R. Some speculations on the psychophysiology of mind. In Jordon M. Scher (Ed.), *Theories of the mind*. New York: The Free Press of Glencoe, 1962.

Johnson, R. C., Ackerman, J. M., Frank, H., & Fionda, A. J. Resistance to temptation, guilt following yielding, and psychopathology. *Journal of Consulting and Clinical Psychology*, 1968, *32*, 169–175.

Johnson, R. C., Dokecki, P. R., & Mowrer, O. H. *Consciene, contract, and social reality: Theory and research in behavioral science*. New York: Holt, Rinehart & Winston, 1972.

Johnson, R. C., & Medinnus, G. R. *Child psychology: Behavior and development*. New York: John Wiley, 1965.

Jolly, A. Lemur social behavior and primate intelligence. *Science*, 1966, *153*, 501–506.

Jones, H. E. The study of patterns of emotional expression. In L. Reymert (Ed.), *Feelings and emotions*. New York: McGraw-Hill, 1950.

Jones, H. E. The study of patterns of emotional expression. In L. Reymert (Ed.), *Feelings and emotions*. New York: McGraw-Hill, 1950.

Jung, C. G. *Psychological types*. New York: Harcourt, 1933.

Kagan, J. Reflection-impulsivity: The generality and dynamics of conceptual tempo. *Journal of Abnormal Psychology*, 1966, *71*, 17–24.

Kagan, J. The determinants of attention in the infant. *American Scientist*, 1970, *58*, 298–306.

Kagan, J. Motives and development. *Journal of Personality and Social Psychology*, 1972, *22*, 51–66.

Kagan, J. Discrepancy, temperament and infant distress. In M. Lewis & L. A. Rosenblum (Eds.), *The origins of fear*. New York: John Wiley, 1974, pp. 229–248.

Kagan, J., & Berkun, M. M., The reward value of running activity. *Journal of Comparative and Physiological Psychology*, 1954, *47*, 108.

Kagan, J., & Lewis, M. Studies of attention in the human infant. *Merrill-Palmer Quarterly*, 1965, *11*, 95–127.

Katz, D., & Stotland, E. A preliminary statement to a theory of attitude structure and change. In S. Koch (Ed.), *Psychology: A study of a science*. Vol. 3, New York: McGraw-Hill, 1959, pp. 423–475.

Katz, P. K., & Ziegler, P. K. Self-image disparity: A developmental approach. *Journal of Personality and Social Psychology*, 1967, *5*, 186–195.

Kelly, G. A. *The psychology of personal constructs*. Vol. I. New York: Norton, 1955.

Kendon, A., & Cook, M. The consistency of gaze patterns in social interaction. *British Journal of Psychology*, 1969, *60*, 481–494.

Kessen, W. An American glimpse of the children of China: Report of a visit. *Social Science Research Council Items*, 1974, *28*, 41–44.

Kety, S. S. Neurochemical aspects of emotional behavior. In P. Black (Ed.), *Physiological correlates of emotion*. New York: Academic Press, 1970.

Khanna, D. A critique of existential guilt. *Psychotherapy: Theory, Research, and Practice*, 1969, *6*(3), 209–211.

Kierkegaard, S. *The concept of dread* (Trans. by W. Lowrie). Princeton: Princeton University Press, 1944. (Originally published in Danish, 1844.)

Kilty, K. M. On the relationship between affect and cognition. *Psychological Reports,* 1969, *25,* 215–219.

King, H. E. Psychological effects of excitation in the limbic system. In D. E. Sheer (Ed.), *Electrical stimulation of the brain.* Austin: University of Texas Press, 1961.

Kinsbourne, M. The minor cerebral hemisphere as a source of aphasic speech. *Archives of Neurology,* 1971, *25,* 302–306.

Kish, G. B. Cognitive innovation and stimulus seeking: A study of the correlates of the obscure figures test. *Perceptual and Motor Skills,* 1970, *30,* 95–101.

Kistiakovskaia, M. I. Stimuli evoking positive emotions in infants in the first months of life. *Soviet Journal of Psychiatry,* 1965, *3,* 39–48.

Klein, G. S. Freud's two theories of sexuality. In M. M. Gill & P. S. Holzman (Eds.), *Psychology versus metapsychology: Psychoanalytic essays in memory of George S. Klein.* New York: International Universities Press, 1976, 14–70.

Klerman, G. Depression and adaption. In R. Friedman & M. Katz (Eds.), *The psychology of depression: Contemporary theory and research.* Washington: Winston and Sons, 1974.

Klinger, E. *Structure and functions of fantasy.* New York: Wiley-Interscience, 1971.

Klinger, E. Consequences of commitment to and disengagement from incentives. *Psychological Review,* 1975, *82,* 1–25.

Kluckhohn, C., Murray, H. A., & Schneider, D. M. *Personality in nature, society, and culture.* New York: Knopf, 1956.

Knapp, P. H. Introduction: Emotional expression—past and present. In P. H. Knapp (Ed.), *Expression of the emotions in man.* New York: International Universities Press, 1963, pp. 3–19.

Koch, S. Behavior as "intrinsically" regulated: Work notes towards a pre-theory of phenomena called motivational. In M. R. Jones (Ed.), *Nebraska Symposium on Motivation.* Lincoln: University of Nebraska Press, 1956.

Koestler, A. *The act of creation.* New York: Macmillan, 1964.

Kotsch, W. E., & Izard, C. E. Experimenter-manipulated facial patterns and emotion experience. In preparation.

Kraines, S. H. *Mental depressions and their treatment.* New York: Macmillan, 1957.

Kron, R. E., Stein, M., & Goddard, K. E. Newborn sucking behavior affected by obstetric sedation. *Pediatrics,* 1966, *37,* 1012–1016.

Kubie, L. S. Theoretical aspects of sensory deprivation. In P. Solomon *et al.* (Eds.), *Sensory deprivation.* Cambridge, Mass.: Harvard Press, 1961, 208–220.

Kubie, L. S. The fallacious use of quantitative concepts in dynamic psychology. *Psychoanalytic Quarterly,* 1974, *16,* 507–518.

Kummer, H. *Social organization of Hamadrya baboon.* Chicago: University of Chicago Press, 1968.

Kuusinen, J. Affective and denotative structures of personality ratings. *Journal of Personality and Social Psychology,* 1969, *12*(3), 181–188.

Kwint, L. Ontogeny of motility of the face. *Child Development,* 1934, *5,* 1–12.

La Barbera, J. D., Izard, C. E., Parisi, S. A., & Vietze, P. Four and six month-old infant's visual responses to joy, anger, and neutral expression. *Child Development,* 1976, *47,* 535–538.

Laird, J. D. Self-attribution of emotion: The effects of expressive behavior on the quality of emotional experience. *Journal of Personality and Social Psychology,* 1974, *29,* 475–486.

Landis, C. An attempt to measure emotional traits in juvenile delinquency. In K. S. Lashley (Ed.), *Studies in the dynamics of behavior.* Chicago: University of Chicago Press, 1932.

Lange, K. *The emotions.* Denmark, 1885. (Trans. by Istar A. Haupt for K. Dunlap (Ed.), *The emotions.* Baltimore: Williams and Wilkins, 1922.)

Lanzetta, J. T., & Kleck R. Encoding and decoding of facial affect in humans. *Journal of Personality and Social Psychology*, 1970, *16*(1), 12–19.

Lazarus, A. A. Learning theory and the treatment of depression. *Behavior Research and Therapy*, 1968, *6*, 83–89.

Lazarus, R. S. Emotions and adaption: Conceptual and empirical relations. In W. Arnold (Ed.), *Nebraska Symposium on Motivation*, Lincoln: University of Nebraska Press, 1968.

Lazarus, R. S. Cognitive and coping processes in emotion. In B. Weiner (Ed.), *Cognitive views of human motivation*. New York: Academic Press, 1974.

Lazarus, R. S., & Averill, J. R. Emotion and cognition: With special reference to anxiety. In C. D. Spielberger (Ed.), *Anxiety: Contemporary theory and research*. New York: Academic Press, 1972.

Lazarus, R. S., Averill, J. R., & Opton, E. M., Jr. Towards a cognitive theory of emotion. In M. B. Arnold (Ed.), *Feelings and emotions*. New York: Academic Press, 1970.

Learmonth, G. J., Ackerly, W., & Kaplan, M. Relationships between palmar skin potential during stress and personality variables. *Psychosomatic Medicine*, 1959, *21*, 150.-157.

Le Boeuf, B. J., & Peterson R. S. Social status and mating activity in elephant seals. *Science*, 1969, *163*, 91–93.

Leeper, R. W. A motivational theory of emotion to replace "emotion as disorganized response." *Psychological Review*, 1948, *55*, 5–21.

Leeper, R. W. Some needed developments in the motivational theory of emotions. In D. E. Levine (Ed.), *Nebraska Symposium on Motivation*. Lincoln: University of Nebraska Press, 1965, pp. 25–122.

Leeper, R., & Madison, P. *Toward understanding human personalities*. New York: Appleton-Century-Crofts, 1959.

Lester, D. *Explorations in exploration*. New York: Van Nostrand Reinhold, 1969.

Leventhal, H. Emotions: A basic problem for social psychology. In C. Nemath (Ed.), *Social psychology: Classic and contemporary integrations*. Chicago: Rand McNally, 1974.

Leventhal, H., & Cupchik, G. C. The informational and facilitative effects of an audience upon expression and the evaluation of humorous stimuli. *Journal of Experimental Social Psychology*, 1975, *11*, 363–380.

Leventhal, H., & Cupchik, G. C. Sex differences in response to cartoons and slapstick movies. Unpublished manuscript, University of Wisconsin, Madison, Wisconsin, 1977.

Leventhal, H., & Mace, W. The effect of laughter on evaluation of a slapstick movie. *Journal of Personality*, 1970, *38*, 16–30.

Levine, J. Responses to humor. *Scientific American*, 1956, *194*(2), 31–35.

Levine, J. Humor. In *International Encyclopedia of the Social Sciences*. New York: Macmillan, 1968. (a)

Levine, J. Introductory essay. In J. Levine (Ed.), *Motivation in Humor* New York: Atherton Press, 1968. (b)

Levine, J., & Rakusin, J. The sense of humor of college students and psychiatric patients. *The Journal of General Psychology*, 1959. *60*, 183–190.

Levine, J., & Redlich, F. C. Intellectual and emotional factors in the appreciation of humor. *The Journal of General Psychology*, 1960, *62*, 25–35.

Levine, J., & Zigler, E. Humor responses of high and low premorbid competence alchoholic and nonalchoholic patients. *Addictive Behaviors*, 1976, *1*, 139–149.

Levine, R. A. *Culture, behavior and personality*. Chicago: Aldine, 1973.

Levine, R., Chein, I., & Murphy, G. The relation of the intensity of the need to the amount of perceptual distortion: Preliminary report. *Journal of Psychology*, 1942, *13*, 283–293.

Levitt, E. E. *The psychology of anxiety*. Indianapolis: Bobbs-Merrill, 1967.

Lévy-Schoen, A. *L'image d'autrui chez l'enfant*. Paris: Presses Universitaires de France, 1964.

Lewinsohn, P. A behavioral approach to depression. In R. Friedman & M. Katz (Eds.), *The psychology of depression: Contemporary theory and research.* Washington: Winston and Sons, 1974.

Lewis, H. *Shame and guilt in neurosis.* New York: International Universities Press, 1971.

Lewis, M., & Rosenblum, L. A. (Eds.), *The origins of fear.* New York: John Wiley, 1974.

Liberman, R. P., & Raskin, D. Depression: A behavioral formulation. *Archives of General Psychiatry,* 1971, *24,* 515–523.

Liddell, H. The biology of the "prejudiced" mind. In Jordon M. Scher (Ed.), *Theories of the mind.* New York: The Free Press of Glencoe, 1962.

Lindsley, D. B. Emotion. In S. S. Stevens (Ed.), *Handbook of experimental psychology.* New York: John Wiley, 1951, pp. 473–516.

Lindsley, D. B. Psychophysiology and motivation. In M. R. Jones (Ed.), *Nebraska Symposium on Motivation.* Lincoln: University of Nebraska Press, 1957, pp. 44–105.

Lindsley, D. B. Common factors in sensory deprivation, sensory distortion, and sensory overload. In Solomon *et al.* (Eds.), *Sensory deprivation.* Cambridge, Mass.: Harvard, 1961, 208–220.

London, P. The major psychological disorders. In P. London & D. Rosenhan (Eds.), *Foundations of Abnormal Psychology.* New York: Holt, Rinehart, & Winston, 1968.

London, P., Schulman, R. E., & Black M. S. Religion, guilt, and ethical standards. University of Illinois. Undated manuscript.

Lorenz, K. Plans and vacuum activities. In M. Autori et al. (Eds.) *L'instinct dans le comportement des animaux et de l'homme.* Paris: Masson, 1956, pp. 688–800.

Lorenz, K. *On aggression.* New York: Harcourt, Brace, and World, 1966.

Ludwig, L. M., & Ellsworth, P. C. Some effects of observation set on the interpretation of nonverbal cues. Unpublished manuscript, 1974.

Luria, A. R. *Higher cortical functions in man.* New York: Basic Books, 1966.

Luria, A. R. *The working brain: An introduction to Neuropsychology.* New York: Basic Books, 1973.

Luria, A. R., & Vinogradova, I. S. An objective investigation of the dynamics of semantic systems. *British Journal of Psychology,* 1959, *50,* 89–105.

Lynd, H. M. *On shame and the search for identity.* New York: Science Editions, 1961.

Maas, J. W., & Mednieks, M. Hydrocortisone-mediated increase of norepinephrine uptake by brain slices. *Science,* 1971, *171,* 178–179.

MacLean, P. D. Psychosomatic disease and the "visual brain": Recent developments bearing on the Papez theory of emotion. *Psychosomatic Medicine,* 1949, *11,* 338–353.

MacLean, P. D. The limbic system and its hippocampal formation: Studies in animals and their possible application to man. *Journal of Neurosurgery,* 1954, *11,* 29–44.

MacLean, P. D. Contrasting functions of limbic and neocortical systems of the brain and their relevance to psychophysiological aspects of medicine. In E. Gellhorn (Ed.), *Biological foundations of emotion.* Glenview, Ill.: Scott, Foreman, 1968, pp. 73–106.

MacLean, P. D. The limbic brain in relation to the psychoses. In P. Black (Ed.), *Physiological correlates of emotion.* New York: Academic Press, 1970.

Magoun, H. W. Non-specific brain mechanisms. In H. F. Harlow & C. N. Woolsey (Eds.), *Biological and biochemical bases of behavior.* Madison: University of Wisconsin Press, 1958, pp. 25–36.

Maher, B. A. *Principles of psychopathology.* New York: McGraw-Hill, 1966.

Maier, S. F. Failure to escape traumatic shock: Incompatible skeletal motor responses or learned helplessness? *Learning and Motivation,* 1970, *1,* 157–170.

Major, D. R. *First steps in neonatal growth.* New York: Macmillan, 1906.

Mandler, G. Emotion. In R. W. Brown *et al.* (Eds.), *New directions in psychology.* New York: Holt, 1962, 267–343.

Mandler, G. The interruption of behavior. In D. Levine (Ed.), *Nebraska Symposium on Motivation.* Lincoln: University of Nebraska Press, 1964.

Mandler, G. *Mind and emotions.* New York: Wiley, 1975.

Mandler, G., & Watson, D. L. Anxiety and the interruption of behavior. In C. D. Spielberger (Ed.), *Anxiety and behavior.* New York: Academic Press, 1966, pp. 263–288.

Marañon, G. Contribution a l'étude de l'action émotive de l'adrénaline. *Revue Française d'Endocrinologie,* 1924, *2,* 301–325.

Marks, H. L., Siegel, P. B., & Kramer, C. Y. Effect of comb and wattle removal on social organization of mixed flocks of chickens. *Animal Behavior,* 1960, *8,* 192–196.

Marler, P. Communication in monkeys and apes. In I. Devore (Ed.), *Primate behavior: Field studies of monkeys and apes.* New York: Holt, Rinehart & Winston, 1965, pp. 544–584.

Marsella, A. J., Murray, M. P., & Golden, C. Ethnic variations in the phenomenology of emotions, I. Shame. *Journal of Cross Cultural Psychology,* 1977, in press.

Marshall, A. G. & Izard, C. E., Cerebral electrotherapeutic treatment of depressions. *Journal of Consulting and Clinical Psychology,* 1972a, *42*(1), 193–197.

Marshall, A. G., & Izard, C. E. Depression as a pattern of emotions and feelings: Factor-analytic investigations. In C. E. Izard, *Patterns of emotions: A new analysis of anxiety and depression.* New York: Academic Press, 1972b.

Marshall, G. The affective consequences of "inadequately explained" physiological arousal. Unpublished doctoral dissertation, Stanford University, 1976.

Martin, B. The assessment of anxiety by physiological behavioral measures. *Psychological Bulletin,* 1961, *58,* 234–255.

Maslach, C. Negative emotional biasing of unexplained arousal. Unpublished manuscript, University of California, Berkeley, 1976.

Maslow, A. *The farther reaches of human nature.* New York: Viking, 1971.

Masters, W. H., & Johnson V. E. *Human sexual response.* Boston: Little, Brown, 1966.

Masters, W. H., & Johnson, V. E. *Human sexual inadequacy.* Boston: Little, Brown, 1970.

May, R. *The meaning of anxiety.* New York: Ronald, 1950.

May, R. The origins and significance of the existential movement in psychology. In R. May, E. Angel, & H. F. Ellenberger (Eds.), *Existence: A new dimension in psychiatry and psychology.* New York: Basic Books, 1958.

May, R. What is our problem? In Eleanor S. Morrison & Vera Borosage (Eds.), *Human sexuality: Contemporary perspectives.* California: National Press Books, 1973.

McCall, R. B., & Kagan, J. Attention in the infant: Effects of complexity, contours, perimeters, and familiarity. *Child Development,* 1967, *38,* 939–952.

McCary, J. L. *Human sexuality: Physiological, psychological and sociological factors.* New York: D. Van Nostrand Company, 1973.

McClelland, D. C. *Personality.* New York: The Dryden Press, 1951.

McClelland, D. C. Toward a theory of motive acquisition. *American Psychologist,* 1965, *20,* 321–333.

McClelland, D. C., Atkinson, J. W., Clark, R. A., & Lowell, E. L. *The achievement motive.* New York: Appleton-Century-Crofts, 1953.

McDougall, W. *An introduction to social psychology.* London: Methuen, 1923 (First edition, 1908).

McGhee, P. E. Cognitive development and children's comprehension of humor. *Child Development,* 1971, *42,* 123–138. (a)

McGhee, P. E. Development of the humor response: A review of the literature. *Psychological Bulletin,* 1971, *76,* 328–348. (b)

McGhee, P. E. Cognitive mastery and children's humor. *Psychological Bulletin,* 1974, *81,* 721–730. (a)

McGhee, P. E. Development of children's ability to create a joking relationship. *Child Development,* 1974, *45,* 552–556. (b)

McGhee, P. E. Moral development and children's appreciation of humor. *Developmental Psychology,* 1974, *10,* 514–525. (c)

McGrade, B. J. Newborn activity and emotional response at eight months. *Child Development*, 1968, *39*, 1247–1252.

McGrew, W. C. *An ethological study of children's behavior*. New York: Academic Press, 1972.

McKennan, D. Violation of prohibitions. In H. A. Murray, *Explorations in personality*. New York: Oxford University Press, 1938.

Mead, M. Social change and cultural surrogates. In C. Kluckhohn, H. A. Murray, & D. M. Schneider (Eds.), *Personality in nature, society, and culture*. (2nd edition), New York: Alfred A. Knopf, 1956, pp. 651–662.

Meade, M. Some anthropoligical considerations concerning guilt. In M. L. Reymert (Ed.), *Feelings and emotions*, New York: McGraw-Hill, 1950.

Meadows, C. M. Joy in psychological and theological perspective: A constructive approach. Unpublished Ph.D. dissertation, Princeton Theological Seminary, 1968.

Meadows, C. M. The phenomenology of joy: An empirical investigation. *Psychological Reports*, 1975, *37*, 39–54.

Mehrabian, A. *Nonverbal communication*. Chicago: Aldine-Atherton, 1972.

Meskin, B., & Singer, J. L. Daydreaming, reflective thought and laterality of eye movements. *Journal of Personality and Social Psychology*, 1974, *30* (1), 64–71.

Milgram, S. Behavioral study of obedience. *Journal of Abnormal and Social Psychology*, 1963, *67*, 371–378.

Milgram, S. Group pressure and action against a person. *Journal of Abnormal and Social Psychology*, 1964, *69*, 137–143.

Milgram, S. Some conditions of obedience and disobedience to authority. *Human Relations*, 1965, *18*(1), 53–75.

Miller, D., & Swanson, G. The study of conflict. In M. Jones, (Ed.), *Nebraska Symposium on Motivation*. Lincoln Nebraska: University of Nebraska Press, 1956.

Miller, G. Living systems: Structure and process. *Behavioral Science*, 1965, *10*, 337–379.

Miller, G., Galanter, E., & Pribram, K. H. *Plans and the structure of behavior*. New York: Holt, 1960.

Miller, N. E. Studies of fear as an acquirable drive: I. Fear as motivation and fear-reduction as reinforcement in the learning of new responses. *Journal of Experimental Psychology*, 1948, *38*, 89–101.

Miller, N. E. Liberalization of basic S–R concepts: Extensions to conflict behavior, motivation, and social learning. In S. Koch (Ed.), *Psychology: A study of a science*. (Vol. 2), New York: McGraw-Hill, 1959, pp. 196–292.

Miller, R. E., Banks, J. H., Jr., & Ogawa, N. Communication of affect in "cooperative conditioning" of rhesus monkeys. *Journal of Abnormal and Social Psychology*, 1962, *64*, 343–348.

Miller, R. E., Caul, W. F., & Mirsky, I. A. The communication of affects between feral and socially isolated monkeys. *Journal of Personality and Social Psychology*, 1967, *7*, 231–239.

Miller, R. E., Murphy, J. W., & Mirsky, I. A. Relevance of facial expression and posture as cues in communication of affect between monkeys. *Archives of General Psychiatry*, 1959, *1*, 480–488.

Mischel, T. P. Cognitive conflict and the motivation of thought. In T. P. Mischel (Ed.), *Cognitive development and epistomology*. New York: Academic Press, 1971.

Mischel, W. Cognitive appraisals and transformations in self-control. In B. Weiner (Ed.), *Cognitive views of human motivation*. New York: Academic Press, 1974.

Mischel, W., & Baker, N. Cognitive appraisals and transformations in delay behavior. *Journal of Personality and Social Psychology*, 1975, *31*, 254–261.

Mischel, W., & Ebbesen, E. B. Attention in delay of gratification. *Journal of Personality and Social Psychology*, 1970, *16*, 329–337.

Mischel, W., Ebbesen, E. B., & Zeiss, A. Cognitive and attentional mechanisms in delay of gratification. *Journal of Personality and Social Psychology,* 1972, *21,* 204–218.

Mischel, W., & Moore, B. Effects of attention to symbolically presented rewards upon self-control. *Journal of Personality and Social Psychology,* 1973, *28,* 172–179.

Modigliani, A. Embarrassment, facework and eye contact: Testing a theory of embarrassment. *Journal of Personality and Social Psychology,* 1971, *17*(1), 15–24.

Montague, A. *Touching: The human significance of skin.* New York: Harper & Row, 1972.

Montgomery, K. C. A test of two explanations of spontaneous alternation. *Journal of Comparative and Physiological Psychology,* 1952, *45,* 287–293.

Montgomery, K. C. Exploratory behavior as a function of "similarity" of stimulus situations. *Journal of Comparative and Physiological Psychology,* 1953, *46,* 126–133.

Montgomery, K. C. The role of exploratory drive in learning. *Journal of Comparative and Physiological Psychology,* 1954, *47,* 60–64.

Montgomery, K. C. The relation between fear induced by novel stimulation and exploratory behavior. *Journal of Comparative and Physiological Psychology,* 1955, *48,* 225–228.

Moore, B. S. Underwood, B., & Rosenhan, D. Affect and altruism. *Developmental Psychology,* 1973, *8,* 99–104.

Morell, F., Barlow, J., & Brazier, M. Analysis of conditioned repetitive response by means of the average response computer. In I. Wortis (Ed.), *Recent Advances in Biological Psychiatry.* New York: Grune & Stratton, 1960, pp. 459–464.

Morris, D. *The naked ape: A zoologist's study of the human animal.* New York: McGraw-Hill, 1968.

Mosher, D. L. The interaction of fear and guilt in inhibiting unacceptable behavior: *Journal of Consulting Psychology,* 1965, *29,* 161–167.

Mosher, D. L. The learning of congruent and noncongruent social structures. *Journal of Social Psychology,* 1967, *73,* 285–290.

Mosher, D. L. Measurement of guilt in females by self-report inventories *Journal of Consulting and Clinical Psychology,* 1968, 32, 690–695.

Mosher, D. L., & Galbraith, G. G. Effects of sex guilt and sexual stimulation on the recall of word associations. *Journal of Consulting and Clinical Psychology,* 1970, *34*(1), 67–71.

Mosher, D. L., & Mosher, J. B. Guilt in prisoners. *Journal of Clinical Psychology,* 1967, *23,* 171–173.

Mowrer, O. H. *Learning theory and behavior.* New York: John Wiley, 1960. (a)

Mowrer, O. H. Psychotherapy and the problem of guilt, confession, and expiation. In W. Dennis (Ed.), *Current trends in psychology,* X. Pittsburgh: University of Pittsburgh Press, 1960. (b)

Mowrer, O. H. *The crisis in psychiatry and religion.* Princeton, N.J.: Van Nostrand, 1961.

Murphy, G. *Human potentialities.* New York: Basic Books, 1958.

Murray, H. A. *Explorations in personality: A clinical and experimental study of fifty men of college age.* New York: Oxford, 1938.

Myers, A. K., & Miller, N. E. Failure to find a learned drive based on hunger: Evidence for learning motivated by "exploration." *Journal of Comparative and Physiological Psychology,* 1954, *47,* 428–436.

Nathan, P. *The nervous system.* Philadelphia: Lippincott, 1969.

Nevrovich, A. Personal communication, Institute of Pre-school Education, Moscow, USSR, 1974.

Nicholas, O. L. Guilt as related to self-concept and personality adjustment, *Dissertation Abstracts,* 1966, *26*(7), 4080.

Novaco, R. W. *Anger control: The development and evaluation of an experimental treatment.* Lexington, Mass.: Lexington Books, 1975.

Nowlis, V. Research with the mood adjective check list. In S. S. Tomkins & C. E. Izard (Eds.), *Affect, cognition, and personality.* New York: Springer, 1965, pp. 352–389.

Nowlis, V. Mood: Behavior and experience. In M. B. Arnold (Ed.), *Feelings and emotions.* New York: Academic Press, 1970.

Nunnally, J. C. A human tropism. In S. R. Brown & D. J. Brenner (Eds.), *Science, physiology, and communication: Essays honoring William Stephenson.* New York: Teachers College Press, 1972, pp. 255–277.

Nunnally, J. C., & Lemond, L. C. Exploratory behavior and human development. *Advances in Child Development and Behavior,* 1973, *8,* 59–107.

Odom, R. D., & Lemond, L. C. Developmental differences in the perception and production of facial expressions. *Child Development,* 1972, *43,* 359–369.

Ogren, D. J., & Dokecki, P. R. Moral development and behavior disorders in young children. In R. C. Johnson, P. R. Dokecki, & O. H. Mowrer (Eds.), *Conscience, contract, and social reality: Research in behavioral science.* New York: Holt, Rinehart & Winston, 1972, pp. 402–410.

Okel, E., & Mosher, D. L. Changes in affective states as a function of guilt over aggressive behavior. *Journal of Consulting Psychology,* 1968, *32,* 265–270.

Olds, J. Mechanisms of instrumental conditioning. In R. Hernandez-Peon, (Ed.), The physiological basis of mental activity. *Electroencephalographic and Clinical Neurophysiology,* Suppl. 24, 1963, pp. 153–187.

Olds, J., & Peretz, B. A motivational analysis of the recticular activiting system. *Electroencephalographic and Clinical Neurophysiology,* 1960, *12,* 445–454.

Oliver, W. A., & Mosher, D. L. Psychopathology and guilt in heterosexual subgroups of homosexual reformatory inmates. *Journal of Abnormal Psychology,* 1968, *73,* 323–329.

Ornstein, R. E. *The nature of human consciousness.* San Francisco: W. H. Freeman, 1973.

Ornstein, R. E., & Galin, D. Physiological studies of consciousness. In P. R. Lee, R. E. Ornstein, D. Galin, A. Deikman, & C. T. Tart (Eds.), *Symposium on Consciousness* (AAAS, 1974). New York: Viking, 1976.

Osgood, C. E. Dimensionality of the semantic space for communication via facial expressions. *Scandinavian Journal of Psychology,* 1966, *7,* 1–30.

Osgood, C. E. On the why and wherefore of E, P, and A. *Journal of Personality and Social Psychology,* 1969, *12,* 194–199.

Osgood, C. E., Suci, G. J., & Tannenbaum, P. H. *The measurement of meaning.* Urbana: University of Illinois Press, 1957.

Papez, J. W. A proposed mechanism of emotion. *Archives of Neurological Psychiatry,* 1937, *38,* 725–743.

Papez, J. W. Correlation of the Papez mechanism of emotion with the attitude theory of emotion of Nina Bull. In N. Bull, *The attitude theory of emotion. Nervous and mental disease monographs.* New York: Collidge Foundation, 1951, No. 81.

Parisi, S. A., & Izard, C. E. Five-, seven-, and nine-month-old infants' facial responses to twenty stimulus situations. In preparation, 1977.

Paul, M. I., Ditzion, B. R., Pauk, G. L., & Janowsky, D. S. Urinary adenosine 3',5'-monophosphate excretion in affective disorders. *American Journal of Psychiatry,* 1970, *126,* 1493–1497.

Pecjak, V. Verbal synesthesiae of colors, emotions, and days of the week. *Journal of Verbal Learning and Verbal Behavior,* 1970, *9,* 623–626.

Peiper, A. *Cerebral function in infancy and childhood.* New York: Consultants Bureau, 1963.

Peretz, D. Reaction to loss. In B. Schoenberg, A. C. Carr, D. Peretz, & A. H. Kutscher (Eds.), *Loss and grief: Psychological management in medical practice.* New York: Columbia University Press, 1970.

Perry, R. B. *General theory of value: Its meaning and basic principles constructed in terms of interest.* New York: Longmans, Green, 1926.

Perry, R. B. *Realms of value.* Cambridge, Mass.: Harvard Press, 1954.

Persons, R. W. Intermittent reinforcement, guilt, and crime. *Psychological Reports,* 1970, *26,* 421–422. (a)

Persons, R. W. The Mosher Guilt Scale: Theoretical formulation, research, and normative data. *Journal of Projective Techniques,* 1970, *34,* 266–270. (b)

Persons, R. W., & Marks, P. A. Self-disclosure with recidivists: Optimum interviewer–interviewee matching. *Proceedings 77th Annual Convention of the American Psychological Association,* 1969, *4,* 531–543.

Pesso, A. *Movement in psychotherapy.* New York: New York University Press, 1969.

Peterfreund, E. Information, systems, and psychoanalysis: An evolutionary biological approach to psychoanalytic theory (with Jacob T. Schwartz). *Psychological Issues,* 1971, *7,* 1–399.

Peterson, D. R. The insecure child: oversocialized or undersocialized? In O. H. Mowrer (Ed.), *Morality and mental health.* Chicago: Rand McNally, 1967.

Piaget, J. *The origins of intelligence in children* (Trans. by Margaaret Cook). New York: International Universities Press, 1952. Originally published in 1936.

Piaget, J. *Six psychological studies.* New York: Random House, 1967.

Piers, G., & Singer, M. S. *Shame and guilt: A psychoanalytic and cultural study.* Springfield: Charles Thomas, 1953.

Pigareva, M. L. Effect of hippocampal destruction on conditioned reflex switching in albino rats. (In Russian), *Zh. Vyssh. Nervn. Deyat. im. I. P. Pavlova* 1969, *19,* 801–808.

Pigareva, M. L. Facilitation of conditioned reflex switching of dissimilar reflexes in rats following hippocampal lesion. (In Russian), *Zh. Vyssh. Nervn. Deyat. im. I. P. Pavlova,* 1970, *20,* 932–940.

Plutchik, R. The role of muscular tension in maladjustment. *Journal of General Psychology,* 1954, *50,* 45–62.

Plutchik, R. *The emotions: Facts, theories, and a new model.* New York: Random House, 1962.

Plutchik, R., & Ax, A. F. A critique of determinants of emotional state by Schachter and Singer (1962). *Psychophysiology,* 1967, *4*(1), 79–82.

Podell, L., & Perkins, J. C. A Guttman scale for sexual experience—a methodological note. *Journal of Abnormal and Social Psychology,* 1957, *54,* 420–422.

Polanyi, M. *Personal knowledge: Toward a post-critical philosophy.* Chicago: University of Chicago Press, 1958.

Pope, K. S. The stream of consciousness. Unpublished doctoral dissertation, Yale University, 1977.

Pope, K. S., & Singer, J. L. Regulation of the stream of consciousness: Toward a theory of ongoing thought. In G. Schwartz & D. Shapiro (Eds.) *Consciousness and self-regulation: Advances in research.* New York Plenum Press, 1976.

Prange, A., & Vitols, M. M. Cultural aspects of the relatively low incidence of depression in Southern Negroes. *International Journal of Social Psychiatry,* 1962, *8,* 104–112.

Pribram, K. H. Feelings as monitors. In M. B. Arnold (Ed.), *Feelings and emotions.* New York: Academic Press, 1970.

Prideaux, E. Expression of the emotions in cases of mental disorders. *British Journal of Medical Psychology,* 1922, *2,* 45.

Rachman, S. *The meanings of fear.* Middlesex, England: Penguin Education, 1974.

Rado, S. Psychodynamics of depression from the etiologic point of view. (Originally published, 1928). In W. Gaylin (Ed.), *The meaning of despair.* New York: Science House, 1968.

Rank, O. *The trauma of birth.* New York: Harcourt, Brace, 1929.

Rapaport, D. *Emotions and memory.* New York: Science Editions, 1961 (originally published, 1942).

Rapaport, D. On the psychoanalytic theory of affects. *International Journal of Psychoanalysis,* 1953, *34,* 177–198.

Rapaport, D. On the psychoanalytic theory of motivation. In M. R. Jones (Ed.), *Nebraska Symposium on Motivation.* Lincoln: University of Nebraska Press, 1960.

Rasa, O. A. E. Territoriality and the establishment of dominance by means of visual cues in *Domacentrus jenkinsi (pices: pomacentridae)*. *Zeitschriet fur Tierpsychologie*, 1969, *26*, 825–845. (Cited by R. N. Johnson, *Aggression in man and animals*. Philadelphia: W. B. Saunders, 1972.)

Reiss, I. L. *The social context of premarital sexual permissiveness*. New York: Holt, Rinehart & Winston, 1967.

Reymert, M. L. *Feelings and emotions*. New York: McGraw-Hill, 1950.

Rheingold, H. L. General issues in the study of fear: Section I. In M. Lewis & L. A. Rosenblum (Eds.), *Origins of fear*. New York: Wiley, 1974.

Richardson, L. F. *Statistics of deadly quarrels*. Pittsburgh: Boxwood, 1960.

Rodin, J., & Singer, J. L. Laterality of eye-shift, reflective thought and obesity. Paper read at the Eastern Psychological Association, 1974.

Rogers, C. R. *Client centered therapy*. Boston: Houghton Mifflin, 1951.

Rogers, C. R. A theory of therapy, personality, and interpersonal relationships, as developed in the client-centered framework. In S. Koch (Ed.), *Psychology: A study of a science*. Vol. 3. New York: McGraw-Hill, 1959, pp. 184–256.

Rogers, C. R. *On becoming a person*. Boston: Houghton Mifflin, 1961.

Rosenhan, D., & London, P. *Foundations of abnormal psychology*. San Francisco: Holt, Rinehart & Winston, 1970.

Rosenhan, D., Underwood, B., & Moore, B. S. Affect moderates self-gratification and altruism. *Journal of Personality and Social Psychology*, 1974, *30*, 546–552.

Rothbart, M. K. Laughter in young children. *Psychological Bulletin*, 1973, *80*, 247–256.

Rubin, Z. Measurement of romantic love. *Journal of Personality and Social Psychology*. 1970, *16*, 265–273.

Rubinstein, B. B. Explanation and mere description: A metascientific examination of certain aspects of the psychoanalytic theory of motivation. In R. R. Holt (Ed.), *Motives and thought: Psychoanalytic essays in honor of David Rapaport*. *Psychological Issues*, Monograph 18/19, 1967, *5*, 20–77.

Rusolova, R., Izard, C. E., & Simonov, P. V. Comparative analysis of mimical and autonomic components of man's emotional state. *Aviation, Space, and Environmental Medicine*, 1975, *46*.

Russell, B. *A free man's worship*, 1918, (Cited in E. W. Sinnott, *The bridge of life*. New York: Simon and Schuster, 1966.)

Saayman, G., Ames, E. W., & Moffett, A. Response to novelty as an indication of visual discrimination in the human infant. *Journal of Experimental Child Psychology*, 1964, *1*, 189–198.

Sade, D. C. Determinants of dominance in a group of free-ranging rhesus monkeys. In S. A. Altman (Ed.), *Social communication among primates*. Chicago: University of Chicago Press, 1967, pp. 99–113.

Safer, M. A., & Leventhal, H. Ear differences in evaluating emotional tones of voice and verbal content. *Journal of Experimental Psychology: Human Perception and Performance*, 1977, in press.

Sameroff, A. J. Respiration and sucking as components of the orienting reaction in newborns. *Psychophysiology*, 1971, *7*(2), 213–222.

Sanford, N. The effects of abstinence from food upon imaginal processes: A preliminary experiment. *Journal of Psychology*, 1936, *2*, 129–136.

Sanford, N. The effects of abstinence from food upon imaginal processes. A further experiment. *Journal of Psychology*, 1937, *3*, 145–159.

Sarason, S. B. The measurement of anxiety in children: Some questions and problems. In C. D. Speilberger (Ed.), *Anxiety and behavior*. New York: Academic Press, 1966.

Sarason, S. B., Davidson, K. S., Lighthall, F. F., Waite, R. R., & Ruebush, B. K., *Anxiety in elementary school children*. New York: Wiley, 1960.

Sartre, J. P. *The emotions: Outline of a theory.* New York: Philosophical Library, 1948.

Savitsky, J. C., & Izard, C. E. Developmental changes in the use of emotion cues in a concept formation task. *Developmental Psychology,* 1970, *3*(3), 350–357.

Savitsky, J. C., Izard, C. E., Kotsch, W. E., & Christy, L. Aggressor's response to the victim's facial expression of emotion. *Journal of Research in Personality,* 1974, *7,* 346–357.

Savitsky, J. C., & Sim, M. Trading emotions. Equity theory of reward and punishment. *Journal of Communication,* 1974, *24,* 140–146.

Schachtel, E. G. *Metamorphosis.* New York: Basic Books, 1959.

Schachter, J. Pain, fear, and anger in hypertensives and normotensives: A psychophysiologic study. *Psychosomatic Medicine,* 1957, *19,* 17–29.

Schachter, S. The interaction of cognitive and physiological determinants of emotional state. In C. D. Spielberger (Ed.), *Anxiety and behavior.* New York: Academic Press, 1966, pp. 193–224.

Schachter, S. *Emotion, obesity and crime.* New York: Academic Press, 1971.

Schachter, S., & Latané, B. Crime, cognition, and the autonomic nervous system. In D. Levine (Ed.), *Nebraska Symposium on Motivation.* Lincoln: University of Nebraska Press, 1964.

Schachter, S., & Singer, J. E. Cognitive, social, and physiological determinants of emotional states. *Psychological Review,* 1962, *69*(5), 379–399.

Schafer, R. Emotion in the language of action. In M. M. Gill & P. S. Holzman (Eds.), Psychology versus metapsychology: Psychoanalytic essays in memory of George S. Klein. *Psychological Issues,* 1976 *9*(4) Monograph 36, 106–133.

Scher, J. M. Mind as participation. In Jordon M. Scher (Ed.), *Theories of the mind.* New York: The Free Press of Glencoe, 1962.

Schildkraut, J. J., Davis, J. M., & Klerman, G. Biochemistry of depression. In D. H. Efron, J. O. Cole, J. Levine, & J. R. Wittenborn (Eds.), *Psychopharmacology: A review of progress 1957–1967.* Washington D.C.: Public Health Service Publication, 1968.

Schlosberg, H. S. A scale for the judgement of facial expressions. *Journal of Experimental Psychology,* 1941, *29,* 497–510.

Schlosberg, H. S. The description of facial expressions in terms of two dimensions *Journal of Experimental Psychology,* 1952, *44,* 229–237.

Schlosberg, H. S. Three dimensions of emotion. *Psychological Review,* 1954, *61, 81*–88.

Schoenberg, B., Carr, A. C., Peretz, D., & Kutscher, A. H. (Eds.), *Loss and grief: Psychological management in medical practice.* New York: Columbia University Press, 1970.

Schultz, D. K. Fantasy stimulation in the treatment of depressed psychiatric patients. Unpublished doctoral dissertation, Yale University, 1976.

Schutz, W. *Joy: Expanding human awareness.* New York: Grove Press, 1967.

Schwartz, G. E., Davidson, R. J., Maer, F., & Bromfield, E. Patterns of hemispheric dominance in musical, emotional, verbal, and spatial tasks. Paper read at the meetings of the Society for Psychophysiological Research. Galveston, Texas, 1973.

Schwartz, G. E., Fair, P. L., Greenberg, P. S., Freedman, M., & Klerman, J. L. Facial electromyography in the assessment of emotion. *Psychophysiology,* 1974, *11,* 237.

Schwartz, G. E., Fair, P. L., Greenberg, P. S., Mandel, M. R., & Klerman, J. L. Facial expression and depression: An electromyographic study. *Psychosomatic Medicine,* 1974, *36,* 458.

Schwartz, G. E., Fair, P. L., Salt, P. S., Mandel, M. R., & Klerman, J. L. Facial muscle patterning to affective imagery in depressed and non-depressed subjects. *Science,* 1976, *192,* 489–491.

Scott, W. A. Structure of nature cognitions. *Journal of Personality and Social Psychology,* 1969, *12*(4), 261–278.

Sears, R. R. Attachment, dependency, and frustration. In J. L. Gewirtz (Ed.), *Attachment and dependency*. New York: Wiley, 1972.

Sears, R. R., Maccoby, E. E., & Levin, H. *Patterns of child rearing*. New York: Harper, 1957.

Seligman, M. E. P. *Helplessness: On depression development and death*. San Francisco: W. H. Freeman, 1975.

Seligman, M. E. P., & Maier, S. F. Failure to escape traumatic shock. *Journal of Experimental Psychology*, 1967, *74*, 1–9.

Seligman, M. E. P., Maier, S. F., & Greer, J. The alleviation of learned helplessness in the dog. *Journal of Abnormal and Social Psychology*, 1968, *73*, 256–262.

Shaffer, H. R., & Emerson, P. E. Patterns of response to physical contact in early human development. *Journal of Child Psychology and Psychiatry*, 1964, *5*, 1–13.

Shagass, C. Explorations in the psychology of affect. In Jordon M. Scher (Ed.), *Theories of the mind*. New York: The Free Press of Glencoe, 1962.

Shand, A. F. *The foundations of character*. London: Macmillan, 1914.

Sheffield, F. D., & Campbell, B. A. The role of experience in the "spontaneous" activity of hungry rats. *Journal of Comparative Physiological Psychology*, 1954, *47*, 97–100.

Sheffield, F. D., & Roby, T. B. Reward value of a non-nutritive sweet taste. *Journal of Comparative and Physiological Psychology*, 1950, *43*, 471–481.

Sheffield, F. D., Roby, T. B., & Campbell, B. A. Drive reduction vs. consummatory behavior as determinants of reinforcement. *Journal of Comparative and Physiological Psychology*, 1954, *47*, 349–354.

Sheffield, F. D., Wulff, J. J., & Bacher R. Reward value of copulation without sex drive reduction. *Journal of Comparative and Physiological Psychology*, 1951, *44*, 3–8.

Sherfey, M. J. *The nature and evolution of female sexuality*. New York: Random House, 1966.

Silverman, C. *The epidemiology of depression*. Baltimore: Johns Hopkins Press, 1968.

Silverman, I. W. Incidence of guilt reactions in children. *Journal of Personality and Social Psychology*, 1967, 338–340.

Simmel, G. Sociology of the senses: Visual interactions. In R. E. Park & E. W. Burgess (Eds.), *Introduction to the science of sociology*. Chicago: University of Chicago Press, 1921.

Simonov, P. V. On the ratio of the motor and vegetative components in the conditioned defensive reflex in man. *International Symposium on Central and Peripheral Mechanisms of Motor Activity in Animals and Man*. Moscow, 1964.

Simonov, P. V. *Teoriya otpasheniya i psikofizologiya emotsii*. Moscow: Izdatellstvo Hauka, 1970.

Simonov, P. V. On the role of the hippocampus in the integrative activity of the brain. *Acta Neurobiol. Exp.*, 1972, *34*, 33–41.

Simonov, P. V. *Higher nervous activity of man: Motivational–emotional aspects* (In Russian). Moscow: Izdatelstvo Nauka, 1975.

Singer, J. L. *Daydreaming: An introduction to the experimental study of inner experience*. New York: Random House, 1966.

Singer, J. L. *The child's world of make-believe: Experimental studies of imaginative play*. New York: Academic Press, 1973.

Singer, J. L. *Imagery and daydream methods in psychotherapy and behavior modification*. New York: Academic Press, 1974.

Singer, J. L. Navigating the stream of consciousness. *American Psychologist*, 1975, *30*, 727–738.

Singer, J. L., & Antrobus, J. S. A factor analysis of daydreaming and conceptually related cognitive and personality variables. *Perceptual and motor skills*, 1963, Monograph supplement 3-V17.

Singer, J. L., & Singer, D. G. Imaginative play and pretending in early childhood: Some experimental approaches. In A. Davids (Ed.) *Child personality and psychopathology*, Vol. 3. New York: Wiley, 1976.

Sinnott, E. W. *The bridge of life*. New York: Simon and Schuster, 1966.

Sinsheimer, R. L. The brain of Pooh: An essay on the limits of the mind. *American Scientist,* Jan.–Feb., 1971, 20–28.

Skinner, B. F. *Beyond freedom and dignity*. New York: Knopf, 1973.

Smilansky, S. *The effects of sociodramatic play on disadvantaged preschool children*. New York: Wiley, 1968.

Smith, W. J. Messages of vertebrate communication. *Science,* 1969, *165,* 145–150.

Snygg, D., & Combs, A. W. *Individual behavior*. New York: Harper, 1949.

Solomon, R. L., & Corbit, J. D. An opponent process theory of motivation: I. Temporal dynamics of affect. *Psychological Review,* 1974, *81,* 119–145.

Solomon, R. L. Turner, L. H., & Lessac, M. S. Some effects of delay of punishment on resistance to temptation in dogs. *Journal of Personality and Social Psychology,* 1968, *8*(3), 233–238.

Solomon, R. L., & Wynne, L. C. Traumatic avoidance learning: Acquisition in normal dogs. *Psychological Monographs,* 1953, *67,* 1–19 (Whole No. 354).

Speigel, E. A., & Wycis, H. T. Stimulation of the brain stem and basal ganglia in man. In D. E. Sheer (Ed.), *Electrical stimulation of the brain*. Austin: University of Texas Press, 1961.

Spencer, H. *The principles of psychology*. Vol. I. New York: Appleton, 1890 (1st ed., 1855).

Sperry, R. W. Hemisphere disconnection and unity in conscious awareness. *American Psychologist,* 1968, *23,* 723–733.

Spielberger, C. D. Theory and research on anxiety. In C. D. Spielberger (Ed.), *Anxiety and behavior*. New York: Academic Press, 1966.

Spielberger, C. D. (Ed.) *Anxiety: Contemporary theory and research*. New York: Academic Press, 1972.

Spielberger, C. D., Gorsuch, R. R., & Lushene, R. E., *State–trait anxiety inventory test manual for form X*. Palo Alto: Consulting Psychologists Press, 1970.

Spiro, M. Ifaluk: A South Sea culture. Unpublished manuscript, Human Relations Area Files, Yale University, 1949.

Spitz, R. A. *The first year of life*. New York: International Universities Press, 1965.

Spitz, R. A., & Wolf, K. M. The smiling response: A contribution to the ontogenesis of social relations. *Genetic Psychology Monographs,* 1946, *34,* 57–125.

Spranger, E. *Lebensformen* (3rd ed.; Halle: Niemeyer, 1923. Trans. by P. Pigors, *Types of men;* New York: Steckert, 1928.)

Sprague, J. M., Chambers, W. W., & Stellar, E. Attentive, affective, and adaptive behavior in the cat. *Science,* 1961, *133,* 165–173.

Sroufe, L. A., Waters, E., & Matas, L. Contextual determinants of infant affective response. In M. Lewis & L. A. Rosenblum (Eds.), *The origins of fear*. New York: Wiley, 1974, pp. 49–72.

Sroufe, L. A., & Wunsch, J. P. The development of laughter in the first years of life. *Child Development,* 1972, *43,* 1326–1344.

Stamfl, T. Implosive therapy. In D. Levis (Ed.), *Learning approaches to therapeutic behavior change*. Chicago: Aldine Press, 1970.

Stechler, G. The effect of medication during labor on newborn attention. *Science,* 1964, *144,* 315–317.

Sternbach, R. A. *Pain: A psychophysiological analysis*. New York: Academic Press, 1968.

Stone, L. J., Smith, H. T., & Murphy, L. B. (Eds.), *The competent infant*. New York: Basic Books, 1973.

Stotland, E. *The psychology of hope*. San Francisco: Josey-Bass, 1969.

Sullivan, H. S. *The interpersonal theory of psychiatry*. New York: Norton, 1953.

Sutherland, E. W. On the biological role of cyclic AMP. *Journal of the American Medical Association,* 1970, *214,* 1281–1288.

Switzer, D. K. A psychodynamic analysis of grief in the context of an interpersonal theory of self. *Dissertation Abstracts,* 1968, *29*(13), 381.

Szasz, T. S. *Pain and pleasure: A study of bodily feelings*. New York: Basic Books, 1957.

Tart, C. T. *Altered states of consciousness: A book of readings*. New York: Wiley, 1969.

Tart, C. T. States of consciousness and state-specific sciences. In Robert Ornstein (Ed.), *The nature of human consciousness*. San Francisco: Freeman, 1973.

Tart, C. T. Discrete states of consciousness. In P. R. Lee, R. E. Ornstein, D. Galin, A. Deikman, & C. T. Tart, *Symposium on Consciousness* (AAAS, 1974). New York: Viking, 1976.

Taylor, J. (Ed.) *Selected writings of John Hughlings Jackson*. New York: Basic Books, 1958.

Thomas, H. Visual fixation responses of infants to stimuli of varying complexity. *Child Development*, 1965, *36*, 629.

Thompson, J. Development of facial expression of emotion in blind and seeing children. *Archives of Psychology*, 1941, *37*, 5–47.

Tinbergen, N. *The study of instinct*. London: Oxford University Press, 1951.

Tinbergen, N. "Derived" activities: Their causation, biological significance, and emancipation during evolution. *The Quarterly Review of Biology*, 1952, *27*, 1–26.

Tinbergen, N. On war and peace in animals and man. *Science*, 1968, *160*, 1411–1418.

Tinbergen, N. *The animal in its world*. Vol. 2: *Laboratory experiments and general papers*. London: Allen & Unwin, 1972.

Tolman, E. C. *Purposive behavior in animals and men*. New York: Appleton-Century-Crofts, 1932.

Tomkins, S. S. *Affect, imagery, consciousness*. Vol. I. *The positive affects*. New York: Springer, 1962.

Tomkins, S. S. *Affect, imagery, consciousness*. Vol. II. *The negative affects*. New York: Springer, 1963.

Tomkins, S. S. Affect and the psychology of knowledge. In S. S. Tomkins & C. E. Izard (Eds.), *Affect, cognition and personality*. New York: Springer, 1965.

Tomkins, S. S., & McCarter, R. What and where are the primary affects? Some evidence for a theory. *Perceptual and Motor Skills*, 1964, *18*, 119–158.

Tonks, C. M., Paykel, E. S., & Klerman, G. L. Clinical depressions among Negroes. *American Journal of Psychiatry*, 1970, *127*, 329–335.

Triandis, H. *The analysis of subjective culture*. New York: Wiley, 1972.

Triandis, H. C., & Lambert, W. W. A restatement and test of Schlosberg's theory of emotions with two kinds of subjects from Greece. *Journal of Abnormal and Social Psychology*, 1958, *56*, 321–328.

Ulrich, R. E., Hutchinson, R. R., & Azrin, N. H. Pain-elicited aggression. *Psychological Record*, 1965, *1*, 111–126.

Underwood, B., Moore, B. S., & Rosenhan, D. Affect and self-gratification. *Developmental Psychology*, 1972, *8*(2), 209–214.

Unger, J. M. On the development of guilt reactivity in the child. Doctoral paper, Cornell University, 1962.

Van Buren, J. M. Sensory, motor, and autonomic effects of mesial temporal stimulation in man. *Journal of Neurosurgery*, 1961, *18*, 273–288.

Van Hooff, J. A. R. A. M. Facial expressions in higher primates. *Symposium of the Zoological Society of London*. 1962, *8*, 97–125.

Van Hooff, J. A. R. A. M. Facial displays of Catarrhine monkeys and apes. In D. Morris (Ed.), *Primate ethology*. London: Weidenfield and Nicholson, 1967, pp. 7–68.

Vernon, J. A. McGill, T. E., Gulick, W. L., & Candland, D. K. The effect of human isolation upon some perceptual and motor skills. In Solomon *et al.* (Eds.), *Sensory deprivation*. Cambridge, Mass.: Harvard Press, 1961.

Vine, I. The role of facial-visual signalling in early social development. In Von Cranach & Vine (Eds.), *Social communication and movement*. New York: Academic, 1973.

Vinogrado, O. S. The hippocampus and the orienting reflex (in Russian). In E. Sokolov & O.

Vinogrado (Eds.), *Neironnye mekkanizmy orientirovochmykk refleksov*. Moscow: Izdatelstvo Nauka, 1970, 183–215.

Wachtel, P. L., & Schimck, J. G. An exploratory study of the effects of emotionally toned incidental stimuli. *Journal of Personality*, 1970, *38*, 467–481.

Wallace, J., & Sadalla, E. Behavioral consequences of transgression. I. The effects of social cognition. *Journal of Experimental Research in Personality*, 1966, *1*, 187–194.

Walter, W. G. Brain stimulation in behaving subjects. Neurosciences Research Program Workshop. December, 1966. (Cited in J. R. M. Delgado, *Physical control of the mind*. New York: Harper & Row, 1971.)

Walters, R. H., & Parke, R. D. The role of the distance receptors in the development of social responsiveness. In L. P. Lipsitt & C. C. Spikes (Eds.), *Advances in child development and behavior*. Vol. 2. New York: Academic Press, 1965, pp. 59–96.

Washburn, R. W. A study of the smiling and laughing of infants in the first years of life. *Genetic Psychology Monographs*, 1929, *6*, 398–537.

Webb, W. B. "A motivational theory of emotions . . ." *Psychological Review*, 1948, *55*, 329–335.

Wehmer, G. M. The effect of a stressful movie on ratings of momentary mood, experienced anxiety, and plasma 17-hydroxycorticosteriod level in three psychiatric groups. Unpublished doctoral dissertation, Vanderbilt University, 1966.

Wenger, M. A. Emotion as a visceral action: An extension of Lange's theory. In M. L. Reymert (Ed.), *Feelings and emotions*. New York: McGraw-Hill, 1950, pp. 3–10.

Wessman, A. E., & Ricks, J. H. *Mood and personality*. New York: Holt, Rinehart & Winston, 1966.

Wheeler, J. A. The universe as home for man. *American Scientist*, 1974, *62*, 683–691.

Wheeler, L., & Caggiula, A. R. The contagion of aggression. *Journal of Experimental and Social Psychology*, 1966, *2*, 1–10.

White, B. L. *The first three years of life*. Englewood Cliffs, N. J.: Prentice-Hall, 1975.

White, J. C., & Sweet, W. H. *Pain: Its mechanisms and neurosurgical control*. Springfield, Ill.: Charles C Thomas, 1955.

White, R. W. Motivation reconsidered: The concept of competence. *Psychological Review*, 1959, *66*, 297–333. Also in R. W. Fiske and S. R. Maddi (Eds.), *Functions of varied experience*. Homewood, Ill.: Dorsey Press, 1961.

Whiting, J. W. M., & Child, I. L. *Child training and personality*. New Haven: Yale University Press, 1953.

Willingham, C. *Eternal fire*. New York: Vanguard Press, 1963.

Wolff, P. H. Observations on the early development of smiling. In B. M. Foss (Ed.), *Determinants of infant behavior*. II. New York: Wiley 1963, pp. 113–134.

Wolff, P. H. The causes, controls, and organization of behavior in the neonate. *Psychological Issues*, 1966, *5*(1), Whole No. 17.

Wolff, P. H. The natural history of crying and other vocalizations in early infancy. In B. M. Foss (Ed.), *Determinants of infant behavior*. IV. London: Methuen, 1969, pp. 81–109.

Wolpe, J. *Psychotherapy by reciprocal inhibition*. Stanford: University Press, 1958.

Woodworth, R. S. *Experimental psychology*. New York: Holt, 1938.

Woodworth, R. S. *Dynamics of behavior*. New York: Holt, 1958.

Woodworth, R. S., & Schlosberg, H. S. *Experimental psychology*. New York: Holt, 1954.

Wright, S., & McDonald, C. Review of behavioral treatment of depression. *Psychological Reports*, 1974, *34*, 1335–1341.

Wundt, W. *Grundriss der psychologie*. 1896. (C. H. Judd, transl.)

Wynne, L. C., & Solomon, R. L. Traumatic avoidance learning: Acquisition and extinction in dogs deprived of normal peripheral autonomic functioning. *Genetic Psychology Monographs*, 1955, *52*, 241–284.

Young, P. T. *Motivation and emotion: A survey of the determinants of human and animal activity.* New York: Wiley, 1961.

Zigler, E., Levine, J., & Gould, L. Cognitive challenge as a factor in children's humor appreciation. *Journal of Personality and Social Psychology,* 1967, *6*, 332–336.

Zillman, D. Excitation transfer in communication-mediated aggressive behavior. *Journal of Experimental Social Psychology,* 1971, *7*, 419–434.

Zillman, D., & Bryant, J. The effect of residual excitation on the emotional response to provocation and delayed aggressive behavior. *Journal of Personality and Social Psychology,* 1974, *30*, 782–791.

Zimbardo, P. G. The human choices: Individuation, reason, and order vs. deindividuation, impulse, and chaos. Unpublished manuscript, Stanford University, 1969.

Zimbardo, P. G., & Miller, N. E. Facilitation of exploration by hunger in rats. *Journal of Comparative and Physiological Psychology,* 1958, *51*, 43–46.

Zimbardo, P., Pilkonis, P., & Norwood, R. *The silent prison of shyness.* Stanford University, 1974. (Paper distributed by Scott, Foresman College Division, Glenview, Illinois.)

Zimmerman, W. B. Psychological and physiological differences between "light" and "deep" sleepers. *Psychophysiology,* 1968, *4*, 387.

Zuckerman, M. The development of an affect adjective check list for the measurement of anxiety. *Journal of Consulting Psychology,* 1960, *24*, 457–462.

Zuckerman, M. Scales for sex experience for males and females. *Journal of Consulting and Clinical Psychology,* 1973, *41*, 27–29.

Zuckerman, M. The sensation seeking motive. *Progress in Experimental Personality Research,* 1974, *7*, 79–148.

AUTHOR INDEX

SUBJECT INDEX

Activation (reticular)
  and EEG patterns, 28
  and emotion, 27-28
  and "emotional excitement," 28
Activity-affects, 23-24
Adaptive functions, principle of, 105-106
Affect, psychoanalytic conceptions of, 19-25
Affect-cognition interactions, 45-48
Affect induction, and delay of gratification,
    298-300
Affective-arousal theory, 190
Affective attributes, of objects, 156
Affective-cognitive orientation, 50
Affective-cognitive structures, 45-48, 155,
    157-158
  and the sex drive, 184-186
Affects
  and the organization of consciousness, 154-
    158
  patterns of, 92-96
  and special states of consciousness, 156-158
Aggression, dangers of, 352-353
Allocentric perception, 24
Anger
  activation of, 329-330
  antecedents of, 334-335
  causes of, 329-330
  characteristics of, 329-333
  consequences of, 345
  definition of, 87
  experience of, 331-333
  expression of, 330-331
  and psychosomatic symptoms, 351-352
  significance of, 333-334

Anger expression
  effects on perceiver, 347-351
  photo of, 88
Anger situation
  pattern of emotions in, 332-333
  profile of dimensions in, 331-332
  profile of emotions in, 344
Animation complex, and positive emotions,
    249
Anticathexis, 194
Anxiety
  and the corticosteroids, 380
  definition of, 93
  differential emotions theory of, 377-378
  Freudian theory of, 376-377
  norepinephrine-epinephrine ratio in, 380
  see also Affects, patterns of; and Emotions,
    patterns of
"Anxious attachment," 377
Appraisal, 31-32. See also Evaluation of
    context and emotion
Arousal
  determinants of, 199-200
  and emotions, 198-199
  and intrinsic motivation, 198-201
  and learning, 200-201
Attachment, mother-infant, 73-77
Attention as a function of interest, 191-193
Autocentric perception, 23-24
Autonomic nervous system and emotion, 114-
    116

Biochemistry, and emotions, 17
Biological directedness, see "Regulation to ends"